AMERICAN MUSICAL THEATER

AMERICAN MUSICAL THEATER

JAMES LEVE

Northern Arizona University

New York | Oxford

OXFORD UNIVERSITY PRESS

Oxford University Press is a department of the University of Oxford.
It furthers the University's objective of excellence in research,
scholarship, and education by publishing worldwide.

Oxford   New York
Auckland   Cape Town   Dar es Salaam   Hong Kong   Karachi
Kuala Lumpur   Madrid   Melbourne   Mexico City   Nairobi
New Delhi   Shanghai   Taipei   Toronto

With offices in
Argentina   Austria   Brazil   Chile   Czech Republic   France   Greece
Guatemala   Hungary   Italy   Japan   Poland   Portugal   Singapore
South Korea   Switzerland   Thailand   Turkey   Ukraine   Vietnam

For titles covered by Section 112 of the US Higher Education
Opportunity Act, please visit www.oup.com/us/he for the
latest information about pricing and alternate formats.

Published by Oxford University Press
198 Madison Avenue, New York, New York 10016
http://www.oup.com

Library of Congress Cataloging-in-Publication Data
Leve, James, author.
   American musical theater / James Leve, Northern Arizona University.
      pages cm
   ISBN 978-0-19-537960-0 (alk. paper)
   1. Musicals--United States--History and criticism--Textbooks. I. Title.
   ML1711.L48 2015
   782.1'40973--dc23
                                                        2015007675

Printing number: 9 8 7 6 5 4 3 2 1

Printed in the United States of America
on acid-free paper

To Donelle Ruwe and James Quincy Leve

CONTENTS

PREFACE

merican Musical Theater is the culmination of many years of teaching, researching, and writing about musical theater. In the classroom, I have experimented with various pedagogical approaches to the topic, and the framework that I have adopted for this book presents musical theater in an accessible, engaging, and interdisciplinary fashion. In addition to exposing students to the canon, performing repertory, and evolution of the musical theater genre, this book encourages them to think across the disciplines; to draw on their knowledge of music, literature, popular culture, and history; and, most important, to synthesize the study of musical theater into their intellectual development.

American Musical Theater is designed for a one-semester undergraduate or graduate course and primarily for music and theater majors. However, faculty in other areas, especially English and American studies, will find this book easily adaptable to their disciplinary foci. There are some technical musical discussions, but these can be excluded from reading assignments without disrupting the narrative flow of the chapters. The organizational structure that I have adopted allows for flexibility and can serve various pedagogical styles. One can use this text to emphasize the history of the genre, its artistic components, its cultural contexts, or any combination thereof.

ORGANIZATION

American Musical Theater provides a chronological history of the musical theater genre within a cultural context. It covers the major artistic trends, seminal works, and leading figures in the field. Unless otherwise noted, the dates given for the musicals refer to the original Broadway productions. The first chapter is an introduction to the integrated book musical in general and *Oklahoma!* in particular. It provides a foundation for understanding musical theater from several different vantage points. I begin with a detailed analysis of *Oklahoma!* in order to introduce concepts that recur throughout the course, such as the role that musical theater plays in the national dialogue on race relations and the hegemonic role of Jewish writers in the history of Broadway. Beginning the course with *Oklahoma!* and establishing it as both a forward and backward point of reference helps students to understand the evolution of musical comedy from a popular entertainment to a popular art form as well as to measure the impact of Rodgers and Hammerstein on musical theater.

Chapter 2, which is also introductory in nature, takes students back to the nineteenth century and introduces them to the various popular forms of musical theater that influenced the development of the Broadway musical in the early twentieth century. This chapter establishes the two major trends that have informed the entire history of musical theater: story-oriented genres and variety-like formats.

Chapters 3 through 12 progress through the twentieth century decade by decade, and Chapter 13 overviews the first decade and a half of the current century. The remaining four chapters explore issues (Off Broadway, race, rock music, and the star) that encompass more than a single decade, tie into other chapters, and stimulate lively classroom discussion. Instructors can integrate these chapters at various points in the course. For instance, the chapter on the rock musical (16), which encompasses the late fifties through the present, could be assigned in conjunction with the chapter on the sixties (9).

CASE STUDIES

A unique pedagogical feature of this book is the use a case-study musical in each chapter. This feature is predicated on my belief that deep readings of seminal musicals are preferable to an exhaustive but perfunctory examination of the repertory. These case-study musicals have been carefully selected either to exemplify a specific historical moment (e.g., the forties) or to provide a lens through which to examine a particular theme (e.g., the Broadway star). The case studies are identified immediately after their respective chapter's title along with the theaters in which they ran and the length of their runs. Each chapter includes a plot synopsis of the case study, and the majority of photographs represent these case studies and the people associated with them. Each case study is placed into a specific thematic framework as dictated by its respective chapter. For instance, Stephen Sondheim's *Company* (Chapter 10) grounds the discussion of the unique character and historical context of the concept musical, the most important development of the seventies. Moreover, *Company* provides a basis for a discussion of Sondheim's career and his preeminence in the post–Rodgers and Hammerstein era. Lastly, the analysis of *Company* connects to the discussion of *Cabaret* in the previous chapter and to developments covered in subsequent chapters. Instructors can assign addition or substitue titles as they see fit. I have included at least one musical example and some analysis for most of the case studies, although the depth and scope of these discussions vary, depending on the focus of the chapter.

The case studies introduce important figures and works in musical theater history while also illustrating concepts and trends so as to paint a rich and complex picture of the genre. In other words, the repertory is not an ends but rather a means of engaging students in the sort of larger issues that musical theater scholars are investigating today. Instructors are encouraged to augment the reading and assign various audio and video recordings to enhance or expand the scope of each chapter. The important thing is that students grasp the big picture. They should avoid getting bogged down in the minutia and multitude of facts inherent to any genre survey.

This approach also has the benefit of introducing key figures such as Cole Porter and major trends such as the megamusical in an integrated fashion rather than in modular blocks. Further, students receive multiple exposures to certain concepts. For instance, by the time students arrive at Chapter 7, their second contact with the forties, they should be able to analyze the case study, *Brigadoon,* in relation to the musical play, which it epitomizes. Likewise, students first read about the rock musical *Hair* in the context of the sixties (Chapter 9), and they re-encounter it in the discussion of the concept musical (Chapter 10), the Off Broadway musical (Chapter 14), and finally the rock musical (Chapter 16). By examining the same works and issues from different vantage points, students are encouraged to make the sort of intellectual connections that one hopes to foster in a liberal studies education.

Each chapter concludes with a feature called "And Bear in Mind," which introduces a musical that complements or contrasts the primary case study. For example, the chapter on the thirties focuses on *Anything Goes*, a quintessential diversionary musical comedy from the decade; the "And Bear in Mind" section introduces the musical satire *Of Thee I Sing*. These two works—the two longest-running musicals of the decade—represent the two primary musical theater trends of the Depression years.

RESOURCES

The study of musical theater poses some practical challenges because most of the material is still protected by copyright. I have therefore been careful to select case-study musicals for which published scores (full vocal scores as opposed to vocal selections), scripts, recordings, and, in some cases, films are readily available. Most university libraries will already own much of the material. Although an accompanying anthology and set of recordings would be ideal resources, such materials would be prohibitively expensive and highly impractical for any publisher. The Internet can enhance the study of musical theater in ways that only a decade ago would not have been possible. Instructors will find a remarkable range of historical recordings, film footage, live productions, and television excerpts of musicals (such as those originally presented on the Tony Award ceremonies and television variety shows such as *The Ed Sullivan Show*). They can also access unpublished scripts and other archival materials. The New York Public Library of the Performing Arts is a rich repository of such materials. Musical theater leasing companies can be of some, albeit limited, assistance with regard to unpublished materials. The pedagogical apparatus at the end of each chapter consists of a list of names, terms, and concepts as well as prompts for classroom discussion. Annotated bibliographies for each chapter are vailable on the compansion website. The companion website also contains addition readings, test questions, and listening suggestions. Instructors are encouraged to make use of the fast-expanding scholarly literature on musical theater, many titles of which are found in the general bibliography.

ACKNOWLEDGMENTS

To paraphrase a popular childrearing adage, it takes a village to write a good college textbook. One depends on a myriad of scholars, editorial staff, and colleagues, not to mention the patience of friends and family. It is my sincere hope that the people who helped me during the many years that it took to complete this textbook will take pride in the finished product. I would like to thank my editor at Oxford, Richard Carlin, who has shepherded this book through its crucial final phases. I would also like to acknowledge Jan Beatty, who nudged the book along in its early phases, and Norm Hirschy, editor for music books in the Academic and Trade Division at Oxford, who has never denied me a favor when I asked him for one. I am grateful to Emily Schmid and Meredith H. Keffer, editorial assistants at Oxford, for their help in getting this book to press and in preparing the companion website, respectively.

I am indebted to several people from the musical theater world, especially John Kander, Stephen Sondheim, Charles Strouse, Galt MacDermot, David Thompson, Dominic Symonds and André Bishop. George Boziwick and the staff at the New York Public Library for the Performing Arts made much of the research for this book possible. Other archives and institutions that have furnished materials include the British Library, Georgia State University, the Kurt Weill Foundation, and the Wisconsin Historical Society.

I have several professional colleagues to thank. Geoffrey Block, William A. Everett, Raymond Knapp, Paul Laird, James O'Leary, Tom Riis, and Steve Swayne are among the musical theater scholars who were quick to answer my calls. Katharine Weber is a fount of information about Kay Swift, among other things. Special thanks go to Stephen Brown, whose insights inform the musical analyses appearing throughout this book. Students in my musical theater classes at Northern Arizona University were among the first people to read chapters of this textbook and provide feedback.

Lastly, Donelle Ruwe is nearly as much a part of this book as I am. Her contribution, intellect, push back, and push forward have been invaluable from start to the finish.

CHAPTER 1

OKLAHOMA! AND THE INTEGRATED BOOK MUSICAL

(*OKLAHOMA!*, 1943, ST. JAMES THEATRE, 2,212 PERFORMANCES)

Richard Rodgers and Oscar Hammerstein's *Oklahoma!* opened in 1943 and set a new course for the American musical. Although social attitudes and tastes in music have radically changed since the early forties, *Oklahoma!* is still recognized as one of America's major artistic achievements of the twentieth century. It marked the coming of age of the musical theater genre and established a new artistic standard against which subsequent musicals were measured for decades. In his 2007 monograph on *Oklahoma!*, Tim Carter asks, "Why write a book on *Oklahoma!*?" His answer is as good as any: "Because it is a landmark in the Broadway musical, because it is a glorious show, and because it raises important issues about the genre, the theater, and its times." *Oklahoma!* bestowed artistic respectability on a genre that seventy years earlier had still been viewed as frivolous entertainment. Not every musical theater historian subscribes to a before-and-after-*Oklahoma!* model, but there are pedagogical benefits in establishing this seminal work as both a forward and backward point of reference. By beginning our survey of the genre with *Oklahoma!* rather than an earlier work, we can better understand the evolution of musical comedy from a slapdash popular entertainment into a uniquely American popular art form, as well as grapple with the changes that precipitated the decline of musical theater since the early sixties. And so we begin our story in 1943, when the Broadway musical reached its maturity.

OVERVIEW

Theater posters for the New Haven and Boston preview performances of *Away We Go!*, the original title of *Oklahoma!*, advertised a "musical comedy." The label assured theatergoers that the show would be entertaining—nothing too intellectually or emotionally taxing after a hard day's work. One could expect a light romantic plot, an opening number featuring attractive chorines, an assemblage of conventional ballads and comic songs, peppy dances, and a happy ending.

Before the Broadway premiere, however, the producers not only changed the title to *Oklahoma!*, but they also adopted a different genre designation. Posters printed for New York advertised a "musical play." The new label warded off any possible backlash from disappointed patrons who expected something more along the lines of Cole Porter's conventional musical comedy *Something for the Boys*, which had opened just a few months earlier. Many facets of *Oklahoma!* were atypical for a musical in 1943: a simple atmospheric opening number, ballet sequences, a death scene, and a concise and believable plot. Such unusual features, plus the country-western setting and a cast of relatively unknown actors, ran the risk of scaring off potential ticket buyers. The "musical play" label also reflects a reformulation in the minds of the writers and producers about the very nature of *Oklahoma!* They considered other labels, such as folk opera, but the Theatre Guild, the producing organization behind *Oklahoma!*, felt that these might intimidate Broadway's mainly middlebrow audience.

The "musical play" label was not new in 1943. However, after *Oklahoma!* it acquired a more narrow definition and was applied mainly to musicals with serious themes, three-dimensional characters, and more dramatic cohesiveness than found in a typical musical comedy. One of *Oklahoma!*'s achievements is its integration of song and dance into the story. Indeed, all of its artistic components appeared to share a unified vision. As Richard Rodgers quipped, "the orchestrations sound the way the costumes look." After *Oklahoma!*, the old practice of interpolating a musical number for the mere purpose of showcasing a performer's special talent or plugging a song to boost sheet-music sales came to be seen as a violation of the new musical theater aesthetic. Writers began to pay closer attention to how songs functioned within the story. Suddenly, the musical numbers had to grow organically from the dramatic situation and relate directly to the characters.

INTEGRATION THEORY

The "integrated musical" and *Oklahoma!*'s seminal role in propagating it figure large in the historiography of musical theater. *Oklahoma!* forced writers to justify songs on dramatic grounds. Before 1943, several writers, including both Hammerstein and Rodgers, recognized the importance of integrating songs into the plot, but *Oklahoma!* acquired the reputation, rightly or wrongly, of being the first musical to fully put the theory into practice.

Oklahoma!'s reputation as a revolutionary musical coalesced in the days and weeks after its Broadway opening. With rave reviews and long lines at the box office, the producers and writers engaged in what amounted to a well-orchestrated public relations campaign to ensure the production's artistic preeminence as well as its commercial success. They propagated the notion that the creative team had shared a unified artistic vision from the start, an assertion belied by several factors, including the uncertain pre-Broadway tryout period. Rodgers, Hammerstein, the choreographer Agnes de Mille (1905–1993), and the director Rouben Mamoulian

THE BOOK OF A MUSICAL

Technically speaking, the book of a musical refers to the spoken dialogue. Published scripts of musicals contain both the spoken dialogue and the lyrics, which are only rarely by a single person. Historically, the writer of the dialogue has been credited as "book writer," a term that reflects an early attitude that writers of musical comedy did not merit the more esteemed label "playwright." A book writer today might be accorded the distinction of "librettist" (a term borrowed from opera) or "scriptwriter" (a rather nonspecific label) but rarely "playwright." The distinction between "book writer" and "playwright" is not entirely without justification, as book writers do in fact work under a completely different set of conditions than playwrights. In particular, writing musical theater, unlike writing spoken drama, is a highly collaborative process.

(1897–1987) spread the idea—whether they truly believed it or convinced themselves of it—that the show sprang from a purely artistic impulse rather than a commercial one. Their statements helped solidify *Oklahoma!*'s status as the first fully integrated musical.

The evolving rhetoric surrounding *Oklahoma!* in the weeks leading up to its Broadway premiere and continuing well after the initial glow of its success had faded helped to secure the show's legacy, but it also explains the ideology behind the new aesthetic concept of integration, an ideology informed by several factors, including World War II politics; the discourse surrounding lowbrow, middlebrow, and highbrow art; nationalism; and concerns over the propagandistic tendency of American popular culture. It should be noted that the creators of *Oklahoma!* did not publicly employ the term "integrated musical" until after preview performances began. However, once the term became associated with *Oklahoma!*, musical theater writers embraced it and all that it connoted. Critics, too, became "'integration' conscious," to quote Rodgers, and it did not take long before their descriptive use of the term became prescriptive. The term "integration" thereby quickly came to symbolize a new artistic spirit. As James O'Leary observes, it has "remained a regulatory formal ideal that continues to shape how historians and critics have written about the musical theater."

As already noted, before the Broadway premiere of *Oklahoma!*, both its title and generic label remained fluid. The Theatre Guild, which was operating with depleted sums, was determined not to repeat the failure that it had experienced with Gershwin's *Porgy and Bess*, which it produced in 1935, and it struggled with how best to market the show (see Chapter 15). The Guild eventually settled on "musical play" because it emphasized the show's high artistic quality while promoting its entertainment value. The moniker also distinguished *Oklahoma!* from the lighter musical comedy genre and helped to align it with the artistic merits of operetta (see Chapters 2, 3, and 5) but without invoking that genre's European origins. The Guild's publicity staff employed the term "integration" as "a rhetorical emblem of sophistication," according to O'Leary, while at the same time appealing to the country's then-populist fervor. It was Hammerstein, who, when the production headed to Boston, waxed theoretically about the show, which was still called *Away We Go!* He glorified its highbrow achievements and thereby laid the groundwork for the formal concept of the integrated musical, which had been part of his thinking for years. In a 1925 article for *Theatre Magazine*, Hammerstein made the case for "the musical play with music and plot welded together in skillful cohesion." However, *Oklahoma!* surpassed all earlier attempts to weave the disparate elements of a musical into a unified work of art guided by a single ethos, and it ultimately elevated the artistic status of musical theater. No one could ignore the new standards set by *Oklahoma!*, not even established musical comedy writers such as Irving Berlin and Cole Porter (see Chapter 6).

Throughout and long after the Rodgers and Hammerstein era (1943–1960), few commentators questioned the validity or meaning of the term "integrated musical." However, no one codified or articulated a formal aesthetic theory for this sort of musical theater. Several musical theater scholars have recently wrestled with the vagaries and contradictions of the term and the assumptions that it engenders. Their efforts have given greater clarity to our understanding of the integrated musical.

Integration theory points to the realignment of song and spoken dialogue epitomized by shows such as *Oklahoma!* Most commentators today agree that the theory advances the notion that songs progress (or should progress) the plot and that the songs and dialogue flow into each other seamlessly without drawing attention to the shift between singing and speaking. Geoffrey Block, the author of the "Integration" article in *The Oxford Handbook of the American Musical*, lays out five key "Principles of Integration":

> The songs advance the plot.
>
> The songs flow directly from the dialogue.
>
> The songs express the characters who sing them.
>
> The dances advance the plot and enhance the dramatic meaning of the songs that precede them.
>
> The orchestra, through accompaniment and underscoring, parallels, complements, or advances the action.

After 1943, critics trumpeted musicals that adhered to these principles, and it is no coincidence that many of these same musicals make up a substantial portion of the musical theater canon and have remained in the standard performing repertory. For O'Leary, the underlying aesthetic tenet of the integrated musical is "a seamless relationship between the libretto and all other aspects of a production." However, many musicals, including some critically acclaimed works, contain nonintegrated songs and dances. According to Scott McMillin, even *Oklahoma!* contradicts its own sprit of integration with "People Will Say We're in Love," which lacks the logic and tone of the rest of the otherwise integrated score. However, *Oklahoma!*, according to McMillin, is none the worse for it. No musical is entirely without the occasional transgression. After all, even high-minded musical plays seek to entertain, as is the genre's birthright. It is therefore helpful to consider integration as an overarching artistic attitude, a frame of mind, a basic aesthetic of coherency, rather than as a strictly observed dramaturgical approach.

Organic unity, a concept that stems back to nineteenth-century symphonic and opera composers such as Beethoven and Wagner, has figured large in the discourse regarding integration theory. Organic unity can extend to all elements of a musical. Musical organicism involves motivic development and strong thematic connections over the course of an entire composition (e.g., Beethoven's Fifth Symphony). It also refers to connections between the foreground and background structures of a composition. The score for *West Side Story* (1957), which weaves together recurring motives and themes in dramatically powerful ways, is often held up as one of the finest examples of musical organicism in the musical theater repertory. On the other hand, some top-notch musicals, such as *Guys and Dolls* (1950), feature eclectic scores—collections of songs that might have a unity of purpose and spirit but little musical unity.

In fully integrated musicals, the songs and dances grow naturally, organically, from the spoken dialogue, and they either advance the plot or reveal the emotional life of the characters. However, Scott McMillin sees a greater disjunction between song and spoken dialogue than most adherents of integration theory would allow. This difference arises from two orders of time, as McMillin identifies them, one with a relatively realistic unfolding of the action (book time) and one in which the suspension of real time takes hold (lyric time). Language operates differently in lyric time, as word and phrase repetition occurs in ways unheard in spoken dialogue and everyday human social intercourse. Musical numbers do not necessarily progress the action (although they can) but rather tell the audience something about a character or situation. In "Many a New Day" from *Oklahoma!*, which has one of the most repetitive melodies in the repertory, Laurey attempts to convince herself that Curly means no more to her than any other man does. "Out of My Dreams" reveals something to Laurey, and thus to us, about what she is feeling. Neither song moves the action forward in a narrative or dialectical sense, but *Oklahoma!* would lack its psychological texture without them. Lynn Riggs's *Green Grow the Lilacs*, the play on which *Oklahoma!* is based, contains no comparable speeches or interior monologues. Rodgers and Hammerstein instinctively exploited the difference between book time and lyric time. Every song and dance (including "People Will Say We're in Love") "elaborates" what occurs in the book-time segments.

People who disparage musical theater are bothered by the fact that the characters, unlike real people, break out into song at any time and any place. They do not allow themselves the suspension of disbelief that is a prerequisite for all forms of music theater and therefore are unable to experience or appreciate the genre's full emotional sweep. In the early days of musical comedy, the songs and dances

TABLE 1.1. Rodgers and Hammerstein Musicals

DATE	TITLE	TYPE	PERFORMANCES
1943	*Oklahoma!*	musical play	2,212
1945	*State Fair*	movie musical	–
1945	*Carousel*	musical play	890
1947	*Allegro*	musical play (concept musical)	315
1949	*South Pacific*	musical play	1,925
1951	*The King and I*	musical play	1,246
1953	*Me and Juliet*	musical comedy	358
1955	*Pipe Dream*	musical play	246
1957	*Cinderella*	television musical	–
1958	*Flower Drum Song*	musical comedy	600
1959	*The Sound of Music*	musical play	1,443

CONCEPT MUSICALS

Concept musicals tend to maintain a strong separation between song and spoken dialogue (see Chapters 9 and 10). Although concept musicals often achieve organic unity, calling them "integrated" muddies our understanding of the term as it applies to *Oklahoma!* Concept musicals replace "integration" with "concept" (the central thematic idea) as the governing element. They are "integrated" only insofar as they incorporate the various artistic elements in the service of a single directorial (or authorial) vision. By contrast, musical comedies from the early twentieth century interpolate songs willy-nilly and with little dramatic purpose. They reflect the casual attitude toward musical theater dramaturgy that existed prior to the forties, after which the spirit if not the practice of integration theory began to take hold.

interrupted the story without dramatic justification (or, as some historians have described it, the dialogue interrupted the musical numbers on the pretext of having to tell a story). *Oklahoma!* definitively rendered such disregard for continuity unacceptable.

From left, Richard Rodgers, Irving Berlin, Oscar Hammerstein, and the choreographer Helen Timiris at auditions for *Annie Get Your Gun*. *Courtesy Library of Congress Prints and Photographs Division, Washington, DC.*

RODGERS AND HAMMERSTEIN

Richard Rodgers and Oscar Hammerstein first met each other in 1916 at Columbia University and collaborated on a few songs in 1920, but *Oklahoma!* marks the beginning of their legendary collaboration. Other collaborations have endured longer than Rodgers and Hammerstein's, but none of them is venerated with the same degree of reverence or has exerted as much influence on the musical theater genre.

Ironically, although *Oklahoma!* was a blockbuster, it was not at all clear that Rodgers and Hammerstein would collaborate on a second musical, let alone eleven (Table 1.1). However, the untimely death in 1943 of Rodgers's first partner, Lorenz Hart, dispelled any doubts. Rodgers and Hammerstein's next project was the 1945 movie musical *State Fair*. Five of their Broadway musicals occupy an important place in the musical theater canon: *Oklahoma!*, *Carousel*, *The King and I*, *South Pacific*, and *The Sound of Music*. *Allegro* was a valiant early attempt at the concept musical (see Chapters 9 and 10). It traces the life of a small-town doctor who loses his way but eventually finds redemption. This ambitious experiment lasted only 315 performances. Even less successful were *Me and Juliet* and *Pipe Dream*, a backstage musical comedy and a musical play based on John Steinbeck's *Sweet Thursday,* respectively. *Flower Drum Song*, another musical comedy, was a modest hit. Rodgers

RICHARD RODGERS AND OSCAR HAMMERSTEIN

Richard Rodgers (1902–1979) and Oscar Hammerstein (1895–1960) were both born in New York City to well-to-do families, had fathers named William (thus the name Williamson Music Company, which they founded in 1945), grew up in Harlem, attended Columbia University, and participated in collegiate theatrical productions. Otherwise, they were as different from each other as two collaborators could possibly be. Rodgers's grandparents, all of them Russian Jews, arrived in America in 1860. Rogazinsky, his father's original family name, was anglicized before the end of the nineteenth century. Rodgers's father attended City College, worked his way through Bellevue Medical School, and practiced medicine. He was also an observant Orthodox Jew. Richard's mother, Mamie Levy, received a good education and piano lessons, but she became a nervous hypochondriac. The Rodgers household was fraught with tension, due in part to hostilities between William and his overbearing live-in mother-in-law, who chided him for his devout religious beliefs and thick Russian accent.

Richard Rodgers inherited his appreciation of music from his father and quickly developed a passion for musical theater. After seeing Jerome Kern's Princess Theatre musicals (see Chapter 4), he decided to become a theater composer. A mutual acquaintance introduced Rodgers to Lorenz Hart (1895–1943), a lyricist in search of a composer. The meeting took place at the Hart household on West 119th Street, and by the time Rodgers left, he and Hart had agreed to collaborate. In his memoir, *Musical Stages*, Rodgers recalls the "theories" that Hart espoused on that fateful day, that "writers were afraid to approach adult subject matter and that the rhyming in general was elementary and often illiterate." They discovered "a mutual conviction that the musical theatre . . . was capable of achieving a far greater degree of artistic merit in every area than was apparent at the time." Rodgers and Hart's songs figure large in the "Great American Songbook" (a construct that refers to the corpus of popular songs in the Tin Pan Alley tradition written between the twenties and the advent of rock music in the fifties). Hart possessed great facility with interior rhymes and polysyllabic words. His lyrics revel in:

WORDPLAY:	"Hear me hollar / I choose a / Sweet lolla / Paloosa / In thee" (from "Thou Swell")
SEXUAL INNUENDO:	"When he talks he is seeking / Words to get off his chest. / Horizontally speaking / He's at his very best" (from "Bewitched, Bothered and Bewildered")
ERUDITE ALLUSION:	"It is no metropolis, / It has no big Acropolis" (from "Dear Old Syracuse")

UNREQUITED LOVE:	"Unrequited love's a bore / And I've got it pretty bad. / But for someone you adore, / It's a pleasure to be sad" (from "Glad to Be Unhappy")
IRONY:	"It's got to be love! / It couldn't be tonsillitis / It feels like neuritis / But nevertheless it's love" (from "It's Got to Be Love")

Jazz elements, such as syncopation and blue notes, give Rodgers and Hart's songs a sense of modernity and urbanity. Rodgers's music reveals a penchant for scalar melodies ("Dancing on the Ceiling") and embedded scales within melodic lines ("Blue Room").

Rodgers and Hart's first major break came when the comic Lew Fields (half of the famous Weber and Fields duo) (see Chapter 2), who had turned to producing, interpolated some of their songs into his musicals. Field's approbation boosted Rodgers and Hart's confidence, but it took them six more years to get a musical onto Broadway. In the meantime, Rodgers attended the Institute of Musical Arts (later renamed the Juilliard School). Rodgers and Hart's fortune changed in 1925 when the Theatre Guild (the future producer of *Oklahoma!*) mounted the revue *The Garrick Gaieties* and hired them to write the score. Their songs, "Manhattan" in particular, garnered high critical praise. Between 1925 and 1930, Rodgers and Hart wrote fourteen musical comedies. Herbert Fields, Lew's son, wrote the book for half of these. Their musicals are quintessential twenties romantic comedies in tone and style, but they range in subject matter from the Revolutionary War (*Dearest Enemy*, 1925) to psychoanalysis (*Peggy-Ann*, 1926).

After the stock market crash of 1929, Rodgers and Hart went to Hollywood and remained there until 1934. They produced some excellent work, but they missed the creative energy of New York. So when producer Billy Rose offered them the opportunity to write the score for the circus musical *Jumbo*, they returned to New York. *Jumbo* cost nearly $350,000 to produce and closed at a loss, but it appealed to the critics and initiated Rodgers and Hart's most artistically adventurous period.

Nearly every year between 1936 and 1942, one or two hit musicals by Rodgers and Hart opened on Broadway: *On Your Toes* (1936), *Babes in Arms* (1937), *I'd Rather be Right* (1937), *I Married an Angel* (1938), *The Boys from Syracuse* (1938), *Too Many Girls* (1939), *Higher and Higher* (1940), *Pal Joey* (1940), and *By Jupiter* (1942). As Rodgers recalled in his memoir, "It seemed as if nothing we touched could go wrong. We had the freedom to do what we wanted and the satisfaction that what we wanted to do, others wanted to see. We could experiment with form and content not only in our songs but also in the shows themselves."

Pal Joey, Rodgers and Hart's penultimate and most mature work, is based on John O'Hara's epistolary novel of the same name (see Chapter 7). The title character is a cad, and the story deals with adultery, blackmail, and the seamy side of show business. Rodgers and Hart's last musical, *By Jupiter*, is based on the play *The Warrior's Husband* by Julian F. Thompson. All told, Rodgers and Hart collaborated on twenty-eight Broadway musicals and six movie musicals.

(Continued)

By the early forties, Hart's habit of disappearing without a word, excessive drinking, and erratic work habits had begun to take a toll on Rodgers. Had Hart's mental and physical health improved, he and Rodgers might have continued working together for years. However, even before Hart died, Rodgers had found a partner on whom he could depend. By contrast, when Hammerstein died eighteen years later, a search for his replacement proved exceedingly difficult. This, the third phase of Rodgers's career (1960–1979), was his most disappointing. He wrote his own lyrics for his first and most successful show from this period, *No Strings*, but thereafter collaborated with various lyricists, all of them much younger than he, including Stephen Sondheim (*Do I Hear a Waltz?*), Martin Charnin (*Two by Two* and *I Remember Mama*), and Sheldon Harnick (*Rex*). Despite working with a younger generation of lyricists, Rodgers never abandoned the book musical format.

Oscar Hammerstein II grew up at the epicenter of New York's frenetic theater world. His paternal grandfather, Oscar Hammerstein I (1847–1919), was an opera impresario, whom the Metropolitan Opera, his chief rival, paid over a million dollars to abstain from producing any operas for ten years; Oscar's father, William Hammerstein, managed a theater; and his uncle, Arthur Hammerstein (1872–1955), was a Broadway producer. The young Oscar was raised Episcopalian, but his paternal grandfather was a German Jew. At his family's urgings, he went to Columbia University to study law. He wrote lyrics and librettos for theatrical productions on campus, and after his father and grandfather died, he abandoned law for a career in the theater and went to work for his uncle as an assistant stage manager. That same year he wrote his first play, *The Light* (1919), which closed out of town. By 1920, Hammerstein was collaborating with the composer Herbert Stothart (1885–1949), and within three years they had written four musical comedies. He also wrote three more spoken plays, all of which closed quickly, as well as a musical with the composer Dudley Wilkinson (1897–1991).

Hammerstein's first major success was the 1923 musical *Wildflower*, which featured music by Stothart and Vincent Youmans. It ran for an impressive 477 performances. *Mary Jane McKane*, also with music by Stothart and Youmans, opened the same year and played 151 performances, a respectable run in 1923. In 1924, Hammerstein, along with the more seasoned Otto Harbach, wrote his first operetta, *Rose-Marie*, which had music by Stothart and Rudolf Friml (see Chapter 5). Hammerstein learned a great deal about lyric writing from Harbach. For the remainder of the decade, he maintained a busy pace, swinging between operetta and musical comedy, and collaborating with Jerome Kern, George Gershwin, Sigmund Romberg, and Emmerich Kalman. Hammerstein and Romberg's 1926 operetta *The Desert Song* has the distinction of being the first Broadway musical made into a movie.

Hammerstein and Kern's first joint effort was the 1925 musical comedy *Sunny*. The writers shared a vision for an indigenous musical theater, which they came closest to realizing with *Show Boat* in 1927 (see Chapter 5). In the early thirties, Hammerstein gave Hollywood a try, but he found it unrewarding and quickly returned to New York. His Broadway work in the thirties was lackluster, and by 1942 he and most of the Broadway establishment considered his career to be over.

and Hammerstein also wrote the first major television musical, *Cinderella*, whose initial broadcast was seen by over 100 million viewers. In addition, they produced *Annie Get Your Gun* (1946) and a few spoken plays. Hammerstein died of stomach cancer in 1960, shortly after the Broadway premiere of *The Sound of Music*.

THE EVOLUTION OF *OKLAHOMA!*

Oklahoma! was the least likely of musicals to become a hit in 1943. The United States had officially entered World War II in late 1941, and most theatergoers at the time preferred musical comedy to anything with a serious tinge. Riggs's *Green Grow the Lilacs* had been only a modest success. Moreover, the Theatre Guild—which was founded in 1919—was on the brink of financial collapse. From the start, the Guild's main founders, including Lawrence Langner (1890–1962) and Theresa Helburn (1897–1959), wanted to foster American drama. They produced plays by Eugene O'Neill, Thornton Wilder, and Maxwell Anderson, among others. They also spearheaded musical adaptations of spoken plays produced under their auspices. Their most momentous project of this sort had been George Gershwin's *Porgy and Bess* (1935), which was based on DuBose Heyward's 1925 novel *Porgy* and subsequent stage adaptation thereof in 1927. The production of *Porgy and Bess* inspired Helburn to develop other musicals with American themes.

Helburn held high ideals for musical theater and argued that dance should be as integral to the story telling as song. She felt that *Show Boat* and *Porgy and Bess* portended a shift in musical theater toward opera and envisioned what she called "grand operetta" as a potential uniquely American genre. She identified several plays appropriate for musical treatment, including Ferenc Molnár's *Liliom*, which the Guild had produced in 1921. She approached the composer Kurt Weill (see Chapter 7), who was interested in the project, but the Guild could not obtain the musical rights for Molnár's play. (When the Guild did acquire the rights a couple of years later, it hired Rodgers and Hammerstein to write the score and titled the show *Carousel*.) Helburn eventually settled on Riggs's *Green Grow the Lilacs*, which the Guild had produced in 1931. The play featured dialect and real folk songs of the American heartland. These local-color elements responded to the populism of the moment, but the play was forgotten soon after its sixty-four performances on Broadway. Helburn offered the show to Rodgers and Hart, whose career the organization had helped launch in the twenties, but only after considering several other composers, including Jerome Kern, Irving Berlin, Cole Porter, Aaron Copland, Ferde Grofé, and the folksinger Woody Guthrie. Rodgers needed no convincing; Hart, on the other hand, was indifferent to the idea. A year earlier, Rodgers, increasingly worried about Hart's alcoholism and erratic behavior, approached Hammerstein about working together. Hammerstein privately agreed to step in should Hart bow out of the Guild project. Now, however, before giving the nod to Hammerstein, Helburn considered other lyricists and librettists, including Ira Gershwin. With so much uncertainty surrounding the members of the creative team, the press erroneously announced that the musical would have a score by Rodgers and Hart and a book by Hammerstein. By late 1942, all contracts had been signed, the Guild was in full production mode, and Rodgers and Hammerstein were immersed in their first collaboration.

Oklahoma!'s artistic unity was not easy to achieve, and some of the show's major accomplishments came about by pure happenstance. Even assembling the artistic staff posed some challenges. Rouben Mamoulian was hired to direct the show only after more established directors had turned down the assignment. The choreographer Agnes de Mille lobbied for the assignment; her work on Aaron Copland's ballet *Rodeo* in October 1942 convinced the producers that she was ideal for the job. For the set designer, the Guild considered Oliver Smith, who had created the scenery for *Rodeo*, but they ultimately hired Lemuel Ayers. Miles White was the Guild's first and final choice to design the costumes. Rodgers tapped the esteemed arranger Robert Russell Bennett (1894–1981) to do the orchestrations.

THE ARTISTIC COMPONENTS

Book and Lyrics

With *Oklahoma!*, Hammerstein established a new literary standard for musical theater. His book remains a model of efficient and sound musical theater dramaturgy. He created psychologically complex characters and offset the relatively static nature of the plot by maximizing the emotional potential of the story. Humor, romance, and pathos are in perfect balance. The humor, moreover, emanates from the characters and situations, as opposed to being one-liners, as was generally the case in earlier musical comedies. The songs and dances arise naturally from the story, and the dramatic tension builds and resolves effectively.

Audiences found the show's realistic dialogue, character development, and plot refreshing and superior to the conventions of musical comedy. Hammerstein retained the basic structure of Riggs's play (two acts, each containing three scenes), but he opened up the action to include a greater variety of physical locations. In particular, he set the box social beneath the stars at the Skidmore Ranch, which provided a natural spot for the song "The Farmer and the Cowman Should Be Friends" and its attendant rousing square dance. He added the character of Will Parker, whom Riggs's play merely mentions, and thereby created a love triangle between Will, Ado Annie, and Ali Hakim that parallels the one between Curly, Laurey, and Jud. He also altered several details involving the resolution of the story. In *Green Grow the Lilacs*, Curly is detained in jail while awaiting trial for the murder of Jud. His innocence remains in question, and he escapes from jail and turns up at Aunt Eller's house. When a posse comes looking for him, Aunt Eller buys Curly and Laurey enough time to consummate their marriage. Hammerstein lessened the tension surrounding Jud's death. Rather than dwelling on the possibility that Curly could go to jail for murder, he emphasized the festive mood of the wedding night and the bright future of the Oklahoma Territory. Aunt Eller convinces—coerces is more like it—the judge to acquit Curly right then and there in the middle of her kitchen *cum* makeshift courtroom, so that Curly and Laurey can get on with their life together. This change serves *Oklahoma!*'s utopian vision. Jud's death (he falls on his own knife) is just punishment for someone who lives outside the conventions and mores of the community.

Hammerstein's dialogue is natural and unassuming without becoming prosaic. He gave the characters rich psychological lives defined by their actions and speeches. No scene illustrates Hammerstein's ability to create character and conflict better than the opening. The parallel scene in Riggs's play takes place inside Aunt Eller's kitchen. Hammerstein moved the action outdoors, and Lemuel Ayers designed an evocative backdrop for the scene. As Aunt Eller calmly churns butter, Curly sings "Oh, What a Beautiful Mornin'" from off stage, at first a cappella and then, while he saunters into full view of the audience, accompanied by orchestra. Curly has come to ask Aunt Eller's niece, Laurey, to the box social. He claims, though, not to have any serious designs on Laurey, who soon comes out of the house, singing the opening strain of his song. Laurey, with feigning nonchalance, quips, "Oh, I thought you was somebody," and then resumes her singing. Thus, with a short song and a few lines of dialogue, Hammerstein establishes the locale, the main characters, and the central conflict of the story. Curly and Laurey play a game of cat and mouse because they are too proud, and perhaps immature, to express their feelings for each other in any other way.

Riggs deserves credit for the basic framework of this scene. His play opens with Curly singing a real song, "Git Along, You Little Dogies," from offstage, followed by a lengthy exchange between the cowboy and Aunt Eller. The playwright hoped to capture "in a kind of nostalgic glow (but in dramatic dialogue more than in song) the great range of mood which characterized the old folk songs and ballads" that he had heard as a child growing up in Oklahoma. As Riggs wrote in the preface to the published script, "The people in a room, agreeing or not agreeing, are to me truly dramatic." Hammerstein transformed Riggs's opening into an extended scene anchored by the song "Surrey with the Fringe on Top," which borrows the Western imagery and even some lines directly from Riggs's dialogue. Curly serenades Laurey and Aunt Eller with his lyrical description of the surrey. Countering Laurey's verbal assaults, he shifts almost imperceptibly from spoken dialogue ("If I was to ast you, they'd be a way to take you, Miss Laurey Smarty," to which Laurey replies, "Oh, they would?") into song, starting with the verse, which is only slightly more stylized than prose: "When I take you out tonight with me, / Honey, here's the way it's goin' to be." Hammerstein reserves the most poetic language for the refrain, the music of which relies on repetition at the melodic level as well as from one phrase to the next. Moreover, the refrain occurs three times, with dialogue and musical underscoring intervening between statements (Example 1.1).

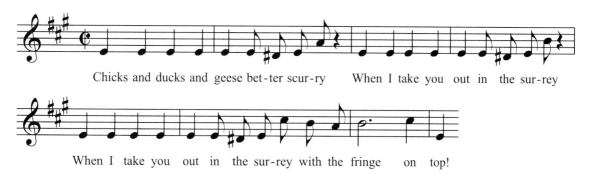

EXAMPLE 1.1. "Surrey with the Fringe on Top," refrain, first phrase

This scene epitomizes Rodgers and Hammerstein's ability to weave together speech and song in the service of the story. Laurey, unable to respond to Curly, has no option but to listen, and so she (as well as the audience) is lulled into his romantic vision of the surrey. It is difficult—no, impossible—for her to ignore the emotional stirrings that she experiences when Curly is near, even though she is too vainglorious to admit it to him or to herself. Curly's musical performance sweeps her, Aunt Eller, and us into his fantasy. The musical and poetic rhythms of the refrain create the lilting gait and hypnotic clip-clop of horses pulling a surrey. The number has an understated romantic charm. Curly relies on his charisma, and in the third and final stanza, as the music quiets down to a wisp of sound, smooth rhythms replace the clip-clop accompaniment of the first two verses, a lyrical string line provides a soft cushion for the melody, and the lyrics describe an idyllic return trip home beneath a starlit sky. When the song is over, Laurey regains her composure and snaps out of the dream state into which Curly has lulled her. The scene ends like the parallel scene in Riggs's play, but the musical version makes a deeper emotional imprint on the audience. Laurey will attend the party with Jud, either to spite Curly or because she is confused or both, but she has revealed her true feelings (at least to the audience) in musical theater terms.

PLOT OF OKLAHOMA!

The ranchers and the farmers of the Oklahoma Territory have not yet achieved the degree of civility required to become a thriving and lawful state of the Union. One of these ranchers, a cowboy named Curly McLain, loves Laurey Williams, an orphan who lives on her farm with her Aunt Eller, and hopes to take her to the local box social but is too proud to tell her directly. Laurey, who would accept if Curly would only ask her, agrees instead to go to the box social with Aunt Eller's farmhand, Jud Fry, a dark, menacing loner. On the way to the party, Jud frightens Laurey, and she runs to find Curly. Curly and Laurey openly confess their love for each other and plan to get married. Will Parker, a kind but slow-witted cowboy, returns from Kansas City with a bag full of presents for his sweetheart, Ado Annie. While Will was away, Ado Annie, who enjoys the attention of almost any man, kept company with a Persian peddler named Ali Hakim. Hakim avoids a shotgun wedding with Annie by helping Will to get her back. At Laurey and Curly's wedding, Jud attempts to fight Curly, but he ends up falling on his own knife and dies. In Aunt Eller's kitchen, Curly receives a quick trial and is acquitted. He and Laurey leave for their honeymoon, eager to begin their brand-new life in a brand-new state.

TABLE 1.2. Musical Structures in *Oklahoma!*

"Oh, What a Beautiful Mornin'"	AB (verse + refrain) (16+16)
"The Surrey with the Fringe on Top"	verse | AABA (8+8+8+12)
"Kansas City"	verse | AA' (16+28)
"I Cain't Say No"	verse | ABA' | CD | ABA' (16+16+24 | 8+9 | 16+16+24)
"Many a New Day"	verse | ABA' (monothematic) (12+8+8)
"It's a Scandal"	verse | AA'A'' (16+16+16)
"People Will Say We're in Love"	verse | AABA' (16+16+8+8)
"Pore Jud Is Daid"	AA | recitative |AAA-- (8+8 | -- | 8+8+12)
"Lonely Room"	ABB'CAD (8+8+8+8+8+10)
"Out of My Dreams"	AA' | BB' | AA' (16+28 | 16+18 | 16+30)
"The Farmer and the Cowman"	ABB | CC | AB | CC | A | CC | B (16+8+8 | 16+16 | 16+8 | 16+16 | | 16 | 16+16 | 8)*
"All Er' Nothin'"	verse | ABA' (16+8+12)
"Oklahoma!"	verse | AA'BA'' (16+16+8+16)

*Dialogue occurring between some sections is not indicated.

Music

The score for *Oklahoma!* marks a striking change in Rodgers's compositional style. In addition to the historical and geographical settings of their musicals, Rodgers and Hammerstein's working arrangement made an impact of the music. With Hart, Rodgers usually wrote the music without having any lyrics to guide him. Like most Tin Pan Alley and Broadway composers at the time, Rodgers favored the thirty-two-bar AABA song form. Songs of this type commonly began with a verse in free form that sets up the situation and establishes the mood for the refrain. Hammerstein, in contrast to Hart, typically worked out a complete set of lyrics before Rodgers composed a note. Hammerstein clearly preferred the expressive freedom that this arrangement afforded him, and his lyrics in turn inspired Rodgers to compose his most dramatically effective music. More than ever before, Rodgers gave his scores an authentic-sounding historical and geographical patina. Content dictated musical style and form, as opposed to the conventions of commercial music. Rodgers mined a wider range of expressive devices to depict settings as diverse as nineteenth-century Siam and New England, and the Pacific Rim and Austria during World War II. The melodies, rhythms, and harmonies of *Oklahoma!* suggest a bucolic Western setting without ever feeling derivative or dull. One finds less stylistic range among Rodgers's earlier scores, despite their high quality.

For *Oklahoma!*, Rodgers and Hammerstein experimented with a variety of musical forms. Only two songs have an AABA structure, "The Surrey with the Fringe on Top" and "People Will Say We're in Love," and even these are not the conventional thirty-two-bar variety. A few numbers, including "I Cain't Say No," have more expansive structures.

The structurally diverse yet stylistically unified score reflects *Oklahoma!*'s ideology of community and helps convey the message that the inhabitants of Oklahoma must embrace the effects of modernity on their lives (modernity being synonymous with a civil society and the values of the new century). "Oh, What a Beautiful Mornin'" adopts an archaic strophic verse-refrain structure, which is appropriate for what is intended to sound like a real (diegetic) folk tune that Curly sings while approaching Laurey's house in the early morning hours. Both this song and "Out of My Dreams" are waltzes. The former evokes the West through a simple melody, pastoral imagery, and spacious Coplandesque orchestrations. Laurey's "Out of My Dreams" has the dreamy, romantic quality associated with European operetta. Both waltzes stand in relief to the "modern" character of "Kansas City" and the folksy strains of "The Farmer and the Cowman." On the other hand, Jud's "Lonely Room," the most operatic number in the show, has a free form, a metaphor for his willful disposition. In "Pore Jud Is Daid," Curly sings recitative and a hymn-like melody as he mocks his rival. Like "Oh, What a Beautiful Mornin'," "Pore Jud, " and "The Farmer and the Cowman" also function as "real" music. Their melodic and harmonic simplicity evokes folk music and creates the appearance of authenticity.

When the curtain went up on *Oklahoma!*, audiences saw a mostly bare stage and heard someone singing off stage. This opening announced a new type of musical. Musical comedies usually began with a chorus number and featured attractive chorines in flashy costumes. "Oh, What a Beautiful Mornin'" has a deceptively simple melody in three-quarter time. The orchestra enters almost imperceptibly midway through the first verse. The melodic construction and harmonic tension are masterstrokes. The first phrase of the refrain reaches its apex note, a startling lowered seventh scale degree, on "morn[in']." This pitch, an appoggiatura, forms a dissonant fourth that resolves to the third on the second syllable of the word (Example 1.2).

Appoggiatura

A non-harmonic tone occurring on a strong beat and usually forming a dissonance with the predominant harmony. Appoggiaturas are often approached by leap (an interval larger than a step), and they resolve by step on the subsequent weak beat. Also called a "leaning-note."

In the twenties and thirties, white composers such as George Gershwin and Harold Arlen incorporated the flat seventh from the blues scale, but here the pitch carries no apparent blues association. Curly, inspired by the natural beauty surrounding him, expresses himself with self-assurance, but the music hints at the impending trouble that lies ahead. The next phrase ("I got a beautiful feeling") replicates the first, except that it replaces the D-natural with a D-sharp, which resolves upward to E, the highest note in the song, rather than downward as in the first phrase. The last leg of the song lazily descends a full octave. As demonstrated here, Rodgers's melodies express Hammerstein's words with seeming

EXAMPLE 1.2. "Oh, What a Beautiful Mornin'," refrain

effortlessness. Hammerstein's lyrics avoid manufactured emotion and easy laughs. They approach a level of poetry and emotional realism rarely heard in musical theater and are as integral to the story as the spoken portions of his librettos.

Choreography

Helburn, Langner, Rodgers, and Hammerstein sought a choreographer with the background and vision to capture the Western milieu through movement. Rodgers alone doubted de Mille's ability to transfer her ballet training to the Broadway stage, but the others ultimately prevailed. Like the music, de Mille's choreography functioned on two levels. Will Parker's tap sequence in "Kansas City" demonstrates a popular dance that he picked up on his trip, and the square dance at the Skidmore Ranch calls for "real" folk dancing. Other dances use the artifice of choreographed ballet to advance the story. One of *Oklahoma!*'s high points is the extended dream ballet sequence (titled "Laurey Makes Up her Mind") at the end of Act I. A Ballet segment also occurs in "Many a New Day." Ballet was not new to Broadway in 1943, but de Mille made it more integral to the dramatic foundation of a show. She struck a delicate balance between classical ballet and popular dance, articulating the dramatic and emotional content of the story while providing vivid local color. (De Mille recreated her original choreography for the 1955 film version of *Oklahoma!*)

As early drafts of the script reveal, Hammerstein and Rodgers identified several places for dance but did not always specify the content. De Mille developed these ideas once she was on board. Her dances portrayed psychological aspects of the characters and reinforced the show's themes. For instance, in "Kansas City" Will Parker announces the coming of modernization to a backwoods territory that hopes to become a state. He makes his point through dance, showing off a two-step and a rag that he picked up in Kansas City. These newfangled steps are a stark contrast to the square dance in the second act, not to mention the stylized ballet segments.

The dream ballet reifies Laurey's indecision and emotional turmoil through modern dance movement. Hammerstein's second draft mapped out the ballet as a fantasy. "Laurey's contemplation of her problems will be played against the background of the world she lives in. . . . Aunt Eller . . . advises Laurey to do whut's natchrel and ride to the party with Curly. . . . Jud comes in and challenges his right. Curly starts firing shots at Jud but they make no sound. . . . It looks as if Jud will kill Curly." The mortal threat to Curly startles Laurey. As she regains her composure, the real Jud brusquely orders her to prepare for the dance. Although sketchy, Hammerstein's description established the dramatic arc of the ballet. De Mille followed the basic outline of Hammerstein's scenario but explored a darker sexual side of Laurey's imagination. She insisted on using trained dancers to represent the leads in the dance.

De Mille created the dream ballet without the benefit of music, which Robert Russell Bennett subsequently pieced together using melodies from Act I as specified by the choreographer (Table 1.3). She later claimed that there was some discussion about featuring a circus ballet at the end of Act I but that she argued for something more threatening and psychologically realistic: "Girls don't dream about the circus. They dream about horrors. And they dream dirty dreams." Whether or not de Mille actually raised this point during rehearsals, the fact that she later made the statement suggests that she was concerned that her full contribution to *Oklahoma!* would not be rightly acknowledged. She also boasted about introducing more sexual energy into the show than Hammerstein had planned.

The dream ballet exposes a psychological dimension of Laurey otherwise unavailable to the audience. Words alone, whether sung or spoken, could never have achieved this psychological depth with such grace or immediacy. The ballet heightens the dramatic tension of the story by juxtaposing Laurey's imagined violently sexual scene with the actual appearance of Jud in the brief book scene that closes the act—an intriguing way to send the audience out to the lobby for intermission.

The dream ballet elevated the role of dance in musical theater. In fact, the published score of *Oklahoma!* includes a detailed description of it. (Each action is printed above the corresponding music.) In recent years, productions have deviated from de Mille's original choreography, and some versions use the actors playing Curly, Jud, and Laurey instead of classically trained lookalike dancers.

Sets and Costumes

The Theatre Guild reserved a third of *Oklahoma!*'s $83,000 budget for the sets and costumes—$16,588 and $18,890, respectively. This considerable investment reflects the importance that the producers placed on the visual aspect of *Oklahoma!* The sets and costumes had to accomplish more than merely present an authentic image of the Oklahoma Territory; they had to communicate the spirit of the story.

Riggs's script begins with a vivid description:

> It is a radiant summer morning several years ago, the kind of morning which, enveloping the shape of earth—men, cattle in a meadow, blades of the young corn, streams—makes them seem to exist now for the first time, their images giving off a visible golden emanation that is partly true and partly a trick of imagination focusing to keep alive a loveliness that may pass away.

TABLE 1.3. "Dream Ballet"

MELODIC SEGMENTS	DESCRIPTION OF THE ACTION IN THE PUBLISHED SCORE
"Out of My Dreams"	The dream figures of Laurey and Curly dance ecstatically.
"Oh, What a Beautiful Mornin'"	"Laurey" and "Curly" keep on dancing. A young girl enters and soon others dance on. Two of Curly's cowboys.
"Kansas City"	A little girl presents "Laurey" with a nosegay. More girlfriends dance on and embrace her.
"Oh, What a Beautiful Mornin'"	A bridal veil floats down from the skies and they place it on "Laurey's" head.
"The Surrey with the Fringe on Top"	"Curly" and the boys enter, in the manner of cowboys astride their horses. "Curly" awaits his bride, who walks down an aisle formed by the girls. [This section is titled "The Wedding."] "Jud" walks slowly forward and takes off "Laurey's" veil.
connecting music	"Laurey" is left alone with "Jud."
"Pore Jud Is Daid"	Three dance-hall girls enter.
"I Cain't Say No"	The women dance with "Jud" and the boys.
"Pore Jud Is Daid"	
connecting music	
"I Cain't Say No"	
"Pore Jud Is Daid"	"Laurey" and "Jud" are left alone. "Curly" enters and fires at "Jud" with an imaginary pistol.
"Lonely Room"	
"The Surrey with the Fringe on Top"	"Jud" chokes "Curly" to death and carries "Laurey" off.
"People Will Say We're in Love"	The real Jud awakens Laurey from her dream and [she] starts to go mechanically with him. The real Curly enters expectantly, and seeing them leave, he stands alone, puzzled, dejected and defeated, as the curtain falls.

Lemuel Ayers captured the essence of this description in a painted backdrop. His designs evoked the style and iconography of regionalist artists from the thirties, especially Thomas Hart Benton, Grant Wood, and John Steuart Curry. The Depression years and the war inspired a grassroots interest in the American heartland, and

"The Farmer and the Cowhand" dance at the box social in *Oklahoma! Courtesy KB Archives.*

many artists responded by creating murals and canvases filled with folk imagery and populist themes. Benton's paintings relied on simple, isolated images, a windmill, a haystack, a corn silo. Ayers's sets evoked the bucolic imagery and populism that had made the ballet *Rodeo* and similar works so appealing. Attentive to the spatial requirements for the dances, he employed three-dimensional scenery sparingly— a chair, a butter churn—and instead he poured his creative energy into the backdrops. In part because of the wartime shortage of materials, the set was plain, but the colors were evocative, and the perspectives created a sense of expanse. Black-and-white photographs of the original production of *Oklahoma!* do not do justice to the understated charm of the sets and costumes (see Fig. 1 in the color insert). Nor do they effectively convey how well the scenery's variegated colors and near-Impressionistic rendering of the territory added to the atmosphere of the musical.

Miles White's costumes aimed for the same effect as Ayers's sets, but he and Helburn understood that authentic clothing would be too bland for an upbeat musical. There were also practical matters to consider, such as the requirement that the costumes not constrict the dancers and that accessories such as hats and fringe not be an encumbrance. White sought inspiration from a 1904–1905 Montgomery Ward catalogue, which showed how people from the era and region actually dressed. He based the costumes for the can-can dancers in the dream ballet on vintage cigarette cards featuring pictures of women in provocative poses. White gave most of the cowboys chaps, boots, hats, and fringed gloves, and the women shawls and flowers. He ordered that polka dots be sewn onto the cowboys' shirts, although he ended up removing these, with de Mille's help, and eliminating other accessories. What remained was a minimalist, suggestive couture.

INTERPRETATION

The most traditional reading of *Oklahoma!* emphasizes the fragmented community—ruled by two opposing factions, ranchers and farmers, and vulnerable to lawlessness—that is struggling to achieve unity and statehood. For most commentators in the forties and for decades beyond, *Oklahoma!* expressed the renewed American nationalism resulting from World War II and embraced the notion that individual desires must be sublimated to the needs of the community. Once the people of the Oklahoma Territory discover a common goal and live by a system of laws, they can join the Union as a full-fledged state. This view of the musical played into the groundswell of patriotism during the war. Further, it received the stamp of legitimacy by those associated with the production who were quick to draw a strong connection between the musical's success and the nationalist sentiments that it aroused. *Oklahoma!* celebrated American ingenuity and inclusiveness. For Richard Rodgers, it was the exemplar of a genre that itself manifested an American spirit: "We've got what we think is a lusty, American kind of musical, a glorification of the American ability to invent its own musical forms and rhythms."

Recent scholarship on *Oklahoma!* has shifted attention to how race, assimilation, and isolationism play out in the musical. Rodgers and Hammerstein were both strong supporters of Jewish causes, and the latter was an outspoken interventionist. One interpretation of *Oklahoma!* maps the bitter dispute between isolationist and interventionist camps prior to America's entry into the war onto the farmers and the cowmen. *Oklahoma!* reconciles the tension between these two factions by combining the populist conservative ideology with the assimilationist agenda of liberal New Dealers. In *Oklahoma!* the two factions learn to coexist.

Oklahoma! also explores personal identity. In *Making Americans: Jews and the Broadway Musical*, Andrea Most argues that "The Broadway stage was a space where Jews envisioned an ideal America and subtly wrote themselves into that scenario as accepted members of the mainstream American community." Ali Hakim and Jud Fry, both outsiders and a potential threat to the community, provide the underlying dramatic tension of the story. Riggs described Ali as a "swarthy Syrian" and Jeeter (Jud) as having a "curious earth-coloured face and hairy hands." Both descriptions suggest a racial "other." Andrea Most sees Ali, whom Hammerstein described simply as a "Persian peddler," as the Jewish immigrant who assimilates into American society through the traditional paths of marriage and community, and Jud as the dark (read African American) loner who threatens the peace of the community and is literally eliminated. Originally, Hammerstein intended to pair Ali with a south-of-the-border female character named Lotta Gonzales, who, like Ali, would have represented an exotic and sexually open character. Most's reading applies best to the original production, which featured the Yiddish comic actor

Joseph Buloff (1899–1985) in the role of Ali. Each stanza of his only song, "It's a Scandal, It's an Outrage," contains two jokes, both with a classic setup-punchline construction, reflecting its vaudeville (and perhaps Jewish theater) influence. Buloff played the role without attempting to mask his thick Yiddish accent. In fact, his outward Jewishness raised concerns among the production staff about anti-Semitism. Their consternation was unfounded, as audiences, like the Oklahoma folks themselves, welcomed the lovable, nonthreatening foreign salesman. At one point, the Theatre Guild considered the Jewish comic Groucho Marx for the role of Ali, and one of Hammerstein's early drafts makes the peddler Armenian and gives him the name Kalenderian Kalazian. The film version of *Oklahoma!* whitewashed Ali by casting All-American Eddie Albert (born in Illinois in 1906) in the role. The 2002 Broadway revival of *Oklahoma!* (directed by Trevor Nunn) reestablished Ali as a swarthy outsider of some sort by featuring the Indian-born Muslim actor Aasif Mandvi (né Aasif Mandviwala) in the role.

In contrast to Ali, Jud, Most argues, embodies society's worst stereotypes of the black man. (Incidentally, the original Jud was also played by a Jewish actor, Howard Da Silva [see Chapter 8].) Jud is violent and sexually threatening, and he nearly rapes Laurey. Curly's proprietary instinct to save Laurey from Jud evokes Jim Crow images of white violence against black men suspected of touching or simply desiring a white woman. As Curly claims in "Pore Jud is Daid," Jud is a dark and savage man who literally lives among the rats in a smokehouse (African Americans were sometimes called "smokies"). In the same song, Curly suggests that Jud should hang himself, a chilling reference to lynchings. A rubric in the published score of *Oklahoma!* instructs Curly and Jud to sing "Pore Jud is Daid" "like a Negro at a revivalist meeting."

Oklahoma! espouses the utopian ideal of a diverse and inclusive America, but, as it turns out, such a vision has its limitations. Whereas Ali is the nonthreatening ethnic other—a comic figure—who assimilates, Jud is the racialized ("dark"), dangerous other. This disparity between ethnicity and race in *Oklahoma!* mirrors the complicated history of Jews and African Americans during the twentieth century. Jewish performers such as Al Jolson, Sophie Tucker, and Eddie Cantor often appeared in blackface, in effect hiding their own ethnicity behind a black exterior (see Chapter 17). Likewise, in *Oklahoma!* the latent xenophobia of the white locals toward Ali is displaced onto Jud Fry because he threatens the peace and security of the community. Hammerstein would have further complicated things had he gone through with his plan to feature Ali in a blackface performance of a "coon song" entitled "Peddler's Pack."

According to Bruce Kirle, Rodgers and Hammerstein's utopian world also excludes Native Americans, the only group that legitimately belonged to the Oklahoma Territory. The othering of Jud in *Oklahoma!* is achieved by projecting onto him stereotypical traits also ascribed to Native Americans: drunkenness, dumb-wittedness, predatory sexuality, untamed and uncultured nature (in need of civilizing by Western society). However, actual Native American characters are conspicuously absent from *Oklahoma!*, even though Lynn Riggs, who was himself

AND BEAR IN MIND

Kiss Me, Kate *(1948, New Century Theatre, 1,077 performances)*

Music and lyrics by Cole Porter
Book by Samuel and Bella Spewack

Alfred Drake and Patricia Morison as Fred Graham and Lilli Vanessi, former husband and wife, playing Petruchio and Katherine in *The Taming of the Shrew*, the play-within-the-play of *Kiss Me, Kate*. *Courtesy KB Archives.*

The composer-lyricist Cole Porter never abandoned his interest in musical comedy for more serious musicals (see Chapter 6), but his musicals after *Oklahoma!* achieve a greater degree of integration than his earlier ones, with *Kiss Me, Kate* arguably being his greatest artistic achievement. *Kiss Me, Kate*, Porter's fourth Broadway work after the premiere of *Oklahoma!*, is a backstage musical involving the actors appearing in a musical version of Shakespeare's *The Taming of the Shrew*. The influence of *Oklahoma!* is evident in the show's well-drawn characters, humor derived from the dramatic situations, and overall integrity. Porter had great fun composing what amounts to a double score, one part book songs for the contemporary story and one part songs for the fictional musical version of *The Taming of the Shrew*.

part Cherokee, alludes to the fact that the white territorial population often intermarried with the native population. During the trial scene in Riggs's play, the territory folks declare that they are all "full of Indian blood" as a way of legitimizing their right to the land and declaring themselves to be true Americans, unlike the federal marshal who tries to arrest Curly. In effect, Riggs dramatizes the formation of a new society, a diverse mix of Native Americans, whites, and Jews. His utopian vision permits, even encourages, intermarriage and miscegenation as a positive expression of melting-pot ideology. Hammerstein and Rodgers's pot is smaller: the territory folks are white, except for Jud, who remains isolated by his refusal to accept the laws of the land.

EPILOGUE

Lorenz Hart attended the Broadway opening of *Oklahoma!* and, according to Rodgers, led the cheering. Within weeks, Rodgers and Hart were rewriting their

1927 musical *Connecticut Yankee* for a Broadway revival. Meanwhile, Hammerstein oversaw the production of *Carmen Jones*, a project that he had begun a few years earlier (see Chapter 15). Rodgers hoped that working on a show would help Hart to overcome his troubles, but the lyricist died tragically just days after the *Connecticut Yankee* revival opened. Hart's death paved the way for Rodgers and Hammerstein's nascent collaboration to continue. Within months, they began work on the movie musical *State Fair* and their next Broadway musical, *Carousel*. By this time, no one could ignore the dawning of a new era on Broadway.

NAMES, TERMS, AND CONCEPTS

Ayers, Lemuel	integration theory
book time versus lyric time	*Kiss Me, Kate*
de Mille, Agnes	Mamoulian, Rouben
diegetic music	*Oklahoma!*
Green Grow the Lilacs	musical play versus musical comedy
Hammerstein II, Oscar	Riggs, Lynn
Hart, Lorenz	Rodgers, Richard
Helburn, Teresa	Theatre Guild
integrated musical	White, Miles

DISCUSSION QUESTIONS

1. Discuss integration theory as it applies to musicals of the Rodgers and Hammerstein era.

2. Why is *Oklahoma!* held up as a model of the integrated musical?

3. According to Scott McMillin, how do "book time" and "lyric time" operate in musical theater?

4. Compare and contrast the musical comedy and the musical play around the time of *Oklahoma!*

CHAPTER 2

MUSICAL THEATER IN NINETEENTH-CENTURY AMERICA

(*A TRIP TO CHINATOWN*, 1891, MADISON SQUARE THEATRE, 657 PERFORMANCES)

The historic boulevard called Broadway (originally the Wickquasgeck Trail) slices diagonally across the entire length of Manhattan. In the early twentieth century, the Broadway Theater District—the "Great White Way," as Shep Friedman dubbed it in 1902—ran along Broadway between 14th Street and 34th Street. Today, all but a few Broadway theaters, the majority of them erected during a theater construction boom that ended with the Great Depression, lie within an area circumscribed by 42nd Street and 52nd Street at the south and north ends, respectively, and by 8th Avenue and Broadway on the west and east sides.

Broadway did not become the primary purveyor of musical theater until the early twentieth century. Before 1900, the musical theater industry was not concentrated in any one urban center. Popular genres such as the minstrel show, burlesque, and variety played in every corner of the country and appealed to different socioeconomic classes. At the turn of the century, urbanization, theater business practices, and technological advances led to the centralization of the musical theater industry in New York. Today New York remains the heart and soul of the American musical.

The Broadway musical emerged in the early twentieth century as a consolidation or melding of several popular nineteenth-century forms. These precursors of the modern musical invariably followed one of two basic trends: employing music and dance in the service of telling a story (operetta, melodrama, burlesque, and farce-comedy) or featuring songs, dances, and comedy without a unifying storyline (minstrel shows, extravaganzas, revues, and variety). These two fundamentally different types of musical theater have never been mutually exclusive, and they have shaped the history of the Broadway musical to the present day.

PLOT-CENTERED GENRES

The Black Crook: "The First Musical Comedy"

For years, *The Black Crook* (1866) had the dubious distinction of being called the first musical. It did constitute the first unequivocal hit of the American music theater stage, but to call it a "musical" distorts our understanding of the term. *The Black Crook* (1866) provided enough story and entertainment to please both devotees of drama and fans of song and dance. It was an "unprecedented blend of art and bodily allurement," as one commentator describes it, which came about entirely by chance. William Wheatley, the manager of the fashionable Niblo's Garden, had arranged to present a melodrama by Charles M. Barras called *The Black Crook*, which had music by Thomas Baker. Two other producers, Henry C. Jarrett and Harry Palmer, had engaged a French ballet troupe to perform *La Biche aux Bois* at a different theater, but when the theater burned down they convinced Wheatley to interpolate the ballet into his production of *The Black Crook*. What seems like a peculiar request was in fact an accidental stroke of genius in that the two works complemented each other. The initial production ran 474 performances.

Barras based the premise for *The Black Crook* on Carl Maria von Weber's *Faust*-inspired opera *Die Freischutz* (1821). The eponymous Black Crook, a nefarious sorcerer whose real name is Hertzog, is losing his powers, so he makes a pact with Zamiel in which he earns a year of life for every soul that he delivers to the devil. He pursues Rodolphe. Rodolphe is in love with Amina, but he has a rival, the villainous Count Wolfenstein, who hopes to marry Amina. Stalacta, the Fairy Queen, seeks vengeance against Zamiel. She assists Rodolphe in defeating Hertzog and Wolfenstein and eventually in reuniting with Amina.

Although critics considered *The Black Crook* stereotypical nineteenth-century melodrama, they admired the lavish spectacle and ballet segments, which included dancing demons, a masked ball, and a dance of the Amazons. Sophisticated stage machinery created supernatural effects. The score was a mishmash of songs and dances by a committee of composers, but this and all other imperfections were overshadowed by the show's flagrant display of the female body, which the advertisements audaciously publicized. One critic described the "symmetrical legs and alabaster bosoms so lavishly presented to our view." The prurient features of the show boosted ticket sales. Productions of *The Black Crook* appeared in American cities for a quarter of a century. In New York alone, no less than seven revivals took place between 1868 and 1892.

Burlesque

Lydia Thompson and her "British Blondes"

In its mixture of German opera and French ballet, *The Black Crook* was a uniquely American phenomenon and prefigured the coexistence of the profound and profane in the Broadway musical. American musical theater continued to borrow from European models even as it developed its own unique character. Burlesque (also called travesty and extravaganza), originally a distinctly English genre, appeared in

Members from the cast of the 1893 production of *The Black Crook*, which incorporated women in a variety of trouser roles. *Courtesy Library of Congress Prints and Photographs Division, Washington, DC.*

New York by 1868. The genre satirized popular plays and novels, and music usually played a dominant role in the proceedings. Like *The Black Crook*, burlesque exploited the female body in order to lure a large male clientele. Burlesque rose to great popularity following the Civil War. The craze began with British actress and entrepreneur Lydia Thompson (1838–1908) and her "British Blondes," who first appeared in America in *Ixion, ex-King of Thessaly Ixion* (1868).

As a teenager, Thompson performed in pantomimes in Britain and then on the Continent. She eventually became a featured burlesque performer in London. Because of burlesque's controversial nature, Thompson encountered considerable resistance in America, but interest in her troupe of "British Blondes" did not wane. Thompson continued to appear on stage until 1904.

Ixion, a bastardization of the Greek myth, became a *cause célèbre* and aroused moral indignation, much of it leveled against Thompson. One newspaper's crusade against her was so fierce that she accosted the editor, who subsequently brought her to court. The case bestowed only more attention on the show in the form of free publicity. Within a year, several theaters were offering similar *divertissements* with performers dressed in tights.

Evangeline

One of the first works billed as a "musical comedy" was a more homegrown and more chaste example of burlesque. *Evangeline, or the Belle of Acadie* (1874) took its inspiration from Henry Wadsworth Longfellow's recitation poem *Evangeline, a Tale of Acadie* (1847). The composer Edward E. Rice (1848–1924) and writer J. Cheever Goodwin (1850–1912) intended *Evangeline* as an antidote against Lydia Thompson's lurid brand of burlesque, although they, too, featured women in tights in several roles, even the male protagonist.

Longfellow's poem is set in 1655 in the idyllic land of Acadia, a French colony in Nova Scotia. Evangeline is betrothed to Gabriel, the son of a blacksmith. Gabriel and Evangeline are separated from each other when English soldiers arrive and announce that all inhabitants of Acadia must cede their land to England. Evangeline spends her days searching for her lost lover. Her travels take her as far south as Louisiana. She becomes a Sister of Mercy and aids the afflicted. By the time she finds Gabriel, he is at death's door. He soon dies, and she too succumbs.

Rice and Goodwin's burlesque bears little resemblance to Longfellow's poem. The writers added a villain, political humor, travels to distant lands, and a happy ending. As the story begins, Evangeline and Gabriel are about to wed. Le Blanc, a notary, rejoices at the fact that once Evangeline is married, he will be able to claim the fortune left by her uncle:

> She was to have his provided she—
>
> Remains from matrimonial fetters free
>
> But if she married then the wealth that he
>
> Designed for her would straight revert to me
>
> And I become in turn, sole legatee.

A Hessian army captain discovers two soldiers that Evangeline has hidden and arrests her. She dissembles, "Oh sir, I never knew that I did wrong. They asked protection." The captain interrupts in a thick Hessian accent, "Why did you not send them to McKinley? That's what the matter with Hanna." (The "McKinley" reference is to William McKinley, the 25th President of the United States; "Hanna" refers to Marcus Alonzo Hanna, a Republican industrialist who managed McKinley's first presidential campaign.) Such topical jokes appeared throughout the show, and when they became stale they were replaced with more timely ones. Evangeline is led away before Le Blanc is able to obtain her signature on the wedding contract.

Act II opens in Africa, where Evangeline has been taken. Le Blanc arrives in pursuit of her, and Le Blanc's beloved, Catherine, has followed him. Soon, and without any explanation whatsoever, Gabriel also appears. Meanwhile, the captain and his men gather diamonds, but policemen enter and arrest them along with Evangeline and the other Acadians. After the prisoners attempt an escape, the king orders that they be beheaded, but as the axe is raised he discovers that Le Blanc is a fellow Mason. Evangeline and Gabriel's wedding, which was interrupted in Act I, now resumes. Le Blanc thinks that the fortune that Evangeline was supposed to receive from her uncle is now his, but he has lost the document that spells this out. Catherine agrees to marry him despite his lack of wealth.

The dialogue, most of it in rhyming verse, revels in puns and irrelevant jokes. For instance, Le Blanc commands Hans, "Go soldier, go! Get thee to a gunnery" (a pun on Hamlet's famous line to Ophelia, "Get thee to a nunnery"). In Africa, when explaining his unusual manner of dress to Catherine, he declares, "I wear this Roman toga 'cause 'twixt me and you / When you're a Roman (roaming) you must do as Romans do. Ha! Ha! That's very good." At times, dramatic propriety is abandoned entirely for the sake of a cheap joke. While arguing with Catherine, Le Blanc inquires, "Do you take me for a Chinaman because I work for Rice?" (the play's composer). The most celebrated moment in *Evangeline* was a cow dance in Act I. Gabriel appears with a cow and exclaims: "Confound that heifer, me she nearly spilled / When once we're married I shall have her (heifer) killed." Evangeline responds, "Anyone who loves me must love my cow." The wedding guests arrive, and the cow, besought by Evangeline, performs a dance.

Evangeline epitomizes the amalgam of dance, comic business, and specialty acts that were typical of burlesque entertainment. As described in the introduction to a facsimile edition of the script, *Evangeline* "drew on all the most familiar forms of public entertainment of the era: its special effects ran from homespun to exotic; it was topical and fresh, silly and profound, serious and outrageous all at the same time." It was a winning combination of elements, for *Evangeline* enjoyed a thirty-year life on the stage. Rice and Goodwin went on to write other works, but *Evangeline* remained their primary source of income and greatest triumph. Its success helped to keep pantomime, spectacle, burlesque, and comic opera popular.

Weber and Fields

Joe Weber (1867–1942) and Lew Fields (1867–1941) specialized in burlesque entertainment and German dialect comedy (also called "Dutch" comedy). They were a popular comedy team in vaudeville and later on Broadway. They specialized in ethnic humor, with an emphasis on German-Jewish stereotypes. Their contrasting physiques—Weber was short and dumpy and Fields tall and bearded—gave their act a degree of visual humor. They first appeared together on stage when, at only sixteen years of age, they were hired to perform at Miner's Bowery Theatre. In 1896, they leased a theater, renamed it Weber and Fields' Broadway Music Hall, and began producing two-part burlesque shows, the first part featuring a travesty based on a current play and the second an "olio" or variety show. Their parodies took titles such as *Cyranose de Bricabrac* (1898), which was a musical spoof of Edmond Rostand's 1897 play *Cyrano de Bergerac*. Fields and Weber's partnership ended abruptly in 1904, but their influence continued well into the twentieth century.

In the early twentieth century, the growing middle class sought family-oriented entertainment with less risqué content. As mainstream musical theater became more respectable, burlesque filled the void, thereby relegating itself to adult, mostly male, entertainment. Since the thirties, the term "burlesque" has connoted little more than striptease.

Operetta

Opera in America did not always resemble the nonprofit, highbrow institution that it is today. In the nineteenth century, impresarios presented European opera in American cities in the original language as well as in English translation. These productions were subject to the same rules of the marketplace as other forms of entertainment. Scholars disagree over opera's influence on the modern American musical. Raymond Knapp notes, "opera had throughout provided an important model both from 'above' and 'below,' that is, both as a standard to aspire to and as a genre whose traces and influence may be found in virtually all of the nineteenth century 'entertainments' from which the musical developed (especially operetta)." However, at the turn of the century, operetta was enormously popular, and it influenced musical theater as much if not more than opera did. Only later, can it be argued, did opera become the ideal against which certain "highbrow" musicals (e.g., *Porgy and Bess*) were measured.

The generic term "operetta" (some history books prefer "comic opera") encompasses satirical operas such as W. S. Gilbert and Arthur Sullivan's *H.M.S. Pinafore* (1878) and romantic works such as Franz Lehár's *The Merry Widow* (1905). The "operetta" article in the *New Grove Dictionary of Music* begins: "A light opera with spoken dialogue, songs and dances. Emphasizing music rich in melody and based on 19th-century operatic styles . . ." Notwithstanding the loaded term "light opera," the definition is sufficiently vague to apply to the full range of operettas produced in America. They were popular entertainment and as such reflected middle-class tastes and values. In later decades, commentators reappropriated the term "operetta" for musicals such as *My Fair Lady* (1956) and *A Little Night Music* (1973).

Operetta has its origins in France. Adolphe Adam and Jacques Offenbach specialized in one-act works satirizing contemporary society. These were intended to counter the pretensions of *opera comique*, which was usually, but not always, comic and included spoken dialogue. Gilbert and Sullivan rethought the French genre in English terms, satirizing British society and spoofing Italian operatic conventions such as coloratura passages and contralto villainesses. The Viennese composers Franz von Suppé and Johann Strauss also took their inspiration from the French. Viennese operetta favored stories of romance. Both the English and Viennese schools modeled their music on operatic practices and incorporated spoken dialogue.

Operetta arrived in America in the mid-nineteenth century and quickly caught on as a popular form of entertainment. In fact, operettas and musical comedies were rarely differentiated: they shared producers, writers, performers, and patrons. The New York premiere of Gilbert and Sullivan's *H.M.S. Pinafore* took place in 1879 and unleashed a frenzy of *Pinafore* productions (mostly unauthorized). American audiences could readily relate to Gilbert and Sullivan's wit and appreciate their artistry. That English society was the main brunt of the joke only fueled America's love affair with their work, which has continued up to the present. *Pinafore*'s popularity opened up the floodgates for the importation of other operettas, and these gates did not close for nearly forty years.

Before long, American composers started to write their own operettas. Reginald de Koven (1859–1920), for instance, teamed up with the librettist Harry B. Smith (1860–1936) to write *The Begum* (1887). He had more lasting success with *Robin Hood* (1891), a work with more serious operatic pretentions than the typical operetta. The composer Woolson

Harry B. Smith (1860–1936) was the leading musical theater lyricist and book writer of his day. He is credited with over 300 stage works.

Morse wrote *Wang* (1891) with J. Cheever Goodwin, the wordsmith for *Evangeline*. Set in Siam, *Wang* epitomizes the popularity of orientalist stories at the time. Morse attracted the attention of Gilbert, who, after terminating his partnership with Sullivan, invited him to be his collaborator; but the composer remained in New York and continued to work with Goodwin. John Philip Sousa, otherwise known as the "March King" and the director of the United States Marine Band, composed fifteen operettas, none more popular than his first, *El Capitan* (1896).

Toward the end of the century, operetta suffered a decline in both quality and popularity, but it enjoyed a resurgence around 1907 (see Chapter 3). Today, operetta from this era is held in low esteem due to its mawkish charm, dated music, and implausible plots. Because of the dearth of old operettas in the standard performing musical theater repertory, our exposure today to the genre is severely limited; however, operetta was so popular in the early twentieth century that several silent film versions were made, as incredible as that may seem. Hollywood continued to churn out film adaptations of operettas until well after the genre's halcyon days on Broadway, usually taking immoderate liberties with the material and exaggerating the sentimentality of what was already perceived as a corny genre. Operetta on film peaked during the Depression, during which it provided downtrodden Americans a much-needed escape from the harsh realities of daily life. The similarities between most of these films and the stage versions on which they were based amount to the title and a few songs. Today, several opera companies include an operetta or two in their repertory.

American-Made Musical Comedy

The Mulligan Guard Plays

Toward the end of the century, farcical story-centered musicals began to appear with increasing frequency. As Gilbert and Sullivan were delighting American audiences with stories about British upper-class society, Edward Harrigan was entertaining immigrant working-class audiences with stories about themselves. Harrigan was born in 1844 on New York's Lower East Side. In the late 1860s, he began appearing in music halls, billing himself as "Ned Harrigan, the Irish comic singer." He also performed blackface routines as a member of the Manning's Minstrels. In 1871, Harrigan formed an act with the Chicago actor Tony Hart (born Anthony J. Cannon). They started out in variety, performing comic skits created by Harrigan. Harrigan expanded some of these into full-length plays with songs, for which he wrote the lyrics, and his father-in-law, the English-born David Braham (1834–1905), composed the music. Harrigan is best known for a series of musicals written between

1879 and 1881 collectively called the "Mulligan Guard plays." They represent an important step in the direction of the modern musical comedy genre.

Harrigan, who grew up in one of the poorest and most ethnically diverse neighborhoods of New York, wrote about tenement life. His plays portray the nitty-gritty, daily grind of New York's burgeoning ethnic populations. In addition to featuring Irish, German, and African-American characters, Harrigan's plays also included Italians, Chinese, and Jews. Harrigan had little interest in the upper classes. As he claimed:

> Polite society, wealth, and culture possess little or no color and picturesqueness. The chief use I make of them is as a foil to the poor, the workers, and the great middle class. The average gentleman is so stereotyped that he has no value except in those plays where he is a pawn on the chess-board of melodramatic vice or tragic sin. He does very well in *Camille* and *Forget-me-not*, but I can't imagine him at home in a happy tenement-house or enjoying himself at a colored ball.

Harrigan's musicals are devoid of the romantic plots of latter-day musical comedy. Instead, they focus on urban life, politics, and social mores. He strove to capture the social milieu of tenement neighborhoods on the Lower East Side. The dramatic conflicts reflect real-life situations of immigrant enclaves and typically involve Irish and German rivalries or other intra-immigrant squabbles. Although exaggerations of the truth, his plays are far closer to real life than historical drama or upper-class farce. Harrigan achieved a degree of realism through local color, urban slang, dialects, costumes, and real locales, such as McSorley's Saloon (which is still standing). According to Jon Finson, the "ethnic conflicts" constituted the most realistic element of Harrigan's plays: "Neighborhood gangs, ethnic boundaries, and confrontations were just as much a fact of city life then as now."

Harrigan believed that his depictions of life on the street "served a real social need." He sympathized with his fellow Irish Americans but was not afraid to dwell on their propensity for drink. In fact, Dan Mulligan, the character he regularly played, was the proprietor of a saloon. Harrigan's African American characters relied on minstrel show stereotypes. Tony Hart specialized in playing Rebecca, a recurring black character. She and her boyfriend, Palestine Puter, are usually embroiled in some sort of comic antics and spend much of their time bickering. The following exchange from *The Mulligan Guard Nominee* is typical:

PUTER: Do you want my love to turn to hate?

REBECCA: I'd hate to see it, but my mother was a Hayti lady and I can
            hate myself.

Harrigan's urban black dandies had a proclivity for playing the numbers racket. However, they are proud of their heritage, enjoy a sense of empowerment, and feel superior to other ethnic groups. Jewish characters in Harrigan's plays, based on the German-born Jews with whom he had grown up, were typically "clever at dealing with money" (e.g., a secondhand clothing merchant).

Like latter-day situation comedy, the Mulligan plays take place in the same location, the Lower East Side, and feature recurring characters, usually played by the same actors, and similar farcical plots, which include some sort of conflict between Dan Mulligan and his nemesis, the German butcher Gustavus Lochmuller. Both men have Irish wives, Cordelia and Bridget, respectfully. Many of Harrigan's plays build to a climax involving some sort of skirmish between Mulligan and the black Skidmore Guard, a paramilitary group led by barber Simpson Primrose and the Reverend Palestine Puter. Invariably, the Mulligan Guard and the "Skids" reserve the same dance hall or venue for the same date and time, which eventually leads to a chaotic on-stage melee.

In *The Mulligan Guard Nominee* (1880), Mulligan, the proprietor of the Wee-Drop Saloon, runs against Lochmuller for the office of Alderman. His campaign strategy includes courting the black vote, as an early song in the show explains (see Example 2.1 below). As the play begins, Bridget Lochmuller has just returned from a visit to Sligo, Ireland. Following her trail is an English detective who is suspicious of secret meetings held at the house where she was staying. He has seen letters written by her containing a reference to the F.N.A., which he interprets as the Fenian National Association (a revolutionary nationalist organization of Irish and Irish American citizens that plotted to capture Canada). The intrigue builds when a women's group led by Cordelia, and coincidentally also called the F.N.A., secretly meets in back of the Wee-Drop. This meeting confirms the detective's suspicions about Bridget Lochmuller's connections to the Fenian National Association. In the final

EXAMPLE 2.1. "Hang the Mulligan Banner Up," refrain

scene, a victorious Mulligan, the Skidmore Guard, and the Lochmullers are on a boat sailing toward Albany. The detective learns that the letters "F.N.A." are merely a reference to the Florence Nightingale Association (named after the famed American nurse), not the Irish paramilitary group, as he had assumed.

The songs incorporated into the Mulligan plays (approximately eight in each) are generally superfluous to the story, but they were part of the attraction and sometimes involved the audience in a sing-along. Braham's music reflects the popular song types of his day. They adopt a long verse–short chorus format. The melodies consist of short, mostly syllabic phrases, and the harmonies are unadventurous, with the exception of some surprising chromaticism. The occasional romantic song is invariably a waltz. Minstrel show influences are evident in the inclusion of spirituals and cakewalk two-steps.

By the mid-1890s, Harrigan's brand of ethnic comedy had lost its social relevance. Irish immigration had subsided, and a wave of Italians and Eastern Europeans began to arrive on American shores. The Irish no longer occupied the bottom rung of the economic ladder, as they had entered the political establishment in several major American cities. Harrigan died in 1911, but he had lived to see the ascendency of George M. Cohan, whose own brand of comedy is indebted to him (see Chapter 3).

Farce-Comedy

The Brook

The farce-comedy is arguably the most immediate precursor to the modern American musical comedy. Similar to Harrigan's plays, it took the form of a stage comedy or farce with songs. In 1877, Nathan Salsbury brought his Salsbury's Troubadours, which he had founded in London two years earlier, to St. Louis, where they performed a farce-comedy titled *The Brook*. The plot amounts to little more than an excuse to perform a variety of songs: five characters (played by the five Troubadours) go on a picnic outing. They travel by small boat to the chosen destination (Act I), spend a pleasant afternoon there (Act II), and return home (Act III). *The Brook* stood out from the exotic operettas and fanciful burlesques of the period. In Salsbury's own words, "The main object which we strive to attain is the natural reproduction of the jollity and funny mishaps that attend the usual picnic excursion." Farce-comedies provided decent-quality family entertainment. The writers interpolated vernacular songs, eccentric dances, and jokes—the same sort of material found in variety shows. Moreover, farce-comedies were relatively inexpensive to produce and easier to cast than more lavish forms of entertainment.

A Trip to Chinatown

Charles Hoyt's *A Trip to Chinatown* appeared on Broadway in 1891 and subsequently enjoyed an enormously successful nationwide tour. It held the record for being the longest-running Broadway musical for twenty-eight years. *Chinatown* is set in San Francisco and rests on a simple premise: Rashleigh Gay wishes to attend a masquerade ball along with his sister, Tony; his friend Wilder Daly; and Wilder's house girl, Flirt; but he fears that his uncle, the wealthy bachelor Ben Gay, will not permit it. Rashleigh and Wilder offer to accompany the girls to Chinatown, but only as a pretext for attending the ball. Instead, the young men and women dine at a fancy restaurant, the Riche, retrieve masks that were left there for them in advance, and proceed on to the ball. A young widow by the name of Mrs. Guyer has agreed to chaperone the youths, but a letter that she has written to explain the ruse to Rashleigh inadvertently finds its way into the hands of Ben Gay, who interprets it as an invitation to a *tête-à-tête* at the restaurant. The rest of the action, such as it is, involves the performance of songs and dances. Act II, which takes place in the restaurant and involves a lot of hiding behind curtains, anticipates the Harmonia Gardens scene from *Hello, Dolly!* (1964) (see Chapter 9). Act III occurs on a balcony during the ball. When the uncle arrives at the Riche for the rendezvous with the widow, she embarrasses him in front of everyone and teaches him to let the young have their day.

Poster for an 1899 production of *A Trip to China*, featuring various images of the widow, Mrs. Guyer. *Courtesy Library of Congress Prints and Photographs Division, Washington, DC.*

A Trip to Chinatown featured some popular preexisting songs as well as original ones by Hoyt and the composer Percy Gaunt. The songs ran the gambit from a romantic duet called "The Widow" to the drinking ditty "Out for a Racket" to the comic "Reuben and Cynthia" to the famous waltz clog "The Bowery." They served no real dramatic purpose but provided plenty of entertainment. For instance, during the restaurant scene, the widow performs for Welland Strong, an old, sickly friend coerced by Ben Gay into accompanying his nephew and his entourage to Chinatown.

WIDOW: Mr. Strong, this isn't the first time you've been out for a pleasant evening. I see by the way you handle that bottle.

STRONG: When I was on earth I was not obtuse to the redeeming features of wine, women, and song.

RASHLEIGH: Well, be a boy again. We have the wine and women. Give us the song.

And with no further prodding, Strong launches into "2:15." Later, as Ben Gay waits alone at his table for the widow to return, she and her young friends enjoy themselves at a nearby table.

WIDOW: Please pass the salt.

RASHLEIGH: With all my heart.

WIDOW: Just the salt, please.

TONY: Well, here's to all of us!

ALL: Drink hearty.

They toast and then sing:

> Reuben, Reuben, I've a notion
> If the men were sent away,
> Far beyond the stormy ocean,
> Female hearts would all be gay.
> Cynthia, Cynthia, I've been thinking,
> If the men should take that trip,
> All the women in creation,
> Right away would take that ship.

"The Bowery," which predates the show, has nothing whatsoever to do with the plot. It describes an incident in New York's Bowery, infamous as a district of ill repute.

VERSE 1

> Oh! the night that I struck New York,
> I went out for a quiet walk;
> Folks who are "on to" the city say,
> Better by far that I took Broadway;
> But I was out to enjoy the sights,
> There was the Bow'ry ablaze with lights;
> I had one of the devil's own nights!
> I'll never go there anymore.

The catchy refrain (Example 2.2), a waltz clog, is a typical respite from the more detailed narrative of the verse. It is reasonable to assume that, during the long run of *A Trip to Chinatown*, audiences joined in during the singing of the refrain. Despite the show's San Francisco setting, the inclusion of "The Bowery" anticipates the New York–centric nature of musical comedy beginning in the next decade.

Gaiety Theatre Musicals

Musical comedies associated with London's Gaiety Theatre appeared in New York starting in the 1890s and continuing well into the new century. The Gaiety Theatre opened in 1868 and during the first two decades of operation housed a wide range of entertainments. In the early 1890s, George Edwardes (1852–1915), who had worked as an assistant at Richard D'Oyly Carte's Savoy Theatre, home to Gilbert and Sullivan's operettas, took over the management of the theater. He eschewed burlesque in favor of works of a more genteel nature, structurally similar to farce-comedy. The first musical of this type, *In Town*, opened in 1892 at the Prince-of-Wales Theatre (the Gaiety was unavailable). The next year, Edwardes presented *A Gaiety Girl*, also at the Prince-of-Wales Theatre, marketing it as a "musical comedy." In 1894 *The Shop Girl* premiered at the Gaiety Theatre, establishing it as the main venue for this type of musical.

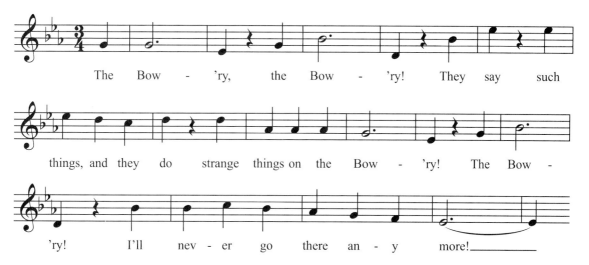

The Bow - 'ry, the Bow - 'ry! They say such things, and they do strange things on the Bow - 'ry! The Bow - 'ry! I'll nev - er go there an - y more!_____

EXAMPLE 2.2. "The Bowery," refrain

A Gaiety Girl had a book by Owen Hall (pseudonym of Jimmy Davis), music by Sidney Jones, and lyrics by Harry Greenbank. The British embraced its outspokenness and modernity. The show depicts a clash between the new social order and the old one, as personified by, respectively, the Gaiety chorus girls (young, attractive actresses dressed in the latest fashion) and a group of haughty single aristocratic women. The latter hope to find suitable husbands among the soldiers stationed at a nearby military barracks. Unbeknownst to each other, both groups of women have been invited to a party by the officers. The ladies of privilege are no match for their alluring nonconformist counterparts, who end up carrying themselves with more dignity than their alleged social betters.

Greenbank and Jones's score owes much to Gilbert and Sullivan. It contains concerted numbers, choral interjections within solos, light arias, and comic numbers. Many songs shift between the meters 2/4 and 6/8 and between major and minor keys. The lyrics revel in feminine rhymes, social commentary, and the insouciant humor associated with Gilbert. The setting, a British military barracks, suggested the sort of rousing opening male chorus found in *H.M.S. Pinafore*. A divorce judge named Sir Lewis is also a guest at the base. Upon his entrance, which is announced by the chorus ("And with all the row that the laws allow, give a hip, hip, hip, hooray!"), he sings the patter song "I'm a Judge of the Modern Society Sort" backed by the chorus.

The Gaiety Theatre repertory appealed to the British middle class and reflected its values. The Gaiety Girls' *joie de vivre* struck a chord with a society on the brink of modernity. The repertory appealed to American audiences for the same reasons. *A Gaiety Girl* played in several major American cities, and a flood of similar works appeared on Broadway between 1895 and 1910, including *The Geisha* (1896) and *Floradora* (1900). Their popularity helped to establish the rising meritocracy as a common subject for musical comedy. They attacked nineteenth-century religious, legal, and political institutions and thereby announced the end of Victorian mores. They also created a vogue for rags-to-riches plots.

The musical theater genres surveyed thus far all center around some sort of linear dramatic narrative. But shows featuring songs and comedy skits with little or no connective story were just as ubiquitous. An assortment of variety entertainments, the forerunners of vaudeville, thrived during the second half of the nineteenth century, none more popular, and disreputable, than the minstrel show.

Minstrel Show

The institution of blackface minstrelsy emerged from theatrical lampoons of the dress, speech, and mannerisms of black slaves and free blacks. White America could not get enough of such caricatures, as well as the harmonies, banjo playing, and shuffle dancing associated with black music. Thomas Dartmouth Rice (1808–1860), a white song-and-dance man, rose to prominence for his performance of Jim Crow, a black character he regularly performed, and popularized blackface impersonations. His Jim Crow act developed around the song "Jump, Jim Crow," which he first sang while appearing in *The Rifle* in 1828. Rice began to write skits and plays that incorporated blackface performers, "Negro" plantation songs, and black dialect. His success led to a proliferation of black impersonators during the 1830s. Soon Rice was writing longer entertainments, which he called "Ethiopian operas." The earliest professional minstrel troupes consisted entirely of white performers who, like Rice, used burnt cork to blacken their faces (a practice referred to as "corking") (see Chapter 15). They performed satirical skits, songs, and dances, claiming to depict urban African Americans as well as rural plantation life.

Variety

Other popular venues that featured variety acts of one kind or another included the circus, showboat, and concert saloon. In the 1840s, theaters were erected expressly to house variety acts. Before long, variety began to emphasize risqué, male-oriented entertainment. Tony Pastor—a former variety performer—responded by presenting "family entertainment." He converted the Bowery Minstrel Hall in New York into Tony Pastor's Opera House. His efforts to "bourgeoisify" variety (make it more appealing to middle-class audiences) led to the professionalization of the genre and eventually gave rise to vaudeville. Harrigan and Hart and the Four Cohans (see Chapter 3) were among the many entertainers who worked for Pastor. Pastor remained in the variety business until 1909. His only serious competition came from B. F. Keith and E. Albee's Union Square Theatre, which offered nonstop vaudeville.

Vaudeville

Vaudeville was the most popular form of entertainment in America at the turn of the twentieth century, playing in nearly 3,000 theaters nationwide. Vaudeville performers led an itinerant existence, traveling from city to city. Organized vaudeville circuits, facilitated by a well-functioning railroad system, ensured the dissemination of the form to all parts of the country. Although vaudeville's heyday was over by 1910, its influence lasted well into the twentieth century, as performers and writers went on to work in radio, movies, and eventually television. Being the most democratic and racially integrated show business institution, vaudeville introduced the country to a wide and diverse range of talent, including George M. Cohan (Irish) (see Chapter 3), Bert Williams (African American) (see Chapter 4), and Al Jolson (Jewish) (see Chapter 17). Vaudeville also helped to homogenize popular entertainment by introducing the same songs and dances to different parts of the nation. Performers worked closely with music publishers to plug songs, an arrangement that continued on Broadway well into the twentieth century.

Song Plugger

Music publishing houses employed song pluggers to sing songs for potential customers, including entertainers looking for fresh material. Both Irving Berlin and George Gershwin worked as song pluggers early in their music careers. The job title still exists, but the duties have evolved over the years.

CONCLUSION

Throughout its history, American musical theater has been a highly eclectic genre, ranging from operatic works to revues to acrobatics. Even today, song-and-dance entertainment and story-driven musicals still comfortably coexist on Broadway. All of the forms examined in this chapter contributed to the birth of musical comedy at the dawn of the twentieth century. Attempting to privilege any one of them as the primary model is not only futile, but it also disregards historical reality. The Broadway musical is an intrinsically American phenomenon in that it resulted from the melding of several diverse forms. It is also a site where art and commerce intersect, not to mention highbrow and lowbrow, white and black, and rich and poor.

NAMES, TERMS, AND CONCEPTS

Black Crook, The	Harrigan, Edward
black face	Hoyt, Charles
burlesque	minstrel show
Emmett, Dan	Mulligan plays
Evangeline	Operetta
farce-comedy	Pastor, Tony
Gaiety Theatre shows	*Trip to Chinatown, A*
Gilbert and Sullivan	vaudeville

DISCUSSION QUESTIONS

1. Identify the influences of nineteenth-century musical theater entertainment on musical theater during the twentieth century.

2. Discuss the historical legacy of the minstrel show and its lingering impact on American popular culture.

CHAPTER 3

BROADWAY AT THE TURN OF THE CENTURY

(*LITTLE JOHNNY JONES*, 1904, LIBERTY THEATRE, 52 PERFORMANCES)

New York at the turn of the twentieth century was poised to become America's cultural capital and main economic engine. In 1898, the five boroughs that make up New York City today (Manhattan, the Bronx, Brooklyn, Queens, and Staten Island) came together to form a single metropolis with a population of nearly three and a half million people. New York's meteoric rise coincided with the dawn of the modern era and epitomized all that it entailed, a vibrant middle class, a shift from the industrial age to an era of corporate consolidation of wealth and power, and an unprecedented intermingling of different classes and ethnicities. The new, bourgeoning metropolis was home to a third of the country's major companies. Immigrants were streaming into the city in record numbers (the vast majority of immigrants coming to the U.S. came by way of New York, and many settled there). The Interborough Rapid Transit System (IRT) was under construction. New York, like its skyscrapers, symbolized the actualization of the American Dream and the audacious belief in America's destiny. For the first time, theatrical producers could count on New York to generate the sort of profits that they could heretofore count on only through touring productions.

Before the advent of sound recordings, radio, and film, live musical theater entertainment dominated America's cultural landscape, and it was as diverse as the American-born and immigrant audiences that attended it. The corporate consolidation of the means of theatrical production at the start of the century and the attendant centralization of the theater industry in New York transformed musical theater into a more homogenous form of entertainment. Revues, musical comedies, and operettas emerged as the most popular forms, and each one relied on conventions and patterns that made the rapid mass production of musicals possible and profitable. It was at this time that "Broadway" became a major space of cultural production.

MUSICAL COMEDY

Musical comedy at the dawn of the new century was a slapdash, unrefined affair, for the most part incapable of meeting the artistic demands and critical standards of good theater. The quality of musical comedy production had declined so much that critics lamented the death of the genre. Book writers remained indifferent to dramaturgical concerns, treating stories as mere scaffolding for the performance of songs, dances, and comedy routines. The stories, which mostly dealt with modernity and contemporary values, aroused a passing interest, but the songs and dances were interpolated without dramatic justification.

Thus was the state of musical comedy when a young George M. Cohan began his career as a vaudeville entertainer in 1889. Around 1900, Cohan turned to writing and within a few years ushered in a new era for the Broadway musical. Musical comedies from England, especially works associated with the Gaiety Theatre (see Chapter 2), continued to enjoy sustained popularity in New York. They centered on young lovers who overcome some authoritarian figure's objections to their union. Cohan Americanized this type of plot and created shows that captured the country's strong sense of individualism and democratic ethos.

George M. Cohan

Background

"Hero of the footlights," "Yankee Doodle Boy," "ultimate showman," "first auteur of the American musical," "Yankee Doodle Comedian"—these are just some of the honorifics ascribed to George M. Cohan (1878–1942). Cohan personified the meritocratic ethos of his age. The critic Arthur Hornblow wrote in 1919 that Cohan "represents the restless American spirit, the cheeky, go-aheadedness of the hustling Yankee." Adjectives such as "brash," "abrasive," and "patriotic" describe both Cohan and his brand of musical comedy, which provided a refreshing contrast to the more genteel English farce-comedies. Cohan embraced modern, New World values and rejected the Victorian sense of decorum, but he paid a price for his insouciance. Critics accused him of vulgarity and crassness. They found him, to quote Cohan's own words, "a swaggering, impudent, noisy vaudevillian, entirely out of place in first-class theatres," but he found comfort in the approbation of his adoring fans.

Cohan was born in Providence, Rhode Island, to Jerry and Nellie Cohan (Helen Frances Costigan), both Irish American variety performers. Jerry Cohan had served as an orderly during the Civil War and appeared as "The Ethiopian Comedian" in minstrel shows before entering vaudeville in the 1870s. He soon met and married Nellie, who, being a good storyteller, began to appear alongside her husband. In 1889, George and his sister Josie (Josephine) joined the act. Originally called the "Cohan Mirth Makers," the family foursome became one of the most sought-after attractions in vaudeville. Renamed the Four Cohans, they played this program for a total of six hundred one-night stands.

Their act featured George's buck-and-wing dancing (a precursor to tap dancing) and an original comedy with songs and dances called *Goggles Doll House*. Cohan's dancing covered the entire width of the stage and sometimes continued up the

The Four Cohans, *l to r*: Helen (Nellie), Josephine (Josie), Jerry, and George. *Courtesy Library of Congress Prints and Photographs Division, Washington, DC.*

proscenium. He sang with great confidence, but he produced a distinct nasal timbre and tended to speak-sing rather than vocalize on sustained pitches.

George soon turned to writing skits and composing songs. Lacking any formal writing training, he developed his craft through trial and error, paying close attention to audience response. In 1892, he had the opportunity to observe firsthand the evolution of Henry Guy Carleton's *A Guided Fool* from rehearsal to opening night. The play starred the comic actor Nat Goodwin, whose acting style influenced Cohan's. Cohan recalled: "It was the first time I had ever got a slant on how plays were doctored and pulled together." Later that year, Cohan encountered the playwright Dion Boucicault. Forgotten today, Boucicault's plays appealed to audiences through a mixture of sentimentality, humor, and spirited song. Cohan appeared in two of them and later acknowledged Boucicault's influence on his own dramaturgical formula: "[Boucicault] tells a story quickly, he gives you some basic, exciting emotion, good plot twists, with a *lot* of laughter and some charming songs. And, above all, thank God above all, Boucicault is fun." George had no more background in songwriting than in playwriting, but in short order he discovered his voice and achieved tremendous success. A typical Cohan song features vernacular lyrics, an upbeat melody in the major key, non-fussy harmonic progressions, and an anti-elitist sentiment.

When Cohan turned twenty, he met his soon-to-be wife, Ethel Levey. She joined the act as soon as they were married. He assumed greater control over the family's professional activities and wrote short plays for the Four Cohans to perform. The legitimate theater world of Broadway beckoned, and George was ready to answer the call.

Cohan's conversion from actor to writer coincided with the formation of Broadway as a special site of cultural production, the result of a concentration of wealth coupled with a rising professional class that Cohan himself personified. For this expanding group of eager, upwardly mobile Americans, mostly university-educated men and their wives, theater became one of the cultural rituals that confirmed their identity within the social fabric of New York and the nation, an act of self-fulfillment, and a way of preserving a sense of middle-class identity and expressing their sense of entitlement. Musical theater, as a highly collaborative art form dependent on the close cooperation of experts, skilled laborers, and thinking practitioners (director, scenic designer, orchestrator, and actor), mirrored successful corporate models of operations. Cohan, the consummate Broadway professional, embodied the new habitus of America's emerging middle class. He also personified the patriotic spirit embraced by immigrant and native-born Americans.

Cohan's first musical for New York was *The Governor's Son* (1901), which was merely an expanded version of a vaudeville skit that he had written for the Four Cohans. The plot was "a confusing narrative labyrinth," according to Gerald Bordman. Although the show closed prematurely in New York, it turned a decent profit on the road and brought Cohan a degree of respect. George's next Broadway venture, *Running for Office* (1903), also based on an earlier vaudeville sketch, centers on parallel romances between a widow and widower and their two children. Despite having a better script, *Running for Office* played only slightly longer (forty-eight performances) than *The Governor's Son*.

Little Johnny Jones

Having achieved a modicum of success as a writer, the young Cohan felt confident enough to create a musical from scratch, and a newspaper account about the American jockey Tod Sloan inspired the plot. *Little Johnny Jones* (1904) epitomizes Cohan's brand of musical theater. Not only does the boy get the girl, but he also reaffirms his faith in American justice. The romantic storyline has roots in British musical comedy, but Cohan infused it with an American sense of fair play and egalitarianism. Establishing the formula for his subsequent musicals, the score features up-to-the-minute popular musical styles and vernacular dialogue. Rousing marches in 2/4 expressed Cohan's love of America, and waltz ballads tapped into the sentimentality and lyric traditions of Irish nationals and American-born Irish. In *Little Johnny Jones* and subsequent musical comedies, Cohan expressed his exuberant love of America in rousing, upbeat numbers, some of which weave together snatches of traditional tunes and original material. Critics complained about Cohan's vainglorious patriotism, but he proudly defended it as a means of reaching the common people. He similarly defended his flagrant use of slang, another source of consternation for Cohan's detractors. Cohan's image and popularity relied on the patriotic narrative that he himself cultivated.

Little Johnny Jones exemplifies Cohan's signature brisk-moving action. A chorus of ladies and gentlemen opens the show by announcing the time and place ("The Cecil in London Town"). The taut exposition that follows wastes little time in establishing the protagonists, antagonists, and dramatic conflict. Characters appear, announce who they are and why they are present in a couple of lines (or a song), and then make way for the action to advance. *Little Johnny Jones* is in three acts, the first set in London, the second in Southampton, and the third in San Francisco's Chinatown. About halfway into the first act, Anstey, Jones's dastardly nemesis, delivers an aside that reveals his motive. His sinister demeanor comes straight out of nineteenth-century melodrama.

> Laugh on my proud beauty. He who laughs screams with delight. You'll close up 'Frisco's china Lottery, will you? Cheat me out of one hundred thousand dollars a year, will you? Wait till you are Mrs. Anstey. I'll soon teach you and your crusading band of fool women to stay at home and mind your own damn business. McGee wants Jones. He shan't have him. I'll pay that jockey more money than any man of the American turf.

Shortly thereafter, the energy builds as Jones's first entrance nears. Jones greets his pal, Timothy McGee, exclaiming that he is "fine and dandy. Boston nobby. Fat and fine and splendid." When a throng of young American ladies arrives, Johnny gives them a friendly racing tip: "Pawn your jewelry, go into hock, and play Yankee Doodle to win!"

PLOT OF LITTLE JOHNNY JONES

The musical opens at the Cecil Hotel in London. The villain, Anthony Anstey, who controls the gambling scene in San Francisco, has gotten engaged to a wealthy American widow and president of the San Francisco Female Reformers, Mrs. Kenworth, in order to put a stop to her activist social agenda. He also hopes to marry off her niece, Goldie Gates, to the wealthy Earl of Bloomsbury, but she has fallen in love with the jockey Johnny Jones during a race in San Francisco. Jones returns her affection.

Goldie has traveled to England to see Jones race in the Derby. In order to avoid detection from her aunt, Goldie disguises herself first as a Parisian woman and then as the very man she is supposed to marry. Anstey tries to get Jones to pull the race, but the jockey loses fair and square. Anstey accuses Jones of rigging the race and intentionally losing. Anstey, Mrs. Kenworth, Goldie, and Johnny's friends debark on a ship for New York, but Johnny stays in England in order to clear his name. A detective working for the racing commission turns up evidence that proves Anstey's guilt. Back in San Francisco, Goldie has been kidnapped by Anstey, and an extensive search ensures. Johnny eventually finds her, and all ends well for the couple.

Cohan starred in *Little Johnny Jones,* but he allowed the other actors (including the members of his family) some show-stealing moments. For instance, Tom Lewis (b. 1860), a former blackface minstrel show entertainer, played a detective and delighted audiences with his droll delivery and simulated intoxication. Of course, Cohan reserved some of the best songs for himself, "A Yankee Doodle Dandy," "Give My Regards to Broadway," and "Life's a Funny Proposition," a philosophical rumination on life's unpredictabilities and pitfalls.

Jones's spirited flag-waving barely disguises a certain anti-English sentiment. In his first appearance, Jones launches into "Yankee Doodle Dandy," singing a brisk eighth-note pattern that brazenly quotes the main theme of the Revolutionary-era tune "Yankee Doodle" (Example 3.1). The borrowed line was meant to evoke the long-standing American and Irish hostility toward the British. In the 1700s, the British redcoats taunted American colonists by singing "Yankee Doodle" set to derogatory lyrics, but when the tide of the Revolutionary War turned against them, the colonists returned the insult by using the same song to mock the British. Cohan answers the quoted phrase with an original melody (mm. 4–7). This phrase lands heavily on the rhymes "am" and "Sam," which occupies the highest note of the melody up to this point in the song. Jones next sings a strain from "Dixie" and, to round off the verse, the opening of "The Star-Spangled Banner." The refrain (ABAC) echoes the sentiments of the verse, beginning "I'm a Yankee Doodle Dandy" on a catchy march tune. The final phrase is another "Yankee Doodle" quote, set a fourth higher. "Yankee Doodle Dandy," which is arguably more integrated into the story than most musical comedy songs at the time, defines who Johnny Jones is and explains what he is doing in England: he has come to defend himself and his country against Old World snobbery.

EXAMPLE 3.1. "Yankee Doodle Dandy," (a) verse, first eight measures (b) refrain, first eight measures

The second-act finale of *Little Johnny Jones* is the stuff of musical theater legend. The scene, taking place at Southampton Pier, features "Give My Regards to Broadway," an homage to America as embodied by Broadway. Johnny, who has decided to remain in England in order to clear his name, watches from the pier as the ship carrying his bride-to-be departs for America without him. Whitney Wilson, seemingly an aimless drunk but actually a private detective in disguise working for the racing commission, has discovered that Anstey rigged the Derby and suspects that he framed Johnny. He informs Jones that he will shoot a flare into the air from the deck of the ship as soon as he has obtained Anstey's confession of his crime. As Jones awaits Wilson's signal, he sings a slow, melancholy version of "Give My Regards to Broadway," but after he sees the sky light up, he delivers a spirited, up-tempo reprise.

"Give My Regards to Broadway" epitomizes the combination of sentimentality and swagger found in many of Cohan's songs. The memorable tune moves primarily by step, reserving wider intervals for key points in the lyric (Example 3.2). The largest interval occurs in the last phrase (C), effectively preparing the listener for the final cadence. This phrase ("Give my regards to old Broadway and say that I'll be there ere long") not only occupies the highest range of the song but also contains the only non-diatonic pitches. The underlying harmony tonicizes the subdominant and helps to drive the song to its satisfying conclusion.

Little Johnny Jones played only fifty-two performances during its initial run on Broadway, but Cohan brought a revised version back to New York several times over the next couple of years. The show marked the beginning of Cohan's long professional association with the producer Sam H. Harris. Harris and Cohan complemented each other temperamentally and professionally, and together they built a theater empire.

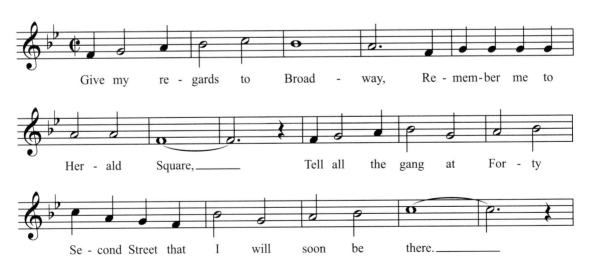

EXAMPLE 3.2. "Give My Regards to Broadway," refrain, first sixteen measures

Cohan's Career During the Twenties and Thirties

The most acrimonious period of Cohan's career occurred in 1919 when New York actors staged a four-week strike, which eventually led to the formal recognition of Actors' Equity Association as the official bargaining unit for professional thespians. Cohan sided with management, which drew the ire of many show people, some of whom never forgave him for siding with the opposition. The strike caused the suspension of sixty productions, including Cohan's *The Royal Vagabond*. Cohan suffered emotional scars from the personal attacks leveled at him. None of the threats or aspersions hurt him more than the opposition he faced from members of the Lambs and Friars, two professional theatrical clubs from which he felt pressure to resign. Cohan eventually rejoined the clubs, but he never joined Equity. As a producer, Cohan, who had always felt a close affinity for his fellow actors, never recognized Actors' Equity's legitimate right to organize. His anti-union stance also led to the dissolution of his partnership with Harris.

Cohan's first play following the strike, *Genius and the Crowd* (1920), did poorly. He interpreted its failure as a sign that the theater he once knew was a thing of the past: "I guess people don't understand me anymore, and I don't understand them. It's got so that an evening's entertainment just won't do. Give an audience an evening of what they call realism and you've got a hit. It's getting to be too much for me, kid." Cohan felt that Broadway had been "everything in life I've never had: my education, and the friendships, games, adventures, and just plain fun of boyhood and growing up." It was difficult for him to let go and to embrace the changes.

Cohan continued to write new plays and musicals as well as "Cohanize" plays written by others (which amounted to modifying the leading role to accommodate his signature performing style, interpolating jokes, and infusing the dialogue with American idioms). However, by 1920 his best days as a writer had passed, and he was not predisposed to adopting the bleaker sentiments and naturalistic style of American drama during the twenties and thirties. He began to rely on formula and self-referential humor. As one of Cohan's biographers notes, "there are too many convenient telephone calls, too many people eavesdropping, too many characters fortuitously able to come into the core of the action when needed." In *The Merry Malones*, a young actor looks at the audience and sings, "Ev'ry little play has got a plot / So a little plot this play has got." Cohan understood that he could not compete against a new generation of composers that included the likes of Jerome Kern, Richard Rodgers, and George Gershwin, and that he was no match for playwrights such as George S. Kaufman and Marc Connelly. He attempted to revive the innocence and wide-eyed optimism of the days of *Little Johnny Jones*, but Broadway had moved on.

In the early thirties, Cohan gave Hollywood a try, appearing in the film *The Phantom President* (1932), which boasted a Rodgers and Hart score. The next year, he played Nat Miller in the Theatre Guild's production of Eugene O'Neill's *Ah, Wilderness!* In 1937, Cohan appeared on Broadway as Franklin D. Roosevelt in Rodgers and Hart's *I'd Rather Be Right*. He was reluctant at first to depict the then-sitting U.S. president, whom he did not fully support, but he was too shrewd to turn down a good opportunity. During the production, Cohan treated Rodgers and Hart with disdain, a reflection perhaps of his inability to see himself replaced by younger writers.

In 1936, Cohan received the Congressional Medal of Honor for his World War I songs "It's a Grand Old Flag" and "Over There," although it took him nearly three years to appear at the White House to accept his award from President Roosevelt, the man he had begrudgingly portrayed in 1937. Two years later, Warner Brothers released *Yankee Doodle Dandy*, a hagiographic biopic about Cohan. As Cohan stipulated, the film excluded the most personal details about his life. More entertaining than historically accurate, the film earned James Cagney an Academy Award for his portrayal of the great showman. Cohan saw the film shortly before he passed away from colon cancer. A year later, *Oklahoma!* opened on Broadway, and Cohan's light on Broadway dimmed forever.

OPERETTA

Operetta suffered a decline in popularity at the turn of the century, but the downturn reversed itself in 1907, the year in which Franz Lehár's *The Merry Widow* (*Die Lustige Witwe*) made its American debut. Set in Paris, this popular Viennese operetta, based on Henri Meilhac's *L'attaché d'ambassade* (1861), mixes international diplomacy and romance. The plot concerns the future marital status of Hanna Glawari, the widow of the title, who is living the charmed life in Paris. The possibility that she could marry a foreigner and take her fortune out of Pontevedro causes her country's Paris delegation considerable consternation. Their solution is to find her a suitable Pontevedrian to marry. They hope that Count Danilo Danilovich, whom she once loved but was forbidden to marry, will once again sweep her off her feet. He eventually does, but only after protecting his pride and concealing his love for nearly three acts.

The Merry Widow was an unequivocal hit, and it reversed the flagging interest in operetta. Reginald de Koven (see Chapter 2), America's leading native-born operetta composer at the time, publically praised *Widow*: "The dramatic purpose and coherency . . . came like water in the desert after the tawdry musical inanities which have pervaded and infested Broadway for some years. . . . [B]ook and music are welded together into an organic, artistic whole." Of the few operettas still regularly performed today, *The Merry Widow* counts among the most beloved.

Producers, hoping to capitalize on *The Merry Widow*'s success, began to look for similar works. De Koven had shifted his interest from operetta to opera. Filling the void was the Irish-born composer Victor Herbert (1859–1924). Herbert grew up in London and studied music in Germany, but he immigrated to America in 1886 at the age of twenty-seven, originally to play cello in the Metropolitan Opera orchestra. Despite Herbert's birth in Ireland, the literature treats him as an American composer. Herbert had his first Broadway hit with *Babes in Toyland* (1903). His next major triumph, *Naughty Marietta* (1910), was one of the first operettas with an American setting. Waltzes and marches dominate Herbert's scores, but the composer was not averse to writing music in the American vernacular, such as ragtime and comedy songs.

REVUE

Florenz Ziegfeld, Jr. (1867–1932) produced his first *Follies* in 1907. He took his inspiration from a series of annual Parisian revues, the Folies-Bergère, which

The Ziegfeld Girls crowned by Will Rogers in the *Ziegfeld Follies of* 1924. *Courtesy KB Archives.*

featured titillating displays of feminine beauty and satirized the preceding year's cultural, social, and political highpoints with a myriad of specialty acts. Literature on the revue genre emphasizes its mixture of songs, dances, and comic skits, but several early revues were unified by an overriding theme, or at least a sense of purpose. Some revues even had a plot, albeit a flimsy one. As the word implies, a revue (the term "review" was used until producers adopted the French "revue") incorporated topical humor and centered on current events. Revues satirized plays, operas, and "contemporary foibles and follies." Whereas vaudeville and variety (which targeted the male trade) never gained acceptance as "legitimate" theater, the revue, especially the Ziegfeldian type, acquired a degree of legitimacy and enjoyed great success on Broadway for over two decades.

Ziegfeld originally produced his *Follies* as summer entertainment for a mostly male clientele. The first edition of the *Follies* starred his wife, Anna Held, and boasted a book by Harry B. Smith (see Chapter 2). Having discovered his niche, Ziegfeld produced a new *Follies* almost every season until 1931, for a total of twenty-one editions (several later revues borrowed the Ziegfeld name, the last one in 1957). He brought a sense of balance to the revue format. The *Follies* paraded beautiful women in the latest fashions, but it also featured top-notch talent such as Eddie Cantor and W. C. Fields.

Songwriters such as Irving Berlin were among the luminaries who furnished songs for the *Follies*. The designer Joseph Urban began working for Ziegfeld in 1915 and introduced the sleek, modern style of Art Deco to scenic design. The *Follies* faced stiff competition from the Shubert brothers' *Passing Show*, the *George White Scandals* (thirteen editions between 1919 and 1939), the *Greenwich Village Follies* (eight editions between 1919 and 1928), and the *Earl Carrol Vanities* (nine editions between 1923 and 1940). By offering erotic voyeurism in the guise of classy entertainment, these revues transferred the illicit nudity of burlesque into a socially acceptable venue.

The year 1907 was a seminal time for American musical theater. Ziegfeld brought respectability and popularity to the revue, *The Merry Widow* ignited a renewed passion for operetta, and *Little Johnny Jones* played on Broadway for the third time and reaffirmed George M. Cohan's preeminence in the musical comedy domain. By the end of the decade, musical comedy, operetta, and revue were all enjoying great popularity. However, musical comedy was beginning to suffer again from formulaic plots and songs, and it took a new generation of writers led by Jerome Kern to advance the genre toward greater sophistication.

GEORGE LEDERER

George Lederer's Casino Theatre was the first Broadway theater to house revues. Lederer inaugurated his theater during the summer of 1894 with *The Passing Show*, which, unlike most revues, had music, lyrics, and book by a single writer, Sydney Rosenfeld. Rosenfeld's script parodied the popular English play *Sowing the Wind* by Sydney Grundy, which dealt with a father's attempt to keep his daughter from entering into a particular marriage. Rosenfeld's story, such as it was, connected songs and sketches, including one in which Gus Pixley walked with "his head near his heels" and another that featured "Acrobatic Burlesques of the Amazons." Notwithstanding its story-specific material, *The Passing Show* was essentially a variety show, and it had something for everyone. It also established the summer months as an ideal time for variety entertainment.

Building on his success with the *Passing Show*, Lederer joined with Thomas Canary to produce a second revue, *The Merry World* (billed as the "Second Annual Summer Review"), which had a script by Edgar Smith and a score by William Furst. It featured parodies (or "travesties") of popular plays from the previous theatrical season. *The Merry World* drew large Jewish audiences, so much so that a planned "Hebrew" act performed by David Warfield was not included. Lederer and Canary's next revue, *In Gay New York* ("3rd Annual Review"), took audiences on a musical tour of the city. The perfunctory plot, by Hugh Morton, began with a wedding and followed the bride and groom on their honeymoon in New York, with a finale set at Coney Island. *In Gay New York* spawned several imitations and generated demand for similar extravaganzas.

AND BEAR IN MIND

The Chocolate Soldier *(1909, Lyric Theatre, 296 performances)*

Music by Oscar Straus
Original German libretto (*Der Tapfere Soldat*)
by Rudolph Bernauer and Leopold Jacks [Jacobson]
Translation by Stanislau Stange

Edith Bradford as Mascha in the 1909 Broadway production of *The Chocolate Soldier. Courtesy Library of Congress, Prints and Photographs Division.*

The Chocolate Soldier, an operetta based on George Bernard Shaw's play *Arms and the Man* (1894), opened in New York nearly fifty years before *My Fair Lady*, the most famous musical based on one of Shaw's plays. The operetta premiered in Vienna in 1908 and remained popular for decades, with no fewer than six Broadway revivals between 1910 and 1947. Despite its popularity, Shaw detested the operetta and vowed never to allow another one of his plays to be musicalized. Only after his death in 1950 did his estate agree to the musical adaptation of *Pygmalion* (and later *Anthony and Cleopatra*).

The plot of *The Chocolate Soldier* typifies operetta. It takes place during the Serbo-Bulgarian War and involves aristocratic characters and romantic intrigue. The Bulgarian aristocrat Nadina (originally Raina) is engaged to a handsome but supercilious soldier named Alexius Spiridoff, but when a Swiss mercenary in the Serbian army named Bumerli, who carries chocolate instead of ammunition, seeks her help, she hides him in her bedroom and soon falls in love with him. After the war, she loses interest in Spiridoff and marries the less pompous Bumerli.

Straus's score boasted several popular numbers, including the waltz "My Hero," the duet "That Would Be Lovely," the trio "Romanze," and the sextet "The Tale of a Coat." A Hollywood version of *The Chocolate Soldier* was released in 1941, but with most of Shaw's story excised.

NAMES, TERMS, AND CONCEPTS

Actors' Equity Association

Broadway theater district

Chocolate Soldier, The

Cohan, George M.

De Koven, Reginald

Four Cohans, The

"Give My Regards to Broadway"

Herbert, Victor

Interborough Rapid Transit System (IRT)

Lehár, Franz

Little Johnny Jones

Manhattan, Brooklyn, Queens, the Bronx, and Staten Island

The Merry Widow

"Yankee Doodle Dandy"

Ziegfeld, Florenz

Ziegfeld Follies

DISCUSSION QUESTIONS

1. Distinguish between musical comedy, revue, and operetta in the early twentieth century.

2. How did George M. Cohan transform the English farce-comedy and other nineteenth-century musical theater entertainments into his unique brand of musical comedy?

3. Explain why George M. Cohan's musicals resonated with America's sense of patriotism and modernity.

4. How did the centralization of the theater industry in New York City at the turn of the twentieth century influence the production of musical theater?

CHAPTER 4

THE TEENS
(*VERY GOOD EDDIE*, 1915, PRINCESS THEATRE, 341 PERFORMANCES)

By 1910, musical comedy was once again suffering from formulaic plots, bland songs, and stale jokes. George M. Cohan's best days as a musical comedy writer were behind him. When *The Little Millionaire*, his eleventh musical, opened in 1911, critics bemoaned, "same old Cohan." New musicals generated profits, but they offered more of the same in terms of content, as producers preferred reliability to innovation. The most acclaimed and popular musical comedies from the early teens, Karl Hoschna and Otto Harbach's *Madame Sherry* (1910) and Ivan Caryll's *The Pink Lady* (1911), were entirely forgotten by the end of the decade (a silent film version of the former was released in 1917). Many musicals from the period were mere vehicles for box-office stars such as Marie Cahill and Eddie Foy. Vernon and Irene Castle mesmerized audiences with renditions of the Turkey Trot, foxtrot, and Bunny Hug, but the shows in which they appeared were unremarkable.

Operetta fared no better than musical comedy, limping along until the onset of World War I, which doomed the prospects for anything with European associations, especially Viennese. Victor Herbert remained a popular operetta composer, but none of his works from the decade surpassed the popularity of his earlier hits. Rudolph Friml made a name for himself in 1912 with *The Firefly*, and Sigmund Romberg also appeared on the scene, but operetta did not fully regain its former stature until the twenties (see chapter 5).

On the other hand, it was a favorable time for revues. Ziegfeld continued to produce his annual *Follies*, and competitors inaugurated their own yearly series (see Chapter 3). Ziegfeld's comic headliners, opulent scenery and costumes, and displays of feminine beauty—epitomized by the "Ziegfeld Girls"—continued to delight audiences. The Ziegfeld name became synonymous with the motto "glorifying the American girl." The impresario also had an eye for talent, and several of the artists he booked went on to illustrious careers. The 1910 edition of the *Follies* featured the Jewish comedian Fanny Brice (1891–1951), whose life later provided the basis

EARLY BROADWAY STARS

Marie Cahill (1870–1933) started out in vaudeville and made a successful transition to Broadway. She developed a reputation for comic repartee and as a "coon shouter" (see Chapters 5 and 17).

Eddie Foy (1854–1928), famous for his comic skills and acrobatic dancing, also made the leap from vaudeville to Broadway. In 1912, Foy began touring with his children in an act billed as "Eddie and the Seven Little Foys."

Vernon Blythe (1887–1918) and Irene Foote (1893–1969) met in 1910 and married the next year. As the husband-and-wife dance team known as Vernon and Irene Castle, they popularized ballroom dancing in America and Europe and introduced several new dances, including the Castle Walk and the Maxie. Their career might have reached further heights had Vernon not perished in a plane crash during World War I.

ZIEGFELD FOLLIES *STARS*

Bert Williams (1874?–1922) began his stage career in minstrel shows, but he moved on to vaudeville and Broadway. Williams's comic talents are legendary, and he is remembered for his self-deprecating signature song "Nobody." At a time when few black entertainers appeared on Broadway, Williams performed alongside white actors.

The avuncular Will Rogers (1879–1935) built a lasting legacy as a humorist and folk philosopher. Part Cherokee, he began his stage career performing cowboy tricks in a Wild West show. Ziegfeld featured Rogers in the *Follies* between 1916 and 1924. Rogers also performed on the radio, wrote a newspaper column, and appeared in films.

Ann Pennington (1893–1971) was a stage and early screen performer. After appearing in vaudeville, she made her Broadway debut in the *Ziegfeld Follies* of 1913.

Ed Wynn (1886–1966), best known today as Uncle Albert in the 1965 movie *Mary Poppins*, was a popular Broadway entertainer. Shows were constructed around him and his comic affectations, such as his signature lisp and giggle.

for the 1964 musical *Funny Girl*, and the African American comic actor Bert Williams. Over the years, Will Rogers, Marilynn Miller (see Chapter 5), Ann Pennington, and Ed Wynn appeared in the *Follies*; Irving Berlin, Sigmund Romberg, and Jerome Kern were among the celebrated composers to supply the music.

In 1911, the Shubert brothers opened the Winter Garden Theatre with a revue entitled *La Belle Paree*. Ticket sales were so brisk that in 1912 they inaugurated an annual revue called the *Passing Show*, appropriating the name from the venerated 1894 variety show (see Chapter 3). Other producers quickly jumped on the bandwagon and established their own annual revues, with tantalizing titles such as *Hitchy-Koo* and *George White's Scandals*.

It was during this period that Jerome Kern (1885–1945) emerged as the preeminent Broadway composer of his generation. Kern had written songs that were interpolated into shows by other composers, but by the late teens his talents became increasingly in demand. Kern's first publically acknowledged Broadway credit came in 1914 when he and the lyricist Herbert Reynolds (1867–1933) (pseudonym of Michael E. Rourke) wrote five songs for *The Girl from Utah*, a musical about a

George Gershwin (left) and Jerome Kern in 1933. *Courtesy Library of Congress Prints and Photographs Division, Washington, DC.*

woman who flees Utah for London in order to escape a prearranged marriage. One of their contributions to the show, the immortal "They Didn't Believe Me," popularized a new type of song, the moderate foxtrot ballad in 4/4. People admired its "un-Viennese freshness," as one commentator put it. This and other songs from this period mark a distinct shift in Kern's music to longer melodic phrases, motivic development, and goal-oriented lines. The foxtrot ballad replaced the march and waltz as the preferred mode for expressing romantic sentiments.

In 1912 Kern received his first opportunity to compose an entire musical comedy when the Shuberts hired him to write the score for *The Red Petticoat*, a comedy based on Rida Johnson Young's *Next*, a play about gold miners in Nevada. Kern composed ensembles and extended musical scenes, the sort of material typical of operetta, even though the story takes place in American territory and the libretto incorporates vernacular dialogue. Kern's next Broadway assignment, *Oh, I Say!*, had a libretto by the ubiquitous Harry B. Smith based on a

Rida Johnson Young (born Ida Louise Johnson) (1869–1926), who hailed from Baltimore, became one of the few successful women wordsmiths on Broadway in the early twentieth century. She collaborated with several leading operetta composers, including Victor Herbert, Sigmund Romberg, and Rudolf Friml.

French farce (see Chapter 2). The show fared little better than *The Red Petticoat*, although it has the distinction of being one of the first musicals to use saxophones. Kern's third musical, *Ninety in the Shade* (1915), marks his first collaboration with Guy Bolton. Bolton was new to musical comedy, but he shared Kern's views on the state of the genre. Among other things, they objected to the mindless interpolation of songs that had nothing to do with the story. Kern's first opportunity to rid musical comedy of its worst practices came when producers Ray Comstock and Elisabeth Marbury asked him to compose the score for a new type of musical that they planned to produce at the Princess Theatre. Their endeavor coaxed the American musical out of its infancy and moved it in the direction of a mature art form. As Lee Davis observes, "The coming of *Oklahoma!* in 1943 was vividly important to the American musical theater. . . . But the *original* concept, the tightly expressed idea of a contemporary, integrated musical theater, where book and music and lyrics are equal and interdependent, was born in the mind of Jerome Kern, twenty-four years earlier."

PRINCESS THEATRE MUSICALS

The Princess Theatre was designed by the architect William A. Swasey and built for the purpose of housing children's plays and Grand Guignol (graphic horror entertainment). With financial backing from the Shuberts, William Brady, and Arch Selwyn (a founder of Goldwyn Pictures), construction of the theater, which was located at 104 West 39th Street, began in 1912. Swasey fashioned an intimate 299-seat auditorium, a relatively small stage, and a blue and off-white interior. The theater's diminutive proportions fostered a more realistic mode of acting and intimate style of singing than was possible in larger Broadway houses. The Princess opened its doors in 1913 with a group of one-act plays. Because the production was only a modest success, Brady and Selwyn quickly dumped their shares in the theater. Ray Comstock, the manager of the theater, started to book silent movies. Meanwhile, Elisabeth Marbury (1856–1933), one of Broadway's first female producers, was suing Comstock over a plagiarism issue regarding the aforementioned one-act plays. They settled the case quickly and began working on what would become the most important musical comedy venture of the decade.

Like Kern and Bolton, Marbury hoped to elevate the literary quality of musical theater. She observed, "Various societies are doing their best to elevate the legitimate drama. It seems to me that now is the time for some one [*sic*] to do the same thing to musical comedy, which has gone along for years in its poor old way, with its same old jokes, its same old stage settings." She envisioned a series of intimate, sophisticated works modeled on the Gaiety Theatre musicals (see Chapter 2).

The Princess Theatre musicals, as they are collectively called, merit attention because they mark an important step in the advancement of the genre. They portrayed the rarefied world and reflected the refined tastes of the upper-class audience for which they were intended. The books were smart, with modern characters, crisp and urbane dialogue, and swift-moving action set in a respectable and prosperous milieu. These musicals employed a small orchestra (some sources put the number of musicians at eleven). Most important, the songs in these musicals relate to the plot to a degree unheard of in earlier musical comedy. The dramatic tension of the plots stems from the threat of impropriety ("innocence mistaken for vice," as one critic describes it), a favorite theme at the time. Divided into two acts, the action unfolds in a variety of familiar locales such as a department store, a leisure boat heading up the Hudson River, and a private college. The leading characters represent the modern upwardly mobile American. The main couple is young, attractive, and in the throes of early love. The secondary couple is more experienced in the ways of the world. If a third pair of lovers is included, it is comic in nature. The leading male character usually finds himself entangled in some complication. The leading woman is, as one scholar has put it, a "moral guardian" for such a wayward fellow. Some of the female characters hold jobs and enjoy a considerable degree of independence. A colorful array of secondary figures includes a lawyer, a judge, a female detective, newlyweds, divorcées, a college president, and a hotel manager.

Jerome Kern, Guy Bolton, and P. G. Wodehouse deserve much of the credit for the high artistic quality of the Princess Theatre repertory, although only Kern participated in the enterprise from its inception. Scholars put the total number of Princess Theatre musicals at seven, but the size and makeup of the repertory are complicated by two factors (see Table 4.1). First, due to various logistical complications, some of the musicals originally scheduled for the Princess Theatre were forced to play elsewhere. Second, not every musical that did play at the Princess Theatre was of the sort envisioned by Marbury. The first production, *Nobody Home*, featured music by Kern and lyrics by Schuyler Greene and an uncredited Herbert Reynolds. Kern convinced the producers to hire Bolton when it became apparent during previews that the book, by Paul Rubens, needed revising. History repeated itself when, during the production of the second Princess musical, *Very Good Eddie,* Bolton was summoned to rewrite the script. For the third Princess musical, *Have a Heart*, Bolton was engaged from the start, as was Wodehouse. Kern, Bolton, and Wodehouse wrote three more shows for the Princess plus *Sally* (1920) and *Sitting Pretty* (1924). Musical theater scholars venerate their collaboration, and many Broadway composers cite the Kern–Bolton–Wodehouse musicals as a major influence on their work. The conductor John McGlinn wrote that they "were the first . . . to take the musical comedy firmly out of the loosely structured revue format while avoiding the trappings of European operetta. . . . [T]he scores were small-scale wonders, full of charm and delicacy." A poem by the comic playwright and director George S. Kaufman (see Chapter 6) attests to the triumvirate's famed reputation:

> This is the trio of musical fame,
> Bolton and Wodehouse and Kern:
> Better than anyone else you can name
> Bolton and Wodehouse and Kern.
> Nobody knows what on earth they've been bitten by,
> All I can say is I mean to get lit an' buy
> Orchestra seats for the next one that's written by
> Bolton and Wodehouse and Kern.

JEROME KERN

erome Kern's parents, immigrant Bohemian Jews both, enjoyed a comfortable life in America. His father's business acumen afforded the young Kern the opportunity to study music in Europe. His mother, a pianist, bestowed her love of music onto her son. As soon as he was old enough, Kern traveled abroad and studied at a music conservatory in Heidelberg, Germany. Kern harbored ambitions of becoming a composer of concert music, but while later residing in London, he realized that his career lay in the theater. During his twenties, Kern split his time between composition and the publishing business. He regularly visited London, where the producer Charles Frohman (who died in the sinking of the *Lusitania* in 1915) hired him to write songs for the actor Seymour Hicks. While in London in 1910, Kern met and married Eva Leale (in an Anglican church). The couple settled in New York in 1912 and in 1916 moved to Bronxville, a town in Westchester County that was generally off limits to Jews. Shortly thereafter, the Kerns moved to Cedar Knolls, New Jersey, and in the thirties to Hollywood. Their marriage experienced turbulent patches, but it endured until the composer's death.

Kern was a confident and pugnacious composer. The writer Otto Harbach (see chapter 5) called him "the great American Englishman." Kern scholar Stephen Banfield describes him as a mixture of European sophistication and the tough New York Jew. Indeed, Kern's most mature writing represents a synthesis of his European musical training and his affinity for popular American musical idioms.

BOLTON AND WODEHOUSE

uy Reginald Bolton (1884–1979) and P. G. (Pelham Granville) Wodehouse (1881–1975) brought an English sensibility to Broadway, although only one of them was actually English. Wodehouse was British by birth, but he immigrated to the United States in 1915. Bolton was born in England but to American parents. He attended schools in Paris and New York and studied architecture. He became one of the most eminent librettists of the pre-Rodgers and Hammerstein era, collaborating with Cole Porter, George Gershwin, and Richard Rodgers as well as Kern. Although his musicals are too dated for contemporary tastes, in their day they were state of the art.

Wodehouse started out writing short stories and novels and is best known today as the creator of the literary characters Bertie Wooster and his inimitable butler, Jeeves. His first song lyrics were for *Miss Springtime* (1916). Wodehouse raised the standard of musical theater lyrics and influenced an entire generation of lyricists that included Lorenz Hart and Ira Gershwin. However, allegations that he was a Nazi sympathizer tainted his reputation and haunted him until his death.

Written accounts of Wodehouse and Bolton's collaboration play fast and loose with the facts, including their own, *Bring on the Girls!: The Improbable Story of Our Life in Musical Comedy, with Pictures to Prove It* (1953). In any case, Bolton and Wodehouse seem to have avoided the rancor that beset other writing partnerships. They had similar artistic temperaments, and Bolton's dialogue and Wodehouse's lyrics eschewed the "gooey sentiments" of early musical comedy. Wodehouse primarily wrote the lyrics but occasionally worked with Bolton on the dialogue. They collaborated on several librettos but were officially listed as co-authors only twice, for *Oh, Kay!* (1926) and *Anything Goes* (1934) (see Chapter 6).

The Princess Theatre musicals stand out for their freshness in a decade that produced little else of long-range significance. Marbury and Comstock inaugurated the series with an adaptation of the 1904 English musical comedy *Mr. Popple (of Ippleton)*. Retitled *Nobody Home*, the musical centers on a budding romance between Violet Brinton and a society dancer named Vernon Popple. Standing in the way of their happiness and permanent union is her aunt's staunch opposition. Vernon's brother arrives in town and falls in love with a showgirl named Tony Miller. Both couples eventually overcome the obstacles to their happiness. The facts surrounding Kern's and Bolton's participation in this project remain fuzzy. Marbury and Comstock asked Paul Rubens, the librettist and composer of *Mr. Popple*, to adapt his work for the Princess Theatre. The producers were dissatisfied with the results, however, and hired Kern to compose new music and Joseph Herbert to write a new script. Herbert abruptly withdrew from the project, at which point Kern suggested Guy Bolton as a substitute. *Nobody Home* did not fully accomplish the reforms that Kern and Bolton had hoped for, but it ran a respectable 135 performances.

Philip Bartholomae's comedy *Over Night* was the basis for the next Princess musical, *Very Good Eddie*. The plot centers on two pairs of newlyweds who happen to be taking the same Hudson River boat to the same honeymoon hotel. By the end of the musical, the titular protagonist, whose suffragist bride towers over him, discovers his inner man. The musical did so well that after five months of sold-out business, the producers transferred it to the much larger Casino Theatre, then to the 39th Street Theatre, and eventually back to the Princess, for a total of 341 performances. Despite its success, *Eddie* was Marbury and Comstock's last joint venture, as the former left the partnership to produce *See American First* (1916), Cole Porter's first Broadway musical (see Chapter 6).

Comstock forged ahead with *Have a Heart*, which added Wodehouse to Bolton and Kern's already fruitful collaboration. The plot concerns a couple that completes divorce proceedings and then decides to elope. Their second marriage to each other nearly falls apart when a silent movie star catches the husband's roving eye. *Have a Heart* opened at the Liberty Theatre and ran for nearly two months.

TABLE 4.1. The Princess Theatre Musicals and Other Musicals Produced at the Princess Theatre in the Teens

1915	*Nobody Home* (135 performances)	Music by Kern Lyrics by Schuyler Greene and an uncredited Herbert Reynolds Book by Bolton
1915	*Very Good Eddie* (341 performances)	Music by Kern Lyrics by Greene and Reynolds Book by Bolton
1916	*Go to It* (based on Charles Hoyt's *A Milk White Flag*) (23 performances)	Music and book by John L. Golden Lyrics by Golden, Anne Caldwell, and John E. Hazzard
1916	*Have a Heart* (Liberty Theatre, 76 performances)	Music by Kern Lyrics by Wodehouse Book by Bolton
1917	*Oh, Boy!* (Liberty Theatre, 478 performances)	Music by Kern Lyrics by Wodehouse Book by Bolton
1917	*Leave It to Jane* (Longacre Theatre, 167 performances)	Music by Kern Lyrics by Wodehouse Book by Bolton
1918	*Oh, Lady! Lady!!* (219 performances)	Music by Kern Lyrics by Wodehouse Book by Bolton
1918	*Oh My Dear!* (189 performances)	Music by Louis Hirsch Lyrics by Wodehouse Book by Bolton
1919	*Toot Sweet* (premiered in Chicago under the title *Overseas Revue*) (45 performances)	Music by Richard A. Whiting Lyrics by Raymond B. Egan Book by Will Morrissey

Oh, Boy!, the first musical of Bolton and Wodehouse's own invention, also incorporates a newlywed trope. No sooner have the just-married George Budd and Lou Ellen settled into their Manhattan apartment when his Quaker aunt, who is the trustee of his inheritance, announces a visit. George fears that she will cut him off because he has not told her about the marriage. The show ran 463 performances and introduced "Till the Clouds Roll By." The writers wrote the show for the Princess, but they allowed Henry W. Savage to produce it at the Liberty Theatre in order to fulfill a contractual obligation.

Comstock, William Elliott, and Morris Gest co-produced *Leave It to Jane*, which is based on George Ade's *The College Widow*. Arguably the best known of the Princess

Theatre musicals, *Leave It to Jane* captured the youthful vitality of America's rising professional class and initiated the college-musical trend. The titular heroine, the daughter of Atwater College's president, convinces Billy Bingham, the town's finest athlete, to attend the school and play for its football team. A successful Off Broadway revival of *Leave It to Jane* in 1959 gave New York audiences their first exposure to the Princess Theatre repertory in over forty years.

In *Oh, Lady! Lady!!*, Kern's final Princess Theatre show, an heiress named Mollie plans to marry Willoughby Farringdon, but her mother opposes the union (a common dramatic device) and suspects Willoughby when the family jewels go missing. It turns out that the girlfriend of Willoughby's valet, Fanny Weld, is the guilty party in the robbery. The score contained "Bill," one of Kern's most memorable songs, but it was dropped out of town. Ten years later, Kern and Hammerstein interpolated "Bill" into *Show Boat* with new lyrics by the latter (see Chapter 5). Kern had nothing to do with the last two Princess shows, *Oh My Dear!* and *Toot Sweet*.

As there are no original cast recordings of the Princess Theatre musicals and only limited access to the scripts and scores, exposure to this repertory is rather limited. Given the near reverence in which scholars and critics have held these musicals, it is hard to account for why only one of them, *Very Good Eddie*, has ever been revived on Broadway. The production came about in 1975 when the producer

The cast of *Very Good Eddie* posing on the Rip Van Winkle Inn set. *Courtesy Photofest.*

David Merrick transferred a summer production at the Goodspeed Opera House in Connecticut to the intimate Booth Theatre, where it ran for 304 performances. The revival produced a recording and made a performance version of the show possible, but it was not faithful to the original version.

Bartholomae's *Over Night* begins on a pier in Poughkeepsie, New York. Two newlywed couples have separately booked passage aboard the Albany Day Line S. S. Hendrik Hudson. Richard Kettle (changed to Eddie for the musical) cowers in the shadow of his suffragette wife, Georgina. The other husband, Percy Darling, a former classmate of Richard's at Yale, possesses the opposite temperament. He is overprotective of his new wife, Elsie Darling, who, in contrast to Georgina, is subservient to her husband. Both couples board the boat without their luggage, so Georgina, who is more than able to do her own heavy lifting, and Percy go to fetch their respective belongings. With Richard and Elsie standing together on the deck, the boat suddenly sets sail, leaving Percy and Georgina on the dock. With the couples rearranged, a series of compromising situations and comic complications ensues until the newlyweds are reunited at the end of Act II.

Bartholomae himself adapted his play for the musical, which, retitled *Very Good Eddie*, premiered in Schenectady, New York, and then moved on to neighboring Albany. Negative reviews in both cities prompted the producers to bring the show back to New York for revision. It was at this point that Bolton and Herbert joined the creative team, probably at Kern's behest. Bolton took over the scriptwriting duties. He retained some of Bartholomae's lines but restructured the subplots and expunged the political content, including most of the references to the suffragist movement. Bolton's revised script was less confusing, but it lost some of the original's comic intrigue. It retained some of Schuyler Greene's lyrics and included new ones by Herbert. (The 1975 version inexplicably concludes when a message arrives from the reverend who presided over the two couples' weddings stating that neither marriage is valid.)

The opening night of *Very Good Eddie* at the Princess Theatre was a distinguished affair, with the Vanderbilts, Astors, and Pulitzers in attendance. Wodehouse was on hand to review the show for *Vanity Fair*. He and his fellow critics complimented the work as a whole, although they split over Kern's music. Some complained about a "melodious monotony." On the other hand, the *Sun* exclaimed that Kern "had never provided a more tuneful score."

The score's ragtime allusions accord with the plot's American milieu and underscore the encroaching modernity on the lives of the late-Edwardian-era characters. Syncopated dance rhythms pervade several songs as if to announce the dawn of a new era. The exuberant rhythms of ragtime, which suggested uninhibited pleasure and joy, were a welcome and uplifting respite for a war-weary audience. Kern reserved the show's only romantic waltz, "Nodding Roses," for the moment when Elsie Lilly and Dick come together toward the end of the show (the published score includes a second waltz in the appendix, "Alone at Last," which is assigned to Percy and Elsie Darling). "Nodding Roses" coyly quotes the "Presentation of the Rose" motif from Richard Strauss's 1911 comic opera *Der Rosenkavalier*.

Bolton's dialogue flows smoothly into the musical numbers. For example, the first waltz mentioned above emerges naturally from the dialogue:

RIVERS:	That's the second time that confounded clerk has kept me from hearing your answer.
ELSIE:	My answer? Don't you see—I'm wearing a rose!
RIVERS:	Do you mean it? Elsie—my dearest—what do you say?
ELSIE:	[singing] Though my answer you entreat My lips seem helpless to repeat The words my heart would say.

This excerpt, although hardly a major dramaturgical breakthrough, is more convincing than the typical musical comedy song lead-in from this period. On the other hand, even Bolton occasionally stooped to employing cheap humor (as when the clerk announces, "Sounds like a song cue," before "If I Find the Girl"), but his book was a step in the right direction, and the critics, who had been disparaging the lack of integration in musical comedy, signaled their approval. A young Richard Rodgers, who saw *Very Good Eddie*, considered it a turning point for musical theater.

The character of Eddie Kettle evoked the on-screen "Tramp" persona of Charlie Chaplin, who had become a major film star by this time. The character of Tramp, introduced in 1914, was the embodiment of pathos, an underdog with whom audiences sympathized and identified. Eddie too struggles against his own fate and overcomes adversity. His character-defining song "When You Wear a 13 Collar" epitomizes his Chaplinesque disposition. It also achieves a level of dramatic truth rarely encountered in musical theater from this period. The lyrics, by Schuyler Greene, who was never more than a minor figure in musical theater, are exemplary. The wordplay, colloquialisms, and topicality provided a distinct alternative to the verbosity and stiffness of operetta texts, and they paved the way for the sophisticated corpus of popular songs written during the twenties and thirties by people such as George and Ira Gershwin, and Howard Dietz and Arthur Schwartz.

"When You Wear a 13 Collar" (first verse and refrain)

VERSE

I'm a peaceful little person,
But peace is sometimes worse'n
All the wars combined, That histories recall,
I've been pushed around and kicked at,
Stepped upon, abused, and picked at
Till I wonder that I'm anything at all.

Even little flies that flutter
From the sugar to the butter
Command respect because they carry germs:
Their importance seems to teach us,
In this world of all sized creatures,
Half are robins and the other half are worms.

REFRAIN

When you wear a 19 collar,
And a size 11 shoe
You can lead a pirate crew,
Smoke and drink and swear and chew;
But you have to lock ambition up,
And throw away the key,
When your collar's number thirteen
And your shoes are number three.

Instances of enjambment, elided words ("worse'n"), feminine rhymes, and patter underscore Eddie's pusillanimous disposition. All of these features obtain in the first four lines. Eddie expresses his masculine inadequacies through the lexicon of war and compares his situation to the raging conflict in Europe. References to war also occur in the third refrain: "Wifey never thinks of war / But you just live in one constant state of armed neutrality, / when your collar's [etc]." The published score includes three extra refrains, for a total of six, which suggests that Ernest Truex, the actor who appeared as Eddie, performed encores of the song.

"Thirteen Collar" has a conventional verse-refrain format. The verse, a sixteen-bar melody with its own AABA phrase structure, is twice as long as the refrain, which consists of two symmetrical phrases (AB). The short refrain provides a moment of reflection. The verse and refrain have distinct rhythmic characters. The former trips along in dotted eighth note–sixteenth note rhythms, with longer note values occurring at the ends of each phrase (Example 4.1a). Short dotted rhythms and a circle-of-fifths progression help to produce a rushed, nervous quality. The unexpected long-short rhythm (♪ ♪) on "person" and "worse'n"—a stark contrast to the otherwise ubiquitous short-long rhythm (♪♪)—underscores Eddie's skittishness. By contrast, the refrain is dominated by even eighth-note rhythms (Example 4.1b). Its angularity and strict four-part voice leading suggest an ironic air of pomposity, which seems incongruous with Eddie's disposition. The singer must work breathlessly to perform this phrase smoothly (Truex was reportedly no more than an adequate singer with a raspy voice). Further, the harmonic rhythm quickens, and the melody creeps upward, placing further physical demands on the singer. A sagging five-note chromatic run on "throw away the key" encapsulates Eddie's defeatist attitude.

Truex employed physical gestures, such as making double fists and sticking out his elbows on "but you just live in one constant state of armed neutrality." During the interlude between the first and second verse, he produced a folding chair from the footlights, sat down, and addressed the audience directly:

I get awfully tired of sitting
Here alone at night and knitting
I should like to go out one night with the boys
Where they sell cigars and liquors
And where if a fellow snickers
No one glares at you with "Edwin, stop that noise."

EXAMPLE 4.1. "13 Collar," (a) verse, opening phrase, (b) chorus, opening phrase

PLOT OF VERY GOOD EDDIE

On a boat docked at the Hudson River city of Poughkeepsie, Eddie Kettle and his bride, Georgina, wait to embark on their honeymoon. Coincidentally, another pair of newlyweds, Percy Darling, an old classmate of Eddie's, and Elsie, have booked passage on the same boat. Both couples have forgotten to bring their luggage aboard, so Georgina and Percy return to the dock. However, the boat suddenly leaves without them. Seemingly abandoned by their respective spouses, Eddie and Elsie have no choice but to pretend that they are married so as to preserve the appearance of propriety. The same situation holds true for Percy and the overbearing Georgina. A voice teacher named Mme. Matroppo and her students are also passengers on the boat. Another one of Eddie's former college chums, Dick Rivers, has boarded the boat in pursuit of Elsie Lilly, one of Matroppo's students with whom he has fallen in love. When the passengers arrive at the Rip Van Winkle Inn, Eddie and Elsie maintain their charade but try to obtain separate rooms from a very confused hotel clerk. Georgina eventually shows up at with Percy in tow. An already complicated situation becomes more complicated, in part because two people named Elsie are staying at the hotel. In the end, the newlyweds are reunited, and Dick courts Elsie Lilly.

During the fourth line, he stood on the chair.

Today, a character-specific song such as "13 Collar" would most likely occur in Act I, but Truex performed it toward the middle of Act II. For the 1975 revival, the song was relocated to Act I. The original placement of the song, which seems peculiar today, serves as a reminder that *Very Good Eddie*, although of above-average quality, was a product of its age. Indeed, the show relied on stock comic business. Such flaws notwithstanding, *Very Good Eddie* severed ties with the loosely constructed farce-comedy genre and anticipated the more mature musical comedies that Kern, Bolton, and Wodehouse later wrote and inspired others to write.

BEYOND THE PRINCESS THEATRE

During the final years of the decade, postwar prosperity produced a flood of original musical comedies. A new generation of composers was getting its first hearing on Broadway, including Irving Berlin (*Watch Your Step*, 1914), Cole Porter (*See America First*, 1916), Richard Rodgers (*A Lonely Romeo*, 1919), and George Gershwin (*Sinbad*, 1919). Kern inspired these budding composers, and he continued to influence writers for decades to come.

Kern's magnum opus, *Show Boat* (1927), lay nearly ten years into the future (see Chapter 5). Throughout the twenties, he enjoyed success in New York and London, but he suffered a crushing personal setback when he lost a sizable portion of his wealth in the stock market crash of 1929. During the thirties, Kern collaborated with both Hammerstein and Otto Harbach on several Broadway shows. Like any Broadway composer worth his salt at the time, Kern was summoned to Hollywood. His 1936 film *Swing Time*, with book and lyrics by Dorothy Fields, is arguably the finest of the ten Fred Astaire-Ginger Rodgers screen musicals. After America entered World War II, Kern wrote songs (e.g., "The Last Time I Saw Paris") for several patriotic films. He turned down an offer from MGM to compose the songs for *The Wizard of Oz*. After suffering a heart attack in 1937, he returned to writing for the stage.

Hammerstein tried to interest Kern in working on a musical version of *Green Grow the Lilacs*, the source of *Oklahoma!*, but he declined. Kern lived to see *Oklahoma!*, but he allegedly did not care for Rodgers's music. In 1945, he traveled to New York for a planned revival of *Show Boat*. He also agreed to write the score for *Annie Get Your Gun*, Rodgers and Hammerstein's first joint producing venture. Kern cooperated with MGM on *Till the Clouds Roll By*, a biopic loosely based on his life, but he died before its premiere. While antiquing in New York, Kern collapsed on the street from a brain hemorrhage. Because there was no one around who recognized him, Kern was taken to City Hospital on Welfare Island, where he died amidst friends six days later.

AND BEAR IN MIND

Naughty Marietta *(1910, New York Theatre, 136 performances)*

Music by Victor Herbert
Libretto by Rida Johnson Young

*N*aughty Marietta takes place in New Orleans in 1780 against the backdrop of the struggle between France and the United States over Louisiana. Étienne Grandet, the pirate Bras Priqué in disguise, plots to rule Louisiana. He shares his illicitly acquired riches with his father, who poses as Lieutenant Governor Grandet and conveniently protects his son from arrest. A ship arrives bearing several casquette girls, sent by the King of France to be brides for the French colonists. One of them, Marietta (really the Contessa d'Altena), has made the journey in order to avoid an arranged marriage. She poses as the son of an Italian puppeteer. Étienne suspects that Marietta is the contessa and hopes to marry her in order to legitimize his political ambitions, but Marietta is attracted to Dick Warrington, whom the French king has charged with capturing Bras Priqué. At a ball, Dick rebuffs Marietta, who in turn reveals her true identity and declares that she will marry Étienne; but Adah, a courtesan and the

(Continued)

pirate's former lover, discloses his true identity. He will have to answer to the real governor, whom he has imprisoned on the Isle of Pines. Marietta and Dick are united.

Oscar Hammerstein (the uncle of Oscar Hammerstein II) produced *Naughty Marietta*, which starred the Italian singer Emma Trentini (1885–1959). Originally titled *Little Paris*, the work exemplifies the colorful albeit convoluted plots of operetta. It features a contrived array of situations and characters, a masked ball, a courtesan, pirates, and a femme fatale disguised as a man. Moreover, the operetta takes place in an American locale, a rarity at the time. *Naughty Marietta* featured several popular numbers, including "Ah, Sweet Mystery of Life," the tune that only Marietta's true lover knows in its entirety. The *New York Dramatic Mirror* pointed out that Herbert's score avoids "Gallic crispness, Viennese swing, Italian floridness, German simplicity, and English solidity; it is American in phrasing and in orchestrations." The score offsets the book, which is a "necessary evil," a "painfully disjointed . . . spindle-legged comedy."

- -

NAMES, TERMS, AND CONCEPTS

Bartholomae, Philip	*Naughty Marietta*
Bolton, Guy	*Over Night*
Chaplin, Charlie	Princess Theatre
foxtrot ballad	"They Didn't Believe Me"
Herbert, Victor	"When You Wear a 13 Collar"
Kern, Jerome	Wodehouse, P. G.
Leave It to Jane	Young, Rida Johnson
Marbury, Elisabeth	*Very Good Eddie*

- -

DISCUSSION QUESTIONS

1. How do the Princess Theatre musicals prefigure mature musicals of later decades?

2. What do the Princess Theatre musicals teach us about the concerns, values, and dreams of America's upwardly mobile middle class?

3. How does Jerome Kern's music for the Princess Theatre musicals differ from that of earlier musical comedies as typified by George M. Cohan's songs?

CHAPTER 5

THE TWENTIES

(*SHOW BOAT*, 1927, ZIEGFELD THEATRE, 575 PERFORMANCES)

The Roaring Twenties conjures up images of flappers, speakeasies, the Lindy Hop, jazz bands, and rum-running. Americans, having triumphed in World War I, were eager to enjoy the spoils of victory, and postwar economic prosperity led to a period of unbridled self-indulgence. Attending a Broadway musical was one way that the new class of well-educated, upwardly mobile Americans confirmed their social status and exercised their right to pursue the pleasures that their income and place of privilege afforded them. New theaters sprang up in record numbers, as producers scrambled to meet the increased demand for entertainment. Indeed, the twenties were Broadway's boom years in terms of the sheer number of productions. New musical comedies opened at a record rate, sometimes two in a single day.

Musicals from this period boasted exuberant dancing, memorable music, and diverting if mindless scripts. These shows did not attempt to tax the mind, stir up deep emotions, or strive for literary refinement, and few of them made any cultural impact whatsoever beyond their original Broadway run. However, many songs from these shows became standards and left a lasting legacy on American popular music, but the scripts have been collecting dust, and for good reason: they suffer from silly plots, shoddy construction, and sorely outdated humor. Older generations of Americans still recognize Jerome Kern's "Look for the Silver Lining," but few people know that it came from the musical *Sally*. Twenties musicals rarely reached the level of good art because they did not have to. Indeed, no one expected a musical to be remembered after it served the utilitarian purpose of making money, which many did in spades. In fact, musicals that took themselves too seriously usually met with failure.

The easy accessibility of musical theater songs was in the mutual best interest of Broadway and Tin Pan Alley. The symbiotic relationship between these two independent but related industries—musical theater and music publishing—affected the musical theater genre in two ways: (1) it encouraged producers to treat musicals

Several important composers and lyricists realized their early promise in the twenties, the most prominent being George and Ira Gershwin, Richard Rodgers, Lorenz Hart, Cole Porter, Vincent Youmans, Oscar Hammerstein, and Arthur Schwartz. Along with Kern and Irving Berlin, they produced the songs that America danced to and listened to until rock and roll dislodged Broadway as the mainstream popular music idiom.

as commodities for a mass market, and (2) it protected the genre from "avant-garde pretentiousness." The artistic aspirations of the writers were subjugated to the demands and whims of the producers, performers, and audiences. The celebrated songwriters named above hoped to improve the quality of musical comedy, but the conditions for realizing their aspirations lay in the future.

One musical from the twenties towers over all the rest: Jerome Kern and Oscar Hammerstein's *Show Boat* (1927). Given the frivolous nature of most musicals at the time, it is remarkable that Kern and Hammerstein undertook this project, let alone that it was a success. Not only was *Show Boat* the major musical theater event of the decade, but it also marks a milestone in the history of the genre. It is the oldest work in the standard performing repertory. Miles Kruger, the author of the first monograph on *Show Boat*, dubs the show "a majestic musical drama." Gerald Bordman considers it "the first totally American operetta." Florenz Ziegfeld, who produced *Show Boat*, billed it as "An All American Musical Comedy." Some scholars consider *Show Boat* the first "musical play"; others see it as a deliberate step by Kern toward opera—an opinion enhanced by the fact that the work entered the New York City Opera's repertory in 1954, the first Broadway musical to do so. However, *Show Boat* represents a point of convergence of the three most popular musical theater forms at the time: musical comedy, operetta, and revue. Yet it does not conform to any one of them. The musical treatment of the story's principal romantic couple reveals the influence of operetta, but the show's conception, structure, and pervading spirit all point to musical comedy. The showboat entertainment (the show-within-the-show part of *Show Boat*) resembles the variety format of a revue. To fully appreciate the historical importance of *Show Boat*, it will be useful to place the show into the context of twenties musical comedy.

THE CINDERELLA MUSICALS

Irene

Irene opened in late 1919 and set a trend that lasted throughout the twenties. With a libretto by James Montgomery, lyrics by Joseph McCarthy, and music by Harry Tierney, it was the first of several musicals from the period with a modern-day story based on the Cinderella archetype: a young, attractive, and often impoverished woman discovers her Prince Charming and marries upward in class. The show's heroine, Irene O'Dare, is an Irish immigrant and upholsterer's assistant. When she is sent to repair cushions at a Long Island estate, she charms Donald Marshall III, the unattached scion of the wealthy owners. Irene and Donald marry but only after overcoming several obstacles, including his mother's staunch objection to having an immigrant daughter-in-law. The modern-day Cinderellas of these musicals were more liberated and independent than their forebears in literary fairytales and operettas. They improve their fate not through the intervention of a fairy godmother but rather through their own agency and natural charm.

Sally

Producers acted quickly to capitalize on *Irene*'s success. In 1920, *Mary* and then *Sally* followed in close succession. Ziegfeld ventured beyond the revue format to produce *Sally*, which featured Marilyn Miller, one of the brightest musical comedy stars of the decade (see Chapter 17). *Sally* was a Kern–Bolton–Wodehouse collaboration (see Chapter 4), although Ziegfeld brought in Clifford Grey to write additional lyrics and Victor Herbert to compose "The Butterfly Ballet," a vehicle for Miller. The show's heroine, an orphan named Sally Rhinelander, toils as a dishwasher at a Greenwich Village restaurant alongside "Connie," the exiled Duke Constantine of Czechogovinia. A young aristocrat named Blair Farquar (Prince Charming by any other name), of the Long Island Farquars, secures the services of several employees at the restaurant for a private function that he is hosting at his

Irene O'Dare (Edith Day) charming Donald Marshall III (Walter Regan) in *Irene*, the original "Cinderella Musical." *Courtesy Photofest.*

estate. He falls head over heels in love with Sally. Otis Hooper, the theatrical agent in charge of the entertainment for the soirée, convinces Sally to go on stage for his indisposed lead dancer. Hooper later manages to get Sally (who turns out to be a fantastic dancer) into the *Ziegfeld Follies* (Ziegfeld was a shameless self-promoter). She becomes a star as well as the future Mrs. Blair Farquar.

Sally featured sumptuous sets by Joseph Urban, Ziegfeld's favorite designer, and it boasted several hit songs (see Chapter 3). The show ran for 561 performances and returned to Broadway in 1923 along with *Irene*.

The Cinderella-musical craze continued unabated throughout the decade. Even George M. Cohan jumped on the bandwagon with *Little Nellie Kelly* (1922) and *The Rise of Rosie O'Reilly* (1923).

Although the product of Jewish writers, virtually all of the Cinderella musicals avoided Jewish characters, as anti-Semitic sentiments were too virulent for any explicit reference to Jewish life to succeed on Broadway. Indeed, the one exception, *Betsy*, despite having a score by Rodgers and Hart, failed with critics and audiences. On the other hand, by the twenties, the Irish had entered the echelons of respectable society.

Whatever their title—whether *Sunny*, *Poppy*, or the triple title-snatching *Sally, Irene and Mary* (as the Shubert brothers billed one of their productions)—these musicals featured a rags-to-riches story and captured the spirit of an America caught up in

FRED AND ADELE ASTAIRE

The Nebraska-born sister and brother team of Fred (1899–1987) and Adele (1898–1981) Astaire appeared in vaudeville and later on Broadway. During the twenties, the Astaires starred in several musicals in New York and London, but after *The Band Wagon* (1931), Adele left show business to marry Lord Charles Cavendish. In 1932, Fred appeared without her in *Gay Divorce*, after which he went to Hollywood. The film medium transformed Astaire into a major star. Although he possessed a pleasing singing voice, Astaire is best remembered for his elegant and seemingly effortless dancing.

the modern age. They championed the working class and propagated the myth of American egalitarianism and upward mobility. The heroine might be a stenographer, a shop girl, or a flower peddler; most likely she was Irish. She often marries the boss's son after helping to extricate him from some compromising situation. He, on the other hand, is decidedly a member of the privileged Protestant class, a Morgan or Wellington. The stories invariably take place in New York, with excursions to Long Island, the horse races, or a popular show business venue.

OTHER MUSICAL COMEDIES

By Gershwin

George Gershwin built his reputation in the twenties with a different type of musical comedy. His first, *Lady, Be Good!* (1924), did for musical theater what his *Rhapsody in Blue* did for concert music. *Lady, Be Good!* made the jazz-inflected score fashionable on Broadway at a time when operetta was enjoying its last hurrah. Other Broadway composers injected jazz elements into their music, but Gershwin expanded the Tin Pan Alley vocabulary with the angular melodic character, syncopated rhythms, and pungent harmonies of jazz. His brother Ira's colloquial, sharp-witted lyrics were a natural match for George's music. The script for *Lady, Be Good!*, by Guy Bolton and Fred Thompson, epitomizes the zany antics and anything-for-a-laugh plots of the era. The story centers on Dick and Susie Trevers, siblings played by Fred and Adele Astaire, who find themselves living on the street after their landlady, whom Dick has spurned, evicts them. Given the show's preposterous plot, Ethan Mordden rightly considers *Lady, Be Good!* to be "about the treat of seeing the Astaires in an Aarons-Feedley

George Gershwin's *Rhapsody in Blue*, a single-movement concert work for solo piano and orchestra (originally an augmented jazz band), premiered in 1924 during Paul Whiteman's "Experiment in Modern Music" concert at Aeolian Concert Hall and introduced jazz into serious music composition.

musical with a Gershwin score" (see Chapter 6). This is, after all, the musical that introduced "Fascinating Rhythm." As siblings, the Astaires rarely enacted an on-stage romantic relationship with each other, which, in this case, helps to explain the plot's tortuous intrigue (for example, Adele Astaire spent much of the second act impersonating a Mexican widow).

By Rodgers and Hart

Herbert Fields (1879–1958) collaborated extensively with Rodgers and Hart in the twenties (see Chapter 1). During his long career, which continued until the end of the Rodgers and Hammerstein era, Fields wrote the book for over twenty musicals, including *Annie Get Your Gun* (which he co-authored with his sister Dorothy) and several Cole Porter works.

Between 1925 and 1931, Richard Rodgers and Lorenz Hart collaborated on a diverse range of musical comedies, most of them with the book writer Herbert Fields. The trio's first collaboration, *Dearest Enemy* (1925), takes place in New York against the backdrop of the Revolutionary War. A group of women distract the British commander-in-chief, General William Howe, while George Washington prepares for the battle of Washington Heights in upper Manhattan. The musical fantasy *Peggy-Ann* (1926) introduced Freud into the musical theater genre. Next came *A Connecticut Yankee*, based on Mark Twain's *A Connecticut Yankee in King Arthur's Court* (1889). *Present Arms*, the writers' first of two musicals in 1928, is a Pearl Harbor romance between a street-smart Marine and a British aristocrat. The Marine must compete against a wealthy German for her hand. Rodgers and Hart's second show that year, *Chee-Chee*, was based on Charles Petet's *The Son of the Grand Eunuch*. The subject matter was too risqué and bizarre even for twenties audiences. *Spring Is Here* (1929), which did not involve Fields, was a surer bet: a conventional romantic comedy set on Long Island based on Owen Davis's play *Shotgun Wedding*. The last Rodgers–Hart–Fields musical, *America's Sweetheart*, opened in the early thirties. Anticipating the film *Singin' in the Rain*, it dealt with the transition from silent films to talkies: a Midwestern couple moves to Hollywood, and the wife becomes a silent film star; however, she has a lisp, which becomes a liability during the advent of talkies.

THE OPERETTA REVIVAL

Operetta recaptured some of its former glory in the twenties and accounted for some of the biggest hits of the decade. Sigmund Romberg (1887–1951) and Rudolph Friml (1879–1972) dominated the field and wrote more than half of the eleven longest-running works of the period. Whereas in earlier years the labels "musical comedy" and "operetta" were used interchangeably, in the twenties each form carved out a unique identity. As musical comedy started to absorb jazz and other American idioms, operetta maintained its European associations and continued to favor waltzes and other continental forms. Despite operetta's Old World pedigree, its escapist nature appealed to a large segment of Broadway patrons. In contrast to earlier operettas, which usually took place in distant, fairytale-like environs, several operettas from the twenties were set in locales closer to home, even though these, too, evoked the exoticism characteristic of the genre.

Friml, a Czech Catholic by birth who studied with Antonín Dvořák in Prague, immigrated to the United States in 1906. Sigmund Romberg, a Hungarian Jew, arrived in New York in 1909 via Vienna, where, employed at the Theater an der Wien, he got to know Franz Lehár (see Chapter 3). Romberg's first major employment in the States was with the producers Lee and Jacob Shubert, for whom he contributed songs to *The Passing Show* series as well as some musical comedies (see Chapter 3). *Maytime* (1917) was Romberg's first major success in the operetta field. During this period, Romberg wrote several operettas with a bittersweet ending rather than the typical fairytale ending that one had come to expect of the genre, and he invested the waltz with greater dramatic poignancy and the ability to express emotions tinged with loss and nostalgia.

The two most successful operettas during the twenties opened in 1924 within three months of each other: Friml's *Rose Marie* (book and lyrics by Oscar Hammerstein and Otto Harbach) and Romberg's *The Student Prince*. *Rose Marie* takes place in the Canadian Rockies and features a Native American heroine. Friml incorporated several Indianist identifiers, such as drones in "Indian Love Call." *The Student Prince*, which evokes the middle European settings of earlier operetta, is the tale of a young prince who must choose between love and duty (he opts for duty, the basis for the unhappy ending). The reception in New York was so positive that the Shubert brothers backed nine profitable touring productions of *The Student Prince*.

Romberg's later operettas have settings ranging from Maryland during the Civil War to contemporary New York City. Some of them have happy endings and contain lyrical ballads in duple meter. During the same period, Friml gravitated toward stories with French associations, including *The Three Musketeers* (1928). Many of Romberg's scores reflect a sense of American egalitarianism in that they include syncopated musical comedy numbers along with sentimental waltzes. The Depression all but put an end to operetta on Broadway, but Hollywood kept the genre alive well into the fifties.

SHOW BOAT

Plainly put by Joseph Swain, "*Show Boat* is the first American musical that integrates the elements of a [*sic*] musical theater into a credible drama." That *Show Boat* continues to be performed today is a testament to Kern and Hammerstein's vision and the lasting relevance of the show's sweeping story. Although *Show Boat* did not spark an immediate revolution in musical theater, it demonstrated that the musical theater genre could withstand the dramatic weight of serious themes and tragic stories.

Source Material

The novelist Edna Ferber (1885–1968) published *Show Boat* in 1926, first in serial form and then as a single book. Kern, who was eager to work on something with dramatic substance, immediately pursued the rights for a musical adaptation of the novel. He asked Hammerstein to write the book and lyrics. Ferber was reluctant to permit a musical adaptation of her novel, knowing what both Kern and Hammerstein most surely knew: that the story, which spanned fifty years and dealt with racism and spousal abandonment, was the most unlikely basis for a musical comedy. Prior to 1927, musicals based on novels were few and far between, and none had a plot as epic in scope or characters as complex as *Show Boat*. Kern recognized the story's wealth of unique musical possibilities, including presentational (diegetic) songs and the use of changing musical styles to accompany the long march of time. He must have argued his case convincingly, for Ferber soon signed a contract with him and Hammerstein. By then, Florenz Ziegfeld had already decided to produce *Show Boat*.

Kern's selection of Hammerstein over other lyricists was hardly an act of blind faith. He recognized in Hammerstein, with whom he had collaborated on *Sunny* in 1925, a desire to raise the standards for musical theater and to work with more sophisticated dramatico-musical structures. Indeed, *Show Boat* prefigures themes, styles, and concerns of Hammerstein's later musicals and was instrumental in his maturation as a dramatist and lyricist. On the other hand, Ziegfeld's interest in *Show Boat* is more difficult to explain, given that he had built his fortune producing rather frivolous revues. *Show Boat* was more complex and dramatic than any of his previous endeavors, and it came with tremendous risks. Ziegfeld claimed that *Show Boat* was "the opportunity of my life," but exactly what he meant by this statement is not clear. Did he hope to associate himself with a work worthy of the label "art"? Could the audacity of producing a show unlike anything Broadway had ever seen or the sheer insurmountable odds of pulling it off have attracted him? Whatever the reason, Ziegfeld threw his full support behind the project.

Ferber's novel follows the life of Magnolia Hawks, the daughter of Captain Andy and his dour wife, Parthy, operators of a river showboat called the Cotton Blossom. Magnolia, unversed in the ways of the world, is swept off her feet by a ne'er-do-well gambler named Gaylord Ravenal. Before long, they are married and have a baby girl named Kim. They move to Chicago, where they enjoy the high life until Ravenal's lucky gambling streak runs out. Broke and ashamed, Ravenal abandons his wife and daughter. Magnolia, forced to fend for herself, returns to the stage as a "coon shouter" (a white female singer who imitated black characters in the manner of minstrel shows) (see Chapter 17), as she had been on the Cotton Blossom, but this time appearing in a basement cabaret in Chicago. This job paves the way for her to become a major star. By the end of the story, Kim, following in her mother's footsteps, has become a Broadway star. When Parthy dies, Magnolia returns to the Cotton Blossom.

The novel's main subplot centers on Julie Dozier, an actress on the Cotton Blossom and confidante of the young Magnolia. Pete, the boat's engineer and a scandalmonger, informs the local sheriff of Lemoyne, Mississippi, that Julie is "half Negro." The sheriff boards the showboat and accuses Julie and her Caucasian husband, Steve, of breaking local miscegenation laws. So as not to cause Captain Andy any further trouble, they voluntarily leave the employ of the showboat. In

Chicago years later, Magnolia encounters Julie at a brothel while returning money that Gaylord had borrowed from the madam.

Hammerstein intended to incorporate all of the novel's main events, but he ended up eliminating several details lest the musical become too unwieldy. He tamed the sprawling narrative by eliminating the early years of the story. The musical begins in the late 1880s, when Magnolia is already a young woman and easily taken in by Ravenal's dashing looks, debonair charm, and apparent worldly experience. Hammerstein also omitted several characters, including Kim's husband, and conflated others. He raised the dramatic status of Julie Dozier (changed to Julie LaVerne) by promoting her to the top star of the Cotton Blossom. When Magnolia seeks work in a Chicago nightclub, Julie, now an alcoholic and the featured singer at the club, selflessly sacrifices her job for Magnolia.

Hammerstein turned Ferber's original ending on its head. Several characters die in the course of her novel, including Andy and Parthy, and Ravenal is never heard from again after he abandons Magnolia in Chicago. The final portion of the novel focuses on Magnolia and Kim. Joe and Queenie, two black showboat workers who figure prominently in the first half of the story, are long forgotten. Hammerstein, feeling pressure to provide a conventional musical comedy ending, kept Magnolia's parents alive until the end of the show and brought back Ravenal for an entirely unmotivated reunion with Magnolia. Further, in the final scene, Ellie and Frank, two former Cotton Blossom performers who have found success in Hollywood, just happen to be visiting Natchez. As one chronicler of *Show Boat* has suggested, "had *Show Boat* been adapted for the stage one decade later, Hammerstein would have adhered to Miss Ferber's elimination of the gambler and not permitted him to reappear." Hammerstein has been forgiven for this, his only major "immature concession to musical comedy," but no critic has ever felt entirely comfortable with these changes.

Reception

The premiere of *Show Boat* took place in Washington, DC, and lasted until nearly 1 a.m. Ziegfeld demanded that Kern and Hammerstein shorten the show to a more tolerable length. As a result, *Show Boat* lost some exceptional material, including "It's Getting Hotter in the North" and "Mis'ry's Coming' Around," a powerful lament performed by the Cotton Blossom's black workers at a key dramatic moment in Act I. At the Broadway premiere, as audience watched with muted enthusiasm, a dejected Ziegfeld sank on the stairs leading up to the balcony and wept, declaring, "The show's a flop. I knew it would be. I never wanted to do it." The rave reviews the next morning buoyed his spirits, as did the long line in front of the newly constructed Ziegfeld Theatre.

Show Boat gained national exposure rather slowly for a Broadway hit. Ziegfeld delayed the national tour, fearing competition from the movies. The Depression further postponed the widespread attention that the musical might have otherwise enjoyed. However, *Show Boat* eventually received the recognition that it deserved, and it has maintained its status as one of the great American musicals.

The town beaux and their "pretty bevy" of Southern beauties, from the original Broadway production of *Show Boat. Courtesy Photofest.*

A definitive version of *Show Boat* does not exist, for each major stage revival and film version brought about changes to the script and score, often extreme ones necessitated by changes in social attitudes. There have been several major revivals of *Show Boat* plus two film versions, each one unique. Kern and Hammerstein made changes to the show as early as 1928, when they expunged songs, wrote new ones, and rearranged material for the first London production. In particular, they assigned new material to Joe when Paul Robeson, for whom the role was originally written, agreed to play the part. They made additional changes for the 1936 movie version, which starred Robeson, Irene Dunn, and Helen Morgan, and planned some others for the 1946 Broadway revival. Hammerstein made further alterations for the 1951 MGM movie. In Kern's and Hammerstein's absence, directors and producers of *Show Boat* revivals have continued to alter the show based on their own artistic prerogatives or political agendas, using the abundance of material written for the show at one time or another as they saw fit.

Collectively, the various live stage and celluloid incarnations of *Show Boat* reflect the evolution of American attitudes about race. One need look no further than the opening line of the musical, which was originally sung by the black stevedores (boat workers). This line has been subjected to the changing political winds with regard to race: the original phrase was "niggers all work on the Mississippi." London audiences in 1928 heard "coloured folks." The 1936 film substituted the word "darkies," which today seems no less offensive than the original "niggers." For the 1946 Broadway revival, Hammerstein reinstated "colored folks" (American spelling). Some recorded versions of the song favor "Here we all work . . ." A 1966 revival at Lincoln Center at the height of the civil rights movement avoided the problem altogether simply by eliminating the opening portion of the first scene. Harold Prince's 1994 revival reinstated "Colored folks." A 1988 EMI studio recording of *Show Boat* documents the show's rich musical history and includes every surviving song that Kern and Hammerstein wrote for it. The recording also includes some of the spoken dialogue with musical underscoring as in the original production.

Score

The score of *Show Boat* accomplishes several things at once. It depicts the story's passage of time from 1887 to 1927. Indeed, the score encapsulates the history of American popular theater music from the Reconstruction to the Jazz Age. It also distinguishes between the black and white characters and the different social classes represented in the story. Several diegetic numbers are part of the musical's show business milieu. Magnolia, Julie, Elle, and Frank perform songs on the stage of the showboat or a nightclub. Julie's "Bill," the mother of all torch songs, reveals something about her character, even though it was composed for an earlier show, albeit with different lyrics (see Chapter 4). Kern and Hammerstein gave the romantic leads the surging lyricism of operetta (e.g., "You Are Love") and wrote upbeat musical comedy numbers (e.g., "Life Upon the Wicked Stage") for Ellie and Frank.

Show Boat's extended opening scene is one of Hammerstein and Kern's major achievements. This segment, nearly fifteen minutes in length, establishes musical motives, five main characters, three dramatic conflicts, two social realities, and the principal romantic plot while providing more entertainment than the average musical comedy does in twice the time. "Cotton Blossom" and the anthem "Ol' Man River," which serve as bookends to the scene, are different configurations of three basic motives heard throughout the scene (Table 5.1). The A phrase, a virtually pentatonic melody reminiscent of American popular song, moves by step in the first measure and by wider intervals in the second measure (Example 5.1a). Tonic and subdominant harmonies reinforce the ethnic flavor of the melody. The B phrase

TABLE 5.1. Joseph Swain's Comparison of "Cotton Blossom" and "Ol' Man River"

"COTTON BLOSSOM"		"OL' MAN RIVER"	
Verse:	A	Verse:	A
	B	Refrain:	C'
	A		C'
Refrain:	C		B
	C		C'''

consists primarily of motion by thirds, a direct reference to the A theme (Example 5.1b). The first three notes of the C theme (on "Cotton Blossom") (transposed to E major: E-C#-B) are the inversion of the last three notes of the opening motive (B-C#-E, on "Mississippi") (Example 5.1c). The descending motion here contrasts with the ascending motion of the A theme.

"Ol' Man River" evokes the Negro spiritual, but the well-known main theme (C') is an inversion of the first four notes of the "Cotton Blossom" refrain (C). The song exhibits motivic consistency even as it continually evolves. For instance, the opening rhythmic motive (♩ ♩ ♫♪) occurs six times in succession. The first phrase has an arch contour, which peaks in m. 4. The second phrase (A') develops the same idea but reaches a higher peak, which Kern achieves by shifting the fourth measure of A to the third measure of the phrase. The fourth phrase is also a prime form of A (A''), but it ascends higher still and thus forces the final cadence to occur an octave higher than the other A phrases, a fitting climax to the song.

Between "Cotton Blossom" and "Ol' Man River" occur several important musical events, including Gaylord Ravenal's "Where's the Mate for Me?" and his and Magnolia's duet "Only Make Believe," during which they seal their fate. Ravenal and Magnolia's is the most lyrical and romantic music (i.e., similar to that of operetta) in the score. Ravenal's first line in the show, "Who cares . . . ?" (the opening words of "Where's the Mate for Me?"), poses a question that Hammerstein answers with the last words of "Make Believe": "I do." "Only Make Believe" is not merely a lyrical tune; it is a tightly wound emotional scene that establishes the two characters and their relationship in musical terms. Magnolia and Gay, as most of the other characters call him, appear unprepared for the charged sexual tension that unexpectedly overcomes them midway through the song. "Make Believe" is no mere declaration of love for the audience's vicarious pleasure; it stages the very act of falling in love.

In the next scene, Julie LaVerne sings "Can't Help Lovin' Dat Man," which elicits the suspicion of Queeney, who exclaims, "How come y'all now dat song? . . . ah didn't ever hear anybody but colored folks sing dat song. Sounds funny for Miss Julie to know it." The song exposes Julie's secret, but it also establishes her relationship with Magnolia, who, when hearing it, shuffles in an exaggerated fashion along with some of the black characters. The song is a fusion of black music (blues) and white music (Tin Pan Alley), and it reflects the fact that Julie is technically (and legally) a black woman but appears white. The music is marked "Tempo di Blues," and the verse ("Oh, listen, sister") is a twelve-bar blues melody; the refrain adopts the standard AABA form of Tin Pan Alley. Julie gains the audience's sympathy in this scene, which makes the later revelation of her and Steve's forbidden love all the more devastating.

The omnipresent river in *Show Boat* means different things to the different characters. For the black workers, the river is a source of hardship and strife, but it is a source of pleasure for the white patrons of the Cotton Blossom. In Captain Andy's view, the river is like hope that springs eternal. By way of contrast, Joe recognizes that as a black man he must resign himself to suffering as sure as the river will keep on rolling along. The river also carries spiritual significance. In "Ol' Man

EXAMPLE 5.1. *Show Boat*, Opening, (a) mm. 13–16 (A theme), (b) mm. 21–24 (B theme), (c) mm. 37–40 (C theme)

PLOT OF SHOW BOAT

The Cotton Blossom, a showboat owned by Cap'n Andy Hawkes, pulls into the Mississippi River town of Natchez. Before long, the riverboat gambler Gaylord Ravenal and Cap'n Andy's daughter, Magnolia, meet and quickly fall in love. The showboat's featured actress, Julie LaVerne, the daughter of mixed-race parents, and her husband, Steve, who is white, are forced to give up their jobs because the local sheriff has discovered that they are guilty of miscegenation. Cap'n Andy, in need of replacements for his leading actors, permits Magnolia to appear and hires Ravenal to play opposite her. Before long, Magnolia and Ravenal marry, move to Chicago, and have a daughter, Kim. When Ravenal's luck runs out, he deserts his wife and daughter. Magnolia is hired to sing at a nightclub, but, unbeknown to her, only after Julie LaVerne, now an alcoholic and the featured singer at the club, quits so that Magnolia can take her place. Magnolia goes on to enjoy a successful singing career, and after her so does Kim. After Magnolia retires from the stage, she returns to her parents on the Cotton Blossom, where she is reunited with Ravenal.

River," Joe invokes the River Jordan, which, according to the Bible, one crosses in order to get to paradise. Similarly, African Americans could achieve spiritual and personal freedom by crossing the Ohio River during the journey along the Underground Railroad. The weighty symbolism notwithstanding, *Show Boat* ultimately trivializes the racial problems embedded into the plot, despite Hammerstein's best intentions. Joe's song injects a degree of gravitas into the show, but *Show Boat* established a pattern in white-written musicals about race (see Chapter 15).

Critics have always had problems with the second act of *Show Boat*, as it contains too many improbable coincidences, even for musical comedy, and too many song interpolations in the Trocadero nightclub scene. Moreover, the action of the second act reflects certain assumptions about how race relations were to be portrayed on Broadway, namely that black characters had to suffer for the benefit of the white characters and that interracial romances were ultimately doomed to failure. Julie and Steve cannot escape the harsh reality of anti-miscegenation laws, and their marriage cannot withstand the virulent racism of Reconstruction. She must pay for attempting to pass as white. However, even as she slides toward the abyss in Act II, Julie commits an act of altruism and forfeits her livelihood for Magnolia's benefit, after which she disappears, never to be heard from again (except in the whitewashed 1951 MGM film version). This much of the story comes from Ferber's novel. On the other hand, Hammerstein and Kern found it expedient—in fact, they felt obligated—to reunite Magnolia and Gaylord despite the utter incredulity of this reunion.

AFTER *SHOW BOAT*

For all its historical importance, *Show Boat* did not precipitate immediate major changes in musical comedy. How could it have, given the trivial nature of the genre in the late twenties? Kern and Hammerstein's sophisticated approach to Ferber's novel was not easily transferable to the light musicals that followed on the heels of *Show Boat*. Given the choice between producing a musical with serious content and one with appealing music but little in the way of substance, most producers continued to choose the latter, if only because of its greater earning potential. The biggest hits during these years were *Good News!* (1927) and *Whoopee!* (1928). George M. Cohan's last musical, *Billie*, also opened in 1928, and the Marx Brothers appeared in *Animal Crackers*, their last Broadway musical.

For years, *Good News!* was a favorite of amateur and high school drama clubs. It boasted several hit songs, including "The Best Things in Life Are Free," and spawned two movie adaptations. Reminiscent of *Leave It to Jane* (see Chapter 4), it takes place on a football-crazy college campus. *Good News!* was the first of four hit musical comedies by the writing team of B. G. ("Buddy") De Sylva (1895–1950) (book and lyrics), Lew Brown (1893–1958) (lyrics), and Ray Henderson (1896–1970) (music). (Laurence Schwab, one of the show's producers, co-wrote the book with De Sylva.) Their musicals captured the aura and exuberance of the Flapper Age. *Good News!*, *Hold Everything!* (1928), and *Follow Thru* (1929) involve sports—football, boxing, and golf, respectively. *Flying High* (1930), a thinly disguised Charles Lindbergh spoof, involves aviation. *Manhattan Mary* (1927), their least successful musical, was an Ed Wynn (see Chapter 4) vehicle with a backstage-musical plot.

When, in the thirties, the three writers went to Hollywood, De Sylva became head of Paramount Studios and produced a few hit Broadway musicals. Brown and Henderson continued to write, but they never repeated their earlier success with De Sylva.

Before *Good News!*, De Sylva had collaborated with several distinguished composers, including Jerome Kern and George Gershwin, and contributed songs to two Jolson vehicles, *Sinbad* and *Bombo* (see Chapter 17). Brown, who had immigrated to America with his family when he was five years old, dropped out of high school in order to became a Tin Pan Alley writer. Henderson studied music at the Chicago Conservatory and then played piano in a dance band. In the early twenties, he churned out hit songs such as "Five Foot Two, Eyes of Blue" and "I'm Sitting on Top of the World."

Ziegfeld produced the Eddie Cantor vehicle *Whoopee!* Cantor played Henry, a hypochondriac from the East who goes to California, where he helps Sally Morgan avoid a marriage to the local sheriff. She is in love with Wanenis but has been forbidden to marry him because he is part Indian. It turns out in the end that Wanenis has no native blood whatsoever. *Whoopee!* is one of several musical comedies in the repertory that exploit Native American stereotypes. At one point, the Jewish Cantor, disguised as an Indian, spoke in a Yiddish accent. The show also included a gratuitous blackface performance by the Jewish Cantor, a practice he shared with Al Jolson (see Chapter 17). The score, by Gus Kahn (lyrics) (1886–1941) and Walter

Donaldson (music) (1893–1947), boasted several hit songs, including "Makin' Whoopee." *Whoopee!* constitutes their only major Broadway show. Before *Whoopee!*, Donaldson, who was born in Brooklyn, founded a music publishing company and composed a remarkable number of hit songs, including "My Mammy," which Jolson made famous (see Chapter 17). The German-born Kahn worked with several composers during his career, including Vincent Youmans. His hits include "Ain't We Got Fun?" and "It Had to Be You." Shortly after *Whoopee*, Kahn went to Hollywood, where he worked on films such as *Flying Down to Rio*.

By the mid-twenties, Kern was, according to Stephen Banfield, searching for "a better musical return on his investment than musical comedy's conditions could offer him." Kern could have turned to operetta, but his musical comedy skills would have been wasted in that genre. Unlike Gershwin and Rodgers, Kern was not pre-disposed to integrating jazz into his musical vocabulary. With *Show Boat*, he was able to avoid operetta as well as compete against composers who, like Gershwin and Rodgers, were refashioning musical comedy in their own image. He also established "his bid for grandeur, and his retreat into something still novel and integral but more manageable and pregnant with future possibilities."

Show Boat opened during the most prolific season in Broadway history. The following year saw a decline in the production of new musicals, and the downward trend continued until the stock market crash created an entirely new reality for Broadway producers and theatergoers. Moreover, in 1927 the first talkie movies took the entertainment industry by surprise, and by 1929 the first full-length movie musicals were winning over audiences. The Broadway musical has never fully recovered from these events.

AND BEAR IN MIND

No, No, Nanette *(1925, Globe Theatre, 321 performances)*

Music by Vincent Youmans
Lyrics by Irving Caesar and Otto Harbach
Book by Harbach and Frank Mandel

Based on May Edington's story *His Lady Friend* and Frank Mandel's stage adaptation thereof called *My Lady Friend*, the musical *No, No, Nanette* is about a young woman who asserts her independence by having a good time in Atlantic City, but only long enough to teach her ornery boyfriend, Tom, a lesson. Nanette, an orphan, is well provided for by her wealthy Bible-publishing uncle, Jimmy Smith. Jimmy's creed is to spread

(Continued)

happiness, which he does by sharing his wealth, not only with his niece but also with a few women of questionable character. After several complications and misunderstandings, Nanette and Tom make up, and Jimmy, who has given his wife considerable reason to worry, is cleared of any wrongdoing.

No, No, Nanette reflects the preoccupation in the twenties with material wealth and power. Nanette is not really happy until she has some of it. When Tom discovers her with $200, he thinks that her reputation is ruined. The show enjoyed successful runs in both Chicago and London before arriving on Broadway, by which time its prospects for success in New York were high. The show produced the hit songs "I Want to Be Happy" and "Tea for Two." The producer of *No, No, Nanette*, Harry H. Frazee, attempted to repeat the show's success with *Yes, Yes, Yvette* in 1927, but without success.

In 1971, a hit revival of *No, No, Nanette* proved that nostalgia sells. Supervised by Busby Berkeley (1895–1976) and featuring a top-notch cast headed by old-timers Ruby Keeler and Patsy Kelly, the production inaugurated the revival craze that continues to this day.

Nanette, played by Louise Groody, flirting with her uncle Jimmy's lawyer, Billy Early (Wellington Cross), as Pauline the cook (Georgia O'Ramey) looks on, in the original Broadway production of *No, No, Nanette. Courtesy KB Archives.*

. . . .

NAMES, TERMS, AND CONCEPTS

Caesar, Irving

Cinderella musicals

Ferber, Edna

Fields, Herbert

Friml, Rudolph

Gershwin, George

Harbach, Otto

Irene

Lady, Be Good!

"Look for the Silver Lining"

No, No, Nanette

"Ol' Man River"

Rhapsody in Blue

Roaring Twenties

Romberg, Sigmund

Sally

Show Boat

stock market crash

Student Prince, The

Youmans, Vincent

. . . .

DISCUSSION QUESTIONS

1. How do class and gender relate to each other in the so-called Cinderella musicals?

2. Identify the inherent obstacles to adapting Edna Ferber's *Show Boat* as a musical and to bringing it to the stage?

3. Compare and contrast the dramatic and musical treatment of the white female characters and African-American female characters in *Show Boat.*

CHAPTER 6

THE THIRTIES
(*ANYTHING GOES*, 1934, ALVIN THEATRE [TODAY THE NEIL SIMON THEATRE], 421 PERFORMANCES)

The Great Depression and the rise of fascism in Europe cast a pall over Broadway for most of the thirties. With producers' apprehensions running high and discretionary spending for entertainment shrinking, the production of new musicals fell to a mere fraction of what it had been in the twenties. The 1933–1934 theater season hit a record low of thirteen new musicals (the annual average ever since). Moreover, hit musicals ran fewer performances than what had been customary a decade earlier. On the other hand, songwriting on Broadway could not have been in better shape. With George Gershwin and Richard Rodgers in their prime, Jerome Kern and Irving Berlin still in top form, and Cole Porter hitting his stride, American popular song reached a new level of sophistication. In addition to Porter, top-tier lyricists active at the time included Lorenz Hart, E. Y. Harburg, and Ira Gershwin. For downtrodden Americans, the radio and dancing were among the few affordable pastimes, and Broadway supplied the music.

Thirties musicals benefited from two major artistic developments. Dance began to play a more intrinsic dramatic role, and technical advances in scenic design (in particular, the mechanized revolving stage) allowed the action to unfold with greater fluidity. Classical ballet appeared in several shows, as choreographers and dancers from the ballet world began to work on Broadway, including George Balanchine (1904–1983), José Limón (1908–1972), and Agnes de Mille (see Chapter 1). Several musicals included a dream ballet, anticipating *Oklahoma!* One notable example is the "Beggar Waltz" from *The Band Wagon* (1931), which, as choreographed by Albertina Rasch, featured Fred Astaire as a homeless man and Tilly Losch as a ballerina, and made effective use of the revolving stage. By the end of the decade, American-style show dancing merged with European classical traditions to produce the standard Broadway dance lexicon.

Musical comedy continued to dominate Broadway, but it responded to the sour mood of the country in two distinct ways. Whereas musical comedy in the twenties expressed the unchecked euphoria of America after the war, thirties musicals either provided an escape from the dire realities of daily life or satirized important issues of the day, including the war industry, labor rights, political corruption, and racism. Cole Porter's *Anything Goes* and George Gershwin's *Strike Up the Band*, the two longest-running musicals of the decade, epitomize these two trends, respectively.

COLE PORTER

Cole Porter (1891–1964) has been described as an "elegantly polished Brahmin who relished a brash, sometimes raunchy, change of pace." This description accords

Cole Porter at home. *Courtesy KB Archives.*

with the public image that Porter himself cultivated, but it has little to do with who he really was. Porter hailed from a wealthy Episcopalian family in Peoria, Indiana, a stark contrast to the majority of Broadway writers at the time, most of them New Yorkers and Jewish. As a boy, Porter attended Worcester Academy in Massachusetts. Upon graduation, he visited Europe in the manner of "the Grand Tour" and then attended both Harvard and Yale. It was during college that Porter began to gravitate toward music. He wrote his first Broadway musical, *See America First*, in 1916. The show did poorly, and the following year Porter returned to Europe, where he lived, mostly in Paris, until the late twenties. During his years as an expatriate, Porter wrote songs for interpolation into Broadway and West End musicals, but he remained "a very talented dilettante."

Porter was gay, but like many gay men of his era, he married, some believe in order to protect his public image. In Paris, he met the wealthy American socialite Linda Lee Thomas (1883–1954). Eight years his elder, Thomas had been married to the allegedly abusive Samuel Thomas, the owner of the *New York Morning Telegraph*. Porter and Thomas married in 1919. As members of the upper echelons of American society, the Porters became trendsetters, spending the early years of their marriage in Paris and Venice, throwing lavish parties, hobnobbing with nobility, and making the Riviera a fashionable destination for wealthy Americans.

When the couple returned to the States in 1927, Porter wrote several hit musical comedies in rapid succession and quickly rose to preeminence in the field. *Paris* (1928), his first Broadway success, played 195 performances. The French-born actress Irene Bordoni, Broadway's embodiment of Continental chic, starred in the show and introduced the song "Let's Do It." Set partly in France, the plot centers on a romance between a French actress and a wealthy young man from Newton, Massachusetts. His disapproving mother spoils his plans to marry the actress. The next year, Porter's *Wake Up and Dream* opened in London to critical acclaim, but the subsequent Broadway version fared less well in part because it faced stiff competition from Porter's own *Fifty Million Frenchmen* (1929). *Frenchmen* had a book by Herbert Fields (see Chapter 5) and starred William Gaxton and Victor Moore, both of whom later appeared in *Anything Goes*. The next year, Porter and Fields wrote *The New Yorkers*, which included "Love for Sale." Seemingly infallible, Porter next wrote *Gay Divorce*, the musical that introduced "Night and Day" and "You're in Love," and marked Fred Astaire's last appearance on Broadway and his first major one without his sister, Adele.

Having established himself as one of Broadway's leading writers, Porter received a barrage of offers from film studios. In Hollywood, he felt less inhibited about his sexuality and allegedly had relations with several men, which drove Linda to leave him. In 1937, and at the height of his career, Porter suffered a horseback-riding accident. In the ensuing decades, he underwent tens of surgeries to relieve the pain caused by the injury. Linda returned to him after the accident, and they remained together until she died in 1954. After her death, Porter led a rather reclusive existence, and he stopped composing altogether after the amputation of his right leg in 1958. He died in Santa Monica, California, in 1964.

Porter's sophistication, erudition, and glamorous lifestyle made him a natural subject for a biopic. Between the thirties and late fifties, Hollywood churned out

Fred and Adele Astaire in *Funny Face*. *Courtesy KB Archives.*

several films about Tin Pan Alley composers, each one a shameless hagiography that treats facts as inconveniences. Such is the case for the first of two biopics about Porter, *Night and Day*, which, at Porter's own suggestion, starred the debonair Cary Grant. Porter had his hand in the script, for which he received $270,000 from Warner Brothers, but only with the proviso that he absolved the studio from factual accuracy. The studio executives did not feel that Porter's extramarital affairs, social circles, and near-effortless success were the right stuff for a film about one of America's cultural icons; so they insisted on a more "respectable" portrayal of the writer than was the reality, and Porter, who was prone to fabricating facts about his life, put up no objection. The one aspect of Porter's life that met with the studio's approval and served its populist agenda was his horseback-riding accident. The expurgated film version of Porter paints him as a heterosexual who never strays from his marriage and who must struggle for his laurels. It also propagated the myth that Porter was wounded as an enlisted soldier in the French army and the French Foreign Legion. Even Porter's songs did not escape bowdlerizing: Joseph Breen, the enforcer of the censorship rules known as the Hays Code, advised the studio to substitute "hell" in "Blow, Gabriel, Blow" and "cocaine" in "I Get a Kick Out of You" with less suggestive nouns. In the end, the film normalized Porter's life beyond recognition—and audiences loved it.

Nearly sixty years later, MGM released a second Porter biopic, *De-Lovely* (2004), starring Kevin Kline as Porter and Ashley Judd as Linda. Directed by Irwin Winkler, this film acknowledges Porter's homosexuality and presents a more realistic, if not entirely accurate, account of Porter and Thomas's marriage. It craftily recognizes Porter's complicity in the making of *Night and Day* by including a scene in which Cole and Linda attend a private screening of the film.

Porter's Music

The musical theater historian Cecil Smith describes Porter as "a littérateur and genteel pornographer." Indeed, Porter reveled in risqué allusions and treated sex with a delicious sense of naughtiness. Porter's songs engage in all sorts of subjects, from an oyster's journey down and then up the gullet of the wealthy Mrs. Hoggenheimer to Georgia Sand's appearance at a party in trousers, but always from the perspective of the sophisticate.

Porter delighted in pushing the envelope of poetic decorum, but he showed off his erudition by quoting French, Italian, German, and Spanish idioms. He felt just as comfortable writing songs about elevator operators as about the champagne-quaffing crowd. Indeed, he could quote Shakespeare and Shelley in one breath and Mae West and Josephine Baker in the next. Porter's expressions of love encompass a diverse range of possibilities, from flights of ecstasy to sadomasochism.

Porter's romantic ballads stand out for their lusty language and sultry melodies, often in a minor key. His was a tortured, self-effacing brand of love, a love with little redemptive power. When Porter waxes romantic, he acknowledges the heady intoxication of love but also its perverse humanness, and he juxtaposes physical love with spiritual love. Porter was the master of the *double entendre*. Some scholars have drawn a causal connection between Porter's suppressed homosexuality and his risqué lyrics in songs such as "Love for Sale." He kept his homosexual encounters separate from the public part of his life, but he allegedly engaged in sadomasochistic and degrading sexual acts, mostly with men of lower social standing, sometimes rewarding their services with money or gifts.

Porter's lyrics achieve their fullest effect in combination with his inventive, artful music. In art as in life, Porter embraced Europe, and he felt less need than his contemporaries to give his songs an "American" stamp. He could jazz it up when the spirit moved him, but he luxuriated in long, languid minor melodies ("Begin the Beguine" and "I Love Paris"), the result of a conscious effort to write "Jewish music," as he once boasted to a somewhat taken-aback Richard Rodgers. "Blue" notes are rare in Porter's music, a stark contrast to the songs of Berlin, Gershwin, and Arlen. On the other hand, Porter employed chromaticism and harmonic shifts to enhance the emotional impact of the lyrics.

Porter's songs also exhibit tight-knit motivic designs. The music theorist Allen Forte identifies several recurring motivic and large-scale structural connections in Porter's ballads:

1. A tendency for his melodies to unfold from a primary melodic tone, which is usually established in the opening moments of the song.
2. Strategic placement of the apex and nadir of the melody.
3. Decorative tones—especially the incomplete neighbor tone—on key words.

"In the Still of the Night" contains all three features. The lowest and highest notes of the song occur at important structural points, respectively, at the beginning of the melody (on "in") and at the start of the B section (on "do"). The melody also employs motive transferal, which accounts for its strong sense of unity. For example, the descending-third figure in the first phrase on "still of the night" is replicated an octave higher and in an expanded form at the beginning of the B section on "Are you my life-to-be . . . ?" Thus, Porter not only marks the A and B sections with the nadir and apex notes, respectively, but also connects these sections motivically. It should be noted that a half-diminished-seventh chord, one of Porter's favorite harmonies, gives a minor tinge to the word "night."

Whereas Rodgers had *Oklahoma!* and Gershwin *Porgy and Bess* to elevate their artistic stature, Porter never deviated from the brand of musical comedy that he wrote from the start of his career. His late musical comedies are set in the same milieus as his early ones. He preferred European locales, although he also wrote musicals set in New York. In Porter's musicals, the prophetic mingles with the profane; the privileged class rubs elbows with criminals or some other socially dubious element. For instance, in *DuBarry Was a Lady*, a washroom attendant played by Bert Lahr dreams that he is Louis XV and that Ethel Merman is Madame du Barry (see Chapter 17). The producer of the musical described it as "a high-class modern low-brow smut show."

On the other hand, Porter was not blind to the new artistic standards set by *Oklahoma!* In 1948, he wrote what most critics consider to be his masterpiece, *Kiss*

Me, Kate, a backstage musical about a troupe of actors performing a musical version of *The Taming of the Shrew*. The libretto, by Bella and Samuel Spewack, draws clever parallels between Shakespeare's characters and the "actors" who play them. Porter was in his element, as the story mixes highbrow (Shakespearean theater) and lowbrow (gangsters and showgirls) (see "And Bear in Mind" in Chapter 1).

For the remainder of his career, Porter exhibited little interest in serious topics or psychologically complex characters, and he made no attempt to expand his horizons as a composer. He had no need to change. Wealthy from the start, he could afford to write any type of musical that interested him, which was invariably a musical comedy.

Anything Goes

Anything Goes ranks among the most revived musicals from before 1943. Its racy humor, topicality, mixing of social classes, and sassy music make *Anything Goes* a quintessential thirties musical. Audiences today still appreciate Porter's hit-filled score and the book's farcical plot, whose most urgent concern is whether or not the boy will get the girl. That *Anything Goes* still plays so well today surpasses all expectations, given its haphazard and topsy-turvy beginnings. As Raymond Knapp notes, "*Anything Goes* (1934) seems, on the face of it, one of the happiest of accidents, a show that somehow 'works' even though its composer . . . was in effect the third choice (after Kern and Gershwin), and even though its original story and book (by Guy Bolton and P. G. Wodehouse) had to be almost completely rewritten by newcomer Russell Crouse in collaboration with director Howard Lindsay." The architect of this chaotic production was the producer Vinton Freedley.

In 1923, Freedley and Alex A. Aaron formed a partnership and began a ten-year period of producing musical comedies, which they did with stunning success. They championed George Gershwin in particular. An Aarons–Freedley musical is, to quote Ethan Mordden, a "quick, brash, and freaky musical comedy that has everything but a story." Great songs and popular stars outweighed weaknesses in the dramatic design of their shows. In 1927, Aaron and Freedley built a theater on West 52nd Street and christened it the Alvin, an amalgamation of the beginning letters of their first names: al + vin. Their luck ran out with Gershwin's *Pardon My English* (1933), which did poorly and bankrupted their partnership.

Freedley and his wife fled the country in order to avoid creditors. As he recovered in Tobago from the emotional and economic shock of the *Pardon My English* debacle, Freedley came up with an idea for a musical set on a trans-Atlantic liner with several eccentric characters. In late 1933, he returned to the United States and secured commitments from three major stars: Ethel Merman (see Chapter 17), William Gaxton, and Victor Moore. He still had no specific plot in mind, just a basic construct.

Sources vary regarding the details of the production, but the most reliable sources suggest the following sequence of events. With his still-untitled show, Freedley hoped to revive the type of intimate, sophisticated musical identified with the Princess Theatre, so naturally he approached Bolton and Wodehouse to write the book (see Chapter 4). He also contacted Cole Porter. As his creative team went to work on the show, Freedley traveled to London, where he hired Howard Lindsay, a former actor, to direct the production.

When the writers started working on the script, Bolton was living in Sussex, and Wodehouse, who had fled the United States in order to avoid a mounting tax debt, was residing in a not-too-distant French town, so they shuttled back and forth across the English Channel. Porter, who was vacationing in Germany, wrote the songs without even seeing a script. Bolton and Wodehouse used Freedley's idea for a seafaring musical as a pretext for a comedy that disparaged Hollywood, which they disdained. Their first draft, now lost, was a satire about Hollywood mores set aboard an ocean liner. The romantic hero, Jimmy Crocker, has fallen in love with his boss's daughter, Barbara Frisbee, and follows her onto the ship *Columbia*, on which she and her British fiancé, Sir Evelyn Oakleigh, have booked passage to England. Once aboard, Jimmy meets a smalltime crook named Moon, who has disguised himself as a priest. He also runs into Jenny, a nightclub performer who is in love with him, and an ex-screenwriter, Elmer Purkis, who has broken his contract with a film studio. Jimmy lands in the brig, but he escapes when he and Moon win the clothes off two Chinamen in a game of strip poker. They expose Oakleigh

Ethel Merman (center) in the role of Reno Sweeney, performing "Blow Gabriel, Blow" in *Anything Goes*. *Courtesy Photofest.*

as the father of an illegitimate Chinese child, and Jimmy wins Barbara's hand in marriage.

It was at this point in the show's evolution that things started to unravel. Freedley rejected Bolton and Wodehouse's script, lest he antagonize the Hollywood establishment. Bolton and Wodehouse wrote a second version, in which Jimmy and Elmer concoct a fake bomb from a barbell with the intention that Jimmy will toss it overboard, become a hero, and win Barbara's affections. Freedley did not like the new script; however, this time his concerns about a Hollywood satire were overshadowed by a real-life event that precluded any humor involving a bomb, fake or otherwise: in September, the *SS Morro Castle* suffered a devastating fire off the coast of New Jersey, and over 125 people perished.

With the date of the first rehearsal approaching, Freedley began to panic. Bolton had planned to be in New York for rehearsals, but a life-threatening gangrenous appendix kept him from leaving England. Wodehouse would not dare step foot in America, lest the IRS catch up with him. Desperate, Freedley convinced Howard Lindsay to serve as script editor in Bolton's and Wodehouse's stead. Lindsay agreed on the condition that the producer find him a collaborator. Freedley suggested Russel Crouse, who came with little experience but strong recommendations.

Lindsay and Crouse ended up writing an entirely new script. They invented a new character, Reno Sweeney, based on the evangelist Aimee Semple McPherson, and elevated Moonface to "Public Enemy Number Thirteen." By the time the liner reaches England, the romantic heroine, renamed Hope, inherits a fortune and is therefore free to marry Jimmy, renamed Billy. Not a trace of Hollywood or the stage business involving a bomb remained. Bolton and Wodehouse were not pleased with this turn of events, but they were powerless to do anything about it. The Broadway production credited them with the book and recognized Lindsay and Crouse for their assistance. Thereafter until the early sixties, Bolton, Wodehouse, Lindsay, and Crouse shared credit for the book.

PLOT OF ANYTHING GOES

Billy Crocker is in love with Hope Harcourt, but she has agreed to marry the English aristocrat Sir Evelyn Oakleigh in order to rescue her family's failing finances. This romantic triangle works itself out aboard a ship sailing from New York to London. Billy inadvertently becomes a stowaway. Also aboard the ship are Reno Sweeney, who is in love with Billy, and Moonface Martin, a.k.a. Public Enemy Number Thirteen. By the time the ship reaches England, the Harcourts' financial problems have sorted themselves out, Hope and Billy are engaged, Reno has latched onto Sir Oakleigh, and Moonface, to his disappointment, is no longer wanted by the FBI.

Music

Anything Goes features some of Porter's most memorable songs. At the very top of the show, Ethel Merman sang "I Get a Kick Out of You," which Porter had written in 1931 for the unproduced *Star Dust*. It was highly unusual, if not unprecedented, to begin a musical with such a story-specific and emotionally fraught ballad. Musical comedies at the time typically opened with a dramatically neutral song, usually a chorus, that set the tone, lest latecomers miss the exposition of the story. Composers reserved potential hit songs for later in the action, when the audience was more fully engaged. Porter allegedly placed "I Get a Kick" at the top of the show in order to get his friends to the theater on time; he warned them that they would miss a great song were they to arrive late. The curtain goes up on a Manhattan bar, where Billy meets his boss, Elisha J. Whitney, who is about to travel to London abroad the SS American. Billy runs into Reno Sweeney, who chides him for forgetting about a date that they had made. She too is about to board the same ship and asks Billy to join her. He replies, "Guys like me are a dime a dozen. You won't miss me over there." Dejected, she quips, "Why are the cute ones always so dumb," and then sings the memorable song.

Many of Porter's ballads express the exhilaration and despair of love with altitudinal imagery. "I Get a Kick Out of You" is the first of three such instances in *Anything Goes*. In each case, the reference to height informs the range and tessitura of the melody. "I Get a Kick Out of You" masterfully captures Reno's mixed feelings of rejection and resignation. She is too forlorn, and perhaps jaded, to believe for a second that the thrill of modern plane travel, still a novelty in the thirties, could compare to the intoxication of love. Porter illustrates the comparison in musical terms, specifically in the soaring climatic line that contains no less than five interior rhymes (six if one counts "my"): fly[ing], high, guy, sky, i[dea]. Time and time again, Porter achieved such breathtaking yet seemingly effortless songwriting.

The main theme of "I Get a Kick Out of You" consists of an ascending scale connecting the sixth scale degree and the fifth scale degree (A and G) (Example 6.1a). The ascending motion alludes to the lyric "flying so high" in the third A phrase (Example 6.1b). This theme develops throughout the song, which is sixty-four measures long, twice the normal length of the standard AABA ballad. Porter employs a close-knit motivic design throughout. The text shapes the variations of each A section. The sixteen-measure A section divides not into two symmetrical phrases but rather two unequal yet closely related phrases: 4+12 (a+a'). The second and longer phrase (a') develops the triplet figure introduced in the second measure of the first phrase. The final four measures of A round out the a' phrase by paraphrasing the opening scalar theme. The "b" segment is also based on the "a" theme. Table 6.1 illustrates how the main theme evolves throughout the refrain.

A^2 starts out with the infamous reference to cocaine in the lyric. The flow of the melody derives from the original lyric. A^2 begins like A^1, but the note on "even," G, is prolonged for four measures through upper-neighbor and raised lower-neighbor embellishments. After the fitting triple repetition on "even one sniff that would bore me terrific'ly too," the melody descends chromatically to E, as though Reno

EXAMPLE 6.1. "I Get a Kick Out of You," refrain, (a) first phrase, (b) final phrase

gives in to the ennui of her hopeless romantic yearning. The last A (A³) contains one of musical theater's greatest musical phrases. Capturing the feeling of "flying so high," the melody overshoots its goal of G and continues on to D, the highest note in the song. The string of interior rhymes occurring on the downbeats creates a sense of forward momentum. The closing phrase fills in the upper fourth of the scale rather than descending to the tonic as in the first two A sections, thus preparing the final cadence to occur an octave higher than all of the previous ones.

TABLE 6.1. Refrain of "I Get a Kick Out of You"

A¹	a (1–4)	a' (5–16)
A²	a (17–20)	a" (21–32)
B	b (33–40)	b' (41–48)
A³	a (49–52)	a‴ (53–64)

Reception
None of the major revivals of *Anything Goes* faithfully replicated the original 1934 version; each one employed a revised script and interpolated popular songs from other Porter shows. The 1962 Off Broadway version was the basis for the available performance version until the 1987 Lincoln Center revival replaced it. The latter is closer to the 1934 production than the 1962 revival, for which Bolton revised the script; it was also used for the 2011 Broadway revival. Hollywood made two movie versions of *Anything Goes*, neither one close to the original stage version.

SATIRICAL MUSICAL COMEDIES AND REVUES IN THE THIRTIES

The struggling economy and rumblings in Europe spurred several writers to move beyond the safe limits of romantic musical comedy and into the realm of satire. Even before the Wall Street crash of 1929, the Gershwins and George S. Kaufman had written *Strike Up the Band* (1927), a satire about war profiteering and the collusion between capitalists and the military. Horace J. Fletcher convinces the U.S. government to declare war on Switzerland so that he can maintain his monopoly on the American cheese market. The show closed out of town, but a revised version with a new book by Morrie Ryskind opened on Broadway two years later and started a trend for political satire. Ryskind substituted Swiss cheese with Swiss chocolate and toned down the war motive. The new version was a hit, albeit a less vitriolic satire than the first version. *Strike Up the Band* was the first of three political satires by Kaufman, Ryskind, and George and Ira Gershwin. *Of Thee I Sing* (1932) and its sequel *Let 'Em Eat Cake* (1933) take aim at the American political system. *Of Thee I Sing* has the distinction of being the first musical to win the Pulitzer Prize for Drama. Gershwin's scores for these works parodies operetta conventions, but the librettos maintain a musical comedy tone, albeit of a zanier nature than usual. The self-contained songs in the score reflect Gershwin's characteristic inventiveness, but the most effective comic moments lie in the extended musical scenes, especially the finalettos at the end of the acts, which involve choral interjections in the style of Gilbert and Sullivan.

Whereas *Of Thee I Sing* radiates a musical comedy spirit, *The Cradle Will Rock* invokes a darker, more Juvenalian form of satire. *Cradle* has a fascinating backstory, which is dramatized in Tim Robbins's 1999 film *Cradle Will Rock*. Marc Blitzstein (1905–1964), who wrote the work, was under the sway of the German composer Kurt Weill and dramatist Bertolt Brecht. In fact, Brecht suggested the theme for *Cradle* when he heard Blitzstein perform "Nickel Under the Foot," a cynical anthem sung by a street hooker and at the time a standalone number. Brecht urged the composer to write a larger work about the various manifestations of prostitution in contemporary society. *The Cradle Will Rock* uses the struggle between labor and management to illustrate various circumstances in which people prostitute themselves. The plot was timely, as several conflicts involving union organizing were engulfing the nation's major industries. *Cradle* evokes the bleakness, political relevance, and dissonance of Brecht and Weill's works, but it ends on a positive note as the common-man hero of the story, Larry Foreman, stands up to the corrupt Mr. Mister and portends his downfall.

The Federal Theatre Project 891, which was overseen by Hallie Flanagan under the auspices of the Works Progress Administration (WPA), included *Cradle* in its planned 1937 season. Orson Welles directed the show, and John Houseman produced it. The Federal Theatre Project (FTP) had the mission of providing relief to creative artists by engaging them for various projects. Flanagan hired John Houseman (1902–1988) and Rose McClendon to head the "Negro Units" of the FTP. Houseman brought Orson Welles (1915–1985) into the fold of the FTP when he

PLOT OF THE CRADLE WILL ROCK

T he action is set in Steeltown, USA, which is controlled by Mr. Mister, a self-serving businessman who dominates the press, the churches, and the anti-union Liberty Committee until Larry Foreman organizes the steelworkers to rise up against him. When Foreman is thrown into jail, Mr. Mister offers him a bribe to cease his union activities. By refusing, Foreman precipitates the greedy power broker's downfall.

hired him to direct *Macbeth* ("Voodoo Macbeth"). Flanagan had the difficult task of negotiating congressional demands and the artists' desire to work without the fear of censorship. When the FTP sponsored educational plays that criticized institutions such as the Supreme Court, Congress cut off funding.

While *Cradle* was in rehearsals, strikes and protests intensified and grew more violent, especially in Northern cities. A forty-four-day strike of the United Auto Workers at General Motors in Flint, Michigan, from late December 1936 until the following February resulted in the first contract between the union and the company. On May 30, Chicago witnessed a brutal police offensive against striking Republic Steel workers. Meanwhile, conservative factions in Congress sought to dismantle the arts programs sponsored by the WPA. In June, the government, pressured by the House Un-American Activities Committee, announced a devastating 30% reduction in funding for the New York Federal Theatre Project. A memorandum issued from Washington in early June prohibited any new production to open before July 1. The cast of *Cradle*, although shaken by the news, went through with a planned dress rehearsal at the Maxine Elliott Theatre on 39th Street on June 15, the night before the scheduled opening.

The next day, Welles and Houseman arrived at the theater only to find it padlocked and blocked by armed guards charged with ensuring that the sets and costumes not be moved. Welles and Houseman announced that they would present the show without costumes or sets at some theater to be announced. When they found an available venue, the Venice Theatre on 59th Street, they led the cast, crew, and ticket holders on a twenty-block march up Broadway. Ironically, the actors' and musicians' unions prohibited their members from performing on the stage of the non-union Venice Theatre, so Blitzstein appeared alone on the bare stage and began to play the score on an upright piano. Suddenly, the actors, forbidden to perform "on stage," stood up from their seats and delivered their lines and sang their songs. *Cradle* played this way for eighteen more performances. Subsequent productions have attempted to recapture the Spartan original production, even though the creators had originally called for a large orchestra and lavish sets and costumes.

Welles, who left the Federal Theatre Project over the handling of *Cradle*, and Houseman, who was let go for insubordination, formed the Mercury Theatre and inaugurated it with a production of *Cradle*. The drama critic George Jean Nathan wrote that the show was "little more than the kind of thing Cole Porter might have written if, God forbid, he had gone to Columbia instead of Yale." His was a minority view: a Broadway production opened in early 1938 and ran for 108 performances.

Irving Berlin's *Face the Music* (1932) is a satire about the Depression and police corruption told in the form of a backstage musical. With a book co-written by Kaufman and his long-term writing partner Moss Hart, the show was bound to be zany. The plot centers on Kit Baker and her friend Pat, both of whom dream of appearing in a Broadway musical. The wife of the chief of police, Martin Van Buren Meshbesher, decides to invest money in a Hal Reisman musical, *Rhinestones of 1932*. The producer gladly accepts the money, unaware that it is stolen and that Meshbesher is trying to launder it. Critics pan *Rhinestones*, but Meshbesher takes over as producer and turns it into a hit by adding nudity and other racy material. The police decide to hold an inquiry into the revised show. Reisman, who had dropped out and become a waiter, decides to produce the inquiry as a show called *Investigations of 1932*.

Even Rodgers and Hart tried their hand at satire. *I'd Rather Be Right* (1937) had a script by George S. Kaufman and Moss Hart. George M. Cohan made a comeback playing FDR in the show. *I'd Rather Be Right* expressed optimism about the New Deal and the president's efforts to balance the federal budget. Cohan was anti-Roosevelt and accorded little respect to Rodgers and Hart, but he knew a good role when he saw one (see Chapter 3).

Kurt Weill (1900–1950) immigrated to America in 1935 after fleeing the Nazis. He quickly established himself as a major presence on Broadway (see Chapter 7). As soon as he settled in New York, Weill wrote *Johnny Johnson* (1936), which is based on the antiwar play *The Good Soldier* Švejk. Paul Green wrote the libretto, Lee Strasberg directed, and the progressive Group Theatre produced. *Johnny Johnson* follows a confused pacifist whose fiancée convinces him to enlist in the army. While serving in Europe during the war, he befriends a frightened German soldier; gets wounded; sneaks into a meeting of the Allied High Command and sprays laughing gas on the generals in order to get them to sign a peace treaty; gets arrested; undergoes psychiatric evaluation and is committed to an insane asylum, where he organizes the patients into a type of League of Nations; is released; and becomes a toy maker and street merchant.

Weill's next musical, *Knickerbocker Holiday* (1938), was a collaboration with the playwright Maxwell Anderson. It is an allegory involving the historical figure of Pieter Stuyvesant, who imposed a type of dictatorship on New Amsterdam (New York City) in 1647. Anderson wrote it as a critique of the concentration of power and FDR's overreaching during the New Deal. The show did poorly, but it boasted "September Song," a perennial favorite ever since.

The revue genre, which continued to flourish during the thirties, also provided satirical entertainment, beginning with *Strike Me Pink* in 1933. In 1935, the Theatre Guild produced *Parade*. Its left-leaning skits took aim at the Depression and the "Aryanization" of Germany. Critics were not amused, and they complained about the show's anti-establishment position. The Federal Theatre's *Sing for Your Supper* (1939) was more successful, featuring spoofs of *The Cradle Will Rock* and the 1939 New York World's Fair. Hitler made an appearance in a skit entitled "The Last Waltz." Harold Rome, working under the pseudonym Hector Troy, contributed "Papa's Got a Job."

Rome also provided the score for the decade's longest-running revue, *Pins and Needles* (1937). Starting out as a modest entertainment presented by the International Ladies' Garment Workers' Union, *Pins and Needles* opened at the old Princess Theatre, renamed the Labor Stage Theatre when the ILGWU used it as a meeting hall. During its 1,108 performances, *Pins and Needles* remained current through the addition of new songs and skits. For instance, a sketch called "The Red Mikado" was devised when two all-black versions of *The Mikado* competed on Broadway in 1939 (see Chapter 15). The sketch included the lyric "Three Little D.A.R.s [Daughters of the American Revolution] are we/ Full to the brim with bigotry," a reference to the society's infamous refusal to permit the African American opera singer Marian Anderson to sing in Constitution Hall.

OTHER REVUES

Most revues of the decade avoided satire. Some of the best ones were intimate, sophisticated entertainments with some connecting thread, featuring a score by a single composer and lyricist, a unifying theme or point of view, and a cast of players that appeared throughout the proceedings. *The Little Show* (1929) set the trend for this type of entertainment. The composer Arthur Schwartz and lyricist Howard Dietz (see Chapter 7) provided six songs, including the urbane "I Guess I'll Have to Change My Plan." Max Gordon, one of the most successful producers of his day, presented *Three's a Crowd* in 1930. It, too, boasted sophisticated skits and songs by Schwartz and Dietz. Gordon also produced what is arguably the most renowned revue of the decade, *The Band Wagon* (1931), which featured skits by the ubiquitous George S. Kaufman and a top-notch Schwartz and Dietz score. Also noteworthy is the double revolving stage that the designer Albert Johnson devised. The ensemble cast included Fred and Adele Astaire in their last joint appearance.

OTHER NOTABLE EVENTS ON BROADWAY

Whereas Porter dominated the first half of the decade, Rodgers and Hart produced an impressive array of hits in the late thirties, most of which incorporated dance in various novel ways. Noted ballet choreographer George Balanchine worked on four of these shows: *On Your Toes* (1936), *Babes in Arms* (1937), *I Married an Angel* (1938), and *The Boys from Syracuse* (1938). *On Your Toes* addressed an issue on many people's minds at the time, the distinction between low art and high art. Act I included an imitation of classical Russian ballet, "La Princess Zenobia," and Act II the jazzy "Slaughter on Tenth Avenue."

"Slaughter on Tenth Avenue" is one of the most memorable sequences in *On Your Toes*. George Balanchine's choreography, which represents a seminal moment in the history of musical theater dance, and Richard Rodgers's score are equally famous for their mixing of jazz and modernist elements. The dance, a violent tale involving dancers and gangsters, functions as part of a show-within-a-show. The music, orchestrated by Hershy Kay (1919–1981) and Hans Spialek (1894–1983), is still a part of the repertory of popular American symphonic music, along with Gershwin's *Rhapsody in Blue* (see Chapter 5). The New York City Ballet and other dance companies have incorporated "Slaughter on Tenth Avenue" into their repertories as a standalone ballet, usually employing Balanchine's choreography.

Babes in Arms is the prototypical let's-put-on-a-show musical. A group of can-do kids, the children of out-of-work vaudevillian performers, stages a show in order to raise money. Balanchine's second-act ballet, "Peter's Journey," is a fantasy sequence in which a one-time leftist character wins a raffle and imagines his new life of wealth and privilege. *I Married an Angel*, based on a Hungarian play by János Vaszary, is about a man soured on women and romance. The most noteworthy dance sequence was the "Honeymoon Ballet" in Act I. *The Boys from Syracuse* has the distinction of being the first Broadway musical based on a Shakespeare play, *The Comedy of Errors*. George Abbott wrote the script and directed the production. Balanchine interpolated an extended dance sequence—involving a prophecy that the Dromio of Syracuse sees in a crystal ball—into the fast-moving action of Act II. Rodgers and Hart also wrote *Jumbo*, a circus entertainment by any other name. Billy Rose produced the show with live animals in the cavernous Hippodrome Theatre.

In 1937 George Gershwin was struck down by a brain tumor at the age of thirty-eight. The enormous strides in Gershwin's creative growth during the thirties makes his premature death particularly tragic and an immeasurable loss to American music and Broadway. One need only compare his first work of the decade, *Girl Crazy* (October 1930) (see Chapter 17), with his last, his magnum opus, *Porgy and Bess* (1935) (see Chapter 15). *Porgy and Bess* is based on DuBose Heyward's 1925 novel *Porgy*. Heyward and his wife, Dorothy, collaborated on a stage adaption of the novel, which the Theatre Guild, caught up in the momentum of the folk-play movement, produced in 1927. Writers no less in stature than Kern and Hammerstein expressed interest in turning *Porgy* into a musical (it would have starred Al Jolson in blackface [see Chapter 17]), but Gershwin beat them to it, signing a contract with the Theatre Guild in 1933. Gershwin's score blends musical theater and operatic idioms, and contains several extended passages and choruses.

World War II engulfed Europe in 1939. As America remained on the sidelines for three years, Broadway produced revues and mostly formulaic musical comedies, the most popular being Porter's *DuBarry Was a Lady*, Rodgers and Hart's *Too Many Girls*, and Lew Brown's *Yokel Boy*. However, musicals with more serious themes began to appear in 1940, such as Rodgers and Hart's *Pal Joey* and Kurt Weill and Moss Hart's *Lady in the Dark* (1941). These shows helped pave the way for *Oklahoma!* in 1943. Porter remained detached from politics and other serious matters, at least artistically. He went straight from *DuBarry* into a triptych of similarly frothy musical comedies: *Panama Hattie* (1940), *Let's Face It* (1941), and *Something for the Boys* (1943). The country entered the war in late 1941, and Americans soon gained a newfound sense of confidence and optimism. *Oklahoma!* spoke to this optimism and marked the beginning of a new era in musical theater.

AND BEAR IN MIND

Of Thee I Sing *(1931, Music Box Theatre, 441 performances)*

Music by George Gershwin
Lyrics by Ira Gershwin
Book by George S. Kaufman and Morrie Ryskind

O*f Thee I Sing* follows the presidential campaign of John P. Wintergreen. William Gaxton starred as Wintergreen and Victor Moore as his hapless vice president, Alexander Throttlebottom. Wintergreen wins on a platform of love, pledging to remain faithful to Mary Turner, who bakes the best corn muffins, even after the Southern belle Diana

The First Lady, Mary Turner (center, Lois Moran), presents her husband, John P. Wintergreen (bending towards her, William Gaxton) the First Twins in *Of Thee I Sing. Courtesy Photofest.*

(Continued)

Devereaux wins the honor of becoming the First Lady in an Atlantic City beauty contest. When Devereaux, "the illegitimate daughter of an illegitimate son of an illegitimate nephew of Napoleon," causes a diplomatic stir between the United States and France, Congress impeaches Wintergreen, but it reverses its decision upon learning that Mary is with child. Diana marries Throttlebottom, who, as vice president, must assume the obligations of the president in the event that he is unable to fulfill his duties.

The sequel, *Let 'Em Eat Cake*, begins as Wintergreen and Throttlebottom are running for re-election. They are defeated by Tweedledee, after which Wintergreen and Mary move to New York and start to sell blue shirts. Inspired by an agitator named Kruger, Wintergreen leads a revolution. The revolutionaries defeat Tweedledee, and Wintergreen becomes a dictator of the proletariat. In order to collect war debts, he proposes a game of baseball between the League of Nations and the Supreme Court justices to settle accounts. His plans go awry, and a military tribunal sentences Throttlebottom and Wintergreen to the guillotine. Mary helps lead the resistance against the new dictator, Kreuger, and saves her husband, who restores the republic. Throttlebottom becomes president.

Whereas Herbert Hoover's fumbling administration provided an easy target for *Of Thee I Sing*, events in Europe were so dire that audiences were unable to appreciate *Let 'Em Eat Cake*, which lacked a love story and painted a depressing scenario of a theoretical fascist America. It played only ninety performances and for decades existed only in the memories of those fortunate enough to have seen the original production. On the other hand, the script for *Of Thee I Sing* was published in hardcover (1932), a first for a musical.

NAMES, TERMS, AND CONCEPTS

Aaron, Alex, and Vinton Freedley

Anything Goes

Balanchine, George

Blitzstein, Marc

The Boys from Syracuse

The Cradle Will Rock

Federal Theatre Project

Great Depression

Houseman, John

"I Get a Kick Out of You"

Kaufman, George S.

Kiss Me, Kate

Of Thee I Sing

Porter, Cole

Strike Up the Band

Welles, Orson

Works Progress Administration (WPA)

. . . .

DISCUSSION QUESTIONS

1. How did musical theater respond to national events and world affairs in the thirties?

2. Identify the hallmark features of Cole Porter's music and lyrics.

3. In what ways do Gershwin's three satires borrow from operetta?

CHAPTER 7

THE FORTIES

(*BRIGADOON*, 1947, ZIEGFELD THEATRE, 581 PERFORMANCES)

N ot all musical theater historians hail the premiere of *Oklahoma!* in 1943 as the beginning of the American musical theater's Golden Age. Some prefer an earlier date—for instance, 1927, the year of *Show Boat*—but no one denies the profound influence that *Oklahoma!* had on the musical theater genre. After 1943, the practice of interpolating songs into a musical without a logical reason or dramatic justification was primarily used by older musical comedy writers who were out of step with the new artistic standards introduced by Rodgers and Hammerstein, which demanded that songs, dances, and dialogue be fully integrated. Even musical comedies were subjected to these standards. Moreover, as musical theater plots began to encompass a greater geographic and historical range—from the Civil War–era town of Cicero Falls (*Bloomer Girl*) to fourteenth-century China (*Lute Song*)—composers went beyond the limited traditional musical vocabulary and thirty-two-bar form of generic Tin Pan Alley songs. Richard Rodgers, for instance, endowed each of his scores with a distinct sound evocative of the time and place in which the story occurs without slipping into pure pastiche. Not every composer was as adept as Rodgers in this regard, but in general musical theater scores became more responsive to the specific setting of a story and in the process became more distinctive. Audiences, although still flocking to musical comedies, also welcomed the new psychological maturity, complexity, and range of emotions of the musical play.

Oklahoma! did not open in a cultural vacuum, however, and it was hardly the first musical to address serious issues. In the years immediately preceding *Oklahoma!*, several thought-provoking musicals appeared on Broadway. And before that, Hammerstein had explored weighty themes. In the mid-thirties, George Gershwin was moving in the direction of serious musical theater, and his score for, *Porgy and Bess* makes one wonder how he would have responded to the Rodgers and Hammerstein revolution had he not been stricken at such an early age. Although the German-born Kurt Weill had absorbed the American popular vernacular into his composition, from the moment he landed in America, he instinctively approached musical theater as a high art genre. Weill and Moss Hart's *Lady in the Dark* (1941) was as daring as it was unique. Even Rodgers and Hart were gravitating toward serious subjects in the late thirties. Viewed in this context, *Oklahoma!* appears to have emerged from a growing artistic trend that Kim Kolwalke has characterized as "idiosyncratic experimentation" or risk taking. *Oklahoma!* responded to the mood of a country enmeshed in a world war and reeling from a grueling economic depression, and it came about at a time when theatergoers were growing weary of frivolous musical comedies.

Not every attempt to achieve the dramatic coherence and integration of dialogue and music of the Rodgers and Hammerstein model succeeded or met with approval. Moreover, some established writers were indifferent to the new type of musical that *Oklahoma!* represented, and their musicals from this period are largely indistinguishable from those that they wrote in the thirties. For example, Porter's *Mexican Hayride* (1944), a farce involving a female bullfighter in Mexico, featured the sort of songs that one had come to expect from the famed composer-lyricist. Several musical comedies, especially those with a topical wartime setting, lost their relevance and became outdated as soon as they closed.

LERNER AND LOEWE

No musical theater writers from this period emulated Rodgers and Hammerstein more than Alan Jay Lerner and Frederick Loewe. Although Lerner, a lyricist and book writer, and Loewe, a composer, were relative Broadway newcomers in the

Frederick Loewe (left) and Alan Jay Lerner (right) shortly after the opening of *My Fair Lady. Courtesy Associated Press.*

LERNER AND LOEWE

Alan Jay Lerner (1918–1986) grew up in the New York of Jerome Kern and George and Ira Gershwin. By the age of twelve, he had decided on a life in the theater. His father, Joseph J. Lerner, the cofounder of a successful department store chain, left home when the boy was still young. Lerner stayed with his mother but developed a close bond with his father—who was a womanizer, misogynist, autocrat, political conservative, and avowed atheist (the Lerners were Jewish by birth)—took an active role in shaping Alan's worldview. He sent his son to New York's top schools, Bedales School in England and Harvard University. Lerner inherited his father's love of languages and theater. While attending Harvard, he wrote for the Hasty Pudding shows, and shortly after graduation he worked as a freelance writer while living in a series of hotel rooms. Soon, he got married, the first of a total of eight times.

Lerner flunked his induction physical and was thus sidelined from serving in World War II. Although unhappy about having to remain in New York, he was around to witness the revolution that was occurring in musical theater. Musicals such as *Lady in the Dark* made a deep impression on him. Despite his father's pragmatic disposition, Alan grew up a romantic and developed a fascination for fantasy, the occult, and extrasensory perception. He looked for stories set in the past because, he wrote, "Looking back to earlier times may be an escape, but it can also be a reaffirmation." Such stories, he believed, possess an inherent lyricism sometimes lacking in modern stories.

Frederick Loewe (1901–1988) was one of several illustrious Broadway composers who emigrated from Europe. Like Kurt Weill, he was born in Berlin. His father, Edmond, was a famous Viennese tenor, celebrated for appearing as Danillo in the first Berlin production of *The Merry Widow* (see Chapter 3). Frederick attended a music conservatory in Berlin and won the Hollander Medal. In 1924, he traveled to New York with his father, whom the impresario David Belasco had booked for an engagement. While in New York, Edmond died, and the young Frederick decided to remain in the bustling modern metropolis. He announced to no one in particular that he was going to "crash Broadway," but it took him several years to do so. In fact, Loewe practically starved, and during the Depression he performed a series of menial jobs, including delivering mail on horseback in Montana. Upon returning to New York, he took up boxing, among other things. Like his future partner, Loewe enjoyed the male camaraderie of the Lambs Club. Eventually, a few of his songs found their way into Broadway shows.

early forties, their distinguished collaboration spanned nearly the exact same years as Rodgers and Hammerstein's, beginning in 1942 and ending in 1960 (they reunited briefly in 1971 for a movie version of Antoine de Saint-Exupéry's *The Little Prince*). Lerner and Loewe wrote integrated musical plays with picturesque settings, psychologically motivated characters, and serious themes, and thereby helped to propagate the Rodgers and Hammerstein model.

Whereas Rodgers and Hammerstein each had years of experience and a long list of accomplishments before they ever thought of working together, neither Lerner nor Loewe had had even a modest hit before their first meeting, which took place by chance at the Lambs Club in 1942. Returning to his table from the restroom, Loewe spotted Lerner and asked him, "You write lyrics, don't you?" Lerner responded, "I try." Soon they were collaborating, but at first it appeared that they were not destined for greatness. Their first three shows failed, and the fact that none of them has ever been recorded has practically guaranteed their obscurity.

The Lambs Club, the first professional theatrical club in America, was established in 1874 and eventually settled into its permanent home on West 44th Street, a building designed by Stanford White.

Before he met Lerner, Loewe had written two musicals with the lyricist Earle Crooker, but neither one had been a success. *Salute to Spring* (1937) only played outside New York, but the songs attracted enough attention that a year later Loewe and Crooker received an offer to write the score for *Great Lady*, which ran only twenty performances. Three years passed, and then in 1942 the producer Henry Duffy, who was in the process of revising a musical called *Patricia* (based on the 1925 farce *The Patsy* by Barry Conners), which he had produced in San Francisco a year before, asked them to rework their songs from *Salute to Spring* for the purpose of interpolating them into the revised musical. Crooker, who had joined the Navy, was either unavailable or uninterested in the project, but Loewe seized the opportunity. It was at this point that he approached Lerner, enlisting his help with the songs. The revised musical, retitled *Life of the Party* (1942), hardly portended the future triumphs of this newly formed team.

Lerner and Loewe's second musical, *What's Up?* (1943), was a light comedy about an Eastern potentate who makes a forced landing at Miss Langley's School for Girls, where he is detained by a measles epidemic, hardly the sort of material that was going to stick out in a year that included *Oklahoma!* Their next project, *The Day Before Spring* (1945), takes place during a college reunion, which is attended by former lovers who had nearly eloped ten years earlier. The man, now a well-known author, has written a novel that reminds the woman of their relationship. She has read it and wants to reconnect with him. Lerner's erudition found full expression, as the woman receives conflicting advice from Voltaire, Freud, and Plato. She follows Freud's and decides to run away with the writer, but fate intervenes and she returns home with her husband. The score offered some memorable moments, but a weak book, which the *New York Times* accused of being "austere" and lacking "literary sparkle," precipitated the closing of the show after only about five months. Despite the show's poor showing in New York, MGM secured the film rights, although it shelved the project indefinitely. Even though none of these shows yielded a hit, Lerner and Loewe had established themselves as reliable professionals. Their next show would make them the equals of Rodgers and Hammerstein.

Brigadoon

The original marketing materials for *Brigadoon* made no mention of a source. Posters as well as the *Playbill* adopted the generic label "A New Musical." (The *Playbill* for the first revival, in 1950, identified *Brigadoon* as a "musical play.") Shortly after the Broadway opening, the theater critic George Jean Nathan publicly accused Lerner of plagiarism, citing similarities between *Brigadoon* and "Germelshausen," a German fairytale by Friedrich Gerstäcker (1816–1872). Indeed, the plot of *Brigadoon* resembles that of "Germelshausen" in several ways. The town of Germelshausen comes to life only one day every century, a result of a curse cast by the Pope. Gertrud, one of Germelshausen's youthful inhabitants, meets an outsider, an artist named Arnold. They fall in love. Hoping that he will marry her, Gertrud does not warn him that the town will vanish at midnight. However, Arnold's deep love for his mother compels Gertrud to escort him to the town's edge just in time for him to escape. He—along with the reader—learns about the Pope's curse only after the town vanishes. Lerner neither verified nor denied the allegation of plagiarism. He did suggest, perhaps as a diversionary tactic, that James M. Barrie influenced *Brigadoon* more than anyone or anything else. Barrie's play *Dear Brutus* is about a forest that mysteriously appears once a year, and his literary romance *Little Minister* (1891) has a quaint Scottish setting.

In all probability, Barrie's unique mixture of fantasy and realism exerted some influence on Lerner. However, several features of *Brigadoon* stand out for their originality. Lerner set his story in present-day (i.e., forties) Scotland. (The German location of "Germelshausen" would have been unthinkable for a romantic musical produced in 1947.) The plot of *Brigadoon* can be summarized in a few sentences: Tommy and Fiona meet and fall in love. Because Fiona's town comes to life only one day every hundred years, Tommy must decide in haste whether to join her for eternity or to return to his unhappy life in New York. Secondary and tertiary subplots round out the story. A love triangle involving Charlie, Harry, and Jeannie is intertwined with the main plot. Meg's dogged pursuit of Tommy's friend Jeff provides most of the humor, although this plot strand is not fully developed and never reaches a conclusion. What saves *Brigadoon* from becoming saccharine is the intersection of reality and fantasy, and the fact that Tommy must ultimately choose between the two.

Brigadoon's Scottish milieu encouraged the writers and designers to incorporate folk and Celtic elements. David Ffolkes's costumes for the original production incorporated kilts and a variety of colorful plaids. The set designer, Oliver Smith, created vistas of a fictional Scottish countryside. Agnes de Mille choreographed evocative dances, including the sword dance that Harry and others execute at Jean and Charlie's wedding. Peggy Clark's lighting design received as much praise as the work of the other designers. Ted Royal's orchestration used a conventional forties Broadway pit orchestra to imitate the reedy timbre of bagpipes.

Brigadoon was produced by Cheryl Crawford, who capitalized the show at around $160,000. Advance ticket sales surpassed $400,000.

The Highland setting also inspired Loewe's most evocative theater music to date. He incorporated Scottish folk elements, albeit stereotypical ones, and captured the operetta-like ethos of the story, creating a remarkably compact and nonfussy score. Trude Rittman composed the dance music in close consultation with de Mille, although she never received official credit (the *Playbill* listed her as "musical assistant to Miss de Mille"). Open-fifth drones, gigue-like triple meter rhythms, and occasional modal harmonies evoke the mythologized Scotland of travel brochures.

Book

Brigadoon strikes a perfect balance of romance, pathos, and humor. Like any good playwright, Lerner invented psychologically complex characters, each with a distinct voice and disposition. These characters are fully fleshed out in the exposition. The opening scene introduces two American traveling companions, Tommy Albright and Jeff Douglas. The former feels a certain emptiness and questions the wisdom of his impending marriage to his social-climbing fiancée in New York. Jeff is a quintessential New York cynic, drinking heavily and interjecting a dose of sarcasm at every opportunity. His emotional distance makes him the one character able to appeal to Tommy on an intellectual level. Jeff's stinging comments do more than merely interject humor; they provide a necessary oppositional point of view to Tommy's brighter outlook. Fiona is steadfast in her resolve to marry out of love as opposed to necessity. By contrast, her sister, Jeannie, is a dutiful daughter, and she looks forward to becoming Charlie Dalrymple's obedient wife. Charlie, having reveled in the freedom of bachelorhood, has reached that point in a young man's life when he realizes that the time has come to settle down. Harry Beaton, the bitter antagonist, resents the restrictions that the "miracle" has imposed on his life. Not only must he forego his plans to attend Edinburgh University, but he must also bear witness to the marriage of his beloved Jeannie to another man, all of which is more disappointment than he can endure. He threatens the extinction of Brigadoon, but he remains a sympathetic character. Meg is the victim of the overdeveloped libido inherited from her mother. Mr. Lundie, the "dominie" (schoolmaster), the avuncular prophet, watches over Brigadoon. Jane, Tommy's American fiancée, who appears only in the penultimate scene, represents the cosmopolitan woman of Tommy's world. When Tommy breaks off their engagement, she responds with more anger than heartbreak.

Lerner skillfully interwove the various plot strands into a well-unified action. Tommy and Fiona must overcome their own biases as well as external obstacles to their union. The very miracle that has brought them together in the first place can tear them asunder forever. Harry's dilemma, moreover, weighs heavily on their situation, not to mention the existence of Brigadoon. The subplot involving Meg and Jeff provides comic relief, but it remains independent from the rest of the story (the MGM film version of *Brigadoon* further minimizes its importance). However, the events of the day affect Jeff, who, after accidentally killing Harry, becomes the rational voice of reason and forces Tommy to face reality and return to New York.

Resolution of the secondary plot (the Charlie/Jeannie/Harry triangle) is reached by the beginning of Act II, when Harry dies. The wedding continues, and Jeannie and Charlie look forward to a happy future together. The dramatic turning point in Tommy and Fiona's story is marked by Tommy's decision to remain in Brigadoon (Act II, scene 2). However, a reversal occurs when Jeff, momentarily shedding his protective comic façade, pulls Tommy back to the real world of New York. The climax and resolution of *Brigadoon* occur in nearly immediate succession. After passing several miserable weeks away from New York, Tommy decides to return to Scotland. His love for Fiona is strong enough to awaken Brigadoon, thus allowing him to join her for all eternity. Fiona does not appear on stage during the final scene (the reunion of Tommy and Fiona). (In the MGM film, Fiona greets Tommy, and they embrace before the final crossfade.) Instead, Jeff, stunned by Tommy's resolve to remain with Fiona, looks on in disbelief as his best friend disappears forever into the world of Brigadoon. The lingering image of these two friends, who will never see each other again, as they wave farewell to each other is a poignant reminder of the irreversible consequences of Tommy's decision.

PLOT OF BRIGADOON

Tommy Albright and Jeff Douglas, two American tourists, struggle to find their bearings in the Scottish Highlands when suddenly a village that is not on their map appears in the distance. When they arrive in the town, hoping to find a cozy inn, they are puzzled by the strange dress and behavior of the villagers. The town is bustling with preparations for the wedding of Jean MacLaren and Charlie Dalrymple. Fiona, Jean's sister, is attracted to Tommy, and as they get to know each other, Jeff is hotly pursued by Meg Brockie, an uninhibited dairymaid in search of male companionship. As Tommy and Fiona begin to fall in love, Tommy reconsiders his engagement to his ambitious fiancée in New York.

At the MacLaren household, Tommy is puzzled by the date of 1787 written next to the entry for Jean's weeding. Fiona escorts him to Mr. Lundie, the schoolmaster, who explains the "miracle of Brigadoon": two hundred years earlier, the pastor of Brigadoon made a pact with God in which the town would come alive only once every one hundred years so as not to be influenced by the relative values of any given age. As a condition for the miracle, no one from the town can ever leave. At Jean and Charlie's wedding, Harry Beaton, who burns for Jean and cannot bear to see her marry someone else, threatens to run away. A chase ensues, during which Harry is accidentally killed, by Jeff, it turns out.

As the strangely blessed and tragic day draws to a close, Tommy asks Fiona if there is any way for him to remain with her. Mr. Lundie explains that anything is possible if he truly loves Fiona. Jeff, shaken by the events of the day, convinces Tommy to return to America.

(Continued)

Upon arriving home, Jeff starts drinking more than usual, and Tommy quits his job and steals away to New Hampshire. After four miserable months, he breaks off his engagement and announces to Jeff that they must return to Scotland, unsure of what he will find when he gets there. When the two friends arrive at the spot where Brigadoon first appeared to them, they find nothing. Mr. Lundie suddenly appears, as Tommy's love has awoken Brigadoon just long enough for him to join Fiona. As the mist enfolds the town and Tommy, Jeff is left standing alone and dumbfounded.

Score

Lerner and Loewe wrote one of the repertory's most endearing scores for *Brigadoon*, and several songs from the show became crossover hits. The distribution of songs is somewhat unorthodox, though. Fiona and Tommy sing one solo each and share three duets, for a total of five numbers. Jeff is one of musical theater's few non-singing major characters. He does not seem particularly interested in women, at least not the libidinous Meg, even though she gives him plenty of encouragement. Perhaps he is too emotionally detached from his life to sing in this, the most romantic of musicals. On the other hand, Jeff, in contrast to Tommy, remains an outsider to Brigadoon, unable to appreciate fully its magical charms. Jeannie, too, is a non-singing role but, like Simple Susan in the contemporaneous *Finian's Rainbow*, she expresses herself through dance. Meg and Charlie sing two solos each. Meg's two songs, one in each act, provide comic relief (neither song was included in the film version). Charlie expresses his feelings for Jeannie in his two songs. Jane does not sing, and her brief appearance toward the end of show is dominated by Tommy's mental recollection of songs that he (or the audience) associates with Brigadoon. Nor does Mr. Lundie have a song, although his loquacious, patriarchal nature and knowledge of the miracle might have provided a good basis for one. Following the Rodgers and Hammerstein model, *Brigadoon* makes effective use of the chorus and corps of dancers (still separate entities in the forties). The men's chorus and women's chorus have one number each. The full choir sings three numbers, including the hymn "Brigadoon."

Instead of a traditional Broadway overture, *Brigadoon* begins with a brief orchestral passage taken from the wedding dance sequence at the end of Act I. This music, evocative of Scottish folk music, segues directly into the "Prologue," which creates a fitting fairytale aura. With narrative lyrics ("Once in the Highlands, the Highlands of Scotland . . .") and sweet homophonic harmonies, this number is the aural equivalent to the visual device at the beginning of many old Hollywood films: a book magically opens to reveal the first scene. The "Prologue" melts into Tommy and Jeff's protracted spoken scene. Sensing the mysterious power of the woods, Tommy observes, "There's something about this forest that gives the feeling of being in a cathedral." Despite having a good career and attractive fiancée in New York, Tommy feels a certain emptiness and discontent. This scene ends with "Brigadoon," another homophonic choral number. The town suddenly springs to life and draws in Tommy and Jeff. It is only the second day of the "miracle," and the citizens of Brigadoon must be reminded of their obligations, especially that no one leave Brigadoon lest the spell be broken. Allusions to faith and religion hang in the air of *Brigadoon*. Two centuries earlier, Mr. Forsythe made a grand bargain with God because, as Mr. Lundie explains, "the Highlands of Scotland were plagued with witches; wicked sorcerers who were taking the Scottish folk away from the teachings of God an' puttin' the devil in their souls."

The first scene draws a stark contrast between Tommy and Jeff's contemporary world and the archaic, eighteenth-century aura of Brigadoon. Lerner included a few pointed references to the atomic age and the Cold War. When Jeff notices Angus's astonishment after Tommy gives him a coin minted in the twentieth century, he exclaims, "What did you give him, a hunk of uranium?" Later, Jeff tells Meg that his ex-fiancée "fell in love with a Russian"; she asks, "Russia is in Europe, isn't it?" He quips, "Yes, more and more." Lundie tells Tommy that he hears the voices of the modern world: "There mus' be lots of folk out here who'd like a Brigadoon." This line must have cut deeply, coming just a few years after World War II and on the cusp of the Cold War.

Tommy and Fiona's solos and duets carry the romantic weight of the story, yet theirs are the most conventional songs in the score, all of them adopting the standard AABA song form (mostly of the thirty-two-bar variety). Each song begins with a short verse that economically establishes the dramatic framework for the refrain. Fiona's wanting song, "Waitin' for My Dearie," features a thirty-two-bar refrain, but a trio, during which the women's chorus (the lassies) joins the heroine, intervenes between the first and second statements. The lassies challenge Fiona, who protests that she prefers waiting for the right lad to marrying the wrong one. Her friends, by contrast, would rather marry the wrong man than no man at all. The trio shares features with the verse: four-measure phrases, which contrast the long-breathed eight-measure phrases of the refrain, and a median harmonic relationship. The reprise of the refrain occurs one step higher than the first statement.

With the exception of the trio, the structural, melodic, and harmonic features of "Waitin' for My Dearie" figure large in Tommy's songs and Fiona's other songs. Their first duet, "Heather on the Hill," adopts a Hammerstein-like approach to courtship in that the would-be lovers coyly hint at their attraction for each other but avoid openly declaring their feelings. A jaunty refrain theme slowly ascends, evoking a sun rising through the mist, with the long notes in mm. 2, 4, and 6 slowly unfolding a subdominant harmony (A^b-C-E^b). It features a graceful dotted rhythm of a sort rarely heard in musical theater. After arriving on E-flat in the sixth measure of the first phrase, the melody reverses direction and gently falls back to G. The second A phrase replicates the first except that the concluding descending phrase continues on to E-flat. This tonic note (respelled as D-sharp) functions as the leading tone to the first chord of the bridge, which wanders from F-flat major (enharmonically spelled as E major) to G-flat major. Following some spoken dialogue underscored by the orchestra, the reprise of the refrain unites Tommy and Fiona musically for the first time. They sing together first in unison, then in alternation, and finally in note-against-note harmony.

"Almost Like Being in Love," the most popular song from *Brigadoon*, interjects the jazzy ethos of Tommy's contemporary New York into the archaic Brigadoon soundscape. The bridge of the song moves to the submediant, exemplifying Loewe's fondness for modulations by thirds. The restatement of the refrain includes a refreshing metric shift from *alla breve* (cut time) to common time, marked *andante*; the second half of the refrain restores the original meter of *alla breve*. There is yet another surprise in store: the final A begins directly in the bright key of D, a major third higher than the original key. As already observed, Loewe creates excitement late in a song by modulating to a higher key, sacrificing tonal closure for an effective climatic ending. Here, too, Tommy and Fiona sing alternating phrases as well as two-part harmony.

Tommy's "There But For You Go I" is a deceptively simple number that verges on art song. The text is a highly stylized poetic lyric, and the music has a soulful quality, as befitting the tone of the dramatic situation. The A phrase consists of a soaring melody with little internal repetition, more typical of operetta than musical comedy. The B section moves into the minor mediant key, underscoring the forlorn sentiment of the text ("Lonely men around me"). A sequence of this phrase leads to an augmented-sixth chord, which resolves to V^7 just before the return of A. A partial restatement of the refrain occurs one step higher than the opening presentation.

Three outstanding musical features account for the dramatic intensity of Tommy and Fiona's parting duet, "From This Day On." The verse, despite its parsimonious nature, has the emotional weight of a dramatic aria. From the very first measure, the music expresses Fiona's distress, as she, reaching a high F, fervently implores, "Dinna ye know, Tommy, that ye're all I'm livin' for?" (Example 7.1). The phrase structure of the refrain is unusual. The A phrase contains twelve measures instead of the standard eight, and a rather long opening grammatical unit: "You and the world we knew will glow till my life is through," followed by "For you're part of me from this day on." The A phrase divides into three overlapping subunits (4 + 4 + 6), which creates the

(Continued)

EXAMPLE 7.1. "From This Day On," (a) verse, first four measures, (b) refrain, first twelve measures

TABLE 7.1. Overlapping Phrase Structure of "From This Day On"

A Section											
Phrase 1	m. 1	m. 2	m. 3	m. 4							
Phrase 2				m. 4	m. 5	m. 6	m. 7				
Phrase 3							m. 7	m. 8	m. 9	m. 10	m. 11	m. 12
	You	and the world we	knew will	glow	till my life is	through; For	you're	part of me from	this day	on.		

impression that the characters are overcome by their emotions (Table 7.1). The B section shifts to the minor mediant key and, like the verse, begins on a high note, thereby heightening the sense of urgency on "these hurried hours were all the life we could share." During the final A section, sequences of the A theme force the singer into a higher range. Like the town that vanishes into the mist, the music dissolves into the "Brigadoon" choral hymn (marked "Farewell Music" in the score). The final cadence of the hymn is followed by the "Mystic Theme," the most chromatic melody in the score, first heard during the transition between Tommy and Jeff's opening dialogue and the audience's first glimpse of MacConnachy Square in Act I.

"The Chase" strikes an appropriately menacing tone, but the narrative lyrics, delivered by the men's chorus, is hopelessly prosaic and overly conversational: "Lads, say a prayer, I'm afraid Harry Beaton is dead! / Looks like he fell on a rock and it crushed in his head." Lerner and Loewe wrote a similar type of chorus for Lancelot's rescue of Guinevere in *Camelot*. These sung accounts of events once served an important purpose, but today they have a wooden, melodramatic quality.

With the exception of "From This Day On," Lerner and Loewe's score exhibits a formulaic regularity (Table 7.2). By contrast, Rodgers and Hammerstein's music from this period is more adventurous with regard to structure, harmony, and counterpoint. On the other hand, Lerner and Loewe never sacrifice clarity or appropriateness of tone for complexity; they worked within the conventions of the day. Loewe aimed for an operetta-like sense of phrasing and lyrical line. Lerner's pliant lyrics have a Hammerstein-like simplicity and strike an apt poetic tone. Rarely if ever do they

TABLE 7.2. Common Musical Characteristics in *Brigadoon*'s AABA Songs

Verse that effectively establishes the mood, dramatic context, and key for the refrain
Presence of one or more mediant modulations, especially during the release (B)
B section comprising two parallel four-measure phrases, the second often an exact or varied sequence of the first
Three quarter-note pick-up beats performed with a fermata over each note
Reprisal of the refrain in a higher key than the first statement

draw undue attention to Lerner's erudition or deft facility with language. They are refreshingly romantic at the right times and droll when the moment demands it.

Social and Political Context

It has been argued that *Brigadoon* appealed to audiences in the late forties because it painted an idyllic world removed from the looming existential threats of the time. Americans had grown weary of the country's interventionist actions of the previous decades, and they responded by turning inward. This period marks the beginning of a right-leaning trend in America, which elected one of the most conservative Congresses of the century just a year after *Brigadoon* opened. The show's success, it could be said, expressed some of the postwar period's growing xenophobia and middle-class smugness. The town of Brigadoon represented a safe haven because it is "eternally static, homogeneous, and conformist," according to John Bush Jones. On the other hand, the quaint village resembles a fascist state, "an isolationist utopia, and a pretty scary one at that." The villagers, moreover, exhibit an anti-intellectual streak, and Harry Beaton must forego his plans to attend university and explore the world beyond Brigadoon. Harry serves as the sacrificial lamb because he is a nonconformist who poses a grave threat to the community. In contrast to *Oklahoma!*'s Ali Hakim, Harry refuses to resign himself to the staid life of his village. For audiences today, *Brigadoon* is no more than an enchanted romantic tale set in a distant land like any other fairytale musical. Its message, rather than being political, is simply that love conquers any and all obstacles to happiness.

After *Brigadoon*, Loewe moved to upstate New York to enjoy the fruits of his labors. By contrast, it was not Lerner's nature to pursue such idle pleasures at the expense of furthering his career. They would work together again, but in the meantime Lerner collaborated on projects with other composers.

THE RODGERS AND HAMMERSTEIN GENERATION

Today, the names Rodgers and Hammerstein are as inseparable as Gilbert and Sullivan, but in early 1943 one could have said the same thing about Rodgers and Hart (see Chapter 1). In fact, some people believed that "Rodgers Hart" was an actual person. Moreover, in the early forties Hammerstein's career, which had suffered several setbacks in the thirties, seemed moribund. Even after the premiere of *Oklahoma!*, the future of "Rodgers and Hammerstein" was in doubt. Hammerstein attended to some unfinished projects, and Rodgers managed to cajole Hart into rewriting their 1927 musical comedy *Connecticut Yankee* for a forties wartime audience. The revival, which boasted five new songs, including "To Keep My Love Alive," was a modest success, but Hart died within days of its opening. Hammerstein completed *Carmen Jones*, his adaptation of Georges Bizet's opera *Carmen*, for an all-black cast, which he had begun in the late thirties. By the end of 1943, however, Rodgers and Hammerstein seemed fated to work together again. Hollywood beckoned, and one of several film offers that came their way, a musical adaption of Philip Strong's novel *State Fair*, caught their attention. Twentieth Century Fox released the film in 1945, the same year as the opening of Rodgers and Hammerstein's second Broadway musical, *Carousel*, which is based on the Hungarian play *Liliom* (1921) by Ferenc Molnár. *Carousel* resembles *Oklahoma!* in several ways: rich character development, integrated choreography (including a dream ballet) by Agnes de Mille, a death scene, and a serious theme. The score bursts with originality. Rather than a standard medley overture, *Carousel* opens with a pantomime accompanied by the deftly composed "Carousel Waltz." Billy Bigelow's famous "Soliloquy," a nearly eight-minute rumination about his impending fatherhood, remains one of musical theater's outstanding achievements. The anthem "You'll Never Walk Alone" features a through-composed melody, and yet it became a popular standard. Rodgers and Hammerstein's next show, *Allegro*, represents one of the earliest essays into the concept musical, but it did not fully succeed (see Chapters 9 and 10). In 1949, Rodgers and Hammerstein reestablished their preeminence with *South Pacific*, which garnered the 1950 Pulitzer Prize for Drama.

Kurt Weill

When the Jewish composer Kurt Weill (1900–1950) fled the rising tide of Nazism in Germany in 1933, he first went to Paris and in 1935 immigrated to America. From the moment he arrived in New York, Weill immersed himself in the world of Broadway musical theater. He successfully assimilated the American popular music vernacular into his musical vocabulary, and he wrote several innovative musicals. Kim Kowalke calls Weill Rodgers's "chief rival." During the forties, Weill composed six Broadway musicals, which played a total of 1,758 performances, an impressive record, especially for a German émigré and one-time modernist composer. Also impressive are the wide range of topics and sheer iconoclasm of his works. Weill gravitated toward interesting literary material, and he collaborated with some of the most distinguished musical theater professionals and writers of the decade. *Lady in the Dark* (1941) introduced Freudian psychoanalysis into musical theater. Moss Hart, who wrote the book and directed the show, drew on his own personal experience on the couch with the well-known psychiatrist Gregory Zilboorg (George Gershwin was also one of his patients). *Lady in the Dark* is about a troubled fashion editor, Liza Elliot. The central musical movements occur during her three therapeutic sessions, which take the form of extended dream sequences (Glamour Dream, Wedding Dream, and Circus Dream). The final song in the show, "My Ship," holds the key to Liza's neurosis. She hears part of the tune, which she learned as a child, in her head but cannot complete it until she makes an emotional breakthrough. Gertrude Lawrence starred as Liza, and Danny Kaye, playing a gay photographer, famously sang the patter song "Tchaikovsky" in one of the dream sequences. "The Saga of Jenny" charts Liza's paralysis. By today's standards, the solution to Liza's malady seems essentialist and chauvinistic. Liza comes to the realization that she loves Charley Johnson, after which she can complete "My Ship."

One Touch of Venus is one of several fantasy musicals from the forties. Ogden Nash and S. J. Perelman co-authored the book, which is about a barber who places

Gertrude Lawrence as Liza Elliott and Victor Mature as Randy Curtis in *Lady in the Dark*. *Courtesy KB Archives.*

the engagement ring intended for his fiancée on the finger of a statue of Venus. The statue comes to life, and Venus pursues the barber until she realizes that the real world lacks excitement and turns back into stone. The barber subsequently breaks his engagement. The score produced one durable hit song, "Speak Low." Cheryl Crawford produced, Elia Kazan directed, and Agnes de Mille choreographed. As was becoming a common practice at the time, ballet segments were incorporated into the story, in particular "Forty Minutes for Lunch" and "Venus in Ozone Heights."

The Firebrand of Florence, Weill's one and only failure of the decade, was the second musical adaptation of Edwin Justus Mayer's play *The Firebrand*, which takes place in Renaissance Florence. Like Weill's previous show, it too involved a statue. The Duke of Florence repeatedly threatens to hang Cellini, first for the attempted murder of Count Maffio, then for the actual murder of the count, and finally for stealing away a model named Angela, whom they both covet. With lyrics by Ira Gershwin, *The Firebrand* included several concerted segments in the style of Gilbert and Sullivan. The show starred Lotte Lenya (1898–1981), Weill's common-law wife, but neither she nor the show made an enduring impression.

Street Scene, an adaptation of Elmer Rice's play of the same name, fared much better. Weill's most operatic Broadway musical, *Street Scene* portrays working-class New Yorkers in a relatively realistic way, although the music balances the dour tragic story with flights of romanticism. The action unfolds in front of a tenement house. Anna, the victim of an abusive marriage, enters into an affair. Anna's daughter, Rose, dreams of escaping the dull existence of tenement life, but she cannot decide between her smooth-talking boss and her earnest neighbor Sam. Her dreams inspired some of Weill's most soaring music. Eventually, Anna's drunken husband learns about the affair and kills her and her lover. Rose, feeling alone now more than ever, packs her suitcase and leaves the tenement.

Weill collaborated with Lerner on *Love Life*. Cheryl Crawford suggested the project to Lerner and Loewe shortly after *Brigadoon*, but Loewe was not interested. *Love Life*, the first concept musical after *Allegro*, experimented with form and addressed problems besetting modern marriage. The concept never fully gelled, despite direction by Elia Kazan. *Love Life* is Weill's only Broadway show that has yet to be recorded.

Lost in the Stars, the last show that Weill completed, is a "musical tragedy" based on Alan Paton's 1948 novel *Cry, the Beloved Country*. Maxwell Anderson wrote the book and lyrics. The story takes place in South Africa and deals with the theme of racial prejudice. The protagonist, an Anglican priest of a Zulu tribe, searches for his son, Absalom, who has accidentally killed a white man during an attempted robbery. The victim's father, a white planter named James Jarvis, supports freedom for the black race, but he also subscribes to apartheid. Absalom admits his guilt and faces a death sentence. When Jarvis visits him in jail, they become friends.

The range of Weill's output attests to his eagerness to embrace the issues, musical styles, and themes that characterized America musical theater at the time. His legacy, however, rests more on *Die Dreigoschenoper* (*The Threepenny Opera*), which premiered in Berlin in 1928. The first American production, in 1933, lasted only twelve performances. (Weill was still in Europe at the time and had little to do with the production.) One critic wrote, "*The 3-Penny Opera* is as humorless as Hitler." An Off Broadway production in 1956 established *Threepenny* as one of the most important musical theater works of the century, and several covers of the show's opening number, "Mack the Knife," topped the charts (see Chapter 14). On the other hand, Weill's Broadway musicals helped to shape the perception at the time of musical theater as popular art. Like Gershwin, Weill died young, but in the brief time he resided in his adopted country, he experimented more than anyone else and never repeated himself.

Harold Arlen

The Buffalo-born Harold Arlen (1905–1986) is best known for the songs he composed for the movie *The Wizard of Oz*, including the classic "Over the Rainbow," but he wrote over fourteen Broadway musicals, two of them in the forties. This son of an Orthodox Jewish cantor was one of the most influential songwriters of his generation; yet, ironically, none of his Broadway musicals has achieved canonical status. During the thirties, Arlen composed songs for revues, including the *Cotton Club Parade*. *Bloomer Girl*, which opened in 1944, is arguably the first musical directly influenced by *Oklahoma!* With lyrics by E. Y. Harburg (Arlen's partner on *The Wizard of Oz*), a book by Fred Saidy and Sid Herzig, and choreography by Agnes de Mille, *Bloomer Girl* takes place during the Civil War era at the intersection of the abolitionist and early women's movements. The latter is symbolized by the wearing of "bloomers," named after the reformer Amelia Jenks Bloomer (1818–1894). Celeste Holm, the original Ado Annie in *Oklahoma!*, starred as Evelina Applegate, the fictional niece of Dolly Bloomer (Amelia Jenks Bloomer). Evelina uses the Underground Railroad to free her fiancé's slave. Arlen's affinity for African

Celeste Holm (1919–2012) was an actress of stage, film, and television. Rodgers and Hammerstein remembered her when looking for a replacement for Anna in *The King and I* after Gertrude Lawrence died in 1952. Holm's film roles include Anne Dettrey in *Gentleman's Agreement* (1947), for which she won an Academy Award, and Karen Richards in *All About Eve* (1950).

American musical idioms was on full display here, as well as in his next musical, *St. Louis Woman* (1946), which had lyrics by Johnny Mercer. *St. Louis Woman* was based on Arna Bontemps's 1931 novel *God Sends Sunday*. Bontemps and Countee Cullen (1903–1946) collaborated on the book for the musical, although the latter died before the show opened. Lena Horne agreed to play Della Green, who is in love with Bigelow Brown, the proprietor of a saloon. She leaves him for Little Augie, a jockey on a winning streak. Brown attempts to kill Augie, but he is killed by a jilted lover. Before he dies, though, he casts a curse on Augie. Della leaves Augie, after which his winning streak comes to an end. The lovers reunite at the end of the show. Several problems besieged *St. Louis Woman*, none more devastating than Lena Horne's decision to withdraw from the project because she felt that it demeaned African Americans, and the NAACP agreed with her. *St. Louis Woman* ran only 113 performances, but it featured a top-notch score containing "Any Place I Hang My Hat Is Home" and "Come Rain or Come Shine." Arlen continued to write black musicals in the fifties, but none of these shows achieved the popularity of the decade's major hits (see Chapter 15).

Vernon Duke

The Russian-born Vladimir Dukeksky (1903–1969), who anglicized his name to Vernon Duke when he immigrated to America around 1930, was nearly as active on Broadway as Weill, but his legacy suffers from a lack of hit shows. He had studied classical music at the Kiev Conservatory and composed music for the Ballets Russes. Duke's songs "April in Paris" (lyrics by Harburg) and "Autumn in New York" (lyrics by Duke), both from the thirties, have been singled out for their sophistication, but *Cabin in the Sky* (1940), an all-black musical fantasy about redemption, marks the high point in his musical theater career. The heroine, Petunia, pleads with God to give her dying husband, Little Joe Jackson, a second chance to lead a righteous life. Her prayers are answered, and Joe receives six months to prove himself. Opposing male and female characters vie for Joe's soul. The Lord sends his General to help him, and the Devil sends Lucifer Junior to tempt him, which he does by enlisting the talents of the sexually alluring Georgia Brown. Petunia is inadvertently shot while trying, but failing, to protect Joe. Now ghosts, they arrive in Heaven, but only Petunia is permitted to enter. She argues Joe's case and wins. The Southern writer

John La Touche was chosen to write the lyrics because he could supply some authentic regional charm. Unlike Arlen, Duke felt uneasy about writing about African Americans: "I didn't think myself sufficiently attuned to Negro folklore." In fact, Duke and La Touche traveled to the South to research "southern talk and Negro spirituals," as the composer reported. Todd Duncan, the original Porgy in *Porgy and Bess*, appeared as the "Lawd's General" (as originally listed), and Ethel Waters starred in both the stage version and the 1943 MGM film version.

Duke's *Banjo Eyes*, which also had lyrics by La Touche, was the first of two Broadway musicals based on John Cecil Holm and George Abbott's comedy *Three Men on a Horse*. (The other, *Let It Ride*, opened in 1961.) *Banjo Eyes* starred Eddie Cantor (1892–1964), whose character discovers that he can choose winning horses, but only if he refrains from placing bets himself. A medical emergency sidelined Cantor and forced the show to close prematurely.

Duke's other forties musicals either folded out of town or played only briefly on Broadway. Both *Jack Pot* and *Sadie Thompson*, his two post-*Oklahoma!* musicals, opened in 1944 and played about seventy performances each. *Sadie Thompson*, an adaptation of W. Somerset Maugham and John Colton's play *Rain*, might have played longer had its intended star, Ethel Merman, not quit during rehearsals, allegedly over objections to Howard Dietz's lyrics. The story begins as Sadie and several fellow travelers are quarantined on the island of Pago. A marine named Timothy O'Hara falls in love with her, but their relationship comes under attack from a Christian missionary, who thinks that she is a prostitute. One evening, the missionary pays her a visit and succumbs to her attempts to seduce him. He subsequently commits suicide.

Arthur Schwartz (1900–1984) spent most of the forties in Hollywood working as a producer at Columbia Studies. Before moving to the west coast, he had collaborated with Oscar Hammerstein on *American Jubilee* for the 1939–1940 New York World's Fair. Schwartz's first Broadway musical in the forties, *Park Avenue* (1946), received poor notices, so he returned to California disillusioned. *Inside U.S.A.* (1948) reunited Schwartz and Howard Dietz. Early in his career, Howard Dietz (1896–1983) worked with Jerome Kern on *Dear Sir* (1924). Dietz and Schwartz first collaborated on the 1929 revue *The Little Show*. Like Schwartz, Dietz also spent much of his career in Hollywood, working as director of publicity at MGM.

NEW VOICES

Composers

Leonard Bernstein

Several important writers first appeared on the scene at the dawn of the Rodgers and Hammerstein era and helped to shape the Broadway musical for the next two decades. Leonard Bernstein stands out for his classical pedigree and sophisticated composition characterized by complex textures, cross-rhythms, counterpoint, and inventive harmonies. He attended Harvard and then the Curtis Institute of Music in Philadelphia. Bernstein's renowned conducting career began to take shape in 1943,

BETTY COMDEN AND ADOLPH GREEN

Comden and Green began working together in 1939, writing comic material and performing at a Greenwich Village nightclub. Their signature zaniness served them well in both Hollywood and on Broadway. Their screenplays include *Singin' in the Rain* (1952), *The Band Wagon* (1953), and *Auntie Mame* (1958). Comden and Green felt most comfortable writing stories set in their native city of New York. A typical Comden and Green musical features a madcap plot and a strong dose of silliness. They attempted a few serious musicals, most of which came up short, the main exception being *Applause* (1970), which won the Tony Award for best musical (see Chapter 11).

when he was appointed assistant to the legendary conductor Serge Koussevitzky. Within days of the opening of *Oklahoma!*, Bernstein made his conducting debut with the New York Philharmonic when Bruno Walter fell ill. Bernstein juggled conducting and composing throughout his career. That someone of his Ivy League and conservatory training would even consider writing musical theater says a lot about Bernstein's irrepressible ambition and eclectic tastes. On the other hand, it also says a lot about the rising status of musical theater at the time. That Bernstein excelled in both worlds is a testament to his formidable talents. Although he wrote fewer musicals than most Broadway writers of his stature, the quality of his output is consistently high.

A year after Bernstein made his historic symphonic debut, he composed the ballet *Fancy Free*, which Jerome Robbins conceived and choreographed for the New York City Ballet. By the end of 1944, Bernstein had written his first Broadway musical, *On the Town*, which was based on *Fancy Free*. Robbins choreographed, George Abbott directed, and Betty Comden and Adolph Green wrote the book and lyrics, marking their Broadway debut as writers. The score incorporates five extensive ballet segments that Bernstein composed himself, rather than a dance arranger, as was the standard practice.

Jule Styne

Jule Styne and Frank Loesser both had successful Hollywood careers before they attempted a Broadway musical. Styne (1905–1994) was born in London, but his family moved to Chicago when he was six. He was a child piano prodigy, and in the twenties he led his own dance band. In the thirties, Styne worked as a vocal coach first in New York and then Hollywood. He and Loesser collaborated on songs in Hollywood, including the 1941 hit "I Don't Want to Walk Without You." The next year, Styne and lyricist Sammy Cahn (1913–1993) struck up a collaboration that continued off and on for decades, and in 1944 they wrote *Glad to See You!* It was an ignominious beginning to a highly successful musical theater career, closing during previews in Philadelphia. Three years transpired before they tried Broadway again, but this time they had a hit on their hands. The show was *High Button Shoes*, based on the novel *The Sisters Liked Them Handsome* by Stephen Longstreet (1946). Jerome Robbins's choreography and winning performances by Phil Silvers and Nanette Fabray contributed to a long run of 727 performances. Two years later, Styne returned to Broadway with *Gentlemen Prefer Blondes*, which is based on Anita Loos's 1925 novel. Leo Robins (best known for his lyrics for "That's Entertainment") wrote the lyrics, and Loos co-wrote the book with Joseph Fields. Marilyn Monroe's appearance in the 1953 film version, in which she sings "Diamonds Are a Girl's Best Friend," overshadows the fact that the Broadway version marked Carol Channing's first appearance in a major leading role. Styne maintained a peripatetic pace on Broadway in the fifties and sixties.

Frank Loesser
Frank Loesser (1910–1969) ranks as one of Broadway's greatest composer-lyricists. However, before he found his unique musical theater voice, Loesser worked as a staff writer at Universal Studies, churning out lyrics for top movie composers, including Hoagy Carmichael and Arthur Schwartz. When America entered the war in 1941, Loesser enlisted in the Army and started to compose his own music. After the war, he returned to Hollywood, but he was soon hired by the producers Cy Feuer and Ernest Martin to write the score for *Where's Charley?*, their maiden Broadway voyage. *Where's Charley?* is based on Brandon Thomas's 1892 farce *Charley's Aunt.* It introduced "Once in Love with Amy," which Ray Bolger got the audience to sing along with him. Loesser's best years lay ahead.

Harold Rome
Harold Rome (1908–1993) was the first major Jewish Broadway composer to attend Yale University, Cole Porter's alma mater. After graduating, he settled in New York. The year was 1934, and satirical revues were in vogue. Rome had trained in architecture, but jobs were scarce, so he found employment with the Works Progress Administration (see Chapter 6) and wrote the satirical revue *Pins and Needles*, whose long run lasted into the early forties. Rome's first book musical, *The Little Dog Laughed*, closed out of town. Like Loesser, Rome wrote material for armed services entertainment during the war. The revue *Call Me Mister* (1946) was his most successful show during this period. In 1948, Rome tried his hand again at a book musical, *That's the Ticket!*, which had a book by Julius J. and Philip G. Epstein, the authors of the classic film *Casablanca* and Stephen Sondheim's *Saturday Night. That's the Ticket!*, however, never made it to New York, even with Jerome Robbins at the helm. Rome wrote a few successful book musicals in the fifties and early sixties.

Burton Lane
Burton Lane (1912–1997) also straddled the pre- and post-*Oklahoma!* eras. As a young man, he worked as a song plugger at Remick's along with George

Gershwin, and he wrote material for revues. His first major book musical, *Hold on to Your Hats*, opened in 1940. It was touted as Al Jolson's return to Broadway after an absence of nearly ten years (see Chapter 17). Jolson was himself one of the show's producers, but after nearly five months of performances, he got restless and left the show, forcing it to close prematurely. *Laughing Room Only!* (1944), Lane's first post-*Oklahoma!* show, was a revue. After that, he and E. Y. Harburg wrote the score for *Finian's Rainbow* (1947), which boasted an impressive number of popular songs and a socially relevant plot. Whereas the contemporaneous *Brigadoon* was a romantic fantasy about Americans in Scotland, *Finian's Rainbow* was a satire about an Irish father, his daughter, and a leprechaun in America. It examined race and class relations in a unique and amusing manner.

Lyricists

Several lyricists rose to prominence in the forties, including Johnny Mercer, Howard Dietz, John La Touche, and E. Y. Harburg, who, taken together, wrote lyrics for no fewer than forty-eight musicals, sixteen of them during the forties. These writers divided their time between Hollywood and Broadway. Their influence has never been fully assessed, in part because none of them had the sort of long-term collaboration that would have helped to carve out a unified body of work. Instead, they circulated among the same composers, including Kurt Weill, Vernon Duke, and Arthur Schwartz.

E. Y. Harburg

E. Y. (Yip) Harburg (born Isidore Hochberg) held strong leftist political views, which informed much of his work and occasionally got in the way of his career. Harburg attended Townsend Harris High School and City College of New York with Ira Gershwin. A pacifist, he avoided military service during World War I by taking a job in Uruguay. At the start of the Depression, he wrote songs with Jay Gorney, including "Brother, Can You Spare a Dime?" Soon the duo was under contract in Hollywood, but Harburg continued to provide material for Broadway revues. His first book musical was *Hooray for What!,* which he wrote with Harold Arlen in 1937.

John La Touche

Several of the lyricists working on Broadway in the forties hailed from the South. John La Touche (1917–1956) was born in Baltimore, but he grew up in Virginia. Like many Broadway lyricists, he attended Columbia University. After *Cabin in the Sky* (1940), La Touche continued to work with Vernon Duke, but in 1946 he collaborated with another Duke, Ellington, on *Beggar's Holiday* (1946). La Touche's much-admired *The Golden Apple* (1954) is a modern retelling of Homer's the *Iliad* and the *Odyssey*. La Touche also worked in opera, writing the libretto for Douglas Moore's *The Ballad of Baby Doe* (1956) as well as some of the lyrics for Leonard Bernstein's *Candide*. His career was cut short when he died of a heart attack at the age of thirty-eight.

Johnny Mercer

Johnny Mercer (1909–1976), the lyricist of "Hooray for Hollywood," was born in Savannah, Georgia. He went to New York to pursue a singing career, arriving just in time for the stock market crash of 1929. He started to write song lyrics, some of which were heard on Broadway. In 1931, Mercer, who was not Jewish, married the Jewish dancer Ginger Meehan. The couple lived with her mother in Brooklyn while he struggled to jumpstart his singing career. The next year, he sang with the Paul Whiteman Orchestra, and shortly thereafter he went to Hollywood. Mercer worked on eight Broadway book musicals, two of them in the forties, but he had far more success as a Hollywood songwriter. His popular hits include four Oscar-winning songs: "In the Cool, Cool, Cool of the Evening," "On the Atchison, Topeka and the Santa Fe," "Moon River," and "The Days of Wine and Roses." Mercer's first full-length musical, *Walk with Music* (1940), which had music by Hoagy Carmichael, closed after only fifty-five performances. On Broadway, Mercer also collaborated with Harold Arlen (*St. Louis Woman* and *Saratoga* [1959]), Robert Emmett Dolan (*Texas, Li'l Darling* [1949]), and Gene De Paul (*Li'l Abner* [1956]). Mercer wrote music and lyrics for two Broadway shows, *Top Banana* (1952) and *Foxy* (1964). In 1942, he cofounded Capital Records with Buddy DeSylva (see Chapter 5) and Glen Wallichs.

Robert Wright and George Forrest

Floridian Robert Wright (1914–2005) and New Yorker George Forrest (1915–1999) started to work together around the time of the first "talkies." They carved out a peculiar niche for themselves on Broadway, arranging instrumental music by a single classical composer into discrete numbers, fitting original lyrics to the music, and writing a book that incorporates the "new" gerrymandered songs. This type of show anticipates the now-popular jukebox musical (see Chapters 12 and 13). *Song of Norway* (1944), their first such concoction, is a biographical musical about the life of the Norwegian composer Edvard Grieg (1843–1907). *Kismet* (1953), which is based on Edward Knoblock's 1911 play *Kismet,* uses music by Aleksander Borodin (1833–1887) to tell an exotic fairytale set in what is present-day Iraq. Not all of their efforts were as successful of these, however; and when they tried to write an original score, as they did for *Kean* (1961), the results were lackluster.

Directors

George Abbott

The Rodgers and Hammerstein era was also a propitious time for directors. George Abbott (1887–1995), whose theatrical career spanned nearly eight decades, witnessed firsthand the early formation of the modern Broadway musical, its Golden Age, and its decline. He started out as an actor in the teens and turned to play-writing in the twenties. In the forties, Abbott served as the director, book writer, producer, or some combination thereof for nine Broadway musicals (plus many spoken plays), including *Pal Joey.* In the fifties and sixties, he was even more prolific. Abbott's scripts are structurally sound and dramatically logical, but they lack psychological depth. He himself once boasted, "I helped bring plot and common sense into the musical."

Jerome Robbins

By contrast, Jerome Robbins's artistic reputation is unsurpassed. The demands that he placed on his writers and performers often aroused their enmity, but few ever questioned his genius. Robbins made his Broadway debut in 1939 as a member of the cast of *Your Eyes*. Before long, he was directing and choreographing musicals, beginning with *On the Town* in 1944. Robbins's career includes *The King and I*, *The Pajama Game*, *Gypsy*, *West Side Story*, and *Fiddler on the Roof*.

Hassard Short

The English-born director Hassard Short (1877–1956) receives less attention today than Abbott and Robbins, but he directed some of the most important musicals of the forties, including *Lady in the Dark* and *Carmen Jones*. Also a lighting designer and choreographer, Short helped to revolutionize the visual aspect of Broadway musicals. He substituted footlights with hung lights from the balcony, introduced color to lighting design, and incorporated mirrors. He also employed a revolving turntable and moving platforms, most notably in *The Band Wagon* (1931) (see Chapter 6).

Beyond *Brigadoon*

Brigadoon last appeared on Broadway in 1980. The visual concept for this production, which was directed by Vivian Matalon, attempted to evoke the Grimms' fairytales and gave the show a cinematic fluidity, which would not have been possible with forties stage technology. The scenery, which was budgeted under $200,000, involved a series of rock formations. Today, the budget for the same production would reach into the millions. A revised version of *Brigadoon*, sanctioned by Lerner's daughter, played at Chicago's Goodman Theater in 2014. A different revision, by the playwright John Guare (author of *Six Degrees of Separation*), has been heading toward Broadway since 2008. Guare turned Brigadoon into "a pacificist town that 'disappeared' in 1939 because its inhabitants didn't want to live in a world torn apart by war."

Lerner and Loewe, albeit not as prolific as Rodgers and Hammerstein, rank among the greatest musical theater writers. *My Fair Lady* (1957) broke all previous records and remains a highpoint in the history of the book musical. This brilliant adaptation of George Bernard Shaw's *Pygmalion* has lost none of its luster. A recently planned Broadway revival of *My Fair Lady* (at one point to star Colin Firth and Anne Hathaway) never panned out. The 1964 film version stars Rex Harrison, who originated the role on Broadway. Plans for a new film version featuring a screenplay by Emma Thompson and starring Firth and Carey Mulligan, has been shelved indefinitely. Lerner and Loewe's *Camelot* still holds a firm place in the repertory (see Chapter 9).

AND BEAR IN MIND

Pal Joey, 1940, Ethel Barrymore Theatre, 374 performances

Book by John O'Hara
Music by Richard Rodgers
Lyrics by Lorenz Hart

P*al Joey* is one of the first musicals based on a series of short stories (others include *Guys and Dolls*, *Fiddler on the Roof*, and *Cabaret*), as opposed to a single full-length novel or play. These stories, by John O'Hara, take the form of letters written by a cad named Joey. They were published in *The New Yorker* magazine. The original title for the musical was *Your Pal Joey*, a reference to the way that Joey closes his letters.

O'Hara wrote the book for the musical, rounding out the plot with some newly invented material. The action takes place in Chicago. Joey Evans, one of musical theater's first anti-heroes, is a two-bit nightclub performer who uses anyone he needs to to get to the top. The two women in his life are polar opposites of each other: Linda English, a better and kinder woman than Joey deserves; and Vera Simpson, a wealthy socialite who bankrolls his career—until the situation gets too dicey for her comfort. After Vera drops him, Joey tries to return to Linda, but she has wisely moved on. O'Hara toyed with the idea of a reconciliation between Linda and Joey, but he abandoned it in favor of the more realistic ending.

The collaboration was far from ideal, especially for the assiduous Rodgers. O'Hara delayed completion of the script and stayed away from the production, and Hart, as was his wont, came and went as he pleased. Moreover, Rodgers felt that George Abbott, who was producing and directing *Pal Joey*, had underfinanced the show and lacked the commitment needed to make it a success. Abbott began to take the show more seriously only after Rodgers suggested that he pull out of the project.

Pal Joey opened on Christmas day. The celebratory mood of the opening-night party, which was held at Hart's apartment, was destroyed by Brooks Atkinson's review, which disparaged the "odious" and "ugly topic" of the show and called O'Hara's book "joyless." The oft-quoted conclusion of Atkinson's review is worth repeating: "Although *Pal Joey* is expertly done, can you draw sweet water from a foul well?" Time has been kind to *Pal Joey*, but Atkinson's review devastated Hart, although it did not stop the show from running 374 performances.

Pal Joey is Rodgers and Hart's most mature work; of all their musicals, it comes the closest to achieving the rich depiction of characters and integration of dialogue and music of Rodgers and Hammerstein's musicals. *Pal Joey* pushed musical theater further away from the happy-ending prerogative of musical comedy and toward greater realism. *Pal Joey* defied expectations and did not try to smooth the edges of its seedy characters.

Gene Kelly created the role of Joey, but unfortunately a recording was not made at the time. A 1952 studio recording of *Pal Joey* with Vivienne Segal (who was in the original production) and Harold Lang (who was new to the show) led to a Broadway revival the same year. The 2008 Broadway revival of *Pal Joey* featured a revised book by Richard Greenberg. It was poorly received and closed after eighty-five performances.

NAMES, TERMS, AND CONCEPTS

Abbott, George	La Touche, John
Allegro	Lerner, Alan Jay
Arlen, Harold	Loewe, Frederick
Bernstein, Leonard	*Love Life*
Brigadoon	Mercer, Johnny
Comden, Betty	*Pal Joey*
Duke, Vernon	Robbins, Jerome
"Germelshausen"	Rome, Harold
Green, Adolph	Short, Hassard
Harburg, E. Y. (Yip)	Styne, Jule
Lady in the Dark	Weill, Kurt

DISCUSSION QUESTIONS

1. Identify the similarities between *Oklahoma!* and *Brigadoon*.

2. Explain the appeal of *Brigadoon* during the late forties and early fifties.

3. Discuss Kurt Weill's influence on the Broadway musical.

CHAPTER 8

THE FIFTIES

(*THE MUSIC MAN*, 1957, MAJESTIC THEATRE, 1,375 PERFORMANCES)

By the middle of the century, the public perception of musical theater as popular entertainment had shifted to a perception of musical theater as popular art. During the fifties, the genre attained a higher artistic status and began to receive the sort of serious critical attention previously reserved for spoken drama and opera. Obtaining a ticket for *Guys and Dolls* or *The King and I* was considered "a mark of social distinction," according to theater critic Brooks Atkinson. Musical theater scholar Steve Adler argues that writers during this era "would establish or burnish their reputations and catapult the musical from its prewar anything-goes giddiness to a more sophisticated, sometimes even contemplative state." For the first time, one engaged in serious discourse about a musical theater canon. In 1956, Yale University formed a committee to deal with the preservation of musicals. *The Ed Sullivan Show* regularly featured scenes from Broadway musicals such as *My Fair Lady* and *West Side Story*. Book publishers began to publish musical theater scripts for mass consumption. In 1949, Simon and Shuster issued an anthology of Oscar Hammerstein's lyrics, and a decade later Random House published *Six Plays by Rodgers and Hammerstein*. Indeed, Rodgers and Hammerstein were treated as a national treasure. In 1951, NBC produced *Richard Rodgers' Jubilee Show*. Three years later, a tribute to Rodgers and Hammerstein (*The General Foods 25th Anniversary Show*) aired on all four major networks (ABC, NBC, CBS, and DuMont). Critics held up musical theater as an example of America's ability to compete culturally with Europe. The Broadway musical had achieved international recognition and become one of the country's preeminent cultural exports. The U.S. government even included musical theater in its diplomatic efforts to

The Ed Sullivan Show aired weekly from 1948 to 1971. It regularly featured scenes from Broadway musicals, which helped to boost ticket sales.

curb the spread of communism by teaching the value of a modern, open, and pluralistic society.

The fifties contributed a sizable portion of the standard musical theater performing repertory. Several major writers from earlier decades remained active during the fifties, and those who came of age around the time of *Oklahoma!* sought to elevate the genre to new heights. As Mark Grant has observed, they took "strophic song forms and the harmonic limitations of popular music and [gave] them a dramatic power derived from opera and symphony." Leonard Bernstein created exuberant scores by combining the rhythmic vitality of bebop with the musical sophistication of art music. Frank Loesser mixed the profane and the sacred to create a sense of worldly irony and bemusement. Several respected writers such as Jerome Moross, Gian Carlo Menotti, and John La Touche failed to achieve the same degree of fame of these writers, but they too helped to raise the artistic bar of musical theater. The second half of the decade witnessed the arrival of composers and lyricists of the first post-Rodgers and Hammerstein generation, including Stephen Sondheim. No one at the time seemed to worry much about the new type of music that had caught the imagination of the youth movement. When Broadway did acknowledge rock and roll, it was only in order to parody it. The integrated book musical was in force and seemed impervious to outside influences.

Musical theater writers in the fifties did not try to transform the genre so much as build on the progress of the forties. Engaging stories and interesting characters remained a top priority, and dance became an increasingly important dramatic element. Jerome Robbins and Agnes de Mille were still the dominant choreographers at the time, but Michael Kidd and Bob Fosse joined their ranks. "Director-choreographer" became a more common job description, as several artists with roots in the dance world began to oversee entire productions.

The Broadway and Hollywood choreographer Michael Kidd (1919–2007) is best remembered for infusing his dances with a sense of athleticism. In the late thirties, Kidd joined Lincoln Kirstein's Ballet Caravan and appeared in the title role in Aaron Copland's *Billy the Kid*. In 1942, he joined what is now the American Ballet Theatre and was a featured solo dancer in several works, including Leonard Bernstein's *Fancy Free* in 1946. He made his Broadway debut in 1947 as the choreographer of *Finian's Rainbow*. He choreographed and/or directed over seventeen other Broadway musicals, including *Guys and Dolls* (1950) and *Can-Can* (1953). His film credits include *Seven Brides for Seven Brothers* (1954) and *Hello, Dolly!* (1969). Kidd's work earned him a total of five Tony Awards and an honorary Academy Award in 1997.

Bob Fosse (1927–1987) hailed from Chicago. He started dancing when he was nine and appeared in nightclubs and burlesque houses during his teens. Exposure to the seedy side of show business during his impressionable years made a profound impact on his career. Fosse became a highly successful television, film, and stage choreographer and director. He began as a performer, appearing in Broadway musicals in the mid-forties and in Hollywood musicals in the fifties. In 1954, he made his Broadway debut as a choreographer with *The Pajama Game*. The hallmarks of his style—sexually provocative poses and steps, isolated body movements, heightened theatricality—were present early on. Fosse turned to directing beginning with *Redhead* in 1959. In 1973, he became the first choreographer or director to win an Emmy Award, an Academy Award, and a Tony Award, for *Liza with a Z!*, *Cabaret*, and *Pippin*, respectively. Although a well-respected artist, Fosse earned a reputation for being difficult. Altogether he choreographed, directed, or both choreographed and directed thirteen Broadway musicals, including *Sweet Charity* (1966) and *Chicago* (1975). His film credits include *All That Jazz* (1979), which was based on his first-hand experience as a heart attack victim, and a couple of non-musicals, such as *Lenny* (1974) and *Star 80* (1983).

Despite its improved artistic status, in the fifties the Broadway musical faced several challenges. The cost of production rose precipitously, which in turn drove up ticket prices. Moreover, migration of the middle class to the suburbs and the looming specter of television conspired to keep people at home and away from the theater. By 1953, nearly two thirds of American households owned a television set. The television industry broadcast musicals into living rooms, which did not bolster attendance at live theater. Rock and roll and the widening generation gap turned young people off musicals. In fact, rock threatened the centrality of the musical in American popular culture.

HISTORICAL BACKGROUND

Historical narratives about the fifties emphasize the country's economic prosperity and conservative politics. Americans settled into a period of conformity, feeling a sense of superiority and smugness born out of the victory in World War II and the attendant economic expansion. The Cold War influenced the nation's politics and cultural tastes. Senator Joseph McCarthy (1908–1957) led an insidious congressional fight against the spread of communism, and his nefarious tactics silenced dissent. The term "McCarthyism" refers to the senator's demagoguery and his reckless witch hunts to root out alleged communists and communist sympathizers from government and vulnerable industries, in particular the entertainment industry. The fear engendered by McCarthyism fueled distrust of the Soviet Union and paranoia between neighbors as well as family members. People were afraid to speak out, lest they be accused of having links to communism. McCarthyism had the effect of uniting people from the left, middle, and right against a single enemy, the result being self-censorship.

With Europe vulnerable to Soviet influence, the U.S. government redirected its energy onto the Asian-Pacific region and adopted a strategy of containment, leading to a series of disastrous actions. The Korean War erupted in 1950, undermining the euphoria and optimism that followed World War II. The war increased suspicion of the government and lulled many people into a sense of complacency. According to some historians, the war was the first military conflict that America entered into without a clear-cut justification. Containment extended beyond foreign policy. The rhetoric of containment was not limited to communism. It affected attitudes about race, gender, sexuality, intellectual discourse, and dissent. Indeed, many Americans felt an acute sense of disenfranchisement, in particular women, ethnic minorities, and homosexuals.

Communism was not the only threat facing the nation. Suburban expansion weakened major urban centers, juvenile delinquency posed a new and growing danger, the struggle for civil rights led to violence and instability on American streets, and the arms race fueled existential anxieties. In retrospect, the first underground nuclear tests in 1951, the *Brown v. Board of Education* case in 1954, the Civil Rights Act of 1957, and the launching of the Soviet satellite Sputnik in 1957 stand out as some of the defining moments of the decade. But Americans were too blinded by the pursuit of pleasure to take notice of the internal and external crises eroding the country's sense of confidence. The Eisenhower administration put an avuncular face on the complacent nation during the second half of the decade, but these events signaled a country deeply insecure of its future, and young people eventually responded with greater activism in the sixties.

CULTURAL BACKGROUND

The baby boom reflected the country's moral certitude as well as its cultural, political, and economic optimism after World War II. The economy was expanding at an unprecedented rate, accompanied by an increase in living standards and discretionary income. The five-day workweek was uniformly adopted. Weekly earnings rose every year between 1950 and 1959. Technology made a burgeoning popular culture more available and diverse than ever, and economic prosperity allowed Americans to consume culture like never before. The decade saw the introduction of the credit card, the mass popularization of the martini, drive-in movies, and Hula Hoops.

Musical theater was part of the narrative that defined American popular culture. It helped to bridge the intellectual elites and the common folk and brought low art and high art into contact with each other. The advent of the LP (long-playing) record, which Columbia Records introduced in 1948, could not have come at a more propitious time, as the middle class, the target audience for Broadway musicals, expanded exponentially. With the original cast recording of *Oklahoma!* in 1943, Decca Records set a precedent, and within a couple of years, Capital, Victor, and Columbia had all entered the original cast album business. The LP brought Broadway musicals into the homes of Americans for whom New York and Broadway were practically foreign places and who would otherwise not have had exposure to the genre. For suburban Americans, notes George Reddick, Broadway musicals were "sophisticated cultural products that were not easily available except through cast recording." The business of recording Broadway and Off Broadway musicals has created a lasting aural legacy of the genre, although the years prior to 1943 remain sorely underrepresented. Goddard Lieberson (1911–1977), twice the president of Columbia Records, deserves much of the credit for propagating the cast recording. However, Lieberson was no slave to the written score of a show, and if necessary he made changes in order to create an effective and meaningful experience for the home listener. By the fifties, most Broadway musicals were being recorded for posterity. Columbia Records was *My Fair Lady*'s primary investor, and the company's original cast album of the show became the highest-selling recording of the fifties.

Album cover of the original cast LP of *My Fair Lady* featuring Al Hirschfeld's famous caricature depicting playwright George Bernard Shaw as the master puppeteer, manipulating the character of Henry Higgins, who in turn manipulates Eliza Doolittle. *Courtesy Photofest.*

Television also entered the musical theater business in the fifties. However, like other television genres, television musicals leave much to be desired with regard to quality. Filming what is inherently a live art form posed several problems. Radio had aired musicals, but that medium never had to deal with the visual aspect of the genre. The overriding aesthetic issue pertained to whether television musicals should aim for the polish of a Hollywood film or the spontaneity of live theater. The networks broadcast both classic musicals such as *Anything Goes* and new musicals created specifically for the new medium, such as *St. George and the Dragon* starring Kukla, Fran, and Ollie (1953). *Musical Comedy Time,* a series that presented Broadway classics such as *No, No, Nannette,* ran on NBC in 1950–1951. Rodgers and Hammerstein's *Cinderella* marks the pinnacle of the fifties television musical. First aired live on CBS in 1957 with Julie Andrews as Cinderella, it reached an unprecedented 107 million viewers. Two subsequent television remakes of *Cinderella* (1965 and 1997) were also successful. Television variety shows and specials also included excerpts from Broadway musicals.

JULIE ANDREWS

The stage and screen star Julie Andrews (b. 1935) is best known for her performance in the title role of the movie *Mary Poppins* (1964) and as Maria in the film version of Rodgers and Hammerstein's *The Sound of Music* (1966). She was born in Walton-on-Thames, England, to theatrical parents. Andrew's mature soprano voice was so impressive that she was appearing professionally in London by the age of twelve. She came to America in 1954 to appear on Broadway in the English musical *The Boy Friend.* Two years later, she won the role of Eliza Doolittle in *My Fair Lady*, which brought her instant stardom. While still performing Eliza, Andrews appeared as Cinderella in the first live television broadcast of Rodgers and Hammerstein's *Cinderella* (1957). In 1960, Andrews returned to Broadway as Queen Guinevere in Lerner and Loewe's *Camelot*. She was passed over for the role of Eliza Doolittle in the film version of *My Fair Lady* in favor of Audrey Hepburn but as a result, she was available to appear in *Mary Poppins*, for which she won an Academy Award. In 1959, Andrews married the Broadway and Hollywood scenic designer Tony Walton, whose credits include *Mary Poppins*. Her second marriage was to Blake Edwards, who directed her in several films, including *Victor/Victoria* (1982), which co-starred *The Music Man*'s Robert Preston.

Musicals of the late forties and fifties reflect a middle-class desire for culture that is both entertaining and meaningful. Audiences welcomed the strong sense of purpose of fifties musical theater, but they were not predisposed to the intellectual and aesthetic challenges of high-art institutions like the opera house, and musical theater writers were reticent to confront provocative topics such as the Holocaust, leaving such subjects to more avant-garde writers. Politically speaking, Broadway musicals fell under the influence of the conservatism of the Cold War era. Producers, who were not in the business of spurring political activism, steered clear of intellectually challenging shows that might scare away middle-class suburbanites. On the other hand, Broadway was not as vulnerable to censorial scrutiny as Hollywood, and it never generated a blacklist, even though Broadway writers had good reason to fear the same sort of recriminations that many Hollywood writers suffered under McCarthy's influence. Several distinguished Broadway artists were summoned to appear before the House Committee on Un-American Activities (HUAC), including E. Y. Harburg, Jerome Robbins, Arthur Laurents, and Abe Burrows. Robbins, for one, named names, which marked him for the rest of his life. When musicals addressed social and political themes, they usually did so in light-hearted ways. However, as cultural texts, even musical comedies have something to say about the times. For instance, *The Music Man* expresses nostalgia for a simpler, less complex age. The protagonist, an outsider named Harold Hill, threatens to unravel the moral fabric of the quaint homogenous Iowan town in which the story takes place. The scenario resonated with the country's xenophobia and fear of the growing Soviet threat. *The Music Man* was not the only show that expressed a yearning for a less uncertain world and a less diverse America. *A Tree Grows in Brooklyn* (1951), *Three Wishes for Jamie* (1952), and *By the Beautiful Sea* (1953) all take place in an earlier idealized period of American history. In contrast to these shows, musicals set in Europe provided a different vantage point from which to view America. Paris,

NBC has recently tried to revive the popularity of live musical theater broadcasts, beginning with *The Sound of Music* starring Carrie Underwood in 2013 and *Peter Pan* in 2014.

because of its indelible romantic and cosmopolitan character, was a favorite setting for both Broadway and Hollywood musicals. Cole Porter's *Silk Stockings* and *Can-Can* treated Paris as a gateway to Europe.

"Cold war musicals," as Bush Jones labels them, "used aspects of East-West tensions or America's fear of internal communism as their premise, their setting, or the object of their comedy." On the other hand, Rodgers and Hammerstein's so-called "Orientalist" musicals (*South Pacific*, *The King and I*, and *Flower Drum Song*) reflect the country's policy of containment at the time. Menotti's *The Consul*, a "Broadway opera," stands out as the only work from the period about Soviet-style domestic politics. It tells the horrifying story of a husband and wife who suffer under the authoritarian overreach into the lives of ordinary citizens in some anonymous Eastern European country. The wife, Magda Sorel, tries to obtain a visa in order to leave the country and join her husband, a political dissident who has escaped the secret police. Succumbing to her fear of the repressive government, she eventually commits suicide. The score garnered Menotti the Pulitzer Prize for Music in 1950.

The Consul is a stark contrast to Cold War musical comedies such as Irving Berlin's *Call Me Madam* (1950) (see Chapter 17) and Cole Porter's *Silk Stockings* (1955). Throughout his career, Porter steered clear of musicals with serious themes, and *Silk Stockings*, his last Broadway musical, was no exception. Based on the 1939 film *Ninotchka*, it has no deep political message, only the fact that Russian diplomats are human and easily seduced by the creature comforts of the West. The film, directed by Ernst Lubitsch and starring Greta Garbo, involves three members of the Soviet diplomatic corps who have been sent to Paris to sell jewelry that the government confiscated from aristocrats during the Revolution. When Ninotchka, an agent sent by Moscow, arrives in Paris to rescue her comrades from the lures of the West, she, too, begins to appreciate the gay life of Paris and life beyond the Red Curtain. Brooks Atkinson's review of *Silk Stockings* epitomizes the general attitude on Broadway about communism: "The political satire is secondary to the ironic delight it takes in the follies of the characters, no matter which side they are on."

West meets East in Rodgers and Hammerstein's *South Pacific* (1949), *The King and I* (1951), and *Flower Drum Song* (1958). Hammerstein, an avowed internationalist, believed in world federalism and expressed his politics in his musicals. *The King and I* teaches that all differences can be bridged or transcended by acknowledging a common humanity. The American fascination with the real-life story of Anna Leonowens and the barbaric King of Siam goes back to Margaret Landon's 1944 best-selling novel *Anna and the King of Siam*, the source material for the musical. A film version of the novel was released to great acclaim only two years after it was published. Hammerstein's version plays down the novel's ethnocentric attitude. The King's gradual shift from outmoded tradition to modernity echoes America's patriarchal attitude toward the East. Modernization was a goal of the country's containment strategy. As Christina Klein notes, "by helping 'backward' nations become 'modern,' the U.S. hoped to alleviate the conditions that made communism an attractive option and thus secure these nations' participation in the 'free world' alliance." Anna Leonowens is the voice of compassion in a world tired of war. Rather than relying on violence or political coercion to influence the King, she opts for "the power of love and the tools of culture." She teaches the King's several wives how they can incorporate the ways of Western domesticity into their daily lives. Her insistence that the King honor his promise to provide her with a house of her own is not a mere power play but rather an illustration of why the King must accept a "system of international law" if he is to join the modern world. U.S. officials used *The King and I* as a strategic export to convey America's power while avoiding the sort of negative images of the country that Hollywood sometimes painted.

After *The King and I,* Rodgers and Hammerstein turned away from innovation and toward convention. *Me and Juliet* (1953) was a backstage musical comedy with a traditional romantic plot. *Pipe Dream* (1955) was based on John Steinbeck's novel *Sweet Thursday,* a story about love, redemption, and the acceptance of others. Cultural assimilation, Asian American identity, and the generation gap intersect in *Flower Drum Song* (1958), which, despite its interesting combination of themes, is a conventional musical comedy. It is based on C. Y. Lee's 1957 novel *The Flower Drum Song,* which involves Chinese immigrants in San Francisco. Gene Kelly directed the musical. Despite the show's all-Asian *dramatis personae,* Rodgers and Hammerstein cast actors of different ethnic backgrounds, including some white actors. If these musicals represent lesser Rodgers and Hammerstein, their last show, *The Sound of Music* (1959), reminded people of their formidable talent. Because Hammerstein was dying of cancer at the time, the team of Howard Lindsay and Russel Crouse (see Chapter 6) was engaged to write the book, which is based on *The Trapp Family Singers* by Maria Augusta Trapp and a German film titled *Die Trapp Familie.*

The writer Fred Saidy (1907–1982) shared Harburg's leftist politics and collaborated with him on several musicals, including the still-popular *Finian's Rainbow* in 1947.

Candide, an adaptation of Voltaire's satiric novel (1759), was Lillian Hellman and Leonard Bernstein's response to McCarthyism. Hellman, who had appeared before HUAC in 1952, intended *Candide* as an attack on the complacency that she felt was endangering America. However, many of the political references in her original script were expunged before *Candide* opened on Broadway. Candide and his beloved Cunegonde live, they are told by their mentor Doctor Pangloss, "in this best of all possible worlds." However, as they travel the world they encounter the worst disasters and cruelty that humankind and nature can dish out. Still, they hold steadfastly and blindly to the absurdly optimistic view propagated by Pangloss. Three acclaimed poets contributed lyrics to the show, Richard Wilbur, Dorothy Parker, and John La Touche. The musical was flawed from the start, but theater and opera companies have continued to revive *Candide* because of the combination of Voltaire's darkly humorous plot and Bernstein's effervescent music. The eclectic score, much of it a parody of opera (in particular, Rossinian opera), demands trained singers; in fact, it is one of the few Broadway musicals that the opera world has absorbed into its standard repertory.

Li'l Abner (1956), Broadway's first comic-strip musical, deals with the specter of atomic bomb testing and the federal government's willingness to experiment on its own citizens. Al Capp's comic strip *Li'l Abner,* a popular social and political satire set in a Kentucky hick town, ran in newspapers from 1934 until 1977. The premise of the musical is revealed by a government official who arrives in Dogpatch, U.S.A., and ceremoniously announces that the town has been given the "honor" of being a nuclear test site because it is "the most useless piece of real estate in the U.S.A." Directed and choreographed by Michael Kidd, *Li'l Abner* featured high-voltage dances, a tuneful score by lyricist Johnny Mercer and composer Gene de Paul (1919–1988), and a lusty fast-paced book by Norman Panama and Melvin Frank. The creative team never allowed the serious themes to overwhelm the balletic production and farcical nature of the plot.

E. Y. Harburg's politics, which were far to the left of most Broadway writers', landed him on the Hollywood blacklist. No one more than he understood the power of musical theater to teach while entertaining. He once said, "a musical should be fun, but it should contain truth." In 1951, Harburg partnered with the composer Sammy Fain to write *Flahooley*, a satire about consumerism. Barbara Cook, the future Marian the Librarian in *The Music Man*, made her Broadway debut in *Flahooley*. The book, co-authored by Harburg and Fred Saidy, one of few from the decade with an original premise, blended satire and fantasy, but these two elements worked against each other: Brooks Atkinson dubbed *Flahooley* "the most complicated, verbose and humorless [musical] of the season."

The American business world inspired several musicals during the late fifties and early sixties. *The Pajama Game* (1954) pitted labor against management. It takes a few pointed jabs at communism but is otherwise politically noncommittal. It should be noted that Joseph McCarthy's influence had dissipated by the time *The Pajama Game* debuted, and another Joseph, Stalin, had died in 1953. Moreover, the Eisenhower era was in full swing.

Business-oriented musicals peaked in 1961 with Frank Loesser's *How to Succeed in Business Without Really Trying*. This uproarious satire shifts the focus from the worker to the executive and traces the upward trajectory of a shrewd young man without any readily apparent applicable skills or prospects named J. Pierrepont Finch. By simply following the instructions laid out in a manual about corporate-ladder climbing, Finch becomes the Chairman of the Board in record time. With a book co-authored by Abe Burrows, Jack Weinstock, and Willie Gilbert, *How to Succeed* won the 1962 Pulitzer Prize for Drama and remains popular today.

Black writers saw diminishing opportunities on Broadway during the fifties, but black performers found work in musicals. Black and white performers appeared alongside one another in Harold Rome's 1949 musical *Call Me Mister*, beginning a trend of interracial casts on Broadway. However, mixed-cast musicals waned as white writers became afraid of being accused of creating offensive portrayals of African Americans. Langston Hughes (1902–1967) was one of the most important African American poets and playwrights of the twentieth century. He attended Columbia University and studied engineering, but he turned to writing during the Harlem Renaissance. Hughes's *The Barrier*, an operatic adaption of his 1935 play *Mulatto*, played on Broadway for only a few days in November 1950. Several problems besieged the production, including negative publicity generated by Hughes's objections to forced segregated seating in Baltimore. Hughes's *Just Around the Corner*, from the same year, never reached New York. His 1957 musical *Simply Heavenly* is constructed around the character of Jess Simple, an earlier creation of his. Simple wants to divorce his wife and marry Joyce Lane. The show opened Off Broadway, but shortly after its premiere, the Fire Department closed down the theater, and the musical never rebounded. The protagonists in *Simply Heavenly* embrace their cultural heritage rather than avoid it, as occurs in most white-created black musicals (see Chapter 15).

Harold Arlen wrote two black musicals in the fifties, but he set them in the Caribbean. *House of Flowers* (1954) takes place in and around Madame Fleur's house of ill repute. Fleur faces competition from Madame Tango. One of Fleur's employees, Ottilie, falls in love with a white Frenchman named Royal. To protect her "investment," Madame Fleur plots to have him killed, but her plans go awry. Whereas *House of Flowers* indulged in exotic visions of Caribbean culture, Arlen's next show, *Jamaica*, was a satire played out against the relationship of a fisherman named Koli and Savannah, the woman he loves. Koli is content with life on Pigeon Island, but Savannah dreams of going to New York City. However, after Koli recues her brother from death, she decides to remain with him. *Jamaica* changed directions midstream when Harry Belafonte, who was slated to appear in the show, withdrew from the production. Ricardo Montalban replaced him, at which point the writers shifted the focus of the story onto their female star, Lena Horne. Horne had suffered several setbacks and indignities, including being put on the Hollywood blacklist. She became the target of Hollywood gossip and death threats when she married the white musician Lennie Hayton in 1947. Theirs was the first major public interracial marriage in Hollywood during the postwar years. By appearing in *Jamaica*, Horne felt that she might revitalize her flagging career. The reworked version of the show, however, lacked the satirical sting of the original. Harburg, who wrote the book and lyrics, downplayed the racial complexities of the interracial romance at the center of the story. Some people connected with the show worried that Horne and Montalban's on-stage romance would stir up trouble. Race relations also affected life backstage: the show's producer, David Merrick, clashed with the local stagehand union by challenging them to accept black workers, and he won.

THE MUSIC MAN

The ingenious score and charming story of *The Music Man* account for its popularity more than a half a century after it opened on Broadway. In its nostalgia for the past, the musical expresses the prevailing mindset of Main Street America during the fifties. The story, set in Iowa circa 1912, is about a fast-talking salesman whose powers of persuasion evoke the advertising industry's increased influence in postwar America. The salesman, who calls himself Professor Harold Hill, belongs to a group of conmen, phonies, and charlatans from fifties culture—including Holden Caulfield, the protagonist in J. D. Salinger's novel *The Catcher in the Rye* (1951). Hill is also one of several notable musical theater antiheros, including Joey Evans (*Pal Joey*) (see Chapter 7). In the postwar era, the well-oiled sales pitch became a veritable art form, as celebrated in the recent popular television series *Mad Men*. On the other hand, *The Music Man* evokes a more innocent time, when neither ethnic outsiders nor communists threatened the sheltered life of rural America. American salesmanship and small-town America intersect in *The Music Man*. After all, the main thoroughfare of River City, Iowa, the setting for *The Music Man*, varies little from Disneyland's Main Street, U.S.A., which was conceived as a representation of a turn-of-the-century Midwestern Main Street.

Meredith Willson

Meredith Willson (1902–1984) was not the typical Broadway composer. He hailed from Mason City, Iowa, the heart of the Midwest. When *The Music Man* opened on Broadway, he was nearing sixty, at which point most Broadway writers would already have had a string of shows to their name. However, Willson was no show business neophyte, although his métier was not musical theater. As a young man, Willson left Iowa for New York, where he enrolled in the Damrosch Institute of Musical Arts. He played in the John Philip Sousa Band between 1921 and 1923 and the New York Philharmonic from 1924 to 1929, serving under legendary conductors Wilhelm Furtwängler and Arturo Toscanini. Willson later turned to conducting and composing. He wrote popular songs as well as concert works. He found work in San Francisco and Los Angeles during the Golden Age of radio and hosted his own show, *Good News*.

In art as in politics, Willson was generally conservative. He championed Stravinsky and Gershwin but had little patience for composers who experimented with "a scale with twenty-four quarter tones." In his memoir, published shortly before he undertook *The Music Man*, Willson waxed nostalgic about his small-town childhood and fretted about the cultural leanings of the younger generation: "Just think, tomorrow's kids won't know a thing about the thrill of hearing Sousa's band. I hope the new button-pushing, streamlined, jet-propelled, atomic-powered age won't also eliminate things like hammers and flatirons." Willson's artistic orthodoxy could be a bit precious, as his irony-free description of Sousa marches reveals: "Every part of a Sousa march is inspired—the bass line, the woodwind figures, the trombone countermelodies, and even the peckhorn afterbeats." Willson composed his first symphony, "The San Francisco," in tribute to the Golden Gate Bridge, constructing it "measure for cable, note for rivet" with little sense of musical adventurousness. Among Willson's musical accomplishments is the score for Charlie Chaplin's film *The Great Dictator* (1940).

Willson's initial exposure to musicals came by way of playing in pit orchestras, but this was long before *Oklahoma!* Somehow he managed to absorb the craft of musical theater writing as exemplified by Rodgers and Hammerstein. He understood how to develop character, to evoke a specific time and place, and to use music in the service of the story. Rodgers and Hammerstein' expressed the populist notion of community and American identity, but one cannot imagine these native New Yorkers ever creating the portrait of middle America that Willson did with such deftness. He brought River City and its inhabitants to life with an uncanny specificity of sound, language, and humor.

Evolution

The Music Man took nearly seven years to reach fruition. The project began when Cy Feuer and Ernest Martin, the dynamic young producing team responsible for *Guys and Dolls* (1950), proposed that Willson write a musical comedy about his Iowa childhood. What was at first just a passing suggestion grew into something of an obsession for Willson. Despite suggestions in the literature that he based *The Music Man* on his 1948 memoir *And There I Stood with My Piccolo*, he in fact invented an original story, although he did draw on his memories of playing flute in Mason City's first high school band (circa 1912), which performed without a conductor. The band's meager repertory included Beethoven's Minuet in G, "the one piece we could always manage to get through somehow without stopping." Willson came up with a workable premise: a fast-talking salesman arrives in Mason City and sells its citizens on the idea of funding a school band. Willson also devised a subplot about a "spastic boy" in a wheelchair. The musical was to be called *The Silver Triangle*. Feuer and Martin, already seasoned producers, were not about to commit money to the project until it was dramaturgically sound. As Willson rewrote the show, pressure began to mount as some of the best musicals in the repertory opened on Broadway, including *My Fair Lady*. It would have been hard for any writer to ignore the remarkable achievements and artistic quality of these shows. The producers tried to help Willson iron out the show's lingering flaws. Martin even gave him a copy of Lajos Egri's *The Art of Dramatic Writing*, which emphasizes character development over plot. Slowly but surely, Willson turned what started out as "a play with music" into a musical. The score was coming along fine, but Feuer and Martin continued to have concerns over the book. In 1956, Willson met the writer Franklin Lacey (1917–1988) and asked him for help in revising the book and solving the lingering problems with the subplot. They decided to substitute the "spastic boy" with a boy who lisps, Marian's younger brother, who is troubled by the sudden death of his father. It was too late, however, for Feuer and Martin, who had by then given up on the show, so Willson contacted Kermit Bloomgarden, who had just produced Loesser's *The Most Happy Fella*. Bloomgarden agreed to produce the show, and shortly thereafter Morton Da Costa (1914–1989) signed on to direct.

Book and Score

The idiosyncratic plot of *The Music Man* suggested an array of clever song ideas that Willson managed to conceive not as mere novelties but as fully integrated parts of the score. He adopted a unique approach to the lyrics. "The musical numbers," he felt, "ought to grow out of the dialogue without interruption or jerkiness." He treated the lyrics as though they were part of the dialogue, which led him to write several songs without rhymes: "I want to have an underlying unsuspected rhythm underneath the dialogue when I'm ready for a song, like a cable running along underneath Powell Street—then I can hook on to it any time I wish without the audience realizing it." Rhythmic speech occurs in several places in *The Music Man*, anticipating rap music. The opening number, "Rock Island," replaces melody with spoken rhythms. The euphonic text consists of rhythmic prose rather than metric verse. As performed by a group of traveling salesmen aboard a train bound for River City, the song simulates the acceleration and steady rhythm of the train, starting slowly and graduating speeding up. Several of Harold Hill's songs incorporate spoken patter, most notably the opening section of "Seventy-Six Trombones." Hill begins speaking and almost imperceptibly slides into singing. "Ya Got Trouble" functions as a character song while also advancing the plot. Its tortured logic

French solfège or Italian solfeggio (there are other variants) is a pedagogical system for teaching the reading of music and other musicianship skills such as sight singing. The solmization syllables do, re, mi, fa, sol, la, and ti, which are widely used in English-speaking countries, correspond respectively to the seven notes of the major scale. Modified syllables (e.g., di and me) are used for notes outside of the scale.

and Harold's fast-talking sales pitch establish the salesman's ability to pull the wool over the eyes of the unsuspecting River City citizenry.

Marian's first musical number ("Piano Lesson" / "If You Don't Mind My Saying So") occurs while she is giving Amaryllis her weekly piano lesson. As the young pupil executes an arduous finger exercise—a series of ascending and descending perfect fourths—Marian and her busybody mother engage in what appears to be a recurring argument regarding the librarian's spinsterhood. The opening spoken section flows effortlessly into the singing section. Marian's lyrics blend solfège exercise syllables, her entreaties to Amaryllis about her technique, and the quarrelsome dialogue with her mother. The music is of the most mundane nature, little more than a keyboard finger exercise. The humor emerges from the dialogue, as when Mrs. Paroo refers to Balzac and Shakespeare as "hifalutin' Greeks" or to Marian's perfect man as a "blend of Paul Bunyan, Saint Pat and Noah Webster." The next number, "Good Night My Someone," is also an extension of Amaryllis's piano exercises. A charming waltz lullaby, it functions as Marian's wanting song. Later in the act, the same music is recast as Hill's "Seventy-Six Trombones," a march in 6/8 time. Willson thereby musically associates the two protagonists. Harold and Marian, it is worth noting, are the only characters with songs in a standard AABA thirty-two-bar structure.

The Music Man famously featured a real barbershop quartet, the Buffalo Bills. The quartet's singers played the squabbling members of the town's school board, whose four numbers have little to do with the plot but add to the nostalgic aura of the show. Whenever they sing, the board members, who have not spoken for years, manage to get along just fine, and every time the suspicious mayor charges them with obtaining Hill's "credentials," the slippery salesman tricks them into singing close barbershop harmony and thereby escapes their request for his papers. In one instance, Hill coaxes them into a verse of Edwin Pearce Christy's "Goodnight Ladies," an actual minstrel song published in 1867, which provides a counter-melody to the society ladies' "pick-a-little" patter.

Harold and Marian are closer in disposition to Hammerstein's flawed protagonists than to the traditional musical comedy ingénues. They are outsiders and not comfortable integrating themselves into the community. Hill belongs to no one or no place, recalling the nomadic nature of *Oklahoma!*'s Ali Hakim and *Guys and Dolls*'s Sky Masterson. Marian resists getting too familiar with the people of the insular Midwestern community in which she lives. After all, she is a single, professional woman. Even her mother fails to understand her. Harold and Marian both stand out for their intelligence, hers derived from books, his from life experience. Their initial encounter contains echoes of Laurey and Curly's first meeting in *Oklahoma!* They build a wall of animosity in order to disguise any feelings they might have for each other.

PLOT OF THE MUSIC MAN

A conman by the name of "Professor" Harold Hill travels throughout the Midwest claiming to be able to teach any child how to play a musical instrument. He arrives in a town, promises that he will form a children's band, and then flees with the money that he has collected for instruments and uniforms from the unsuspecting parents. He meets his match, however, when he lands in River City, Iowa, where Marian Paroo, the town's librarian and custodian of its modest intellectual life, challenges his authenticity. Marian has high standards where men are concerned, which helps to explain why she is still single. She lives with her meddling mother and younger brother, Winthrop, who struggles with a lisp. Mayor Shinn also suspects Hill, so he charges the members of the school board, who have not spoken to each other in years, to obtain his "credentials." Hill hoodwinks the mayor, the board, and everyone else, with the exception of Marian. He also helps the mayor's daughter, Zaneeta, overcome her father's objection to her budding relationship with Tommy Djilas, a boy from the wrong side of town. Marian discovers incriminating information about Hill, but before she can deliver it to the mayor, the Wells Fargo wagon pulls into town carrying instruments for the children, including Winthrop. After Marian observes the positive effect of the instruments on her brother, she decides to withhold the damaging information.

Hill has fallen in love with Marian, and she begins to warm to his charms, but she only partially overlooks his transgressions. When Marian questions Hill about his pedagogical methods, he claims to employ a revolutionary "Think System." When one of Hill's jealous rivals arrives in town hoping to bring him down, Marian stops him from reaching the mayor by kissing him. Hill, instead of stealing away with his ill-gotten gains, chooses to stay in town. Marian urges him to flee, but he would rather accept his just punishment than lose her. At a town hall meeting to determine Hill's fate, the children parade into the room dressed in their shiny new uniforms and proudly holding their instruments. Marian convinces Hill to lead the band in Beethoven's Minuet in G, and even though the sounds that emanate from the instruments are hardly recognizable as music, the parents brim with pride.

Getting to Broadway

When the time came to cast Harold Hill, several actors were considered, including Jackie Gleason, Milton Berle, Jason Robards, Andy Griffith, and Laurence Olivier. A good singing voice took second place to an ability to embody the spirit of the role. The film actor Robert Preston (1918–1987), known for Westerns and other genre films, won the part, and no one since has surpassed his acclaimed performance—including the film star Van Johnson, who appeared in the London production, Dick Van Dyke, who starred in the first Broadway revival (1980), and Matthew Broderick, who starred in the 2003 television version. Willson notated the spoken portions of Harold Hill's songs with nonstandard notation (each syllable indicated by an "x")—by contrast, Frederick Loewe notated actual melodies for Henry Higgins in *My Fair Lady*, even though Rex Harrison mostly spoke his songs. The part of Marian the Librarian went to Barbara Cook (b. 1927), Broadway's leading ingénue at the time, with the exception of Julie Andrews, whose English pedigree would not have suited the role.

When *The Music Man* went into rehearsals, Willson still had lingering concerns regarding the character of Marian: "With everything else tightening up as a result of the simplification of the subplot, Marian's lack of dimension loomed up big now. . . . This girl's aloofness from her fellow townspeople, her failure to grab off a boy friend, her apparent snobbishness, remained unsatisfactorily explained." By this time, Willson had composed the first version of Marian's "My White Knight," which consisted solely of the lyrical ballad portion of the final version. As a stand-alone song, this ballad seemed too generic, expressing Marian's "longing for the guy of her dreams" but nothing that made her truly unique. Willson knew that if he could just articulate the qualities of the man with whom Marian would fall in love, he would be able to solve the problem. After months, he thought, "Maybe she just wants a guy who is not too Iowa-Stubborn to love her and to admit it once in a while. A guy who is . . . *not ashamed of a few nice things!*" Initially, he composed a polka section to express this sentiment. Marian reveals her erudition by citing Shakespeare and Beethoven, but the strength of the lyric lies in the expression of what she really desires: "I would like him to be more int'rested in me/ Than he is in himself, / And more int'rested in us than in me." "The tune not only dropped into place in a couple hours," Willson recalled, "but did so with the kind of 'inevitability' you always pray for, to where you could never bring yourself to change a note." The expanded number played well during rehearsals but not during previews in Philadelphia, so Willson continued to rewrite. "Each day, in the middle of everything else, I showed up with a new version of this song. A talking version. A cut version. A lengthened version. An inside-out version. An outside-in version. Why [Barbara Cook] didn't go berserk and stuff it down my throat I'll never know." Willson edited much of the polka version and reordered the various modular sections, transferring the ballad chorus from the end of the song to the beginning. When Willson heard the new version in performance, he was satisfied. The final version is a soliloquy framed by the "My White Knight" refrain (Example 8.1). "Standing in the back [of the theater], I caught up with the true Marian—what she was—who she was. She was a certain girl graduate of the Armour Institute in Chicago circa 1880 who took her appreciation for a few nice things into a little Iowa town and spent her life scattering it among the kids in her Sunday school class, the kids in her kindergarten, and the kids just passing by the house."

THE MUSIC MAN VERSUS WEST SIDE STORY

Because *The Music Man* and *West Side Story*, with music by Leonard Bernstein and lyrics by Stephen Sondheim, opened during the same theatrical season and competed for the Tony Award in several categories, comparison of the two shows,

EXAMPLE 8.1. "My White Knight," refrain, first eight measures

however different from each other they may be, is unavoidable. Together these two disparate shows tell us something about the xenophobic climate in America during the fifties. Each show deals in its own unique way with American youth, a growing problem in the fifties, when juvenile delinquency was on the rise. Viewed side by side, *West Side Story* and *The Music Man* highlight the dichotomy between urban and rural life. Carol Oja calls *The Music Man* an antidote to *West Side Story,* "at once a wistful escape from the social and political perils of the present and a comforting reassertion of old-fashioned musical comedy." However, *The Music Man* relied on nostalgia. By contrast, *West Side Story* confronted the violence that transformed city streets into war zones in the mid-fifties. Willson created sonic and visual images of the past, a roving barbershop quartet, the sound of piano exercises emanating from the screen door of a fatherless household, boys and girls meeting

Debbie Allan as Anita (foreground) in the 1980 Broadway revival of *West Side Story.*

each other clandestinely in the library, contentious town hall meetings, and social gatherings. Willson's 1912 Iowa excluded any trace of racial tension, which is a striking contract to *West Side Story*'s portrait of interracial and inner-city strife. Barbershop singing was ostensibly an all-white pastime. Winthrop Paroo, an awkward boy circa 1912, serves as the foil to the deprived, angst-ridden teenagers of *West Side Story.*

That the Tony Award committee vote reached a tie on the first round of ballot-ing suggests that the momentum that year could have gone either way. Most critics today would agree that both shows espouse the principles of good musical theater and boast extraordinary scores. In the end, *The Music Man* won the Tony Award for best musical.

AN EMBARRASSMENT OF RICHES

Jule Styne

Jule Styne, a nearly ubiquitous presence on Broadway in the fifties, is best remem-bered for his last musical of the decade, *Gypsy* (1959), which had lyrics by Stephen Sondheim (see Chapter 17). Apart from *Gypsy*, Styne gravitated toward musical comedy and wrote several of them with the lyricist team of Betty Comden and

MARY MARTIN

Mary Martin (1913–1990), who hailed from Texas, became a Broadway star just in time to benefit from the improved standards of musical theater. She was known for her high-spirited performances, especially in the roles of Nellie Forbush in *South Pacific* (1949), the gravity-defying title character in *Peter Pan* (1954), and Maria in *The Sound of Music* (1959). Her performance of "My Heart Belongs to Daddy" at a Siberian railroad station in Cole Porter's 1938 musical *Leave It to Me!* is legendary, mainly because it included a comical striptease. The mezzo-soprano timbre of her voice added to the song's sex appeal. Martin did not create the title roles of *Hello, Dolly!* or *Annie Get Your Gun*, but she played them in the London productions.

Adolph Green (see Chapters 7 and 9), beginning with the revue *Two on the Aisle* (1951). Styne's next musical, *Hazel Flagg* (1953), has the distinction of being the first musical based on a film, *Nothing Sacred*, which was itself based on a short story by James Street (1903–1954) called "A Letter to the Editor" published in *Cosmopolitan* magazine in 1937 (see Chapter 13). It is about a woman who, being diagnosed with radium poisoning, decides to spend her final days in New York City and in the process becomes a *cause célèbre*. She eventually learns that the cancer diagnosis was false.

Mark "Moose" Charlap (1928–1974) was a minor Broadway composer, remembered mostly for *Peter Pan*. He wrote three more Broadway musicals, all of them flops. *Kelly* (1965) has the dubious distinction of playing a single performance.

Styne contributed songs to one of three different musical incarnations of James M. Barrie's *Peter Pan* that appeared between 1950 and 1954. The first, a play with music, had songs by Leonard Bernstein. Disney's better-known animated version appeared in 1952 with songs by Sammy Fain and Sammy Cahn. The third version, overseen by Jerome Robbins, started out with a score by Moose Charlap and Carolyn Leigh (see Chapter 9). Styne, Comden, and Green wrote six additional songs for the show, including "Never Never Land." The show starred Mary Martin as Peter Pan and Cyril Ritchard as Captain Hook (and Mr. Darling). NBC broadcast this version live and in color in 1955, 1956, and 1960, all three times with Martin and Ritchard repeating their Broadway roles. The 1960 telecast was rebroadcast in 1963, 1966, 1973, and 1989. NBC presented a live broadcast of a somewhat altered version of *Peter Pan* in 2014.

Bells Are Ringing (1956) starred one of Hollywood's favorite dumb blondes, Judy Holliday. Jerome Robbins directed, and he and Bob Fosse collaborated on the choreography. Styne's showmanship and Comden and Green's madcap sense of humor combined to produce several strong comic songs, but it is the ballads, "Just in Time" and "The Party's Over," that have stood the test of time. The 1960 film version, which costarred Holliday and Dean Martin, was already dated by the time it was released, but it gives one a sense of what Holliday did with the role on Broadway.

Frank Loesser

In the fifties, Frank Loesser, who, like Styne, had made a name for himself in Hollywood, joined the ranks of Broadway's top songwriters. Loesser's first Broadway exposure dates to 1936, when he provided lyrics for a revue entitled *The Illustrator's Show*. Loesser then worked in Hollywood, mainly as a lyricist, supplying words for songs by Hoagy Carmichael, Burton Lane, and Jule Styne, among others. He won an Academy Award for "Baby, It's Cold Outside," which he wrote for the 1947 film *Neptune's Daughter*. Loesser's first full-length Broadway score was for *Where's Charley* (1948), an adaptation of Brandon Thomas's 1892 English drawing-room comedy *Charley's Aunt*. The musical starred Ray Bolger, best known as the Scarecrow in the movie *The Wizard of Oz*. George Abbott directed the show and provided the book. Loesser wrote only three musicals in the fifties (if one includes *Greenwillow*, which opened in early 1960), but all of them earn high marks for originality. His score for *Guys and Dolls* is still among the most beloved in the repertory. *Guys and Dolls* is a romantic comedy without serious pretension, but it is also an artistic gem, the type of show that Larry Stempel calls "literate musical comedy." It is based on stories by Damon Runyon (1884–1946). Runyon virtually invented the paradoxical Hollywood gangster argot, a mixture of proper grammatical syntax and street slang. Loesser's score has a beguiling eclectic range of styles. His penchant for mixing the profane and the sacred is on full display.

In addition to writing musicals, Loesser also enjoyed the theater and music business, and he possessed shrewd business savvy. In 1950, he founded Frank Music Corporation and one decade later Frank Productions. Eager to expand his client list, Loesser encouraged several unsigned young writers, including Jerry Ross and Richard Adler. In 1953 he acquired Music Theater International, which remains one of the major musical theater leasing organizations.

Richard Adler and Jerry Ross

Richard Adler (1921–2012) and Jerry Ross (1926–1955), native New Yorkers both, were ideal collaborators. Adler's father was a concert pianist, but the young Richard gravitated toward popular music. Ross (né Jerold Rosenberg) grew up in the Bronx, acted in the Yiddish theater, and later studied music at New York University. The two writers met in 1950 and began collaborating on pop songs. They scored a hit with "Rags to Riches" (1953), which was recorded by Tony Bennett. Their first Broadway assignment was *John Murray Anderson's Almanac* (1953), shortly after which they wrote two hit musical comedies in quick succession, *The Pajama Game* (1954) and *Damn Yankees* (1955). Both shows surpassed 1,000 performances and boasted a highly inventive score. Richard Bissell's novel *7½ Cents* was the basis for *The Pajama Game*. The show benefitted from a top-notch production team: Frederick Brisson and Harold Price produced, Bob Fosse supplied the choreography, and George Abbott co-authored the book with Richard Bissell and co-directed with Jerome Robbins. Bissell, who had firsthand knowledge of the pajama manufacturing business, attempted to address the conflict between labor and management, but George Abbott steered the project in the direction of romantic comedy. The plot centers on a labor-union dispute at a pajama factory, but the show avoids the sort of divisive issues that informed *The Cradle Will Rock* (see Chapter 6). The tuneful score features "Hey There," "Steam Heat," and "Hernando's Hideaway." During "Hey There," Sid, the new factory superintendent, sings the first verse into a Dictaphone, and as he plays back the tape he sings a duet with himself.

The production team of *Damn Yankees* included most of personnel responsible for *The Pajama Game*. It was the first of five Fosse musicals built around Gwen Verdon, who won her second of four Tony Awards for her seductive portrayal of the devilish Lola. Douglas Wallop and George Abbott co-wrote the libretto, based on the former's 1954 novel *The Year the Yankees Lost the Pennant*, a clever retelling of the Faust legend adapted to the national pastime. Joe Boyd, a middle-aged baseball fan, sells his soul to the devil in return for becoming a young, strapping star slugger for the Washington Senators. But Joe begins to miss his wife and exploits an escape clause in the contract to get out of the deal. The show produced the sultry "Whatever Lola Wants" and the rousing "You Gotta Have Heart."

Adler and Ross's budding partnership ended tragically when Ross died at the young age of twenty-nine from bronchiectasis. *The Pajama Game* and *Damn Yankees* were state-of-the art musical comedies, with clever scores, legendary performances, inventive choreography, and the best production teams that Broadway had to offer. Hollywood turned out faithful celluloid versions of these shows, in 1957 and 1958, respectively. Ross posthumously won the Tony Award for best musical for *Damn Yankees* during what was the first televised Tony Award ceremony (broadcast locally). Adler, left without a partner, struggled to restart his career. He found modest success writing musicals for television. He also produced special events for the Kennedy and Johnson administrations, including the fundraiser held at Madison Square Garden in New York on May 19, 1962, during which Marilyn Monroe famously sang "Happy Birthday" to JFK.

Albert Hague

The composer Albert Hague (né Albert Marcuse, 1920–2001), a name rarely mentioned today, turned out two successful Broadway musicals in the fifties, *Plain and Fancy* (1955) and *Redhead* (1959). After escaping the Nazis, the German-born Hague studied in Rome and then at the University of Cincinnati. *Plain and Fancy*, which Hague wrote with the lyricist Arnold B. Horwitt (1918–1977), is about an Amish community in Pennsylvania. Like *Brigadoon*, it involves a pair of urbanites who stumble into an isolated rural community. Hague's next show is one of the repertory's few musical crime mysteries (along with *Drood* [1985], *Curtains* [2007], and *A Gentleman's Guide to Love and Murder* [2013]). The murder case involves a young actress whose niece falls in love with the victim's stage partner. The sibling writing team of Herbert and Dorothy Fields conceived the show in the early fifties and pitched it to an uninterested Irving Berlin. For the lead, the producers wanted Gwen Verdon, who by then had won three Tony Awards. She agreed to do the show on the condition that Fosse, her husband at the time, direct and choreograph. Before completing the script, Herbert Fields fell ill, so he asked David Shaw to help him. Then Fields died, and Sidney Sheldon joined the book-writing team. That so many writers worked on the book helps to explain why critics found the show confusing. Hague's next project, *The Girls Against the Boys* (1959), also with lyrics by Horwitt, ended his Broadway winning streak. Even such comic talents as Bert Lahr, Nancy Walker, and a young Dick Van Dyke could not keep the show afloat. Its most memorable moment was a rock-and-roll parody performed by Lahr and Walker. Hague was among the pioneering composers of television musicals. His music for the perennial holiday favorite *How the Grinch Stole Christmas* (1966) is better known today than his Broadway scores. Hague's 1969 musical *The Fig Leaves Are Falling* belongs to a sixties fad of musicals about marriage. Even with a book and lyrics by the then-popular song parodist Allan Sherman, it folded after only four performances. *The Fig Leaves*, which opened in 1969, when U.S. divorce rates began to climb, commented on marriage with the tone-deaf one-liners of a bad television sitcom, as opposed to Edward Albee's brutally acerbic play *Who's Afraid of Virginia Woolf?* (1962).

Jerry Bock and Sheldon Harnick

Like Jerry Ross and Richard Adler, Jerry Bock and Sheldon Harnick perfectly complemented each other's talents. Harnick (b. 1924), a Chicagoan, is best known as a lyricist, but he majored in music at Northwestern University. When he moved to New York, he followed the same path that many of his contemporaries had trod, writing sketches for revues and television. He was first heard on Broadway in *New Faces of 1952*. Jerry Bock (1928–2010) first noticed Harnick when he heard that show's "Boston Beguine" sung by Alice Ghostley. Bock, a New Yorker, studied music at the University of Wisconsin. After graduating, he and the lyricist Larry Holofcener wrote material for Sid Caesar's television show *Your Show of Shows*. They placed some of their songs in the 1955 Broadway revue *Catch a Star*. Their first book musical, *Mr. Wonderful*, opened the following year. Conceived and produced by Jule Styne, it starred Sammy Davis, Jr. and was effectively his nightclub act in the guise of a book musical. Bock and Harnick's first joint effort was the boxing musical *The Body Beautiful*, which had a book by Will Glickman and Joseph Stein, the future librettist for *Fiddler on the Roof*. Their next project, *Fiorello!* (1959), traces the political fortunes of Fiorello LaGuardia, the iconoclastic mayor of New York from 1934 to 1945. It was the third musical to win the Pulitzer Prize for Drama.

Bob Merrill

The Philadelphia-born Bob Merrill started out as a nightclub singer and then worked in radio and film. He made a name for himself as a songwriter with hits such as "If I Knew You Were Comin' I'd've Baked a Cake" (1950) (co-authored with Al Hoffman and Clem Watts) and "How Much Is That Doggie in the Window?" (1952). Despite Merrill's attraction to novelty subjects for his popular songs, he selected plays by Eugene O'Neill, regarded as "the father of American drama," as the basis for his first two Broadway musicals. *New Girl in Town*, based on *Anna Christie* (1921), the winner of the 1922 Pulitzer Prize for Drama, employed the same production team responsible for Ross and Adler's hit musicals. Heading the cast were Gwen Verdon and Thelma Ritter, who shared the Tony Award for Best Actress in a Musical (it was Verdon's third Tony). *Anna Christie* is about a reformed prostitute who tries to turn her life around. She agrees to accompany her father, from whom she has been estranged for five years, on a coal barge. That anyone might have found O'Neill's play a promising vehicle for a musical attests to Rodgers and Hammerstein's impact on the serious direction of musical theater. However, it must have seemed like a stretch for George Abbott, who had built his reputation on swift-paced musical comedy. Brooks Atkinson noted, "Mr. Abbott uses 'Anna Christie' as a kind of safe anchorage in a storm of dancing and singing. . . . [His] effort to make a bigtime [*sic*] festival out of a somber theme is not altogether successful." Merrill's score "at best did no harm," hardly the sort of assessment that a first-time Broadway composer hopes to receive. O'Neill's *Ah, Wilderness!* (1933) served as the basis for Merrill's next show. Joseph Stein and Robert Russell adapted the play, and David Merrick produced. *Ah, Wilderness!* was more inherently suited to musical comedy than *Anna Christie*. Set in 1907 Connecticut, it tells the story of a seventeen-year-old boy named Richard, one of six Miller children. Richard's mother has concerns about the literature he has been reading, such as Oscar Wilde's *Salomé*. Richard is in love with Muriel, whose father goes to great lengths to destroy their relationship. Muriel defies her father, though, and reunites with Richard after he unwittingly gets drunk and ends up at a house of ill repute. Robert Morse appeared as Richard, Jackie Gleason as his Uncle Sid, and Walter Pidgeon as his father, a role played by George M. Cohan in the first production of O'Neill's play. Like Irving Berlin, Merrill lacked formal musical training, but he was able to channel his fervid imagination and melodic instincts into musical theater. In an interview, he claimed that he could not read a note of music and that he composed from a toy xylophone. "You can't fool yourself with fancy arranging," he insisted. "All my hits have a very simple, hummable melody. . . . They . . . are all wholesome, and they are all happy." This sentiment is ironic given that Merrill is the only Broadway composer known to have committed suicide. He shot himself in his car at the age of seventy-four. He had suffered from depression and could not bear the thought of spending his last years in a wheelchair.

Harold Rome

After specializing in revues for over a decade, Harold Rome transitioned to book musicals in the fifties (see Chapter 6). He got off to a disappointing start, though: his 1948 musical *That's the Ticket!* closed out of town. He rebounded in 1952 with the hit summer camp musical *Wish You Were Here*. Based on Arthur Kober's play *Having a Wonderful Time*, the musical takes place at a camp for adults in the Catskill Mountains and featured a real on-stage swimming pool. Rome next composed the score for *Fanny*, a musical play in the Rodgers and Hammerstein tradition. In fact, the producer of the show, David Merrick, tried to woo Rodgers and Hammerstein to write the score, but Rodgers refused to work with him. Rome's score was his most lyrical and expressive to date. At the end of the decade, Rome wrote the score for another Merrick production, *Destry Rides Again* (1959), which was based on the story of Max Brand.

CONCLUSION

History books give a mixed impression about the internal affairs of America in the fifties, but scholars agree that musical theater during the decade experienced an embarrassment of riches. When people wax nostalgic about the Golden Age of musical theater, they might as well be referring to 1957, when on any given night one could choose between *My Fair Lady, West Side Story, The Most Happy Fella, The Pajama Game, The Music Man, Li'l Abner,* and *Bells Are Ringing.* And this was a year without a new Rodgers and Hammerstein musical. The last years of the decade saw some top-notch but conventional musicals. The country's complacency and Broadway's seeming imperviousness to rock music would eventually give way to activism and a new aesthetic in musical theater. These changes, however, were still a few years away. Even in the heat of the sixties, many writers continued to write in the tradition of Rodgers and Hammerstein, but their musicals, even the very best ones, began to appear reactionary as the more innovative writers challenged the very aesthetic qualities and dramatic approaches that brought musical theater to its zenith in the fifties.

AND BEAR IN MIND

The Most Happy Fella, *1956,*
Imperial Theatre and then Broadway Theatre,
678 performances

Music and lyrics by Frank Loesser

Frank Loesser returned to Broadway after *Guys and Dolls* with *The Most Happy Fella.* This, Loesser's most operatic musical, is based on Sidney Howard's 1924 Pulitzer Prize–winning drama *They Knew What They Wanted,* which was based on the Italian drama *Paolo e Francesca.* The protagonist, Tony Esposito, a middle-aged immigrant grape grower in the Napa Valley, represents the shift during the Rodgers and Hammerstein era from stock ingénues to older, imperfect, and more complex leading characters. Tony falls in love with a diner waitress named Amy. Instead of a proper tip, he leaves her his amethyst tie pin and a mawkish love note. They carry on a mail correspondence until he convinces her to marry him. But when she asks

Robert Weede as Tony Esposito and Jo Sullivan as Rosabella in the original Broadway production of *The Most Happy Fella*. *Courtesy Photofest.*

him to send a photograph of himself, Tony sends one of Joe, his younger and more handsome foreman. When Amy, whom Tony calls Rosabella, arrives in Napa, she discovers the truth about Tony. While driving to meet his bride for the first time, Tony gets injured in a car accident. Angry and confused, Amy sleeps with Joe and becomes pregnant. At first, Tony threatens to kill Joe, but soon he recognizes that his own dishonesty played a part in Amy's transgression. Despite objections from Tony's selfish, spinster sister, he and Rosabella decide to raise the baby together.

Sidney Howard injected a lot of politics into the story, a turgid statement about modern relationships. Loesser focused on the story's inherent romance. He added two major female roles, Amy's best friend, Cleo, and Tony's lonely sister, Marie, whose voice types—one a Broadway belter, the other a mezzo-soprano— provided variety and operatic depth to both the musical texture as well as the drama. Loesser turned out an impassioned score, full of duets, trios, chorus numbers, extended scenes, and comic songs for the secondary characters. Loesser's Amy is more romantically inclined than Howard's version of her, who has a more mercenary disposition. The composer exploited the operatic potential of Tony's

(Continued)

generous character. The Metropolitan Opera baritone Robert Weede, who was beyond his prime as an opera singer, revitalized by his career by starring as Tony in the original Broadway production. Jo Sullivan sang the role of Rosabella/Amy. (She became Loesser's second wife in 1959.) *The Most Happy Fella* has shown up on opera company programming, and it has been revived on Broadway several times.

By the time *The Most Happy Fella* premiered on Broadway, *My Fair Lady* had already become the hit of the 1956–1957 season. Although much admired by the musical theater community, *The Most Happy Fella* is arguably the least appreciated show of the fifties, with Bernstein's *Candide*—also a work somewhere between musical theater and opera—being a contender for the same distinction.

NAMES, TERMS, AND CONCEPTS

Arlen, Harold	Loesser, Frank
baby boom	LP
Bernstein, Leonard	McCarthyism
Bock, Jerry	Merrill, Bob
Candide	*Most Happy Fella, The*
Cinderella	*Music Man, The*
Cold War	O'Neill, Eugene
Ed Sullivan Show, The	*Pajama Game, The*
Fosse, Bob	*Peter Pan* musicals
Harnick, Sheldon	Prince, Harold
Kidd, Michael	Styne, Jule
King and I, The	*West Side Story*
La Touche, John	Willson, Meredith

DISCUSSION QUESTIONS

1. Discuss the novel features of Meredith Willson's score for *The Music Man*.

2. What evidence supports the notion of an increase in the cultural status of musical theater during the fifties?

3. Chart Rodgers and Hammerstein's career during the fifties.

4. Describe the treatment of politics in fifties musicals.

CHAPTER 9

THE SIXTIES
(*CABARET*, 1966, BROADHURST
THEATRE, 1,165 PERFORMANCES)

I n the early sixties, musical theater experienced a precipitous decline in popularity. The Rodgers and Hammerstein brand of musical theater, which had dominated Broadway for nearly two decades and espoused a utopian view of the world, could not accommodate the uncertainty and anxiety caused by the Cold and Vietnam wars, and rock was replacing Broadway music as the primary popular musical idiom. With few exceptions, established Broadway composers and lyricists at the time were not about to start writing rock music. It fell to younger writers to transform the musical theater genre into a relevant art form for the postmodern age. Some writers experimented with form and content in the hope of reinvigorating the musical theater genre. They created a more ironic, commentative, and self-reflexive form of musical theater, the "concept musical," so called because it is governed by a central theme or directorial concept. (The experimental camp also included a few visionary directors and choreographers.)

"THE AGE OF AQUARIUS"

The sixties was a transformative decade that altered the way that many Americans viewed their government, careers, and personal lives. It also triggered a reassessment of the country's role in the world. In response to the complacency of the fifties, the sixties experienced a rise in activism and a renewed belief that government could function as a powerful instrument for positive change. President John F. Kennedy's commitment to the Peace Corps is just one example of the federal government's efforts to effect change on a global scale. President Lyndon B. Johnson's "Great Society" and "War on Poverty" gave further credence to the belief in government's power to improve the lives of average Americans. The Civil Rights Act of 1964 marked the end of the institutionalized discrimination of the Jim Crow era. The first human moonwalk in 1969 realized a goal that Kennedy had set at the beginning of the decade. The Supreme Court stood up to reactionary factions that railed against the expanded civil rights and civil liberties that the justices had put in place. This period was dubbed the "Age of Aquarius." Anything and everything seemed possible.

The collective optimism of the sixties trickled down to the individual. The decade ushered in a period of self-empowerment and self-reflection. Americans felt that they had a natural right to demand a greater degree of agency in their personal lives. Experimenting with drugs and sex, listening to rock music, and even "sticking it to the man" were expressions of a desire for greater personal fulfillment. Since the sixties, the focus on the self, the "culture of narcissism," as some have labeled it, has influenced each subsequent generation of Americans, from the "me generation" (baby boomers) in the seventies and eighties, to Generation X in the nineties, to today's Generation Y (millennials). Nostalgia associated with the sixties is rooted in the fact that "the twin desires for self-fulfillment and social change," as M. J. Heale has noted, worked in concert, however fleetingly.

By the mid-sixties, a counterculture movement had emerged and was attracting disaffected youths as well as disenfranchised and disillusioned people of all ages. Members of the movement either viewed it as a vehicle for change or were turned on by its alternative lifestyle, or both. However, the counterculture movement was anything but monolithic. It encompassed students, hippies, minorities, feminists, and people on spiritual quests. The phrase "do your own thing" became its credo—which explains why the 1968 hit rock musical based on Shakespeare's *Twelfth Night* adopted the phrase as its title (see Chapter 16). Uniting these factions was a shared desire to undermine the values of "the establishment." Drugs, rock, interracial dating, and collective living all represented the antithesis of mainstream values. Long hair became the counterculture's emblematic dress code, and both men and women let it grow as a political statement. Music and humor became potent weapons of the movement. Rock music drifted further to the left. Bob Dylan's "Blowin' in the Wind" reached the Top 40 chart. The movement shined a light on the hypocrisy of America's policies in Vietnam by employing oppositional binarisms, such as love versus war, sex versus killing, and naked versus clothed. Institutions were to be besmirched as instruments of the establishment. Fueling the movement was a growing demoralization among Americans over the negative direction in which the country was heading. According to Terry Anderson, "without racism, war, campus paternalism, police brutality, the size of hippiedom would have been proportionately about the same as the beatniks in the late 1950s."

The animosity between mainstream America and the counterculture intensified when Nixon was elected in 1968. The campus youth movement provoked violent reaction from university administrators and state and local governments. The violence reached tragic proportions when, on May 4, 1970, Ohio National Guardsmen, called in to quell unrest at Kent State, opened fire, killing four unarmed students and wounding nine more. Conservative factions sowed the seeds of suspicions about the counterculture movement and orchestrated a campaign to squelch the protests. One of their tactics was to stir up irrational fears by lumping hippies together with communists and prostitutes.

WRITERS OF THE RODGERS AND HAMMERSTEIN ERA

Oscar Hammerstein's death in 1960 presaged the end of musical theater's Golden Age, but that news did not immediately reach the musical theater establishment. Indeed, against the tumultuous political and social backdrop of the sixties, Broadway seemed a stuffy, conservative institution. Producers were not in the business of advancing causes and had no stomach for investing money in agenda-driven musicals. Most Broadway writers, young and old, were more acclimated to Tin Pan Alley than to rock music, and they continued to work in the honored tradition of the integrated book musical. It took years before any Broadway composer worked with rock idioms other than to parody rock and roll (e.g., *Bye Bye Birdie*) (see Chapter 16). The increasing popularity of rock music among the young posed an existential threat to musical theater. Whereas in earlier years teenagers danced to the strains of Gershwin and Rodgers, their sixties counterparts regarded Broadway as a conservative institution patronized by their parents' generation. After all, *My Fair Lady, West Side Story, Gypsy*, and *The Sound of Music* were all still running on Broadway in the early sixties. Eventually, the Broadway establishment came to recognize the necessity of attracting young audiences, but change did not happen overnight. Moreover, events occurring on the streets, on college campuses, in average American households, and in government chambers eventually forced Broadway to take notice.

Schwartz and Dietz

Several Golden Age musical writers sang their swan song during the Kennedy years, including Irving Berlin, Vernon Duke, Arthur Schwartz, Howard Dietz, and Frederick Loewe. Few of their efforts registered, however. Schwartz and Dietz's *Jennie*, their final Broadway musical, was a rather lackluster showcase for Mary Martin. Its outdated plot follows a theatrical couple as they tour the country performing in melodramas. *Jennie* premiered about one month before the assassination of John F. Kennedy, and after that fateful event, it had little resonance for audiences, with the possible exception of diehard Mary Martin fans.

Lerner and Loewe

The sensational success of *My Fair Lady* haunted Lerner and Loewe. They knew that their next project would inevitably be compared to what many critics considered the best musical in the repertory. They did not make it any easier on themselves by choosing to adapt the 1958 novel *The Once and Future King*, T. H. White's retelling of Arthurian legend. Loewe, in fact, needed some coaxing. "Who the hell cares about a cuckold?" he exclaimed. Lerner focused on the story's love triangle involving King Arthur, Lancelot, and Guinevere. The plot and score of the musical worked well on stage, but Lerner's transformation of Lancelot into a handsome prig negatively skewed the audience's feelings about Arthur. *Camelot*, which starred Richard Burton and Julie Andrews (see Chapter 8) as Arthur and Guinevere, remains a popular but imperfect work. After *Camelot*, Loewe went into retirement, while the younger, spryer Lerner spent the remaining years of his career collaborating with various composers, although without felicitous results. He collaborated with Richard Rodgers on a show about extrasensory perception and reincarnation, topics about which he was obsessed, but their partnership ended prematurely without producing a show. Lerner eventually managed to bring his ESP musical to fruition in 1965. *On a Clear Day You Can See Forever*, as the show was eventually called, featured some excellent music by Burton Lane (see Chapter 7), but it ran under a year. Katharine Hepburn made her only musical theater appearance in *Coco*, Lerner's last musical of the decade. She played the famed haute couture designer Coco Chanel and, like Rex Harrison and Richard Burton before her, mostly spoke her way through her songs, which were composed by André Previn (b. 1929).

Frank Loesser

Frank Loesser and Abe Burrows reunited in 1961 for *How to Succeed in Business Without Really Trying*, a droll satire about the byzantine path to promotion in corporate America (see Chapter 8). It was the fourth musical to receive the Pulitzer Prize for Drama. Loesser's 1960 folk musical *Greenwillow* (based on B. J. Chute's 1956 novel of the same name) did poorly despite his characteristically inventive score. Loesser languished for the remainder of the decade. *Pleasures and Palaces* (based on Sam Spewack's 1961 play *Once There Was a Russian*) closed on the road in 1965. Loesser failed to complete *Señor Discretion Himself*, an adaptation of a short story by Budd Schulberg. Loesser died in 1969 of lung cancer, feeling that his time had passed.

Harold Rome

Harold Rome's *I Can Get It for You Wholesale* (1962) anticipated several musical theater trends of the sixties: Jewish themes (*Milk and Honey, A Family Affair, Fiddler on the Roof, Cabaret, The Education of H*Y*M*A*N K*A*P*L*A*N*, and several revues), business-oriented stories (*How Now, Dow Jones*), stories with ethnic characters (*13 Daughters, Fiddler on the Roof, Bajour, Illya Darling*, and *Zorbá*), and antiheros (*Do Re Mi, How to Succeed, Stop the World—I Want to Get Off*, and *110 in the Shade*). However, what one most remembers about the show is the appearance of Barbra Streisand, who, making her Broadway debut, famously sang the comic secretarial song "Miss Marmelstein." *Wholesale* centers on a ruthless ladder climber, Harry Bogen, who throws aside anyone who gets in his way, his mother and girlfriend included. Rome's *The Zulu and the Zayda* (1965) tells the story of a Jewish man, originally from Czarist Russian, who moves from London to South Africa, where his son has hired a black man to be his companion. Rome remained active into the seventies, but none of his later projects made it to Broadway. His musical adaptation of *Gone with the Wind* (originally titled *Scarlett*), which had a book by Horton Foote, played to enthusiastic audiences in Japan and London, but the American production never got beyond Los Angeles.

Irving Berlin

Septuagenarian Irving Berlin made his final Broadway foray in 1962. The titular character of *Mr. President* (1962) struggles to control his daughter as well as the Soviets. En route to Russia, he learns that he has been declared *persona non grata* in Moscow, but he belligerently orders the pilot of his plane to land there anyway. The president's provocation causes him to lose his bid for a second term. Berlin, who had gingerly negotiated the Rodgers and Hammerstein revolution, was not about to embrace changing tastes this late in his career. His score contained some entertaining albeit conventional songs. The book, by the team of Howard Lindsay and Russel Crouse (see Chapter 6), relied on formula and stale jokes about life in the White House. The show looked old fashioned next to the work of Broadway newcomers such as Stephen Sondheim, Lionel Bart, and the team of Leslie Bricusse and Anthony Newley. Berlin lived nearly another quarter-century, but he never came out of retirement to write another musical.

Meredith Willson

Meredith Willson returned to Broadway in 1960 with *The Unsinkable Molly Brown*. Like Lerner and Loewe, he faced the formidable task of topping his previous project, *The Music Man* (see Chapter 8). He chose a subject that evoked a similar turn-of-the-century American milieu: Molly Brown. Like *Annie Get Your Gun*, a musical about Annie Oakley, *The Unsinkable Molly Brown* told the story of a real-life strong-willed but poorly educated woman. Molly Brown (1867–1932) is best remembered for

Leonard Bernstein and Alan Jay Lerner's bicentennial musical *1600 Pennsylvania Avenue* also depicted life in the White House, but it had loftier ambitions than *Mr. President*. The production was such a fiasco that Bernstein refused to allow a cast recording to be made.

having survived the sinking of the Titanic in 1912. Her life provided the basis for a quintessential American rags-to-riches story set in rural Colorado, Denver, and various locales in Europe. However, Richard Morris, who wrote the book, ignored some of the most intriguing details of Brown's biography, such as her two failed bids for a seat in the U.S. Senate, her divorce in 1909, and her support of women's rights. His dialogue suffers from too many corny patches, and his handling of the upper-class Denverites smacks of reverse snobbism. Ultimately, Morris's Molly, unlike Annie Oakley, fails to win the full sympathy of the audience. Willson's score did not make up for the weaknesses in the book. The sort of novel ideas that seemed so refreshing in *The Music Man* come off here like dull contrivances, and his homespun humor wears thin at times. However, Tammy Grimes's star-making performance helped to keep the show running for 532 performances. Willson's next musical, *Here's Love* (1963), did not fare much better, despite its beloved source material: *Miracle on 34th Street*. Choreographed by Michael Kidd (see Chapter 8), the show opened with a rousing ten-minute parade scene ("The Big Clown Balloons"), but it was downhill from there. The cast included a young Michael Bennett, the future creator of *A Chorus Line* (see Chapter 10).

Richard Rodgers

No Strings (1960), Richard Rodgers's first show after Hammerstein's death, was the first of several sixties musicals involving an interracial romance. Rodgers, either not yet ready to take on a new lyricist or unable to find someone compatible, decided to write his own lyrics. Samuel A. Taylor (1912–2000) devised the plot, which takes place in Paris, where two expatriates, a white novelist and a chic black fashion model, fall in love; however, faced with the racial tensions back home, they end their romance before returning to America. In interviews, Rodgers down-played the role of race in the show, claiming that the interracial romance was merely the result of casting Diahann Carroll and Richard Kiley as the lovers. The setting and subject matter inspired Rodgers to return to the jazzy idioms of his days writing with Lorenz Hart. The orchestrations, by Ralph Burns, did not incor-porate strings (a musical pun on the title); the orchestra was situated backstage, and sometimes musicians wandered into the action on stage. Running 580 perfor-mances, *No Strings* was Rodgers's most successful work from this period, but a planned film version fell victim to racial politics. Seven Arts Productions acquired the film rights for $2 million but pulled the plug on the project because it feared resistance from Southern film distributors.

Richard Adler

Like Richard Rodgers, Richard Adler also returned to Broadway partner-less (see Chapter 8), and he too wrote a show about an interracial relationship set abroad. *Kwamina* (1961) had several strengths, including choreography by Agnes de Mille and a winning performance by Sally Ann Howes, the composer's wife, but it mus-tered only thirty-two performances. On the other hand, the show's depiction of African culture reveals the same attitude as earlier Orientalist musicals. The story focuses on the conflict between tribal customs and modern science.

Jule Styne

Throughout the sixties, Jule Styne maintained the feverish pace that he had set for himself in the fifties, collaborating extensively with Betty Comden and Adolph Green (see Chapter 7). They began the decade with *Do Re Mi*, a musical comedy that Garon Kanin adapted from his 1955 novella about the payola scandal in the juke-box industry. The story required Styne to write a couple of rock-and-roll parodies in addition to some traditional theater songs, including the ballad "Make Someone Happy." Phil Silvers and Nancy Walker appeared as Hubie Cram, a pathetic and unscrupulous dreamer of grandeur, and his dutiful but exasperated wife, Kay, who simply wants him to find an ordinary job.

Edmund G. Love's *Subways Are for Sleeping*, a book about people who have given up on the rat race and are living hand to mouth, provided the basis of Styne, Comden, and Green's next show. The legacy of this musical rests less on its artistic merits than on the producer David Merrick's infamous publicity stunt in which he published favorable quotes from average New Yorkers who happened to share names with the city's major theater critics. The musical failed on several accounts,

DAVID MERRICK

David Merrick, whose career in the theater spanned nearly five decades (1942–1990), earned the reputation of being a nefarious, divisive, and manipulative operator on Broadway, traits not uncommonly ascribed to theatrical producers but in his case particularly pronounced. The only major Merrick biography (unauthorized) is titled *The Abominable Showman*, one of his nicknames. "The Undertaker" was another. Upon the occasion of his death in 2000, *The New York Times* printed the following editorialized eulogy:

> He possessed a keen commercial and artistic sensibility and an almost hostile business acumen, as well as a flair for publicity that will link his name forever with the likes of P. T. Barnum. . . . Tales of Mr. Merrick's acerbity are rife, yet they are offset not only by the popularity of the shows he produced but also by the high artistic merit of many of them.

Merrick's infamy notwithstanding, he achieved the best hit-to-flops ratio in the business, 60:40, far better than the century's rough average of 20:80.

but the score featured some good material, such as a song in Act I in which several subway riders sing imitative counterpoint as they argue over the best route for the female protagonist to reach her destination.

Styne collaborated with Bob Merrill on the 1964 hit *Funny Girl*, the musical that transformed Barbra Streisand into a bona fide star. The show continued to run after Streisand departed for Hollywood, becoming Styne's longest-running Broadway musical. Styne and Merrill, a strong composer in his own right, collaborated twice more in the seventies.

Bob Merrill

In the early sixties, Bob Merrill, with two recent hits to his name, was in high demand (see Chapter 8). David Merrick moved quickly to commission him to write what became one of the major hits of the decade, *Carnival. Carnival* is remembered not only as a well-crafted musical but also as the beginning of the long, albeit contentious, relationship between Merrick and the choreographer-director Gower Champion (1920–1980). Champion directed seven musicals for Merrick, four of them in the sixties. *Carnival* was a traditional book musical with a heartwarming story. Although inspired by MGM's 1953 film *Lili*, which starred Leslie Caron, *Carnival* required an entirely original score.

THE FIRST POST–RODGERS AND HAMMERSTEIN GENERATION

Several writers who came of age during the Rodgers and Hammerstein era made their first mark on Broadway amidst the rock revolution. As rock displaced Broadway as America's mainstream popular music, the idiom in which these composers were accustomed to writing began to lose its cultural relevance. Therefore, achieving both artistic success and commercial viability required a creative solution. Most writers worked within the nearly passé traditional Broadway musical style. Only a few young composers, most notably Charles Strouse, attempted to incorporate rock idioms into their music.

Traditional Book Musicals

Oliver!

Lionel Bart's *Oliver!* premiered in England in 1960 and arrived on Broadway in 1963. It was the third hit from the London stage to transfer to Broadway in as many years, preceded by *Stop the World—I Want to Get Off* and the spoken satire *Beyond the Fringe*. An English presence of this magnitude was not seen again on Broadway until the surge in megamusicals in the late eighties (see Chapter 11).

Bart took his inspiration from David Lean's 1948 film version of *Oliver Twist*, not from Charles Dickens's novel, which he claimed not to have read. He eliminated several characters, such as Rose Maylie and Monks, and concentrated on Oliver's encounters with Fagin, Nancy, and his beneficent uncle. Bart wrote simple melodies, in many cases starting diatonically and introducing chromatic pitches to heighten the lyrics, as is the case in "Where Is Love." In some instances, a character's gait became the rhythmic basis for his or her songs. The triple-meter rhythms of "Oliver," for instance, are based on Mr. Bumble's heavy stride.

The Broadway production of *Oliver!* deviated from the London version in several respects. David Merrick, who won a bidding war over the American rights, did not open *Oliver!* right away. Instead, he waited a couple of years in order to build buzz for the musical. Merrick's second-to-none business savvy paid off in spades. He forestalled possible backlash from the Jewish community by eliminating the anti-Semitic elements of the novel. One feature that was retained from the London production was the Jewish inflection of Fagin's music, which, according to Bart, had the character of "a Jewish mother-hen clucking away." Although a hit, *Oliver!* was not without its critics, one of whom described the less overtly Jewish Fagin as "Aryanised" and another as a "complacent low comedian." The production weathered these and other complaints, and it won several Tony Awards. It did not hurt business that scenes from *Oliver!* appeared on the same 1964 episode of *The Ed Sullivan Show* (see Chapter 8) that introduced the Beatles to America.

Many commentators point to 1964 as the end of the Golden Age of musical theater, but more musicals opened that year than in any other year of the decade, including nearly twenty open-ended Broadway productions, over thirty

LIONEL BART

L ionel Bart (1930–1999) was born and raised in London, the youngest of seven children of a poor Jewish family. He never received formal musical training and required an amanuensis to transcribe his music. He began his music career writing popular songs such as "Living Doll" and "Rock and the Caveman." He gained his first theatrical experience at Britain's Unity Theatre, which had emerged from the leftist Worker's Theatre Movement. Bart did not shy away from political or polemical topics. According to his biographers, David and Caroline Stafford, at the Unity Theatre Bart "learned the power of simplicity in composition and theatrical effect . . . [and] witnessed at first hand the atavistic spell that those old, belting, oom-pah music hall styles could weave over an audience." He wrote several shows for the Unity Theatre, including a satirical version of *Cinderella* with songs such as "The Class Slipper" (1953). Bart's musical theater career took off when he collaborated with the composer Laurie Johnson on *Lock Up Your Daughters*, an adaptation of Henry Fielding's eighteenth-century play *Rape Upon Rape*. The musical ran for 328 performances in London, but the 1960 American production closed before getting to Broadway. Four musicals by Bart followed in quick succession. The first, *Fings Ain't Wot They Used T'Be* (1960), a comedy by Frank Norman, featured rough-and-tumble Cockney-speaking characters. *Oliver!* opened the same year, erasing any lingering doubts about Bart's future in musical theater. Indeed, with the success of *Oliver!* Bart became England's premiere musical theater writer, following in the footsteps of Ivor Novello (1893–1951) and Noël Coward (1899–1973). Bart next wrote two political works, the antiwar *Blitz* (London, 1962) and *Maggie May* (1964), which tells the story of a prostitute and a dockworker in Liverpool, the latter of whom gets killed while attempting to stop a shipment of arms intended for the police in apartheid South Africa. Neither work reached America. Bart's next two shows, *Twang!* (1965), a spoof of the Robin Hood legend, and *La Strada* (1969), based on Fellini's movie of the same name, failed to live up to expectations.

Bart's life might have been a charmed one had his rapid success in the early sixties not led him astray. He rubbed elbows with British royalty as well as show-business royalty, such as the Rolling Stones and the Beatles. But Bart did not handle his success well. Reckless with his wealth and health, he made devastating financial decisions and battled with alcoholism. He died of liver cancer in 1999, never coming close to repeating the success he had found with *Oliver!*

JERRY HERMAN

Jerry Herman, who was raised in Jersey City by working-class Jewish parents, is one of the few successful Broadway composers of his generation without formal music training. When it was time for college, Herman spent a year studying design and architecture at Parsons School of Design, but the next year he transferred to the University of Miami to study theater. He never made any pretensions about his music: he favored direct, memorable melodies and uncomplicated harmonies and eschewed complex formal structures. His lyrics are rarely fussy or belabored. Indeed, Herman intentionally sought to recapture the days when songs by theater composers such as Irving Berlin, his professed model, were the popular music of the day. Herman succeeded to a certain extent, although by the sixties show tunes rarely crossed over into the mainstream commercial market. According to ASCAP, "Hello, Dolly!" is one of the most performed songs of the twentieth century. Herman never stretched himself as a composer. He relied on formula, but he possessed sound theatrical instincts and a good ear for melody.

Off Broadway productions, and a variety of limited-run productions at City Center and on Broadway.

Two traditional book musicals, both of them blockbuster hits, began their record long runs in 1964: *Hello, Dolly!* and *Fiddler on the Roof.* Lastly, several B-list musicals, few of which register today (e.g., *Bajour, Ben Franklin in Paris,* and *I Had a Ball*, all of them also from 1964), enjoyed runs of over two hundred performances, still a respectable number in the sixties.

Hello, Dolly!

Jerry Herman, the composer and lyricist of *Hello, Dolly!*, is the most reactionary songwriter of his generation. In the eighties, Herman overtly championed gay causes, but even then he remained within the parameters of traditional musical comedy. Although *Hello, Dolly!* was an unqualified hit in the sixties, commentators today are divided over its artistic value. Mark Grant views *Hello, Dolly!* as a decisive turning point in the loss of literary quality of musical theater, noting that the production inverted the relationship between the written and visual aspects of a musical. It made "spectacle-as-content" an artistic imperative for future generations. Grant blames the show's director and choreographer, Gower Champion, who subordinated plot, character, and the narrative function of songs to visual spectacle. Champion achieved his first directorial success in 1960 with *Bye Bye Birdie*, the musical that marked the Broadway debut of composer Charles Strouse and lyricist Lee Adams (see Chapter 16). Herman's next show, *Mame* (1966), practically replicated *Dolly!* in all but plot. It too revolved around a larger-than-life woman who

A weary Tevye (Zero Mostel) rests right before he address God in "If I Were a Rich Man" in *Fiddler on the Roof. Courtesy KB Archives.*

rejects society's rules for how she should behave. Ethan Mordden calls this type of star vehicle the "big woman" musical, better known as the diva musical.

Tenderloin, She Loves Me, Fiddler on the Roof, The Apple Tree, *and* The Rothschilds

Herman's brand of musical theater changed little over the course of his career. By contrast, Jerry Bock and Sheldon Harnick cultivated a wider stylistic range and gravitated toward more serious stories. At the beginning of the decade, they faced what could be called the "*My Fair Lady* dilemma". After *Fiorello!* (1959), which won the Pulitzer Prize for Drama in 1960, all eyes were on Bock and Harnick's next project,

for which they chose another New York story, this one set in the city's infamous red-light district during the Gay Nineties (see Chapter 8). *Tenderloin*, based on Samuel Hopkins Adams's 1959 novel of the same name, pits good against evil as personified by, respectively, the social reformer Reverend Brock (based on Charles Henry Parkhurst) and the police, politicians, and prostitutes of the neighborhood nicknamed the Tenderloin. Its 215 performances, a respectable albeit not particularly profitable run at the time,

Charles Henry Parkhurst (1842–1933), a minister and social reformer, is credited with exposing the corruption of Tammany Hall, the seat of New York City politics in the nineteenth century. The Tenderloin district ran from the low 20s to 42nd Street and from Fifth Avenue to Seventh Avenue.

CHARLES STROUSE AND LEE ADAMS

Charles Strouse (b. 1928) and Lee Adams (b. 1924) met in the early fifties and formed a collaboration that continued uninterrupted until the early seventies. When Strouse decided to work at Green Mansions, a summer resort in the Adirondacks with a vibrant theater tradition, he took Adams with him. They wrote sketches, short musicals, and novelty numbers, collaborating extensively with Michael Stewart, the future book writer for *Bye Bye Birdie* (see Chapter 16) and *Hello, Dolly!* By the end of the summer, Strouse had abandoned his previous aspirations of becoming a classical composer in favor of a life in musical theater. Strouse and Adams attracted the attention of producers with their revue material for three consecutive editions of Ben Bagley's *Shoestring Revue* (1955–1957) and *The Littlest Revue* (1956). Around this time, Strouse and Adams wrote their first full-length book musical, *A Pound in Your Pocket* (book by S. I. Abelow and Robert Cenedella), which is based on Charles Dickens's *The Old Curiosity Shop*, and a few years later a one-act opera called *The Cozy*. Shortly thereafter, they received an offer from Ed Padula to write the score for *Bye Bye Birdie*. When Adams relocated to Connecticut in the early seventies, Strouse began working with other lyricists, but he reunited with Adams whenever the lyricist was willing and available. Strouse wrote *Annie* (1977), one of his most popular musicals, with lyricist Martin Charnin and book writer Thomas Meehan.

paled in comparison to *Fiorello*'s 795. Bock and Harick's next musical, the highly admired *She Loves Me* (1963), initially ran for only 302 performances but has risen in esteem ever since. *She Loves Me* is based on Ernst Lubitsch's film *Little Shop Around the Corner* (1940), itself based on Miklós Lászlo's Hungarian play *Parfumerie* (also the source of the popular 1998 film *You've Got Mail*). Harold Prince made his directing debut with *She Loves Me*. Joseph Masteroff, who wrote the show's book, balanced the story's romance and humor and expertly handled the original source's charming array of impetuous, naïve, opportunistic, and romantic characters. Barbara Cook, still Broadway's favorite ingénue in the sixties, played the role of Amalia Balash (see Chapter 8). Bock and Harnick's score solidified their reputation for insightful character-driven songs, skills that would help make their next show the biggest hit of the decade.

Bock and Harnick's magnum opus, *Fiddler on the Roof*, has an endearing score and engaging script, by Joseph Stein, but it owes much of its success to the director-choreographer Jerome Robbins. Robbins exerted no less directorial authority over *Fiddler* than Champion did over *Dolly!*, but he escapes the sort of criticism that Grant levels at the latter. In fact, Grant writes, "Perhaps no other director-choreographer could have so brilliantly devised sectarian communal ritual dances to express universal human truths." Robbins's visual style and thematic approach to the material have led several commentators to call *Fiddler* a concept musical, but the plot and integrated score essentially follow the Rodgers and Hammerstein model. Whereas Champion strengthened the adequate writing of *Dolly* by subordinating it to, according to Grant, "gestures of staging," Robbins enhanced what was intrinsically good material in the first place. After *Fiddler*, Robbins, only forty-six years old at the time, retired from musical theater in order to concentrate on ballet. His departure might explain why some musical theater historians emphasize 1964 as the beginning of the end of the Golden Age.

Bock and Harnick followed *Fiddler* with a light-hearted musical comedy called *The Apple Tree* (1966), which comprises three separate one-act musical comedies based on, respectively, Mark Twain's short story "The Diary of Adam and Eve," Frank R. Stockton's "The Lady or the Tiger?," and Jules Feiffer's "Passionella." Barbara Harris, Alan Alda, and Larry Blyden starred in each segment, and Mike Nichols directed. *The Apple Tree* ran a respectable but unremarkable 463 performances. "Passionella" contains Bock and Harnick's singular rock-and-roll song, a rock waltz parody called "You Are Not Real," sung by a solipsistic rock star who accuses Passionella of insincerity.

Bock and Harnick's next and final collaboration, *The Rothschilds,* is based on Frederic Morton's book *The Rothschilds: A Family Portrait* (1962). The musical traces the history of the Rothschild family from its humble beginnings in Germany, to the founding of their financial empire and growing political influence under the guidance of patriarch Mayer Rothschild, to their assistance in funding Napoleon's defeat, to how they secured a declaration of rights for European Jews. *The Rothschilds* was a noble albeit unsuccessful effort, and it was negatively compared to *Fiddler*. Although at times striking, the music lacks the warmth of *Fiddler*, but so, too, does the story. According to Philip Lambert, Bock listened to "Handel, Mozart and Beethoven, German lieder and Viennese folk songs" in preparation for writing the show. Indeed, Bock invoked eighteenth-century European musical opulence, eschewing the ethnic musical idioms that inform *Fiddler*. Gilbert and Sullivan and Johann Strauss inspired some of the lighter moments in the score.

Events surrounding the production of *The Rothschilds* put such a strain on Bock and Harnick's collaboration that it fell apart forever. Neither writer ever commented much on their falling-out other than suggesting that after *The Rothschilds* they simply drifted apart. They both harbored anger, but it was not over a specific incident or event; years passed without their talking.

Wildcat, Little Me, *and* Sweet Charity

Cy Coleman (1929–2004) was a jazz musician before becoming a musical theater composer. His most effective scores are those composed for stories that lend themselves to his jazz background. (He occasionally dabbled in rock idioms.) Colman's first major foray on Broadway, *Wildcat* (1960), was a star vehicle for Lucille Ball. With an original story by N. Richard Nash, it takes place in 1912 along the Mexican border, although one would not know it from the contemporary sound of Coleman's music. Ball played Wildcat Jackson, who hopes to strike it rich in oil so that she can take care of her physically disabled sister. The requisite love story involved Ball's character and Joe Dynamite, with whom she spars for almost two acts until the oil-gushing happy ending. Carolyn Leigh, with whom Coleman had written the hit singles "Witchcraft" and "The Best Is Yet to Come," wrote the lyrics. Other than "Hey, Look Me Over!," an upbeat march in 6/8, the show made little impression. Ball, who bankrolled the entire production herself, relied on her old comic gags to make up for the weak script.

Coleman and Leigh reunited for *Little Me* (1962), which was based on Patrick Dennis's satirical confessional novel *Little Me: The Intimate Memoirs of That Great Star of Stage, Screen and Television, Belle Poitrine* (1961). In his first musical theater venture, the comedy writer Neil Simon wrote the book. Simon suggested that the seven male roles around whom the story revolves (four husbands and three lovers) be played by a single actor: Sid Caesar. Bob Fosse, who was in great demand at the time, codirected the show with Cy Feuer as well as supplying the choreography. *The New York Times* called Simon's book "a flimsy contrivance," Leigh's lyrics "lively, if not brilliant," and Coleman's music "functional." The show ran an unimpressive 257 performances.

Four years later, Coleman, Simon, and Fosse reunited for *Sweet Charity* (1966), a musical based on Fellini's *Nights of Cabiria* (1957). It was the first of three musicals on which Coleman collaborated with the lyricist Dorothy Fields (see Chapter 2). Fosse and Gwen Verdon (see Chapter 8), his wife at the time, who played Charity, gave the show its athleticism and sexual energy. Verdon, who excelled in roles that epitomized what has been called the "Madonna-whore complex," brought pathos to the role of Charity, whose vocation as a call girl in Fellini's film was changed to a less disreputable dance-hall hostess. The critics applauded the score but found Simon's book wanting. *The New York Times* equated the show's obsequious desire to please with Charity's need to be loved.

Although not Cy Coleman's longest-running musical, *Sweet Charity* features one of his best scores. Coleman incorporated sixties-style rock and jazz while paying tribute to traditional Broadway musical theater. With songs such as "Hey Big Spender," "There's Gotta Be Something Greater than This," "The Rhythm of Life," and "If My Friends Could See Me Now," the score showed off Coleman's wide stylistic range. Ralph Burns's orchestration gave the music an electricity rarely heard on Broadway.

Sweet Charity is invariably referred to as a "Fosse musical" rather than "a Coleman musical." Ethan Mordden calls the show "a first-class piece of writing that nevertheless could not have existed without [Bob] Fosse and [Gwen] Verdon." On the other hand, *Charity*, like many of Fosse's shows, has been accused of lacking heart. Clive Barnes wrote that his choreography is "slick and clever and yet perfectly empty of true choreographic interest." Fosse was a master of style over content. His method, Barnes suggests, was "to reduce movement to robot simplicity and have a whole group of dancers performing eccentric, often jerky movements with the mechanized perfection of a Swiss cuckoo clock." When the material inherently suited Fosse's icy sensibilities and angular gestures, the results were

NEIL SIMON

Neil Simon (b. 1927), the most popular and successful American comic playwright during the last third of the twentieth century, has written over thirty-five works for the stage and over twenty movies, some of them based on his plays. Simon got his start in television writing for NBC's *Your Show of Shows* starring Sid Caesar and Imogene Coca. In the sixties, and with only one Broadway credit to his name, Simon turned his comic genius to musical theater, eventually writing the books for five works: *Little Me*; *Sweet Charity*; *Promises, Promises*; *They're Playing Our Song*; and *The Goodbye Girl* (adapting his own screenplay). Simon's joke-oriented style of comedy dates some of his plays, but at the peak of his career, he enjoyed tremendous popularity. His most acclaimed works for the stage include *The Odd Couple* (1965) and his autobiographical trilogy: *Brighton Beach Memoirs* (1983), *Biloxi Blues* (1985), and *Broadway Bound* (1986). Simon has served as "play doctor" on an untold number of Broadway-bound musicals, including *A Chorus Line* (see Chapter 10).

stunning (e.g., *Chicago* [1975]). Proving the adage that imitation is the sincerest form of flattery, several choreographers have attempted to emulate Fosse's distinct style. Fosse, who had danced in Chicago strip clubs in his youth, excelled at sleazy, slithering, and sexually charged choreography, and he gravitated toward stories about charlatans, murderers, uneducated losers, and self-deluded dreamers.

After its initial Broadway run, *Sweet Charity* played in London and Paris. The first Broadway revival (1986), for which Fosse recreated his direction and choreography, starred Debbie Allen, Bebe Neuwirth, and Michael Rupert, and ran for 369 performances, and the second revival (2005), which starred Christine Applegate, ran for 279 performances. A 2009 production at the highly admired Menier Chocolate Factory in England borrowed Neil Simon's concept for *Little Me* of featuring a single male actor as all three of Charity's romantic interests. Fosse directed the 1969 film adaptation of *Charity*, which was an unmitigated failure, despite Shirley MacLaine in the title role.

Innovative and Experimental Musicals

The surging popularity of rock music during the sixties pushed the Broadway musical further to the margins of popular culture. With the major exceptions of *Oliver!*, *Dolly!*, and *Fiddler*, the most noteworthy musicals of the decade were innovative in nature: *Stop the World—I Want to Get Off*, *Man of La Mancha*, *Cabaret*, *Hair* (see Chapter 16), and the Off Broadway hit *The Fantasticks* (see Chapter 14). Each one unique, these musicals tapped into the experimental ethos of sixties theater by exploring new modes of presentation and nontraditional content. They responded to the changing times, not monolithically, but decisively.

Anyone Can Whistle

Despite being hailed a wunderkind in the fifties for his lyrics for *West Side Story* and *Gypsy*, Stephen Sondheim was not content with being just a lyricist. Before joining the creative team of *West Side Story*, Sondheim had written both music and lyrics for *Saturday Night*, but due to the death of the show's main producer, the production never panned out (see Chapter 8). Sondheim finally heard his music and lyrics on Broadway with the 1962 farce *A Funny Thing Happened on the Way to the Forum*. This hilarious romp blended a plot based on the comedies of the Roman playwright Plautus (251–183 BC) with a vaudeville sensibility. The sheer wit and inventiveness of Sondheim's score, influenced by such disparate sources as Igor Stravinsky and burlesque, placed him at the vanguard of his generation, although *Forum*'s farcical nature gave little indication of the artistic breakthroughs that his later musicals would achieve (see Chapter 10).

A few years later, Sondheim reunited with Arthur Laurents (the book writer for *West Side Story* and *Gypsy*) to write *Anyone Can Whistle* (1964), arguably the most experimental and abstruse musical of the decade. The poster for the show aptly announced "a wild new musical." Laurents's absurdist book, which he originally titled *The Natives Are Restless* and then *Side Show*, satirizes the relativity of mental health in the nuclear age and explores the potential dangers of psychiatry. The plot, divided into three acts, concerns a corrupt "mayoress," Cora Hoover Hooper, of a town on the verge of bankruptcy. She concocts a fake miracle in the hope that tourists will flock to her town. They do, but they get lost among the inmates of the local Cookie Jar, "a rest home for non-conformists," according to Sondheim. Angela Lansbury played the mayoress, making her musical theater debut and appearing in her first of several Sondheim musicals (see Chapter 17). Like many musicals before it, *Anyone Can Whistle* included a dream ballet (choreographed by Herbert Ross), although, in typical Sondheim fashion, the dream is a nightmare. Opening the same year as *Dolly!* and *Fiddler*, *Anyone Can Whistle* stood out for its eccentricities and quixotic plot. Although a flawed work that closed after a mere nine performances, it has achieved cult status.

Anyone Can Whistle provided Sondheim his first opportunity to experiment with the ways that songs function in musical theater:

> I had begun to feel, way back during "*Gypsy*," that the whole notion of Broadway musicals depending on "integrated" songs—numbers that spring from the dialogue and further the plot—ought to be re-examined, and perhaps changed. Though the tone of "Anyone Can Whistle" was off, the songs did break with tradition: they commented on the action instead of advancing it, and I think their relation to the book was excellent.

Sondheim described the show as "a perfectly respectable attempt to present something unconventional in the commercial musical theater." One year later,

THE SHERMAN BROTHERS

The Sherman brothers, Robert B. (1925–2012) and Richard M. (b. 1928), had a virtual songwriting monopoly on children- and youth-oriented film musicals during the sixties and seventies. The Shermans were born in New York. They both served in the military and attended Bard College. Disney Pictures hired them to write songs for the film *The Parent Trap* (1961) and *Mary Poppins* (1964), and thereafter they served unofficially as the studio's songwriters in residence. They also wrote the music for several non-Disney projects, most notably *Chitty Chitty Bang Bang* (1968). The Shermans' only original Broadway musical, *Over Here!* (1974), starred Patty and Maxene Andrews (the two surviving members of the Andrews Sisters) and featured an original score in the Big Band–era style of World War II. The two sisters, practically playing themselves, go to Europe to entertain the troops, but they end up discovering that the singer whom they have engaged to be the third voice in their act is a German spy. The show picked up where the Sherman's earlier *Victory Canteen* left off. Although *Over Here!* played 341 performances and was a top-grossing musical in 1974, it did not lead to a more active Broadway career for the brothers. Their musical *Busker Alley*, which they wrote in the late sixties (A. J. Carothers wrote the book), was headed for Broadway in 1995, but its star, Tommy Tune, suffered an injury on the road, which precipitated the cancellation of the New York run. In recent years, both *Mary Poppins* and *Chitty Chitty Bang Bang* were adapted into Broadway musicals. Despite the Shermans' successful collaboration, the brothers had a contentious relationship. The 2009 film documentary *The Boys: The Sherman Brothers' Story*, made by their sons, Gregory and Jeff Sherman, attempts to explain this aspect of their lives.

Sondheim and Laurents collaborated with Richard Rodgers on *Do I Hear a Waltz?*, which turned out to be an unpleasant experience for all concerned, although the score is as good as any third-period (i.e., post-1960) Rodgers musical. Thereafter, Sondheim was absent from Broadway until *Company* opened in 1970 (see Chapter 10) and inaugurated his most productive period.

Stop the World—I Want to Get Off *and* The Roar of the Greasepaint—The Smell of the Crowd

The English writer and composer Leslie Bricusse (b. 1931) has not received the critical attention that someone with his track record deserves. Like the Sherman brothers, Bricusse is best known for movie musicals, especially *Doctor Doolittle* (1967) and *Willy Wonka and the Chocolate Factory* (1971).

However, in the early sixties Bricusse had three stage musicals playing simultaneously in London and New York. Bricusse and Anthony Newley (1931–1999) co-authored the music, lyrics, and book for two offbeat sixties musicals: *Stop the World—I Want to Get Off* (1962) and *The Roar of the Greasepaint—The Smell of the Crowd* (1965). Newley also starred in these shows. (Bricusse also collaborated with several other notable composers, including Michel Legrand.) *Stop the World* focused on marriage and career building in the postwar era, and *Greasepaint* addressed the English class system.

These Bricusse–Newley musicals anticipated several defining aspects of the mature concept musical. They both employed a novel theatrical approach and, despite their considerable flaws, fostered a climate of experimentation in musical theater. *Stop the World* takes the form of a circus. Littlechap, the show's only male character, is a clown—a common symbol of alienation in twentieth-century art and theater—in his own life's circus. Littlechap recalls Charlie Chaplin's Tramp (see Chapter 4) and, to a lesser extent, the mime Marcel Marceau. Like Rodgers and Hammerstein's *Allegro*, *Stop the World* encapsulates a single life: as Newley described it, "It's the seven ages of man roughly and sketchily put inside a [circus] tent." Despite its popular score and strong performances, *Stop the World* met with hostility from the critics. David Merrick, who produced all of Bricusse's shows in the sixties, advertised "a new-style musical," but many critics accused it of being all gimmick and no content. The cool reception is understandable, as Littlechap is a two-dimensional everyman, and not a very nice one at that. Both he and the main female characters (his wife and three lovers, all played by the same actress) are sorely underdeveloped. Littlechap's boss and father-in-law is portrayed by a disembodied reedy bassoon in an engaging bit of verbal-musical dialogue with the cowering Littlechap. Also objectionable was what one critic called "excess paraphernalia," such as music-hall routines and a Greek chorus made up of women in leotards. Instead of content and form coming together in a meaningful way, the novel concept, according to Howard Taubman, eventually "evaporates into mannerism." The critical drubbing did not stop the show from becoming an international hit.

In the sixties, Leslie Bricusse also wrote lyrics for *Pickwick*, a musical based on Dickens's *The Pickwick Papers*. With music by Cyril Ornadel and a book by Wolf Mankowitz, *Pickwick* was David Merrick's second Dickens musical. The producer hoped to repeat his success with *Oliver!*, but the show ran only fifty-six performances.

The Roar of the Greasepaint—The Smell of the Crowd was an allegory about the British class structure. Differing from *Stop the World* in theme only, *Greasepaint* adopted the same tone, loose narrative structure, and stick-figure characters. The set was a nebulous playing area, a circus ring by any other name. A group of ragtag urchins takes the place of *Stop the World*'s leotard-clad Greek chorus. Corresponding to the allegorical story, the characters have names such as Sir, Cocky, Girl, and Negro.

Man of La Mancha

Man of La Mancha has been mischaracterized as an adaptation of *Don Quixote*. Several musical adaptations of Cervantes's epic novel exist (ballet, tone poem, opera), some dating back to the seventeenth century, but *Man of La Mancha* is a different type of work. In 1959, the writer Dale Wasserman was in Madrid when he read an article announcing that he was there to write a dramatization of *Don Quixote*. Although apocryphal, the article encouraged him to contemplate such an adaptation. However, he was more drawn to the novelist than to his novel. As Wasserman thought about the project, one line from the novel kept coming to mind: "I know who I am, and who I may be if I choose." These words suggested a play-within-a-play

Dale Wasserman (1914–2008) received little formal education. Before *Man of La Mancha*, which constitutes his entire musical theater output, he adapted Ken Kesey's *One Flew Over the Cuckoo's Nest* (1963) for the stage. The play ran only eighty-two performances but the 1975 film adaptation won five Academy Awards.

concept. The plot of the musical sprang from the fact that the novel's protagonist is the novelist's alter ego: "Both of them were actors, fantasists, dreamers of impossible dreams." He concluded, "to catch him [Cervantes] at the nadir of his career, to persuade him toward self-revelation which might imply something of significance concerning the human spirit—*there*, perhaps, was a play worth writing." The result was a teleplay called *I, Don Quixote*, which aired in November, 1959, as part of *The DuPont Show of the Month*. The story begins as Cervantes (1547–1616) finds himself in prison facing the Inquisition. He acts out his novel *Don Quixote* for the other prisoners in order to stop them from destroying his manuscript. Twenty million viewers tuned in to see *I, Don Quixote*. Despite the positive response, Wasserman remained unsatisfied with the play, so he decided to rework it for the stage. At the time, the director Albert Marre and the composer Mitch Leigh were looking for musical theater projects. Marre felt that the metatheatrical device of Wasserman's play, a story within a story, provided a sound basis for such a project, so he contacted the writer and convinced him to convert his teleplay into a musical.

The poet W. H. Auden agreed to write the lyrics for the musical. Wasserman felt honored that a poet of Auden's stature would agree to work on the show, but he was also reticent. Indeed, the material that Auden wrote for the project was formidable, but most of it was too poetic or literary to work as song lyrics. According to Wasserman, it was "gall-and-wormwood attacks on the vulgarity of an inimical society—not the society that Don Quixote railed against, but our own. Some possessed inspired lyricism—eloquent on the page but unsingable on stage. . . . Auden's words sing on the page. The addition of music creates a fatal redundancy." It soon became painfully clear to Wasserman that Auden felt "a profound disagreement with the play's philosophy and the consequent impulse, conscious or otherwise, to sabotage it." When the poet suggested that Cervantes recant his quest, Wasserman had no choice but to end the collaboration. Joe Darion replaced Auden on the project.

Man of La Mancha premiered during the summer of 1965 at the Goodspeed Opera House. It reopened in New York at the Anta Washington Square Theatre in November and played for an impressive 2,328 performances. The Anta (which seated 1,136 people) was not a typical Broadway theater. Rather than a proscenium, it had a thrust stage, more suitable to Shakespeare than musical comedy. *La Mancha*

MIKE LEIGH

Mitch Leigh (b. 1928–2014) studied composition at Yale with Paul Hindemith. He achieved early success writing television jingles, including the ubiquitous "Nobody Doesn't Like Sara Lee." Leigh's legacy rests squarely with *La Mancha*. Although the four Broadway revivals of *La Mancha* collectively ran for only 672 performances, the show continues to be performed all over the world, including in Turkey in 2013. Steven Suskin writes that Leigh "entered the musical theatre with the instant classic *Man of La Mancha*. . . . [H]is output has been overwhelmingly bleak, with *La Mancha* followed by nine fiascos." Albert Marre directed these shows, most of which starred his wife, Joan Diener (1930–2006), whose earthy rendition of Aldonza in *Man of La Mancha* had impressed the critics. *Cry for Us All*, an adaptation of William Alfred's *Hogan's Goat*, played a mere nine performances. *Home Sweet Homer* (originally titled *Odyssey*) (1976), which co-starred Yul Brynner, did even worse, closing after a single performance. Diener did not appear in *Halloween* (1972), an experimental musical (involving dwarfs), even though Marre directed. Starring Barbara Cook and Jose Ferrer, it premiered at the Bucks County Playhouse, received scathing reviews, and closed before reaching New York.

played about half of its run there and then moved to the Martin Beck Theatre when the Anta was marked for demolition. The show ranks as the third-longest-running Broadway musical of the sixties and currently the 25th of all time. It has been translated into over forty languages.

La Mancha incorporates several defining characteristics of the concept musical: metatheatrical plot device, fragmented narrative, a fine line between reality (life) and illusion (theater), single-unit set, and central of theme. Wasserman observed, "The most interesting aspect of the success of *Man of La Mancha* is the fact that it plows squarely upstream against the prevailing current of philosophy in the theater," by which he meant the Theater of the Absurd and Black Comedy, both of which were in vogue in the sixties. By contrast, *La Mancha* presented a more positive spiritual tale centered on the human imagination.

Mitch Leigh's music for *Man of La Mancha* blends the rhythmic vitality of Spanish music with a musical theater sensibility. Shifts between major and minor keys, irregular and mixed meters, and hemiolas give the score its propulsive energy and Iberian flavor. The use of guitar further adds to the score's Spanish aura. "The Quest" (often erroneously called "The Impossible Dream"), one of the most popular and covered musical theater songs from the sixties, incorporates the repeated ostinato pattern of the bolero.

CONCEPT MUSICAL

Features

The label "concept musical" applies to an array of works, mostly from after the mid-sixties, that deviate from the traditional book musical model. No show has ever been advertised as a concept musical, a term mostly used in academic circles. In fact, the writers of these shows tend to disavow the label. Moreover, no two definitions of the concept musical are exactly alike; some commentators have opted for more idiosyncratic labels such as "metaphorical musical" and "fragmented musical." Whatever the preferred nomenclature, critics and scholars agree that concept musicals privilege theme over narrative. They reject the linear storytelling mode of book musicals like *Oklahoma!* in favor of a more fragmentary structure and self-referential mode of presentation, and some lack a plot altogether. The structure, book, score, staging, and visual elements all serve a central concept governed by a thematic metaphor or point of view. Concept musicals are capable of moving back and forth in time; presenting multiple locations, timeframes, and points of view simultaneously; and shifting between the interior and exterior life of the characters. Some works achieve an almost cinematic style. Character dominates over plot, and the internalized individual becomes the point of focus—a radical departure from the Rodgers and Hammerstein model, in which the protagonists' actions have real ramifications for the society in which they live.

Sondheim's *Assassins* (Off Broadway in 1990, Broadway in 2004) opens at a carnival shooting gallery. The game represents the belief that everyone in America has a right to achieve fame, whatever the cost. The rest of the musical consists of vignettes based on the long list of presidential assassins and would-be assassins, from John Wilkes Booth to John Hinckley, Jr. (the show leaves out Richard Lawrence, who attempted to assassinate Andrew Jackson in 1835, as well as anyone since the early eighties). John Weidman, who wrote the book for the musical, takes considerable artistic license with the historical chronology. For instance, John Wilkes Booth, accompanied by the other assassins, visits a hesitant Lee Harvey Oswald at the Texas School Book Depository in Dallas, and they all urge him to carry out his plans to kill President Kennedy, if only to preserve their infamous place in history. Many concept musicals adopt a circular structure, and *Assassins* is one of several that begin and end with the same musical number, "Everybody's Got the Right." By the end of *Assassins*, so much has transpired that the reprise of the number takes on an entirely different meaning than it had earlier.

Origins

The theater critic Martin Gottfried coined the term "concept musical" in the late sixties in reference to John Kander and Fred Ebb's *Zorbá*. For Gottfried, the experimental musicals at the time were "left-wing" shows, by which he meant progressive and experimental. Sondheim, when asked about the concept musical label, associated the term with "directorial style." Indeed, the concept musical has involved the director in the creative process to a degree unheard of in earlier musicals, but

Sondheim's response fails to account for the writers' contribution. In point of fact, concept musicals have redefined the relationship between the writers and the director. As musical theater historian Larry Stempel emphasizes,

> a concept may precede the writing of a script or it may bring a certain stylistic consistency to bear on a given reading of a script. Whose reading? Nowadays, clearly the director's—though the emergence of the independent director in the modern sense, one who is neither also an actor nor an author, is largely a twentieth-century phenomenon.

Before the fifties, the interpretive authority of the text rested primarily with the writer, and occasionally the actor. In the decades that followed, however, Jerome Robbins, Bob Fosse, Gower Champion, Harold Prince, Michael Bennett, and Tommy Tune elevated the role of the director and choreographer to the level of auteur. The emergence of the concept musical is best understood within the context of this shift to the "super-director." Stempel notes, "their [the directors'] point of departure was not an existing script to be realized onstage so much as a vision or stage idea that in turn helped shape the script's development." Without Michael Bennett, *A Chorus Line* would never have come into being, thus explaining why he demanded credit for the musical's conception as well as the choreography and direction (see Chapter 10). Bob Fosse co-wrote the book for *Chicago* with Fred Ebb, and he was the sole author of the book for his last musical, *Big Deal* (1986), in which he avoided working with a composer and lyricist altogether by using pre-existing songs (in the manner of the jukebox musical [see Chapters 12 and 13]). The most effective concept musicals are informed by a single artistic vision. Boris Aronson's set for *Company*, which was overseen by Harold Prince, was an abstraction of the cold urban environment in which the action takes place (see Chapter 10). Aronson incorporated steel platforms, Plexiglas panels, walkways, and stairs. Robert Ornbo's lighting design and D. D. Ryan's costumes for *Company* echoed the feeling of alienation that the character of Robert experiences.

The modular nature of many concept musicals gives them the semblance of a theme-oriented revue—"revues in disguise," to quote Stempel. Indeed, concept musicals reify the revue of yesteryear by investing it with a metaphorical power generally absent in book musicals. The revue-like structure and a Brechtian influence help to explain concept musicals' metadramatic nature. They draw attention to themselves as theater by self-consciously differentiating between book time (spoken dialogue) and lyric time (songs and dances) (see Chapter 1). They often break down the fourth wall that traditionally separates the onstage action from the audience. Musicals such as *Hair* (see Chapter 16) and *Assassins* confront the audience in ways unheard of in traditional musical theater. Many concept musicals adopt theatrical metaphors as a way of drawing attention to the thin line between theater and real life. For example, *Chicago* takes the form of a vaudeville, a metaphor for the American criminal justice system. It illustrates how the press creates celebrities out of criminals and draws a parallel between a trial lawyer's performance and that of a stage actor. The characters perform themselves as they appear in their various vaudeville turns. This doubling or mirroring of character also occurs in *Cabaret, Follies,* and *A Chorus Line.*

Allegro

Rodgers and Hammerstein's *Allegro* (1947) and Kurt Weill and Alan Jay Lerner's *Love Life* (1948) represent the earliest attempts at the concept musical, but neither one fully achieved the marriage of form and content that the form demands. *Allegro* covers the first three-and-a-half decades of the life of Joe Taylor, Jr., a kind of Everyman (see Chapter 7). The story begins in 1905 with Taylor's birth. The action encompasses the pivotal moments in his life: he falls in love, earns a medical degree, and moves from his small hometown to Chicago. His initial dream of helping the needy is supplanted by the superficial rewards of tending to wealthy but vapid urbanites. When Taylor's assertive wife has an affair in order to promote his career, he leaves her and the hospital and returns to his hometown to set up a general practice, his intention from the start. Hammerstein borrowed theatrical devices from the playwrights Thornton Wilder, Luigi Pirandello, and Bertolt Brecht to frame the sprawling narrative, including a Greek chorus that comments on the book scenes and constantly reminds the audience of the story's universal theme. Agnes de Mille, who directed and choreographed *Allegro*, achieved a fluid, balletic production, with seamless choreographed transitions between scenes. The stage was mostly bare, with locations suggested with lighting and platforms rather than literally depicted.

Although not a box-office hit, *Allegro* set the stage for the experimental musicals of the sixties and seventies. It anticipated the devices found in seminal concept musicals such as *Cabaret, Company, Follies,* and *Chicago*: rear projections, a recurring theme song, lighting effects, cinematic devices, and a chorus or characterless singers that provide commentary. A seventeen-year-old Stephen Sondheim was a production assistant on *Allegro*. He has often commented on the influence of working on such an innovative project and has quipped that he has spent his whole career rewriting *Allegro*.

Love Life

Love Life opened a year later, and it too addressed the subject of marriage. It took the form of a vaudeville show, anticipating *Chicago*. Lerner and Weill mapped the story of a single marriage onto American history, beginning in 1790 and continuing to the present (1948). A magician appears at the opening and transports the audience back to 1790, recalling a happy time in the marriage of Sam and Susan Cooper. The scenes that follow trace the Cooper's marriage in thirty-year increments, although the wife and husband never age. As the centuries come and go, the couple is forced to confront the challenges that each new era presents. Their marriage gradually collapses from the weight of events beyond their control. Vaudeville numbers performed between the scenes comment on the action. The final vignette, a minstrel show, suggests that the Coopers are unhappy living apart but realistic about the poor prospects of reviving their marriage. Like later concept musicals, *Love Life* dealt with issues of alienation and self-deception in contemporary America.

Joey Grey performing "If You Could See Her" in the original Broadway production of *Cabaret*. *Courtesy Photofest.*

It lacked the warmth and optimism of musicals like *Brigadoon*, and audiences, still celebrating the victory of World War II, were put off by the show's cynicism. The set designer of *Love Life,* Boris Aronson, went on to design *Cabaret, Company,* and *Follies.*

CABARET

When interviewed about *Cabaret* in 1966, Fred Ebb, the show's lyricist, said, "We're looking for a new form of musical theater, one that'll break away from what's become stale and static, and self-imitative." A few weeks later, *Cabaret* opened on Broadway and ran for 1,166 performances. It won seven Tony Awards during what was the first nationally televised Tony Awards ceremony. The 1972 film version of *Cabaret* garnered Academy Awards for its director, Bob Fosse, and leading lady, Liza Minnelli. *Cabaret* is still performed all over the world today, in high schools and colleges and on professional stages.

Cabaret was as innovative in structure as its subject matter was shocking, and it is as relevant today as when it opened in 1966. The plot intertwines two parallel love stories, both of which unravel amid the early rumblings of Nazism in thirties Germany. Harold Prince, who produced and directed *Cabaret*, initially conceived of a traditional book musical, but he eventually came up with the idea of alternating traditional book scenes and expressionistic scenes set in a Berlin cabaret called the Kit Kat Klub.

Evolution

Source Material

Cabaret is based on Christopher Isherwood's *The Berlin Stories*, which bears witness to the rise of the Nazi Party in Berlin during the decline of the Weimar Republic. Isherwood, an English novelist, lived in Berlin from 1929 to 1933. *The Berlin Stories*, which was published in 1945, comprises two novellas, *The Last of Mr. Norris* and *Goodbye to Berlin*. The latter contains six interconnected stories, including "Sally Bowles," the basis for *Cabaret*. The stories involve several inconsequential characters from the dark niches of Berlin society: petty thieves, prostitutes, and wannabe revolutionaries. *Goodbye to Berlin* is unified by a single point-of-view character, a homosexual English writer living in Berlin whom Isherwood named after himself. He claims to operate with the objectivity of a camera lens, merely recording what he

HAROLD PRINCE

Harold Prince (b. 1928) is associated in one way or another with many seminal musicals from the second half of the twentieth century, including *Fiddler on the Roof* and *Phantom of the Opera*, not to mention no fewer than ten Sondheim musicals. After serving in the Army, Prince began his illustrious theater career as a stage manager for George Abbott (see Chapter 7). In the mid-fifties, he started producing musicals with Frederick Brisson and Robert E. Griffith. In 1962, Prince replaced Word Baker (see Chapter 14) as the director of *A Family Affair*, John Kander's first Broadway musical. It was an inauspicious directorial debut.

sees: "I am a camera with its shutter open, quite passive, recording, not thinking. . . . Some day, all this will have to be developed, carefully printed, fixed."

Isherwood explores the unraveling moral fabric of German society through the banalities of everyday life. The opening segment, titled "A Berlin Diary," introduces Christopher Isherwood, his landlady, Fräulein Schroeder, and the other tenants at her boarding house. The next section is about the narrator's relationship with Sally Bowles. In "On Ruegen Island," Isherwood, during a seaside sojourn, observes a homosexual relationship between Peter Wilkson and Otto Nowak. Otto also figures in "The Nowaks"; Isherwood, hard up for cash, rents a room from Otto's family, who lives in a squalid district of the city. "The Landauers" is about a wealthy Jewish family, the daughter of which takes English lessons from Isherwood.

In 1951, the English playwright John Van Druten adapted *The Berlin Stories* as a spoken play entitled *I Am a Camera*. He gave the episodic plot of Isherwood's novel greater continuity by focusing on Sally Bowles and limiting the action to four months and to the boarding house of Fräulein Schroeder, whom he renamed Schneider. Van Druten's plot centers on Sally's relationship with the homosexual narrator of *The Berlin Stories*. They are fond of each other, but they never become sexually involved. The play is in essence a love story without the physical attraction. At the end of the play, Christopher and Sally part company as he decides to return to England. Van Druten invented a subplot involving two Jewish characters from *The Berlin Stories*, Fritz Wendel and Natalia Landauer. Fritz conceals his ethnic identity until late in the play, when an anti-Semitic attack against the Landauer family business impels him to reveal the truth and to confess his love for her. *I Am a Camera* has been overshadowed by *Cabaret*, which paints a more vivid and complex picture of the corrupting forces that undermine the morality and daily life of German society.

Concept

When Harold Prince and his creative team started work on *Cabaret*, they thought of the story in terms of a traditional book musical. Musical theater convention dictated a love story and a related subplot, so the book writer, Joseph Masteroff, altered the nature of the relationship between Christopher Isherwood (changed to Clifford Bradshaw) and Sally Bowles by making them lovers, and he invented a romance between Fräulein Schneider and Rudy Schultz, a character of Masteroff's own invention. Neither relationship ends in marriage. The parallel unhappy endings were bleak for a Broadway musical in 1966, but they were a powerful expression of what the writers wanted to say about the intersection of politics and private life in Berlin at the time.

The turning point in the development of the project occurred when Prince decided to intersperse the book scenes with expressionistic cabaret vignettes. He made the cabaret a metaphor for the German psyche during the years leading up to the election of Hitler as chancellor of Germany. It took the creative team some time to settle on what would transpire in the cabaret, but they eventually agreed on incorporating skits and songs that commented on the book scenes. The character of the emcee, whom Joel Grey memorably created for both the original stage production and the film, is based on real nightclub performers whom both Prince and Kander had seen in Europe after the war. Their memories gave birth to the grotesque, androgynous, Mephistophelian emcee who has ever since been synonymous with *Cabaret*.

The power of *Cabaret* (a hybrid between a traditional book musical and a concept musical) to achieve its full dramatic effect resulted from a unified artistic vision among the members of the creative team. The set, lighting, and costume designers distinguished between the book scenes and cabaret episodes by giving the former a realistic style and the latter an expressionistic aura. Boris Aronson hung a giant mirror over the cabaret stage and tilted it at strategic moments in order to reflect the theater audience.

Music and Lyrics

With *Cabaret*, Kander and Ebb found their unique voice. The dark material and the dual dramatic structure inspired them to write two parallel scores, one consisting of traditional book songs, one of novelty numbers for the cabaret, thereby articulating Prince's bifurcated structural framework. The original score contains a nearly equal number of cabaret numbers (eight, plus a kick line dance) and book songs (seven).

Before Kander and Ebb committed anything to paper, they listened to period recordings of Berlin jazz. Although commentators often cite Kurt Weill as an influence on *Cabaret*, Kander insists, "I very consciously didn't listen to Kurt Weill. . . . Kurt Weill was doing very early on what I was doing many years later. . . He was really using the vernacular of that period." The cabaret songs capture the ironic mixture of sentimentality and sarcasm of authentic German cabaret songs. The first thing Kander and Ebb wrote was a series of songs that collectively create the decadent milieu of Berlin in the late 1920s. These numbers, which they called the

JOHN KANDER AND FRED EBB

ohn Kander and Fred Ebb first met in 1962 at the suggestion of Tommy Valando, their mutual publisher. They started working together almost immediately, and only Ebb's death in 2004 ended their partnership, making theirs the longest composer–lyricist collaboration in the history of musical theater. Since 2004, Kander has shepherded to Broadway three musicals that he and Ebb had completed before the lyricist's death—*Curtains* (2006), *The Scottsboro Boys* (2010), and *The Visit* (2015)—bringing the total number of their Broadway musicals to 14. (*All of Us*, their musical based on Thornton Wilder's play *The Skin of Our Teeth*, has had two productions outside of New York but has never reached Broadway.) Kander and Ebb literally wrote together in the same room at the same time, a remarkable feat given that they were as different from each other in temperament as two collaborators could possibly be.

Kander was born in Kansas City on March 18, 1932. His was a close-knit Midwestern family. He attended Oberlin College, earning a bachelor's degree in music in 1949, and then entered the master's program in composition at Columbia University, receiving his degree in 1954. Fred Ebb, born on April 8, 1928, grew up in New York City with his two sisters. Their parents were undemonstrative and never took them to the theater. Ebb recalled, "Looking back, I can honestly say I don't believe my mother and father ever touched each other in my presence. I never saw them kiss or embrace. . . . They stayed together with their children as their only common interest." Ebb saw theater as an escape from his home life and started to attend plays and musicals whenever he could afford a ticket. A bright student, Ebb graduated from DeWitt Clinton High School ahead of his class and as valedictorian. He earned a bachelor's degree from New York University in record time and, according to him, a master's degree in English literature from Columbia University in 1957.

In the years immediately before they met, Kander and Ebb each worked with various writers in the hope of finding a suitable collaborator. In 1962, Kander wrote *A Family Affair* with his boyhood friends James and William Goldman. It was a light-hearted satire about the trials and tribulations of mounting a Jewish wedding. Around the same time, Ebb wrote the Off Broadway musical *Morning Sun* with the composer Paul Klein. Set in the post–Civil War era, *Morning Sun* centers on the execution of a young man named Rome, who leaves home in search of excitement and is falsely accused of killing a man in a barroom brawl. Rome's Bible-thumping mother brings his siblings to see their older brother hang for his alleged crime, hoping to use the experience as an object lesson on righteousness.

With *A Family Affair* and *Morning Sun* behind them, Kander and Ebb poured their creative energy into their collaboration, which took off when their introspective song "My Coloring Book" was nominated for a 1963 Grammy Award. Their

(Continued)

first full-length musical, *Golden Gate*, which is set in San Francisco following the devastating earthquake of 1906, never found a producer, but it led to their first Broadway assignment, *Flora, the Red Menace* (1965). *Flora* was not a hit, but it began their affiliation with Harold Prince, who was on the verge of becoming a major Broadway director, and Liza Minnelli, who won a Tony Award for her performance in the title role.

The settings of Kander and Ebb's musicals range from Depression-era New York to the island of Crete. They viewed the modern world through the lens of theater and more often than not adopted a play-within-a-play format. For example, *The Act*, which starred Liza Minnelli, shifts between the nightclub where the female protagonist is staging her professional comeback and book scenes that reveal the problems in her personal life. Kander and Ebb's scores reflect their different personalities and artistic predilections: the composer is well known for his romantic sensibilities and lyrical tendencies, whereas the lyricist's reputation is built on cynicism and an acerbic sense of humor. The opposing qualities that they bring to the table produce the dramatic tension of Kander and Ebb's scores. Nowhere is this feature more apparent than in the songs of survival that Kander and Ebb wrote for female stars. Liza Minnelli's rendition of *New York, New York* is a quintessential example.

"Berlin Songs," were going to be sung throughout the show by an array of disenfranchised Berliners: a fat man, an aging operatic tenor, a streetwalker, two Chinese singers, a group of college boys. The "Berlin Songs" explored a wide variety of topics, including economic hardship, prostitution, and sexual adventurism. When the emcee was added to the mix, it was decided that he alone should sing the "Berlin Songs" as a single musical set. But the writers eventually rejected this idea, and the emcee ended up performing a variety of songs at strategic points throughout the show.

In the most inflammatory song in *Cabaret*, "If You Could See Her Through My Eyes," the emcee likens a gorilla to a Jew. The number comes on the heels of Fräulein Schneider and Herr Schultz's engagement party and anticipates the collective reaction of the guests, which pressures Schneider to break off the engagement. The song is a particularly powerful example of Kander and Ebb's knack at entertaining the audience while advancing a thematic point. The music has the easygoing gate of a vaudeville softshoe *pas de deux*. In the middle of the song, the emcee dances with a female gorilla in an apron to the strains of a waltz variation of the main theme. The full impact of the number is achieved on the final line, which starts, "If you could see her through my eyes." On "eyes," the emcee reaches the highest note in the song and holds it out for several seconds on a sugarcoated falsetto as the orchestra drops out. After a long pause, he lets loose with the most devious line in musical theater: "she wouldn't look Jewish at all." On the surface, the dancing gorilla and unctuously sentimental emcee seem like broad comedy (with a hint of bestiality), but the "racist"

EXAMPLE 9.1. "Willkommen," vamp and first four measures.

humor is subversive. The emcee's crooning and dancing give the appearance of a vaudeville turn, but the number, one eventually learns, is Nazi propaganda.

Cabaret dispenses with the traditional Broadway medley overture. In the famous opening scene, the emcee welcomes the cabaret audience as well as the theater audience. The first sound heard is a drumroll crescendo followed by an anemic cymbal crash. A long pause follows, and then the plodding vamp of the opening number, "Willkommen," emerges, evoking a decadent cabaret atmosphere, something sinister and unsettling. The opening harmony, a tonic added-sixth chord, and repeated eighth notes on the offbeats simultaneously suggest the seedy milieu of the cabaret and the ominous cloud looming over Germany (Example 9.1). With a smirk on his lipstick-smeared lips, the emcee sings the opening strains, which end with a chromatic appoggiatura gesture consisting of three elements (approach by downward leap, strong-beat dissonance, and resolution upward by half step) on the word "welcome," the English translation of the German "willkommen" and the French "bienvenue." The non-harmonic pitch on the downbeat beckons the audience, teasingly seducing it into the decadent pleasures of the cabaret. The appoggiatura motive recurs on "Glücklich zu sehen" and again on "happy." This figure reappears throughout the score.

The title song of *Cabaret* foreshadows the sad ending of Sally and Cliff's relationship. As Sally performs "Cabaret" at the Kit Kat, she remains painfully aware of her life (double life), and in this moment she is living it on stage. Prince experimented with the placement of "Cabaret" but settled on the dramatic highpoint of the story, when Sally faces the decision of whether or not to abort her unborn child and thereby destroy her relationship with Cliff. It is the only song in the show that bridges the real world of the main story and the surreal world of the cabaret. As Sally sings about Elsie, a dying prostitute and friend, we understand that she is singing about herself. In the middle of the song, immediately after the line "I remember how she'd turn to me and say," Sally walks into an abstract space, which Prince called "Limbo," and disappears into her own thoughts. Kander and Ebb distinguish this portion of the song from what precedes and follows it. The tempo slows, and the accompaniment doubles the melody with staccato chords in stop time. An accelerando slowly returns the music to its initial tempo and the orchestra begins to pulsate with syncopated eighth notes. On "When I go I'm going like Elsie," the music slows down dramatically and modulates up a half step. Sally launches into a "cakewalk" version of the tune on "start by admitting, from cradle to tomb," and then the music drives toward its desperate conclusion. Sally belts out the final high B-flat for seven measures as the orchestra plays a frenetic, tightly wound version of the "Willkommen" vamp followed by an ascending string of chromatic chords.

1972 Film Version

For the film version of *Cabaret,* the director Bob Fosse and the screenwriter Jay Presson Allen drastically altered the story and entirely reconfigured the music. They expunged Masteroff's secondary plot, incorporated more of Isherwood's novel, and rethought the role of Cliff in more "Isherwoodian" terms, renaming him Brian Roberts and repatriating him to England. Brian still sleeps with Sally, but he also has sex with a wealthy German character named Maximilian von Heune. Sally also sleeps with Max, and in one scene the three of them appear to be on the verge of a *ménage a trois*. This scene gives new (or literal) meaning to the song "Two Ladies," which follows this encounter. In place of Schneider and Schultz's courtship, Natalia and Fritz's romance from Van Druten's *I Am a Camera* is reinstated. Sally and Brian's relationship cannot bear the weight of their narcissism, inaction, and political passivity. In stark contrast, Fritz and Natalia's love will endure, which makes their likely extermination all the more tragic and poignant.

The film incorporates only the diegetic songs from Kander and Ebb's original score. All of the songs are performed inside the cabaret with the exception of "Tomorrow Belongs to Me," which is sung in a beer garden. In this way, Fosse achieved the verisimilitude of a non-musical film and thereby presented a relatively "realistic" rendering of Germany around 1930. Kander and Ebb supplied

PLOT OF CABARET

Cabaret begins in 1930, as Clifford Bradshaw (Cliff), a writer from Pennsylvania, arrives by train in Berlin, where he hopes to find inspiration for his second novel. During his first taste of Berlin's nightlife, Cliff meets Sally Bowles, a cabaret singer from England working at the Kit Kat Klub. After flirting with Cliff, Sally is fired from the club. With nowhere else to go, she shows up at Fräulein Schneider's boarding house, where Cliff has rented a room, and convinces him to take her in as a roommate. Their relationship becomes intimate, and Sally gets pregnant. Faced with the responsibility of supporting a family, Cliff accepts an offer from his German friend Ernest to help smuggle contraband from Paris, but he is unaware that Ernest is a member of the Nazi party and that his black market exploits are politically motivated. In a parallel subplot, Fräulein Schneider and one of her tenants, Herr Schultz, a Jewish proprietor of a fruit shop, decide to marry, but when anti-Semitism in Berlin escalates, she breaks off the engagement. Cliff, disgusted by the events happening around him, leaves Germany, hoping against hope that Sally will join him in Paris.

three new cabaret songs for the film, "Maybe This Time," which they had written years earlier; the Marlene Dietrich-like ballad "Mein Herr"; and "Money" to replace "Sitting Pretty." Like the Broadway version, Fosse's film associates the decadence of German culture with the downfall of the Weimar Republic, but it emphasizes sexual deviance above all else. Ironically, this aspect of the film helps to explain why it resonated so loudly with American audiences, but it also blamed the very thing that it seemed to be celebrating. The film seems to be both an endorsement and condemnation of sexual deviance.

1998 Broadway Revival

A radical reworking of *Cabaret* by the director Sam Mendes and choreographer Rob Marshall opened on Broadway in 1998. With a respectful nod to Fosse, Mendes placed the book scenes into the cabaret milieu and created an even more conspicuously decadent and campy cabaret. For example, the suggestive "Two Ladies" is performed not by the emcee and two cabaret girls, as was the case in the original production, but by the emcee, a cabaret girl, and a cabaret boy in drag. Whereas the 1966 production used the rise of the Nazis as a warning about the moral decline of America in the sixties, and the film seemed to blame Hitler's triumph on sexual deviance, Mendes's version focused on how the Nazis and the Holocaust could have happened at all. He used every means at his disposal to remind the audience that it was partaking of a theatrical event. For instance, he had members of the audience sit at small round tables close to the stage, ensuring that they were not mere

AND BEAR IN MIND

Fiddler on the Roof (1964, Imperial Theatre, 3,242 performances)

Music by Jerry Bock
Lyrics by Sheldon Harnick
Book by Joseph Stein

P rior to 1950, musical theater writers, the majority of whom were Jewish, avoided outward expressions of Jewishness and eschewed Jewish characters and themes. However, the discovery of the Holocaust brought unparalleled attention to the historical plight of Jews, and during the fifties, as American Jews were beginning to shed their status as "ethnic whites," Broadway writers began to depict Jewish characters, not as ethnic others but as integrated members of American middle-class society. By the time *Fiddler on the Roof* opened in 1964, what it meant to be a Jewish American had shifted, and third- and fourth-generation Jews had begun to lose a connection to their ethnic heritage.

Although Jewish life became a more acceptable topic for musicals in the fifties, serious topics remained off limits until the end of the decade. *The Sound of Music* (1959) reinforced a self-imposed ban on stories about Jewish persecution. However, after 1959, Broadway saw a proliferation of Jewish musicals. *Fiddler on the Roof* was only one of five Broadway musicals with Jewish characters and Jewish themes that opened in 1964.

Set in Czarist Russia, *Fiddler on the Roof* is based on four short stories by the Yiddish writer Sholem Aleichem (Sholem Naumovich Rabinovich, 1859–1916) about a poor Jewish dairyman named Tevye. Joseph Stein, who wrote the book for *Fiddler*, created a unified plot about an observant Jewish peasant who stubbornly trudges into the modern era as his daughters decide for themselves whom they will marry. Tevye's faith and paternal identity are severely tested when his third eldest, Chava, elopes with a non-Jew.

Fiddler on the Roof had its detractors, including Jewish intellectuals such as Irving Howe, who attacked it as a "tasteless" reflection of the "spiritual anemia . . . of the middle-class Jewish world." Howe warned, "Jewishness as we have understood it is reaching an end and that much is consequently being lost to us." Indeed, Stein's book replaced Aleichem's worldview with a Jewish American, not to mention commercially viable, outlook. During the 2004 Broadway revival of *Fiddler*, audiences never bothered to question the authenticity of the portrayal of Tevye by the non-Jewish actor Alfred Molina. The fifth Broadway revival of *Fiddler*, which opened in late 2015, starred Danny Burstein, who had played Herr Schultz in the 2014 revival of *Cabaret*. Burstein's mother was a Catholic from Costa Rica, his father "a nice Jewish boy from the Bronx."

observers safely distanced from the stage and protected by an imaginary fourth wall. By being forced to feel physically part of the cabaret, the audience was practically made complicit participants in the action. The emcee was omnipresent, observing, participating, indicting. In the final *coup de théâtre*, the cabaret morphed into a Nazi death camp, as the emcee took off his coat to reveal striped prison clothes with a yellow star and a pink triangle, Nazi labels for Jew and homosexual, respectively.

Explicitly bisexual, Mende's version of Cliff is the closest theatrical incarnation of Christopher Isherwood's original character in *The Berlin Stories*. The collapse of Cliff and Sally's relationship is brought on as much by his sexuality as her decision to have an abortion. Mendes expunged "Why Should I Wake Up?", Cliff's only song in the original 1966 *Cabaret*. Cliff's meager musical role underscores his self-denial about Sally's self-destructive nature as well as the horrific events taking place around him. Although he goes through the motions of making love to Sally, his suppressed sexuality, or confused sexual orientation, runs counter to the traditional musical theater leading man, which helps to explain why Kander and Ebb could never come up with an effective declaration of love for him to sing. In Mendes's version, Cliff, now essentially a speaking role, is the objective camera lens observing life around him, not unlike what the original writer in Isherwood's novel professes to be.

Hoping to raise greater self-awareness, Mendes forced the audience to consider the role that everyday Germans played in the social and political inertia that enabled the Holocaust. His version of *Cabaret*, which was revived on Broadway in 2014, warns against enjoying the cultural trappings of a society without considering the moral consequences. It also illustrates the potential interpretive open-endedness of the concept musical in general and *Cabaret* in particular.

Cabaret is no mere history lesson. It relies on characters and events of seemingly little consequence to express what mere historical facts cannot. Like every successful concept musical that followed, *Cabaret* has its own internal logic and metaphorical devices. In its perfect marriage of content and form, the musical achieves in theatrical terms the same effect that Isherwood's novel does in literary terms. Its interweaving of plot and commentary, book scenes and revue vignettes, and political history and cultural critique exposed an entire generation of writers to a new approach to musical theater. *Cabaret* sustains, even benefits from, multiple directorial interpretations and ranks among the most important shows of the twentieth century.

THE NIXON ERA

The 1969 hit *1776* was an ironic postscript to the politically tumultuous decade. Opening at such a particularly volatile moment in American history, it was a reassuring tonic for Broadway's most conservative audiences, but *1776*'s male-dominated cast, patriotic theme, and flag waving flew in the face of feminism and the burgeoning anti-government sentiments of the late sixties. The demand for tickets for both *1776* and the more radical *Hair* (see Chapter 16), which had opened a year earlier, underscored the lack of political consensus at the beginning of the Nixon era. *Cabaret* obliquely reflected America in the sixties (Harold Prince certainly thought it did), but *1776* and *Hair* addressed American ideologies directly. Whereas *1776* depicted events that led to the founding of the country, *Hair* questioned what the country was becoming. John Adams, the protagonist of *1776*, who forges a consensus against the most adverse of odds, provided a stark contrast to the shady figure of Richard M. Nixon, and his integrity spoke to conservatives and liberals alike. *Hair* was more cynical, but it, too, referenced history to comment on contemporary America. The concurrent popularity of *Hair* and *1776* at the end of the decade reflects the uncertain state of Broadway, which was, like the country, being pulled in opposite directions by progressive imperatives and conservative values.

SELECTIVE BIBLIOGRAPHY

. . . .

NAMES, TERMS, AND CONCEPTS

1776

Adams, Lee

Allegro

Anyone Can Whistle

Assassins

Bart, Lionel

Berlin Stories, The

Bricusse, Leslie

Bye Bye Birdie

Cabaret

Camelot

Carolyn Leigh

Chicago

Coleman, Cy

concept musical

Darion, Joe

Fiddler on the Roof

Hello, Dolly!

Herman, Jerry

I Can Get It for You Wholesale

"If You Could See Her"

Isherwood, Christopher

Leigh, Mitch

Love Life

Man of La Mancha

Masteroff, Joseph

Newley, Anthony

No Strings

Oliver!

The Roar of the Greasepaint—The Smell of the Crowd

Stop the World—I Want to Get Off

Strouse, Charles

Sweet Charity

Wasserman, Dale

"Willkommen"

· ·

DISCUSSION QUESTIONS

1. How did cultural, social, and political developments in the sixties create an inhospitable climate for the traditional Broadway book musical?

2. Identify the role of plot and narrative in concept musicals.

3. Compare the original stage version of *Cabaret* with Bob Fosse's film version.

4. Analyze the diminishing musical role of Cliff.

5. What are the metatheater devices of *Cabaret*?

CHAPTER 10

THE SEVENTIES
(*COMPANY*, 1970, ALVIN THEATRE, 706 PERFORMANCES)

The seventies is arguably the least understood decade in the history of the Broadway musical. Framed by the escalation of the Vietnam War and the Iran hostage crisis, the decade was a time of great upheaval and uncertainty, and Broadway was not impervious to the economic stagnation, political insecurity, and social woes that were crippling the nation. For musical theater it was a time of radical artistic, technological, and operational changes; colossal hits and resounding flops; increasing diversification; diminishing resources; and dwindling audiences. Doomsayers at the time warned that musical theater was fated to become an irrelevant cultural artifact.

The gloomy outlook on musical theater was fueled by the dilapidated state of New York City itself. An economic slump brought New York to the brink of bankruptcy in 1975 and caused a sharp spike in crime. Broadway, as the nation's premiere theater institution, had to contend with realities on the streets. The Time Square area had degenerated into a seedy, squalid, red-light district. Adult entertainment venues existed alongside legitimate theaters. As one historian notes, "going to a Broadway show now involved an element of very real danger." The continuing middle-class exodus to the suburbs posed a real existential threat to Broadway. By the middle of the decade, the League of New York Theatre Owners and Producers began to mobilize in an effort to improve the situation.

Before proceeding any further, it is necessary to determine what constitutes "decline." Disheartened critics and fans explain the perceived decline of musical theater during the seventies in purely artistic terms, decrying the negative impact of rock music on the genre, the cultural shift in importance from the word to visual content, and a decrease in the "entertainment value" of musical theater. They blame the seventies for hastening the decline in the quality of Broadway. On the other hand, producers and bean counters measure the genre's health in terms of audience attendance and ticket sales. In this regard, musicals in the seventies outstripped those of earlier decades, for the hits actually ran longer and made bigger profits than ever before, a trend that continues today. Of course, raw data do not tell the whole story; for instance, several of the decade's most esteemed works, including *Company* and *Chicago*, did not enjoy particularly profitable runs. As Harold Prince would claim, they were successes but not hits, a distinction intended to distinguish between a work's intrinsic artistic value and its financial success, the two of which do not always go hand in hand.

Broadway has always defied the pessimistic prognosticators and has weathered multiple storms. As Prince acknowledged in the mid-seventies, "for the last 3,000 years people have been saying the theater is dying." Nostalgia plays a big role in shaping attitudes about the state of Broadway. Gerald M. Merkowitz reminds us, "It is a truth universally acknowledged, [*sic*] that this Broadway season (whatever year this is) is the worst ever, that fewer plays are being produced than ever before, and fewer of them are of any quality." On the other hand, some of the upheavals that musical theater experienced during the seventies caused irreversible damage and did not bode well for the health of the genre.

One event in the sixties stands out as a harbinger of the maladies influencing the negative perception of the genre in the seventies: rock music definitively replaced Broadway as the mainstream popular music idiom, which meant that Broadway composers could no longer count on songs from their shows to become crossover hits and generate additional income. Some critics see the seventies as precipitating a steep decline in the literary substance of musical theater. According to Mark Grant, the 1964 musical *Hello, Dolly!* made "spectacle-as-content" an artistic imperative for future generations (see Chapter 9); however, most theater chroniclers believe that musical theater suffered even greater harm in the seventies. Denny Martin Flinn unapologetically blames *Annie* (1977) for being "the show which begot the downfall." In point of fact, musical theater in the seventies was more vibrant than in the sixties. Seventies musicals account for nearly 20% of the 100 longest-running Broadway musicals ever, nearly double the percentage of the previous decade. However, the converse is also true. Whereas hit shows ran longer, flops often closed after a single performance and lost record sums of money.

What distinguishes musical theater in the seventies most from that of the preceding decade is its sheer diversity of offerings and rising production costs. The old Broadway business model reached its obsolescence as union demands, artistic exigencies, and technology drove up costs well beyond the rate of inflation. The dire economic situation led to a mad rush to judgment about shows even before they officially opened. Jittery producers began pulling the plug on musicals before the public could weigh in, sometimes after a single performance, no longer willing to wait and lose money while hoping that positive word of mouth would boost business.

There is one notable exception that complicates the idea that musical theater in the seventies was in a state of decline: Stephen Sondheim established his preeminence on Broadway. Between 1970 and 1979, Broadway played host to five Sondheim musicals (not including the 1977 revue *Side by Side by Sondheim*), each one critically acclaimed.

SERIOUS AND COMIC TRENDS IN THE SEVENTIES

A dizzying array of musicals opened in the seventies, including an extraordinary number of what John Bush Jones calls "issue-driven" or "in-your-face message" musicals. The list is long, and the primary source material ranges from Leon Uris's *Exodus* to William Inge's *Bus Stop*. Some serious musicals were based on historical subjects, including the Rothschild financial empire (*The Rothschilds*), Saint Joan (*Goodtime Charlie*), and the Civil War (*Shenandoah*). The vast majority of these works flopped, and for good reason. Eighteen of the most unsuccessful serious musicals collectively played a grand total of 220 performances—or an average of 12.2 performances per show. This figure represents a loss of millions of dollars.

Familiar Voices

Established Broadway writers were just as likely to write about serious subjects as younger writers were. Richard Rodgers collaborated with Sheldon Harnick on *Rex*, which dramatized Henry VIII's quest to produce an heir. Jule Styne worked on *Look to the Lilies*, an adaptation of the film *Lilies of the Field* (1963). The show closed after twenty-five performances, a success compared to Styne's *Prettybelle*, a dark musical about sex and racism, which folded out of town. Another notable flop was Alan Jay Lerner and John Barry's *Lolita, My Love*, based on Vladimir Nabokov's international bestseller *Lolita*, first published in 1955.

Musical comedies in the seventies fared just as poorly as serious musicals. Famous flops include *So Long 174th Street* (16 performances), based on Joseph Stein's play *Enter Laughing*. A few musical comedies with pop-oriented scores fared slightly better. *The Best Little Whorehouse in Texas* incorporated country-western music, and *They're Playing Our Song*, Marvin Hamlisch's first show after *A Chorus Line*, boasted an easy-listening pop score and a workable script by Neil Simon.

Rock Musicals

Rock and roll continued to be an albatross around the necks of musical theater composers and producers. Many writers tried to capitalize on *Hair*'s success, but few succeeded. Even the creators of *Hair* floundered (see Chapter 16). Gerome Ragni and Galt MacDermot wrote the incomprehensible *Dude*. *Via Galactica*, with music by MacDermot and a book by Christopher Gore and Judith Ross, did no better. MacDermot scored a major hit with *Two Gentleman of Verona*, which won the 1971 Tony Award for best musical. Its multiracial cast, slangy dialogue, and pop musical style, all of which seemed hip at the time, date the show today. *Grease* is the only successful rock musical from the decade not to take itself too seriously. An unexpected hit, it was the right musical at the right time for a baby boomer generation feeling nostalgic about its relatively harmless teenage transgressions: close dancing, smoking cigarettes, and necking at the drive-in movies. The score affectionately parodied the defining features of fifties rock and roll: the I-vi-IV-V^7 chord progression, driving triplet rhythms in the accompaniment, doo-wop and male falsetto vocals, car motifs, and sentimental lyrics. The twenty-something wunderkind Stephen Schwartz took Broadway by storm with three rock-oriented musicals: *Godspell* (1971), *Pippin* (1972), and *The Magic Show* (1974) (see Chapters 13 and 16).

Revivals

A highly acclaimed revival of the 1925 musical *No, No, Nanette* (see Chapter 6) in 1970 triggered a revival frenzy on Broadway, which eventually forced the establishment of a Tony Award category for best revival in 1977. A specific category for best musical revival was introduced in 1994, as revivals had begun to outnumber new musicals on Broadway. Other notable revivals from the decade include *Irene* starring Debbie Reynolds (1973) (see Chapter 5), *Gypsy* starring Angela Lansbury (1974) (see Chapter 17), and *The King and I* starring Yul Brynner and Constance Towers (1977). Harold Prince directed an extensively rewritten version of Leonard Bernstein's *Candide* in 1974. This revival guaranteed the work's place in the repertory, although *Candide* continues to be a challenging work to stage effectively (see Chapter 8). Detractors complained about the production's substandard musical performances and the failure to fully solve the dramaturgic weaknesses of the original 1956 version. Hoping to capitalize on the success of *The Wiz* (see Chapter 15) and taking their cue from David Merrick's all-black version of *Hello, Dolly!* starring Pearl Bailey and Cab Calloway (1967), producers transformed a few other Golden Age titles into all-black musicals. In 1976, Abe Burrows oversaw a Motown-inflected version of *Guys and Dolls* (see Chapter 8) for an entirely African American cast. Two years later, a new version of the 1953 musical *Kismet* (1953) starring Eartha Kitt and Melba Moore opened under the new title *Timbuktu!* The action, originally set in Baghdad, was relocated to West Africa. Geoffrey Holder (1930–2014), in high demand after his critically acclaimed work on *The Wiz*, provided the choreography and costume designs.

THE SONDHEIM DECADE

Stephen Sondheim (b. 1930) spent his formative years in Doylestown, Pennsylvania, not far from the country home of Oscar Hammerstein, II. His parents had divorced in 1940, and his mother, a fashion designer, kept him from seeing his father, a successful dress manufacturer, by moving with her son from New York to Pennsylvania. Earlier, Sondheim had attended military school, which gave him the discipline he lacked at home. He recalled, "I liked knowing that I had to be here at 10:03, and do that at 11:07." By the age of fourteen, Sondheim had discovered an interest in musical theater. From the start, he wrote both words and music. Over a six-year period, Hammerstein mentored Sondheim in the art of musical theater writing. It was an informal apprenticeship but a profoundly influential one on the young Sondheim. Hammerstein required him to write four different types of musicals: (1) an adaptation of a play he admired, (2) an adaptation of a play he considered flawed, (3) an adaptation of a non-dramatic source, and (4) a musical based on an idea of his own invention. For the first assignment, Sondheim adapted *Beggar on Horseback* and titled the show *All That Glitters*. He fulfilled the second assignment with a musical based on Maxwell Anderson's *High Tor*. Pamela Lyndon Travers's *Mary Poppins* provided the non-dramatic source material for the third assignment. Sondheim devised a semi-autobiographical story about a struggling young composer for the fourth musical, which he titled *Climb High*.

Sondheim entered Williams College in 1946 intending to major in math. However, after taking a course with Robert Barrow, the chair of the music department, he changed his major to musical composition. Upon graduation, Sondheim won the Hubbard Hutchinson Prize, which he used to study with the avant-garde composer Milton Babbitt. They spent most of their time together analyzing popular songs as well as works by the great masters of classical music.

Sondheim's Broadway debut as the lyricist of *West Side Story* is the stuff of musical theater legend, but the experience, however positive for his career, did not alter his ultimate goal of writing both lyrics and music. Before *West Side Story*, Sondheim had written the music and lyrics for *Saturday Night*, a musical based on Julius and Philip Epstein's play *Front Porch in Flatbush*. A Broadway production was announced, but the producer died unexpectedly in 1955, which postponed the project indefinitely. The first time Broadway audiences heard Sondheim's music as well as his lyrics was for *A Funny Thing Happened on the Way to the Forum* (1962), a farce based on the comedies of the Roman playwright Plautus. Directed by George Abbott and choreographed by Jerome Robbins, *Forum* was a hit. Sondheim's next musical, *Anyone Can Whistle* (1964), was a bold but unsuccessful experiment (see Chapter 9). In 1965, Sondheim agreed, albeit begrudgingly, to write the lyrics for *Do I Hear a Waltz?*, Richard Rodgers's first attempt after Hammerstein's death to collaborate with a new lyricist (see Chapter 9). Around this time, television networks, still eager to capitalize on the enormous success of the nationally televised broadcast of Rodgers and Hammerstein's *Cinderella* (see Chapter 8), commissioned new musicals for the airwaves. Sondheim's contribution, *Evening Primrose*, aired in 1966 as part of *ABC Stage 67*. *Evening Primrose* is a peculiar work based on a short story by John Collier about a group of people who live in a department store.

THE SONDHEIM–PRINCE MUSICALS

Sondheim rose to great prominence with a series of six musicals that he developed with Harold Prince between 1970 and 1981:

> *Company* (1970)
>
> *Follies* (1971)
>
> *A Little Night Music* (1973)
>
> *Pacific Overtures* (1976)
>
> *Sweeney Todd* (1979)
>
> *Merrily We Roll Along* (1981)

The Sondheim–Prince musicals, as they are called, represent the concept musical at its most mature stage. They deal with human relationships but reject the romantic idealism that defined musical theater for over half a century.

The Quintessential Theater Composer

Sondheim calls himself a theater composer, as opposed to a songwriter. He conceives each song for a specific time, place, and character. His music is a distillation of a wide range of classical and popular influences. Sondheim received formal musical training, and during his formative years he championed several modernist composers, including Maurice Ravel, Sergei Rachmaninoff, Igor Stravinsky, and Paul Hindemith. One can hear their influence in Sondheim's inventive harmonies, complex rhythms, vamp-oriented accompaniments, counterpoint, dissonance treatment, disjunct melodic contours, and dense musical textures. Motives sometimes emerge tentatively from an accompanimental figure or "vamp" (e.g., "Send in the Clowns" and "Finishing the Hat") and then evolve into a full-blown melody, not unlike the opening of Ravel's Piano Concerto for the Left Hand (1929–1930). Aaron Copland was one of the few American composers who interested Sondheim, who as a college student wrote an essay on Copland's *Music for the Theatre*. Sondheim's motive-oriented melodies can be disorienting to the untrained ear because they contain unusually difficult intervals and move in unpredictable directions ("The Little Things You Do Together"). Like so much intricate music, they reveal their riches with repeated hearings. On the other hand, Sondheim has composed sweeping, lyrical melodies when the dramatic situation calls for them (e.g., "Being Alive" and "Too Many Mornings").

Sondheim arguably ranks as the greatest Broadway composer of waltzes after Richard Rodgers, although several other writers of his generation have also employed the waltz for its sentimental value and hypnotic charm, none of them, however, with the same emotional depth as he. Sondheim's waltzes emulate Ravel's "contrast of dark and romantic color," as he himself describes it. Erik Satie's *Gymnopédies* haunt some of Sondheim's most evocative waltzes, such as "The Miller's Son" from *A Little Night Music* and "The Last Midnight" from *Into the Woods*.

Sondheim's compositional process does not stop with melody and harmony, as is the case for many Broadway songwriters, but extends to the accompaniments and counterpoint. Like opera and art-song composers, Sondheim writes accompaniments that enhance the dramatic and emotional effect of the lyrics. As Steve Swayne notes, Sondheim's music relies heavily on linear counterpoint, in which "multiple musical lines [spin] a web of harmony arrived at in a linear fashion."

As a young man, Sondheim also studied Broadway composers, especially the "Big Six": Jerome Kern, Irving Berlin, Richard Rodgers, Cole Porter, George Gershwin, and Harold Arlen. Sondheim cites Arlen's harmonic richness and structural freedom as major influences on his composition. Gershwin's music informs Sondheim's syncopated accompaniments, rhythmic drive, and predilection for quartal harmonies. Sondheim admires Kern's songs for "that economy indigenous to the best art: the maximum development of the minimum of material." Sondheim shares Porter's fondness for Latin rhythms and Rodgers's ability to develop full melodies from small motives.

What distinguishes Sondheim most from these Broadway giants is the degree to which his music does the work of the drama. Sondheim's musical inventiveness derives from character and dramatic situation. The composers listed above elegantly

CREATING THE MUSIC

The creation of the music for a Broadway musical involves three interconnected tasks: (1) inventing the musical ideas (motives, themes, and
phrases), (2) arranging these ideas into a song with accompaniment,
and (3) assigning the individual components of the accompaniment
(and sometimes the vocal melody) to the instruments of the orchestra.
For a classically trained composer, these three tasks constitute a single creative act of
composition. In the past, no serious composer would have thought of writing a
melody and leaving the other tasks to someone else. Opera and operetta composers
traditionally did their own arranging and orchestrating; so too did Broadway composers until about 1910. Throughout the twentieth century, Broadway songwriters
had little need to write the accompaniments for their songs or to learn the art of orchestration, and many of them lacked the requisite formal training to do so. Some
composers, in fact, could not notate their own melodies, and others could barely play
the piano. They relied on professional arrangers—often staff employees at music publishing firms—to write out the melody and devise the piano accompaniments.

Over the decades, many Broadway composers have written their own accompaniments, and a few, such as Kurt Weill, have also orchestrated their own shows.
When a second party has been involved, he or she has rarely been credited.

captured the general mood of the lyrics in their music, but, as Swayne points out,
"rarely did they use music to comment on the lyrics, to question or contradict them,
or to reinforce them with a musical logic that owes more to classical music and
opera than to popular song." Sondheim's music expresses as much psychological
subtext as dramatic exposition.

The complexity of Sondheim's music underscores the central paradox of his
career. Swayne explains,

> So the decade that witnessed the start of the Rodgers and Hammerstein
> revolution . . . as well as Berlin's *Annie Get Your Gun* and Porter's *Kiss Me,
> Kate*, and that would end with Frank Loesser's *Guys and Dolls*, found
> Sondheim listening to Ravel and memorizing [Bernard] Herrmann, writ-
> ing a term paper about Copland and imitating Hindemith. For someone
> who wanted to write Broadway shows, Sondheim's musical palette seemed
> to be developing at cross purposes to the audience he would have to reach.

Sondheim's musicals evince a postmodern self-reflexivity and cynicism about
contemporary life. They pay homage to Golden Age musical theater while simultaneously rejecting Hammerstein's utopian vision. Sondheim has continued to explore

the possibilities of musical theater as he mourns the genre's slow demise. The most vivid expression of Sondheim's postmodern sensibilities is his ironic use of pastiche (music in the style of a particular composer or milieu). However, Sondheim's pastiche songs go well beyond mere imitation. For instance, Sally's "Losing My Mind" from *Follies* invokes Gershwin's "The Man I Love," but it springs from the surreal follies occurring in her mind and thereby beckons to an earlier, more innocent time in Broadway history. It uncovers the psychological reality of Sally as she really is, a middle-aged woman on the brink of emotional collapse.

As a lyricist, Sondheim considers himself the heir to Frank Loesser and Dorothy Fields. Many would include Cole Porter and Lorenz Hart as influences, although Sondheim is critical of the latter. Like Porter, Sondheim revels in fanciful wordplay, and he has a seemingly bottomless reservoir of verbal invention and wit. A cryptic crosswords enthusiast, he is the ultimate wordsmith. His lyrics brim with an extensive range of poetic resources—irony, *double entendre*, alliteration, opposition, apposition, and interior rhyme. His songs can be didactic, allegorical, paradoxical, satirical, and unsettling. Like Porter, Sondheim is sophisticated and stylized in one moment and earthy in the next.

Although Sondheim's songs can be intellectually challenging, they can also be emotionally stirring. However, a full appreciation of his songs requires that they be heard in their proper dramatic context. Sondheim writes his lyrics "not just to be sung but to be sung in particular musicals by individual characters in specific situations," as he has explained. By contrast, lyricists of an earlier age wrote about generalized sentiments, albeit in clever, often memorable ways. They introduced a conversational offhandedness to popular song, and sold a lot of sheet music as a result. Sondheim searches for deeper meaning in a song. He eschews placeholders and commonplace sentiments such as "I'm in love." In this regard, Hammerstein, who elevated musical theater lyric writing to a more precise and purposeful art, has remained Sondheim's guiding light.

For Sondheim, writing lyrics and music has more to do with craft than inspiration. Finding the correct prosody, meter, register, rhyme, and syntax is paramount to producing good theater lyrics. Sondheim teases out the most arcane and disarming rhymes, and he allows for the "sheer pleasure of verbal playfulness" (e.g., "the hands on the clock turn, / but don't sing a nocturne / just yet" from *A Little Night Music*). However, he always rhymes with a purpose and rarely sacrifices content for cleverness. One is thoroughly convinced, for instance, when the upper-class lawyer in *A Little Night Music* rhymes "just ash" and "mustache." Forever the craftsman, Sondheim insists on pure rhymes (as opposed to slanted, visual, or near rhymes). "Good rhymes and the expression of emotion" are not mutually exclusive, he has stated. Finding the perfect combination is part of the craft: "A good lyric should not only have something to say but a way of saying it as clearly and forcefully as possible."

Subject Matter

Sondheim has spent his entire career challenging the notion of marriage as a sacred institution and questioning the happily-ever-after myth. The romantic characters in his musicals seldom achieve marital bliss. Sondheim banishes this sort of musical comedy ending and instead explores the vicissitudes of relationships romantic or otherwise. Even when his musicals are not careening toward outright tragedy (*West Side Story* and *Sweeney Todd*) or disconsolation and disillusionment (*Follies*, *Passion*, and *Road Show*), they end in ambiguity (*Gypsy*, *Company*, and *Sunday in the Park with George*). When marriage is the goal, the focus is on what actually happens after happily-ever-after.

Because Sondheim deconstructs the marriage trope, as Raymond Knapp calls it, of musical comedy, his scores exclude the type of love duet that was *de rigueur* in traditional book musicals. Before the sixties, musicals espoused a belief in love at first sight followed by marriage. Hammerstein writes declarations of love (e.g., "Some Enchanted Evening"); Sondheim writes tortuous examinations of love and marriage. The lovers in Sondheim's musicals maintain "the boundaries of [their] individualism in unison singing." By contrast, lovers in earlier musicals sing together and just happen to know the same lyrics. Sondheim is more interested in the "I" than the "we" that is central to musical theater's thick catalogue of love duets. Critics often have accused him of being coldhearted and antiromantic, but his songs, instead of painting false pictures, are brutally honest essays on human relationships. However, he refuses to subscribe to romantic illusions. The charge of heartlessness originated with *Company*, which, according to the composer, was "my first full immersion in evening-length irony—irony not merely employed as a tone for stray individual songs . . . but as the modus operandi of an entire score."

Company

Background

Company was a daring musical because it rejected the romantic ideal of commitment at a time when cultural, economic, and societal forces were weakening the institution of marriage. It deals with the difficulty of "making emotional connections in an increasingly dehumanized society," as Sondheim has described the show. *Company* also qualifies as a landmark work. In contrast to Kander and Ebb's earlier concept musicals, *Cabaret* and *Zorbá*, which incorporate traditional linear narratives, *Company* is plotless.

It takes place in 1970 New York and explores the problems that were afflicting modern couples. When *Company* opened, the divorce rate was rising precipitously, women were beginning to break down the professional barriers that had held them back for decades, interracial and homosexual relationships were becoming less taboo, and Americans were questioning sacred institutions such as marriage. *Company* did not start out as a musical, though. In the late sixties, the playwright George Furth wrote eleven short vignettes about marriage. Each one featured two people locked in a relationship plus an "outsider." Prince felt that Furth's concept was too cumbersome for a spoken play but that it provided the basis for a musical about modern marriage.

Sondheim has this to say regarding the storyline of *Company*:

Company does have a story, the story of what happens inside Robert; it just doesn't have a chronological linear plot. As far as I know, prior to *Company* there had never been a plotless musical which dealt with one set of characters from start to finish. In 1970, the contradictory aspect of the experiment (a story without a plot) was cause for both enthusiasm and dismay. Audiences kept waiting for something to happen, some incident that would lead to another that would lead to another, and were baffled when nothing did.—Excerpted from *Finishing the Hat*

Concept

Prince, Sondheim, and Furth invented a protagonist named Bobby (known to his friends variously as Robert, Robby, Rob-o, Bob-o, and Bobby bubi), a thirty-five-year-old bachelor, as a unifying device and point-of-view character. Bobby spends most of the show socializing with his "married friends" (five couples), and he dates three different women. Collectively, these vignettes chart Bobby's slowly evolving attitude about marriage (Table 10.1). Early in Act I, Bobby asks one of his friends, "What da'ya wanna get married for?," and he spends the remainder of the show searching for an answer. In the penultimate scene, Bobby confronts his still-nascent feelings about the meaning of commitment, and he recognizes that life without "somebody" is empty. Bobby has made progress, although he has no one in particular in mind. As Sondheim states, "Robert, despite his ultimate song ["Being Alive"], never became sufficiently alive [to satisfy the critics]."

The action, as it were, takes place on Bobby's thirty-fifth birthday. In the opening scene, Robert's friends are throwing him a surprise party. A party scene also occurs at the end of Act I, and another at the end of Act II. Prince views these three sequences as representing a single birthday party. Sondheim reasons that "the show takes place not over a period of time, but in an instant in Robert's mind, perhaps on a psychiatrist's couch, perhaps at the moment when he comes into his apartment on his thirty-fifth birthday. The framework is a surreal surprise party for him, which opens and closes each act." At the very end of *Company*, Bobby pauses outside the door of his apartment, aware of what awaits him on the other side, and decides not to enter.

Sondheim understood that the music for *Company* had to function differently from a traditional "Rodgers and Hammerstein kind of song in which the characters reach a certain point and then sing their emotions." Character songs ran the risk of revealing more about Bobby's friends than the fragmented script warranted, not to mention slowing down the action. He therefore decided to use the songs to interrupt the story and reflect on the issues about marriage and commitment raised in the vignettes. Although Sondheim claims to "[hate] Brecht—all of Brecht," he acknowledges *Company*'s debt to the playwright in that nearly all of the songs function as commentary. With the exception of Bobby's songs, they occur outside of the show's dramatic framework and comment on the action rather than reveal subtext

TABLE 10.1. The Vignettes in *Company*

ACT AND SCENE	SCENARIO
Act I, scene 2	Sarah is attempting to lose weight, and Harry is trying to cut back on his drinking. They end up facing each other in a karate match in their living room.
Act I, scene 3	Susan and Peter announce to Bobby that they are getting divorced but will continue to live together.
Act I, scene 4	Jenny and David smoke pot with Bobby. It is her first time.
Act I, scene 5	April confesses to Bobby that she is a dull person. On a park bench, Kathy informs Bobby that she is marrying someone in Vermont. Marta loves the energy of New York.
Act I, scene 6	Just moments before she is to wed Paul, Amy gets cold feet and panics. A conversation with Bobby convinces her to go forward with her wedding.
Act II, scene 2	Following a night of lovemaking, April, an airline stewardess, tries to leave Bobby's apartment in order to catch a flight. Bobby dutifully tries to convince her to stay, but he is not particularly happy when she does.
Act II, scene 3	Bobby introduces Marta to some of his friends. He is surprised to find out that Susan and Peter's divorce has done wonders for their relationship.
Act II, scene 4	Joanne and Larry have taken Bobby to a private nightclub. While Larry is off paying the bill, Joanne expresses bitterness about being a rich man's wife without much purpose. She propositions Bobby.

or a character's inner life. Unlike traditional theater songs, they do not foster a strong emotional connection between the audience and the characters. Some of the numbers are presentational in nature (e.g., "You Could Drive a Person Crazy"), delivered directly to the audience.

Scorching dissonances underscore the cynical outlook, urbane humor, and urban ethos of *Company*. Driving motor rhythms, asymmetrical phrases, repeated notes and chords, and animated bass lines give the score the energy and momentum of rock music, but the musical styles are as varied as the topics of the songs. Sondheim mixes pastiche numbers ("Side by Side") with pop-inflected ballads rich in suspended chords, syncopated rhythms, and mixed meters ("You're Sorry-Grateful"). The lyrics are mosaics of America in the early seventies, with direct references to sex, pot, divorce, feminism, travel, and fads. The tone of the songs derives "from the colloquial, casual bleakness of urban modernism," as Stephen Banfield

The cast of *Company* (minus Bobby) performing the Act II opener, "Side by Side by Side." (Bobby is conspicuously absent from this photograph.) *Courtesy KB Archives.*

observes. The songs depict a sexist culture on the verge of collapse from within. The score includes instances of farce ("Getting Married Today"), biting cynicism ("The Ladies Who Lunch"), and painful yearning ("Someone Is Waiting").

Each member of Prince's creative team was attuned to the singular concept of the show. Michael Bennett, who staged the musical numbers, used choreography to enhance the audience's understanding of what *Company* was trying to say: "What I did in *Company* was to choreograph the characters. . . . I knew it was a chance to do something different because there was so much subtext." In "Side by Side by Side," for instance, the couples and Bobby form a line. Each couple performs a two-measure tap dance break in succession. Bobby gets a turn, too, but, aware that he is partnerless, shrugs instead of executing a dance step.

The orchestrator for *Company*, Jonathan Tunick, incorporated electric keyboards, acoustic and electric guitars, and a group of female pit singers called the "Vocal Minority," all of which helped to give the show a pop recording studio sound similar to what he had created for *Promises, Promises* in 1968. Tunick used combinations of alto flute, flugelhorn, contrabass clarinet, and saxophones to create the mechanical sounds of the city. The show, Tunick recalled, inspired a "lot of penetrating, nasty stinging sounds." For instance, he employed muted trumpets, sometimes doubled by bells, as a recurring timbral motif to underscore the brittle subject matter.

Company looked as sleek and contemporary as it sounded. D. D. Ryan's costumes were stylish and timely. Boris Aronson created an abstract unit set that turned

MICHAEL BENNETT

Michael Bennett (1943–1987) came from a working-class family in Buffalo, where he began taking dance lessons at an early age. He dropped out of high school and went on tour with *West Side Story*. In the sixties, Bennett appeared in several Broadway musicals, including *Subways Are for Sleeping* (1961) and *Here's Love* (1963). *A Joyful Noise* (1966) marks the beginning of Bennett's career as a Broadway choreographer, and *Seesaw* (1973) was the first show that he both directed and choreographed. Bennett's most successful project was *A Chorus Line* (see below), which he followed with *Ballroom* (1978), which did poorly. He rebounded in 1981 with *Dreamgirls* (see Chapter 11). Like Jerome Robbins and Bob Fosse, Bennett had his admirers and detractors, but no one doubted his talent or ability to assess popular tastes. His death from AIDS in 1987 dealt a severe blow to the Broadway community.

contemporary Manhattan into an icy-cold, impersonal, and modular landscape. The basis for the set was a "multi-leveled steel structure indicating various high-rise Manhattan apartments," all connected by elevators and stairs. The vignettes were played out on the various levels, each denoting one of the couples' apartments. Rear and frontal projections revealed skylines and sights of the city.

Score

The dramatic climax of *Company* coincides with Bobby's epiphany at the end of Act II. Expressing in music what is ostensibly an emotional and mental process and inherently undramatic was no easy matter, and Sondheim, Furth, and Prince never reached complete agreement over what the song should say. Sondheim wrote four different versions of the song, beginning with "Marry Me a Little," which developed from a story element that was ultimately not used in the show. In this version of the show, the character of Amy, the hysterical, hyperventilating bride engaged to Paul, fails to overcome her self-doubts and calls off the wedding. Bobby decides to propose to her and makes his case in "Marry Me a Little." The song reveals Bobby's self-deception, that he thinks he can reap the benefits of a committed relationship while maintaining the independence he has enjoyed as a bachelor. A rapid-fire accompaniment with cross-rhythms courses through the song, as a fragmented melody line underscores the mixture of trepidation and exhilaration that Bobby experiences (Example 10.1a). The melody is in 4/4, but the eighth-note groupings superimpose a triple meter onto the accompaniment: five groups of three eighth notes over two measures plus one eighth note left over at the end of the second measure. Consecutive dotted quarter notes in the upper voice of the accompaniment,

"The Farmer and the Cowhand" dance at the box social in the original Broadway production of *Oklahoma! Courtesy KB Archives.*

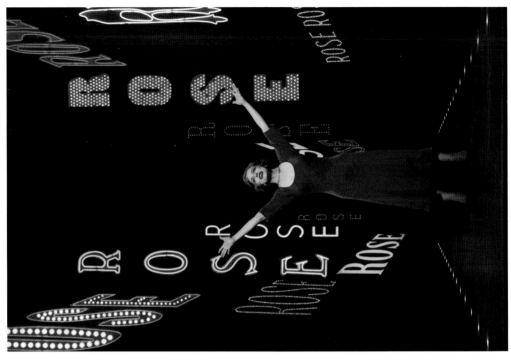

Bernadette Peters performing "Rose's Turn" in the 2003 Broadway revival of *Gypsy*. *Courtesy Photofest.*

Ethel Merman as Mama Rose in the original Broadway production of *Gypsy*. *Courtesy KB Archives.*

"The Farmer and the Cowhand" dance at the box social in the original Broadway production of *Oklahoma! Courtesy KB Archives.*

Sheet music of the fox trot "Babes in the Wood" from *Very Good Eddie. Courtesy of Jason A. Jansen.*

Jean MacLaren (Virginia Bosler), the bride, dances with her father (Edward Cullen) during the wedding scene in the original Broadway production of *Brigadoon*; to the left, Harry Beaton (played by James Mitchell) dances with a woman from his own clan. *Courtesy Photofest.*

Harold Hill (Robert Preston) singing "Marian the Librarian" to Marian Paroo (Barbara Cook) in the original Broadway production of *The Music Man*. *Courtesy Photofest.*

Bob Fosse's signature choreography for "A Secretary Is Not a Toy" from the original Broadway production of *How to Succeed in Business Without Really Trying. Courtesy Photofest.*

The conservative Founding Father performing "Cool, Cool, Considerate Men" in the original Broadway production of *1776*: from the left, Robert Livingston (played by Henry Le Clair), George Reed (Duane Bodin), Lewis Morris (Ronald Cross), James Wilson (Emory Bass), Edward Rutledge (Clifford David), John Dickinson (Paul Hecht), Joseph Hewes (Charles Rule), Dr. Lyman Hall (Jonathan Moore). *Courtesy Photofest.*

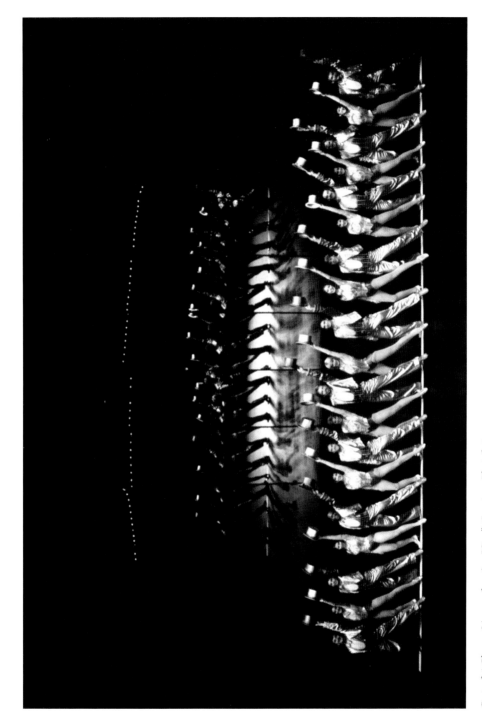

Cast of *A Chorus Line* performing "One". *Courtesy Photofest.*

Terrence Mann as Rum Tum Tugger in the original Broadway production of *Cats. Courtesy KB Archives.*

Rafiki presents Simba at Pride Rock during "Circle of Life" in the Broadway production of *The Lion King. Courtesy Joan Marcus.*

Mary Poppins (Ashley Brown) arriving at the Banks residence during the live stage version of *Mary Poppins*. *Courtesy Joan Marcus.*

Sheet music of "Come Right In, Sit Right Down, Make Yourself at Home," featuring a photograph of Bert Williams in blackface. *Courtesy BenCar Archives.*

Sheet music of a song from the original Broadway production of *The Wiz. Courtesy of David A. Jansen.*

Teenagers from Sweet Apple perform "The Telephone Hour" in the original Broadway production of *Bye Bye Birdie. Courtesy KB Archives.*

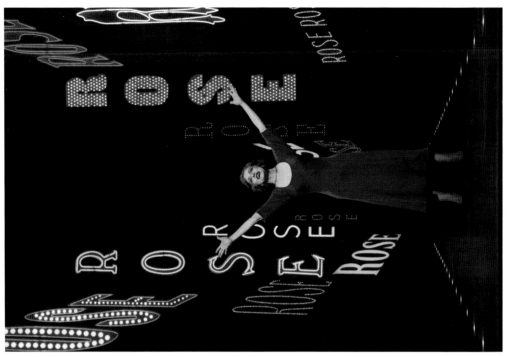

Bernadette Peters performing "Rose's Turn" in the 2003 Broadway revival of *Gypsy. Courtesy Photofest.*

Ethel Merman as Mama Rose in the original Broadway production of *Gypsy. Courtesy KB Archives.*

Angela Lansbury as Rose performing "Rose's Turn" in the 1974 Broadway revival of *Gypsy. Courtesy KB Archives.*

Patti LuPone as Rose performing "Rose's Turn" in the 2008 Broadway revival of *Gypsy. Courtesy Joan Marcus.*

JONATHAN TUNICK

onathan Tunick (b. 1938), Broadway's preeminent orchestrators for over four decades, possesses remarkable technical proficiency and an innate ability to use the orchestra to enhance the drama. Since 1970, Tunick has orchestrated all of Sondheim's musicals with the exception of *Sunday in the Park with George*. In the late fifties, Tunick attended Juilliard as a clarinetist, but after hearing Red Ginzler's sassy orchestrations for *Bye Bye Birdie* (1960), he decided to become a Broadway orchestrator. Tunick's big break came in 1968, when he was hired to do the orchestrations for Burt Bacharach's *Promises, Promises*, which introduced the studio sound of pop music to Broadway. Tunick included amplified pit singers and electronic instruments in order to enhance the contemporary rhythms, meters, and urbane style of Bacharach's music. He gave *Company* a similar, albeit even brassier, sheen. Tunick's orchestration for Sondheim's *Follies* captured the nostalgia and haunting glamour of the *Ziegfeld Follies*. His use of the synthesizer helped to create a ghostly and surreal mood without ever sticking out as a contemporary electronic instrument. *A Little Night Music* evoked the lush string sound of Broadway operetta of an earlier era. *Pacific Overtures* features one of Tunick's most delicate and transparent orchestrations, although when necessary it evokes the raw, primitivistic force of Stravinsky's *The Rite of Spring*. The unusually large orchestra for *Sweeney Todd* consisted of twenty-one different instruments plus a large arsenal of percussion. For *Merrily We Roll Along* Tunick featured a tuba. *Into the Woods* incorporated a smaller ensemble and some exposed solos for the bassoon. Tunick reverted to a more string-dominated sound for *Passion*. Tunick also provided the orchestrations for the film versions of *Sweeney Todd* and *Into the Woods*.

harmonizing the tenor line, accent the triplet cross-rhythms of the driving eighth-note pattern. Bobby's pleas come in short two-measure phrases, suggestive of his reticence (the music is marked "rubato"). The song contains two large-scale units (ABAB). Neither A-section achieves tonal closure; instead, the final line of A ends unexpectedly on what proves to be the tonic of the new key with an unresolved fourth dissonance. This chord interrupts Bobby's momentum, stopping him dead in his tracks. At the end of the song, Bobby cries out, "Amy, I'm ready!" The melody drops from F-sharp, the apex note of the song, to the third scale degree, leaving Bobby up in the air, as the vamp drives to the end. Sondheim recalls, "I was halfway through writing ["Marry Me a Little"] when I realized I'd run into a problem that often arises in playwriting: the character who knows too much too soon. . . . I realized that if Robert could articulate such thoughts aloud to someone he cared for, he would indeed have nowhere to go for the rest of the show."

(Continued)

(b)

Molto rubato ($\bullet$ =120)

Mul-ti-tudes of A - mys_____ Crowd the streets be-low. ___

_____ Av-en-ues of A - mys, Of-fice-fuls of A - mys

Ev - 'ry-where I go._____

(Continued)

EXAMPLE 10.1. Bobby's four finales (opening phrases): (a) "Marry Me a Little," (b) "Multitudes of Amys," (c) "Happily Ever After," (d) "Being Alive"

"Multitudes of Amys," the song that Sondheim wrote to replace "Marry Me a Little," stands out for its unbridled exuberance. As Bobby searches for Amy so that he can propose to her, he returns to the set locations where he encountered his other friends. Eventually, he arrives at Amy's kitchen and pops the question. The main theme, consisting of six notes (first heard on the trochaic lyric "multitudes of Amys") or the five-note variant (used for the truncated trochaic lines such as "crowd the streets below"), occurs in one form or another thirty-five times, not including ten statements of a related five-note melodic unit ("I know what it means") (Example 10.1b). The musical repetition suggests the crowding of Robert's mind with thoughts and images of Amy. Sondheim composed an instrumental break in order to give Robert time to travel from one location to another, seeing Amy everywhere he goes, as the music makes clear. The main theme of the song eventually evokes the pealing of wedding bells. However, the decision was ultimately made that Amy would go through with her wedding to Paul at the end of Act I, thus rendering "Multitudes of Amys" unusable.

Sondheim next wrote "Happily Ever After," Bobby's "defiant summary of what he thinks he's learned from the evening's experiences." Despite its jaunty jazz-waltz rhythms, "Happily Ever After" smacks of irony and belies the suggestion that Bobby has made a breakthrough (Example 10.1c). Harold Prince felt that "Happily Ever After" was "the bitterest, most unhappy song ever written." As originally planned, though, the song would not have been the musical's final word; there was to have been an epilogue set in Central Park, where Bobby, who in despair has abandoned his friends, encounters thirteen different characters, played by the same actors who played his friends. As Sondheim describes the scene, "determined to take a step forward, [Bobby] finally makes a gesture of open and needful connection to one of them, a distracted and lonely young woman." The epilogue, though, was not used, the result being that "Happily Ever After" occurred just moments before the final curtain, not the sort of upbeat ending that audiences were used to hearing. The song remained in the show during previews in Boston, but the audience response was negative.

Having to come up with a replacement, Sondheim wrote the more optimistic "Being Alive," using the opening lines of "Happily Ever After" as a springboard: "Someone to hold you too close, / Someone to hurt you too deep" (Example 10.1d). During the first verse of "Being Alive," Bobby's friends, looking on from behind, urge him on to the realization that making a commitment is necessary if one is not to be alone (George Furth wrote their spoken lines). In the second chorus, Robert substitutes "someone" with the more affirmative "somebody" and the second-person "you" with the first-person "me." These subtle shifts in pronouns accompany a change of tone from "complaint to prayer" between the two choruses, as Sondheim has explained. For this, his fourth effort, Sondheim eschewed irony. "Being Alive" is the most soul-searching song of the four finales. During the course of the number, Bobby gradually discovers what everyone else already knows. To capture Bobby's tentative mood as he searches for what it means to connect to another human being, Sondheim devised an ostinato, which at first sounds in the background in virtually every measure and eventually comes to the foreground in the form of a jubilant fanfare at the end of the song. Because "Being Alive" occurs late in the show and has a high tessitura, it tests the emotional and physical stamina of the actor playing Bobby, but the challenge of performing the song is an analogue for Bobby's mental struggle. "Being Alive" strikes an affirmative tone and ends with an exultant musical climax. However, it does not signify resolution or the obtainment of a romantic objective. Moreover, some commentators have trouble accepting Bobby's "instantaneous transition from habitual bemused distance" to emotional pleading. Prince and Furth preferred "Being Alive" to "Happily Ever After," but Sondheim felt that it was a "cop-out." "Being Alive" perhaps expresses a happy medium between marriage and outright nihilism.

Too good a song to waste, "Marry Me a Little" eventually found its way back into *Company* when Scott Ellis, the director of the 1995 revival, inserted it at the end of Act I (in place of the second birthday-party scene). Sondheim approved of the addition: "because Amy has turned Bobby down, it works well as an internal monologue of despair and self-deceptive determination. It has remained there ever since."

Several commentators have suggested that the character of Bobby is gay, but, as Ethan Mordden, a gay writer, has pointed out, it is unlikely that a gay Bobby would seduce April, a quintessential seventies stewardess. That Bobby is unattached is more likely due to his inability to make a meaningful human connection than to a repressed desire for men. Another common misperception about *Company* is that it is anti-marriage. On the contrary, *Company* recognizes, and even celebrates, the fact that although marriage is difficult, most people prefer it to the alternative. The musical dealt more honestly with the realities of marriage than any musical before it, perhaps with the exception of Weill and Lerner's *Love Life* (1948) (see Chapters 7 and 9). In the twenty-first century, it is conceivable that Bobby is a heterosexual guy who just does not want to get married.

In 2013, it was reported that Sondheim and the director John Tiffany were working on a version of *Company* in which Bobby is "a gay man with commitment issues and multiple boyfriends." As Sondheim explained at the time, "It's still a musical about commitment, but marriage is seen as something very different in 2013 than it was in 1970." This version has not yet reached the stage.

Happily Ever After?

Follies, which opened during *Company*'s initial run, stages a reunion of ex-performers of the fictional Weismann *Follies* (read *Ziegfeld Follies*). The surreal, intermissionless action takes place on the stage of the *Follies* theater, which is scheduled for demolition in order to make room for "yet another parking lot." The guests are haunted by ghosts of their former selves, and they obsess over how their lives have turned out. A *succès d'estime*, *Follies* has been revived several times. The continued interest in *Follies* attests to its emotional depth, extraordinary score, and innovative dramatic structure.

A Little Night Music is based on Ingmar Bergman's film *Smiles of a Summer Night* (1955), a deft comedy of manners. In an attempt to write a musical of waltzes,

The tableaux at the end of Act I of *Sunday in the Part with George* (the artist, Georges Seurat, is played by Mandy Patinkin and Dot, the women with the monkey, by Bernadette Peters). *Courtesy KB Archives.*

Sondheim composed every song in three-quarter time or triple meter (6/8, for example). *Pacific Overtures*, Sondheim's most overtly political show, was overshadowed in 1975 by *A Chorus Line* and *Chicago*. Cowritten with John Weidman, it was a stinging indictment of the Westernization of Japan that began with the arrival of Commodore Matthew Perry near Edo (former name of Tokyo) in 1853. Harold Prince employed Kabuki theater techniques and featured an all-Asian cast, and Sondheim composed original haiku poetry and incorporated Eastern musical elements. Sondheim himself initiated *Sweeney Todd*, as opposed to his earlier collaborations with Prince. It is a macabre tale of a barber who, having been wrongfully convicted of a crime and sent to Australia to serve a long prison sentence, returns to London to seek vengeance on his accusers. *Merrily We Roll Along* started with a request from Prince's wife that he develop a musical about teenagers. Based on the 1934 play of the same name by George S. Kaufman and Moss Hart, *Merrily* traces the devolving relationship of three friends, but it does so in reverse chronological order, ending when they first meet as optimistic young adults. The musical, with a script by *Company*'s George Furth, updated the story and changed the primary protagonist from a Broadway playwright to a Broadway composer. Despite its tuneful, tight-knit score, *Merrily* displeased the critics: it closed after two weeks and precipitated the dissolution of Sondheim and Prince's remarkably fruitful partnership. Sondheim has rewritten *Merrily* several times in an effort to solve the dramaturgical problems that plagued the original version. Its ebullient optimism, moving score, ad relevant story make *Merrily* a popular musical.

In the eighties and nineties, Sondheim entered a more self-reflexive phase. He worked extensively, but not exclusively, with the playwright and director James Lapine. *Sunday in the Park with George* (1984) explored the difficulties of making art in an increasingly commercial and corporate environment. *Into the Woods* (1987) interweaved several classic fairytales around an original one. *Passion* (1994) delved into the dark side of love. It is based on the Italian film *Passione d'Amore*, itself an adaptation of I. U. Tarchetti's novel *Fosca*. Sondheim reunited with John Weidman to write two musicals: *Assassins* (1990) and *Bounce* (2003) (currently titled *Road Show* [see Chapter 13]). Sondheim is currently collaborating with the playwright David Ives on an adaptation of some of the plays in his *All in the Timing* (1994). He has also written music for films, most notably *Reds* (1981) and *Dick Tracey* (1990).

Critical Reception

Sondheim has paid a high price for his art. Despite his unrivaled artistic reputation, most of his musicals have done poorly at the box office, and Broadway has not produced a new Sondheim musical in years. In addition to their difficult subject matter, Sondheim's musicals contain denser musical textures and more dissonances than the average theatergoer is used to hearing. Critics have long admired Sondheim's lyrics, but they have exhibited remarkably little technical insight into his music. They routinely call his songs "un-hummable," a maddening criticism for any composer. After all, a tune's "hummability" is directly related to the number of times one hears it as well as its intervallic content and internal repetitiveness. "The Surrey with the Fringe on Top" quickly imprints itself on the ear because its nine-note main theme contains only three different pitches and occurs three times in the course of eight measures. By accusing Sondheim of writing "dissonant" and "unmelodic" tunes, his critics not only expose their musical ignorance, but they also propagate the myth that if one cannot hum a tune, it must not be any good. Like any great art, Sondheim's music contains layers of beauty and complexity that reveal themselves upon repeated exposure. Sondheim has never stopped evolving as a composer, and his music has not become any easier to grasp. His melodies are more winding and his harmonic palette is richer.

MUSICAL THEATER BEYOND BROADWAY

In the seventies, Regional and nonprofit theaters started to have a measurable impact on musical theater production. These institutions gave many young writers their start and helped to cultivate theater audiences at a time when Broadway was struggling with declining tickets sales. In 1973, the Theatre Development Fund opened a half-price ticket booth (TKTS Discount Booth) smack in the middle of the Broadway Theater District (the booth and surrounding area—Duffy Square—underwent a makeover between 2006 and 2008). Moreover, the New York tourist trade and national touring companies of Broadway musicals continued to expose musical theater to people from all regions of the country. Such signs of life dispel

AND BEAR IN MIND

A Chorus Line (1975, Shubert Theatre, 6,137 performances; premiered earlier the same year Off Broadway at the Public Theater)

Music by Marvin Hamlisch
Lyrics by Edward Kleban
Book by James Kirkwood and Nicholas Dante

Michael Bennett's *A Chorus Line* was the first Broadway musical to hit 4,000 performances. As the choreographer of *Company* and *Follies*, Bennett learned how to employ movement to develop character and create fluid stage transitions. Indeed, *A Chorus Line* owes its character-driven orientation and plotless format to these earlier concept musicals.

A Chorus Line takes the form of an audition for an unnamed Broadway musical: several hopeful gypsies (the show-business term for dancers) are put through an arduous audition during which they must bare their souls to the director, who is part father figure, part "shrink," and part masochist. Metaphorically speaking, the dancers are auditioning for an opportunity to fulfill their life's dream. At the end of the audition, the director announces his selection, which splits what was a unified group of performers into dejected losers and elated winners.

Bennett developed the show over the course of several workshops during which he conducted interviews with a group of professional dancers. He and his scriptwriters then molded this material into a cohesive book. The character of Paul, a gay dancer, delivers a speech late in the show about what it felt like to get caught by his father while performing as a female impersonator. This speech and a former romantic relationship between the director and one of the dancers, Cassie, accounted for *A Chorus Line*'s strong emotional undercurrent.

Bennett's use of cinematic techniques gave *A Chorus Line* a flowing rhythm and dramatic unity, and it helped the audience time travel with the characters to earlier moments in their lives. The simple set design featured a row of eight periaktoi (three-sided columns) along the upstage wall, which allowed the action to crossfade between the present and past. In the blink of an eye, the audience was transported from a rehearsal hall to an empty stage to a silver-and-gold fan design that suggested a sunburst during the finale ("One"). The actors wore naturalistic leotards, leg warmers, and other rehearsal gear. The ensemble made a lightning-fast costume change for the finale, during which the members of the cast entered one at a time dressed in a sparkling gold top hat and tails. In addition to taking their bows, the cast performed a magnificent synchronized chorus line routine. Tharon Musser brought the art of musical theater lighting to new heights. Using computerized lighting cues, she helped the audience to follow the show's quick transitions between the present and past as well as between the public (the audition) and private (the actors' interior thoughts) space in which the story takes place. In addition to Marvin Hamlisch's memorable contemporary music, these elements collectively helped to realize Bennett's strong vision for *A Chorus Line.*

the notion of musical theater's demise. In fact, during the 1978–1979 theatrical season, gross revenues for shows playing on the road surpassed revenues from Broadway theaters by $19 million.

On the other hand, at the end of the seventies the future of musical theater seemed as uncertain as the future of the country. When Ronald Reagan took office in 1981 as the fortieth president, the country feared the threat of another oil embargo and was reeling from inflation and the Iran hostage crisis. Crime and drugs continued to blight urban areas, and the AIDS crisis loomed in the not-too-distant future. America was about to experience the rise of an entirely new type of music: rap. Moreover, the so-called British invasion of Broadway, the subject of the next chapter, brought long-term consequences.

· ·

NAMES, TERMS, AND CONCEPTS

"Being Alive"	"Happily Ever After"
Bennett, Michael	*Little Night Music, A*
Chicago	"Marry Me a Little"
Chorus Line, A	"Multitudes of Amys"
Company	Prince, Harold
concept musical	*Promises, Promises*
Follies	Sondheim, Stephen
Furth, George	Tunick, Jonathan
Hamlisch, Marvin	*Two Gentleman of Verona*

. . . .

DISCUSSION QUESTIONS

1. How does *Company* represent the coming of age of the concept musical?

2. Identify and discuss the commentative songs in *Company*.

3. Explain the increased number of musicals with serious topics in the seventies.

4. Compare the music, lyrics, and dramatic effect of the four finales that Sondheim composed for the character of Bobby.

5. Discuss the treatment of marriage and relationships in Sondheim's musicals.

CHAPTER 11

THE EIGHTIES

(*THE PHANTOM OF THE OPERA*, MAJESTIC THEATRE, REACHED 10,000 PERFORMANCES ON FEBRUARY 11, 2012)

*L*a Cage aux Folles (1983) won six Tony Awards, including one for best score. While accepting his statuette, Jerry Herman, who wrote the score for *La Cage*, declared, "There's been a rumor that the simple hummable show tune is dead on Broadway. Well, it's alive and well at the Palace [Theatre]!" Some people interpreted Herman's speech as a disguised dig at Stephen Sondheim, whose *Sunday in the Park with George* was poised to win the Tony Award that year. In point of fact, *La Cage* and *Sunday* were both major achievements, the latter a traditional musical comedy about a middle-aged gay couple with a timely message about gender, tolerance, and love, the former a postmodern examination of the intersection of art and commerce. *La Cage*'s subject matter and the politics of the AIDS era helped to swing the Tony Award vote in its favor. Sondheim and his collaborator James Lapine were subsequently awarded the 1985 Pulitzer Award in Drama and the New York Drama Critics' Circle Award for *Sunday*.

Sunday and *La Cage* notwithstanding, the dominant story of the eighties concerns neither Herman nor Sondheim: it was the advent and looming dominance of the megamusical and the composer most associated with it, Andrew Lloyd Webber (b. 1948). Lloyd Webber posed much stiffer competition to Sondheim and Herman than they did to each other, and the popularity of his musicals threatened the very existence of their respective brands of musical theater. As it turned out, shortly after *La Cage*, Herman stopped writing altogether (he learned in 1985 that he had contracted AIDS). Sondheim continued to write musicals (he still does), and critics began to frame their discussions about the health of the genre in binary terms: Lloyd Webber represented the philistine who stood in opposition to Sondheim, the authentic genius who never compromised his art.

Gene Barry as Georges and George Hearn as Albin in the original production of *La Cage aux Folles*. *Courtesy Photofest.*

MEGAMUSICAL

Megamusical Defined

Critics and scholars adopted the term "megamusical" during the eighties for a specific type of work originating in England and attributed to Lloyd Webber and the lyricist Tim Rice. As the term suggests, the megamusical privileges spectacle. Its unmitigated commercialism, for which it makes no apologies, and sphere of influence helped to make the megamusical a cultural phenomenon. The megamusical has enjoyed unprecedented popularity on both sides of the "pond," and its pop-rock musical style and business model continue to influence musical theater today. The onslaught of megamusicals on Broadway was dubbed the "British invasion," a not-so-subtle reminder that non-American writers were beginning to dominate a field that had been the domain of American writers for decades.

Megamusicals feature plots of immense, often epic or historical, scope (e.g., the battle between good and evil during the French Revolution), archetypal characters (the hero, the fiend, the waif, the dictator), and outsized emotions (obsession, irrepressible desire, unbearable self-sacrifice). (*Cats* lacks a dramatic narrative, but it otherwise epitomizes the megamusical.) Lofty themes such as freedom, suffering, redemption, and altruism help to make megamusicals easily readily relatable, translatable, and transferable across geographic, linguistic, and cultural borders.

Befitting the term "megamusical," the music, sets, costumes, marketing campaigns, merchandizing, reception history, and hype associated with the genre reach mega-proportions. John Napier, the designer of *Cats, Starlight Express, Les Misérables,* and *Sunset Boulevard*, established visual hugeness as a requisite of the megamusical. Indeed, megamusicals have relied on lavish, complex, computerized, and automated scenery. The plummeting chandelier in *The Phantom of the Opera* and the three-dimensional helicopter that touched down on stage at the end of *Miss Saigon* (Broadway, 1991) epitomize the spectacle that one has come to expect from megamusicals. Critics of megamusicals take issue with the fact that they favor spectacle over substance. As Clive Barnes quipped, "you come out humming the scenery."

Most megamusicals feature through-sung scores alternating between formal closed numbers and transitional dialogical passages (recitative, for a lack of a better term). A commercial pop-rock style is typical, but some works feature an eclectic mix of traditional musical theater, music hall, operetta, and any number of popular musical styles. Several of Lloyd Webber's scores also contain pastiches of one kind or another. Moreover, megamusical composers reach across the divide between musical theater and opera, borrowing the latter's grand sense of lyricism, emotional intensity, and penchant for histrionics. The epic stories; passionate, often zealous, characters; and universal themes of megamusicals demand emotional ballads that build in intensity as they rise in pitch and volume; marches that recall the opulent tableaux of nineteenth-century grand opera; and uplifting choral anthems. Megamusicals call for both "legitimate" vocalization and belting, depending on the character. During the anthems, the chorus can reach a degree of intensity and volume unheard in early musicals. An overly amplified sound manipulated by the sound engineer has robbed the megamusical of a sense of musical spontaneity and subtlety. The unintended result is that the ubiquitous pop-dominated, rock-inflected, over-engineered sound of megamusicals has become the international hallmark of the "new" Broadway.

Tim Rice, Andrew Lloyd Webber's first and most eminent collaborator, had as much to do with fostering the megamusical as anyone else. It was Rice's idea to exclude spoken dialogue. Starting with *Joseph and the Amazing Technicolor Dreamcoat*, Rice simply conceded that the continuous through-sung approach was preferable to trying to compete with the music, which, he believed, inherently dominates over the text. Rice's approach suited Lloyd Webber, who desired artistic control over his shows. The composer remarked, "if you have any dialogue, no matter how brilliant, that interrupts the flow, it means the composer is not in the driver's seat." Today, Rice's artistic posture seems like a self-fulfilling prophecy, as he and other megamusical lyricists stand in the shadow of the composers. They rarely earn the critics' approbation, in part because they seldom move beyond the generalities of pop songs to the specificity of memorable musical theater lyrics. Their lyrics rarely if ever match the poetic subtlety of Hammerstein, the effortless colloquialism of Loesser, the naughty fun of Porter, or the sheer technical brilliance and intellectual

RECITATIVE

Recitative, invented for opera around 1600, can be thought of as sung speech in that, in its simplest form, the vocal line is primarily syllabic, and the rhythms follow the natural pattern of the text. Many recitatives composed in the early seventeenth century approach the expressivity and lyricism of formal arias, but after 1650 composers began to distinguish more concretely between recitatives and arias. Eighteenth-century opera composers relied on melodic and harmonic formulas, and avoided melismas and vocal ornaments, reserving the most expressive and lyrical music for the arias. Before the megamusical, recitative was rare in musical theater, limited to so-called Broadway operas such as *Porgy and Bess* (1935) and *Street Scene* (1947). Frank Loesser gave the gangsters in *Guys and Dolls* recitative to sing, a fitting musical parallel to the arched speech that Damon Runyon devised for his lowbrow characters (see Chapter 8).

depth of Sondheim. Further, monosyllabic rhymes and generic sentiments abound, which helps to ensure the secondary importance of their lyrics. It should be noted, however, that the prosaic quality of their lyrics is an intended goal, for they lose little in translation.

Producers of early megamusicals challenged traditional methods of doing business and established new marketing paradigms. They ultimately decentralized musical theater and helped to transform the genre into a global industry. They developed strategies to build advance ticket sales to the point of neutralizing negative reviews. Some productions have enjoyed runs in New York and London of which earlier writers could only have dreamed. The staggering profits from these behemoths have generated further interest in them and in the merchandise connected to them (coffee mugs, shirts, snow globes, coasters, and refrigerator magnets, for instance). Indeed, the megamusical ushered in a period of corporate franchising.

The Mega Producer

The British producer Cameron Mackintosh (b. 1946) (*Cats, Les Misérables, The Phantom of the Opera, Miss Saigon*) deserves much of the credit for putting the "mega" into megamusical. Borrowing marketing techniques from other industries, Mackintosh branded his productions with a distinct, easily recognizable logo. In the sixties and seventies, Broadway marquees and posters spelled out titles of musicals with a distinct font and bold color scheme—*Zorbá, 1776, Company, A Chorus Line, Chicago*—but Mackintosh imprinted the titles of his musicals on the collective consciousness of theatergoers and non-theatergoers alike with a simple wordless image that became an internationally recognized icon for the show. These logos were ubiquitous, appearing on buses, taxicabs, and billboards, in train stations and other public gathering grounds, and on a vast array of merchandise. Songs from megamusicals often received radio airtime prior to the opening of the show, creating, along with the logo, a sense of inevitability of the show's success: "Don't Cry for Me, Argentina" (*Evita*), "Memory" (*Cats*), and "Do You Hear the People Sing" (*Les Misérables*). In addition, Mackintosh saturated the airwaves and printed advertising media with commercial slogans: *Cats* had "now and forever" and *Les Misérables* "the world's most popular musical."

> Pastiche refers to music, art, or a literary work created in the style of a specific historical period or of a certain composer, artist, or writer. Stephen Sondheim's *Follies* is a veritable feast of pastiche songs associated with the early decades of Broadway.

The Growing Gap Between Critics and Audiences

One of the great ironies surrounding the megamusical's phenomenal success is that American critics have been unwaveringly negative in their appraisal of the genre, often exhibiting a degree of animosity and hostility that borders on bigotry and xenophobia, much of it leveled directly at Andrew Lloyd Webber. They have accused Lloyd Webber of plagiarism and excoriated his work in vitriolic tones. The critical reception of the composer in England has been less negative, although Lloyd Webber's life has often served as grist for the tabloid mill. Olaf Jubin, who has studied the international reception of Lloyd Webber, suggests that American critics "bear some sort of grudge against him, presumably because of his international success in an art form they consider to be predominantly (or even totally) American." If Lloyd Webber has not deliberately courted media attention, he has certainly basked in it, and he has taken pleasure from the knowledge that his shows have proven to be critic-proof at the box office. Only the most critically acclaimed musicals in the past, such as *My Fair Lady*, achieved a level of cultural saturation comparable to that of megamusicals. Moreover, successful megamusicals run for decades and generate profits in the billions.

FROM ROCK OPERA TO MEGAMUSICAL

The term "rock opera" came into existence around the time of The Who's *Tommy* (1969), a concept album conceived around characters and a linear narrative. Influenced by the Beatles' *Sgt. Pepper's Lonely Hearts Club Band* (1967), *Tommy* told a story through a series of songs, but it otherwise had nothing in common with traditional opera. In fact, *Tommy* was never intended for the stage, but in 1975 a film version of *Tommy* directed by Ken Russell was released, and in 1992 a live stage version directed by Des McAnuff opened on Broadway. The original recording of *Tommy* self-identified as a "rock opera," and similarly conceived albums followed suit.

The vocal numbers in *Tommy* serve one of three dramatic functions, as David Nicholls has identified. Kinetic songs progress the story, similar to traditional musical theater songs. Static songs suspend time while allowing characters to reflect on the action. Both types of songs fill the same purpose as operatic arias and traditional musical theater songs. The third type of song entails the performance by an anonymous, sometimes narrative, voice. Recitative passages, which are ubiquitous in megamusicals, are rare in the earliest rock operas.

When *Tommy* first appeared, critics failed to fully comprehend the artistic and sociological implications of the "rock opera" label. They objected to the adoption of the "rock opera" label for works such as *Tommy* and harped on the inherent contradictions of the term. Rock thrives on spontaneity and the heat of the moment, something inimical to opera composition. In reviewing the 1977 concept album *Evita*, which bore the rock opera label, music critic John Rockwell wrote, "if this is a rock opera, it is likely to offend real rock fans," who harbor a "residual prejudice against the high-society connotations of the word 'opera.'" However, even more central to the problem, he noted, "is that rock at its best is a pure, driving, simple music best suited for the exposition of blunt sentiments." Lloyd Webber, he argues, negates any "real rock impetus" in his attempt to express the "intellectual complexities of Rice's text." On the other hand, *Evita* engendered a similar reaction from opera enthusiasts, who tend to be, according to Rockwell, "too conservative to accept a radical shift in style. And the more sophisticated public will be rightly offended by the simple vulgarities of 'Evita's' [sic] clumsily colloquial text, its confusions of viewpoint . . . and its musical incoherence."

The mad rush to adopt the "rock opera" label represents one of several possibilities: an attempt by composers (and record producers) to bestow a degree of artistic gravitas upon their concept albums; a conscious effort to combine the high-art aspirations of opera and the raw energy and counter-cultural impulse of rock music; or a deliberate attempt to mock the high-art pretensions of the operatic world. Whichever the case, the term quickly outlived its intended usefulness. Starting with Rice and Lloyd Webber's *Jesus Christ Superstar*, works inspired by the first wave of concept rock albums but conceived explicitly as dramatic works for the stage acquired certain distinguishing features that rendered the "rock opera" moniker obsolete. When this occurred, critics began to adopt the term "megamusical" to identify works that emulated the Lloyd Webber–Rice brand of through-sung, pop-rock musical. "Megamusical" has the advantage of avoiding the inherent paradoxes of the term "rock opera" for musicals that are neither opera nor rock.

One need only consider *Jesus Christ Superstar* to understand why the term "rock opera" was insufficient to describe stage works generated by the first wave of rock concept albums, which were mostly sociological critiques aimed at young and working-class people in England. *Jesus Christ Superstar* and the works that it inspired feature dramatic, historic, and epic stories. They did not depend on the identifying sound (and/or physical appearance) of a specific rock band to give them a unique identity.

Lingering confusion regarding the megamusical's rock opera pedigree has given rise to other generic labels—such as pop opera and poperetta—that only serve to further confuse the matter. As these appellations suggest, many critics, especially those with a music history background, have trouble discussing rock opera outside the context of the European operatic tradition. Given their limited cultural understanding of rock opera, they have perpetuated the false notion that works such as *Jesus Christ Superstar* are *de facto* operas simply because they are through-sung. Rockwell expressed this view in his wholly unworkable definition of "rock opera" in *The New Grove Dictionary of Music*:

> An operatic work in which the musical idiom is rock and roll. Such works have little direct connection to the opera as traditionally understood. They do not use operatically trained singers; the sound is amplified; some of the more interesting examples were never intended for live performance.

A narrower definition by the rock scholar Martina Elicker accounts better for the historical and cultural basis for the term: "song cycles in the mold of popular music concept albums." However, her definition has its limitations in that (1) few rock operas that conform to her description have been presented on stage in a full-fledged theatrical production (and those that have been staged existed first as an album) and (2) the live concert performances of rock opera (e.g., *Tommy*) usually featured the composers and performers of the concept album. David Nicholls proposes the term "virtual opera" for such works, arguing that they are a distinct genre in their own right rather than merely a subcategory of either opera or rock. The "ideal performances take place in the minds, and between the ears, of individual listeners." Therein lies the primary distinction between rock opera and megamusical. "Virtual opera" derives its narrative plot from the traditional opera genre and its "organizational module of extended verse and chorus" as well as its instrumental forces from the rock world. For the most part, these works exclude recitative. Nicholls states: "Individual songs frequently mirror no more than the characters' thoughts and emotions." The band members do not individually perform the characters but collectively sing the lyrics and music assigned to each character. Like operas and traditional musicals, rock operas contain static and kinetic songs, but they also incorporate songs performed by an "anonymous narrator." For example, the four members of The Who sing together during most of *Tommy* (more similar to the mode of oratorio than of opera).

ANDREW LLOYD WEBBER

Andrew Lloyd Webber and Tim Rice gained quick notoriety for three musicals that they wrote in the seventies: *Joseph and the Amazing Technicolor Dreamcoat* (West End production in 1973), *Jesus Christ Superstar* (Broadway production in 1971), and *Evita* (concept album in 1976, West End production in 1978). (Prior to *Joseph*, they had written some standalone songs and one unproduced musical, *The Likes of Us*.) As their titles suggest, these works deal with unconventional and rather explosive subject matter and do so in ways that depart from traditional practices. Like the American composer-lyricist Stephen Schwartz (see Chapter 16), Lloyd Webber and Rice brought a rock sensibility to musical theater at a time when the genre was still

Lloyd Webber and Tim Rice's first musical, *The Likes of Us*, is in the style of a Lionel Bart musical (see Chapter 9). It tells the story of the famous Victorian philanthropist Dr. Barnardo.

struggling with how to respond to the rock revolution. (Coincidentally, Schwartz and Lloyd Webber were born within days of each other in March 1948.)

Joseph and the Amazing Technicolor Dreamcoat came about when the choir director at Colet Court (the preparatory school for Saint Paul's School in London) requested a short concert work on a religious theme. In its earliest incarnation, *Joseph* amounted to no more than a twenty-minute "cantata." Andrew's years at Westminster coincided with the emerging British rock scene, which made a profound impact on his compositions. Nowhere is this influence more apparent than in *Joseph*, which features a mélange of eclectic soft-rock tunes and pastiche numbers. The short work premiered without much notice, but Andrew's father arranged for a second performance, which the press covered because the event was promoted as a fundraiser to battle drug addiction. Several concerts of *Joseph* followed, each one containing more music than the previous, and in 1969 Decca Records issued a well-received recording of the work. A third version of *Joseph* appeared at the Edinburgh Festival in 1972, by which time Rice and Lloyd Webber's *Jesus Christ Superstar* had brought the duo considerable fame and fortune. A fourth version of *Joseph* premiered in America at the Brooklyn Academy of Music in 1976. *Joseph* finally reached Broadway in 1982 in what now stands as the "official" version. It has remained popular ever since, particularly in community theater.

Jesus Christ Superstar shook up both the theater and religious communities. Rice drew a parallel between rock's cult of the superstar and the aura surrounding Jesus Christ. Like *Joseph*, *Superstar* also traveled an unusual path, beginning as a single-track recording of the title song, then being expanded to a two-disk concept album, and finally appearing as a full-length stage production. *Jesus Christ Superstar* also showcased Lloyd Webber's ability to work in a diverse range of styles. David Walsh, the author of *Andrew Lloyd Webber: His Life and Works*, calls *Superstar*'s musical idiom "a semiconscious agglutination of rock, show music, and classical influences."

Evita charts the rise and fall of Eva Perón, the infamous Argentine first lady. The show treats her life as a rags-to-riches story, using the metaphor of a rainbow that eventually fades to nothing. Eva's anthem "Don't Cry for Me, Argentina" was released as a single on the MCA label in 1976. A two-disk concept album of *Evita* followed in short order, and soon a stage version was planned. Harold Prince, who was at the height of his powers (see Chapters 9 and 10), signed on to direct the production a few weeks before the release of the album. He toyed with the idea of using three different actresses for the title role, each one representing a single side of Eva, but the writers preferred a single actress. *Evita* premiered at the Prince Edward Theatre in 1978. The score, a mixture of pop, folk, rock, and Latin elements, was eclectic enough to attract traditional theatergoers as well as young audiences. Several critics accused Lloyd Webber and Rice of glamorizing an immoral, self-promoting, power-hungry woman, but audiences clamored for tickets. For the Broadway production, the composer, with the orchestrator Hershy Kay's assistance, toned down the harshest rock elements of the original recording. The Broadway production also favored theater singing over the London production's rock vocal style. The New York

ANDREW LLOYD WEBBER AND TIM RICE

Andrew Lloyd Webber's humble origins contrast starkly with the fabulously wealthy, tabloid-scrutinized life that he has led since the seventies. He grew up in the comfortable middle-class London neighborhood of South Kensington. His father, William Webber, attended the Royal College of Music and later became the director of the London College of Music, where Andrew and his brother, the cellist Julian Lloyd Webber, studied. Andrew's mother, Jean, was a music teacher and social activist.

Andrew and Julian's parents gave them an extensive musical education but encouraged them to determine their own direction in life. Andrew developed a passion for historic architecture and, at the age of seven, declared his intentions of becoming the Chief Inspector of Ancient Monuments in Britain. The same year, he also began composing. In 1960, he attended Westminster, and in 1962 he took the Challenge Scholarship examination to be a Queen's Scholar and won on the basis of an essay on Victorian architecture. Despite having a mediocre academic record at Westminster, Lloyd Webber won an Exhibition Scholarship to Magdalen College in Oxford.

Andrew Lloyd Weber sitting at an antique keyboard around the time of *The Phantom of the Opera*. *Courtesy KB Archives.*

(Continued)

Tim Rice (b. 1944) attended school in Tokyo, Lancing College in England, and the Sorbonne in Paris. He planned to go into law but abandoned his studies in jurisprudence for a job at the music publishing and recording company of EMI. He wanted nothing more than to become a rock star. When he met Lloyd Webber, Rice had never even attended a musical, but he welcomed the opportunity to work with the industrious young composer, who, after six months at Oxford, dropped out and moved back in with his parents. Rice rented a room in the Webber household so that he and Andrew could start collaborating.

critics lavished praise on Hal Price and the actors Patti LuPone, Mandy Patinkin, and Bob Gunton, who starred as Evita, Che, and Peron, respectively, but they were characteristically dismissive of Lloyd Webber and Tim Rice.

The musical *Cats* is based on T. S. Eliot's *Old Possum's Book of Practical Cats* (1939). Most of the lyrics were taken from Eliot's book, but Richard Stilgoe and Trevor Nunn wrote the words for "Jellicle Songs for Jellicle Cats" and "Memories," respectively.

The eighties marked the beginning of a new phase in Lloyd Webber's career. He stopped working exclusively with Tim Rice and wrote what became the two longest-running musicals in Broadway history: *Cats* (1982), which did not require a lyricist, and *The Phantom of the Opera* (1988), which required two. Lloyd Webber also composed *Starlight Express*, whose characters are anthropomorphized trains. Directed by Trevor Nunn, the production featured actors on roller skates who zipped around a labyrinthine set of ramps. *Starlight Express* played for almost two decades in England but only two years on Broadway (1987).

Trying to pigeonhole Lloyd Webber as a rock, theater, or opera composer is to ignore his strongest suit—the ability to combine a sundry array of styles into a commercially popular musical theater score. Many of his scores contain an eclectic, if sometimes uneven, mix of pop-rock ballads, music hall ditties, and popular dance music, especially Latin dances. Pastiches of popular styles ranging from blues to country-western to rock and roll feature large in *Joseph*, *Cats*, and *Starlight Express*. Lloyd Webber's ballads (e.g., "Memory") have a simplicity about them that helps to account for their mass appeal. His well of musical ideas runs deep, but neither counterpoint nor harmonic complexity is his *métier*. His greatest gift lies in melodic invention, but his scores often suffer from a lack of dramatic proportion and seemingly random musical recurrences. Indeed, he often reuses melodies in different dramatic contexts and with different lyrics within the same show. Generally speaking, these recurrences neither function as a literal reprise of a song nor invoke a character, thematic idea, or specific emotion. Like most rock musical composers, Lloyd Webber cares more about the popular appeal of his music than about its sense of authenticity with regard to the historical and geographic settings of his shows. Indeed, in *Joseph* and *Superstar*, rock songs give the biblical stories a contemporary spin and appeal to young audiences. In other Lloyd Webber shows (*Evita*, *The Phantom of the Opera*, and *Sunset Boulevard*), quasi-operatic melodies and popular musical elements combine to produce powerful dramatic musical theater.

The Phantom of the Opera

Background

By the end of the seventies, Lloyd Webber was a trans-Atlantic phenomenon, fabulously wealthy, and a lightning rod for the paparazzi. In 1977, he founded the Really Useful Group Ltd., which gave him a corporate entity with which to control the considerable income generated by his musicals. During this period, Lloyd Webber began to collect expensive wines and Victorian art, especially Pre-Raphaelite canvases. He divorced his first wife, Sarah Hugill, and married Sarah Brightman, dubbed "Sarah II" by the British tabloids. Notwithstanding Lloyd Webber's elevated stature and enormous wealth, in the mid-eighties he still felt that he had something to prove as a composer, and he chose *The Phantom of the Opera* as a means to accomplish this goal.

The Phantom of the Opera epitomizes every feature ascribed to the megamusical. The sweeping plot takes place in the late nineteenth century mostly on the stage and in the dark chambers and underground passageways of the Paris Opera House. The musical's success stems from its ability to draw audiences into the romantic tale and to arouse sympathy for the broadly drawn characters. There is little subtle characterization or humor to get in the way of the Gothic narrative, although the opera pastiches and diva-like demeanor of the opera singers invite an occasional chuckle.

In London, *Phantom* was an immediate hit. Cameron Mackintosh pulled out all of the stops. The setting inspired an ornate set design and period costumes from Maria Björnson. The show's logo, the half-mask worn by the Phantom, did as much to sell tickets and make *Phantom* an easily recognizable commodity as the pair of feline eyes had done for *Cats*. Two songs from *Phantom* became popular hits even before rehearsals began. Advance ticket sales generated hype, which translated into further ticket sales. The press fixated on any and all gossip involving the show. In New York, audience demand for tickets overshadowed the negative reviews. *Phantom* is a timeless piece of middlebrow culture that opened on Broadway at the height of the Reagan–Thatcher era and is still playing to sold-out houses.

Cameron Mackintosh navigated *Phantom* through every storm, even while overseeing the production of *Les Misérables*. There was some question as to who would direct the show. Trevor Nunn, who helped to make *Cats* an international hit, expected to be handed the job. Lloyd Webber, however, wanted Harold Prince, who was hesitant at first but eventually warmed to the idea of a romantic musical. Tim Rice, whom Lloyd Webber considered for the lyrics, was occupied with *Chess*. Alan Jay Lerner, the revered lyricist of *My Fair Lady* and *Camelot* (see Chapter 7), agreed to write the lyrics, but health problems forced him to withdraw from the project, at which point Richard Stilgoe (b. 1943), the lyricist of *Starlight Express*, came onboard. Stilgoe's strengths lay in plot development, so Lloyd Webber also engaged a twenty-four-year-old Charles Hart to write lyrics for the romantic songs of the show.

Michael Crawford as the Phantom and Sarah Brightman as Christine Daaé in *The Phantom of the Opera. Courtesy Photofest.*

Lloyd Webber hoped to accomplish two goals with *Phantom*: to create a vehicle for his wife Sarah Brightman and to write about real human emotion. After all, his previous protagonists (a biblical figure, a power-hungry peasant, an animal, and an inanimate object) were a far cry from the edifying heroes and heroines of traditional musical theater. However, whether the son of God, a deeply flawed human, a cat, or a train, all of them share something with the Phantom in that they "search for immortality, deliverance and redemption from some real, imagined or self-imposed darkness," according to Paul Prece and William Everett. Lloyd Webber emphasized the beauty-and-the-beast element of the story, even though the kiss at the end does not produce any transformative magic. His emphasis on the novel's romantic element was a departure from earlier Hollywood incarnations of *The Phantom of the Opera*, especially the famous 1924 silent film starring Lon Chaney, which turned the tale into a horror story.

Lloyd Webber relied more on Gaston Leroux's novel (*Le Fantôme de l'opéra*), which takes the form of a journalistic report that documents a ghost sighting at the famous Paris Opera House. The fictional account lacks the supernatural element that had become associated with the story; in fact, the novel provides logical explanations for the various incidents ascribed to the ghost. The "phantom" is a mysterious man named Erik, who served the Shah of Samarkand and became entangled in a political assassination. Instead of adopting Leroux's literary device, Lloyd Webber framed the story as a flashback seen through the eyes of no one in particular. The opening scene, set in 1911, takes place at an auction of artifacts from the opera house.

THE MANY LIVES OF THE PHANTOM

Lloyd Webber's was one of three musical adaptations of *The Phantom of the Opera* in the eighties. Only fate, timing, and Lloyd Webber's clout ensured that his version reached Broadway before either of the other two could (neither one ever did).

A 1984 version of *Phantom* by Ken Hill employed the music of several opera composers, such as Verdi, Gounod, and Offenbach. (It was Hill's second adaptation; the first, written in 1976, used original music by Ian Armi.) Lloyd Webber's interest in the story was sparked by Hill's version, which he only saw because his soon-to-be second wife, Sarah Brightman, received an offer to play Christine Daaé, although she was unavailable at the time. Lloyd Webber together with Cameron Mackintosh approached Hill about collaborating on a West End production. They envisioned a piece of high camp in the vein of *The Rocky Horror Picture Show* (1973). The collaboration failed to materialize, but soon Lloyd Webber came across an English translation of Gaston Leroux's 1911 novel, which further fanned his interest in the Phantom's story. It was at this point that he began writing his own version. He planned on using real opera quotes as Hill had done and string them together with original music, but in the end he opted to write an entirely original score. Meanwhile, the African American director Geoffrey Holder (1930–2014), who had secured the American rights to the novel in 1983, was also at work on a musical adaptation with the composer Maury Yeston and playwright Arthur Kopit. However, in 1986, the American rights entered the public domain, thereby making it possible for Lloyd Webber to rush his version onto Broadway. After Lloyd Webber's *Phantom* became a hit in London, any momentum behind Yeston and Kopit's version slowed to a standstill.

However, the flashback device is no more than a pathway into the past, and the action never returns to the starting point. When the theater's chandelier arrives on the auction block, the audience is transported back to 1881, a time when the embers of Romanticism were still smoldering and gory plots were all the rage. On the other hand, Lloyd Webber opted for a more mysterious ending than the novel, in which Erik allegedly dies from heartbreak. In the musical, after freeing the imprisoned Raoul and releasing Christine from her promise to remain with him, the Phantom simply vanishes (only to reappear in the 2010 sequel to the musical, described below).

Score

Lloyd Webber's score for *Phantom* features several lyrical ballads with soaring melodies, large-scale choral scenes, and three "imaginary operas" (*Hannibal*, by a fictional French composer named Chalumeau; *Il muto*, by a fictional Italian composer named Albrizzio; and the Phantom's *Don Juan Triumphant*). These "operas" are inspired pastiches, the first in the style of French Grand Opera (e.g., Giacomo Meyerbeer's *Les Huguenots*), the second Italian opera buffa (e.g., Gioachino Rossini's *Il barbiere di Siviglia*), and the third Mozart's *Don Giovanni*. By contrast, the melodramatic title song stands out for its driving hard-rock style and descending and ascending parallel chromatic minor chords played on what was intended to evoke the massive theater organs used during the days of silent films. Although an effective song, especially as brilliantly staged by Prince, "The Phantom of the Opera" invited two lawsuits against Lloyd Webber, who had to defend himself in court against charges of plagiarism.

The romantic ballads from *The Phantom of the Opera* incorporate many of the same features found in many of Lloyd Webber's earlier songs: a wide vocal range, large leaps that carry the voice into a high tessitura followed by a descent by step or jump to a vocal region close to the tonic, substitute harmonies borrowed from the rock genre, metrical shifts shortly before the concluding cadence, and sumptuous orchestrations.

Lloyd Webber musically links Christine, the Phantom, and the Vicomte de Chagny (Raoul), who make up the plot's love triangle. "Think of Me" marks Christine's entrance into the story and reveals her vocal talents. Imbedded into the opening theme is a three-measure descent from F-sharp to D (Example 11.1). The three structural pitches—F-sharp, E, and D—are supported by a I-V-IV harmonic progression over a D pedal. An octave leap prepares a half-cadence on A. The bass does not move until the ninth measure of the song (the beginning of the B phrase), at which point a more animated melody in the submediant region takes over. A meter change to 12/8 occurs in the measure immediately before the first full cadence.

The Phantom's first song, "The Music of the Night," incorporates the same structural underpinnings as the opening measures of Christine's "Think of Me. (Example 11.2)" The song is in D-flat major, which Lloyd Webber considers to be the key of "resonance." The $\hat{3}$-$\hat{2}$-$\hat{1}$ descent, however, occurs in half the time as in "Think of Me." The second measure begins with an ascending scale followed by a leap to A-flat. The animated melody consists of eighth notes and quarter notes, but the basic structural pitches mirror those of "Think of Me." The song begins in a low tessitura but ultimately covers a wide vocal range. Starting at m. 5, a gently undulating melody links B-flat and E-flat, which are supported by IV and I⁹, respectively. Like "Memory," "The Music of the Night" has occasioned Lloyd Webber's critics to accuse him of

EXAMPLE 11.1. "Think of Me," first four measures

PLOT OF THE PHANTOM OF THE OPERA

*I*t is 1881. Carlotta, the prima donna of the Paris Opera Populaire, is rehearsing an aria when a backdrop crashes to the stage, causing fear that the Phantom is present. When the diva refuses to go on, the theater's proprietors replace her with a young woman named Christine Daaé, who has been taught how to sing by a mysterious man she knows only as "Angel of Music." Raoul, Vicomte de Chagny, a patron of the opera, attends the performance and recognizes Christine as a playmate from his childhood. When he invites her to dinner, a jealous Phantom leads Christine to his underground realm. She discovers the Phantom's disfigured face beneath his mask.

The Phantom overhears Christine telling Raoul about her visit to his subterranean haunt and is seized by jealousy. A series of disasters besets the opera house.

Six months pass, and Raoul obtains a promise of marriage from Christine. The Phantom has composed an opera and insists that it be produced with Christine in the lead role. During the performance, the Phantom steals away to his lair with Christine. Raoul arrives and is ensnared by the Phantom. The Phantom will free Raoul only if Christine agrees to remain with him. When she shows him kindness and proffers a kiss, the Phantom releases them both. A mob storms the lair only to find that the Phantom has vanished.

musical grave robbing. This passage constitutes a conspicuous "Puccinism," a term coined by the critic Frank Rich to describe Lloyd Webber's alleged borrowings from Puccini. The melodic and harmonic scaffolding derives from Puccini's "Quello che tacete" from *Fanciulla del West* (*The Girl of the Golden West*) (1910) (which prompted another lawsuit against the composer). The condemnation notwithstanding, the artless beauty of "The Music of the Night" and its slowly rising melody enraptures Christine as well as the audience. The second section begins in the bright key of E major. The song ends unexpectedly in the mediant key of F major, suggesting a positive change in Christine's perception of the mysterious Phantom.

Raoul's "All I Ask of You" shares features with "Think of Me" and "The Music of the Night," although the opening measures involve less harmonic movement than Christine's or the Phantom's opening theme. The song begins with an accented upper neighbor tone sounding a ninth above the bass (Example 11.3). This non-chord tone recalls the second measure of "Think of Me" and the third beat of "Music of the Night." The descending leap from F to A-flat on the third beat echoes the first two beats of "Music of the Night." The theme unfolds over a D-flat pedal point until m. 4, which begins on a ♭VII harmony (a common rock chord). The second phrase of "Music of the Night" (the one reminiscent of Puccini) contains the same chord, albeit with a different resolution. The bass slides up a half

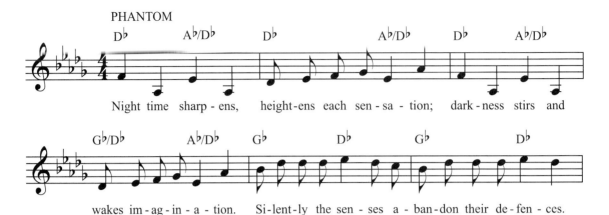

EXAMPLE 11.2. "The Music of the Night," first six measures

EXAMPLE 11.3. "All I Ask of You," first four measures

step, thus paving the way for a smooth transition back to the beginning of the theme. The B section leans toward the subdominant and features a tonic added-ninth chord. It begins with the same note as the opening theme but transferred up an octave and occupying two-and-a-half beats. The resolution to D-flat occurs not by half-step but by a leap of a major ninth. This and a leap of a major seventh in the next measure recall the Phantom's first notes in "The Music of the Night."

Reception

One cannot fully appreciate the sustained popularity and global reach of *Phantom* without taking into account its pre-opening hype and post-opening press coverage, not to mention the gossip, scandal, and intrigue surrounding the show. By the mid-eighties, everything that Lloyd Webber did on and off stage was fodder for the press. That he was purportedly writing *Phantom* for his wife ("Sarah II") only helped to fuel the media circus. On the other hand, the buzz spurred ticket sales well before *Phantom* opened at Her Majesty's Theatre in London in 1986. The cast recording, released a few months later, went platinum in only ten days.

Reviews of the London production were decidedly mixed. Many critics lauded Lloyd Webber's score as his best and most sophisticated work up to that point, but several accused him of selling out and avoiding music capable of expressing the story's grotesqueness. The English reviews were positively glowing compared to the assessment of Lloyd Webber's score by American critics two years later. Reviews of the Broadway production dismissed the composer's work outright: catchy pop tunes that shine little light on the characters, generic lyrics, too many senseless reprises, pastiche, and recycled Puccini. The New York critics barely disguised their contempt for the composer, even stooping to name-calling. Michael Feingold of the *Village Voice* referred to him as "a secondhand music peddler, whose pathetic aural imagination was outpaced years ago by his apparently exhaustive memory." He accused the composer of blatant plagiarism, although he provided no specific examples to support his claim. Frank Rich conceded that some of the songs were "lovely" but that the score is so "generic that most of the songs could be reordered and redistributed among the characters (indeed, among other Lloyd Webber musicals) without altering the show's story or meaning." John Simon, the obstreperous theater critic of *New York Magazine,* noted Lloyd Webber's desire to be taken seriously as a composer, only to rob him of the acknowledgment that he had achieved it. Not every American critic was out for blood. Coming to his defense, Liz Smith acknowledged that Lloyd Webber bashing was "fashionable" (in a review of a mere 300 words). Jack Kroll's review for *Newsweek* noted, "Lloyd Webber provides the most seductive, romantic score heard on Broadway in a long time." Clive Barnes called the show "Phantastic!"

Despite the mixed reception on both sides of the Atlantic, Mackintosh remained sanguine about the show's future. He had little reason to worry about the London production given the million pounds' advance from ticket sales. That the musical won the Laurence Olivier Award (England's equivalent of the Tony Award) for best new musical further boosted the producer's optimism. The London advance, though, was a mere pittance compared to the $16 million from pre-sales for the Broadway production. When the time came to bring *Phantom* to America, the decision was made to feature the three leads from the London cast, only one of whom, Steve Barton, was American. Both Michael Crawford and Sarah Brightman required special dispensation from the American Council of the Actors' Equity Association (see Chapter 3). Crawford received quick approval, but the petition for Brightman was rejected. Prince and Lloyd Webber challenged the ruling, and the composer threatened to cancel the New York production, which would have robbed hundreds of American actors, musicians, and backstage personnel of secure long-term employment. Actors' Equity eventually caved in but stipulated that Brightman could appear for only six months. The scandal, as interpreted by Frank Rich, came down to "ego, marital devotion, xenophobia, [and] labor-management negotiating tactics." It also helped to boost ticket sales.

In the end, even Lloyd Webber's fiercest critics recognized, or were resigned to the fact, that *Phantom* would run for years. The press, admitted Robert

Brustein, had been declawed by a culture that values "scarcity." *Phantom*, he declared, was a "critic-proof event," a "Schlepic . . . not a musical play so much as the theatrical equivalent of a corporate merger." He predicted a sequel—rightly so, it turns out. The producer David Merrick, famous for his publicity stunts, moved the curtain time of his hit *42nd Street*, which was playing directly across the street from *Phantom*, to 8:15 in an effort to attract disappointed ticket buyers unable to score *Phantom* tickets. His ad campaign billed *42nd Street* as "Broadway's l-a-t-e-s-t hit."

Phantom lives on and on. In early 2006, it surpassed *Cats* as the longest-running musical in Broadway history. To break *Phantom*'s record, a new musical today would have to run well beyond 2040, and *Phantom* would have to close immediately. On the other hand, not every production of *The Phantom of the Opera* has met with the same success of the original stage version. An abridged, intermission-less version opened in Las Vegas in 2006. The owner of the Venetian Hotel and Casino built a theater for the express purpose of housing the show, betting that it would become a permanent fixture, but the show closed in 2012. Joel Schumacher's 2004 film version of *Phantom* did abysmally. Film critics were just as dismissive about Lloyd Webber's music as their theater counterparts had been. A. O. Scott felt that the film medium negatively magnified Lloyd Webber's brand of musical theater: "This kind of spectacle might work onstage, where numb enervation can sometimes be mistaken for exhilaration, but this screen version, for all its wailing emotionalism and elaborate production design, lacks both authentic romance and the thrill of memorable spectacle." Lloyd Webber's music, he added, "afflicts this movie like a bad case of swollen lymph nodes."

Lloyd Webber began work on the sequel, *Love Never Dies*, in the early nineties, but the show did not open until 2010. Predictably, it too suffered great indignities at the hands of the press, although there are still rumblings about a future Broadway production. The hype built steadily, as Lloyd Webber planned to open three productions of the work simultaneously, in London, Toronto, and Shanghai, with a Broadway production to follow. In the sequel, the Phantom has taken up residence in Coney Island (where he has founded a venue called Phantasma), of all places. Christine, who is now married to Raoul, receives an invitation to perform in New York, so the couple and their son, Gustave, journey to America. One evening, when Raoul is out drinking, the Phantom pays Christine a visit and insists that she perform for him, threatening that she might otherwise lose Gustave (who is actually the Phantom's son). Raoul prepares to return to Paris without Christine. Meg, Christine's friend from the Paris Opera, abducts Gustave with the intention of drowning him. When caught and confronted, she accidentally shoots Christine, who, before she dies, reveals to Gustave who his real father is.

Ben Brantley flew to London to see the show and wrote one of his snarkiest reviews:

> To think that all this time that poor old half-faced composer hasn't been dead at all, just stewing in his lust for greater glory. Being the title character of "The Phantom of the Opera," the most successful musical of all time,

wasn't enough for him. Oh, no. Like so many aging stars, he was determined to return—with different material and a rejuvenated body—to the
scene of his first triumph. . . . And he might as well have a "kick me" sign
pasted to his backside.

The blogosphere exploded with negative comments about the show as well as
tacky puns (e.g., *Paint Never Dries*). This time, the Lloyd Webber musical could not
overcome the critical thrashing, and it closed in less than eighteen months. After
the London debacle, Lloyd Webber canceled the planned Broadway production.
A subsequent production in 2011 at the Regent Theatre in Melbourne, Australia,
was received favorably. Lloyd Webber fans can view the sequel on a DVD of the
Australian production.

Lloyd Webber next adapted the MGM movie *The Wizard of Oz* (2011) for the
stage. He reunited with Tim Rice to write several new songs to add to Harold Arlen
and E. Y. Harburg's beloved score. A reality television talent show titled *Over the
Rainbow* was launched for the sole purpose of casting the role of Dorothy for the
2011 British production, which had a short run. After the show closed in London, a
similar contest was held on Canada's CBC TV that launched a production in Toronto.
It ran from 2012–13, followed by a North American tour. However, the show created little buzz in the press, an anomaly for Lloyd Webber.

Lloyd Webber wrote the music for *Stephen Ward: The Musical* 2013; book and
lyrics by Don Black and Christopher Hampton), based on the political sex scandal
known as the Profumo Affair, which brought about the resignation of the British Secretary of State for War in 1963. His most recent musical, based on the popular Jack
Black film *School of Rock* (2003), is scheduled to premiere on Broadway in late 2015.

AMERICAN MUSICALS IN THE EIGHTIES

The extraordinary success of *Cats*, *Les Misérables*, and *The Phantom of the Opera*
overshadowed most homegrown musical theater during the eighties. With a few
exceptions, notably *Sunday in the Park with George*, American musicals reflected
reactionary thinking, a bankruptcy of original ideas, and the aversion of American
producers to bankrolling risky projects and unproven writers. The inability of
American musicals to compete against the British megamusical imports portended
a continued decline of the genre, but a few rays of hope broke through the dark
cloud looming over the New York musical theater establishment.

Notable Works

Dreamgirls

New voices to emerge in the eighties included Henry Krieger and Murray Yeston.
Kreiger's *Dreamgirls* will forever be remembered as a Michael Bennett musical,
but it was the brainchild of Krieger and Tom Eyen. Krieger, a white composer,
gravitates toward contemporary black musical idioms. *Dreamgirls*, a musical about
race politics in the music industry, centers on an African American female vocal
trio called "The Dreams." Their meteoric rise from the ghetto to the national stage

causes pain and heartbreak. Bennett employed computer-controlled moving light towers to give the show a cinematic kineticism with simulated crosscuts. The writers adopted the megamusical's use of sung dialogue (little of which made it onto the Broadway cast album or into the 2006 film version) in alternation with formal set pieces (songs). *Dreamgirls* received thirteen Tony Award nominations and won six awards. The song "And I Am Telling You I'm Not Going" counts among the few musical theater crossover hits since the sixties.

Nine

Nine, based on Federico Fellini's 1963 film *8½*, is about a famous Italian movie director suffering a personal and artistic midlife crisis. The composer and lyricist of *Nine*, Murray Yeston, conceived it as an exploration of the important roles that women play in men's lives (mother, lover, wife, whore, muse). Yeston majored in music at Yale University, received a master's degree from Cambridge University, and returned to Yale to pursue a Ph.D. in musicology. His musical erudition is evident throughout the score for *Nine*, which includes a Mozart pastiche, poignant ballads, and a sultry seduvction number. Raul Julia (1940–1994) starred as Guido Contini and won a Tony Award for his performance, one of five that the show garnered. *Nine* also marked a major triumph for the director-choreographer Tommy Tune. Rob Marshall's 2009 film version of *Nine* reduced Yeston's score to a fraction of its former self. At the end of the eighties, Yeston and Tune reunited for *Grand Hotel*, a work begun in 1958 by Robert Wright and George Forrest (see Chapter 8). Their efforts resulted in a run of over 1,000 performances and five Tony Awards.

Big River

Big River: The Adventures of Huckleberry Finn was the big story of the 1984–1985 theatrical season. The combination of Mark Twain's controversial novel, adapted for the stage by William Hauptman, and an appealing country-western score by Roger Miller (1936–1992) drew several good reviews. Miller's previous musical theater experience had amounted to composing and performing the songs for the 1974 Disney film *Robin Hood*, but the producer of *Big River*, Rocco Landesman (who later served as director of the National Endowment of the Arts during the first Obama administration), felt that Miller's background would serve the story. Indeed, Miller, who was born in Texas and raised in Oklahoma, gave the score a rare sense of authenticity by incorporating folk idioms, such as the blues and spirituals.

Musicals Produced by the Public Theater

Joseph Papp's Off Broadway Public Theater remained a dynamic force in musical theater production during the eighties, beginning with a zany postmodern production of Gilbert and Sullivan's *Pirates of Penzance* at Central Park's Delacorte Theater (1980), which the Public operates. Wilford Leach, directing a cast that included the irrepressible Kevin Kline, the inimitable British comic actors George Rose and Patricia Routledge, and rock stars Linda Ronstadt and Rex Smith, brought a circus-like athleticism and postmodern self-referentiality to the Victorian satire about British duty to the Crown. The production transferred to a Broadway theater, where it played 787 performances. In 1984, the Public Theater produced a musical based on William Saroyan's *The Human Comedy*, with lyrics and book by William Dumareq and music by Galt MacDermot, the composer of *Hair* (see Chapter 16). MacDermot lived up to his reputation for eclecticism. He wanted the score "to be like the kind of music a family plays at home." The cast functioned like a Greek chorus, "observing each other the way people do in a small town." After a successful run at the Public Theater, *The Human Comedy* transferred uptown, but the redemptive story was not well served by the larger Broadway venue.

In 1985, another Public Theater summer offering at the Delacorte Theater became a major Broadway hit. *The Mystery of Edwin Drood* (today titled simply *Drood*), based on Charles Dickens's unfinished novel *The Mystery of Edwin Drood* (published in 1870), was the brainchild of Rupert Holmes (b. 1947), who provided the book, music, lyrics, and even orchestrations. The versatile Holmes had begun his career in the pop music business, producing several albums for Barbra Streisand and composing hit songs such as "Escape (The Piña Colada Song)" (1979). Holmes cast Dickens's mystery story in the form of a British music hall entertainment, which gave it a more lighthearted tone and style than a straightforward adaptation of the bleak novel would have done. He devised a clever way to conclude the story, which Dickens left in limbo: he created several different endings, and during a break in the action toward the end of each performance, the audience voted for the version to be performed. Critical reception was so positive that *Drood* transferred to Broadway for an open-ended run and won five Tony Awards (two for Holmes).

FAMILIAR VOICES

A combination of Jerry Herman, Tommy Tune, and the Marx Brothers was behind a quirky musical called *A Day in Hollywood/A Night in the Ukraine*. The show originated in England, without the participation of Herman or Tune, who joined the project for an expanded Broadway version. Act I—the Hollywood part—was a revue spoofing old Hollywood movie musicals. New songs by Herman were combined with pre-existing songs by Harold Arlen and E. Y. Harburg, Cole Porter, and Frank Loesser. Act II—the Ukraine part—was an adaptation of Anton Chekhov's comedy *The Bear* as performed by the "Marx Brothers" (the real Marx Brothers successfully sued the production for copyright infringement).

Kander and Ebb's *Woman of the Year* won the 1981 Tony Award for best musical. Lauren Bacall and Harry Gardino starred in this musical adaptation of the Katharine Hepburn–Spencer Tracy battle-of-the-sexes film (1942). Peter Stone's book updated the story to the present but did little to recognize the impact of the National Organization for Women and its feminist agenda. His heroine, a tiger on the outside, was a nonthreatening feminist on the inside, reflecting some of the reactionary social politics of the early Reagan era. *Woman of the Year*, Kander and Ebb's least edgy and least audacious musical, did well in part because Lauren Bacall played Tess Harding (after she left the show Raquel Welch took over the role, and after her Debbie Reynolds).

Cy Coleman began and ended the decade with a hit. *Barnum* (1980) traces Phineas Taylor Barnum's journey from small-business owner to the presenter of the

"Greatest Show on Earth," as he called his circus. Jim Dale received a Tony Award for his portrayal of the plucky Barnum, and Glenn Close brought intelligence and warmth to his wife, Charity. Joe Layton, who directed the show, worked effectively with a minimal set and a small, multitalented ensemble of actors to simulate the controlled chaos of a three-ring circus, and Cy Coleman wrote a bouncy and eclectic score (lyrics by Michael Stewart) without ever sounding derivative. *City of Angels* (1989) provided Coleman another opportunity to draw on his jazz background. Larry Gelbart's book contains two parallel stories—one about a Hollywood writer, the other about the characters in his detective novel, which he hopes to sell to a movie studio. Because *City of Angels* blends the world of Raymond Chandler and the film noir genre, the designers used strong colors for the scenes with "real" characters and black and white for the scenes with "fictional" ones.

INTERESTING FLOPS

Carrie

In 1992, Ken Mandelbaum published a book entitled *Not Since Carrie: Forty Years of Broadway Musical Flops.* The book's cover bears a photograph of the eponymous lead of the 1988 musical *Carrie* dripping with thick, scarlet-red stage blood. Ever since, *Carrie*, an adaptation of Stephen King's popular literary thriller, has been synonymous with Broadway disaster, fiasco, bomb, or failure. Allegedly, audiences liked *Carrie*, but the show received devastating reviews and closed after seven performances. *Carrie* has since acquired cult status, which eventually emboldened the Off Broadway theater MCC (Manhattan Class Company) to pour $1.5 million into a revival in 2011. This production, however, did little to reverse the original critical consensus about the show.

A Doll's Life and Grind

The Phantom of the Opera helped to revitalize Harold Prince's flagging career after the demise of *Merrily We Roll Along* in 1981 (see Chapter 10). Between *Merrily* and *Phantom*, he directed (and produced) two musicals by the composer Larry Grossman, *A Doll's Life* (1982) and *Grind* (1985). *A Doll's Life* (1982) was an ambitious work and one of Betty Comden and Adolph Green's few attempts at a serious musical. The story, a sequel to Henrik Ibsen's seminal play *A Doll's House* (1879), explores what happens to Nora from the moment she leaves her husband Torvald with the famous door slam heard around the world. Nora learns how to use powerful men, sex, money, and power, but, it is suggested, she eventually returns to her husband. Frank Rich praised Grossman but considered the show a "perplexing curiosity" and Nora "merely a symbol of The Unliberated Female."

Grind explores a serious topic within a seedy show-business milieu, similar to Kander and Ebb's *Cabaret* and *Chicago*. The script, by Fay Kanin, was based on an unproduced screenplay that she had written for Universal Studios. Ellen Fitzhugh wrote the lyrics. Rich noted, "The ironic juxtaposition of the entertainer's escapist act with the racial violence beyond the theater's walls is all heavily didactic—and all too familiar." A top-notch cast was headed by Ben Vereen and Stubby Kay, the original Nicely-Nicely Johnson in *Guys and Dolls*. Leilani Jones played a stripper named Satin and earned a Tony Award.

A *Doll's Life* and *Grind* anticipated the excess of the megamusical: elaborate and expensive sets and costumes, big scores with blaring anthems, and noble ideas. Although Grossman escaped direct blame for the failure of these shows (Prince received the lion's share of it), the closing of *Grind* spelled an end to his Broadway career. *Minnie's Boys* (1970), the first of two musicals that Grossman wrote in the seventies, is about the relationship between the Marx Brothers and their mother, played by Shelley Winters. *Goodtime Charley* (1975) offers a humorous interpretation of events involving the Dauphin of France and Joan of Arc, played by Joel Grey and Ann Reinking. Both shows have lyrics by Hal Hackady. Grossman's four Broadway musicals combined played a total of 188 performances and lost millions of dollars. He found more success as a composer for *The Muppet Show*. Grossman's Off Broadway musical *Snoopy! The Musical*, which premiered in San Francisco in 1975, has remained popular in regional and amateur theater.

REVIVALS AND RETROSPECTIVES

The revival craze that caught fire in the seventies raged throughout the eighties. The number of revivals during the decade topped twenty-five. Yul Brynner returned to Broadway with *The King and I* (see Chapter 17). It was the final leg of a long national tour that culminated with Brynner's 4,625th and final performance as the King. In 1980, Richard Burton reprised his role as Arthur in a revival of *Camelot* at Lincoln Center's oversized (2,779 seat) New York State Theater (today called the David H. Koch Theater). Lerner streamlined his original script and used a flashback framing device to tell the story. A year later, another revival of *Camelot* (essentially the same version) opened at the Winter Garden Theatre, this one starring Richard Harris, the Arthur of the poorly received 1967 movie of *Camelot*. Whereas Burton, twenty years older than he was when he originated the role of Arthur, brought a new sense of authority to the King, Harris turned in a more dour, humorless, passionless performance, "at odds with the very essence of the show's appeal," according to Frank Rich.

David Merrick's production of *42nd Street*, directed and choreographed by Gower Champion, reimagined the 1933 Busby Berkeley movie classic for a nostalgia-crazed eighties audience. Champion died on the day of opening night. In what many perceived as the latest example of Merrick's brazen opportunism and heartlessness, the producer withheld the news of Champion's death until after the thunderous ovation at the end of the show that evening, infamously appearing center stage and announcing the news to both the audience and cast. A media circus ensued, as did a monumental run of 3,486 performances. Something about the show-business hero of *42nd Street*, an ailing director struggling to stage a hit at the height of the Depression, and the female ingénue straight out of Scranton, Pennsylvania, who might be "going out a youngster, but [has] got to come back a star!," reverberated with older audiences who had witnessed the devolution of Broadway during the seventies.

The revue format helped to promote the rediscovery of forgotten African American composers (see Chapter 15), a trend begun in the late seventies with *Ain't Misbehavin'*. Two successful retrospectives provided fitting bookends to the decade. *Sophisticated Ladies* (1980) featured an interracial cast and surveyed the illustrious career of Duke Ellington. *Black and Blue* focused on black culture in Paris between the wars. Squeezed between these two hits were several less vibrant entertainments. *Blues in the Night* (1982) had no dialogue but implied a story about three women involved with the same man, a snake charmer. *Uptown . . . It's Hot* (1986), conceived by Maurice Hines (Gregory's brother), attempted to survey black music in America.

THE LEGACY OF THE MEGAMUSICAL

Blondel and *Chess* generated the sort of the hype emblematic of megamusicals but were box-office failures. *Blondel* was Tim Rice's first show without Lloyd Webber. With music by Stephen Oliver and set in the year 1189, the musical is about a court minstrel. The show played in England in 1983 but never reached Broadway. *Chess* was the official reason that Rice gave for not accepting Lloyd Webber's offer to collaborate on *The Phantom of the Opera*. The show has a contemporary love story with lots of geopolitical intrigue involving a rivalry between the Russian and American chess champions, who are in love with the same woman, Florence. Two musicians from the Swedish pop group ABBA composed the music for *Chess*. Michael Bennett signed on to direct but withdrew due to poor health (see chapter 10), after which Trevor Nunn took over. Originally released as a concept album, *Chess* had gained a large American following. The show was considerably revised for the 1988 Broadway production. A tragic ending replaced the uplifting ending typical of megamusicals. Jessica Sternfeld attributes the early demise of the production to the cultural and political malaise of the eighties: "By the end of *Chess*, we are left with a man who has been forced through a series of despicable deceptions to return to a loveless marriage and an oppressive country, and a woman who has lost, within minutes, her true love and the father who turns out not to be her father after all. Most important, both have lost—been betrayed by, and abandoned by—their countries."

Sunset Boulevard, Lloyd Webber's only successful new work in the nineties, incorporated the elements that one had come to expect from his shows, with one notable exception: it contained spoken dialogue, devised by the playwright Christopher Hampton. Don Black wrote the lyrics. John Napier designed large, complex sets, as he had done for *Cats* and *Starlight Express*. In his typical attention-getting antics, Lloyd Webber broke contracts with some of his leading ladies. Patti LuPone played Norma Desmond in the London production and was slated to open the show on Broadway. However, after the American premiere, which took place in Los Angeles and starred Glenn Close, Lloyd Webber decided that she should appear in the Broadway production and broke his contract with LuPone. Crushed and humiliated, LuPone sued and received a settlement of between $1 million and $2 million (see Chapter 17). Faye Dunaway was scheduled to replace Close in the Los Angeles production, but Lloyd Webber closed it down after Close left for New York.

AND BEAR IN MIND

Les Misérables *(Broadway production, 1987, Broadway Theatre, 6,680 performances)*

Music by Claude-Michel Schönberg (b. 1944)
Lyrics by Alain Boublil (b. 1941)
Additional lyrics by Jean-Marc Natel
English adaption by Herbert Kretzmer
Book by Claude-Michel Schönberg, Alain Boublil, Trevor Nunn, and John Caird

*L*es Misérables is the most successful megamusical not by Andrew Lloyd Webber. The original Broadway production of *Les Mis* (or *Miz*), as the show is affectionately called by its fans, ran just over sixteen years (1987–2003). Since it closed, the show has continued to play around the world and returned to Broadway in 2014. A long-awaited film version was released in late 2012.

The show's lyricist, Alain Boublil, and composer, Claude-Michel Schönberg, were both born to Jewish émigrés. Boublil's family emigrated from Egypt to Tunisia, where he spent his early years, and Schönberg emigrated from Hungary. They both went to Paris to study business, but they gravitated toward music. Boublil, who was awestruck by the musical revolution taking place in Paris during the sixties, became versed in contemporary styles. By contrast, Schönberg wanted nothing more than to write opera; however, when he completed his studies, he received an offer to work as a trainee artistic director at the recording company Pathé-Marconi. The writers first met in 1968 and quickly discovered a mutual passion for works such as *West Side Story* and a shared impatience with the short format of popular songs. Boublil, after attending the premiere of *Jesus Christ Superstar* in New York, enlisted Schönberg in a project about the French Revolution, which resulted in the concept album *La Revolution Française* (1973). Before long, they were working on a stage version, which opened the same year. They returned to the subject after Boublil saw Cameron Mackintosh's 1978 revival of *Oliver!* in London.

Although written by two Frenchmen, *Les Misérables* fits the mold of an Andrew Lloyd Webber musical and, as produced by Cameron Mackintosh, has all the trappings of a British megamusical: conceived as a concept album (released in 1980), through-sung score, and direction by Trevor Nunn. Indeed, *Les Misérables* was part of the "British invasion" and helped to solidify the megamusical's hegemony on Broadway. Following the release of the concept album in 1980, the first live stage production opened in Paris. Two years later, Mackintosh decided to produce the show in England.

(Continued)

Marquee of the original Broadway production of *Les Misérables* and a full-building image of the iconic waif logo. *Courtesy Photofest.*

Boublil and Schönberg's musicals appeal to audiences of all ages, nationalities, politics, and artistic tastes. The key to their success, according to Margaret Vermette, has to do with the level of emotional engagement they demand from the audience.

Meanwhile, the advance for the Broadway production reached an all-time record high (over $37 million). Ironically, even though the critics turned in their most levelheaded reviews of a Lloyd Webber musical, the production barely surpassed the two-year mark and failed to recoup its investment.

In 1992, Lloyd Webber was knighted. He is the recipient of seven Tony Awards, seven Olivier Awards, and the 2006 Kennedy Center Honors. The mixture of vitriol, disdain, admiration, and jealousy that Lloyd Webber engenders makes it difficult to arrive at a full and objective assessment of his career and of the megamusical. Paul Prece and William Everett address the matter with an evenhandedness rarely afforded Lloyd Webber:

The megamusical is arguably the most influential musical genre of the late twentieth century. The pioneering shows of the 1980s have a strong progeny—creating breathtaking effects for theatrical audiences has become part of the art of musical theater thanks to the genre's profound influence. . . . [M]egamusicals have given their fans unashamedly romantic, lush and expansive music. . . . The inherent danger, however, is that these powerful blockbusters can easily overshadow other worthy efforts . . . and thus limit the reputations of their creators . . . , individuals . . . whose efforts keep the great legacy of the musical theatre alive and flourishing.

Lloyd Webber's musical style has not evolved much from the early days of his career. The business of musical theater, on the other hand, has virtually reinvented itself, moving much closer to Lloyd Webber's way of doing things. His influence is inestimable and will continue to make an impact on the genre and the business for years to come.

NAMES, TERMS, AND CONCEPTS

"All I Ask of You"

Boublil, Alain

Brightman, Sarah

Cage aux Folles, La

Cats

Dreamgirls

Evita

Grossman, Larry

Holmes, Rupert

Jesus Christ Superstar

Joseph and the Amazing Technicolor Dreamcoat

Krieger, Henry

Leroux, Gaston

Les Misérables

Mackintosh, Cameron

"Memory"

"Music of the Night, The"

Nine

Nunn, Trevor

Rice, Tim

Schönberg, Claude-Michel

Sunday in the Park with George

"Think of Me"

Webber, Andrew Lloyd

Yeston, Murray

DISCUSSION QUESTIONS

1. Identify the musical and dramatic features that distinguish the megamusical from the traditional Broadway book musical.

2. Describe the relationship between Andrew Lloyd Webber and the press.

3. What accounts for the remarkable international success of megamusicals?

CHAPTER 12

THE NINETIES

(*RENT*, 1996, NEDERLANDER THEATRE, 5,123 PERFORMANCES)

The British megamusical's hegemony on Broadway extended well into the nineties. Some American musicals adopted the style and visual spectacle associated with first-wave megamusicals, and American producers borrowed marketing strategies from Cameron Mackintosh's playbook. In addition, several corporate behemoths, both from and beyond the entertainment industry, expanded into Broadway. Disney in particular established a foothold on Broadway, bringing to the stage live versions of its beloved animated films as well as some new musicals. As Broadway came to resemble more and more a corporate industry, the theater district experienced a major rehabilitation under the auspices of Mayor Rudolph Giuliani's Times Square redevelopment project. These changes spelled the end of Broadway as a New York-centric industry. They also helped to drive up ticket costs to levels well beyond the rate of inflation. Producers began to take national and international markets into greater account, which had a numbing effect on the development of new musicals and drove established writers such as Stephen Sondheim to Off Broadway venues and nonprofit theatrical institutions. Off Broadway also provided many young writers their only opportunity to get their work produced.

THE INCREDIBLE STORY OF *RENT*

Puccini on Broadway

Giacomo Puccini's operas *La Bohème* (1896) and *Madama Butterfly* (1904) inspired the two most successful musicals of the nineties, *Rent* and *Miss Saigon*, respectively. *Miss Saigon* (1991), Claude-Michel Schönberg and Alain Boublil's first musical after *Les Misèrables* (see Chapter 11), faithfully followed the formula that had propelled megamusicals to prominence in the eighties. *Rent*, the only major work by the American writer Jonathan Larson, is a threadbare rock musical. Musicals based on opera appeared as early as the forties (those based on operetta go back even further), but the earliest examples merely updated the plots and set new lyrics to the original music. For *Carmen Jones* (1943), Oscar Hammerstein transferred the action of Bizet's opera *Carmen* to World War II America and wrote new lyrics to fit the composer's popular score (see Chapter 15). While *Miss Saigon* and *Rent* also project the original opera plots into a contemporary context, they feature original rock scores.

Jonathan Larson

Jonathan Larson (1960–1996), the creator of *Rent*, was a middle-class Jewish kid from White Plains, New York. In high school, he played in band, sang in choir, and acted in theater productions. He admired singer-songwriters such as Elton John and Billy Joel, but he fell in love with theater and the works of Stephen Sondheim. He majored in acting at Adelphi University, but he also composed musicals. After graduating, Larson moved to New York. It was the early eighties, and he embraced the life of a struggling downtown artist, waiting tables at the Moondance Diner, sharing a grungy apartment in lower Manhattan with a revolving door of room-mates, participating in the ASCAP Musical Theatre Workshop, performing a one-man autobiographical cabaret act, and slowly earning respect from the theater community. Larson wanted to write a musical version of Orwell's *1984* but, like several writers before him, could not obtain the rights, so he devised his own premise for a sci-fi musical. The result, *Superbia*, was, in Larson's words, "my own dystopia. . . . I imagined a futurist, bottom-line oriented society that was much more user friendly than Orwell's, much more like our own Madison Avenue world." Larson presented scenes from *Superbia* at the 1985 ASCAP Musical Theatre Workshop when Stephen Sondheim happened to be appearing on the panel of experts. Larson's work caught the attention of Sondheim, who subsequently encouraged the young composer. *Superbia* garnered a couple of prestigious writing awards for Larson, but the show never received a full-scale production. In 1991, Larson wrote and performed a one-man "rock monologue" called *30/90*, later retitled *Boho Days*. As Larson explained it, the project "was my attempt to come to grips, like others of my generation, with the diminishing opportunities all around us." Years later, long after *Rent* had become a hit, *Boho Days* was turned into a four-person musical titled *tick, tick. . . BOOM!*

The Road to *Rent*

In the early nineties, Larson received a call from Ira Weitzman, who was in charge of musical theater development at the Off Broadway theater Playwrights Horizons. Weitzman felt that Larson's melodic gifts were stronger than his word craft. He therefore introduced him to the playwright. . . . Aronson and Larson wrote three songs, but their collaboration quickly fizzled out. By this time, though, Larson was committed to the project, and so he decided to work on it alone. He saw the show as a vehicle for addressing social issues close to his heart. Larson had witnessed several friends die of AIDS and therefore felt a duty to confront the crisis in his show. By dealing with the disease along with sexual identity, class, and race, he expressed the concerns of young Americans eager to see a more compassionate country than the one associated with the Reagan era.

PLOT OF RENT

The story takes place in New York's East Village between two consecutive Christmas seasons. Mark, a struggling filmmaker, and his roommate, Roger, a rock musician, try to avoid Benny, their former friend turned landlord, who demands the rent. Mark's ex-lover Maureen arrives and seeks his technical expertise for a live performance piece she is rehearsing. When Mark leaves the apartment, Roger, who is HIV positive, takes his AZT medicine and attempts to compose a song that will give meaning to his life. Mimi, a stranger and junkie, shows up at his doorstep and asks for a candle because of a power outage. She, too, is HIV positive. They are instantly drawn to each other.

Angel, a transvestite and street musician, helps Collins, who has just been mugged. They are both HIV positive, which fuels their mutual attraction. Before Maureen's concert, Mark meets her new lover, a yuppie lawyer named Joanne. Maureen's performance is intended as a protest against Benny's capitalist enterprises. Eventually, Joanne becomes fed up with Maureen's demands and leaves her. Roger and Mimi decide to move in together, but he is overtaken with jealousy and eventually walks out on her.

Several months later, the couples reconcile, but their happiness is fleeting. Angel dies, Joanne and Maureen squabble, Mimi flirts with Benny, Mark considers taking a job with a tabloid television show, and Roger moves to Santa Fe.

At Christmas, a reconciled Maureen and Joanne arrive at Mark and Roger's apartment with the dying Mimi. She succumbs but miraculously returns to Roger.

The subsequent events surrounding the production of *Rent* stand out as one of the most tragic stories in the annals of musical theater history. Larson submitted *Rent*, as the show was then titled, to several Off Broadway and Off Off Broadway theaters, and in 1993 the New York Theatre Workshop put up the money for a reading of the show. The following year, Larson received a Richard Rodgers Studio Production Award to present a workshop of the show, which Michael Grief directed. Before long, two young producers, Jeffrey Seller and Kevin McCollum, took an interest in the show. Bolstered with a check from a Wall Street investor, they put up money for a full-scale workshop in exchange for the rights of first refusal for a commercial production. In late 1995, Larson quit his restaurant job and prepared to enjoy the fruits of his labors. A few days before dress rehearsals, however, he experienced chest pains, which persisted up to the night of the final dress rehearsal. He went to Cabrini Medical Center, where doctors diagnosed food poisoning. A couple of days later, Larson landed in the emergency room at St. Vincent's Hospital with "a viral infection," according to the doctors on duty. Larson attended the final dress rehearsal and returned home. He made himself a cup of tea and looked forward to the opening. Sometime after midnight, he collapsed and died from an aortic aneurysm. *Rent* opened the next evening to great acclaim and, partly because of the tragedy associated with it, became the musical that everyone wanted to see. About a month after the Off Broadway run, the producers rushed *Rent* onto Broadway, where it remained for nine years. *Rent* won the Tony Awards for Best Musical, Best Book, and Best Score; the Drama Desk Award for Outstanding Musical and Outstanding Book; and the Pulitzer Prize for Drama.

Larson had a lanky frame, dressed in black, and cultivated an unkempt appearance, but beneath the grunge-chic exterior existed an irrepressible idealist. He exuded youthful energy, and he ultimately found success through sheer perseverance, though most of his success came posthumously. He earnestly believed that he could rescue the American musical from oblivion, and he felt an obligation to make his musicals as relevant to young audiences as possible. He said,

> Although I am a sentimental romantic who loves old fashioned musicals, I am a member of a very unsentimental, unromantic generation who basically think musicals are too corny. . . . If I want to try to cultivate a new audience for musicals, I must write shows with a score that MTV ears will accept.

Indeed, his score for *Rent* exudes the raw energy of eighties and nineties rock genres. Nevertheless, the producers shunned the term "rock musical," but critics and Larson himself proclaimed it "a *Hair* for the nineties. (see Chapter 16)"

The similarities between *Rent* and *Hair* are numerous. Both shows take place "downtown" and celebrate nonconformity. Drugs, race, sexual freedom, community, and death all figure large in both musicals. The adult characters in *Rent* are the epitome of conformity and, like their counterparts in *Hair*, two-dimensional cartoon figures. *Hair* features a highly eclectic score influenced by rock music. *Rent*, too, has an eclectic rock score, but it was never marketed explicitly as a rock musical. It is largely through-sung, whereas *Hair* contains several miniature songs plus some extended musical sequences. Both shows employed an onstage rock band. The actors in *Rent* sang into standing microphones and wore radio microphones in full view of the audience. There are also some significant differences between the two musicals. *Rent* features a character-driven plot that unfolds in a traditional linear way. *Hair*, on the other hand, has the fragmented action of a concept musical and incorporates several theme-oriented vignettes. Finally, the monosyllabic title *Rent* rings hollow compared to *Hair*, which carries great political significance.

La Bohème and Verismo Opera

Puccini's *La Bohème*, one of two Italian operas based on Henry Murger's novel *Scènes de la vie de bohème* (1851), ranks today among the five most frequently performed operas in the world. Murger's *Scènes* initially appeared in serial form, then as a full-length novel, and eventually as a stage play. The plot centers on a romance

A scene from an English production of *Rent*. © *Jane Hobson / Alamy.*

between a struggling poet named Rodolfo and a frail, consumptive woman named Mimi. Rodolfo and Mimi meet by chance, fall in love, separate, and then reunite just before Mimi succumbs to tuberculosis. Rodolfo's bohemian roommates play a significant role in the story and provide some intrigue for readers with little patience for unadulterated romance. The opera ends with Mimi's death, as Rodolfo cries out, "Mimì! Mimì!" on four high G-sharps. Murger's novel extends beyond Mimi's tragic death to show how the friends grow apart as they reject the threadbare existence that they once passionately embraced in favor of a more comfortable bourgeois lifestyle.

When the novel entered the public domain, both Puccini and Ruggero Leoncavallo (1857–1919), the composer of *Pagliacci* (1892), announced that they were writing an opera based on the story. The ensuing competition between them played out in public. Puccini's opera, conducted by a young Arturo Toscanini, premiered in Turin on February 1, 1896 (exactly one century before the world premiere of *Rent*). A year later, Leoncavallo's version, which spends more time on Musetta and Marcello's romance, premiered.

The plot of *Rent* retains the key events of Puccini's *La Bohème*, and most of the characters are modern equivalents of their operatic counterparts (Table 12.1). Larson and Billy Aronson originally intended to set the story on the Upper West Side, but Larson eventually opted for the seedier, less gentrified East Village. Other details are drawn directly from Murger's novel. To incorporate the AIDS crisis into the story, Larson created homosexual and bisexual parallels for some of Murger's bohemians. He concocted a rather contrived *mélange* of friends: a cross-dresser; a middle-class filmmaker attracted to the downtown bohemian life; his ex-girlfriend, who is currently romantically involved with a female lawyer; an S&M nightclub dancer; and a former-friend-turned-capitalist landlord. Four of these characters are HIV positive. Larson also opted for a more upbeat ending than Murger and Puccini: the HIV-positive Mimi returns to life and to Roger, a rock musician. Feeling the need to include at least one death, Larson devised a tragic ending for Angel, the cross-dressing modern-day equivalent of Schaunard. He expanded the character of the landlord, a one-joke figure in Puccini's opera. Benny plays a more significant role in the lives of the main characters and appears in many more scenes than *La Bohème*'s Benoît.

Verismo, an Italian literary movement of the late nineteenth century, inspired a parallel operatic movement. Verismo literature emulated several tenets of French naturalism, but its two leading authors, Giovanni Verga and Luigi Capuana, rejected its political and social associations, focusing more on human passion. Verismo opera portrays ordinary people in everyday situations, as opposed to the historical or mythological figures of earlier opera. The characters toil and embrace the joys, tragedies, passions, and violence of the real world. As in verismo operas of old, the bleak lives, deprivation, and abject suffering of the characters in *Rent* are far more realistic than anything earlier musicals ever depicted. Michael Greif's direction of *Rent* was, according to Scott Miller, the "theatrical equivalent to *cinema vérité*," which aims for the same gritty realism of verismo opera. Indeed, the actors seemed to be "making it up as they go."

TABLE 12.1. Main Characters in *La Bohème* and *Rent*

LA BOHÈME		RENT	
Gustave Colline	philosopher	Tom Collins	computer teacher
Marcel	painter	Mark	filmmaker
Schaunard	musician	Angel	–
Rodolphe	poet	Roger	rock musician
Mimì	–	Mimì	dancer at S&M club
Musetta	–	Maureen	performance artist
Benoît	landlord	Benny	landlord

A scene from *Miss Saigon.* © *Paul Brown / Alamy.*

Music

Larson adopted the sung-through nature of megamusicals, which alternate between sung dialogue and formal numbers. On the other hand, the music, although eclectic, achieves a more consistent rock style than most megamusicals. And yet, Larson's love of traditional musical theater is evident at nearly every turn. "One Song Glory," although sung in the raspy, throaty style of a rock singer, is essentially a standard musical theater wanting song. "Light My Candle" corresponds quite literally to Puccini's "Oh! Sventata." "Tango Maureen" evinces a musical comedy sensibility. The anthem "Life Support" recurs at several points during the show. Roger and Mimi's "Another Day" constitutes one of the most dramatic musical segments in the show. It incorporates two recurring themes, the "I should tell you" segment and the song "Life Support." "La Vie Bohème," the rousing Act I finale, draws attention to the conflict between Benny and his former friends and thereby sums up the show's posture. It is one of several list songs in *Rent* and the most autobiographical. The "La Vie Bohème" sequence includes recitative-like passages (e.g., the waiter's recitation of the food order and a brief exchange between Maureen and Joanne). In the tradition of Cole Porter name-dropping, Larson cites as many trends and celebrities as possible, including Allen Ginsberg, Langston Hughes, Uta Hagen, Susan Sontag, Stephen Sondheim, *The Wizard of Oz*, Pee-wee Herman, Gertrude Stein, Ecstasy, and Vaclav Havel. Maureen and Joanne's "Take

Me or Leave Me" features a repeated gospel piano ostinato and blues-inflected melody.

Mimi's miraculous survival at the end of the show reveals the distance between *Rent* and nineteenth-century Italian opera. It also suggests that Larson, like Oscar Hammerstein, viewed the world and musical theater through rose-tinted glasses. The frequent vocal melismas in *Rent*, however, are more typical of opera than musical theater or rock. Melismas contribute to the playful character of "Santa Fe," along with the unusual 6/8 meter. "Santa Fe" also features harmonic shifts between D and B and between major and minor. Triple meter and melismas also occur in "I'll Cover You"; however, for Colline's reprise of the song when Angel dies in Act II, Larson incorporated meter and tempo changes to create the mood of a lament.

Two consecutive Christmas seasons serve as bookends to the story. The cycle of a year helps to underscore *Rent*'s theme of death and renewal. However, Larson scapegoats Christmas as a symbol of American conformity and consumerism. He sardonically quotes well-known Yuletide ditties, and his original melody for the line "Christmas bells are ringing" is intentionally moronic.

Rent's soaring rock melodies take their inspiration from the operatic source material. Larson came to composition by way of theater. His composition technique, however, was influenced by both popular and classical music. He quotes Puccini's score for *La Bohème*, but he does so sparingly and only for dramatic effect. He references three famous themes from the opera:

> Rodolfo's "Talor dal mio forzie" (Act I)
>
> "Musetta's Waltz" (specifically, the melody in the accompaniment on "Quando me'n vo," Act II)
>
> Mimi's "Sono andati" theme (Act IV)

Early in Act I, Roger plucks out the accompaniment of "Musetta's Waltz" on his electric guitar as he attempts to complete a song that he hopes will bring him "glory." As revealed in the final scene, this song turns out to be "Your Eyes," which Roger sings to Mimi as she lies on her deathbed. The song ends with an ecstatic statement of "Musetta's Waltz" in the guitar. The association of Musetta's music with Mimi seems incongruous; after all, the flirtatious and free-spirited Maureen is Musetta's counterpart in *Rent*, not Mimi. Puccini associated Musetta with the waltz, the most physical and sensual social dance in nineteenth-century high society, for it literally brought men and women physically closer together. A century later, Larson opted for the more contemporary Latin tango to characterize Maureen's provocative nature. Larson understood that the downtown ambience of *Rent* was no place for a meek, helpless femme like Mimi, so he transformed her into a provocative Latina dancer, although he reserved the tango music for Maureen. Why, then, does Roger (and Larson) invoke Musetta's waltz theme for Mimi?

Prior to this scene occurs a lighthearted vignette, parallel to the one in *La Bohème*, involving Roger and his friends. The mood and musical texture change abruptly when Maureen and Mimi arrive. Larson weaves melodies from earlier songs into the musical underscoring beneath Roger's and Mimi's spoken declaration of love. Finally, Roger sings "Your Eyes," the song that he has been struggling to complete since the beginning of the show. During Mimi's death scene in *La Bohème*, the music modulates to the minor key. By contrast, "Your Eyes" remains in the major key, foretelling the fact that Mimi will not succumb. Ian Nisbet argues that Larson intentionally prepares the audience for this musical conclusion. "Your Eyes" hovers between C major and the relative A minor. The melody edges gradually into a higher register. A slight variation of the opening melody is heard an octave higher just before the line "and before the song dies." Attention is drawn to the word "dies" through a substitution of the anticipated C harmony with a B-flat added-sixth chord. A quote of "I Should Tell You" in G major interrupts the natural flow of the song. As this line reaches a cadence on C major, an extended statement of "Musetta's Waltz," recast in common time, sounds in the electric guitar. Believing that Mimi has left him forever, Roger cries out "Mimi!" at the top of his register, a direct quote from Puccini's opera. The number ends in the major key, as Mimi suddenly returns to life. The corresponding scene in Puccini's opera is saturated with descending semitones. By contrast, Nisbet observes, Larson's music contains upward resolutions of the semitone: "Larson's motif appears to cycle up and down by semitone, first symbolizing death and then, presumably, the opposite of death—life." Whereas Puccini focused on Mimi's death and the pain that it causes Rodolfo, Larson opted to celebrate life and "its ability to aid those 'living with / Not dying from disease'," This shift in focus helps to explain the transfer of Musetta's waltz theme to Mimi, who has greater self-agency than her counterpart in Puccini's opera.

"Seasons of Love," the most popular song from *Rent*, expresses the optimism and communal spirit with which Larson invested the story. The song is the least integrated number in *Rent*, but its pleasing melody, reminiscent of sixties folk-rock, made "Seasons of Love" a crossover hit. Sung by the entire cast directly to the audience immediately after intermission (the film version of *Rent* relocates the song to the beginning), the song sets the mood for the second act. The lyrics strike a happy medium between musical theater specificity and pop-song generality. "Seasons of Love" adopts the verse-chorus structure typical of rock and pop music since the sixties. This form concentrates the most important lyrics in the verse and presents a hummable "hook" in the chorus. The verse consists of four statements of a simple theme over a repeated four-chord progression (ostinato). A preponderance of speech-like rhythms and chords with added tones (notes lying outside of the basic triadic harmony) account for the song's catchy nature and commercial appeal. The opening repeated note functions as the ninth of a IV chord. Each statement of the theme ends on a different chord, which helps to counter the repetitive nature of the verse melody. A contrasting melody begins on "in daylights" over the same basic four-chord progression. A surprising "blue note" occurs on "laughter." The "hook," which features a graceful melisma on "love," emphasizes the subdominant, another feature borrowed from the blues. The title line rounds out

THE BLUES SCALE

The "blues scale" contains two lowered scale degrees, the third and seventh (in practice the fifth is also sometimes lowered), commonly referred to as "blue notes." There are a few different permutations of the blues scale, but all of them contain these two primary blue notes. In popular music (rock, jazz, and pop), blue notes occur as borrowed pitches within an otherwise diatonic framework. The African American song genre known as the blues uses the blues scale, but it also has a twelve-bar form and emphasizes subdominant harmony. A song can contain blue notes without conforming to the blues genre. The musical theater repertory includes many examples by white as well as black composers (e.g., George Gershwin's "I'll Build a Stairway to Paradise").

the refrain as the four-chord ostinato returns underneath the extended melismas in the vocal line.

Reception

Rent benefitted from savvy marketing and a nearly unprecedented level of hype, which fed on Larson's highly publicized death and the lawsuits that followed the tragedy. Moreover, *Rent* became a pop-culture sensation in the manner of a megamusical, but it had a decidedly American stamp and eschewed the spectacle associated with the British-style megamusical. Young people flocked to *Rent*, taking advantage of rush tickets that the producers shrewdly set aside for each performance. Television commercials advertised *Rent* as "the musical for people who hate musicals." No doubt, *Rent*'s liberal politics appealed to a young demographic and gave the show enough cultural cachet to make it a must-see event. The show even spawned a designer fashion line at the upscale Bloomingdale's department store.

Larson's estate became embroiled in several lawsuits in the wake of *Rent*'s incredible success, sometimes as the plaintiff, sometimes the defendant. The family filed a wrongful death suit against Cabrini Medical Center for the misdiagnosis of Larson's life-threatening condition. *Rent*'s critics attacked Larson for trivializing everything that *Rent* claimed to champion: performance art, AIDS awareness, homosexuality, lesbian relationships, and so on. Sarah Schulman, a gay writer, claimed that Larson based several aspects of *Rent* on her 1987 novel *People in Trouble*. She lambasted him for portraying oversimplified gay characters and for the commodification of gay culture in general and AIDS in particular. Schulman objected to Larson's depiction of Maureen and Joanne as bitchy lesbians and the general attitude that gay female relationships are "unstable" and "emotionally pathological."

She also argued that *Rent* was just another narrowly conceived product of a straight, white man and that it commits the usual offense of depicting the Other from a position of privilege. Schulman felt that the show's disenfranchised characters are "simultaneously omnipresent and ignored." Further, she objected to the show's "liberal veneer" and its seemingly gratuitous racial, sexual, and political inclusiveness. Lynn M. Thomson sued twice for royalties as co-author; her case was settled out of court in 1998.

Rent's legacy remains an unsettled question. Indeed, the passage of time has rendered *Rent* a period piece about a small faction of urban life in the nineties. It has a self-referential quality, and the point-of-view character, Mark, reflects Jonathan Larson's outlook on life. Several unanswered questions remain: Was *Rent* exploitative? Did it pander to a generation looking for a cause to champion? For mainstream audiences, the marginalized characters were like exotic others or trendy hipsters. The critic Robert Brustein accused Larson of exploiting AIDS, and Francis Davis labeled the show "victim kitsch." Finally, people argued that Larson's death, rather than the show's artistic merits, accounted for *Rent*'s success.

AMERICAN MEGAMUSICALS

More than any other American composer, Frank Wildhorn (b. 1958) has affiliated himself with the megamusical. His career on Broadway peaked in the late nineties with *Jekyll & Hyde* (1997) and *The Scarlet Pimpernel* (1997). *Jekyll & Hyde*, with a libretto by Leslie Bricusse (see Chapter 9), lasted 1,543 performances. *The Scarlet Pimpernel*, like many megamusicals before it, began as an anthem-rich concept album. Since 1997, though, Wildhorn has racked up a long list of critically disparaged and unprofitable musicals. His last two shows on Broadway, *Wonderland* (2011) and *Bonnie and Clyde* (2009), played a combined total of sixty-seven performances.

Wildhorn came to musical theater from the pop world and, like Andrew Lloyd Webber, brought a populist philosophy to the musical theater genre. According to Wildhorn, were George Gershwin still alive today, he would "be trying to write for as many millions of people as, well, I am. . . . [I]f the future of American musicals is going to be a healthy one, it has got to combine the vocabulary of popular music of today with theater music." Like Lloyd Webber, Wildhorn has also suffered the scorn of New York theater critics, who have accused him of commercialism and opportunism. According to Ethan Mordden, Wildhorn "speaks to people who don't know what music and theatre were, and will thus accept anything sung on a stage, especially a scream-the-theatre-down! score."

Wildhorn has found approbation outside New York, especially overseas, which explains why, despite his dismal track record, he has continued to attract investors for his projects. His megamusicals have played in places such as Prague, Takarazuka, Budapest, Osaka, and St. Gallen. Wildhorn has maintained a hectic pace, writing a new show nearly every year, usually about a fictional or real larger-than-life character: Dracula, Rudolf Valentino, the Count of Monte Cristo, the

WILLIAM FINN

William Finn (b. 1952) studied music at Williams College, Stephen Sondheim's alma mater, and received the Hutchinson Fellowship, as did Sondheim before him. Finn, a product of the Off Broadway scene, writes offbeat musicals, often of a semi-autobiographical nature and with mature themes. They involve "Jewish urbanities with a strong sense of family, even if the families are usually dysfunctional," as Thomas Hischak characterizes them. Finn's so-called Marvin Trilogy propelled him into the spotlight in the early eighties. After surviving a brain disorder in 1992, Finn wrote about his experience in *A New Brain* (1998). *A New Brain* was part of the 2015 *Encores! Off-Center* season. *The 25th Annual Putnam County Spelling Bee* (premiered Off Broadway in 2004), his most commercially successful work, ran on Broadway for 1,136 performances. The scores of Finn's musicals, which are mostly through-sung, vary in quality. They achieve a sense of spontaneity but sometimes at the expense of technical craft. Finn's musical adaptation of the film *Little Miss Sunshine* opened Off Broadway in 2013.

French sculptor Camille Claudel, F. Scott and Zelda Fitzgerald, and Bonnie and Clyde. He has also added to the growing list of musicals based on Edmond Rostand's 1897 play *Cyrano de Bergerac*.

BEYOND THE MEGAMUSICAL

With *Rent* and *Miss Saigon* dominating Broadway in the nineties, several other critically acclaimed musicals vied for media attention. These works represent writers from several generations and with vastly different tastes.

Falsettoland

Rent was not the first musical to recognize the AIDS crisis. William Finn's *Falsettoland,* the third work in his continuing saga about a gay man named Marvin, takes place in 1981, the year in which AIDS was first identified. A sequel to Finn's musical *In Trousers* (1979), *Falsettos* tells the story of a married man and father who one day realizes that he prefers to be with men. With a book by James Lapine and Finn and direction by Lapine, *Falsettos* was revolutionary in that its protagonist is not the clichéd suffering or exuberantly campy homosexual of earlier, closeted days. Whizzer, Marvin's lover, contracts AIDS, although the disease does not yet have a name. Finn intertwines Whizzer's illness with the Bar Mitzvah preparations of Marvin's precocious son, Jason. Finn added lesbian characters to his world of screwed-up New Yorkers, to whom the show seems pitched. To its credit, *Falsettoland* explored serious themes and aroused sympathy for its characters: neurotic, Jewish, gay, or some combination thereof. In 1992, *March of the Falsettos* and *Falsettoland* were combined into a single Broadway musical titled *Falsettos*.

The Secret Garden

The 1991 musical *The Secret Garden*, based on Frances Hodgson Burnett's 1911 children's novel, stands out for its nearly all-female creative team. Lucy Simon (b. 1943), the sister of Carly Simon, wrote the music, and Marsha Norman (b. 1947) the book. Susan Schulman directed, and Heidi Landesman designed the set as well as served as the lead producer.

Simon and Norman's musical has completely overshadowed Sharon Burgett and Alfred Shaughnessy's version of *The Secret Garden*, which is closer in style to a Rodgers and Hammerstein musical than to something likely to appeal to contemporary audiences. This version never reached Broadway, but it was recorded in 1986 with a top-notch cast headed by Barbara Cook.

Since *The Secret Garden,* Lucy Simon and Norman have written, *Doctor Zhivago*, which premiered in California in 2006 and opened and closed on Broadway in 2015 amid a flurry of other new musicals set abroad (*An American in Paris*, *Finding Neverland*, *Gigi*, *Something Rotten!*, and *The Visit*). It received scathing reviews. *The New York Times* critic Charles Isherwood called the show "a turgid throwback to the British invasion of Broadway in the 1980s" and added that "even as it shares similarities with those long-running hits, 'Doctor Zhivago' is inferior in most respects to the musicals it is emulating." Marsha Norman has written the book for *The Red Shoes* (1993), *The Color Purple* (2005), and *The Trumpet of the Swan* (2011), which is based on E. B. White's 1970 children's novel of the same name.

Repackaging and Repurposing

The practice of making a book musical by repackaging or repurposing preexisting popular music goes back decades. Many early Hollywood musicals were made in this way. The musical biopic, for example, tells the story (however bowdlerized or far from the actual truth) of a classical composer, a popular songwriter, or a beloved performer using music associated with him or her (e.g., George Gershwin). Another popular type of film musical interpolates preexisting songs into an original plot unrelated to the origins of the music (e.g., *An American in Paris* [1951], which interpolated Gershwin songs into a love story set in Paris). Broadway has also produced musicals of this nature (including the 2015 stage version of *An American in Paris*), as well as revue-retrospectives. Whereas earlier revues such as the *Ziegfeld Follies* mostly incorporated original music by multiple songwriters (see Chapters 3 and 4), today's revue-retrospectives feature the back catalogue of a single songwriter (Billy Joel), singer (Janis Joplin), vocal group (the Shirelles), or band (the Beatles). These shows drop the pretense of having a narrative or plot and simply present the music in an entertaining way. In the nineties, these three types of musicals proliferated to such an extent that the term "jukebox musical," which had only been used sporadically, became almost universally adopted by critics to describe them. Other labels employed include "non-revival revival," "catalogue musical," "anthology musical," and even "jukeboxical," but none as regularly or universally as "jukebox musical." Whether the term "jukebox musical" should be applied to all three categories remains an unsettled matter. For instance, some commentators exclude the first and third types. According to Larry Stempel, the songs of today's jukebox musicals such as *Jersey Boys* "reflect the popular music of the mainly white, middle-class, and aging baby-boom generation." The nostalgic appeal of jukebox musicals explains why many of them have run for years on Broadway and have drawn crowds wherever they play.

Today's jukebox musical craze can be traced back to the 1983 musical *My One and Only*, a star vehicle for Tommy Tune and Twiggy, which interpolated popular Gershwin songs into a "new," albeit derivative, musical comedy story. Nearly a decade later, *Crazy for You* repeated the same stunt, only with better results. The producers, one of whom was the owner of a high-end mail-order catalogue (The Horchow Collection), marketed the show as a "new Gershwin musical comedy," which was not far from the truth. The book, by Ken Ludwig, is based on the real Gershwin musical *Girl Crazy* (1930) (see Chapter 17), but the creative team felt free to include any Gershwin song they pleased. Although not particularly original, *Crazy for You* won the 1992 Tony Award for Best Musical. Susan Stroman garnered her first of five Tony Awards for her choreography. Broadway's third posthumous "new Gershwin musical" took its title from the composer's song "Nice Work If You Can Get It" (originally "They All Laughed"). It opened in 2012 and starred Matthew Broderick and Kelli O'Hara. The book, by Joe DiPietro, is based on material by Guy Bolton and P. G. Wodehouse (see Chapter 4).

The most unusual bio-musical from the nineties told a story based on the life of jazz musician Jelly Roll Morton (1885–1941). *Jelly's Last Jam* stands out from the typical jukebox musical because it required new lyrics and extensive manipulation of Morton's music. The show did much more than celebrate an African American jazz artist through his music, as many revues did. It explored, among other things, what it meant to be African American during the early days of jazz and the tension between internalized racism and ethnic identity, all seen through the eyes of Jelly Roll Morton. Morton (born Ferdinand Joseph LaMothe) was a "Creole of Color," one of New Orleans's diverse ethnic groups. In nineteenth-century New Orleans, race and class were intertwined, and Creoles enjoyed a higher status than blacks. Some of them even owned slaves. By the turn of the century, Creoles had seen a decline in their social status and began to suffer the same sort of discrimination as ex-slaves. Classical music was a status symbol for well-educated Creoles. In *Jelly's Last Jam*, the character of Morton receives a solid musical education. Some of the real Morton's music reveals a knowledge of classical music, but this aspect of his life remains undocumented. What is clear is that Morton gravitated toward jazz, and, being a shameless self-promoter, claimed to have invented it.

African American cultural identity has figured large in playwright George C. Wolfe's
writing and directing. He first confronted
the issue in his breakout play *The Colored
Museum* (1986).

George C. Wolfe (b. 1954), who created and
directed *Jelly's Last Jam*, presented Morton's life's
story as a confession. Morton denies his black
heritage and its impact on his music. The musical
was, to quote Frank Rich, "a Judgment Day inquisition into the meaning of a life." Morton eventually acknowledges his heritage but, like Dickens's
Scrooge, only after he is forced by a character
named Chimney Man to revisit the seminal events in his life and confront his
past. The story begins on the eve of Morton's death, and he finds himself in
Limbo. The action that ensues charts Morton's life, starting with his early years
in New Orleans. As the moment of his death from stab wounds nears, Morton,
speaking from his deathbed, accepts his black ancestry and then takes his right-
ful place among other jazz legends.

The African American music arranger Luther Henderson (1919–2003) and
white lyricist Susan Birkenhead carved out well-defined book songs from
Morton's music. The cast included Keith David as Chimney Man; Tonya
Pinkins as Anita, Morton's lover, whose toughness is no match for him; Savion
Glover as the young Morton; and Gregory Hines as the adult Morton. Because
of Hines's tap-dancing skills, the musical incorporated more dance than it
otherwise would have done.

Revivals

The 1991–1992 theatrical season was a milestone in Broadway history: for the first
time revivals outnumbered new musicals. The proliferation of revivals spelled a bad
omen for musical theater, but several of them were standout productions, including
the 1992 version of *Guys and Dolls* starring Nathan Lane and Faith Prince. Several
revivals featured a substantially rewritten script, a practice that persists today (see
Chapter 13). In many cases, the new script is the key to making a show that would
otherwise seem out of step with the times—especially regarding attitudes about
feminism, racism, and the LGBT community—resonate with contemporary audiences. For example, Peter Stone's new script for the 1999 revival of *Annie Get Your
Gun* gave the story a refreshing post-feminist twist and expunged the offensive depiction of the Native American characters.

MUSICAL THEATER AT THE END OF THE MILLENNIUM

Jonathan Larson was not the only composer of his generation with serious artistic
aspirations. Several prodigiously talented writers appeared in the nineties, but
few of them have gained the sort of Broadway exposure that composers of earlier
eras enjoyed (see Chapter 13). That many writers gravitated toward dark, dangerous, or divisive topics did not make it any easier for them to build a following.
Other developments toward the end of the century conspired to keep this generation of writers out of the limelight. Live readings and workshops of new musicals

in front of invited audiences began to replace the out-of-town tryout. With Broadway effectively off limits to most of these writers, Off Broadway (and regional theater) became their only real hope of getting heard.

Proving the adage "necessity is the mother of all invention," young writers poured their energy into small-scale musicals suitable for the austere budgets and physical spaces of Off Broadway theater (see Chapter 14). The minimalist Off Broadway musical has come to define an aesthetic and to represent an alternative to the bloated, overly commercial Broadway musical. Several Off Broadway theater organizations have been instrumental in the development of new musicals, especially Playwrights Horizons, Manhattan Theatre Club, the Public Theater, and the Vineyard Theatre. Without the support of these organizations, some important musicals would never have seen the light of day or made it to Broadway.

Even Harold Prince, once the wunderkind of Broadway, co-founded an organization called New Musicals, a "laboratory," to work on shows away from the pressure and sometimes toxic atmosphere of commercial Broadway theater. He located the organization at Purchase College in upstate New York. He and Marty Bell, his partner in the endeavor, chose Kander and Ebb's *Kiss of the Spider Woman* to inaugurate the project. Although the show eventually had a successful Broadway run, the production at Purchase was a costly disaster, and it spelled the end of Prince and Bell's experiment.

To fully understand the hurdles that this generation of writers has faced, one must take into account the widening chasm between nonprofit theater and commercial Broadway during the nineties. As Broadway producers turned more and more to commercially safe projects, not-for-profit theaters stepped in to fill the void. The history of new musicals outside New York City has yet to be written, but as Broadway has closed its doors to risk, many writers have found a more welcoming environment at the not-for-profit theaters away from Broadway. It is endemic of an industry in crisis that top-tier artists such as Sondheim have flocked to nonprofit venues.

Kiss of the Spider Woman (1993) bears all the hallmarks of a Kander and Ebb concept musical: direction by Harold Prince, a show-within-a show format, and a serious theme. Kander and Ebb's second musical of the decade, *Steel Pier* (1997), featured an original story by David Thompson, loosely based on the Orpheus myth. It involves the participants of a Depression-era dance marathon in Atlantic City.

Lynn Ahrens and Stephen Flaherty

The lyricist Lynn Ahrens (b. 1948) and composer Stephen Flaherty (b. 1960), arguably the most successful and artistically conservative writers of their generation, met in 1983 at the BMI Musical Theater Workshop. They garnered considerable attention for their musical comedy *Lucky Stiff*, which played Off Broadway in 1988. Their first Broadway musical, *Once on This Island*, began at Playwrights Horizons in 1990. Based on Rosa Guy's 1985 novel *My Love, My Love*, it tells the story of a dark-skinned Caribbean peasant girl who saves the life of a young mixed-race aristocrat. Because he is obliged to accept an arranged marriage to someone else, she drowns herself in the ocean. The unfulfilled love story, exotic setting, treatment of class, and miscegenation theme connect *Once on This Island* to earlier race-conscious musicals by white writers such as Harold Arlen and E. Y. Harburg's *Jamaica* (1957). In these shows, the mixed-race romance is invariably doomed. The creative team of *Once on This Island* adopted a light-hearted, folkloric storytelling style. The music (which Frank Rich called "trans-cultural light"), Post-Impressionistic sets, costumes, and lighting gave the piece a fairytale quality, which made the shocking ending all the more gut wrenching.

Ahrens and Flaherty's *Ragtime* premiered in 1997. It was produced by Garth Drabinsky, whose Livent Entertainment Corporation was poised to become a major player on Broadway until he was convicted of fraud and forgery in Ontario Superior Court in 2009 after years of legal proceedings.

Michael John LaChiusa

Michael John LaChiusa is more prolific but less mainstream than most of his peers. LaChiusa (b. 1962) hailed from Westfield, New York, and took advantage of the host of cultural events presented each summer at the nearby Chautauqua Institution. Situated on Chautauqua Lake in southwestern New York State, the Chautauqua Institution was founded in 1874 as a retreat for Sunday school teachers. Eventually, its mission expanded to include music, theater, arts, and education.

LaChiusa's desire to write musicals began early in his life. He dreamed of attending Juilliard, but family finances would not permit it, so he ended up at Graham Junior College in Boston, where he majored in television. When he landed in New York, LaChiusa performed at clubs such as CBGB and attended the BMI and ASCAP musical theater workshops. LaChiusa's taste for idiosyncratic subject matter was evident from the start. In 1984, he wrote a musical based on Carson McCullers's *Ballad of the Sad Café*, but he could not interest a producer in the project. In 1991, Playwrights Horizons presented four one-act musicals: *Break*, *Agnes*, *Eulogy for Mister Hamm*, and *Lucky Nurse*. These mini-works portended the offbeat nature of LaChiusa's later musicals. For instance, in *Break*, two construction workers are visited by the Virgin Mary during their lunch break. For the past twenty years, LaChiusa's career has been a whirlwind of activity on and off Broadway. *Marie Christine*, a retelling of Euripides's tragedy *Medea*, opened in 1999, marking the first time that LaChiusa saw his name on a Broadway marquee. He set the story in New Orleans at the end of the nineteenth century and wove voodoo ritual into the classical myth. The show dealt with mixed-race relationships and ended tragically. Musicals involving a death are nothing new (e.g., *Oklahoma!*), but LaChiusa has written a disproportionate share of them, and *Marie Christine* was particularly bloody. The subject matter unleashed some of the composer's most dissonant music. The technical difficulty of the score has led some critics to call *Marie Christine* an opera, a label that LaChiusa eschews. In fact, he once referred to opera as "what Europeans used to write."

Outspoken by nature, LaChiusa has caused some controversy in the theater world. In 2005 he published a scathing opinion piece in *Opera News* that took aim at his peers. Titled "The Great Gray Way," the article argued that musical theater was dead and lamented the fact that the financial situation of musical theater had severely stymied the creative process.

> It shouldn't take that much time to write a musical. It shouldn't take much longer than a year. Musicals should be here and now and that's that. Musicals have to have spontaneity. When you hear it, sitting there in the audience, it has to catch you, as if it's being created in that moment. I think if you keep working and working on a musical, it loses that spark. . . .

The commercial Broadway writer Marc Shaiman (b. 1959), the composer of *Hairspray* (2002), fired back. He posted an online retort accusing LaChiusa of trying to be Stephen Sondheim. The fracas reflects tensions between old Broadway and new Broadway. As the balance between art and commerce has tilted in favor of the latter, opportunities for writers have narrowed along with the stylistic range of musical theater. Broadway has become a hostile place for writers of LaChiusa's artistic temperament. Yet LaChiusa remains active, although he still has not had a major commercial hit.

Adam Guettel

Family dynasties are rare on Broadway. Adam Guettel is a third-generation Broadway composer, the grandson of Richard Rodgers and the son of Mary Rodgers. His output, which is far smaller than LaChiusa's, is highly regarded. As a young boy growing up in New York, Guettel sang with the Metropolitan Opera and New York City Opera. His interest in jazz, though, provided him with a compositional outlet. Guettel attended Yale University, and upon graduation he focused on musical theater composition. Richard Rodgers, who died when Guettel was fifteen, has not been a powerful influence on his work. In the nineties, Guettel established himself with two major book musicals. His first, *Floyd Collins* (1996), is based on an actual event from 1925. A cave explorer named Floyd Collins (some sources misidentify Collins as a coal miner) became trapped in an underground passageway between two caves and died after all attempts to rescue him failed. Collins's story caught Guettel's attention when he read about it in a *Reader's Digest* publication. The musical takes the audience deep into Floyd's emotional world as he waits to be rescued. This part of the show is contrasted by the media circus that unfolds above ground: "The musical language that I came up with for Floyd underground felt very freeing for me. It didn't come out of the music above-ground, it was Floyd's separate magical universe—though the two were somewhat related." Guettel's score emulates the folksiness of Appalachian music without sounding derivative. Guettel blends bluegrass, musical theater, and art music influences. He writes for trained, supple voices capable of negotiating large intervals and sustaining long-breathed lines. He composed a nearly eight-minute opening monologue for Floyd to sing ("The Call") as he searches for gold in the dark cave. *Floyd Collins* never played on Broadway, but it established Guettel as a formidable new voice in musical theater.

Jason Robert Brown

Jason Robert Brown (b. 1970) studied music at the Eastman School of Music. A friendship with Harold Prince's daughter, Daisy, led to an introduction with the famous director and eventually the assignment to compose *Parade* (1998). With a book by Alfred Uhry, *Parade* examines the Leo Frank case. Frank (1884–1915), a Jew and Southerner by birth, was raised in Brooklyn. He migrated to the South in 1907 when he accepted a job at the National Pencil Company. In 1913, Frank was accused of brutally murdering Mary Phagan, a fourteen-year-old employee of the company. The case pitted Jews against blacks, and white Southerners against both groups. Against the ubiquitous popular family entertainment on Broadway at the time, *Parade* stood out for its depressing story and complex theme. Brown's *The Last Five Years* played Off Broadway in 2002 and has since developed an enthusiastic following. An Off Broadway revival opened in 2013, and a film version was released in 2015. Brown's *The Bridges of Madison County* opened on Broadway in 2014 and earned him Tony Awards for Best Original Score and Best Orchestrations. His latest Broadway musical, *Honeymoon in Las Vegas*, opened less than a year later.

Andrew Lippa

The English-born Andrew Lippa (b. 1964) grew up outside Detroit. He studied voice at the University of Michigan and prepared for an opera career, but the composer William Bolcom encouraged him to focus on composition. Lippa's first major musical, *jon & jen*, opened Off Broadway in 1995. His most recent Broadway musical was the short-lived *Big Fish* (2013). Lippa has written various types of musical compositions, including an oratorio about the life of Harvey Milk, one of the first openly gay men to be elected to public office. A year after winning a seat on the San Francisco Board of Supervisors, Milk was assassinated by a disgruntled former colleague on the board.

Jeanine Tesori

Like the other performing arts genres, musical theater has historically relegated women to the stage. The credit line "music by" has only rarely been followed by the name of a woman; and women lyricists on Broadway have been only slightly more numerous than women composers. (Kay Swift was the first woman composer to write an entire Broadway musical, *Fine and Dandy* [1930] [see Chapter 17].) This situation began to reverse itself in the nineties. Lyricists Lynn Ahrens and Susan Birkenhead have filled the void left by Betty Comden, who died in 2006 (see

THE MAGIC KINGDOM ON BROADWAY

The success of the animated film *The Little Mermaid* in 1989 reversed the Disney Company's flagging interest in film musicals during the eighties. Two years later, after the positive reception of *Beauty and the Beast*, Disney's president, Michael Eisner, decided to expand the company's activities into live Broadway theater. Within a couple of years, producing live versions of its catalogue of animated musicals became a part of Disney's resurgence strategy, starting with *Beauty and the Beast* in 1994. Disney dedicated a reported $12 million to the project, and the investment paid off in spades. The film version boasted a score by Alan Mencken and Howard Ashman. The subsequent Broadway version added seven new songs. Ashman had succumbed to AIDS in 1991, so Menken teamed up with Tim Rice to write the additional songs (see Chapter 11). Several critics complained that the stage adaptation was too literal, leaving little to the imagination. David Richards wrote that the production "belongs right up there with the Empire State Building, F. A. O. Schwarz and the Circle Line boat tours. It is hardly a triumph of art, but it'll probably be a whale of a tourist attraction. It is Las Vegas without the sex, Mardi Gras without the booze and Madame Tussaud's without the waxy stares. You don't watch it, you gape at it, knowing that nothing in Dubuque comes close. . . . [I]t is clearly the product of a company that prizes its winning formulas." Menken and Rice also wrote the score for Disney's next show, *King David*, an original idea intended to commemorate the 3,000th anniversary of Jerusalem. More an oratorio than a full-fledged musical, *King David* inaugurated the renovated New Amsterdam Theatre, where it played a limited run of nine performances.

Walt Disney Theatrical Productions, as the Broadway branch of Disney is called today, was founded in 1993, initially headed by Peter Schneider (president) and Thomas Schumacher (vice president). Schneider, who had been with Disney since 1985 and served as the first president of the Feature Animation division during the company's renaissance in the animated film musical field, was partly responsible for *The Little Mermaid* and *Beauty and the Beast*. Schumacher arrived at Disney in 1988. The two were not directly involved with the first two live theatrical projects; in fact, they were initially skeptical about the entire enterprise. Their first project, *The Lion King*, is still running on Broadway.

After *The Lion King*, Schneider and Schumacher turned their attention to an original musical: *Aida*. *Aida* is a megamusical–Disney hybrid, featuring a multiracial cast and a soft-rock score. It recounts the story of Verdi's *Aida* (1871) as told in Leontyne Price's *Aida Story*. The musical premiered in 1998 at Atlanta's Alliance Theatre. The Broadway version opened in 2000 and ran for 1,852 performances.

(Continued)

It, too, featured a rock score by Elton John and Tim Rice. By this time, Disney musicals had joined megamusicals as a punching bag for American critics who were soured by the declining status of the traditional American musical. As Ben Brantley wrote in his review of the show, "Like many Broadway megamusicals today, [*Aida*] has the disconnected, sterile feeling that suggests it has been assembled, piecemeal, by committee."

In recent years, Disney has looked beyond its animated feature films as source material for live musicals. The company teamed up with Cameron Mackintosh to produce the live version of *Mary Poppins*. In 2013, Disney closed *Mary Poppins* in order to make way for a live version of *Aladdin*, which opened in 2014.

Chapter 7). Jeanine Tesori (b. 1961) stands out as the most prominent woman composer to emerge in the nineties.

Tesori attended Barnard College with the intention of pursuing medicine, but she quickly changed her focus to music. Her first Broadway job was composing dance arrangements for *The Secret Garden*. Her breakthrough musical, *Violet*, based on Doris Betts's short story "The Ugliest Pilgrim," opened at Playwrights Horizons in 1997. With a book and lyrics by Brian Crawley, *Violet* is set in the seminal year of 1964 (Betts's story, which was first published in 1969, does not indicate the precise year) and tells the story of a Southern teenage girl who, scarred since birth, goes in search of a televangelist who, she believes, possesses healing powers. Before composing a note, Tesori, as Gershwin had done while working on *Porgy and Bess* and Vernon Duke on *Cabin in the Sky,* traveled to the South to soak up the local flavor.

Tesori's career took off in the new millenium. She received the assignment of writing the songs for *Shrek the Musical* (2008). In 2013, she became the first artistic director of the newly established *Encores! Off Center*, a summer musical theater series at City Center. The first season included two musicals by women, *I'm Getting My Act Together and Taking It on the Road* and *Violet*, which inspired a Broadway production in 2014. In 2015, Tesori's musical *Fun Home* opened on Broadway to rave reviews and won five Tony Awards, including for Best Original Score and Best Musical. Based on the 2006 graphic memoir *Fun Home: A Family Tragicomic* by Alison Bechdel (recipient of a 2014 MacArthur "Genius" Award), the musical brings a surprising degree of humor and pathos to a story of family dynamics, sexual identity, and suicide. *The New York Times* theater critic Ben Brantley wrote, "Much of the music . . . has the interrogative restlessness of thought in pursuit of certainty, and the ambivalent mix of anger and affection that pervades our relationships with our nearest and dearest. There's a delicate dissonance in the multiple-part songs, which are all the more affecting for their implicit yearning for harmony."

DAWN OF THE CORPORATE PRODUCER

The ascendency of the megamusical coincided with the new era of globalization at the end of the millennium (referred to by some economists as the third era). It spelled the end of the New York–centric musical. By the end of the century, producers of the megamusical and the Walt Disney Company had imposed a corporate framework onto the production of Broadway musicals. This model has franchising as its primary goal. The Broadway musical, a commodity with greater national and international reach than ever before, assumed a more homogenous look and generic sound. Musically speaking, there is little stylistic difference between one musical and another; a production of a jukebox musical such as *Mamma Mia* in Las Vegas sounds virtually the same as the Broadway production. Pop singing (heavy use of chest voice, scooping, and an overt use of vibrato—the preferred vocal style of television programs such as *American Idol*) has replaced legitimate musical theater singing as the dominant performance mode. The "authentic" experience of Broadway can be purchased everywhere, thus the term "McMusical." Moreover, like spectators at rock concerts, musical theater audiences expect the live experience to replicate the cast recording (whereas the opposite used to be the case). These changes set a new course for musical theater in the new millennium.

AND BEAR IN MIND

The Lion King *(1997, New Amsterdam Theatre, as of 2015 the fourth-longest-running musical in Broadway history)*

Music by Mark Mancina, Elton John, Lebo M [Lebohang Morake],
Jay Rifkin, and Hans Zimmer
Lyrics by Mark Mancina, Lebo M [Lebohang Morake], Julie Taymor,
Jay Rifkin, and Tim Rice
Book by Roger Allers and Irene Mecchi

The Disney Corporation surprised the Broadway establishment with its stage incarnation of *The Lion King*, which opened at the newly refurbished Amsterdam Theatre on 42nd Street and thereby became identified with the renewal of the Times Square District. Unlike Disney's previous stage adaptations, *The Lion King* did not try to replicate the animated film with live actors. Instead, the company gave the director and puppeteer Julie Taymor freedom to bring her unique artistic vision to the material. Taymor, who hailed from the nonprofit *avant-garde* theater world, employed puppets, African-based music, exotic costumes, and an all-black cast.

(Continued)

Taymor's strong vision transformed the animated film into a surprisingly original live stage musical, but the score, which includes several new songs, lacks a unified voice, the result of being the product of a committee of seven writers, six of whom worked on the film in one capacity or another plus Taymor, who provided some new lyrics. The musical discontinuity between Elton John and Tim Rice's five songs retained from the film ("Circle of Life," "I Just Can't Wait to Be King," "Be Prepared," "Hakuna Matata," and "Can You Feel the Love Tonight") and the atmospheric "African" music written for the live version is particularly pronounced. Hans Zimmer, whose African-inflected underscoring for the film earned him an Academy Award, oversaw the music for the stage version. Because Taymor desired a greater African presence in the score, the African musician Lebo Morake, a native of Soweto, was commissioned to supply the show's authentic sound. Morake had composed much of the film's background music as well as most of the music on a recording entitled *Rhythm of the Pridelands* (music inspired by Disney's *The Lion King*). The film composer Mark Mancina, who had produced the animated film's soundtrack, worked with Taymor to combine these various sources into a single score. Taymor exclaimed, "What I love about the music is that the South African sound and the orchestrations pull all of the pieces together so that it's not one eclectic mess. *Lion King* successfully builds a bridge between Western pop, South African pop, and South African traditional music."

The Lion King qualifies as a megamusical in several ways. The marketing, merchandising, international success, and long run resemble a Cameron Mackintosh megamusical production. The story, based on Shakespeare's *Hamlet*, has the universality of megamusical plots. What perhaps distinguished *The Lion King* from an Andrew Lloyd Webber musical is the fact that the critics shared the audience's enthusiasm.

. . . .

NAMES, TERMS, AND CONCEPTS

Ahrens, Lynn

Brown, Jason Robert

Falsettoland

Flaherty, Stephen

Guettel, Adam

Kiss of the Spider Woman

La Bohème

LaChiusa, Michael John

Larson, Jonathan

Lion King, The

Puccini, Giacomo

"Seasons of Love"

Secret Garden, The

Tesori, Jeanine

Verismo opera

Wildhorn, Frank

Wolfe, Charles

DISCUSSION QUESTIONS

1. How do the labels "rock opera," "megamusical," and "book musical" apply to *Rent*?

2. In what ways, if any, does *Rent* pay homage to the traditional book musical of the Rodgers and Hammerstein era?

3. Consider the topicality of *Rent* in the context of the twenty-first century. What relevance does the show have for today's audiences?

4. Discuss the recent increase in the portrayal of gay characters in musical theater.

CHAPTER 13

THE NEW MILLENNIUM
(*THE LIGHT IN THE PIAZZA*, 2005, VIVIAN BEAUMONT THEATER, 504 PERFORMANCES)

The terrorist attacks on September 11, 2001, thrust America into two expensive and protracted wars and ushered in an era of crippling political discord and profound uncertainty about America's future. Adding to the country's woes, in 2008 the worst economic slowdown since the Great Depression beset the country. Broadway, as it had done during previous national crises, provided some much-needed diversion from the hardships that many Americans experienced. On the day that the world Trade Center Towers collapsed, Broadway responded by canceling all performances, but in the days immediately after the attacks, New York's mayor, Rudolph Giuliani, used Broadway and the ideals it symbolized as a means for confronting the tragedy and for ensuring the vitality of New York's tourist trade.

One casualty of 9/11 was the planned Broadway premiere of Stephen Sondheim's *Assassins*, a musical about presidential assassins that had played Off Broadway over ten years earlier (see Chapter 9). The dark subject matter was deemed too disturbing for the painful recovery period. Based on historical events, *Assassins* explored the underbelly of the American Dream of fame and fortune (see Chapter 9). Audiences, however, flocked to see farcical, uplifting, and nostalgic musicals such as Mel Brook's *The Producers*, *The Full Monty*, and a revival of *42nd Street*.

Before long, Broadway rebounded from the tragedy of 9/11, and by 2006 attendance had reached a record high of nearly 12.5 million. During the 2010–2011 season, Broadway became a billion-dollar-a-year industry, with musicals accounting for the majority of ticket sales. In the years since, however, attendance declined, though profits have risen. A 2013 survey published by the National Endowment for the Arts found that attendance at Broadway musicals between 2008 and 2012 was down, more in fact than for any other artistic category. However, the market for Broadway musicals has expanded internationally, and musical theater has acquired new cultural capital, as reflected in the popularity of films and television shows such as *Glee*, Disney's *High School Musical* series, and even the disparaged television "dramady" *Smash*. Theaters in major cities continue to offer subscription series for touring productions of Broadway musicals. Book publishers have released an array of novels and memoirs about musical theater; and a virtual cottage industry of children's and young adult books involving musical theater has sprung up in recent years. Musical theater studies as an academic field has expanded, and a refereed journal entitled *Studies in Musical Theatre* was founded in 2007. *The Phantom of the Opera* celebrated its 27th anniversary on Broadway in 2013. Finally, the downward trend in ticket sales on Broadway has reversed itself since 2013, with attendance rising 3.3% and setting a new record of over 13 million people.

The bursting of the housing bubble and the attendant economic recession of 2008 coincided with the election of the first African American president in U.S. history. Barack Hussein Obama's election in 2008 has shaped the political discourse ever since, generating hope and optimism on the Left and representing a harbinger of undesired change and new challenges for the Right. Obama promised a brighter future for average Americans and, despite forceful opposition from the Republican Party, passed a sweeping health care bill (Patient Protection and Affordable Care Act of 2010) and attempted to tackle several divisive issues such as the legalization of gay marriage, immigration reform, and gun control. Obama also extricated the nation from two unpopular wars that began during the Bush administration. It is difficult to ignore the preponderance of musicals about racial identity or racial conflict during Obama's first term, two in 2009 alone. *Memphis* involves an interracial relationship. *Fela!* tells the story of the African musician and political activist Fela Kuti. *The Scottsboro Boys* (2010) served as a powerful reminder of the miscarriage of justice that characterizes the history of race in America. Broadway also saw revivals of three musicals with racial themes, *Finian's Rainbow*, *Ragtime*, and *Porgy and Bess*.

> In 1976, George Wallace, the governor of Alabama, granted a pardon to the last surviving member of the Scottsboro Boys. Almost four decades later, the Alabama State Legislature granted posthumous pardons to the other eight, much too late to placate those who believed that all nine boys were innocent and therefore should have been exonerated.

CORPORATE PRODUCING

Even without the 9/11 tragedy and the "Great Recession" of 2008, the economics of Broadway musicals would have experienced a seismic shift. During the new millennium, the cost of doing business on Broadway has far outstripped inflation, and a spike in corporate producing has rendered the freewheeling independent producer a thing of the past. Ticket prices have skyrocketed. In the "age of McMusicals," as Mark Grant has dubbed this era, musicals operate like "corporately franchised staged happenings that are actually music videos packaged for theater." This trend can be traced back to the advent of the megamusical in the eighties (see Chapter 11) and the arrival of Disney on Broadway in the nineties (see Chapter 12). Corporate producing has fueled the global musical theater market and, many argue, diminished risk taking on Broadway. Corporate players have altered the methodology of producing musicals and have had an impact on the content and character of commercial musical theater. The "jukebox musical" epitomizes the risk-averse nature of corporate producing by repackaging previously released popular music in the hope of holding down production costs, minimizing the threat of failure, and maximizing revenues. Critics of corporate producing disparage its consensus-driven decision-making process, lack of imagination, and reliance on focus groups. Independent producers fear that the looming corporate presence will lead to more "pandering to the lowest common denominator," notes Steven Adler, "and the greater whitewashing of Broadway fare by the corporate brush." By contrast, in earlier decades, an iconoclastic musical might catch the interest of a single independent producer willing to invest the time, energy, and capital to see it staged.

Disney has rightly or wrongly received most of the blame for the homogenization, some would say "Disneyfication," of Broadway. The company denies the charge and claims that the term "Disneyfication" "wrongly casts Disney in the role of the mustache-twirling villain whose corporate imperative demands nothing less than the complete homogenization of the American theater scene." However, the charge is difficult to shake off, for Disney has had a deep and lasting effect on Broadway. The playwright and director Charles Wolfe notes that the "corporate thought process defining the artistic journey results in mediocrity becoming the standard." Wolfe agrees with many who believe that good musicals often arise not from corporate structures but from individual artists working together. The impact of corporate producing extends to virtually every aspect of musical theater. The musical arrangements and overall sound production have become homogenized. Synthesized instruments and digital technology dominate pit orchestras and threaten to replace live musicians or at least limit their numbers.

No consensus has been reached regarding the long-term consequences of the corporate incursion on Broadway. Pundits lament an irreversible decline of musical theater. Most critics would agree that commercial considerations have shaped the content and style of Broadway musicals to a degree unheard of in previous eras. For example, test marketing has had the unintended consequence of narrowing the stylistic range of the music to something between pop and rock, and sound engineers have become nearly as important as orchestrators. Market targeting has also led to a staggering increase in jukebox musicals, which attract young audiences as well as baby boomers willing to pay for an opportunity to revisit their formative years (see Chapter 12). The reliance on tourists, moreover, has limited the type of stories and themes that investors are willing to back. The tourist market tends to avoid "weighty subject matter that is not leavened by glib irony, a bleating pop score, or sentimental sugar coating," to quote Adler.

Corporate producers have presided over a decline in the organic integration of songs and dialogue that was musical theater's major achievement during its Golden Age. For the playwright Arthur Laurents,

there was great value in deriving songs "from that initial framework for narrative and character, which, even if inadvertently, ensures that the musical will be about something. The strongest musicals, regardless of the genre or style, have adhered to the basic precept, but writing workshops and classes [see Chapter 12] teach young artists to compose songs without a libretto as a point of departure.

Ironically, the lack of dramatic integrity and purposeful incorporation of songs today is more reflective of the pre–Rodgers and Hammerstein era than of the age of the well-made book musical. As Adler observes, "songs are shoehorned into a show without an eye to the precise matching of character, situation, and song style."

In addition to jukebox musicals, corporate producing has driven up the number of musicals based on films. Disney entered the Broadway market specifically because it recognized the potential profit that its catalogue of existing films could generate. Thomas Schumacher of Disney acknowledges, "Because we're a corporation, we must invest our time and money to work [a production] for its greatest return, not just *a* return. . . . [W]e need to create shows that are franchisable and large enough to justify the level of support we have to give them on a continuing basis." As a musical theater–producing organization, Disney subscribes to a mutual-fund philosophy, juggling many projects at once, honing them, drawing from a general reservoir of money, and cherry picking some to move forward.

Another major player in the musical theater business is Clear Channel, which enjoys a controlling interest in the national touring musical theater market. Clear Channel's predecessor did not invest in new musicals but acquired the rights to present national touring productions of hit Broadway shows and established subscription seasons in various American cities. Clear Channel expanded into the production of new Broadway musicals to ensure that there was ample product to book into its theaters (theater owners at the turn of the twentieth century did the same thing). National tours of musicals generate handsome earnings, as they attract millions of people who might otherwise not attend musicals. Clear Channel, therefore, has a major stake in the commercial viability of Broadway musicals. Unless they are "franchisable," the reasoning goes, they will not turn a profit beyond the original Broadway production.

Corporations such as Clear Channel must compete against today's easy access to a myriad of entertainment options, including videogames, Netflix, concerts, movies, live and televised sporting events, amateur theater, and even live broadcasts of musicals. Because Americans are bombarded by more choices than ever, producers must remain hypervigilant about the market. They eschew an "eat-your-spinach" approach to theater programming and care about musical theater as "art" only insofar as doing so advances the goals of its shareholders. This attitude, many believe, has led to a "growing tide of mediocre, assembly-line shows." However, some theater insiders are more sanguine about the effects of corporate producing, especially the infusion of cash it has brought to the industry and the expanded audience base that it has created.

The corporate hegemony on Broadway has meant bad news for musical theater writers. For composers and lyricists, the increase in jukebox musicals, revivals, and screen-to-stage musicals has meant fewer opportunities and a considerable loss of prestige. For instance, whereas Broadway composers used to be treated as cultural icons (e.g., George Gershwin and Richard Rodgers), today's theater marquees, promotional posters, and even the covers of CD recordings of musicals omit the names of the composers and lyricists, forcing anyone interested in knowing who they are to search the *Playbill,* the recording booklet, or the Internet for the information. Getting a new musical produced on Broadway, let alone one without major commercial potential, has become exceedingly difficult. Productions at nonprofit and Off Broadway theaters have accounted for the most innovative musicals in recent years. *Spring Awakening* and *Next to Normal* both originated Off Broadway. Even someone of Stephen Sondheim's stature has had to revert to Off Broadway and regional theater venues. Young writers hope against hope that they will get their work seen on Broadway. In the meantime, they submit manuscripts and demo recordings to nonprofit theaters and musical theater festivals and contests.

MUSICAL THEATER IN THE TWENTY-FIRST CENTURY

Since the turn of the century, screen-to-stage and jukebox musicals have accounted for the majority of musicals on Broadway. Revivals continue to figure large in most theatrical seasons, and British-style megamusicals (*The Phantom of the Opera, Mamma Mia, Wicked*), although no longer the dominant form, have remained popular. Even concept musicals (*The Scottsboro Boys*) show up occasionally. During the first decade of the century, satire experienced something of a renaissance on Broadway, arguably a defensive response to perceived biases against the musical theater genre, a marginalization of musical theater fans, and an uneasiness about musical theater's exuberant campiness and irrepressible optimism (*Urinetown, The Book of Mormon*). In response, writers have adopted an ironic stance toward musical theater, in effect criticizing the genre from within. Lastly, several highly trained writers have followed in the footsteps of Stephen Sondheim, writing intellectually and musically challenging musicals, often operatic in nature, but with limited commercial appeal. Their musicals rarely make it to Broadway.

The Rock Hegemony

The major story on Broadway in the new millennium is the musical's complete capitulation to rock music. In fact, rock music is the one unifying aspect of Broadway musicals today. For decades, Broadway treated rock as an interloper (see Chapter 16). Critics were dismissive or disdainful of and often downright hostile to musicals that attempted to incorporate rock music. For decades, critically acclaimed rock musicals such as *Hair* (1968), *Grease* (1972), *The Wiz* (1975), and *Rent* (1996) were few and far between. However, in a stunning reversal, rock music now accounts for nearly all of the musical theater categories identified above. It took fifty years for rock to replace traditional Broadway music as the primary idiom for musical theater, but now that it has, more traditional styles of music seem out of step with Broadway tastes. Rock music itself has become a standard musical theater plot element, as many jukebox musicals take their stories from the annals of rock and roll.

Hairspray

Turning John Waters's campy 1988 film *Hairspray* into a commercially successful musical comedy required little rethinking. Given the film's exuberant dancing, youthful appeal, and upbeat message, the only surprise is that the musical took nearly fifteen years to materialize. It boasts a Tony Award–winning score by Marc Shaiman and Scott Wittman and book by Thomas Meehan and Marc O'Donnell. *Hairspray* tells the story of breaking the racial barrier on television. Behind the integrationist theme, however, lies a subversive critique of white America's sense of female beauty and attitudes about gender.

Memphis

Memphis (2009) also combines a story about the popular music industry with race politics, but it is a more realistic and darker musical than *Hairspray*. A white deejay named Huey Calhoun, a fictional character reminiscent of Dewey Phillips, falls in love with black music and an African American singer named Felicia. In an early version of *Memphis* presented at three regional theaters, Huey is beaten for going out with a black woman, but the Broadway version toned down the violence sparked by the interracial relationship. David Bryan, one of the founding members of Bon Jovi, composed the music, and Joe DiPietro wrote the book and lyrics. The score is a pastiche of fifties rock-and-roll styles. The backstage plot ensures entertaining musical numbers, but the interracial story offers nothing new about a topic that musical theater had been dealing with for decades (*South Pacific*, *Jamaica*, *No Strings*, *Golden Boy*). The predictably unhappy ending (Huey and Felicia's interracial relationship cannot withstand society's prejudices) seems like warmed-over Hammerstein.

Dewey Phillips (1926–1968) was a radio disc jockey and an early proponent of rock and roll. His radio career got its start in 1949 on WHBQ/560 in Memphis. He caused shock waves by transmitting both white and black music.

Film-to-Stage Musicals

Musicals based on films date back to the early fifties, but in recent years they have propagated to the point of becoming a distinct genre. Martin Kohn coined the term "movical" to describe this category of musical. A major boon for producers, these musicals come with a built-in "marketing bonanza," a developed storyline, and sometimes a preexisting score. Disney created an entire division dedicated to bringing its animated and live-action films to the stage (see Chapter 12), and MGM followed suit in 2003, founding "MGM on Stage," which was behind the stage version of *Chitty Chitty Bang Bang* (2005). Today, movie studios are mining their catalogues for adaptable films, for the potential revenue stream from such musicals can be greater than that of the original films. Some historians have argued that movicals are a tonic to "*Cats*-itis" (a reference to Andrew Lloyd Webber's long-running musical *Cats*) and that they can compete with megamusicals by featuring impressive scenery, costumes, and lighting (see Chapter 11). This explanation might explain the trend in the nineties, but it does not fully explain the phenomenon today, as even modest-budget films with little in the way of visual spectacle are being adapted as musicals. For example, *Once* incorporated the minimalist approach of the source, a low-budget Indie film about two lonely musicians in Ireland who become unlikely friends.

The "movical" craze reflects a postmodern consciousness, which theater scholar Judith Sebesta defines as "an aesthetic and critical stance shaped by nostalgia, mediatization of culture, suspicion of both the real and grand narratives, inter textuality, pastiche, self-reflexivity, dual coding, parody, and fragmentation." The replacement of literature (novels, novellas, short stories, spoken drama) by film as the primary source material for musicals mirrors a shift in postmodern culture from the word to the visual image. Producers of the earliest film-inspired musicals, which date back to the fifties, instinctively limited themselves to spoken films, acknowledging the futility of trying to compete with the conspicuous opulence of Hollywood musicals. After all, a typical Broadway pit can accommodate around twenty musicians, whereas a film studio can accommodate many times that many. The earliest Broadway adaptations of Hollywood musicals, *Gigi* in 1973 (revived in 2015) and *Singin in the Rain* in 1985, were far and few between. Two factors eventually helped ease the trepidation about adapting Hollywood musicals: (1) producers discovered that audiences would pay handsomely to see their favorite movies in the flesh, and (2) the technical capabilities of live theater began to make it possible to effectively reproduce Hollywood musicals on stage. In the theater, Mary Poppins and Chitty Chitty Bang Bang both flew, perhaps not as realistically as in the films but with enough theater magic to delight audiences.

Adapting animated films for the stage comes with additional challenges. The usual method, as exemplified by *Beauty and the Beast*, is simply to replicate the animated version with real actors. By contrast, the stage version of *The Lion King* reimagines the original film with such ingenuity that it creates its own sense of awe (see Chapter 12). The Broadway-bound stage adaptation of *The Hunchback of Notre Dame* expands on the film through the addition of new songs and a change in tone.

The increase in screen-to-stage musicals is a response to the story saturation and "filmic consciousness," to use Sebesta's term, of today's audiences, which the Internet has only served to reinforce. Movicals essentialize the familiar and reflect the most universal postmodern phenomena: nostalgia and intertextuality. Audiences today suffer from the "saturated self," according to Kenneth Gergen. The "vertigo of unlimited multiplicity" causes one to seek comfort in familiar stories and avoid new ones, which poses a daunting challenge to writers. Live musicals based on popular films have become a ritualistic, communal experience in which everyone shares the same knowledge.

The Producers

The Producers rolled into New York like a tidal wave in early 2001. The prospect of seeing a musical based on Mel Brooks's 1967 cult film *The Producers* sent New Yorkers into a ticket-buying frenzy. In the film version, a crooked Broadway producer ropes his spineless accountant into a get-rich-quick scheme. They plot to overcapitalize a musical comedy that is in such bad taste that it is sure to fail, close the show as soon as the critics pan it, and then flee to Rio with the remaining cash. To ensure that their scheme comes off without a hitch, they select the most outlandishly offensive play they can find: *Springtime for Hitler*, the work of a neo-Nazi who hopes to glorify the "Führer." To their dismay, audiences mistake the show for a satire, and it becomes the hit of the season. The producer and accountant attempt to blow up the theater but wind up in prison. For the musical, Brooks cut the character of Lorenzo St. Dubois, the actor who impersonates Hitler. Instead, the flamboyant director of *Springtime for Hitler*, Roger de Bris, plays the role. Brooks also eliminated Max and Leo's attempt to destroy the theater. Max is arrested, found "incredibly guilty," and goes to prison, while Leo absconds with their Swedish secretary/receptionist, Ulla, and the ill-begotten money to Rio.

The appearance of Nathan Lane as the money-grubbing producer Max Bialystock and Matthew Broderick as his milquetoast accountant Leo Bloom made the critics giddy. As a comic duo, Lane and Broderick became a Broadway sensation overnight. That Brooks's score was a bag of clichés did not stifle enthusiasm for the show. On the contrary, the traditional musical comedy style of the songs enhanced the show's nostalgic appeal. Altogether, *The Producers* won 12 Tony Awards, one of several records that the show either broke or set. At the 2001 Tony Awards ceremony, Mel Brooks could barely contain his mounting glee during each return trip to the podium.

Today *The Producers*'s brand of satire is practically the default mode on Broadway—ubiquitous to the point of becoming platitudinous—but when Brooks's film appeared in 1967, it had a refreshing satirical edginess. The musical version employs the tools of parody, pastiche, and irony to draw attention to the homoerotic nature and pageantry of Nazi culture. Jonathan Burston attributes the musical's success to the "transgressive thrill of its political incorrectness." Even more than the film, the musical traffics in offensive jokes, especially at the expense of homosexuals, African Americans, and women, but it tries, somewhat feebly, to absolve itself from charges of homophobia, racism, or misogyny by hiding behind the smug fifties milieu in which the story is set.

The musical *The Producers* received the near-total approbation of the New York press, which suggested that the show heralded the return of the former glory days of Broadway musical comedy. Indeed, critics and audiences embraced the show's nostalgia fueled by the traditional musical comedy style and New York setting. By 2001, musical theater had lost some of its ties with New York, had become a more homogenous art form, and had suffered a blow delivered by the overwhelming popularity of the megamusical. The New York critics felt that *The Producers* helped to reverse these trends. On the other hand, the prototypical New York roots of *The Producers* explain why sales slowed considerably once local Broadway patrons who wanted to see the show had done so.

Other Notable Film-Inspired Musicals

Brooks's film is not a musical, but it cried out for musical treatment. Not all nonmusical films, however, translate so readily into a musical. For example, the 2002 musical based on the searing 1957 film noir *Sweet Smell of Success* failed in part because Marvin Hamlisch's strong but derivative score overwhelmed the cool plot with its romantic sweep. The film, written by Clifford Odets and Ernest Lehman and starring Burt Lancaster and Tony Curtis, charts the evil machinations of the newspaper columnist J. J. Hunsecker, a role presumably modeled on Walter Winchell, as he sets out to destroy a jazz musician who is in love with his sister. The musical, with a book by John Guare and lyrics by Craig Carnelia, lasted only 109 performances. In her postmortem, Margo Jefferson argued that giving songs of the heart to a nasty character like J. J. only adds to the problems inherent in musicalizing this terse story. By contrast, Sondheim immortalized a mass murderer and his accomplice in *Sweeney Todd*, but he never absolves them from their sins. *Sweet Smell of Success* nearly sentimentalizes its rotten characters.

If musical theater is any indicator, American audiences seem to take great delight in stories about the economic hardships of the British working class. Since 2000, three British films, one about unemployed steel workers (*The Full Monty*, 1997), one about unemployed coal miners (*Billy Elliot*, 2000), and one about employees at a struggling shoe factory (*Kinky Boots*, 2005), have served as the basis for successful Broadway musicals. *The Full Monty* was Americanized by the playwright Terrence McNally, who transferred the action from Sheffield, England, whose once-flourishing steel industry has faced a radical retrenchment, to economically depressed Buffalo, New York, whose steel industry had suffered a similar fate. *The Full Monty* is about a group of mostly laid-off workers who, to make ends meet, perform a striptease at a local club. *The Full Monty* was the first of three screen-to-stage musicals with a score by David Yazbek. The show ran nearly two years but got lost amid the excitement over *The Producers*.

David Yazbek attended Brown University, wrote for the *David Letterman Show*, and has composed songs for children's television. He comes from a rock background but has adapted well to the exigencies of the musical theater genre.

The other two musicals retained the original English setting of the source films. *Billy Elliot*, an adaptation of Stephen Daldry's 2000 film, takes place during the 1984–1985 miner's strike in Margaret Thatcher's England. Billy, a nine-year-old boy who finds his calling in ballet, overcomes the prejudices and personal preoccupations of his father and brother, both of them participants in the coalminers' strike, and wins a full scholarship to attend the Royal Ballet School in London. The father–son relationship overshadows the economic hardships against which the story takes place, and the musical explores prevailing attitudes about dance, gender, class, and sexuality through a combustible combination of ballet and the violent skirmishes between the police and the miners. Elton John, who has moved remarkably successfully between the rock and musical theater worlds, composed the music, and Lee Hall adapted his screenplay and wrote the lyrics. In a bit of novelty casting, three different boy actors played Billy in rotation (the 2012 musical *Matilda* adopted the same arrangement). At the 2009 Tony Awards ceremony, when the winner in the category of Best Male Lead in a musical was announced, the three boys appeared together on stage to accept the award, which was jointly awarded to them (for which the Tony committee had made special allowances—although it refused to extend the same opportunity to the girls who shared the title role in *Matilda*).

Kinky Boots (2013) focuses on the lingering effects of the postindustrial decline in England. It, too, deals with timely issues related to the LGBT community. With a sentimental book by Harvey Fierstein and an easy-listening rock score by Cyndi Lauper, *Kinky Boots* solicits the audience's approbation. According to *The New York Times* theater critic Ben Brantley, "It's a shameless emotional button pusher, presided over—be warned—by that most weary of latter-day Broadway archetypes, a strong and sassy drag queen who dispenses life lessons like an automated fortune cookie." Lola, the major drag-queen role, is the latest addition to an expanding list of sympathetic and campy LGBT roles in the musical theater repertory (*Billy Elliot*'s Michael Caffrey is another). In a year in which the Supreme Court struck down the Defense of Marriage Act, the timely main theme of *Kinky Boots* resonated with fans.

Grey Gardens (2006) stands out for its unusual source material: Albert and David Maysles's award-winning documentary of the same name (released in 1976) about the lives of Edith Bouvier Beale and her daughter, nicknamed Little Edie. The film incorporated and popularized a technique called "direct cinema." Had the Beales not had family ties to Jacqueline Kennedy Onassis, the film would still be a fascinating, albeit voyeuristic, study of a bizarre family dynamic. That anyone could have imagined adapting this documentary into a musical is astonishing; that the writers—Scott Frankel (music), Michael Korie (lyrics), and Doug Wright (book)—succeeded defies all expectations. They preferred pathos to derision and thereby bestowed a sense of dignity on the unfortunate real-life characters and their lives. Christine Ebersole (b. 1953) played Edith in Act I and Little Edie in Act II and won a Tony Award for her performance; Mary Louise Wilson, who portrayed the mother in Act II, also took home a Tony. The writers devised a fictional scenario for the first act that suggests the reasons for the women's later destitution and reclusiveness, the focus of the second act. Set in 1941, the first act centers on an engagement party for Little Edie and Joseph Kennedy at the East Hampton showplace Grey Gardens. The action spans a single "fateful afternoon" and provides an almost mythologized portrait of the Beales as society ladies, the glamorous version of themselves that they maintained in their own twisted version of reality. Act II takes place in 1973, as the mother and daughter are living in squalor in the now-derelict, cat-ridden mansion. The two acts have parallel dramatic arcs. At the end of the first act, Little Edie musters the courage to leave her mother, but she fails to do so at the parallel point in the second act. The score, especially the diegetic songs, evokes music of the forties, but it also achieves a postmodern sense of fragmentation, as the past and present merge inside the minds of the characters. Frankel and Korie have recently collaborated with the playwright Richard Greenberg on a musical adaptation of Todd Haynes's 2002 film *Far From Heaven*, which is about a closeted gay man and his wife in suburban America during the fifties.

Similar to French "cinema vérité," direct cinema, which was popular in the seventies, relied on lightweight hand-held cameras and aimed to capture life as it happened by doing away with the omniscient narrative voiceover (which has enjoyed a revival in recent years) and staged interviews typical of documentaries. The Maysles brothers were among the pioneers of direct cinema.

Jukebox Musicals

The jukebox musical has a precedent in the eighteenth-century *pasticcio*, an opera assembled by weaving a new plot around pre-existing arias either appropriated from earlier operas (by a single or multiple composers) or discarded from the operas for which they were originally composed (in musical theater jargon, "cut-outs"). Today, reusing pre-existing songs as a score for a musical is an expedient and relatively inexpensive way of attracting large audiences and generating enormous profits. However, the very premise of building a musical around repackaged songs runs contrary to the spirit of the integrated musical, but when expertly handled (e.g., *Ain't Misbehavin'* [1978]), a jukebox musical provides good entertainment. Jukebox musicals appeared on Broadway well before the turn of the twenty-first century, but since *Mamma Mia!* opened in 2001, their numbers have surged. The worldwide success of *Mamma Mia!* removed any doubts about the commercial viability of the jukebox musical. With a book by British playwright Catherine Johnson (b. 1957), *Mamma Mia!* employs songs associated with the seventies Swedish rock group ABBA to tell the story of a young woman, Sophie Sheridan, who attempts to discover who among three of her mother's ex-lovers is her biological father. The action just happens to take place on a picturesque Greek island, where her mother, Donna, a former lead singer in a girl group, runs a hotel. The contrived plot notwithstanding, *Mamma Mia!* played to near-capacity crowds for well over a decade and was made into a film in 2008. Ben Brantley equated the show with instant pudding and Hostess cupcakes: "smooth, sticky and slightly synthetic-tasting." Like the critic-proof megamusical, *Mamma Mia!* suffered little at the box office from such snarky criticism. When the show lost its lease on the Winter Garden Theatre in 2013, audience demand was still high enough to warrant transferring the production to the smaller Broadhurst Theatre. Attendance of the Broadway production was unaffected by the film version, in which Meryl Streep

TABLE 13.1. Twenty-First Century Broadway Musicals Based on Films

MUSICAL	FILM SOURCE
The Full Monty (2000)	*The Full Monty* (1997)
The Producers (2001)	*The Producers* (1968)
Hairspray (2002)	*Hairspray* (1988)
Sweet Smell of Success (2002)	*Sweet Smell of Success* (1957)
Thoroughly Modern Millie (2002)	*Thoroughly Modern Millie* (1967)
Urban Cowboy (2003)	*Urban Cowboy* (1980)
Chitty Chitty Bang Bang (2005)	*Chitty Chitty Bang Bang* (1968)
Dirty Rotten Scoundrels (2005)	*Dirty Rotten Scoundrels* (1988)
The Color Purple (2005)	*The Color Purple* (1985)
Mary Poppins (2006)	*Mary Poppins* (1964)
The Wedding Singer (2006)	*The Wedding Singer* (1998)

MUSICAL	FILM SOURCE
High Fidelity (2006)	*High Fidelity* (2000)
Grey Gardens (2006)	*Grey Gardens* (1976)
Young Frankenstein (2007)	*Young Frankenstein* (1974)
Xanadu (2007)	*Xanadu* (1980)
Legally Blonde (2007)	*Legally Blonde* (2001)
Cry Baby (2008)	*Cry Baby* (1990)
Billy Elliot (2008)	*Billy Elliot* (2000)
Shrek the Musical (2008)	*Shrek* (2001)
The Little Mermaid (2008)	*The Little Mermaid* (1989)
9 to 5 (2009)	9 to 5 (1980)
Women on the Verge of a Nervous Breakdown (2010)	*Women on the Verge of a Nervous Breakdown* (1988)
Elf (2010)	*Elf* (2002)
Catch Me If You Can (2011)	*Catch Me If You Can* (2002)
Priscilla Queen of the Desert (2011)	*The Adventures of Priscilla, Queen of the Desert* (1994)
Sister Act (2011)	*Sister Act* (1992)
Ghosts (2012)	*Ghosts* (1990)
Newsies (2012)	*Newsies* (1992)
Once (2012)	*Once* (2007)
Bring It On (2012)	*Bring It On* (2000)
Christmas Story (2012)	*Christmas Story* (1983)
Leap of Faith (2012)	*Leap of Faith* (1992)
Kinky Boots (2013)	*Kinky Boots* (2005)
Big Fish (2013)	*Big Fish* (2003)
Aladdin (2014)	*Aladdin* (1992)
The Bridges of Madison County (2014)	*The Bridges of Madison County* (1995)
Rocky (2014)	*Rocky* (1976)
An American in Paris (2015)	*An American in Paris* (1951)
Finding Neverland (2015)	*Finding Neverland* (2004)

gave "the worst performance of her career," according to film critic A. O. Scott. Echoing Brantley's sentiments, Scott called the film a "mindless, hedonistic assault on coherence."

In contrast to *Mamma Mia!*, *Jersey Boys* (2005) brings form and content together into almost perfect harmony. It is a smart biomusical detailing the true story of Frankie Valli and the Four Seasons and featuring many of the songs that they made famous, such as "Sherry." *Jersey Boys* targeted baby boomers but also appealed to younger fans of classic rock. The original cast looked and sounded remarkably like the Four Seasons. John Lloyd Young's imitation of Frankie Valli's distinctive tenor voice was uncannily accurate. Young, whose performance earned him a Tony Award for Best Actor in a Musical, reprised his role for the 2014 film version of *Jersey Boys*, which remained faithful to the stage version but, despite several good performances, came and went with little notice.

The musical *Fela!* (2009) recounts the true saga of the musician and political activist Fela Kuti (1938–1997). In the seventies, Fela's popularity threatened the security of the military dictatorship in Nigeria. The musical, as directed by Bill T. Jones, featured as much dancing as singing, often literally in the aisles of the theater. The female dancers who represented the polygamist Fela's twenty-seven wives gave the show a propulsive momentum. The score's multicultural style captured the persona, politics, and biography of the rebellious protagonist. *Fela!* had the financial backing of several influential show-business personalities, including Jay-Z (Shawn Carter) and Will and Jada Pinkett Smith.

Frankie Valli and the Four Seasons in *Jersey Boys. From l to r*: J. Robert Spencer as Nick Massi, John Lloyd Young as Frankie Valli, Daniel Reichard as Bob Guadio, and Christian Hoff as Tommy DeVito. *Courtesy Joan Marcus.*

Revivals

Revivals have accounted for nearly half of the musicals produced on Broadway since 2000. Revivals of the Sondheim canon, even his lyrics-only musicals *West Side Story* and *Gypsy*, outnumber those by any other Broadway composer. *Into the Woods* returned to Broadway in 2002. The Scottish director John Boyle staged *Sweeney Todd* and *Company* in 2005 and 2006, respectively, and his revival of *Passion* played Off Broadway in 2013. A 2009 revival of *A Little Night Music* directed by Trevor Nunn starred Catherine Zeta-Jones as Desiree Armfeldt and Angela Lansbury (see Chapter 17) as Madame Armfeldt. By contrast, Broadway has not seen a new Sondheim musical since 1994, although both *Assassins*, which had opened at Playwrights Horizons in 1990, and *Frogs*, which had premiered at Yale University in 1974, played on Broadway in 2004.

In the past, revivals required minor revisions to the original material, but it has become customary for revivals to replace the original script with an entirely new one and to heavily amend the score. In fact, revivals that leave the original material intact (e.g., *South Pacific*) have become the exception. In some cases, the work is so extensively rewritten that it constitutes a new musical altogether, leading some critics to argue that using the original title is tantamount to dishonest marketing. Critics and scholars have begun to adopt the label "revival" (or "revisical") to describe these radical makeovers. The label first appeared in reference to the 1931 revival of Romberg's *The Student Prince* (see Chapter 5), but, like "jukebox musical," it has practically become an official genre designation.

From a producer's perspective, it makes perfect business sense to treat old musicals, even canonical ones, as raw material. Why allow a work to collect dust when it can be updated or entirely transformed into something socially relevant and perhaps profitable? For instance, the 1999 revival of *Annie Get Your Gun* removed the potentially offensive material of the original (i.e., the stereotypical portrayal of Native Americans). Moreover, the estates and literary executors that control these musicals welcome the "revisionist" productions, for they can generate revenue as well as pay homage to the deceased writers that the estates represent. That said, only a few of the most aggressively bowdlerized musicals have earned the approbation of critics and theatergoers. The recent Broadway revivals of Rodgers and Hammerstein's 1957 television musical *Cinderella* and their 1958 musical comedy *Flower Drum Song* employed a new script and reconstructed score. For the latter, the Chinese American playwright David Henry Hwang (*M Butterfly*) transformed the meek, pidgin-English–speaking heroine of the original version into a confident Maoist youth who "might be auditioning for the new, improved Charlie's Angels team," according to Ben Brantley. By contrast, the orthodox revivals of *South Pacific* in 2008 and *The King and I* in 2015 left the Asian stereotypes in place and were solid hits. The 2013 production of *Cinderella* approached the classic fairytale with a postmodern hipness and attitude about gender and social responsibility. In this version, Cinderella loves the Prince, but she holds him to a high moral standard and agrees to marry him mainly to effect positive change in the lives of his subjects. The 2011 revival of Alan Jay Lerner and Burton Lane's *On a Clear Day You Can See Forever* turned the original boy/girl/girl love triangle into a boy/boy/girl love triangle (heterosexual psychiatrist/homosexual male patient/woman [the patient's earlier self]). The new script, by Peter Parnell, replaced the psychiatrist's female patient, Daisy, with a gay florist named David. David's alter ego is a forties-era band singer, as opposed to the eighteenth-century English dame of the original version. Neither critics nor audiences embraced the up-to-date gender politics of the story.

The 2012 revival of *Porgy and Bess* (oddly titled *The Gershwins' Porgy and Bess* to distinguish it from the original version) ranks as the most divisive musical theater production in recent memory. The all female, mostly African American, creative staff responsible for the production (namely, the director Diane Paulus, the playwright Suzan-Lori Parks, the music arranger Diedre L. Murray, and the actress Audra McDonald, who played the part of Bess) attempted to give *Porgy* a new, allegedly more realistic ending, richer back stories, and a greater balance between Porgy and Bess. The Gershwin and Heyward estates sanctioned the changes supposedly because they hoped to attract African American audiences. The production, which premiered at the American Repertory Theater in Cambridge, Massachusetts, and then transferred to Broadway, raised the hackles of admirers of Gershwin's iconic work. Paulus, Parks, and McDonald were drawn into a public debate over their decision to radically alter what many people consider to be America's greatest contribution to the opera repertory. *The New York Times* published a rebuke by Stephen Sondheim that accused Paulus and Parks (as well as the Gershwin and Heyward estates) of arrogance and "willful ignorance". In response to Parks's claim that Gershwin would make changes to the ending were he alive today, Sondheim wrote,

> It's reassuring that Ms. Parks has a direct pipeline to Gershwin . . . and that she thinks he would have taken one of the most moving moments in musical theater history—Porgy's demand, "Bring my goat!"—and thrown it out. Ms. Parks (or Ms. Paulus) has taken away Porgy's goat cart in favor of a cane. So now he can demand, "Bring my cane!" Perhaps someone will bring him a straw hat too, so he can buck-and-wing his way to New York. Or perhaps in order to have her happy ending, she'll have Bess turn around when she gets as far as Philadelphia and return to Catfish Row in time for the finale, thus saving Porgy the trouble of his heroic journey to New York.

By the time the revival reached Broadway, the original ending had been reinstated, but the production, however meritorious, lacked the majestic musical sweep and even pathos of the original.

Satires

Musical theater satire experienced a renaissance at the beginning of the twenty-first century. The works in this category, however, have a markedly different stamp from the satires of the thirties (see Chapter 6). The new satires seem to want it both ways, simultaneously targeting and celebrating the musical theater genre itself. One trend is to ridicule the intrinsic contradictions and idiosyncratic conventions of musical theater. The other is to employ a parody of musical theater to draw attention to a controversial issue.

Urinetown

Urinetown began life in 1999 at New York's edgy Fringe Festival, but after receiving favorable reviews, it transferred to Broadway and won the 2002 Tony Award for Best Original Score. The 965 performances that *Urinetown* tallied on Broadway grossed over $34 million, a tidy sum for such an offbeat show. *Urinetown subsequently* found its niche in regional and university theater; the academic year 2007–2008, for instance, saw 152 productions.

Urinetown (2001) is a futuristic dystopia in the form of a musical comedy parody. It attempts to raise consciousness about ecological irresponsibility and the excesses of a capitalist and consumer society. The plot involves a water shortage that forces the citizens of Urinetown to pay for access to public toilets, which are owned by a corrupt corporate giant, Caldwell B. Cladwell. Anyone unable to pay is exiled to some undisclosed location. When Cladwell arranges the murder of his future son-in-law, his daughter leads a revolt against him. *Urinetown* recalls earlier political satires, especially the Brecht-inspired *The Cradle Will Rock* from 1938 (see Chapter 6). The show's self-referentiality, indebtedness to Brecht and Kafka, and postmodern political agenda set it apart from other musical theater parodies. It denies the musical comedy convention of the happy ending and thereby leaves the spectator to face the as-yet-unresolved problem of overconsumption. The score, by Mark Hollmann (music and lyrics) and Greg Kotis (lyrics), represents a wide range of song genres, including the spiritual and romantic ballad.

Avenue Q

Avenue Q examines contemporary life, especially that of its target audience— young, urban, college-educated professionals. The action, as it were, takes place in New York City in a fictional residential area far from New York's high-rent neighborhoods. The characters struggle with very real social and economic concerns, especially sexual orientation and unemployment. The pleasure of *Avenue Q* derives from hearing adult dialogue emanating from the mouths of Muppet-inspired puppets who interact with human actors as well as with each other (the puppet operators appeared in full view of the audience; one of them, John Tartaglia, was even nominated for a Tony Award).

Robert Lopez and Jeff Marx's score parodies the unrelenting upbeat diatonic music of children's television shows such as *Sesame Street*. The incongruous combination of easy-listening songs and politically liberal lyrics was a winning formula, even though the music did not amount to much more than what it parodied. In 2004, *Avenue Q* surprised the theater community by beating out *Wicked* for the Tony Award for Best Musical. Tony voters sided with the offbeat show-that-could and its unknown writers over the lavishly produced *The Wizard of Oz* prequel and its seasoned composer, Stephen Schwartz.

Some of the puppet characters and their operators in *Avenue Q*. Actors shown from left, John Tartaglia, Ann Harada, Jennifer Barnhard, and Rick Lyon. *Courtesy KB Archives*

Avenue Q looked, sounded, and behaved like an Off Broadway musical (see Chapter 14), and actually was one before transferring to Broadway. The show's humor was urbane, urban, and of a decidedly liberal bent. Like *The Producers*, it helped to reinstate New York as the epicenter of musical comedy. Not only is the musical set in New York, but its logo borrowed the city's subway system's letter-in-a-circle train signs. *Avenue Q* was the first Broadway musical to fully harness the power of the Internet, which the show's savvy target audience felt comfortable using. Although the location-specific material and contemporary themes distinguished *Avenue Q* from the megamusical, the show borrowed many of the megamusical's marketing techniques, such as the aforementioned logo. Merchandising (tote bags, T-shirts, and even earmuffs) helped to brand the show.

Avenue Q's identification with New York had diminishing returns, for the show had limited appeal elsewhere. The producers eschewed the typical national tour in favor of an open-ended run in Las Vegas. The real estate developer Steve Wynn even constructed a Broadway-style theater in the hotel bearing his name and planned to inaugurate it with *Avenue Q*. The theater held 1,200 people, a third more than the John Golden Theatre, where the show played on Broadway. Wynn's bet did not pay off, so he commissioned an abridged one-act version in the hope of attracting attention-challenged Las Vegas tourists. When that strategy failed, he closed the show after a mere five months. *Avenue Q*'s edgy

New York humor did not translate to the more conservative Nevada milieu. Las Vegas audiences did not respond to the show's irony regarding racism and homosexuality. As Hilary Baker notes, the sexuality associated with "Sin City" remains "heteronormative, with little to no tourism catered to queer visitors." In fact, disappointed audiences felt that they had been duped into buying tickets for "liberal propaganda." Moreover, an intimate show such as *Avenue Q* stood little chance of succeeding in an environment practically designed for jukebox musicals and megamusicals, such as *Jersey Boys* and *Mamma Mia!* Back in New York, in 2009 when, audiences for the Broadway production started to taper off, the producers took the unprecedented step of transferring the musical back to an Off Broadway theater.

Spamalot

Monty Python's *Spamalot* (2005) is an adaptation of the 1975 film *Monty Python and the Holy Grail*, itself a spoof of Arthurian legend. Although *Spamalot* had an original score, Ben Brantley lumps the show together with "jukebox karaoke" and "Disney cartoon" musicals, all of which "reconstruct elements from much-loved cultural phenomena and wide fan bases," and therefore constitute an "expanding

Glinda (Kristin Chenoweth, left) and Elphaba (Idina Menzel, right) join the Ozians in singing "One Short Day" in *Wicked*. *Courtesy KB Archives.*

Broadway genre of scrapbook musical theater." Indeed, audiences laughed at the jokes before hearing the punchlines. The Monty Python source film reveled in the surrealist humor, scatological tastes, and verbal innuendos of the British comedy troupe Monty Python. The musical's title, a portmanteau, derives from a Monty Python sketch from 1970 about Spam, the precooked canned-meat product, and the musical *Camelot*.

The comic group Monty Python consisted of six members: five Oxbridge men, Eric Idle, John Cleese, Graham Chapman, Terry Jones, and Michael Palin, plus the American Terry Gilliam. Monty Python gained a following when its television series, *Monty Python's Flying Circus*, aired on BBC from 1969 to 1974. The group gained a faithful American following when the Public Broadcasting System (PBS) presented the series in the mid-seventies. *Monty Python and the Holy Grail* (1975) and the subsequent *Life of Brian* (1979) and *The Meaning of Life* (1983) were all popular movies.

Eric Idle, the creative force behind *Spamalot*, translated the film's sendup of Arthurian legend and the cinematic medium into a self-reflexive parody of musical comedy, interweaving the original film plot with the king's quest to reach the magical land called "Broadway." *The Phantom of the Opera* is the brunt of several jokes. One number, "The Song That Goes Like This," brings Lloyd Webber's penchant for melodic repetition to an absurd level. Sir Galahad and the Lady of the Lake performed the song in a boat beneath a candelabrum. *Spamalot* also jests about the Jewish hegemony on Broadway. The Broadway production grossed over $175 million, but it fell victim to the 2008 recession.

The Drowsy Chaperone

The Drowsy Chaperone was the sleeper hit of 2006. As the curtain goes up, a character named Man in Chair addresses the audience and begins to recount his favorite musical, a comedy from 1928 called *The Drowsy Chaperone*. This opening provides a postmodern framework for the musical-within. Man in Chair produces a recording of *The Drowsy Chaperone* from his dusty musical theater collection and places it on his phonograph (the recording is an anachronism, as original cast recordings of musicals were not made until 1943). Suddenly, the cast of *The Drowsy Chaperone* appears and performs the show, which is about a Broadway star, Janet van de Graaff, who wants to trade in her life in the theater for a life of marital bliss. The escapades that ensue include a producer's attempts to derail the marriage with the help of gangsters who disguise themselves as pastry chefs.

Curtains

Kander and Ebb's *Curtains* (2007) combines the backstage musical and detective story genres. The show went through a protracted gestation period that began in the mid-eighties when Peter Stone proposed a show called *Who Killed David Merrick?* After Stone's death in 2003, Rupert Holmes (see Chapter 11), whose many talents include detective fiction, rewrote the script (see Chapter 11). The Broadway production starred David Hyde Pierce, who won a Tony Award for his portrayal of a charming Bostonian detective and wannabe musical theater star. Holmes set the action in 1959, which allowed Kander and Ebb to work within a traditional musical theater idiom. Like *The Producers* (which is also set in 1959) and *The Drowsy Chaperone*, *Curtains* also paid homage to Golden Age musical comedy, but it was "musical comedy" inside quotation marks. The *dramatis personae* encompassed a colorful array of backstage-musical stock characters along with a few new ones: contentious and suspecting producers, an estranged husband-and-wife songwriting team, the perky and unflappable female ingénue, the flamboyant director, and the idealistic daughter of one of the producers. The requisite romance involves the ingénue of the musical within, *Robbin' Hood!*, and the detective in charge of solving the murder of the show's talentless prima donna. When Stone first conceived the show, Broadway was a different place, independent producers such as David Merrick were still around, and megamusicals such as *The Phantom of the Opera* seemed like a fleeting anomaly. However, by the time *Curtains* opened on Broadway in 2007, the show's humor had lost some of its satirical edge. *Curtains* tapped into the same musical theater nostalgia as *The Producers*, poking gentle fun at the genre while mourning its death, but it commented tacitly on what ails musical theater in the new millennium rather than adopting the exploitative, derisive, and cynical attitude of other satires.

[title of show]

In *[title of show]* (2008), a snarky self-referential musical about a self-referential musical, four friends create an original work to submit to a musical theater contest (the title derives from the space on the application form to identify the name of the show submitted). As the most Spartan and "meta" of musicals, *[title of show]* functions as commentary on the spectacle-over-content bias of today's commercial musical theater. The entire cast consists of only four actors dressed in plain street clothes plus an onstage piano player. *[title of show]* contained more than a grain of truth about the difficulty of being a musical theater writer in today's cultural and economic climate. By contrast, the defunct NBC television series *Smash* conveyed little sense of reality in its treatment of the same topic, preferring hyperbole, platitudinous emotion, and a soap opera plotline. On the other hand, taking a page from *Seinfeld* and *Curb Your Enthusiasm*, *[title of show]* blurred the line between reality and fiction in that the actors in the show, which included the show's creators, were essentially playing themselves. The musical got its start in 2004 at the New York Musical Theatre Festival and then transferred to Broadway. The move was counterintuitive (not to mention ironic, given that such a move epitomized the very commercialism that the show seemed to criticize), as only people with an intimate knowledge of the culture of musical theater, which excludes the average tourist, could fully appreciate the show's meta-references. *The New York Times* review began, "Calling all show queens!," underscoring the self-referential nature of the material.

The Book of Mormon

The Book of Mormon (2011), a satire about Mormon mission life, is the work of Matt Stone (b. 1972) and Trey Parker (b. 1969), the creators of the sardonic television series *South Park* (the first episode of which aired on the Comedy Central channel in August 1997), and Robert Lopez, one of the songwriters of *Avenue Q*. The story begins at the LDS Church Missionary Training Center in Salt Lake City, where a new crop of young Mormon men wait to receive their mission assignments. The handsome Elder Kevin Price and the nerdy Elder Arnold Cunningham are paired together, forming the winningest comic buddy team since *The Producers*' Bialystock and Bloom. Elder Price hopes to fulfill his two-year mission duty in sunny Orlando, Florida, but he and Elder Cunningham are assigned to Uganda. Despite their efforts, they fail to recruit a single African, and a frustrated Price leaves his assignment in despair. Cunningham takes matters into his own hands. Urged by Nabulungi, the daughter of a villager, he preaches *The Book of Mormon* to the locals. However, because they cannot relate to it, Cunningham begins embellishing the parables and soon wins them over. Nabulungi and other villagers allow Arnold to baptize them, but when the truth emerges that he has made up his own version of the holy book, Nabulungi turns against him. She forgives him after she learns that his lies were metaphors. Price, who has been haunted by the Devil, rejoins Cunningham, and the villagers defeat the local warlord. A new army of the church rises up to spread the message of the prophet, as is written in the "Book of Arnold."

The Book of Mormon has the trappings and structure of a Rodgers and Hammerstein musical but with the snarky attitude of a postmodern satire, and therein lies its phenomenal popularity. The show may have also benefited from the increased presence of Mormons in American politics and Mormonism in popular culture. With regard to religion, *The Book of Mormon* wants it both ways: it skewers the inherent contradictions of organized religion but suggests that having faith in something—however preposterous it may be—is better than believing in nothing at all.

Adaptation of Literary Sources

Wicked

Wicked is based on Gregory Maguire's 1995 novel *Wicked: The Life and Times of the Wicked Witch of the West*, which pits a misunderstood Elphaba (Witch of the West) against the self-righteous Glinda (Witch of the North). Book critics accused the novel of being "relentlessly politically correct." The Wizard is essentially an ethnic-cleansing dictator. Frank Baum's Dorothy and her three traveling companions intersect with Maguire's plot but remain peripheral characters. The musical received mixed notices, but it has done blockbuster business on Broadway, on the road, and overseas, and it is currently the eleventh-longest-running musical in Broadway history. Young women in particular relate to the contemporary girl–girl friendship that lies at the core of *Wicked*.

Art Musicals

Like a personal scrapbook, the movical, jukebox musical, revival, and satire satisfy the desire to relive one's past. On another level, they represent an effort, particularly on the part of producers, to attract contemporary audiences suffering from cultural saturation. By repackaging the familiar—a popular film, songs from the past, a classic Broadway musical—these various musical subgenres tap into a collective nostalgia. They feature entertaining, upbeat stories, but they generally require little intellectual engagement. Even their music, invariably a blend of rock and pop, encourages a passive mode of listening. In many cases, the audience enters the theater already knowing the songs.

Not all musical theater writers, however, gravitate toward this type of theater and contemporary rock idioms, and not all new musicals pander so readily to commercial tastes. Since the increase in corporate producing in the nineties, Broadway has also seen works of a more traditional nature. "Traditional" in this case signifies a work that pays homage to the musical theater tradition stretching from Kern and Hammerstein to Sondheim and his contemporaries. The proliferation of rock musicals on Broadway has relegated these works—and those who write them—to the margins, where they struggle in a highly competitive environment. In an ironic twist, these musicals occupy the same place once reserved for rock musicals, which used to be treated with suspicion and even contempt by the Broadway establishment. Today, the emulation of the musical theater tradition forged by Rodgers and Hammerstein marks a writer as being out of step with mainstream popular tastes.

These new musicals, although each one is unique, have enough in common with each other to constitute a distinct subgenre. Intellectually and musically challenging, they appeal to the discriminating theatergoer by featuring an unusual story and a thought-provoking theme. "Art musical" is as good a term as any to describe them, if only because they have many things in common with the "art film." The art film movement, which emerged after World War II, provided an alternative to mainstream cinema. *The American Heritage College Dictionary* defines the art film as "a serious film intended to be artistic, often experimental and not for mass appeal." Likewise, if anything on Broadway can be said to be "art for art's sake," it is these musicals. However, whereas art films have art-film houses, art musicals lack a dedicated venue. They aspire to be on Broadway but can rarely survive there.

By adopting the term "art musical," one can discuss these musicals, as well as those who write them, as a group and place them in an historical context. People will object to the term's built-in highbrow bias, and they will disagree over which works qualify as art musicals. However, the point of the term is not to demean successful commercial musicals or to imply that they lack artistry, but rather to recognize a unique trend among a certain group of writers. Collectively, art musicals provide a much-needed alternative to commercial musical theater. Without them, Steven Adler notes, "it is questionable whether the integrity of the work seen on-stage will be able to withstand the banality of the theme-park sensibility at play on the street."

The art musical is the product of a generation of writers that grew up during the last gasp of the American musical's Golden Age, before rock had replaced the traditional Broadway idiom as America's popular music. These writers were around to attend Richard Rodgers's last few musicals as well as to witness the ascendency of Stephen Sondheim and the coming of age of the rock musical. Barry Singer, in a 1997 *New York Times* article titled "True Believers in the Future of the Musical," identified several thirty-something writers dedicated to traditional musical theater at a time when the corporate musical was beginning to dominate Broadway:

Adam Guettel

Michael John LaChiusa

Jeanine Tesori

Brian Crawley

Randy Courts

Mark St. Germain

Arthur Perlman

Jeffery Lunden

Since Singer's article appeared, the list has grown, and some of the writers, now middle-aged, have achieved a modicum of success or at least notoriety.

The musicals by these writers do not represent a heterogeneous body of work. In fact, in several respects, the writers have more in common with each other than their musicals do. They tend to be intellectual and artistically restless. Most of them attended top universities. The composers received formal musical training, and their scores emphasize storytelling over easy listening. They would not self-identify as "art musical" composers, but they would not refer to themselves as songwriters either. They view themselves as theater composers, writing for specific dramatic situations and characters. Above all, they value the nuance of words and the enchanting combination of music and lyrics. Lastly, they attended the ASCAP or BMI musical theater workshop or both.

In the honored traditional of the best Golden Age book musicals, art musicals use songs to reveal the interior emotional life of the characters. Moreover, the musical styles are specific to the material and suggestive of the story's ambiance. Indeed, art musicals favor a unified score as opposed to an assemblage of songs. By contrast, commercial musicals such as *Hairspray* and *Kinky Boots* are dominated by high-octane group numbers, which explains why critics have likened these sorts of musicals to MTV videos. Generally speaking, on Broadway self-referential irony has replaced interiority. Self-reflective monologues—once *de rigueur* for musical theater—are mostly limited to "wanting songs" and generic declarations of love.

Although art musicals emulate the tradition of the integrated book musical, they are neither reactionary nor old-fashioned. Indeed, they evince the writers' postmodern sensibilities rather than express the optimistic point of view of Golden Age musicals. The plots eschew the unearned sentimentality and dramaturgical expedients of frothy commercial musicals such as *Mamma Mia!*, the visual pageantry of megamusicals such as *Spider-Man: Turn Off the Dark*, and the ubiquitous glossy pop-rock scores of the majority of Broadway musicals today. Art musicals cover a diverse range of provocative and offbeat subject matter, such as disability, single parenthood, and sexual identity. As cultural texts, they are more "writerly" than "readerly," as Roland Barthes would describe them, and some of them are based on important literary sources, such as Edna Ferber's *Giant*.

The writers of art musicals face a particularly harsh economic reality. Similar to art films, which are developed and distributed outside the traditional Hollywood studio system, they rarely receive the backing of a commercial Broadway producer. Most of them begin life away from Broadway, be it in a regional theater, an Off Broadway theater, a college theater, or a theater festival (although the same is often the case for commercial Broadway musicals). Although some art musicals transfer to Broadway (e.g., Jeanine Tesori's *Fun Home*), they find it difficult to complete against splashy musicals such as *Wicked* and *Aladdin*.

The art musical exposes one of the great ironies of commercial theater: that critical reception and box-office performance do not always correspond to each other. Many megamusicals have received devastating reviews but have turned enormous profits (see Chapter 11). Art musicals often experience the reverse effect. Since 2000, approximately one third of the principal theatrical awards for Best Musical, Best Score, and Best Book (Tony Award, Drama Desk, Critics' Circle) have gone to art musicals, although few of these works lasted on Broadway for much more than a year, and some of them were planned as limited runs in the first place. In several instances, the composers and lyricists of art musicals have garnered awards even when their musicals lost out to more commercial titles. Of course, it is nothing new for a critically acclaimed musical to do poorly at the box office (e.g., *She Loves Me* [1963]), but for someone with the artistic temperament of Michael John LaChiusa (see Chapter 12), the most prolific composer of the art musical, the situation is maddening. He and other noncommercial writers have found a more receptive home in regional and educational theater.

Caroline, or Change

Tony Kushner's 2004 semiautobiographical musical *Caroline, or Change* explores the complex relationship between African Americans and Jews during the civil rights era as personified by an eight-year-old Jewish boy named Noah Gellman and his family's black maid, Caroline Thibodeaux. Noah, having lost his mother to cancer, turns to Carolyn for emotional comfort. The story, set in the South in the early sixties, takes place at the intersection of race and economics. Early in the show, two working-class black women at a bus stop learn about the assassination of President Kennedy, which is intended to mark the moment that the country left the conformist days of the fifties behind to face the terrifying uncertainty that has haunted America for the past fifty years. The mostly through-sung show incorporates elements of fantasy into the domestic story. Objects such as a washing machine and the moon are singing characters. Ben Brantley called the show a "postmodern collage" that captures "the swirl and disjunction of patterns of thought." Conspicuously absent from the score are "the usual anthems of uplift and self-empowerment" of many musicals about race. *Caroline, or Change* premiered at the Public Theater and transferred to Broadway at the end of a theatrical season dominated by *Wicked* and *Avenue Q*. Next to these popular shows, the serious musical about race did not stand a chance, and it closed after only 136 performances.

Despite the short run, Kushner was sanguine about the Broadway production, observing that it gave the work greater exposure and allowed it to become part of a wider serious conversation.

The Light in the Piazza

The Light in the Piazza won six Tony Awards, including for Best Original Score, and five Drama Desk Awards, but with only 504 performances, a respectable run even in the twenty-first century, it does not qualify as a major hit. However, the work has since entered the standard musical theater repertory. Based on a novella by Elizabeth Spencer, *The Light in the Piazza* stands out for its disability theme, richly detailed book by Craig Lucas, and lush score by Adam Guettel, Richard Rodgers's grandson. Spencer's novella appeared in *The New Yorker* in 1960 and was made into a film in 1962. Set in postwar Italy, the musical has one of the most romantic plots that Broadway has seen in years. A young Southern woman named Clara Johnson and her repressed and protective mother, Margaret, are touring Italy. While in Florence, Clara falls in love with an Italian, Fabrizio, who is just barely beyond his teenage years. (The Italian "Clara" is derived from the adjective "chiara"—the feminine form of "chiaro," which means bright or clear. In the musical, the name "Clara" both has metaphorical significance and alludes to the novella's title.) Guettel and Craig Lucas remained faithful to Spencer's plot, but they brought her characters to life in unexpected ways. The dramatic conflict of the story stems primarily from Margaret's concern over her daughter's intellectual disability, the result of an accident she suffered as a child. Clara's disability is only gradually revealed to the audience and never to the Italian characters.

Source Material

Elizabeth Spencer was born in Mississippi in 1921. She published her first novel, *Fire in the Morning*, in 1948 and her latest collection of short stories, *Starting Over*, in 2012 at the age of ninety-one. Spencer set her early stories in her native Mississippi, but after winning a Guggenheim Fellowship in 1953 and living in Italy for several years, she wrote several works set in cities on the peninsula. In Italy, Spencer met and married John Rusher, and in 1958 the couple moved to Montreal. It was at this time that she wrote *The Light in the Piazza*. The story pits Italy's evolving culture after World War II against what Frank Rich describes as "the naïve, rather self-satisfied 1950s America of the Johnsons' suburban upper-middle class."

Victoria Clark as Margaret sightseeing in Rome in the original Broadway production of *The Light in the Piazza*. *Courtesy Joan Marcus.*

Margaret, the point-of-view character, undergoes a personal transformation as she slowly arrives at the decision to allow Clara's wedding to go forward. Clara and Fabrizio's unmitigated love for each other provides a stark contrast to Margaret's decaying relationship with her husband. In the end, Margaret acts in accordance with her daughter's wishes rather than with what social propriety—and her overbearing husband—demands of her.

Following the literary tradition of writers such as Henry James, Spencer writes about Americans abroad and thereby sees the world through a distinctly American lens. In *The Light in the Piazza*, the contrast between the Johnsons from Winston-Salem and the Florentine Naccarelli family is a fount of humor, but it also reveals things to Margaret about herself and about America. According to Robert Phillips, the Americans are "open and honest," the Italians "scheming and devious." The end of the story constructs a happy façade, but the insightful reader understands that the marriage will inevitably lead to disaster, at least for the two young lovers. When Fabrizio's overbearing father inevitably discovers that Clara is not a fully functioning adult woman, he will surely insinuate himself into his son's life. Margaret fails to comprehend, or she chooses to ignore, the likely consequences of leaving her daughter in his clutches. Clara will be expected to raise several children, but she will not be able to fulfill her role as mother, for she lacks the emotional maturity to do so. Guettel and Lucas did not attempt to modify the story's ignorance-is-bliss outlook. They intensified the novella's romanticism and resisted the impulse to ironize. In fact, the end of the musical evokes the same uncertain mood hanging over Nellie Forbush and Emile de Becque's relationship at the end of *South Pacific*.

Adam Guettel

Adam Guettel has not led the typical life of a contemporary musical theater composer. As a third-generation Broadway composer, he has had to negotiate the pressure stemming from the high expectations made of someone of his pedigree. His prodigious talent notwithstanding, Guettel finds it difficult to feel optimistic about the current state of musical theater:

Adam Guettel's mother, Mary Rodgers (1931–2014), is best known as the composer of the 1959 musical *Once Upon a Mattress*, which starred Carol Burnett. She also wrote children's literature, most notably *Freaky Friday* (1972), which Tom Kitt and Brian Yorkey (see Chapter 16), the creators of *Next to Normal*, are currently adapting as a musical.

> Musical theater in the abstract I'm sort of in love with. I have an uneasy fascination with it and it's really satisfying when it works out. I'm in love with the idea of writing for live human beings who are singing their emotions and moving a story forward through music. But that's so theoretical. Musicals are also a completely marginalized, scoffed at, sort of contemptible field that gets no respect. And they shouldn't have any, for the most part—I don't think musicals have gotten an unfairly old-fashioned reputation. They are old fashioned in most cases. Plus they are a very difficult thing to do well, and they're very seldom done well.

As a teenager, Guettel listened to rock musicians such as Jimi Hendrix and Jethro Tull rather than Irving Berlin and Cole Porter, and he played bass guitar in a rock band. He gravitates toward unorthodox and difficult topics (although he briefly worked on a musical adaptation of *The Princess Bride*), and he incorporates sophisticated harmonies and arduous melodies into his writing. Like his grandfather, Guettel is first and foremost a theater composer. He respects Rodgers's gift to "encode his melodies with essential emotional information about character, about mood and desire."

Adam Guettel's innate talent as a theater composer is on full display in the songs of *Myths and Hymns* (originally titled *Saturn Returns*), a plotless revue, considered by some as a song cycle. Each song stands on its own. One song in particular, "Come to Jesus," constitutes a musical drama in miniature. Inspiration for the song came from a Presbyterian hymn that Guettel came across in a bookstore. Guettel created a dramatic scenario involving a rupture in the relationship between a young man and woman. During the first half of the song, the woman, Martha, writes to Michael, her estranged lover, from the waiting room of an abortion clinic (although she never explicitly states where she is or what she is doing). In the second half, Michael writes Martha a letter from an airport. Each character recites his or her prosaic letter and then sings the hymn text to a haunting original musical setting. The music imparts the characters' religious fervor as well as their emotional pain stemming from their decision to end Martha's pregnancy and, apparently, their relationship. The vocal lines, typical of Guettel, wind their way upward into the upper reaches of the singers' ranges. The epistolary framework of the song effectively presents the characters' thoughts, sometimes separately and sometimes simultaneously.

Book and Score

On the surface, *The Light in the Piazza* is a straightforward adaptation of a short work of fiction, but, like *My Fair Lady*, it has greater emotional depth than its source material and is therefore bound to overshadow it. Most musical adaptations of nonmusical sources eliminate plot elements and sometimes even entire characters, lest there be no time for songs. Guettel and Lucas managed to add texture to Spencer's story rather than lose large chunks of information. The novella's swimming pool scene, during which Fabrizio and Clara splash about like school kids, would have been particularly difficult to stage, as would the *calcio* (soccer) scene. Guettel's songs give full expression to the subtext of the novella. The secondary characters come to life in ways that they do not on the page. For instance, when Signor Naccarelli discovers Clara's age during the wedding rehearsal, he storms out of the church in a grand, somewhat ridiculous, operatic gesture. The music deepens the emotional and psychological world of the characters. Spencer treats Clara and Fabrizio's relationship with a certain emotional disinterest. By contrast, Lucas and Guettel highlight the underlying sensuality of the young lovers' first moments together as well as the latent humor of their situation. Lucas also gives more substance to the interactions between Clara and the Naccarelli family. Giuseppe and Franca, Fabrizio's brother and sister-in-law, are in a perpetual state of squabbling, and the tension surrounding their strained marriage provides a dissonant but amusing counterpoint to Clara and Fabrizio's as yet untainted love. In one scene, Clara overreacts when Franca tries to provokes Giuseppe by kissing Fabrizio. Franca's subsequent song, "The Joy You Feel," strikes a more dissonant tone than any other song in the score. In the novella, Signora Naccarelli wears black as a sign of mourning for her mother's death. Her counterpart in the Broadway production of the musical was fashionably attired in a golden polka-dotted dress. She also acquired a few humorous touches, such as her habit of intentionally stirring up discord among the members of her family. Lucas also added depth to Margaret's marriage, although her husband, Roy (Noel in the novella), is only seen at the end of a telephone line. He is a cigarette-industry executive with little affinity for art or travel. His absence in Florence is due to a business obligation. Roy and Margaret's conversations are strained, as he tersely dictates his demands to her.

Guettel's score taxes the performers' vocal abilities. His rhapsodic melodies reflect his background as a singer as well as the fact that he composes the music before writing the lyrics. The music achieves a timeless quality, with little specific reference to the story's time and place. Nor is there anything inherently Italianate about the score, except, perhaps, its shimmering lyricism—and the fact that the Italian characters sing in Italian. As Frank Rich pointed out, "it aspires to leave behind such diurnal specifics and soar to the realm of pure emotion. In that, it echoes Clara and Fabrizio, who can only come together if they find a language of love that transcends all cultural, social, and linguistic barriers." Lucas and Guettel decided to use Italian in order to put the audience into the same linguistic frame of mind as the main characters. As Guettel notes, the language barrier is both an asset and curse for Fabrizio and Clara, whose deep feelings for each other transcend language but whose future life together will no doubt be hampered by it. Guettel incorporates melismas (textless vocal lines) into several of the songs. In these instances, pure sound and emotion take on the dramatic function of words.

Clara's intellectual disability does not hold her back vocally. Guettel gave her a wide vocal range and a richer emotional life than her literary counterpart. During Clara's occasional moments of confusion or hysteria, her singing becomes shrill, but she otherwise produces a refined, pleasing lyric soprano quality. Clara delivers the show's title song early in Act II after arguing with her mother over her relationship with Fabrizio. Margaret has accompanied Clara to Rome in order to keep her away from Fabrizio. The argument leads to an outburst by Clara: "Daddy doesn't love you," and Margaret reacts by slapping her across the face. Clara responds in a song about what Fabrizio means to her, "The Light in the Piazza." It marks the turning point in the show, for Margaret begins to understand what she must do: return to Florence and prepare for the marriage.

The music features a purely diatonic melody in C major. The sparse chromaticism is strictly limited to contrapuntal inner voices in the accompaniment. Tension between melody and harmony—a common feature in Guettel's music—here helps to convey Clara's underdeveloped intellect and excitable emotional state. The song consists of two main sections plus a long extension of sustained whole notes. The opening section presents two parallel eight-measure phrases (AA') (Example 13.1a).

Pandiatonic music freely uses all seven degrees of the diatonic scale in a harmonic, melodic, and contrapuntal context. Triads with added tones (especially the sixth, seventh, and ninth) are one common element of pandiatonicism. The absence of chromatic pitches helps to create a strong sense of tonality.

The first phrase bears the full emotional weight of the lyric: "I don't see a miracle shining from the sky. / I'm no good at statues and stories. I try." The opening phrase unfolds slowly with no internal repetition, forming a long-breathed phrase: a slowly ascending scalar line with embedded downward leaps. The second phrase begins like the first, but it rises a step higher. The fifth measure of this phrase features the first sustained nondiatonic harmony ($V4^2$/IV), which announces the title-line refrain: a hymn-like phrase with a quarter-note harmonic rhythm supported by pandiatonic harmony over a pedal point in an inner voice (Example 13.1b).

The B section abandons the parallel phrase structure of the A section. It begins with a metrical shift to 3/2 and features upward leaps of large intervals. "The light in the piazza" refrain recurs but in a higher range. Guettel's fondness for high-arching lines that never seem to reach their goal is evident here. A final statement of the refrain brings the song to its peaceful conclusion. The final two words, "my love," are accompanied by chromatic chords, the second of which resolves to the tonic.

The Light in the Piazza *on Broadway*

The premiere of *The Light in the Piazza* in 2003 was a joint venture between the Intiman Theatre in Seattle and the Goodman Theatre in Chicago. The New York premiere took place in 2005 at Lincoln Center's Vivian Beaumont Theater, which, although technically a Broadway theater, presents plays and musicals in limited runs and serves a subscription audience. The nonprofit venue allowed the show to play on

PLOT OF THE LIGHT IN THE PIAZZA

Margaret Johnson and her daughter, Clara, are enjoying the sights of Florence when a gust of wind blows Clara's hat across the piazza. A young Florentine man named Fabrizio gallantly retrieves it and returns it to her. Although he speaks little English and she no Italian, the two fall in love. Margaret has grave concerns about the chance encounter and attempts to make sure that Clara and Fabrizio's courtship develops no further. She worries about the future because as a little girl Clara suffered a kick to the head by a Shetland pony that left her intellectually disabled. Matters are not helped by Signor Naccarelli, Fabrizio's father, who encourages the young couple. Margaret's husband, who has remained in America, demands that she intervene, but as she watches her own marriage crumble, she gains clarity and gives Clara her blessing.

EXAMPLE 13.1. "The Light in the Piazza," (a) first phrase, (b) second statement of "The light in the piazza" refrain

Since *The Light in the Piazza*, Guettel has written music for plays and films as well as new musicals, including an adaptation of H. G. Wells's *The Invisible Man*. Guettel's output includes an unproduced opera based on Dr. Seuss's *The Butter Battle Book*, for which he has been unable to secure the rights from the Seuss (Geisel) estate.

Broadway without competing directly against more commercial musicals such as *Jersey Boys*. The production was visually breathtaking, featuring costumes designed by Catherine Zuber, lighting by Christopher Akerlind, and scenery by Michael Yeargan, each of whom won a Tony Award for his or her efforts. The action shifted from one famous Italian landmark to another, such as Florence's Piazza della Signoria and the Uffizi. Zuber's costumes revealed the psychological progression of the characters. For instance, Margaret donned an elegant but conservative dress in Act I; in Act II, as her emotional defenses begin to give way to the romantic lure of Italy and her daughter's happiness, she appeared in a persimmon dress with a plunging neckline.

Critics admired *The Light in the Piazza*, but some of them felt unfulfilled and complained that details of Clara's injury are revealed too late. However, the disability theme failed to spark any discussion whatsoever, although Ben Brantley objected to the sophisticated portrayal of Clara, "who voices her thoughts in metaphorically dense and sexually resonant songs that seem beyond the reach of a little girl, even one trapped in a woman's body." He approved more of the handling of Margaret, who "has the virtue of being a convincingly ordinary person who finds extraordinary self-expression in song." Such characters stand out from the "singing cartoons and dancing robots that are multiplying on Broadway like flu germs."

BROADWAY TODAY

New York remains a major force in musical theater, if only because Broadway musicals reach more domestic and international markets than ever before. What opens on Broadway therefore shapes the tastes and expectations of theatergoers the world over. For this reason, the Tony Awards and other theater honors—although tending to be self-congratulatory exercises—have a disproportionate effect on the tastes and expectations of theatergoers. What takes place on Broadway shapes the perception that people have of the musical theater genre. As the record shows, movicals, jukebox musicals, and revivals remain the dominant categories in the second decade of the century. Musicals with original scores have become increasingly rare on Broadway. Since 2010, of the twenty musicals to receive a Tony Award nomination for Best Musical, only twelve featured a new score. The good news is that in each year, the award went to one of these.

Musical theater has established a strong online presence. The Internet today plays an important role in the dissemination of musical theater news and the expansion of musical theater culture. It has also become a resource for musical theater fans, scholars, and even writers. (Stephen Schwartz, the composer of *Wicked*, communicates with his fans through his own website.) Online musicals have reached a critical mass sufficient enough to constitute a subgenre, although these are mostly parodies and have not yet made a major impact on live musical theater. On the

ART VERSUS COMMERCE

Tony Award voters include theater owners, producers, and writers, all of whom tend to vote in their own self-interest. The Tony Awards help to locate the pulse of a given theatrical season, but the competition is capricious and rife with politics. As a result, the Tony for Best Musical has not always been bestowed upon the most meritorious work, and the Best Musical winner has not always also received the award for Best Score, which would seem logical and regularly used to be the case. Since 2000, only six Broadway musicals have won the Tony Award in both categories. In fact, the millennium's first Tony Award for Best Musical went to a show that had neither original music nor singing: *Contact*, which, as conceived by Susan Stroman and John Weidman, consisted of three unrelated tales told in dance accompanied by recorded pop hits and familiar classical pieces.

In the past fifteen years, rock musicals have been the favorite for the Best Original Score and Best Musical Tony Awards. Since 2000, six of the winners for best musical were based on popular films; one was a jukebox musical; two were adaptions of literary sources; and three featured original stories, two of these satires. By contrast, during the previous fifteen years, pop- or rock-oriented musicals accounted for only three best musical winners, as did film-inspired musicals.

RELIGION ON BROADWAY

Reflecting the growing presence of religion in American popular culture, a number of musicals on religious themes have opened on Broadway in recent years. Not since the early seventies, when *Jesus Christ Superstar* and *Godspell* made Jesus and Christianity acceptable topics for musical theater, has Broadway seen such a surge in religion-oriented stories. However, the majority of these musicals have been colossal failures, including revivals of *Godspell* (2011) and *Jesus Christ Superstar* (2012). The main exception is *The Book of Mormon*, which is a satire.

Leap of Faith (2012) was based on a 1992 Steve Martin film about a faith healer con artist. The music was pumped full of ersatz gospel energy, but the faithful were not buying it. *Scandalous: The Life and Trials of Aimee Semple McPherson* (2012) did just as poorly. According to Charles Isherwood, *Scandalous* "reduces McPherson's remarkable life to a cliché-bestrewn fable about the wages of fame." That the show made it to Broadway is likely due to the celebrity status of Kathy Lee Gifford, who wrote the book and lyrics.

other hand, the Internet provides a public forum for anyone to weigh in on a show. Bloggers can smear a work-in-progress before it has had a chance to work out its kinks. As lyricist Lynn Ahrens, whose *Seussical* generated such negative buzz during out-of-town previews that by the time the show reached Broadway it was dead on arrival, lamented that today anyone can "broadcast [his or her opinion] across America. Nobody can be safe anymore, learning from their mistakes in private." The snarky, unchecked online commentary is not conducive to good art, and it sets a dangerous precedent. Out-of-town previews used to afford writers an opportunity to work on a show away from the high-pressure and unforgiving nature of New York. Tweaking a show on the road was an inherent part of the development process of musical theater. The economics of Broadway make it hard enough for new musicals to survive any early signs of weakness without the indiscriminate and unverifiable online opining. Even the television series *Smash* acknowledged the increasing impact of the Internet on musical theater.

Commercial musical theater today shows no signs of moving away from recent trends, such as the repackaging of pre-existing material. Broadway will most likely survive well into the future, but the institution is becoming a de facto museum similar to the not-for-profit opera house (which relies on familiar canonical titles to fund its daily operations and to finance the occasional new opera). A thriving musical theater requires original ideas, new voices, and greater variety. As *The Wall Street Journal* theater critic Terry Teachout believes, "having fun" is the *raison d'être* of Broadway theater, and "the best way to do something fun is to do something that has not been done before."

AND BEAR IN MIND

In the Heights *(2008, Richard Rodgers Theatre, 1,184 performances)*

Book by Quiara Alegría Hudes
Music and lyrics by Lin-Manuel Miranda

*I*n the Heights (2008) takes place in a Dominican American neighborhood in the upper reaches of Manhattan and depicts a family crisis that unfolds over the course of three days. Kevin and Camila Rosario, owners of a taxi company, personify the immigrant struggle to achieve the American Dream. Their daughter, Nina, is home visiting from Stanford University. She is in love with Benny, an African American and the only non-Latino character in the show. Their relationship causes a rift between Nina and her obdurate father. Usnavi, the point-of-view character and the owner of a neighborhood bodega, provides the basis for a subplot involving a winning lottery ticket and his decision to remain in New York rather than escape to a more exotic clime south of the border.

In the Heights provided an alternative to popular culture's essentialist depictions of Latino Americans as poor laborers, Roman Catholic, superstitious, having a tendency toward criminality, and excelling on the dance floor—stereotypes epitomized by *West Side Story*. Latina women, so it goes, are sensual, curvaceous, and impetuous, and the men are passionate lovers. *In the Heights* opened two years after the premiere of the television series *Ugly Betty*, which brought more diversity to the meaning of Latina beauty. *In the Heights* is also one of the first major Broadway musicals written entirely by Latino Americans (*West Side Story* is the work of four white Jewish artists). Lin-Manuel Miranda's score includes a variety of Latino styles but is informed by a musical theater sensibility. Miranda, who grew up in the ethnically diverse neighborhood of Inwood, also played Usnavi.

The critics were generally enthusiastic, although Charles Isherwood quipped that the show was "basically a salsa-flavored soap opera, and if there is an equivalent of schmaltz in Spanish, this musical is happily swimming in it." He called Miranda "a sprightly new Harold Hill from the barrio," a positive albeit somewhat dismissive comparison. In any case, *In the Heights* appealed to a broad demographic because, like *Fiddler on the Roof*, it explored the universal themes of family, community, and self-determination. Directed by Thomas Kali and featuring practically nonstop choreography by Andy Blankenbuehler, the musical received thirteen Tony Award nominations and won four.

Lin-Manuel Miranda (b. 1980), who is of Puerto Rican decent, attended Hunter College Elementary School and High School. He began writing *In the Heights* when he was a sophomore at Wesleyan University. His most recent musical, which is based on Ron Chernow's acclaimed biography *Alexander Hamilton*, uses anachronistic hip-hop music to tell the story of one of America's founding fathers. An early version, titled *Hamilton* and produced at the Public Theater, featured Miranda, who rapped as the title character. He co-wrote the score for the Broadway musical *Bring It On: The Musical* and worked on the Spanish portions of the 2009 bilingual revival of *West Side Story*. In 2009, Miranda, who is not Jewish, received an honorary degree from Yeshiva University, which is situated in Washington Heights.

NAMES, TERMS, AND CONCEPTS

9/11

art musicals

Avenue Q

Billy Elliot

Book of Mormon, The

Brooks, Mel

Caroline, or Change

Grey Gardens

Guettel, Adam

Hairspray

In the Heights

Jersey Boys

jukebox musical

Light in the Piazza, The

Lucas, Craig

Mamma Mia!

Memphis

Movical

Next to Normal

postmodernism

Producers, The

Revisal

Spamalot

Urinetown

Wicked

DISCUSSION QUESTIONS

1. Discuss recent trends in musical theater on Broadway.

2. Is the portrayal of characters with disabilities inherently different in a musical than in a spoken play?

3. How has the corporate presence on Broadway affected artistic choices?

MUSICAL THEATER OFF BROADWAY

(*THE FANTASTICKS*, 1960, SULLIVAN STREET PLAYHOUSE, 17,162 PERFORMANCES)

he Fantasticks holds the record for the world's longest-running musical. It opened Off Broadway on May 3, 1960, at the Sullivan Street Playhouse in New York's Greenwich Village and remained there until it closed on January 13, 2003, after its 17,162th performance. The theater contained only 149 seats (augmented to 153 during the run), so the maximum potential audience for *The Fantasticks* was close to 2,700,000. By contrast, the New York production alone of *The Phantom of the Opera* (at the 1,645-seat Majestic Theatre), Broadway's longest-running musical, has surpassed 12,000 performances, for a potential audience of nearly 20 million, and the number continues to rise. The staggering contrast between these numbers says a lot about the difference in scale between Broadway and Off Broadway theater. However, these numbers are misleading, for the long-term cultural impact of *The Fantasticks* is as significant as that of any Broadway musical. Indeed, *The Fantasticks* has been performed at one time or another by virtually every high school, college, community theater, and professional theater in the country, not to mention in other countries, including Kenya, Israel, Saudi Arabia, and China.

With a relatively small initial capitalization of $16,500, a modest weekly operating budget, and Spartan production values, *The Fantasticks* is *the* quintessential Off Broadway musical. More than five and a half decades after its world premiere, the musical remains a popular work, with nearly 250 productions mounted annually. *The Fantasticks* reopened in New York in 2006, just three years after the original production closed, and seven years later it is still running. In early 2015, a closing date for the revival was announced, but two wealthy anonymous donors pledged enough funds to keep it running indefinitely. In its faithfulness to its own vision, *The Fantasticks* has a rare timeless quality. It enacts a simple, romantic story on a small stage with no more than a platform, a cast of eight (at one time nine), a bench, a few props, and a harp and piano. The universal theme of *The Fantasticks* knows no temporal or geographic boarders. The show belongs to no particular historical moment, and yet audiences of all ages and from all corners of the world can relate to it. Throughout the show's initial run, the producer Lore Noto, librettist Tom Jones, composer Harvey Schmidt, and director Word Baker took care never to let their precious gem dull, and they turned down several offers to transfer the show to a Broadway theater, where it would have been diminished by the larger physical production and would have most likely fizzled out amid the suffocating commercial pressure.

THE OFF BROADWAY SCENE

"Off-Broadway is a state of mind, a set of production conditions, a way of looking at theater at every point at odds with Broadway's patterns," or so it has been written. The term "Off Broadway" appeared as early as 1915 and became associated with a civic theater movement in New York. "Off Broadway" as a designation was widely adopted in the thirties. The early pioneers of Off Broadway—the Washington Square Players and the Provincetown Players—had established themselves in the mid-teens as an alternative to Broadway. These organizations mounted old and new plays deemed unsuitable for the commercial theater. World War II halted most Off Broadway activity, but in the late forties a host of new organizations formed, such as Circle in the Square. By 1949 the growth of the Off Broadway movement made it necessary for Actors' Equity and theater management to bargain over contractual matters. Other theater unions followed suit, and city officials began to regulate Off Broadway theater spaces. Because city fire regulations required any theater with greater than 299 seats to have an asbestos curtain, 299 became the de facto maximum seating capacity, although this figure later increased to the current 499. Today regulations dictate that Off Broadway theaters be located in Manhattan but outside the Broadway Theater District.

In its heyday from the late fifties to the early eighties, Off Broadway was the venue for experimentation, for challenging conventional notions about theater, for confrontation and political protest. However, Off Broadway has also offered conventional, even mainstream, plays as well as avant-garde works, and everything in between. The increasingly commercial trend of Off Broadway in the late twentieth century led theater historian Arnold Aronson to call it Broadway's "low-budget clone." However, at least since the sixties, Off Broadway has proven commerically popular. Some of the earliest Off Broadway musicals were minimal, no-frills revivals of classic Broadway musicals such as *Anything Goes* (Orpheum Theatre, 1962). In recent years, Off Broadway (along with regional theater) has virtually replaced the expensive out-of-town pre-Broadway tryout, which used to be *de rigueur* for a new musical, offering producers a relatively inexpensive venue for testing out a musical in front of a live audience before pouring millions of dollars into a full-fledged commercial production.

The first major Off Broadway production of a musical was the 1956 revival of Kurt Weill and Bertolt Brecht's *The Threepenny Opera* at the Theatre de Lys.

Running a then record-breaking 2,707 performances, this production, which employed an English translation by Marc Blitzstein (see Chapter 6), thrust *Threepenny* into the American spotlight. Starting in the late fifties, original musicals began to proliferate Off Broadway.

Off Broadway musicals constitute such a diverse body of work that for all practical purposes the "Off Broadway" label denotes little more than a small-scale production, a modest budget, and certain contractual regulations. These facets give Off Broadway musicals their distinct look and sound. By necessity, most Off Broadway musicals employ a relatively small cast and small orchestra or instrumental combo. Many productions have employed a single piano accompaniment, although today electronic enhancement of the live instruments is not uncommon. Ironically, several early recordings of Off Broadway musicals feature an augmented orchestra, giving a false impression of how the shows actually sounded in the theater. Even the original 1960 recording of *The Fantasticks* incorporates a second piano, a cello, and drums, none of which were actually used in the theater, although these additions are insignificant compared to recordings that add a full orchestra to what was originally a keyboard accompaniment.

Off Broadway musicals from the late fifties until the eighties encompass four distinct categories: (1) revivals of old Broadway musicals; (2) spoofs of musical comedy, operetta, and movie musicals; (3) musicals based on classic literature; and (4) unconventional or experimental musicals.

Revivals of Broadway Musicals

Off Broadway revivals, despite their modest production values, rescued many early musicals from obscurity, such as Jerome Kern's *Leave It to Jane* (1917) (see Chapter 4). In the early days of Broadway, producers and writers typically did not preserve the written records of a show (scores, scripts, orchestrations) once these materials had served their utilitarian purpose. This lack of concern for posterity means that today anyone wishing to revive a show from this era must first piece together a script and score from materials existing at scattered locations and in various states of completeness. Such revivals, however, rarely represent the musicals as they were originally performed. Either by choice or necessity, the compilers, directors, and producers of these revivals have paid scant attention to authenticity: rewriting the books, sometimes radically; rearranging and reorchestrating the music, typically for a small ensemble or a piano plus rhythm section; and interpolating songs from other musicals by the same composer. On the other hand, several of these revivals have yielded performing editions of musicals that would otherwise remain unperformed.

Musicals Based on Classic Literature

In the sixties, musicals based on classic drama and literary novels proliferated Off Broadway, probably spurred on by the popularity of Lerner and Loewe's *My Fair Lady* (see Chapter 8). One of the first such works was a musical version of Oscar Wilde's *The Importance of Being Earnest* called *Ernest in Love*, which opened the day after *The Fantasticks*. The music, by Lee Pockriss, emulates the quasi-operetta style of *My Fair Lady* and thereby imparts a sense of (British) decorum, but today the score seems wooden and derivative. The script, by Anne Croswell, hews closely to Wilde's play and represents his pithy wit, but it lacks the first-rate dramaturgy of *My Fair Lady*. The opening scene, which has no equivalent in the play, takes place on a London street during a chance meeting between the butlers serving Jack Worthing and Algernon Moncrieff. Their dialogue is expository in nature, hinting at future plot events that anyone familiar with Wilde's comedy would know. Before long, several merchants appear, a boot-maker, a greengrocer, and so on, and complain to the butlers, in thickly etched English commercial-class accents, about their respective employers' outstanding bills: "Not that 'is credit 'ere ain't good." A piano teacher and a tobacconist arrive and voice the same complaints until the latter expresses what is on everyone's mind: "Well, I say it's come to a pretty pass when gentlemen consider it the thing *not* to pay their debts." This is the cue for the first song, an ensemble for the various creditors called "Come Raise Your Cup," a paean to upper-class hypocrisy. Were the aristocracy to pay its debts, the song suggests, the British economy would collapse from the confusion that it would cause bankers and accountants, who have never had to balance their ledgers. The music is a brisk march of the British variety. The lyrics are full of three-syllable words and double rhymes reminiscent of Gilbert and Sullivan's commentaries on British manners. The number is serviceable, but Pockriss and Croswell missed a musical opportunity suggested by Wilde himself. As the curtain rises on *The Importance of Being Earnest*, Algernon is playing a piano offstage. He enters and dissertates on his performance. His well-mannered manservant claims not to have been listening, as it would have been unseemly. Algernon replies, "I'm sorry for that, for your sake. I don't play accurately—anyone can play accurately—but I play with wonderful expression. As far as the piano is concerned, sentiment is my forte." *Ernest in Love* earned the critics' approbation, although Croswell and Pockriss, better known for *Tovarich* (1963), their only Broadway musical, could neither fully get out from under Wilde's shadow nor escape comparison with *My Fair Lady*.

Spoofs and Satires

Little Mary Sunshine (1959), an original musical by Rick Besoyan, spoofed twenties-era operettas such as *Rose Marie* (1924) (see Chapter 5). The plot centers on the female proprietor of a Rocky Mountain inn, which she is in danger of losing, but the captain of the Forest Rangers saves the day and wins her heart. *Dames at Sea* (Off Off Broadway production in 1966; Off Broadway production in 1968), another genre sendup, parodied 1930s Hollywood musicals—in particular, their tendency to paint a fantasy world ignorant of the widespread economic suffering caused by the Depression. The show incorporated a cast of only six people, including a very young Bernadette Peters (see Chapter 17), and an orchestra of three. The writers turned the meager physical aspects of the production into a comic asset by using them ironically to draw attention to the empty opulence of Depression-era Hollywood musicals. Like Busby Berkeley's signature musical films, *Dames at Sea* is a backstage saga about overcoming adversity. A theatrical producer named Hennessey is about to have his thirteenth flop in a row. Ruby, a star-struck hoofer from Utah who has just arrived in town, lands a part in the show and saves it from failure. The premise of the songs—with titles such as "Wall Street" and "Good Times Are Here to Stay"—are recognizable to any devotee of the Hollywood musical. But the composer Jim Wise and lyricists George Haimsohn and Robin Miller gave the clichés enough irony to render the songs entertaining in their own right. A Broadway production of *Dames at Sea* has been announced for late 2015.

Musicals such as *Little Mary Sunshine* tapped into a latent nostalgia for light-hearted musical comedy. However, one also senses in these works an increasing uneasiness about the future of musical theater. The humor of these shows anticipated the postmodern sense of irony and self-referentiality that informs many commercial musicals today (see Chapter 13). By the end of the sixties, the vogue for musical theater spoofs had waned. *A Chorus Line*, which premiered Off Broadway in 1975, rethought the backstage musical convention in contemporary terms and treated musical theater with loving affection rather than with irony. The show examined real problems facing performers at a time when musical theater was on the decline. David Merrick's 1981 production of *42nd Street* was a faithful stage adaptation of the famed Busby Berkeley film of the same name. Other than an occasional knowing wink to the audience, the show glorified the backstage musical of the past without irony. A year after *42nd Street* opened on Broadway, the musical theater satire *Forbidden Broadway*, a campy revue created by Gerald Alessandrini, began a twenty-seven-year run Off Broadway. In the tradition of earlier annual revues, Alessandrini wrote several new editions, thereby maintaining the show's relevance and providing fresh material for returning audience members. *Forbidden Broadway* offered an insider's view of musical theater (as well as spoken theater), satirizing current shows and poking fun at several stage legends. Although entertaining, it served as a bitter reminder that by the early eighties the Broadway musical was in steep decline. The *Forbidden Broadway* franchise was revived in New York in 2012.

Innovative Musicals

The works in the final category best embody the iconoclastic spirit associated with Off Broadway theater. They cover a diverse range of topics, from Charles Schultz's *Peanuts* (*You're a Good Man, Charlie Brown* [1967]) to biblical fanaticism (*Morning Sun* [1963]) to the Gospel of Matthew (*Godspell* [see Chapter 16]) to Christina Rossetti's poem "Goblin Market" (*Goblin Market* [1985]). *The Fantasticks*, notable for its austere physical production and universal theme, also belongs in this category. It tells an archetypal coming-of-age story though a mixture of narration, song, poetry, and movement.

THE FANTASTICKS

Background

The history of *The Fantasticks* begins with Tom Jones's days as a drama student at the University of Texas in Austin. B. Iden Payne, one of his theater professors and a former director of the Shakespeare Memorial Theatre in Stratford-on-Avon,

Early photograph of Harvey Schmidt (left) and Tom Jones. *Courtesy KB Archives.*

impressed upon the young Jones that the purest kind of theater was the open-space approach of the Shakespearean tradition. One needs only golden words to make theater come alive, not the trappings of adjunct props, scenery, and costumes. Payne insisted that theater need not be realistic, and he instilled in Jones a taste for drama built on pure theatricality, such as the plays of Thornton Wilder in which characters speak directly to the audience. It was musical theater's innate theatricality that attracted Jones to the genre: "If people try to use linguistic magic in a regular play, they get nervous. . . . But in musicals, that's what you expect."

Jones (b. 1928) started to collaborate with Harvey Schmidt (b. 1929), an art major who also composed music. They wrote songs for a campus revue called *Hipsy-Boo!*, which their friend Word Baker directed. The revue was a hit, but the Korean War was in full swing, and the budding writers were both drafted. While serving their country, they continued to collaborate by mail and to solicit advice from Word Baker.

As soon as Jones was discharged, he moved to New York for what he told himself would be a six-month tryout period. He received an offer to work on an original musical with John Donald Robb, a former lawyer, a composer, and the dean of the School of Fine Arts at the University of New Mexico. They decided to adapt Edmond Rostand's *Les Romanesques*, which Jones had encountered in Payne's directing classes. The play smiles at the naïveté of youthful love while celebrating its inherent poetic tendency. Rostand, best known as the author of *Cyrano de Bergerac* (1897), based the premise of *Les Romanesques* on *Romeo and Juliet* but gave the plot a comic twist. He employed colorful language in an attempt to counter the prosaic dullness of the realistic drama in vogue at the time. The plot springs from the desire of two neighboring fathers to see their children marry each other. Because the fathers assume that children will do the opposite of what they are told, they fabricate a family feud and forbid their children to talk to each other. As predicted, the boy and girl instinctively rebel against the imposed ban and fall in love. To end the façade, the fathers employ the services of a ruffian, who stages an abduction of the girl. The boy impulsively saves her and thereby provides a reason for the two families to reconcile. The remainder of the play explores what happens after the first blush of falling in love wears off. The girl and boy are disheartened to learn that their fathers orchestrated their marriage. The boy goes off to seek adventure and romance, and the girl nearly flees with the ruffian, who has tricked her into thinking that he wants to take her on a romantic adventure. The play ends with the reunion of the somewhat older and wiser girl and boy.

Rostand specifies neither the time nor place for his play. Jones and Robb decided to set the musical in the American Southwest and to center the action on a conflict between Mexicans and the white Northerners. Robb produced the musical, which they called *Joy Comes to Dead Horse*, at the University of New Mexico in 1956. Jones was unsatisfied with the show, so the two writers agreed to go their separate ways. Jones returned to New York and convinced Schmidt and Baker to work on a new version of the musical. Schmidt took a year's hiatus from his flourishing art career to complete the project. Jones made no major changes to the story, retaining both the large scope and Southwestern milieu of his original concept. Reaction from friends and potential backers was mixed, and the project stagnated. Then, in 1959, a turn of events radically altered Jones and Schmidt's vision for the musical.

Word Baker was in the process of directing three one-act plays for a summer theater at Barnard College, including William Inge's *The Mall* and Jack Dunphy's *The Gay Apprentice*. He wanted a musical to round out the triple bill and thought of *Joy Comes to Dead Horse*. He offered his friends a production of the musical with the proviso that they shorten it to one act. The need to downsize the musical freed Schmidt and Jones's imagination and ultimately unlocked the secret to its success. They abandoned their big-production ideas and essentialized the story and characters, adopting a neutral setting and time period. They renamed the musical *The Fantasticks*, the title of George Fleming's (a.k.a. Constance Fletcher) English translation of *Les Romanesques* on which Jones had based his script. Jones then recalled what Payne had taught him about the presentational style of Shakespearean theater: "we decided to do all the things we always wanted to do, celebrating the restrictions of the theater and the artificiality of it, rather than trying to disguise it in any way."

Baker invited an aspiring producer named Lore Noto to the premiere of *The Fantasticks* at Barnard. Noto fell in love with the musical and offered then and there to produce it Off Broadway, pledging to give the writers complete artistic control plus a $250 advance. He purchased the rights for $500 plus 6% of the gross receipts and began the grueling task of raising a production budget of $16,500, a steep figure for an Off Broadway musical in the early sixties. Noto's artistic team elevated the limitations of the production to an aesthetic concept. Off Broadway theaters were in short supply at the time, so Noto felt lucky to obtain the Sullivan Street Playhouse, even though it was small, grimy, and stale-smelling. In the end, the rundown theater became yet another asset for the ever-increasing minimalist nature of the show. Within a few months, *The Fantasticks* reopened in an expanded two-act version. Reviews were mixed, and it took several months, a bit of luck, and some clever marketing before positive word-of-mouth about the show spread.

PLOT OF THE FANTASTICKS

Agirl and boy, Luisa and Matt, fall in love. Their fathers had forbid them to see each other and erected a wall to separate them. It turns out, though, that the feud is feigned, for the fathers want their children to marry and know that they will do so only if they forbid it. The fathers hire El Gallo to stage an abduction of the daughter, knowing that Matt will come to her rescue and thereby bring the families together happily ever after. End of Act I. As the second act opens, ennui has overtaken the lovers and their fathers. Matt goes out to see the world, and Luisa falls in love with El Gallo. Their experiences are not all happy ones, and eventually they recognize that they have all they need in each other.

El Gallo (Jerry Orbach) singing "I Can See It" to Luisa (Rita Gardner) in the original production of *The Fantasticks*. *Courtesy KB Archives.*

Style and Structure

The Fantasticks draws attention to itself as theater, using a myriad of metatheatrical devices including songs and speeches delivered directly to the audience. The musical unfolds as a ritualistic play-within-a-play, as the overture and opening scene make clear. As the published script describes, "the members of the Company arrive and prepare to do the play. They take down the lettered drape, set out the Wooden Bench, and put the finishing touches on their costumes." El Gallo (the ruffian) then steps out of the frame of the story and sings "Try to Remember" directly to the audience, following which he explains,

> Let me tell you a few things you may want
>   to know
> Before we begin the play.
> First of all, the characters:
> A Boy.
> A Girl.
> Two Fathers.
> And—a Wall.

The stark theatricality of *The Fantasticks* is partially the result of a purposeful avoidance of realism. Jones and Baker drew from, in the former's words, "primitive presentational stage devices from around the world": Shakespeare (open-stage technique, contrast of day and night, verse, and rhyming couplets), Carlo Goldoni (*Arlecchino*), *commedia dell'arte* (makeshift platforms and slapstick comedy), the musical *Candide* (the songs "Glitter and Be Gay" and "Quiet"), *Green Grow the Lilacs* (the source material for *Oklahoma!*), Thornton Wilder's *Our Town*, Japanese theater, and even Ronald Coleman's performance in the 1947 film *A Double Life*. Rostand's play consists entirely of Alexandrian verse, which Fleming's English translation substitutes with rhymed iambic pentameter. Jones created a fanciful mixture of stylized blank verse, measured poetry, and prose. Other metadramatic devices included a prop box that remains in full view throughout the show and from which two of the actors make their entrance, and a Mute who helps with props and denotes the wall by holding up a stick.

In the song "It Depends on What You Pay," El Gallo recites a virtual catalogue of the possible "rapes" (or abductions) that he can perform for a price. The fathers agree on a "first class" rape "with trimmings," which requires a large cast. El Gallo thus summons two mummers to assist him: Henry Albertson, an old classical actor from the school of crisp pronunciation and grand gestures, and his companion, Mortimer, a Cockney who has been performing death scenes for forty years. Jones based the part of Henry on Payne and played the role during the initial period of the production using the stage name Thomas Bruce.

El Gallo literally stages the abduction scene for the benefit of Matt (the boy) and Luisa (the girl).

Three decades after *The Fantasticks* opened, "It Depends on What You Pay" became a cause of concern because of the offensive implications of the word "rape." Therefore, for the thirtieth-anniversary tour of the show Schmidt and Jones wrote a new song Abduction, to replace it.

Henry begins by signaling, "Orchestra! Accelerando con molto." The "Rape Ballet" music accompanies the ensuing slapstick action, which is reminiscent of silent movies. At the end of a long fight involving makeshift sabers from wooden sticks, Henry "dies in so grand a manner" that even Mortimer is impressed, and El Gallo "dies like a diva in the opera, rising again and again from the floor to give one last dramatic, agonized, twitch."

The score for *The Fantasticks* is marked by a strong bebop influence, especially in its turgid dissonant harmonies and jagged, percussive rhythms. The music is idiomatically pianistic and rich in Stravinskian propulsive rhythms and metrical irregularities. For instance, the piano introduction to "Much More" features dissonant chords and a repeating driving rhythmic pattern that is interrupted by hemiolas just before the vocal entrance (Example 14.1). Only two of the score's eleven numbers ("Soon It's Gonna Rain" and "They Were You") conform to the standard thirty-two-bar song format. Some of the songs are practically through-composed, including "Much More," whose unexpected shifts in texture and rhythm capture the mercurial changes in Luisa's mood. Schmidt and Jones framed the show with two evocative waltzes, both meant to hark back to a purer, simpler time: "Try to Remember" and "They Were You." Neither number incorporates the sort of jazz elements or dissonant harmonies found in the rest of the score. The fathers' two numbers, "Never Say No" and "Plant a Radish," have the

EXAMPLE 14.1. "Much More," piano introduction

simplicity befitting characters of the older generation. They are presentational vaudeville-like numbers and therefore add to the theatrical nature of the musical. The addition of the harp, which was suggested by the show's musical director, Julian Stein, provides flowing accompaniments for the more lyrical moments and percussive reinforcement for the accented rhythms.

Interpreting *The Fantasticks*

Ironically, Schmidt and Jones were writing *The Fantasticks* as "a big Broadway musical in the Rodgers and Hammerstein mode" until Word Baker offered to produce a substantially pared-down version of the show. The limitations imposed on the writers forced them to trim the show to its bare essentials so that every gesture, note, and word counted. The result was a musical that seemed right for the moment and for all times. *The Fantasticks* remains popular today, but several aspects of the musical reflect attitudes dominating American culture in the late fifties. The plot is predicated on the rejection of authority and conventionality. Luisa and Matt yearn for self-realization amid the pressure to conform to the institutions of their parents. They feel alienated from their family, society, and even each other. According to Scott Miller, *The Fantasticks* marks the "end of romanticism and the embrace of cynicism"—in other words, the demise of the idealized book musical. This is the opposite of what Schmidt and Jones originally intended. Indeed, *The Fantasticks* was a harbinger of the more confrontational musicals that followed, such as *Cabaret* (see Chapter 9) and *Hair* (see Chapter 16), but it was less provocative than those shows. Its cynicism is a warning, not a posture. *The Fantasticks* adopts a harsh view of the world because it seeks universal truths. If being honest causes pain and disappointment, it also leads to maturity. The work also recognizes the need for beauty and fantasy in order to offset life's hardships.

In the foreword to the thirtieth-anniversary edition of his script, Jones refers to a section from Fleming's translation of *Les Romanesques* in which Sylvette (the girl) "comes forward and addresses the audience, asking them to turn their backs on these dreary realistic plays invading the stage and seek instead for gossamer and romance." Perhaps Jones meant the following passage during the boy and girl's final dialogue:

SYLVETTE: See, poetry is in the hearts of lovers;
Not in adventures only, nor for rovers.

PERCINET: 'Tis true; for my adventures were authentic,
And, O Sylvette, they weren't at all poetic . . .

SYLVETTE: And those our crafty fathers made arise,
They were poetic, though they were just lies.

PERCINET: They built the framework, but our spirits know
On a false trellis still true flowers may grow.

SYLVETTE: Poetry, love, but we were crazy, dear,
To seek it elsewhere. It was always here.

In the last line of this exchange, Sylvette implores the audience not to abandon the poetic language of Rostand's brand of theater. *The Fantasticks* retains the basic romantic framework of *Les Romanesques*, but, according to Jones, it also teaches that one must have realistic expectations about love. Jones wants to have it both ways, however. Reality must be paired with art—for it is through art (e.g., theater) that truth is revealed. Yet poetry is needed in order to keep love alive.

Jones and Schmidt's Legacy

After Jones and Schmidt's distinguished debut, David Merrick, the most opportunistic of producers, tapped them for a musical adaptation of N. Richard Nash's play *The Rainmaker* (which began as a television play in 1952) (see Chapter 9). If the writers' unconventional music concerned Merrick, it did not seem to matter, as he felt that their Texas origins made them a perfect match for the material. Schmidt was about to set off for Iran to produce a series of paintings for *Sports Illustrated* magazine, but Merrick's offer was one that the young composer could not refuse. Merrick steered the musical, titled *110 in the Shade*, in an increasingly commercial direction. Schmidt and Jones produced a beautiful score, but the show ran for less than a year.

Still wanting a return on his investment in the writers, Merrick rehired Schmidt and Jones to work on a musical based on Jan de Hartog's play *The Fourposter* (1951). That the project would require a small budget and a cast of only two appealed to Merrick's avaricious side. Moreover, modern marriage was becoming a hot topic, and the producer figured that if he could sign two major box-office stars, he would have a hit on his hands. The show's marquee read, "David Merrick presents Mary Martin / Robert Preston / 'I Do! I Do!'" The show was a modest hit, but it became a staple of dinner theater and community theater.

Jones and Schmidt's score for *I Do! I Do!* boasted the crossover hit "My Cup Runneth Over," a waltz reminiscent of *The Fantasticks*'s "Try to Remember." Like *Love Life* (see Chapters 7 and 9), *I Do! I Do!* chronicles a typical marriage through five decades. However, the storms that the couple must weather never rise above cliché. Walter Kerr called the show, which had a book by Michael Stewart, "a carefully condensed time capsule of all the clichés that have ever been spawned by people married and/or single." *I Do! I Do!* reinforced conservative views of marriage with a smugness more attuned to the fifties than the sixties. After seeing a revival of the musical in 1996, Ben Brantley observed, "This [the sixties] was, after all, the era of Edward Albee's 'Who's Afraid of Virginia Woolf?,' and August Strindberg had suddenly replaced James M. Barrie as the model for domestic portraiture." Audiences had to wait for Sondheim's *Company* for a more incisive interrogation of marriage (see Chapter 10).

In the late sixties, Schmidt and Jones converted a brownstone building on West 47th into a theater workshop, which they called the Portfolio Studio, for the explicit purpose of experimenting with new musical theater forms. *Celebration*, the only musical developed at the space that transferred to Broadway, was a bold but problematic attempt at another experimental musical. Clive Barnes called *Celebration* "chic and heartless . . . an unpretentiously pretentious fairy tale for adults." The show takes the form of an Edenic ritual: an orphan boy who is banished from the idyllic garden of his orphanage goes on a journey of self-discovery and love. The characters are allegorical stick figures (Orphan, Angel, a cynic named Potemkin, Mr. Rich), and the plot, as it were, reflects the soul-searching fad of the sixties. The score paid lip service to rock music, but, as Barnes warns, "don't worry, you musical conservatives, Mr. Schmidt's music is not *too* rocky, it just shudders rather nicely once in a while." The prosaic metaphorical elements, primitivistic score, and minimalist unit set were little more than ornaments on a thin story. *Celebration* tried to capture the countercultural and anti-establishment ethos of the day, but, in contrast to *Hair*, it fell short of achieving its goal, and it put an end to Schmidt and Jones's Broadway career.

A revised version of Jones and Schmidt's *Colette*, which had run Off Broadway for 101 performances in 1970, nearly opened on Broadway in 1982. Based on Claudine Colette's autobiographical *Earthly Paradise*, this show held Jones and Schmidt's interest for many years, and they rewrote it several times. (Colette born Sidonie Gabrielle, lived from 1873 to 1953.) The Broadway-bound version starred the British actress Diana Rigg, but it closed out of town. A recording of *Colette Collage*, the latest incarnation of the show, was released in 1994.

Accepting the fact that they "were not Broadway writers," Schmidt and Jones turned to creating smaller, more intimate works in the vein of *The Fantasticks*. *Philemon*, set in 287 AD during the Roman Empire, is about a clown named Cockian who is forced to impersonate the Christian leader Philemon. PBS broadcast a television version of *Philemon* in 1976, and a brief Off Broadway revival took place in 1991. Since the mid-seventies, Schmidt and Jones have written several more musicals, including an adaptation of Thornton Wilder's *Our Town*, but none of these ever reached Broadway. Perhaps the writers were stuck between two traditions, the book musical of their youth and the concept musical that emerged during the sixties.

THE HALCYON DAYS OF OFF BROADWAY MUSICALS

In the sixties, Off Broadway experienced a wave of experimental musicals, including rock musicals. Few of these shows, however, left much of a legacy, although *Man of La Mancha* (see Chapter 9), one of the few exceptions, transferred to Broadway and remains a part of the standard repertory. Off Broadway cultivated a wider demographic and expanded geographically from Greenwich Village to other areas of the city, thereby providing more opportunities and venues for a larger range of musical theater. Off Broadway has played host to some conventional musical comedies (such as *The Sap of Life* and *Madame Aphrodite*) and a wide range of revues, including *Oh! Calcutta!*, which brought erotica to mainstream musical theater. New Off Broadway producing organizations sprouted up in record numbers, most notably the Roundabout Theatre Company (1965), the New York Shakespeare Festival (which moved into its current venue, the Public Theater, in 1967) (see Chapter 11), Manhattan Theatre Club (1970), and Playwrights Horizons (1971), all of which have produced important new musicals.

AL CARMINES

Al Carmines (1936–2005) stands out for his interest in esoteric social and political satire. An ordained minister as well as a composer, Carmines worked as a pastor at the Judson Memorial Church in Greenwich Village. He founded the Judson Poets' Theater in 1961 and presented several original musicals there. Carmines won a total of five Obie Awards (the Off Broadway equivalent of the Tony Awards) for Best Musical, the first for *In Circles* (1967), a musical based on Gertrude Stein's *A Circular Play* (1920). *Promenade*, Carmines's best-known work, premiered at the Judson Poets' Theater in 1965 and reopened in 1969 at an Off Broadway theater on the Upper West Side (the Promenade, which took its names from the show, its first production,). With a book by Maria Irene Fornes (b. 1930), the musical is an absurdist romp about two escaped convicts who are on a circular adventure that leads them back to prison. The madcap humor, unusual songs, such as one about naked ladies, and characters with names like 105 and Miss Cake account for the show's zany nature. Leading the top-notch cast were Alice Playten, George S. Irving, Gilbert Price, and Madeline Kahn. The theater critic Clive Barnes detected hints of Friml, Gershwin, Puccini, Coward, Weill, and Jacques Brel in Carmines's kaleidoscopic score. In the seventies, the prolific Carmines, who was gay, wrote *St. Joan* (1972) and *The Faggot* (1973), one of the first musicals to address homosexuality.

A recently published index of Off Broadway musicals, which ends with 2009, identifies sixty-five titles from the sixties. In subsequent decades, the number of musicals produced Off Broadway grew only slightly. What has changed significantly is the number of Off Broadway musicals that have transferred to Broadway. In the sixties, just a handful of works moved to a commercial Broadway venue, including the blockbuster *Hair* (see Chapter 16). By comparison, in the first decade of the new century, twelve Off Broadway musicals reopened on Broadway, including four Tony Award winners for Best Musical and five for Best Score.

For this reason, one can no longer talk about "Off Broadway musicals" as a distinct artistic body of work. Since the eighties, even major Broadway writers such as Stephen Sondheim, John Kander, and Charles Strouse have had to resort to Off Broadway. For instance, when in 1992 Strouse's *Annie Warbucks*, the sequel to *Annie* (see Chapters 9 and 10), experienced trouble during out-of-town tryouts, the producers canceled the Broadway booking. Strouse and his collaborators were committed to a New York production, so in 1993 they opened the show at the Off Broadway Variety Arts Theatre. Sondheim's *Sunday in the Park with George* and Kander and Ebb's *The Scottsboro Boys* premiered Off Broadway, at Playwrights Horizons and the Vineyard Theatre, respectively, and later transferred to Broadway.

Still, Off Broadway retains some of its original character and mission. Off Broadway's least commercial esoteric offerings, such as *Promenade* and *Adding*

AND BEAR IN MIND

Little Shop of Horrors *(1982, Orpheum Theatre, 2,209 performances)*

Music by Alan Menken
Lyrics and book by Howard Ashman

*L*ittle Shop of Horrors is based on the 1960s cult movie of the same name. It blends the sci-fi genre, horror movie campiness, the Faust and Frankenstein legends, and an infectious doo-wop score. The composer Alan Menken (b. 1949) and lyricist Howard Ashman (1950–1991) developed *Little Shop* while participating in the BMI Musical Theater Workshop (see Chapter 12). By Off Broadway standards, the original production, which played at the Orpheum Theatre, was indulgent. Its production values were practically better than its B-movie source material, and the giant human-eating plant, Audrey II, stole the show. *Little Shop* exuded an Off Broadway quirkiness,

Rick Moranis and Ellen Greene in a scene from the film version of *Little Shop of Horrors. Courtesy KB Archives.*

(Continued)

and, like *Grease*, it exploited nostalgia for early rock and roll while mocking fifties era conformity. Opening in 1982, it also functioned as a critique of the conservative ethos of the early Reagan era.

The 1986 film version of *Little Shop* captures the musical's charm and lunacy in celluloid terms and remains very faithful to the stage version except for one concession to Hollywood commercialism: Seymour kills the plant, and he and Audrey live happily ever after. The film also contains a new song for Audrey II called "Mean Green Mother from Outer Space."

Machine (2008), and Broadway's most monumental crowd pleasers, *The Phantom of the Opera* and *The Lion King*, are unlikely ever to invade each other's territory. Production budgets for Off Broadway musicals are a fraction of what they are for Broadway musicals, the result being rather modest sets and costumes, simple lighting designs, and single-piano accompaniments or very small orchestras. The stages and auditoriums are smaller than those of Broadway (and some are quite shabby). Moreover, entering an Off Broadway theater is an entirely different visceral experience from entering a plush Broadway theater. From the smell, to the lighting, to the amenities, to the staff, Off Broadway theaters have their own distinct character. Moreover, unlike Broadway, Off Broadway continues to take risks on unknown writers, noncommercial voices, and occasionally edgy subject matter. Topics of recent Off Broadway musicals include mental illness, Imelda Marcos, and the coming of age of a lesbian.

These differences notwithstanding, rather than providing an alternative to Broadway, Off Broadway increasingly serves as a testing ground for the commercial viability of a musical. The trappings and potential rewards of Broadway are so enticing that even the slightest critical praise of an Off Broadway musical can send producers into a frenzy to rush the show onto Broadway, the result being that many works that would be better served by the artistic milieu of Off Broadway end up with meager Broadway runs and are thereafter quickly forgotten (*Lysistrata Jones*, [2011]). The production history of *The Fantasticks* serves as an important object lesson in this regard. On the other hand, some iconic Off Broadway musicals, such as *In the Heights* and *Spring Awakening*, have benefitted from the widespread exposure that results from playing on Broadway.

One could make the argument that the increasingly cozy relationship between Broadway and Off Broadway is not in the best artistic interests of the musical theater genre. As Off Broadway becomes a "little Broadway," it runs the risk of losing sight of its original mission of providing an alternative to Broadway. The musical theater genre will have lost its primary venue for experimental work and for aspiring writers. A healthy and vibrant Off Broadway is needed for the genre as a whole to thrive and survive.

NAMES, TERMS, AND CONCEPTS

299 seating capacity

Ashman, Howard

Baker, Word

Carmines, Al

Dames at Sea

Ernest in Love

Fantasticks, The

Godspell

"It Depends on What You Pay"

Jones, Tom

Les Romanesques

Little Mary Sunshine

Little Shop of Horrors

Menken, Alan

Noto, Lore

Rostand, Edmond

Schmidt, Harvey

Sullivan Street Playhouse

"They Were You"

"Try to Remember"

You're a Good Man, Charlie Brown

DISCUSSION QUESTIONS

1. What aspects of *The Fantasticks*'s concept, book, and score account for its continuing popularity?

2. Discuss the changing relationship between Off Broadway musicals and Broadway musicals.

CHAPTER 15

THE "BLACK MUSICAL"
(*THE WIZ*, 1975, MAJESTIC THEATRE, 1,672 PERFORMANCES)

The history of the black musical mirrors the struggle of African Americans to overcome the insidious effects of institutionalized racism. Throughout the twentieth century, black writers and performers found success on Broadway, as white audiences enjoyed the music, dancing, and clowning of black artists, but white producers, publishers, and performers shamelessly exploited them and reinforced the racist attitudes of white America. African Americans who wanted to participate in mainstream musical theater had little choice but to propagate stereotypes derived from the minstrel show. When they attempted to explore authentic African American issues and cultural identity, they met with resistance from white critics and audiences.

The generic label "black musical" is ahistorical and misleading. The musicals that historians have lumped together under this label hardly constitute a monolithic body of work. Most of them were performed by all-black casts, but there are exceptions. Many black musicals played to black audiences only, whereas others were intended for predominantly white Broadway audiences (and occasionally segregated white and black audiences [e.g., *In Dahomey*]). There are "black-performed," "white-created," and "black-created" black musicals, to resort to Allen Woll's overly explicit but arguably necessary nomenclature to distinguish among these types, to which one can add musicals by biracial creative teams. The indiscriminate application of the term "black musical" to such a diverse body of work has in effect rendered the term meaningless. In the early twentieth century, the label "Negro musical" was used to identify musicals by black writers and with black performers from mainstream musicals, similar to the term "Negro Baseball League." Today, encyclopedia entries on the subject adopt "African American musical" as an umbrella term for all of the possible permutations of the black musical. As one surveys the black musical, one must attempt to account for the different historical circumstances surrounding the shows and distinguish between those onto which racial stereotypes were projected and those that present African American culture in a more authentic light.

EARLY YEARS

American popular entertainment incorporated aspects of African American culture long before the rise of blackface minstrelsy in the 1840s (see Chapter 2). In the 1830s, Thomas Dartmouth Rice (1808–1860), a white performer from New York, achieved fame and fortune by doing impersonations of an old black man he identified as Jim Crow and singing the song bearing the character's name, "Jump, Jim Crow." Rice allegedly modeled his performance on slaves that he had observed in Kentucky. He started to "blacken up" (appear in blackface), a practice that he propagated as he toured the country. By the early 1840s, Rice's popularity fueled the creation of formal minstrel shows.

In 1843, Dan Emmett (1815–1904) founded the Virginia Minstrels, which consisted of four male performers, all of them appearing in blackface. They debuted in New York City and toured several American cities as well as England. Over the years, Emmett performed in various troupes and composed music for the "walk-around" (parade around the stage), including "Dixie," his most popular song. He also devised the variety-show format that became the model for minstrel shows for the remainder of the century. The actors formed a semicircle, on either end of which were positioned Mr. Bones (thusly named because he played a percussion instrument made from bones) and Mr. Tambo (who played a tambourine). An Interlocutor, located at the midpoint of the semicircle, editorialized the proceedings. The performance consisted of two parts, the first focusing on Negro plantation life, the second on urban life.

During the 1840s and 1850s, minstrel acts acquired a third part, became more formulaic, employed a larger assemblage of performers, and proliferated in number. The first section featured genteel songs. The newly added segment, the "olio," occupied the second position in the show and featured songs and skits satirizing pretentious upper-class society, Shakespeare, and opera, as well as slaves and free blacks. The third section consisted of an extended scene about plantation life. A "walk-around" concluded the show. A popular feature was the dialect song, which after 1880 took on the label "coon song." The offensive stereotype depicted in Sam Lucas's "Coon's Salvation Army" (1884) was typical:

De melon patch am safe today,
No Coons am dar in sight,
De chickens dey may roost in peace
Wid in der coops tonight.

During the Reconstruction era, black performers formed their own minstrel troupes, many at the behest of white managers, who profited substantially therefrom. Of the many ironies surrounding black minstrels, the most disturbing is that the black performers had to appear in blackface and perform the same degrading sort of material as their white counterparts. Today, their willingness to participate in such a demeaning enterprise seems to run counter to their best interests, but black performers had no other professional outlet, and some of them used the minstrel show as an opportunity to dispel racist attitudes. The experience, though, must have been gut-wrenching, all the more so given that postwar minstrel shows embodied an even more odious form of racism than earlier ones.

That such a morally reprehensible institution could also be America's most popular form of entertainment reflects the degree to which racism penetrated all aspects of society. By the end of the century, minstrelsy as an institution was moribund, but the image of blacks "as thoughtless, shuffling, superstitious, devious, and servile," as one historian describes, was ingrained in the consciousness of white America and persisted throughout the twentieth century.

A vibrant black theater emerged at the turn of the twentieth century. Black entrepreneurs began acquiring theaters and marketing musicals to black audiences, and by 1909 the first black-run theater circuits were in operation. (White theater owners also booked black entertainment.) Black writers wrote shows for the black-circuit theaters, but they also aspired to see their work on Broadway. Achieving this goal, however, meant creating material that white audiences would accept: songs, dances, and skits rooted in minstrelsy.

During the first decade of the twentieth century, African American writers sought to distance the black musical from the legacy of blackface minstrel shows. However, the black musicals that reached Broadway at the time were invariably presented for all-white audiences by white producers, who compelled the writers to incorporate coon songs and stereotypical black characters. Nevertheless, some black writers managed to avoid degrading material even though they met with resistance from white critics, producers, and audiences. *The Creole Burlesque Co.* (1890) was one of the earliest shows to take this important step. Sam T. Jack, a white theater owner in the burlesque business, backed the production, which starred several former minstrel entertainers but expunged the formal aspects of the minstrel show, including the semicircle and the plantation backdrop. The show spawned several similar entertainments, some of which featured black female performers and even opera, traditionally the domain of white singers.

For black writers who deliberately tried to break free from the shackles of minstrelsy, complete emancipation was not easy to achieve. Robert Allen "Bob" Cole and Will Marion Cook were among the first black musical comedy writers who moved away from minstrel show stereotypes. Will Marion Cook (1869–1944) received a classical music education. He attended the Oberlin Conservatory of Music at the age of thirteen and later studied in Germany with the famed violinist Joseph Joachim. He also studied composition with Antonín Dvořák at the National Conservatory of Music in New York, but he grew discouraged with his lessons and redirected his energies toward the theater. Cook's first musical of note was *Clorindy, the Origin of the Cakewalk* (1898), which he wrote with the eminent African American poet Paul Lawrence Dunbar (1872–1906). Edward Rice (of *A Trip to Chinatown* fame [see Chapter 2]) produced *Clorindy* at his Casino Theatre Roof Garden, but with most of Dunbar's book expunged.

Before long, Cook became the principal composer for the duo of Bert Williams (see Chapter 4) and George Walker, who helped to break the color barrier on Broadway (they billed themselves as "Two Real Coons"). In 1896, the white producer George Lederer (see Chapter 2) interpolated Williams and Walker's vaudeville act into *The Gold Bug*, hoping to give a boost to what was a failing venture. Four years later, Williams and Walker returned to Broadway in their own show, *The Policy Players*. In 1903, Cook co-authored the libretto and provided the music (Dunbar wrote the lyrics) for the duo's greatest success, *In Dahomey*, the first black musical booked into a major Broadway theater. *In Dahomey* played in New York for seven weeks and then in London for seven months (including a command performance at Buckingham Palace), after which it went on a forty-week American tour. The producers earned between a 300% and 400% return on their investment, proving again that black on Broadway made economic sense. Although Walker and Williams dreamed of elevating the status of black artists in American culture, they continued to pander to the expectations of white audiences. In their subsequent musicals, Walker and Williams strove to present more favorable portrayals of black characters. However, the premature death of Walker put an end to their promising collaboration. Ziegfeld hired the now partner-less Williams to appear in the *Follies*.

Bob Cole (1869–1911) attended Atlanta University and then headed north to pursue a theater career. White producers hired him to write material for their shows, but Cole grew frustrated with the meager pay and miserable working conditions, and in the 1890s he founded a black production company. The company's first full-length musical comedy was Cole's own *A Trip to Coontown* (1897–1898). Despite its name (a twist on the hit musical *A Trip to Chinatown*), this musical represented another step forward for black writers. It was the first musical written by blacks, performed by blacks, and produced by blacks, and it was a sensation. The plot centers around a con artist named Jim Flimflammer, who puts one over on "an old Negro" named Silas Green. Cole, in the part of Willie Wayside, saves Green from being cheated out of his pension. The show played briefly on Broadway and then toured the country. Whereas Cook demonstrated that black musicals could turn a handsome profit, Cole proved that black writers could complete with white writers. Broadway audiences for their shows included black and white patrons, albeit in segregated seating.

Cole went on to form a songwriting partnership with the brothers John Rosamond Johnson (1873–1954) and James Weldon Johnson (1871–1938). Many of their songs, including "Mandy" and "Under the Bamboo Tree," reached such a level of popularity that famous white performers agreed to pose with the writers for photographs featured on the covers of the sheet music. Cole and John Rosamond Johnson also became a successful performing duo. They eschewed black stereotypes and gave their act a sense of dignity. In Cole's own words, "What we aim to do . . . is evolve a type of music that will have all that is distinct in the old Negro music and yet which shall be sophisticated enough to appear to the cultured musician. We want the Negro spirit—its warmth and originality—to color our music." They appeared in one of their own shows, *The Shoo-Fly Regiment*, which James also helped to write. Featuring an all-black cast, *Shoo-Fly* concerns a graduate of Tuskegee Institute who interrupts his plans to become a schoolteacher in order to fight in the Spanish–American War. *Shoo-Fly Regiment* included serious romantic scenes played by black performers. However, white audiences showed little interest in the realistic portrayal of black characters and refused to accept any on-stage depiction of sexually charged relations between them. They liked the novelty of all-black musicals, but they rejected anything that did not meet their expectations of black entertainment. White critics not only did nothing to prepare their readership for a more genuine expression of African American culture, but they reinforced their worst prejudices. Misappropriating Cole's own words, one commentator insisted that audiences wanted a "genuine negro spirit," not ambitious art. In 1907, a critic berated the creators of *The Shoo-Fly Regiment* for attempting to compete artistically against white writers: "colored authors have much to learn before they can instruct or entertain our public. They may reach a certain standard, but, for the present, such performances are futile. If they are to advance, they must advance in a direction of their own. In the direction of imitation they will accomplish nothing, or nothing that is their own." That the mainstream press regularly sanctioned and disseminated such patronizing views made it easy for white theatergoers to continue believing that black writers should stick to material harkening back to minstrelsy. Whether racist propaganda or condescension, such attitudes persisted for decades, making it nearly impossible for black writers to achieve professional parity with their white counterparts. Broadway might have been open to African Americans, but white tastes, whether dictated or merely articulated by the critics of the country's leading presses, continued to impede black writers from competing in mainstream musical theater without making concessions to old stereotypes. Cole and the Johnsons did much to combat this attitude. However, Cole's health began to fail, and in 1911 he committed suicide at the age of forty-three.

THE TWENTIES

After 1910, the presence of black musicals and black talent on Broadway suffered a decline. Black artists either died or moved on to other pursuits. Black musicals played to mostly all-black audiences in venues away from Broadway. Things changed in 1921 when *Shuffle Along* opened on Broadway and initiated what became the heyday of the "Negro musical." Apart from its incandescent score by the black composer Eubie Blake (1883–1983) and lyricist Noble Sissle (1889–1975), *Shuffle Along* helped to desegregate Broadway theaters. It played 504 performances and remains one of the most successful black musicals of all times. It also spawned several imitations. The African American playwright

Shuffle Along of 1933 (Flournoy Miller as Steve Jenkins, left). *Courtesy KB Archives.*

and director George Wolfe (see Chapter 12) is currently developing a backstage musical involving *Shuffle Along* which is scheduled to open in 2016.

During the twenties, the revue genre provided a showcase for black performers and featured lots of African American dance forms such as tap and the Black Bottom. *Dixie to Broadway* (1924) initiated a string of all-black revues. The white producer Lew Leslie (1986–1963) made a career out of producing black revues. His "ownership" of this type of black entertainment underscores the paradoxical nature of the black musical's mainstream appeal: the more popular the black musical became, the more it morphed into white entertainment, usually controlled by white producers and writers. Ironically, the widespread popularity of black musicals during the twenties undermined the influence of black writers, the opposite of what Harlem Renaissance writers experienced. It also led to a gradual resegregation of Broadway theaters.

The Harlem Renaissance refers to the flourishing of African American literature and other creative endeavors from the late teens until the late thirties. The movement helped to define an African American identity and culture apart from white stereotypes.

Attitudes about race among white critics evolved little during the early decades of the century. A review of *Put and Take*, the first black revue after *Shuffle Along*, is all too typical:

> There is too much effort to be dressed up and dignified. . . . Colored performers cannot vie with white ones, and colored producers cannot play within an apple's throw of Ziegfeld and try to compete with him. . . . And here the colored folks seemed to have set out to show the whites they're just as good as anybody. They may be as good, but they're different and, in their entertainment, at any rate, they should remain different, distinct, and indigenous.

A year later *Variety* published an equally offensive opinion about *The Chocolate Dandies* (1924):

> It is a negro piece for the most part uninspired by the native spirit. . . . The white business is "white folks" material of which there is plenty and then some in the show world, and not good darky entertainment, of which there is little enough of the best.

Sometime in the teens, Jewish composers, most prominently Irving Berlin, began incorporating jazz elements into their songs—which Jewish entertainers sang and Jewish music publishers sold—and thereby exposed white America to the sound of black music. However, any benefit that African Americans might have derived from the exposure of their music to white commercial markets is overshadowed today by accusations that Jews exploited black talent. Jewish jazz is now seen as an extension of Jewish blackface (see Chapter 17). These practices represent a willingness among Jews to channel "elements and perceptions of black culture that few other ethnic groups . . . were willing to acknowledge or confront," as Jeffrey Magee has argued. Historians have accused Jews, some of whom were the resolute voices of racial tolerance on Broadway, of willful cultural thievery. However, in the twenties, white music critics argued that there was a natural affinity between Jews and blacks and by extension Jews and jazz. This narrative gave rise to the notion that Jews were the natural mediator for African American culture. In fact, Irving Berlin acquired the title "Broadway's king of jazz"; and rumors circulated about his keeping "a little colored boy" in his closet for inspiration. The public discourse about the musical affinity between blacks and Jews disguised the one-sided nature of their relationship. Magee raises questions about Berlin's authenticity as a jazz composer, noting his "mixing black and white signs . . . with a distinctively assimilative Jewish sensibility in a period when racial boundaries in the public sphere were being policed more intensively, and sometimes more violently, than ever."

THE THIRTIES

The Depression dealt a severe blow to black writers and performers. When leaders of the black community voiced concern about the lack of opportunities for black talent, the Federal Theatre Project, an arm of the Works Progress Administration (WPA) (see Chapter 6), formed the "Negro Unit" to showcase black performers and to celebrate African American culture. The Negro Unit preferred spoken plays, but it produced some musicals, beginning with *Swing It* (1937), written by Eubie Blake, Cecil Mack, and J. Milton Reddie. *Swing It* had trouble completing against the positive legacy of Blake's *Shuffle Along*. The Negro Unit's most successful musical was an all-black production of Gilbert and Sullivan's *The Mikado*. As improbable as combining African American performers and Gilbert and Sullivan operetta may have seemed, it was neither the first nor last effort to do so, and it generated a lot of attention. *Swing Mikado* (1939), as the Unit's version was titled, relocated the action from Japan to the South Sea Islands, "swung" several numbers from the score, and infused the text with black dialect. It opened in Chicago to such acclaim that several producers competed for the opportunity to bring it to New York, all of them unaware that both Michael Todd and Alfred de Liagre were developing their own jazzed-up versions of *The Mikado*. In the casting coup of the decade, Todd signed Bill "Bojangles" Robinson to appear as The Mikado, hoping to draw audiences away from *Swing Mikado*, which had opened in New York three weeks earlier. At this point, de Liagre abandoned his project, unable to compete against the other two black *Mikado*s. Todd called

Bill "Bojangles" Robinson as The Mikado, tap dancing up and down the stairs in the original 1939 Broadway production *Hot Mikado. Courtesy Photofest.*

his version *Hot Mikado* to emphasize the fact that it interpolated more jazz into Gilbert and Sullivan's Victorian-era score than the Negro Unit's version. Todd's instincts paid off, as *Hot Mikado* outshone *Swing Mikado* at the box office and was a popular attraction at the 1939 New York World's Fair.

Soon people were turning all sorts of classic titles into all-black musicals. Oscar Hammerstein's *Carmen Jones* (1943), a retelling of Georges Bizet's 1875 opera *Carmen*, opened shortly after *Oklahoma!* Hammerstein relocated the action of the opera, which takes place in Seville around 1820, to the American South during World War II. Olin Downes's well-intentioned but tainted review of *Carmen Jones* reveals just how entrenched, condescending, and outright racist attitudes about blacks on Broadway were even as late as 1943:

> We were considerably disappointed in one thing of which we had expected a great deal. This was the prevailing self-consciousness and a degree of restraint in much of the acting and nearly all of the dancing. A performance by Negroes—yes—and they do a highly creditable job! But it was not a Negro performance in the natural creative way of that race of born actors and musicians that we had expected to see. There was evidence of too much white man's training in it all . . .

Backhanded compliments such as these continued to appear in print well into the civil rights era.

George Gershwin (see Chapter 5) and Harold Arlen (see Chapters 7 and 8) synthesized the rhythms and harmonies of jazz into their musical vocabulary more than any other white composers at the time, and they exhibited a genuine interest in African American culture. *Porgy and Bess* (1935), Gershwin's crowning achievement, depicted black life in Catfish Row, a fictional black neighborhood in Charleston, South Carolina (see Chapter 6). Gershwin hoped to use *Porgy and Bess* to fulfill a commission from the Metropolitan Opera in 1930, but the prohibition of black singers at the Metropolitan precluded this from happening. The original 1935 Broadway production of *Porgy and Bess*, which featured Will Marion Cook's wife, Abbie Mitchell, in the role of Clara, was not a major hit, but a revival in 1942 produced by Cheryl Crawford reached 286 performances and ensured the work's canonicity and artistic reputation.

Gershwin fans find it difficult to fathom the hostility and criticism that *Porgy and Bess* engendered (and continues to engender, for that matter). Music critics complained about the score's reliance on popular songs; theater critics derided the work's operatic flights; and black critics accused Gershwin and Dubois Heyward, who adapted the libretto from his novel and subsequent play *Porgy* (Ira Gershwin also wrote some of the lyrics), of propagating black stereotypes. The African American social historian Harold Cruse wrote, "*Porgy and Bess* belongs in a museum and no self-respecting African American should want to see it, or be seen in it. . . . It portrays the seamiest side of Negro life—presumably the image of black people that white audiences want to see." Today, *Porgy and Bess* continues to incite debate over authenticity, cultural ownership, and the white exploitation of black culture, even though the work continues to be performed all over the world and returned to Broadway as recently as 2012 (see Chapter 13).

POSTWAR BLACK MUSICALS

Black writers and performers continued to endure setbacks during and after World War II. Racial barriers limited the opportunities available to black artists, and casting based on minstrel stereotypes persisted. African Americans played a typically narrow range of roles: "comic servants, urban vagabonds, Caribbean exotics, and jungle savages." Duke Ellington (1899–1974), the most visible black composer on Broadway after the war, attempted to counter this trend. He wrote a musical based on *The Beggar's Opera* called *Beggar's Holiday* (1946) and another based on the film *The Blue Angel* called *Pousse Café*. Neither work did well on Broadway, but they both found favor elsewhere. The African American poet, playwright, and activist Langston Hughes struggled to make African American cultural heritage an important element of the black musical. In 1947, he collaborated with the Jewish émigré composer Kurt Weill on a musical adaptation of Elmer Rice's *Street Scene* (see Chapter 7). He changed Rice's Swedish janitor, a minor role, to a black janitor, but his other efforts to introduce more black characters into the story met with Rice's objections. Hughes also wrote a couple of operas, including one with the African American composer William Grant Still called *Troubled Island* (1949). However, Hughes grew frustrated with the white domination of American theater and argued that African American talent would not be fully appreciated until black artists took control of the production of their work. He urged black writers to adapt black sources and write for all-black audiences. His first effort, *Simply Heavenly* (1957), addressed the discrimination that black soldiers faced during World War II. Even Hughes, though, incorporated some features associated with earlier black musicals, such as malapropisms and tap dancing.

White-created black musicals fared much better at the box office. Vernon Duke, Harold Arlen, and Kurt Weill created a string of popular black musicals, including *Cabin in the Sky* (1940), *St. Louis Woman* (1946), and *Lost in the Stars* (1949). The lyricist E. Y. Harburg stands out for his serious treatment of black issues in *Finian's Rainbow* (1947) and *Jamaica* (1957). *Jamaica* is one a several musicals about race set outside of the United States. Such works, according to Allen Woll, "used black characters as a form of exotica, and Caribbean locales often allowed librettists and songwriters to escape the tremendous problems of American race relations."

At the height of the civil rights era, black-created musicals on Broadway continued to decline in number. African American writers preferred spoken theater as a vehicle for protest, as they felt that the musical theater genre did not have enough gravitas to serve their serious cause. Black playwrights tapped into the anger of militant groups such as the Black Panthers over the slow progress of the civil rights movement. Three black-created Off Broadway musicals, all of them incorporating gospel music, appealed to African American audiences: Irving Burgie and Loften Mitchell's *Ballad for Bimshire* (1963) and two works by Langston

Hughes, *Tambourines to Glory* (1963) (based on his 1958 novel of the same name) and *The Prodigal Son* (1965). Generally speaking, though, musicals by black writers from the era tended to be "ethnomusicological replications of black life and music," according to Woll. They held little interest for white audiences and made little contribution to the cause of civil rights.

Several musicals by white writers reflected the new consciousness ushered in by the civil rights movement. These shows belong to a long tradition of Jewish-written musicals about discrimination, the plight of African Americans, and miscegenation. Despite their good intentions, the writers could not escape approaching civil rights from a white perspective. Even Oscar Hammerstein, whose liberal politics made him sensitive to issues of prejudice and whose idealism made him predisposed to stories involving cross-racial relationships, never permitted the interracial romances in his shows to reach a happy conclusion. For example, *Show Boat*'s Julie, a person of mixed race and the victim of miscegenation laws, becomes an alcoholic and sacrifices her career for her white friend Magnolia (see Chapter 5).

In the sixties, mixed-race relationships continued to figure large in musicals by white writers. Richard Rodgers's *No Strings* (1962), his first musical after Hammerstein's death, involved a relation between a black woman and white man, both of them American expatriates living in Paris. When faced with returning to America, they decide to go their separate ways rather than confront resistance from friends and family back home. Rodgers denied that the show was about race, but the casting of the black actress Diahann Carroll and white actor Richard Kiley made it impossible not to interpret the work as a statement about race. Richard Adler's *Kwamina* (1961), another musical set in Africa, concerned a romantic relationship between a black man and white woman, but it too was safely removed from the racial conflicts in America, and it ran only thirty-two performances. *Golden Boy* (1964) was the first musical to reflect changing attitudes about interracial relationships in the United States. The source material, Clifford Odets's 1937 play *Golden Boy*, is about an Italian American who aspires to become a violinist. The producer Hillard Elkins conceived the musical as a vehicle for Sammy Davis, Jr. and turned the protagonist into a black man from Harlem. In one scene, Davis and his white lover, played by Paula Wayne, sang a steamy, sexually charged duet called "I Want to Be with You" and then went to bed together. When the show opened in 1964, the lynching of Emmett Till, a black youth who allegedly whistled at a white woman, was still a controversial matter, and miscegenation was still taboo if not outright illegal in several parts of the country. During previews of *Golden Boy* in Detroit, Davis and Wayne received hate mail and required a police escort to and from the theater.

Hallelujah, Baby! (1968) also centered on the civil rights movement. With music by Jule Styne, lyrics by Adolph Green and Betty Comden, and a book by Arthur Laurents, the show told the story of a black woman, Georgina, who dreams of having a singing career. The obstacles she faces reflect the real struggles that African American performers had in negotiating an industry controlled by whites. The writers superimposed Georgina's life over the most active decades of the civil rights movement, from the Great Depression to the late sixties, in order to illustrate the slow pace of progress in eliminating all vestiges of Jim Crow while simultaneously creating sympathy for the show's heroine. When Georgina arrives at the present—1968—she joins the civil rights movement. *Hallelujah, Baby!* trod too lightly on its serious themes and failed to capture the reality of the African American experience in 1968.

Arthur Laurents conceived of *Hallelujah, Baby!* for Lena Horne, but when she abruptly withdrew from the project, a then-unknown Leslie Uggams took her place. Like Horne, Uggams too had married a white man, although she escaped the scandal that surrounded Horne's marriage (see Chapter 8). Uggams's costar, the African American actor Robert Hooks, was active in the civil rights movement, and he brought his political views to bear on his character.

The most outstanding aspect of the show was not its gritty story or political agenda; it was its experimental form. *Hallelujah, Baby!* uses show business to exemplify how segregationist laws held back African Americans. Styne wrote some effective pastiche songs to denote the early decades of the story, but he made no attempt to emulate contemporary popular music styles for the final portion of the show, which takes place in the fifties and sixties.

The all-white creative team approached the material through a musical comedy lens, which did not serve the musical's serious message. Moreover, they seemed oblivious to the inherent difficulties they would face in trying to write about African Americans in the mid-sixties. Betty Comden confessed, "We never thought of ourselves as white people writing about black people. . . [S]uddenly it was not a happy time between the races. We were looked on as quite suspect and it was sort of uncomfortable." Walter Kerr took the writers to task and complained that the characters were two-dimensional and spoke "in an idiom that seemed suitable enough when playwrights were first discovering the Negro and, out of a perfectly genuine goodwill, offering him a hand up." Kerr felt that the show was behind the times and wondered whom the writers had in mind as the show's target audience:

"Hallelujah, Baby!" can't really be talking to Negroes, who have long since ceased to think of themselves as perennial patsies who need to be escorted by loving, liberal white hands across streets to near-safety. And it can't very well be talking to white liberals, either, not at this late date, not when do-gooders have seen the folly of being patronizing to all God's chillum, not when the Invisible Man has ceased being invisible and has become a face, a force, and even a fury to be reckoned with.

As Kerr hastened to point out, events such as the Watts incident in 1965 (six days of riots in South Central Los Angeles sparked by racially biased police brutality) proved that the movement still had a long way to go. In retrospect, Laurents agreed with Kerr. On the occasion of a new production in 2004, he conceded, "I don't think [the show] had much to say." According to the critic Trey Graham, after Lena Horne dropped out, the show "become a simplistic message piece, out of step with a world listening warily to Stokely Carmichael's black-power rumblings and a theater that would soon be moving ecstatically to the rhythms of 'Hair'."

THE SEVENTIES

In the seventies, black-written musicals reemerged as a force on Broadway, as a younger generation of African Americans were less reticent about using musical theater as a medium for exploring black themes and celebrating black culture. Popular plays by black playwrights inspired a number of successful musicals. For instance, *Purlie*, a musical based on Ossie Davis's *Purlie Victorious*, employed a targeted marketing campaign in an effort to build a black audience. *Raisin* (1973), an adaptation of Lorraine Hansberry's 1959 play *A Raisin in the Sun*, has symbolic significance, as it was one of the few Broadway musicals by an interracial collaboration of writers (see *St. Louis Woman* in Chapter 7): Hansberry's former husband, Robert Nemiroff (1930–1991), and Charlotte Zaltzberg (1924–1974) co-wrote the book, Robert Brittan (?–1996) wrote the lyrics, and Judd Woldin (1925–2011) composed the music. The African American choreographer Donald McKayle (b. 1930), who had worked on *Golden Boy*, directed and choreographed the production.

Ain't Supposed to Die a Natural Death

Black-written musicals during this period fall into one of two categories: statements of protest or celebrations of black pride. *Ain't Supposed to Die a Natural Death: Tunes from Blackness* opened on Broadway one year after *Purlie*. The most provocative black musical from the era, it took the establishment completely by surprise and intentionally attempted to rile audiences. Melvin Van Peebles (b. 1932), who had helped to launch the blaxploitation film industry with *Sweet Sweetback's Baadasssss Song* (1971), wrote the music, lyrics, and book. The show exposed black and white audiences to the despair of urban blacks by parading realistic characters drawn from the ghetto—a prostitute, a pimp, a beggar, a homosexual, and a bag lady, to name a few. Van Peeples confronted the critics and white audiences about their complicity in the plight of African American. He set out to make them feel uneasy, and the critics took the bait, responding defensively and in some cases with hostility. T. E. Kalem called the show "a jumbled-up, quasi-Brechtian Harlem re-do of Elmer Rice's *Street Scene*" and charged that the seedy characters "would be promptly denounced as racist stereotypes if a white playwright dared to suggest their existence. . . . In their self-indulgent militancy, black playwrights of Van Peebles' frenzied stamp like to think that they are raising welts of The Man's conscience. Actually, they are catering to a masochistic *mea culpa* claque and assorted liberal breast beaters." Only Martin Gottfried brought some historical perspective to his critique of the show:

> Melvin Van Peebles has finally done what was lying there, waiting to be done. He has taken . . . the very spirit of urban black ghetto existence and thrown it upon the stage. And he has done it without creating some kind of freak show—the minstrel show with real black faces that is mainly what Broadway black theater has been. Van Peebles' "Ain't Supposed to Die a Natural Death" IS the black people and it is magnificent. It is also brutal, a condemnation of the white world for having created the prison of misery, frustration and

indignity that it is now being forced to see. For unlike virtually all black theater that I have seen in the white marketplace, this production belongs only
there. . . . It is not an "artistic play" brought downtown for white approval
condescension. The black theater of our crude past was produced by white
people, showing off the blackbirds, the black Mikado's, the Porgy's and Besses.
The black theater of today is little better, now created by black people but still
essentially exhibitions of black bodies, black "soul."

Ain't Supposed to Die managed to find its audience, in part through Van Peebles's
marketing ingenuity. The show also received free publicity from the attendance
of several black celebrities such as Shirley Chisholm, who announced her historic
candidacy for president of the United States from the stage. One commentator
suggested that "white-guilt foundation money helped keep [the show] going for
325 performances."

In the seventies, black theater was the beneficiary of public funding. Vinnette
Carroll's Urban Arts Corps fostered musicals such as *Don't Bother Me, I Can't Cope*
(1972) and *Your Arms Too Short to Box With God* (1976), both of which incorporated gospel scores by Micki Grant. These were upbeat, mostly sung-through shows,
and a stark contrast to Van Peebles's confrontational brand of theater.

The Wiz

By the late seventies, the focus of black musicals had begun to shift from agitating
for change to celebrating African American culture—to put it another way, they
went from political protest to pure entertainment. *The Wiz* avoided the smugness
of *Purlie* and preachiness of *Ain't Supposed to Die*. It rejoiced unapologetically in
the speech, music, dancing, and fashions of black culture, and did so in a way that
was welcoming to white as well as black audiences. *The Wiz* was the product of an
all-black creative team with the exception of the book writer. The sets, costumes,
orchestrations, and dialogue embraced modern black life. Dorothy's "over the
rainbow" is a contemporary urban world. The music was funky and upbeat.

Music

The composer of *The Wiz*, Charles Smalls (1943–1987), studied at the Juilliard
School of Music, but his career path led to jazz and rock. Indeed, critics noted that
the spirit of "soul" infused his score. The deliberate use of the term "soul" helped to
associate *The Wiz* with black music and differentiate it from other rock musicals
from the era. By the seventies, the term "rock" had come to connote music mainly
by white composers and for white listeners; "soul," on the other hand, was identified
with the black power movement. The album jacket for *The Wiz*, which was issued
on the Atlantic Records label, announced a "super soul musical," lest anyone had
any doubts.

The Wiz's accompaniments, vocal arrangements, and orchestrations emulate
the Motown sound. There are vocal and instrumental rhythmic riffs, honkytonk piano,
long sections with pedal point, gospel call-and-response arrangements, pit singers,

blue notes, and a preponderance of dotted-quarter-note eighth-note rhythms. The unusually large orchestra featured brass choir, high slow-moving string lines against animated vocals, Fender Rhodes electric piano, vibes, and "Shaft" guitar. Moreover, the original cast recording of *The Wiz* employed fadeout endings rather than the full-stop endings used in the theater.

"Ease on Down the Road" (the counterpart to "Follow the Yellow Brick Road" from MGM's *The Wizard of Oz* movie) epitomizes the black ethos of the score. The song, one of few musical theater crossover hits of the seventies, incorporates funk, an offshoot of soul. Funk relied on hard-driving bass lines and repeating rhythms. "Ease on Down the Road" begins with a syncopated riff introduced by the bass and Fender Rhodes piano (Example 15.1a). A Moog synthesizer, acoustic piano, and electric guitar join in on the first repeat. The snazzy, syncopated repeated pattern lies almost entirely between the lowered-seventh and lowered-third degrees of the blues scale. The vocal line is simple and repetitive, centering on a falling minor third between the blue note D-flat and B-flat (Example 15.1b). The harmony, also derived from the blues, oscillates between I^{b7} and IV^{b7}. Starting in m. 18 ("Don't you carry nothin'"), the harmonic rhythm doubles in speed as the melody spins out a variant of the main theme. This phrase involves pungent sharp ninth chords and a circle-of-fifths progression, and it cadences on a bluesy I^{b7}. Accented chords in the brass choir punctuates the phrases. The "Pit Singers" also join in, singing "doot, doot, doot" in three-part harmony.

"'Shaft' guitar" refers to the novel effect created with a wah-wah pedal famously employed by Isaac Hayes in the "Theme from *Shaft*" composed for the 1971 blaxploitation film *Shaft*. Harold Wheeler, the orchestrator for *The Wiz*, wrote "'Shaft' guitar" directly into the score to indicate the effect.

Book

William F. Brown's book for *The Wiz* revels in slang, black cultural references, and self-deprecating humor. The characters occasionally step outside of the story to comment on the action and occasionally to acknowledge the irony of turning a story long identified with populist views of white middle America into a soul-inspired all-black version with a hip, street-smart, and contemporary swagger.

EXAMPLE 15.1. "Ease on Down the Road," (a) recurring vamp, (b) opening phrase

PLOT OF THE WIZ

Dorothy lives with her Aunt Em and Uncle Henry on their farm in Kansas, but she yearns to see the world beyond her home. A tornado carries Dorothy and her house to the Land of the Munchkins. Addaperle, the Good Witch of the North, informs Dorothy that her house landed on and killed the Wicked Witch of the East. Dorothy wants to return to Kansas, so Addaperle directs her to the Wizard of Oz and gives her the dead witch's silver shoes. During her journey to Oz, Dorothy befriends Scarecrow, Tinman, and Lion. When the four friends arrive in the Emerald City, they have an audience with the Wizard, who agrees to grant them their wish, but only if they kill the Wicked Witch of the West, who has enslaved the Winkies. As the four companions near the land of the Wicked Witch, they are attacked by her flying monkeys, which carry Dorothy and Lion to the witch's castle. Dorothy eventually melts the witch by throwing a bucket of water on her. The Winkies, grateful to Dorothy, restore Scarecrow and Tinman. When the four companions return to the Wizard, he refuses to honor his promise. When the Wizard is discovered hiding behind a screen, he discloses that he is merely a simple man from Omaha. He gives Dorothy's friends tokens that represent the things they desire and agrees to accompany Dorothy back to Kansas. As he addresses the citizens of the Emerald City, his balloon takes off without Dorothy. Addaperle suddenly appears and summons her sister, Glinda, the Good Witch of the South, who tells Dorothy that the silver shoes will take her home.

The Wiz manages to celebrate blackness and African American culture while avoiding the politics of protest. It does not attempt to change hearts and minds so much as to entertain with an entirely African American aesthetic and point of view. The humor is neither vulgar nor subtle. For instance, when Dorothy and her companions come across the poppies, the Lion sniffs (or snorts) the airborne pollen and explains, "I suddenly have the urge to do a little cross-pollinating." When Addaperle, the Good Witch of the North, bestows the slippers on Dorothy (silver ones, as in Baum's novel), she remarks, "I hope you don't mind second-hand shoes." Evillene, the Wicked Witch of the West, orders Dorothy to "polish the silver, vacuum the rugs," and she adds, "You *do* do windows, don't you?" The dialogue evokes "the Almighty Himself" and the "Lord" with zeal, and the Wiz's speeches have the euphony and lexical brashness of a Baptist preacher's sermon: "Check this out! I come floating down out of the clouds, I make my maiden message on the multitude, and I whip up the grand-daddy of all revival meetings." Smalls's lyrics are similarly idiomatic and entertaining. For example, he rhymes "tryin'" with "lion" without a hint of self-consciousness. The phrase "Ease on Down the Road" is a jivey substitute for "follow the yellow brick road."

Reception

The theater critic of the *New York Amsterdam News*, a paper written for New York City's African American community, lauded *The Wiz* for reclaiming the American musical theater for black America:

> It is not only food for the soul, but a theatrical version of the impulse that created soul food. Just as Black people took cast offs from white kitchens and turned them into something uniquely theirs so William F. Brown and Charles Smalls have taken a mediocre story . . . which has been canonized by the memory of Judy Garland, and created something uniquely Black.

Most white critics waxed enthusiastic, but those in the minority took the opportunity to air their grievances about the pressure to cater to the politically correct proponents of black culture. Rex Reed, who was at his most influential at the time, wrote the following:

> just because something is black does not make it automatically beautiful. To attack any black-oriented entertainment is to tempt the fates. One has nightmare visions of being denounced as an Archie Bunker, then chased through the streets of Harlem by the Furies with their Afros on fire. Well, I say bunk to all that. Garbage is garbage, no matter what color it is, and this all-black sacrilege is at the top of the rubbish pile. . . . This is a musical for drug freaks creating a mythology inhabited by androgynous monsters, celebrating not the wonders of childhood fantasy, but the profane vulgarity of cruelty and ugliness.

Reed's diatribe was meant to expose the double standard of critics such as Clive Barnes, who went out of his way to find merit in any work by a black writer, whether he liked it or not. Barnes wrote that *The Wiz* "has obvious vitality and a very evident and gorgeous sense of style. I found myself unmoved for too much of the evening, but I was respectfully unmoved, not insultingly unmoved."

The *New York Amsterdam News* came to the musical's defense:

> Contrary to the ambivalent, negative, "maybe I like it, maybe I don't" reporting of the mainstream [i.e., white] reviewers, we take a positive stand and recommend this most unusual satire highly. . . . The music is spirited[,] vigorous and rhythmic. The story of "the Wizard of Oz" is accented by a creative satire with musical renditions easily appreciated and understood by the predominantly Black audience. . . . This play is one which should be supported by the Black community since its demise may come as a result of the inability of the "mainstream play killers" to respond to a white story satirized by Blacks, produced by Blacks, sung by Blacks and seen predominantly by Blacks on opening night.

As the heated rhetoric continued, *The Wiz* became a major hit and won seven Tony Awards. In 1978, it was made into a movie starring Diana Ross, Michael Jackson, and Lena Horne. The wealth of talent was wasted on what was a critical and commercial debacle. A Broadway revival of *The Wiz* opened in 1984 but closed after only thirteen performances. The City Center *Encores!* presented *The Wiz* in 2009, and the general consensus was that the musical had not aged well. NBC plans to broadcast a live version of *The Wiz* in December of 2015, marking the network's third such special event in as many years. The white playwright Harvey Fierstein is reworking the original book. Cirque du Soleil's new theater division is co-producing the event with NBC and will present a subsequent Broadway revival of the show.

Tragedy struck members of *The Wiz* team. Charles Smalls died during surgery for a ruptured appendix at the young age of forty-three. *The Wiz* was his only foray into musical theater, although at the time of his death he was working on an adaption of H. G. Wells's *The Man Who Could Work Miracles*. The producer, Kenneth Harper (1940–1988), died of cancer a year after Smalls. He had been developing a musical for Diana Ross called *Bamboo*, based on a ninth-century Japanese fairytale.

POST–CIVIL RIGHTS ERA

Several retrospectives of important black musicians appeared on Broadway in the late seventies and early eighties. *Ain't Misbehavin'* (1978) was a joyful revue featuring material associated with Fats Waller, and *Sophisticated Lady* (1981) celebrated the music of Duke Ellington with an interracial cast. *Porgy and Bess* also returned to New York in 1976, and Broadway saw several all-black versions of classic musicals, most notably *Guys and Dolls* (1976), *Kismet* (1978), and *Stop the World—I Want to Get Off* (1978). Unlike *The Wiz*, these shows retained the original book and music, albeit with new musical arrangements.

Beginning in the eighties, several new issues facing the African American community replaced the preoccupations of earlier black musical theater, in particular racial and ethnic identity, the rising black middle class, and African American cultural heritage. *Dreamgirls* (1981) had an all-white creative team headed by the director-choreographer Michael Bennett (see Chapter 10). The score is by the composer Henry Krieger (b. 1945) and lyricist Tom Eyen (1940–1991). The plot of *Dreamgirls* exists at the intersection of Motown's influence on mainstream popular music and the exploitation of black artists by both white and black record producers. It is a Faustian tale about a black music promoter who signs a 1960s-style girl group. In an attempt to cross the color barrier, he ruthlessly eliminates the features most associated with African American music and in so doing loses his moral compass. Krieger's *The Tap Dance Kid* (1983), a traditional book musical based on Louise Fitzhugh's novel *Nobody's Family Is Going to Change* (1974), explores black-on-black prejudice. *Jelly's Last Jam*, the first successful black musical of the post-Reagan era, deals with similar issues while also immortalizing an important black musician (see Chapter 12).

The election of Barack Obama as the first African American president was followed by a surge of Broadway musicals with African American themes (see Chapter 13). One of these, John Kander and Fred Ebb's *The Scottsboro Boys* (2010), presciently anticipated the posthumous pardoning of the Scottsboro Boys on November 21, 2013. Because the musical, which has a book by David Thompson,

AND BEAR IN MIND

In Dahomey *(1903, New York Theatre, 53 performances)*

Music by Will Marion Cook
Lyrics by Paul Laurence Dunbar
Book by Jesse A. Shipp

*I*n Dahomey* has great historical significance as the first all-black musical produced on Broadway. The show belongs to a group of "back-to-Africa" musicals, as Allen Woll labels them. *In Dahomey*'s success in New York and subsequently in London fueled demand for mainstream black entertainment. As John Graziano notes, "there is an underlying reality beneath the clowning and pratfalls of the characters; in this show, it is the romance of returning to Africa, which was being hotly debated in the Africa American community during the first decade of the twentieth century." *In Dahomey* did not avoid all traces of minstrel-show entertainment, but it dealt with issues of great concern to African Americans and spoke to black audiences as much as it entertained white ones.

Skylock Homestead (played by Bert Williams [see Chapter 4]) and Rareback Pinkerton (played by George Walker) arrive in Florida pretending to be detectives. They accept a case to find a silver casket owned by the wealthy Cicero Lightfoot. When they fail, they trick Lightfoot into giving them the $500 reward anyway. Lightfoot, a member of the African Colonization Society, discovers a pot of gold and takes all of his friends as well as Shylock and Rareback to Africa. The Americans have a difficult time adapting to the customs of Dahomey and decide to return to America. Only Skylock and Rareback remain in Dahomey, where "evah dahkey is a king."

The script, which is loaded with colorful dialogue, exhibits an acute political and racial self-awareness. In a confrontation with Henry Stampfield ("letter carrier, with an argument against immigration"), Lightfoot, a black character, rails against the "colored race":

STAMPFIELD: Hello Moses. What are you kicking about?

MOSE: Ain't kicking at all. Got both feet restin' right on the ground whar they belong. I'se just naturally disgusted with the frivolities of the colored population of dis country.

STAMPFIELD: You shouldn't let trifles annoy you. I'll dare say you'll find the colored population of Dahomey quite as much a source of annoyance as the colored population of this

(Continued)

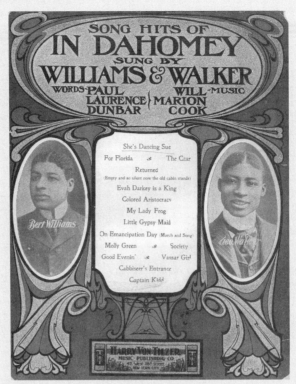

Sheet music for *In Dahomey*, featuring photographs of Bert Williams and George Walker. *Courtesy Photofest.*

country. Your exalted opinion of the ideal life to be found in a barbarous country is beyond my comprehension.

MOSE: It's alright for you to argue that way, 'cause you specs to live an die amongst these white folks here in the United States, but the colonization society that leaves the country for Dahome takes a different view of the matter.

The jaunty score, mostly by Cook, featured "On Emancipation Day," "Swing Along," and "I'm a Jonah Man" (by Alex Rogers). Williams and Walker interpolated other songs during the run of the show. The score was published, a first for an all-black musical.

adopts a minstrel-show format, protestors gathered nightly in front of the theater. Thompson, without identifying himself, asked some of the protestors if they had seen the show, to which they replied that they had not. The brouhaha was a stark reminder of the inherently political nature of black musicals and the important role that they play in the dialogue on race in America.

· ·

NAMES, TERMS, AND CONCEPTS

Ain't Misbehavin'	minstrel show
Ain't Supposed to Die a Natural Death	*Porgy and Bess*
Blake, Eubie	*Purlie*
Brown, William F.	Rice, Thomas Dartmouth
Cabin in the Sky	*Shoo-Fly Regiment, The*
Carmen Jones	*Shuffle Along*
Cole, Bob	Sissle, Noble
Cook, Will Marion	Smalls, Charles
coon song	*St. Louis Woman*
"Ease on Down the Road"	*Swing Mikado*
Ellington, Duke	*Trip to Coontown, A*
Hot Mikado	Van Peebles, Melvin
Hughes, Langston	Virginia Minstrels
In Dahomey	Walker, George
Jim Crow	Williams, Bert
Johnson, James Weldon	*Wiz, The*
Johnson, John Rosamond	

· ·

DISCUSSION QUESTIONS

1. Chart the portrayal of African Americans and the treatment of African American themes in musical theater. Take into account white as well as black writers.

2. How did Broadway perpetuate negative stereotypes of African Americans?

3. Describe the role that the press played in shaping attitudes about African American writers and performers on Broadway.

4. How does *The Wiz* distinguish itself from earlier black musicals?

CHAPTER 16

ROCK ON BROADWAY

(*HAIR*, 1968, BILTMORE THEATRE, 1,742 PERFORMANCES; FIRST OPENED OFF BROADWAY IN 1967 AT THE PUBLIC THEATER)

Broadway may be the final place in America, if not the known universe, where rock still registers as rebellious. In the decorous little jewel boxes that are Broadway's theaters, raunch seems raunchier, and rock musicals flaunt four-letter words and lascivious simulations.
—Jon Pareles, *New York Times*, May 16, 2010

*F*on Pareles wrote these words during the lead-up to the 2010 Tony Awards, when for the first time all of the nominees for Best Musical were rock musicals. Indeed, the awards ceremony that year capped the rock musical's most robust decade to date. Between 2000 and 2009, a record number of rock musicals achieved both commercial success and critical acclaim. Pareles, a diehard rock enthusiast and popular music critic for *The New York Times*, lauded the "arrival" of the rock musical but also expressed an opinion long held by rock critics: rock musicals can never match the visceral impact of live rock concerts. For their part, theater critics have always felt that most rock musicals fail to live up to the standards of good musical theater. For over forty years, the rock musical had suffered attacks from both camps, but by 2010 it had become clear that its moment had finally arrived.

When *Hair* opened on Broadway in 1968, it was billed as a "rock musical," marking the first official use of the term for a mainstream commercial production. *Hair*'s success shocked the Broadway establishment. Prognosticators foretold that all future musicals would be rock musicals, but it took four decades for their predictions to come true. Despite *Hair*'s popularity and profitability, Broadway composers, producers, critics, and audiences remained hostile to rock musicals. Traditional writers viewed rock as intrinsically incompatible with the musical theater genre in that the music's repetitive groove was too inflexible and the lyrics too generic for the nuances of a dramatic scene. Furthermore, they felt that the intentional sound distortion, shouting, and competition between the voice and amplified instruments made it difficult to understand the lyrics. The fixed identification of rock with youth culture and its anti-establishment posture severely limited the music's ability to represent the myriad of settings, historical periods, and dramatic situations of musical theater. Furthermore, rock music had a difficult time crossing the generational divide.

Producers shunned the "rock musical" label lest it scare away average theater-goers (i.e., mostly from a pre-rock generation). They reserved the moniker for those works that targeted younger audiences or people who might not otherwise attend a Broadway show. The 1972 musical *Grease*, for instance, tapped into feelings of nostalgia by announcing itself as "a new 50's rock 'n roll musical." But *Grease* was an exception: its score consisted entirely of pastiche numbers, and it premiered Off Broadway, which was less reticent about adopting the rock label.

For decades, the rock musical genre was held back by the perceived incompatibility of rock music and musical theater. Rock critics mostly viewed Broadway with suspicion and the rock musical as being inauthentic and contrary to the ideology of rock culture. Today's critics do not treat rock musicals with such cynicism. The rock critic Peter Marks recently noted that the rock musical "has evolved

High school hop scene from the original Broadway production of Grease. (Barry Bostwick as Danny Zuko is in the center). *Courtesy KB Archives.*

from novelty on the stage into an all-but-official musical language and that composers of musicals such as *Next to Normal* have begun to tackle subtle emotions and serious subjects and have reified the rock musical as a more sophisticated form." Indeed, one can argue that rock music has definitively transformed musical theater into a genre governed and judged by the aesthetics of rock. Even straightforward book musicals have capitulated to the tastes of audiences reared on rock. Broadway's acquiescence to rock music is the inevitable result of "attrition via demographics, shifting tastes and musicians' ambitions," notes Pareles. Plainly put, the first rock generation is now the target demographic for Broadway. Today's young theatergoers are more likely to have heard of *Rent* and *Wicked* than *Anything Goes* and *Oklahoma!*, and they consume musicals differently than older generations did. Moreover, many aspiring musical theater composers gravitate toward rock music, and established rock composers are more willing than ever to attempt a rock musical (Bono and the Edge's *Spider-Man: Turn Off the Dark* is one of several recent examples). In 2011, *The New York Times* posed a question to a group of young (unidentified) musical theater composers: "What song do you wish you had written?" Of the ten respondents, three cited songs by Stephen Schwartz (one of Broadway's first and most successful pop-rock composers), but five cited rock songs not associated with musical theater, including Bruce Springsteen's "Born to Run." Only three of those polled cited songs by Stephen Sondheim. With the exception of Ray Nobel's 1934 hit "The Very Thought of You," not a single song from the Golden Age of musical theater was mentioned. For the first time in fifty years, one can confidently make the claim that rock on Broadway is, as the song goes, "here to stay."

THE ROCK MUSICAL

Definition

To understand the history of the rock musical, one must first grapple with the meaning of the term, which has been used for more than four decades to describe a widely diverse body of work. In 1979, the first anthology of rock musical scripts was published to commemorate the rock musical's so-called coming of age. The eight scripts contained therein were chosen to represent a cross-section of the subgenre: *The Wiz, Two Gentlemen of Verona, Grease, Jesus Christ Superstar, Your Own Thing, Hair, Tommy,* and *Promenade*, only two of which had been marketed as rock musicals. The compiler of the anthology, Stanley Richards, offered the following description:

> [The rock musical] is more freewheeling, less confined, and even when set in a specific period, manages to evoke an expressive topicality, an implied contemporaneousness [more than traditional musicals]. Frequently, it is also more generous in its utilization of lights and audiovisuals and, of course, there is the beat and the amplified sound.

Richards intentionally left the definition vague enough to account for most rock musicals up to 1979, but today his and similar descriptions are virtually meaningless.

The definition appearing in the *Oxford Companion to the American Musical* (2008) also pertains primarily to works prior to the eighties:

> [U]nconventional and more experimental than traditional shows, not only in subject matter but also in structure and presentation. The music is often more pounding, with more emphasis on the beat and less on the lyrics, and the musical usually is a free-flowing celebration, protest, or both. The rock shows are usually less literary and more anachronistic and rely on a variety of audiovisual effects. Most significantly, the orchestrations for rock musicals require a good deal of electronic instruments so mechanical amplification is a must.

By the late seventies, the rock musical had lost some of its countercultural cachet. The scores for what people considered rock musicals are best described as eclectic pop. Even in the early seventies, young rock-oriented composers, in particular Andrew Lloyd Webber and Stephen Schwartz, liberally mixed rock and pop idioms with traditional musical theater elements. Eventually, rock became viewed as just one of several styles available to Broadway composers. The very concept of the rock musical crumbled under the weight of so many forms of self-expression, not unlike rock music itself. Commercial music trends, global hybridization, and advances in technology began to affect the entire sonic landscape of Broadway, the result being a ubiquitous, homogenized, pop-dominated, rock-inflected, and over-engineered sound, what is the international hallmark of musical theater today.

It is understandable that Elizabeth Wollman, the author of *The Theater Will Rock*, does not even attempt to provide an authoritative definition of the rock musical. Instead, she includes virtually every rock- and pop-oriented musical since the early sixties. Scott Warfield distinguishes four categories of rock musicals: (1) works explicitly identified as rock musicals by the writers and producers (*Hair*); (2) works that began as concept albums (*American Idiot*, based on Green Day's 2004 punk rock album of the same name) (see Chapter 11); (3) works that incorporate some rock features but are not marketed as rock musicals (*Godspell*); and (4) works that pay homage to or parody early rock styles (*Grease*).

Common to all rock-and-roll–oriented musicals are several basic features associated with rock music. The accompaniments are heavily dominated by electric instruments, especially guitar, bass, organ, piano, and, since the seventies, synthesizers. Strong accents occur on beats two and four ("backbeats"). The actors adopt the rock singer's reliance on back-phrasing and a less refined manner of vocal production, and they take advantage of (some might say milk) the microphone, which over time has moved from the stage floor to the actor's body. Broadway actors today wear wireless headset microphones in full view of the audience. Rock musicals have also boosted the average decibel level. Whereas real rock relies on improvisation, spontaneity, and performance, musical theater makes relatively few allowances for musical freedom and more than ever encourages the faithful recreation of the same performance night after night.

Social and Political Framework of the Rock Movement

The ideology behind rock music extends to the rock musical. Rock emerged as the music of youth culture, and it played a defining role in the identity formation of entire generations. The advent of rock and roll in the early fifties coincided with the recognition of a new social category, suburban youths, and an increase in adolescent angst epitomized by the tension between teenagers' desire for freedom and their continued dependence on their parents and the social safety net of their communities. In the fifties, rock and roll spoke directly to the anxiety caused by this perpetual state of ambivalence between freedom and conformity, between the natural stages of childhood and adulthood. Rock continues to thrive on this anxiety, and it articulates attitudes about sex, drugs, and social change.

The belief that rock should be an agent for change dominated the rhetoric surrounding the youth movement of the sixties, rock's countercultural phase. The political left embraced rock (along with folk) as a means for reshaping society into something better: rock as revolution. For the political right, rock music fomented civil unrest and moral corruption. In the seventies, rock became as diversified as the social and economic subgroups that the shrinking economy in the post–civil rights era created. As rock music became increasingly mainstream, it lost much of its shock value. Rock purists mourned the diminished capacity of rock to affect political discourse, while rock's opponents continued to suspect rock of threatening middle-class social and artistic values. Conservatives continued to sound the alarm about rock's negative impact on attitudes about sex, death, and Satanism.

Early rock supporters in the press propagated the belief that rock music should be a pure and authentic artistic expression unadulterated by commercialism. As Wollman writes, this ideology of authenticity "implies that as artists who bare their souls in composition and performance, rock musicians somehow transcend the influences of the music industry." This myth went hand in hand with the increasing individualism of the performer. Sincerity (or the appearance thereof) became an aesthetic imperative. Pop music, on the other hand, romanticizes everyday existence and anesthetizes the listener-consumer. Rock critics have accused rock musicals of producing the same effect: they abhor the corniness and inauthentic emotionalism often associated with musical theater.

Musical Impact of Rock Music on Musical Theater

Since the late sixties, young musical theater composers have fallen under the spell of rock's "groove" and "motor-driven rhythmic impulse," as Mark Grant identifies them. Amplification, the emphasis on backbeats, earsplitting decibel levels, and electric guitars are employed in the service of this groove. The rhythmic ostinato of rock not only pervades the accompaniments but also substitutes for melody. Rock musicians privilege rhythm and rhythmic patterns over melodic development. Irregularly subdivided rhythms in the melody float on an unvarying repetitive pulse in the bass and drums.

Composers trained in the classical tradition find the repetitive groove of rock music antithetical to the musical theater genre. The persistent pulsating beat and the accentuation of off-beats restrict the ability of the music to respond to subtleties and the psychological progression of musical theater lyrics. Moreover, the relative stasis in texture, harmony, and volume of rock music undermines the periodization of musical phrases, upon which good traditional dramatic composition depends. The AABA song structure of traditional musical theater telescopes the development, climax, and resolution of a well-made dramatic scene. From the late twenties onward, the AABA song form, or some variation thereof, provided a satisfying listening experience based on repetition and contrast, and departure and return. As Grant has written, rock music "[flattens] the three-dimensional feeling of story-reversal-denouement [of the AABA structure] into one plane."

Like the music, rock lyrics also differ considerably from that of musical theater. They typically avoid the contextual specificity and character-related details of musical theater lyrics. Moreover, rock songs, by their very confessional nature, treat the "I" differently than music theater songs, which are rooted in character. Rock singers project the "I" of their songs onto the individual listener. As Bono said in reference to writing the lyrics for the musical *Spider-Man: Turn Off the Dark*: "Writing for characters [is] a holiday from the first person, having spent a life of songwriting in the first person." The powerful bond that rock performers forge with their fans is mostly foreign to musical theater, which depends on the fourth wall and the suspension of disbelief. Audiences might identify with, say, Curly in *Oklahoma!*, but they also maintain a certain distance. These distinctions are not merely aesthetic or theoretical: they pertain to the very mode in which the audience perceives and reacts to what is happening onstage.

EARLY ROCK MUSICALS ON BROADWAY

In the fifties and sixties, several musicals included parodies of rock songs and took aim at the youth movement. For example, "Too Young to Live" from *The Girls Against the Boys* (see Chapter 8) asked, "Why can't we share the passion / That thrills us through and through, / Though we be adolescent / And adenoidal too?" The relatively conservative Broadway audience found the song amusing, especially as performed by Nancy Walker and Bert Lahr (both old-style comic Broadway stars), who gyrated their way through it.

These sendups of rock songs were nothing compared to *Bye Bye Birdie*, a full-length musical comedy parody of rock culture. The show marked the Broadway debuts of Charles Strouse (music), Lee Adams (lyrics), and Michael Stewart (book). *Birdie* featured a few presentational rock-and-roll song parodies, sung by Conrad Birdie, a rock idol who, like his real-life model, Elvis Presley, has been drafted into the Army. Birdie's manager, Albert Peterson, the real protagonist of the story, has been putting off marrying his long-term and increasingly impatient fiancée, Rosie Alvarez. She wants him to settle down once and for all, become an English teacher, and live the American Dream with her at his side. But he loves show business, not to mention his overbearing, meddling mother, who will do just about anything to derail his plans to marry Rosie. Albert and Rosie concoct a publicity stunt in which Birdie will appear live on *The Ed Sullivan Show* and give a farewell kiss to a teenage girl selected from members of his fan club. The lucky winner is the daughter of repressed conservative parents from Ohio. Her hormonal and jealous boyfriend barges onto the television set, punches Conrad in front of millions of viewers, and eventually wins back her affections. *Bye Bye Birdie* made light of the widening generation gap, gently poking fun at adults and kids alike. The rock-and-roll songs stand out from the rest of the score, especially the numbers sung by the adult characters. Around this time, critics debated whether or not rock was compatible with the Broadway musical, and for a while *Birdie* provided the answer. Conrad's intentionally banal rock songs emphasize driving triplet accompaniments, rhythmic repetition, simple rhymes, and unearned mawkish emotions—all designed to titillate the mostly white adult Broadway audience. The songs send up the sentimentality and pelvis-grinding rhythms of Elvis Presley's brand of rock and roll. By contrast, the book songs, even those performed by the teenagers, bear the stamp of traditional musical comedy.

Bye Bye Birdie was a major hit, but it did not spur a rock musical craze on Broadway. Producers remained apprehensive, composers eschewed the rock idiom altogether, and the establishment as a whole neglected to cultivate the young audiences that it so desperately needed. Established composers were only interested in rock music to the extent that they could write parodies of it. For example, in 1963 the septuagenarian Irving Berlin wrote the humorous "The Washington Twist" for *Mr. President.*

HAIR

Conception

The story behind the making of *Hair* is as unusual and chaotic as the musical itself. *Hair* generated a lot of buzz, which not only boosted ticket sales but also helped to elevate it to cult status. Myths about *Hair* circulated for years, such as the notion that the show was the product of creative amateurs. On the contrary, *Hair* was created by consummate theater people. Gerome Ragni (1935–1991) and James Rado (b. 1932), both of whom had Broadway credits, conceived of *Hair* as a portrait of the growing hippie movement. They were familiar with Megan Terry's 1966 protest play *Viet Rock*, which contained some rock songs and a series of sketches united by an anti–Vietnam War theme, but they took their immediate inspiration from a *Herald Tribune* article about a high-school student who had been expelled for refusing to cut his hair to the principal-approved length.

Hippies played a defining role in shaping the mood of the country during the late sixties. They were well-educated, upper-middle-class youths, disenfranchised and disconnected from their place of privilege. They embraced anything and everything associated with the countercultural movement: drugs, experimental sex, mysticism, public nudity, and communal living. They also advocated for spiritual and physical change, personal engagement, a rejection of technology, and nonviolence. Sociologists have explained the rise of the hippie movement as an attack on American imperialism, a rejection of the materialistic values of the older generation, a lack of parental affection, and a reaction to the diminishing number of accessible elite jobs. Whatever the cause, hippies sought to break away from the repressive attitudes of the Cold War era through an intense engagement with physical and psychic sensation. They expressed their beliefs publicly—in their flamboyant dress and long hair, in the way they spoke and carried themselves, in their indulgence in drugs and sex, and in their oppositional interaction with the "establishment." Getting stoned on marijuana and listening to rebellious, confrontational rock music went hand in hand. The hippie movement's inherent theatricality fascinated Ragni and Rado, who frequented hippie hangouts in Greenwich Village and took notes about their observations. They completed a script by 1966 and, on the advice of Jerome Robbins (see Chapters 7 and 8), submitted it to Broadway producers, including Harold Prince, even before the songs were written.

It was 1967, and Prince returned the script to the writers' agent along with a polite note of refusal:

> Returning the unconventional musical.
>
> I wish I cared for it, but I don't. It seems to hit on the same note over and over again, and what is supposed to be unconventional, emerges conventional.
>
> Best,
> Harold Prince.

The writers' agent received a more encouraging rejection letter from the director Robert Brustein:

> I liked Gerry's script very much. It has its flaws: it's diffused; it borrows too freely from "Viet Rock"; and the author is almost utopian in assuming a Broadway production for the play. But it has a real pop contemporary light that I like. The music, of course, would be very important to such a work, and of course one would need millions of dollars in order to mount it, but Gerry has a natural, rather crude, talent which should be encouraged.

Joseph Papp, the maverick producer and founder of the Shakespeare Workshop in 1954, was the only person who took an active interest in *Hair*. He liked the script's gutsiness and political relevance. Papp was in the process of transforming the old Astor Library into a new theater space called the Public Theater (see Chapter 11), which he envisioned as "a modern theater, engaged in producing modern plays dramatizing the potent forces of our time." He selected *Hair* to commemorate the opening of the theater and guaranteed Rado and Ragni an eight-week run with the proviso that they hire a trained and experienced composer to write the songs. The publisher Nat Shapiro introduced the writers to the Canadian composer Galt MacDermot, who had received his formal music training at Capetown University in South Africa. MacDermot's only professional theater credit prior to *Hair* was for the Canadian revue *My Fur Lady* (1957). For *Hair* he drew on his knowledge of African music, in particular the ritualistic rhythms of the Bantu people.

Rehearsals

Ragni and Rado disagreed with Papp over his choice of director, among other things. They wanted either Tom O'Horgan or Joseph Chaikin, but Papp favored his own artistic director, Gerald Freedman. Freedman (who had assisted Jerome Robbins on *West Side Story*) gave the fragmented material a much-needed coherency and sense of purpose, a "narrative unity" based on the thin suggestion of a plotline involving Claude's decision to go into the Army. He incorporated nontraditional staging techniques, tore down the fourth wall, and allowed the cast to commune with the audience, handing them flowers, dancing with them, and conversing directly with them. Additional friction arose over the choreographer, Anna Sokolow, whom the writers had convinced Papp to hire. Her working methods clashed with the undisciplined cast, so Papp, pressured by Freedman, fired her.

Hair opened at the Public on October 29, 1967, to mixed reviews. *The New York Times* theater critic Howard Taubman recognized the show's authenticity and idealism. Clive Barnes lauded its effort "to jolt the American musical into the nineteen-sixties" but acknowledged that it did not entirely achieve that goal. He disparaged the practically nonexistent dramatic structure but expressed guarded praise for the music, if only because it "at least does not sound like a deliberate pastiche of Rodgers and Hammerstein." *Daily News* theater critic James Davis called the music "dull" and sniped that "more exciting dancing can be found at any discotheque. . . . The large company of players, handicapped by the show's creative people, seem mentally retarded—and terribly juvenile." Michael Smith of *The Village Voice* despised *Hair* and called it "phoney."

Concerned with the mixed reviews, Papp decided not to take *Hair* any further, so Michael Butler, the scion of a wealthy Chicago family, decided to bring *Hair* to Broadway. Butler was struck by the musical's secondary title, "the American Tribal Love-Rock Musical," and the image of the original poster, which superimposed Ragni and Rado onto a photograph of Geronimo and Sitting Bull. A staunch liberal with connections to John and Robert Kennedy, Butler, along with his co-producer, Bertrand Castelli, voiced strong opposition against the war in Vietnam. He also cared passionately about the unfair treatment of Native Americans. Because Ragni and Rado wanted to make changes to the show for the Broadway production, negotiations between them and the producer broke down; however, a month later Butler accepted some of the writers' demands, in particular that he replace Gerald Freedman with the avant-garde director Tom O'Horgan (1924–2009). O'Horgan agreed to direct *Hair* because, he claimed, it was an opportunity to challenge Broadway, which he considered a "theatrical dead area."

When it came to booking a Broadway venue, however, Butler and Castelli received the cold shoulder from theater owners, who saw the raw and radical content of the show as anathema to commercial theater. So they opened the show at a Times Square nightclub called Cheetah, but they could only afford to keep it running there for forty-five performances. They eventually secured a Broadway house, but only through the intervention of Butler's well-connected father.

O'Horgan emphasized *Hair*'s concept over its narrative. The Broadway version was, as one commentator put it, more about "picturesque physical activity (writhing pantomimes, subtextual business, human pyramids, and sexual semi-exhibitionism), tableaux, bold anti-illusionistic devices, frantic light effects, amplified music and sound, and gimmickry of various sorts" than about story and character. Clothing and artifacts hanging from the walls inside the theater created an offbeat atmosphere. Ragni, Rado, and MacDermot wrote several new songs and reinstated some of the songs that Freedman had cut from the Off Broadway version, and they continued to experiment with the running order of the songs. MacDermot augmented the onstage rock band with a brass section, in part because union rules dictated a minimum ensemble of twelve players at the Biltmore Theatre. His brass arrangements softened the edgy rock style of the Public Theater production and gave the score a wider color spectrum. The expanded score crowded out much of the original narrative and thereby pushed the show in the direction of a theme-oriented revue. Whereas the Off Broadway production of *Hair* focused on the Vietnam War, the Broadway version encompassed a wider array of issues and expressed anti-establishment views on love, drugs, race, poverty, pollution, sexual freedom, and religion. It also shined a brighter light on the tribal rituals of the hippie movement. Individual characters mattered less than the continuity of the movement and oneness of the onstage tribe. Further, the production portrayed the adult characters as two-dimensional authoritarian figures, straw men for the hippies to belittle. In the Off Broadway production, adult actors played the parents. On Broadway, young male hippies in suits and dresses turned the adult men and women into campy cartoon figures.

People were scandalized by two elements of the Broadway production: brief nudity in the "Be-In" scene and the frequent use of obscenities. Papp and Freedman had rejected the nude scene, but O'Horgan included it as a statement about freedom and liberation. Although the nudity was fleeting, thematically warranted, and nonsexual in nature, it drew widespread condemnation—as well as a lot of free publicity. Wherever *Hair* played, outspoken local politicians and community leaders objected to the nude scene, which only solidified the show's reputation as a *succès de scandale*.

Hair's legacy rests in part on its popular eclectic score. Ragni and Rado's initial script called for rock music:

> The sound will be authentic Rock and Roll, definitely keeping away from the "Broadway-Musical Sound." Our lyrics, however, unlike those of most current songs, will be audible above the sounds of the instruments; this will be accomplished by the use of chest mikes for all the singers. . . . Our sound will include exciting beat music, as well as beautiful, melodic numbers. We are trying for a very fresh and current pop sound in a Broadway theater.

MacDermot was able to realize Ragni and Rado's ideas for the score within a couple of weeks. He brought a remarkably supple melodic inventiveness to the scrappy lyrics, and he gave the script's Beat- and folk-inspired street poetry a sense of cohesion, a formal shape, and humor.

Scene from from the original Broadway production of Hair. Courtesy KB Archives. *Courtesy KB Archives.*

Music

Notwithstanding *Hair*'s reputation as the first genuine rock musical, the score incorporates several other musical idioms, including folk and even classical music. In fact, MacDermot did not "feel like a rock 'n' roll composer"; because of his training, he considered himself an African and West Indian composer. He admitted, "I am not sure what rock 'n' roll really is, and I don't care." MacDermot also acknowledged the need to counter the inherently limited expressive range of rock music: "Most rock composers write one kind [of song], because they know that's what will sell. But you're not selling tunes in a show. You're contributing to the whole show. And that means variety." MacDermot's score lacks the character-specific nature of traditional Broadway musical songs, but it projects a strong sense of purpose. It is theatrical, compact, and at times deeply stirring.

Rado and Ragni's original script (1967) included about twenty-one songs, many of them miniatures consisting of a compact statement expressing a particular point of view. The Broadway production featured thirty-one songs, nearly a third more than the Public Theater version (Table 16.1). Given *Hair*'s loose, theme-oriented narrative, adding and subtracting songs never disrupted the overall effect of the show. In fact, *Hair* has probably never

TABLE 16.1. Evolution of the Score of *Hair*

SONGS	ORIGINAL SCRIPT	PUBLIC THEATER	CHEETAH	BROADWAY (1968)
Abie Baby				✓
Ain't Got No	✓		✓	✓
Air		✓	✓	✓
Aquarius		✓	✓	✓
The Bed	✓			✓
Black Boys	✓	✓	✓	✓
Climax		✓	✓	
Colored Spade				✓
Dead End	✓	✓	✓	✓
Donna				✓

SONGS	ORIGINAL SCRIPT	PUBLIC THEATER	CHEETAH	BROADWAY (1968)
Early Morning Singing Song (later "Good Morning Starshine")	✓	✓	✓	✓
Easy to Be Hard	✓	✓	✓	✓
Electric Blues	✓	✓	✓	✓
Exanaplanetooch	✓	✓	✓	✓*
The Flesh Failures (retitled "The Flesh" and "Let the Sunshine In")				✓
Frank Mills		✓	✓	✓
Going Down		✓	✓	✓
Hair	✓	✓		✓
Hare-Krishna (titled "Be-In")				✓
Hashish				✓
High School Heaven	✓			
[I'm] Hung				✓*
I Got Life	✓	✓	✓	✓
I'm Black				✓
In My Brain	✓			
Initials	✓			✓
Manchester		✓	✓	✓
Mess O' Dirt	✓			
My Conviction				✓
Nelly	✓			
Reading the Writing	✓			
Red, Blue and White (Retitlted "Don't Put It Down")	✓	✓	✓	✓
Sodomy				✓
Three-Five-Zero-Zero				✓
Walking in Space	✓	✓	✓	✓
Washing the World	✓			
What a Piece of Work Is Man				✓**
Where Do I Go?	✓	✓	✓	✓
White Boys	✓	✓	✓	✓

*"Exanaplanetooch" and "Hung" were cut from the Broadway production sometime during the course of the run.

**MacDermot set "What a Piece of Work Is Man" to music between the Public Theater and Broadway productions.

CRISSY

EXAMPLE 16.1. "Frank Mills," first fifteen measures

been done the same way twice. Even the original Broadway production continued to evolve musically during its run, and each subsequent touring production was tailor-made for the specific cast, locale, and year.

MacDermot set some of the prose passages in Ragni and Rado's original script as songs without changing a word. Ragni allowed the composer considerable latitude in musicalizing these speeches because, according to MacDermot, he, Ragni, "did not trust words" alone to convey the overriding meaning of the lyrics. "Frank Mills," for instance, began as a spoken monologue for Crissy (Example 16.1).

The prose text consists of nine sentences of different lengths (Table 16.2). There is no question of a rhyme scheme or poetic meter. The published script of *Hair* presents the text in the form of a traditional song lyric, with subdivisions corresponding to the musical phrases and sections. MacDermot superimposed a ternary musical structure onto the text, each section consisting of sixteen measures (ABA'), adjusting rhythms and small melodic details to accommodate the varying sentence lengths. The changing rhythms and inexact repeat of the A section create a fitting sense of spontaneity for Crissy.

TABLE 16.2. Text and Musical Structure of "Frank Mills"

	TEXT	SYLLABLES	PHRASE	SECTION
1	I met a boy called Frank Mills on September twelfth right here in front of the Waverly, but unfortunately I lost his address.	32	a (8 measures)	A
2	He was last seen with his friend, a drummer.	10	a (8 measures)	
3	He resembled George Harrison of the Beatles, but he wears his hair tied in a small bow at the back.	25		
4	I love him but it embarrasses me to walk down the street with him.	17	b (8 measures)	B
5	He lives in Brooklyn somewhere, and wears this white crash helmet.	14		
6	He has gold chains on his leather jacket, and on the back is written the names Mary and Mom and Hell's Angels.	26	c (8 measures)	
7	I would gratefully appreciate it if you tell him I'm in the park with my girlfriend. [And please]	22	a′ (8 measures)	A′
8	And please tell him Angela and I don't want the two dollars back, just him.	18	a″ (8 measures)	

MacDermot set three other prose texts with equally felicitous results: "Colored Spade," "My Conviction," and "What a Piece of Work Is Man." "Colored Spade" has a through-composed melody set over a soul-music groove. The song builds in energy and intensity as it approaches its call-and-response ending. "My Conviction," *Hair*'s only "adult" number and only waltz, is performed by the "Tourist Lady." The song stands out for its classical music elements, such as its flowery and arpeggiated piano accompaniment and the fact that it calls for a "legitimate" soprano voice. But the number is intended as a joke: at the end of the song, the audience learns that the Tourist Lady is a male in drag singing in falsetto (a bait-and-switch ploy later used in the 1975 musical *Chicago*). "What a Piece of Work Is Man" is the closest thing in *Hair* to a folk song. The lyrics combine a famous speech from *Hamlet* with other lines from the play. Recurring melodic segments give what is essentially a through-composed piece a sense of unity.

Reception

The Broadway establishment was perplexed by *Hair*'s commercial success. The critics generally admired the show, but they continued to struggle with the thin storyline. Clive Barnes applauded the transformation of the Off Broadway version to a

PLOT OF HAIR

Berger, the unofficial leader of a group of hippies living in Greenwich Village, welcomes Claude into the tribe, as the group is called. Other members of the tribe include Sheila, a student and political activist; Woof, an aimless youth searching for an identity; Hud, an African American militant; and Jeanie, who is "hung up" on Claude but pregnant with another man's child. Berger is expelled from school, and Claude receives his draft notice and passes his physical. Claude's parents hope that he will grow up and do what his country asks of him. The hippies get stoned and enjoy a Be-In, during which the men burn their draft cards except for Claude, who struggles with the decision whether or not to join the Army. After returning from the induction center, Claude, encouraged by Berger, goes on an LSD trip and imagines being in Vietnam. George Washington, Ulysses S. Grant, John Wilkes Booth, and Colonel Custer are among the luminaries who appear in Claude's hallucination. Eventually, Claude really does go to Vietnam and is killed.

more thematically oriented musical, but he reversed his earlier positive assessment of the music, feeling that what had been "acid-rock, powerhouse lyricism" at the Public excluded a "cheerful conservatism" and became "merely pop-rock, with strong soothing overtones of Broadway melody." On the other hand, he commended the lyrics for being the "authentic voice of today."

At the 1969 Tony Awards ceremony, *Hair* and *1776*, the most patriotic of musicals, competed against each other. The Tony voters showed their true conservative colors by awarding the Tony for Best Musical to *1776*. *Hair* survived despite the loss. By 1972, the musical had tallied over 1,740 performances, fourteen companies were touring the United States, and many more were playing in foreign cities. Pop artists covered songs from *Hair*, and many of these recordings made the Top Forty list.

Hair created waves wherever it played. The German premiere provoked an official request to remove the most "offensive parts" from the show. The show was allowed to open uncensored, but during the run Ragni and Rado were denied admission to the Amba Hotel because of their "hippielike appearance." In England, *Hair* barely escaped censorship from the Lord Chamberlain's office. After the department rejected the submitted script, the producer presented a revised one and received an invitation to discuss the matter. However, before anyone could officially act, Parliament, as had been anticipated, formally did away with preproduction censorship of theater, and *Hair* went on to play in London for nearly five years. During the Paris run in 1970, the commissioner of the Salvation Army (Armée du Salut), who was dressed in street clothes, interrupted a performance when he stood up and staged a protest using a portable loudspeaker. He and other members of his party climbed onto the stage and chastised the cast and audience. The actors de-clawed the angry demonstrators by dancing with them and hugging them. The manager of the theater welcomed the free publicity that resulted from the incident. Meanwhile, the commissioner asserted, "it is not censorship to forbid a show that abandons 40,000 years of civilization to return to the cave." At an anti-pornography rally, he appropriated the show's title as an acrostic: "H" for hypocrisy, "A" for abo-minable, "I" for impious, and "R" for repugnant. Mexican authorities closed *Hair* down after a single performance in Acapulco and expelled seventeen cast members from the country. Italian audiences got a chance to see *Hair* in late 1970, by which time the jaded critics felt that the script was already outdated. They shrugged off the nudity with a characteristic indifference.

Censorship in certain American cities was just as draconian as anything *Hair* encountered abroad, with the exception of Mexico. In 1970, state authorities in Massachusetts attempted to bring charges of obscenity against the producers of *Hair*. The Massachusetts Supreme Court attended a command performance in Boston, after which the seven judges issued a restraining order, as requested by the district attorney. The court ruled that certain changes be made, particularly in the nude and flag-desecration scenes. The case reached the U.S. Supreme Court, which upheld the production's First Amendment rights. The Supreme Court revisited *Hair* when officials in Chattanooga, Tennessee, banned performances of the musi-cal. It took three years for the court to reach a 5-to-4 decision in favor of *Hair*'s producers. In Buffalo, New York, after the Studio Arena Theatre sponsored a book-ing of *Hair*, the Erie County Legislature voted to withhold designated funds from a grant unless the theater agreed not to present "morally objectionable" work. A spokesperson for the legislature accused *Hair* of being "a principal contributor to the growth of drug-sex culture in the community."

Michael Butler produced a Broadway revival of *Hair* in 1977, but it was too early for audiences to see the show with fresh eyes or affectionately as nostalgia for the sixties. Milos Forman's film version, released only two years later, resonated even less with audiences. Forman broadened the story and filmed scenes across the American landscape. He inexplicably altered the ending so that Berger gets trapped into going to Vietnam in place of Claude. Twyla Tharp's stunning choreography mattered little, as the overall concept was flawed. The latest Broadway incarnation of *Hair* opened in 2009. This revival gave a respectful nod to what many consider a naïve time in American youth culture, but it also served as a reminder of the lost opportunities since those heady days. The tribe of this production appeared "fright-ened of how the future is going to change them and of not knowing what comes next," wrote Ben Brantley.

AFTER *HAIR*

Your Own Thing

After *Hair*, Broadway musicals did not immediately capitulate to rock, as many crit-ics had predicted. In fact, most attempts to capitalize on *Hair*'s success met with disappointment (and a hostile press), even those by the creators of *Hair*. Critics liked

Your Own Thing, an Off Broadway rock musical based on Shakespeare's *Twelfth Night*. That this perky show gets little attention today speaks volumes about its dated music, topicality, and weak book. However, in 1967 *Your Own Thing* (billed as "a new rock musical"), which preceded *Hair*'s Broadway transfer, was a welcome novelty. A rock band played from the stage, and screen projections gave the show a modern patina. The score, however, is as flat and unvaried as *Hair*'s is exciting and eclectic. One scholar has compared the songs to the upbeat sound associated with music producer Don Kirshner and tailor-made numbers manufactured for the ersatz rock band the Monkees. The musical eschewed politics for romance. The story takes place in Illyria (read New York circa 1968) and involved a rock group called the Apocalypse. One of the band's members, Disease, is drafted into the Army (perhaps a reference to *Bye Bye Birdie*, *Hair*, or both). To take his place, the band's manager, Orson, hires Viola, with whom he strikes up a relationship. To Orson's consternation, her twin brother, Sebastian, eventually appears on the scene.

Salvation

The next rock musical of note was a revue called *Salvation* (1969) by Peter Link (b. 1944) and C. C. Courtney. *Salvation* is about a man who searches for validation of his life. He questions the authority of religion, rejects Catholicism, and becomes a sixties-style drug-induced prophet.

Dude: The Highway Life

In the early seventies, Ragni and Rado parted ways. Ragni and MacDermot collaborated on *Dude*, another musical with a lost protagonist on a soul-searching journey, and one of the most incomprehensible works ever to reach Broadway. Even the actors failed to fully grasp what it was about. The writers had no concrete idea in mind, although they wanted to express their frustration over the lack of change in America since *Hair*. The show was really "an exercise in writing new songs," as MacDermot put it. Ragni considered *Dude* to be a "morality play." He gave the characters allegorical names such as #33, Dude, Mother Earth, and Bread. The original poster featured a longhaired young man standing with his back turned toward the viewer and his hands on his hips. An outline of the United States silkscreened on the back of his denim jacket is filled in with a road leading toward the sun. The main drama involves a confrontation between #33, played by Dude ("a man with faith in God, innocence intact and strength to love himself and others genuinely"), and Zero ("a bitter man with no faith in God, innocence lost and strength to hate himself and others deeply"). In #33's opening metatheatrical speech, he welcomes the audience to join him:

> Welcome to the first international Broadway Festival Olympic Apocolyptic [sic], Ringling Brothers, Barnum & Bailey Magic Circus Theatre. I am the sun, moon, stars and sky. I am always in orbit . . . I'm the mother-ship, the sister-ship, the God-starship, the good ship Lollypop-ship. I'm always in orbit and this is my space and that's your space.

Dude's patronizing message was a reductive oversimplification of the quest for self-fulfillment of the "Me generation" in the seventies: "to stand against the evil in our own life and the world around us, we must first love ourselves. Only then, can we love others genuinely." Tom O'Horgan replaced the original director, Rocco Bufano, and adopted an environmental concept, for which the cavernous Broadway Theatre was completely refurbished. The $800,000 affair folded after only sixteen performances.

Shortly after *Dude* closed, an undaunted Ragni tried to interest the producers in a revival of the show. A letter to the writer by one of them documents the precarious state of the rock musical in the years shortly after *Hair*:

> I have inquired in the East here, and the impression is that anything that has to do with Rock and Roll is quite passé. The kids don't go in great numbers any more, but I am still trying to find out, and if this is so and I am mistaken, I would be delighted to talk about reorganizing a tour again and raising the money. . . .

The revival never panned out.

Via Galactica

MacDermot's next musical, the futuristic *Via Galactica*, opened just a month after *Dude* closed and did just as poorly as it had. The thin story, by Christopher Gore (who also supplied the lyrics) and Judith A. Ross, involved a group of rebels living on an asteroid in the distant future. It was so convoluted that the producers inserted a synopsis into the program to assist confused playgoers, but it was of little help. "Via Galactica," it began, "is an all music musical. . . . The story takes place a thousand years from now. Man has explored the entire Solar system and decided there's no place like home. Home is Earth and on Earth everything's perfect. Everyone wears a permanently attached spinning hat to control their [*sic*] emotions." Neither the gimmicky setting, laser beams, nor giant spaceship could keep the show open for longer than seven performances. Ken Mandelbaum, author of *40 Years of Broadway Musical Flops* (see Chapter 11), sniped, "Nothing in *Via Galactica* could possibly have entertained a drug-free audience."

Rainbow

James Rado struck out on his own with an Off Broadway musical called *Rainbow*. Although less pretentious than his ex-partners' post-*Hair* musicals, *Rainbow* also suffered from a confusing, fragmentary plot, which involved a "Man" killed in Vietnam, and a hodgepodge score. Like *Dude*, it employed allegorical characters, such as Man, Comedian, and President, as well as theological ones, Buddha and Jesus Christ. The plot picks up where *Hair* leaves off. After his death, Man finds himself in Rainbow Land, where he tries to figure out who he is and whether he is dead or alive. He visits the White House and confronts the President about his death. The critics were justifiably confused. Walter Kerr asked, "Is the counterculture a cocoon from which only pipe-dreams are ever to emerge?" On the other hand, Clive Barnes accentuated the positive, claiming that *Rainbow* "is the first musical to derive from 'Hair' that really seems to have the confidence of a new creation about it." The show closed after only forty-eight performances.

Several other rock musicals opened Off Broadway, few of which were any better than *Rainbow*. *The House of Leather*, which takes place in a New Orleans whorehouse during the Civil War period, never saw a second performance. On the other hand, two musicals by Nancy Ford and Gretchen Cryer (b. 1035) were well received, *The Last Sweet Days of Isaac* (1970), a satire on the effects of mass media, and *I'm Getting My Act Together and Taking It on the Road*, arguably the most successful feminist musical of the era. *The Me Nobody Knows*, with a score by Will Holt (lyrics) and Gary William Friedman (music), was based on an anthology of poems by children from the New York ghetto (*The Me Nobody Knows: Children's Voices from the Ghetto* [1969]). The show took the form of a theme-oriented revue and tapped into the growing concern over disenfranchised urban youth.

Jesus Christ Superstar

The Beatles' 1967 landmark *Sgt. Pepper's Lonely Hearts Club Band* spurred the proliferation of concept albums. Although never intended for the stage, many of these works involved characters and a dramatic story line (see Chapter 11). A few of them were subsequently turned into stage musicals, none more momentous than Andrew Lloyd Webber and Tim Rice's *Jesus Christ Superstar*. *Jesus Christ Superstar* rode the crest of the emerging Jesus movement and the growing popularity of Christian rock.

In 1969, a musical about the final days of Jesus Christ seemed like a farfetched, potentially offensive, and financially risky idea, so the writers had to content themselves with putting out a single of the song "Superstar," which Decca Records backed. They hired Murray Head, fresh from the British production of *Hair*, to sing the song in the guise of a figure known as Everyman (which later evolved into the role of Judas). The recording featured a fifty-six-piece orchestra, a rock band, backup singers, and a large cast. The single reached America in December 1969, stirred up considerable controversy, and quickly made it into *Billboard*'s top hit singles chart. MCA immediately issued Lloyd Webber and Rice a contract for a full-length recording of the score.

The release of the album, a ninety-minute "rock opera," in October 1970 caused a sensation. The recording included a Moog synthesizer, a rock ensemble, acoustic and electric guitars, and a large orchestra. The through-sung score alternates between discrete closed numbers and loosely structured recitative (dialogue) passages. Rather than crying heresy, religious leaders in America embraced *Superstar* as a pedagogical tool. American sales of the album skyrocketed, and suddenly the idea of a rock musical about Jesus Christ no longer seemed so implausible. Indeed, rumors of a stage version immediately began to circulate.

The Australian producer Robert Stigwood (who had brought *Hair* to London) acquired the stage rights. The first thing he did was to shut down all pirated productions and send out two road companies. Plans for a film version were announced even before the show reached Broadway. The opera director Frank Corsaro signed on to direct the Broadway production, but *Hair*'s Tom O'Horgan eventually replaced him. O'Horgan brought his avant-garde sensibilities to the material, but critics thought that his concept was too abstract and senseless.

Various religious factions protested the show. Rabbi Marc H. Tanenbaum, for instance, objected to what he claimed were anti-Semitic overtones in the interpretation of biblical events and warned that the show would harm Christian–Jewish relations. He objected to the sinister nature of Judas and the fact that he was played by a black actor. On the other hand, many Jews, including the majority of employees at MCA, were fans of the work. Jewish producers had offered to invest in the show, and a successful production played in Israel. Rice and Lloyd Webber denied having any religious agenda and called the charges "laughable." Rice pondered, "I can't understand people complaining the Jewish priests are being shown as the bad guys. Everybody in the show—except Pilate—is Jewish. There are some good Jews and some bad Jews." (A Jewish actor played Pilate on Broadway.)

The Broadway production of *Jesus Christ Superstar* failed to live up to expectations and closed within two years. The politics surrounding the production do not account for its early demise. Several people, including Lloyd Webber, blamed O'Horgan for injecting the action with too much homoerotic energy. Others attributes the poor box-office performance to a weak dramatic structure.

Tommy

The 1969 concept album *Tommy* did not become a Broadway musical until 1993, by which time the work had achieved classic rock status. The Who had given live concerts of *Tommy*, and the edgy director Ken Russell had shot a film version in 1975. Producers of the Broadway production, which was officially called *The Who's Tommy*, were confident that it would appeal to traditional musical theater fans as well as to the sixties rock generation. They were wrong, however, and, like *Jesus Christ Superstar*, the production ran out of steam within two years.

SECOND-WAVE ROCK MUSICALS

Little Shop of Horrors

Little Shop of Horrors was a quirky genre-spoof musical based on Roger Corman's 1960 cult film of the same name (see Chapter 14). The show had at least two things going for it: an upbeat, fifties-rock inspired score by Alan Menken and Howard Ashman, and a bizarre sci-fi plot about a carnivorous plant named Audrey II, who, like Doctor Frankenstein's monster, seeks to destroy its creator, a nerdy shopkeeper named Seymour Krelborn, and Audrey, the woman he loves. Whereas *Grease* had relied on the nostalgia for fifties greaser subculture (mooning, car races, leather jackets, and a Jimmy Dean–like disregard for adults), *Little Shop* spoofed fifties innocence and musical fads. The show featured an all-black "girl group" that functioned like a Greek chorus and performed bop-sha-bop vocals. (Menken employed the same gimmick for the 1997 animated Disney film *Hercules*.)

Rent

Rent, a modern retelling of the plot of Giacomo Puccini's *La Bohème*, was the musical theater sensation of the nineties (see Chapter 12). The show's creator, Jonathan Larson, relocated the story to 1990s Manhattan. Exploring homosexuality, gender identity, drugs, and AIDS, *Rent* spoke to a new generation of theatergoers. It preached tolerance and love at a time when the country was still denying the widespread implication of the AIDS crisis and expressing open hostility toward the LGBT community. Although not marketed as a "rock musical," *Rent* featured a rock-inflected score with enough lyricism to please several traditional theatergoers.

Hedwig and the Angry Inch

Toward the end of the century, the homogenized style and sound of pop music began to dominate Broadway, providing a commercially safe middle ground between aggressive rock music and traditional Broadway musical idioms. Musicals with more authentic-sounding rock music found a more welcoming environment Off Broadway. *Hedwig and the Angry Inch* (1998) stood out for its unusual subject matter. The East German title character, born Hansel Schmidt, is haunted by memories of his sexually abusive father. He becomes romantically involved with an American GI, who takes him back to the States, where he, Hedwig, undergoes a botched sex-change operation. (The Off Broadway musical *The Knife*, which had a book by David Hare and starred Mandy Patinkin and Mary Elizabeth Mastrantonio, explored transsexuality more than a decade earlier.) The GI marries Hedwig but later abandons him. After another failed relationship, Hedwig meets an immigrant drag queen, and they form a rock band named the Angry Inch. The creators of *Hedwig*, John Cameron Mitchell (book) and Stephen Trask (score), told the story in the form of a rock cabaret. An acclaimed revival of *Hedwig* opened on Broadway in 2014 and garnered four Tony Awards, including one for the actor Neil Patrick Harris.

Bright Lights, Big City

Jay McInerney's 1984 novel *Bright Lights, Big City* dazzled readers with its inventive use of the second-person narrative, not to mention its theme of urban alienation. It tells the story of a young man too hooked on cocaine and too emotionally paralyzed by the loss of his mother to save either his marriage or job. He spirals out of control and nearly kills himself. The rocker Paul Scott Goodman decided to adapt the novel as a musical, apparently feeling undaunted by the point-of-view literary device that made the book so appealing. Neither rock nor theater critics lauded the results. The composer's rock sensibilities clashed with the exigencies of musical theater. Goodman, a native Scot, himself played the unnamed narrator, mostly from behind an acoustic guitar, but he was not an effective substitute for the novel's narrator, especially given that he was unable, or unwilling, to shed his Scottish brogue. Further, Goodman improvised to the point of distraction.

ROCK MUSICALS IN THE TWENTY-FIRST CENTURY

In recent years, Broadway has seen a flood of film-inspired rock musicals. Many of these shows epitomize the sugary pop music of the hit Fox series *Glee*, Disney's *High School Musical* trilogy, and reality-based television talent competitions. They suffer from generic, prefabricated songs and a mind-numbing sameness: belt singing, a narrow vocal range, the artificial attenuation and reverberation of studio recordings, and a homogenized stylization that has become the new international language of popular music. By contrast, musicals such as *Spring Awakening, American Idiot*, and *Bloody Bloody Andrew Jackson* exude a more genuine rock aesthetic. They eschew the sanctimony of seventies rock musicals such as *Dude*. Many of them in fact are the product of real rock musicians. Whereas once being associated with a Broadway musical signaled the decline in a rock musician's career or, worse, a lack of artistic integrity, today's rock composers, young and old (e.g., Sting and Cyndi Lauper), treat musical theater as a way of expanding their artistic horizons as well as bank accounts.

Spring Awakening

Spring Awakening is based on Frank Wedekind's terse drama of the same name, which premiered in Germany in 1891 and was immediately banned for its controversial content. The musical reached Broadway in 2006 following seven long years of workshop, regional, and Off Broadway productions. Director Michael Mayer shepherded the show from its early workshops to its Broadway premiere. The choreographer Bill T. Jones worked on the Off Broadway and Broadway productions. Instead of updating the story, as many writers would have done, the creators of *Spring Awakening*, Duncan Sheik (music) and Steven Sater (book and lyrics), retained the play's nineteenth-century timeframe and German setting. The story centers a group of students who feel trapped between childhood and adulthood as they struggle to come to terms with their sexuality in a society that suppresses open discussion of such issues. The young male and female characters are bursting with sexual desire. One of the male students kills himself, two of them have their first intimate sexual encounter, and a female student becomes pregnant and then dies after her mother forces her to have an abortion. *Spring Awakening* was hardly the first musical to use rock music to tell a story set in the distant past; *Jesus Christ Superstar* comes immediately to mind. In the case of *Spring Awakening*, the contemporary hard-driving music helps young audiences relate to the characters, in effect erasing the historical distance between them and their nineteenth-century counterparts. As critic Charles Isherwood noted, Sheik and Sater "invest Wedekind's young boys with the anachronistic souls of would-be rock 'n' roll stars, dreamers and screamers strutting on stages in their minds, even as they insist we see them in their original historical context."

Next to Normal

Next to Normal (2009), the most artistically acclaimed rock musical of the century and the second rock musical to win the Pulitzer Prize for Drama, delves into the emotional world of a suburban family with a bipolar mother, Diana, allegedly the result of her son's untimely death. The show featured music by Tom Kitt, book and lyrics by Brian Yorkey, and direction by *Rent*'s Michael Greif. *Next to Normal* examined mental disability within the mundane domestic milieu of a white, sub-urban, middle-class American household. Haunted by her son's ghost, Diana has hallucinations. Her coming-of-age daughter, Natalie, suffers collateral damage from her mother's mental illness. With drug abuse, suicide, and personal loss all figuring large in the story, *Next to Normal* is one of the repertory's bleakest musicals. However, the show's contemporary eclectic rock score appealed to young audiences and helped them to connect emotionally to the story's serious themes. The music responds seamlessly to the shifts between the external and internal world of the characters. The quiet introspective segments of the show are contrasted with bursts of pain, anxiety, and fear. *Next to Normal* followed the by then well-trodden path of premiering outside New York, reopening at an Off Broadway theater in New York, and then transferring to Broadway.

Bloody Bloody Andrew Jackson

Bloody Bloody Andrew Jackson (2010) also combined rock music and a nineteenth-century story. Despite its historical subject matter—the founding of the Democratic Party—the musical tapped into issues concerning contemporary politics. Portraying Jackson as an Emo rock star, the show oozed with irony and elevated mockery to an aesthetic imperative. It invoked a Brechtian sensibility of political theater. The score tapped into the anger associated with the country's rising populism during the early years of the Obama presidency.

Backstage Rock Musicals

Three categories of backstage rock musicals have proliferated in recent years: the most traditional category features an original score and story (e.g., *Memphis*); the jukebox variety tells a real-life story using pre-existing songs (e.g., *Jersey Boys*); the remaining category is a combination of the other two in that it interpolates pre-existing songs into an original plotline (e.g., *Mamma Mia!*). The reliance on the backstage-musical trope reflects an attitude similar to Hollywood's initial uneasiness with the musical theater genre. Plots with a music- or theater-industry milieu contain natural opportunities for diegetic songs (i.e., songs performed as songs in a nightclub or recording studio) and thereby alleviate some or all of the need for integrated book songs. *Memphis*, an example of the first category, explores the intersection of race, racism, and the music industry in the fifties, recalling the 1981 musical *Dreamgirls*, which dealt with similar issues in the sixties and seventies. Both shows boast original scores. So does *Billy Elliot*, a backstage musical about ballet, which features Elton John's best theater songs to date. Like Hollywood biopics, many jukebox musicals, such as *Beautiful: The Carole King Musical* (2013), center around a musician (e.g., Carole King) and feature popular commercial music (e.g., the music of Carole King). *Fela!* dramatizes the story of Fela Kuti, a Nigerian musician and human rights activist (see Chapter 13). *Jersey Boys* is a biographical musical about Frankie Valli and the Four Seasons and naturally incorporates the songs that they made famous. *Rock of Ages* is a sendup of eighties rock band culture with an original love story told through hit rock songs from the eighties, such as those performed by Night Ranger and Twisted Sister.

The Broadway establishment once welcomed the occasional rock musical such as *Grease* as a novelty and good financial opportunity. By contrast, aspiring theater composers today are more likely to be rock composers than any other kind. They have as much of an affinity for rock idioms as George Gershwin and Harold Arlen had for jazz. The popularity of musicals such as *Mamma Mia!*, *Spring Awakening*, and *Next to Normal* have made rock music the lingua franca of Broadway musicals and elevated the esteem in which the rock musical genre is held. Ironically, new works that emulate a more traditional musical theater aesthetic occupy a shadowy existence on the fringes of mainstream theater, the way that the rock musical once did.

AND BEAR IN MIND

Godspell, *1971, Cherry Lane Theatre, 2,118 performances*

Book and conception by John-Michael Tebelak
Music and lyrics by Stephen Schwartz

*I*n 1976, Stephen Schwartz, only twenty-eight at the time, had three musicals running simultaneously on Broadway: *Godspell*, *Pippin*, and *The Magic Show*. The appeal of Schwartz's music had a lot to do with its eclecticism. His musical theater pastiche numbers appealed to traditional Broadway audiences, while his pop ballads appealed to a diverse demographic, including some people who generally stayed away from the theater. Schwartz's rock music not only attracted young people but also injected musical theater with a much-needed youthful energy. *Godspell*, which requires little more than ten actors, rags for costumes, a few props, a chain-link fence for the set, and a small rock band, remains a perennial favorite with high schools and colleges. Recent Broadway revivals of *Godspell* (which literally played next door to the long-running *Wicked*) and *Pippin* served as a reminder of Schwartz's remarkable ascendency in the early seventies and highlighted the ability of his music still to reach young audiences.

John-Michael Tebelak, a fellow student of Schwartz's at Carnegie Mellon University, wrote *Godspell* for his master's thesis. Framed by Jesus's baptism and crucifixion, the action, as it were, takes place in an urban park. A troupe of ragtag actors performs parables based mostly on the Gospel According to St. Matthew, each one in the form of a vaudeville-like skit, pantomime, or musical number. *Godspell*, at

(Continued)

the time more a "spoken play with music" than a full-length musical, premiered at Carnegie Mellon and then played briefly at La Mama in New York's East Village. Tebelak incorporated songs by his friend Duane Bolick, which he felt would help build an emotional connection between young people and the show. After the run at La Mama, the producers hired Stephen Schwartz to write new songs for the show. Schwartz set some of the hymns and Psalm verses from the original production as well as wrote several original lyrics. He took his inspiration from a wide range of popular music including folk, pop, Tin Pan Alley, and the singer-songwriter movement. In effect, his score pays homage to Joni Mitchell, Laura Nyro, James Taylor, Paul Simon, and Cat Stevens. The heaviest rock segment of *Godspell* occurs when Jesus is tied to the fence during the crucifixion scene. Explosive outbursts from the rock band interrupt Jesus's soft plaints on "Oh God, I'm dying." Finally, the cast sings "Long Live God" on a folksy melody that slowly evolves into a gospel celebration with dancing and hand clapping.

If *Jesus Christ Superstar* was enigmatic, operatic in scope, musically complex, and critical of contemporary culture, *Godspell* was warm, reassuring, approachable, and uplifting. The show's religious or spiritual appeal came down to the portrayal of Jesus as a friend, hippie, and clown. *Godspell*'s groovy retelling of the parables made for good entertainment, and the tuneful score created a positive emotional vibe. The almost childlike energy of the proceedings reverberated with post-hippie culture.

. . . .

NAMES, TERMS, AND CONCEPTS

"Aquarius"

Butler, Michael

Bye Bye Birdie

Dude

"Easy to Be Hard"

"Frank Mills"

Freedman, Gerald

Godspell

"Good Morning Starshine"

Grease

Hair

Hedwig and the Angry Inch

"Let the Sunshine In"

MacDermot, Galt

Next to Normal

O'Horgan, Tom

Papp, Joseph

Public Theater

Rado, James

Ragni, Gerome

rhythmic groove

rock musical as a label

Schwartz, Stephen

Spring Awakening

"What a Piece of Work Is Man"

Your Own Thing

DISCUSSION QUESTIONS

1. Explain Broadway's initial hostility to rock music and its reluctance to adopt the "rock musical" label.

2. Why did writers and critics consider rock music to be unsuitable for the musical theater genre?

3. Discuss the controversies surrounding *Hair*.

4. In what way is *Hair* a concept musical?

CHAPTER 17

THE STAR

(GYPSY, 1959, BROADWAY THEATRE AND THEN THE IMPERIAL, 702 PERFORMANCES)

The star phenomenon of today was born on Broadway over a century ago. In its nascent form, American musical comedy was a performer's medium; it was the writers' job first and foremost to furnish stars with material—songs, skits, and jokes—to showcase their individual talents. It was not unusual for writers to begin writing a musical only after a high-profile performer committed to appearing in it. Musical comedy was not even considered a legitimate dramatic art form at the time. Only later, when musicals began to be taken seriously and writers began to create better roles did the specific vocal, physical, and dispositional requirements of a part begin to matter.

Musical theater fans are familiar with many Broadway stars from a century ago, but they know few if any of the musicals in which they appeared. Who has ever heard of *Bombo* from 1921? It was a hit, but people bought tickets mainly to see its star, Al Jolson. Had Jolson been appearing in something else at the time, they would have attended that instead. Jolson himself cared little about the show beyond its ability to advance his career. Throughout the run he interpolated his favorite songs—so many, in fact, that they eventually outnumbered those by the show's distinguished composer, Sigmund Romberg (see Chapter 5).

Once musicals began to be recognized for their artistic merits, casting the most suitable actor for each role became as important as signing a star. In the forties, improvements in the quality of musical theater and the attendant changes in casting practices precipitated the end of the star-dominated musical comedy. Musical theater and star performers continued to enjoy a symbiotic relationship, but the genre now aimed for the high artistic standards and respectability of legitimate (i.e., spoken) theater. In fact, a weighty musical theater role could transform an obscure actor into a star. For example, few people had ever heard of Yul Brynner (1920–1985) before *The King and I*. However, once word of his winning performance as the King began to circulate, people lined up to see him in the role. For some actors, though, the ownership of a role has led to diminishing returns. The role of the King brought

Brynner fame and fortune, but it also narrowed his career path considerably.

Most of the literature on musical theater's stars is biographical in nature. Discussions of their acting, dancing, and singing tend to be anecdotal. Musical theater performance practice has not been well documented, and it has only recently begun to receive the serious scholarly attention that it deserves. The reason for the lacuna has to do in part with the dearth of early musical comedy recordings. Prior to the forties, record companies had little incentive to preserve musical theater for posterity. However, musical theater songs were popular outside the context of the musicals for which they were written. These songs, once constituting the majority of America's popular music, generated tremendous income for composers and lyricists. These songs were performed in nightclubs and on the radio but were invariably divorced from their original dramatic context.

Therefore, early recordings and covers of show music rarely document what was actually heard in the theater. In fact, they feature different arrangements and instrumentation. Many recordings, moreover, reveal the limitations of early recording technology. They suffer from poor fidelity, which leaves modern listeners with a false impression of the quality of the performances. Legitimate (i.e., operatic) voices can come across as shrill and the vibrato sounds unnaturally rapid. For instance, Edith Day's recording of "Alice Blue Gown" from *Irene* (1919) has a thin timbre and narrow frequency spectrum, but it is difficult to discern whether the anemic quality of her performance is the result of early recording technology, a conscious interpretive choice, Day's natural singing technique, or some combination thereof.

Yul Brynner as the King of Siam in the original Broadway production of *The King and I. Courtesy Photofest.*

Several actors have been limited by their success in a role. For instance, Robert Preston's obituary led with his performance as Professor Harold Hill in *The Music Man*, which eclipsed the rest of what had been a long, successful career.

SINGING AND STARDOM

Today, belting dominates American popular culture, from Broadway to the singing of the national anthem at sporting events, to television talent shows such as *American Idol*. However, in the early decades of musical comedy, "legitimate" singing was as standard as belting is today. Originating in opera and other classical genres, legitimate singing privileges well-placed tones over clear enunciation, vocal training over a more instinctive mode of vocal production, the ability to sustain long lines

ORIGINAL CAST RECORDINGS

The early lack of interest in sound recordings of musicals changed in 1943 following the success of the first major original cast recording. The show was *Oklahoma!*, and the recording—originally released in the cumbersome 78 rpm format—established the practice of recording a Broadway show with its original cast shortly after opening night. For both technical and commercial reasons, the earliest original cast recordings excluded a lot of the music that was actually heard in the theater, including the dance arrangements. Today, by contrast, even flops and musicals still in the development stage get recorded. Professional video recordings of musicals, however, are few and far between, as the filming of live performances is impractical and prohibitively expensive. In 1970, the New York Public Library for the Performing Arts began making and preserving live videotape recordings of Broadway musicals (and plays), but these recordings are reserved for scholarly research and remain inaccessible to the general public. In recent decades, bootleg video and audio recordings have surfaced, but these are of varying quality and illegal.

Compact disc technology has allowed for the inclusion of a musical's reprises and incidental music, sometimes to the point of excess. For example, the recording of the 2011 Broadway revival of *How to Succeed in Business Without Really Trying*, which starred Daniel Radcliffe, includes four reprises, "Entr'acte" (to Act II), "Bows," "Exit Music," and an extended version of "Pirate Dance." Likewise, the double-CD soundtrack of the 2014 film *Into the Woods* contains virtually all of the underscoring, for a total of fifty tracks.

Yodelers intentionally manipulate the larynx muscles and use heavy glottal stops to heighten the difference between the chest voice and head voice or falsetto.

on open vowels, measured vibrato, and the development of the head voice. Trained singers learn to negotiate the natural breaks (*passaggio* events) between registers, especially the chest voice and head voice, so as to minimize the changes in timbre and musculature. Legitimate singers roll their r's, form and maintain pure vowels, eschew any hint of regional accent, and rarely if ever vocalize in a full chest voice.

In the early decades of the twentieth century, audiences on Broadway as well as outside of New York embraced both European operetta and American musical comedy. Both genres called for legitimate singing—although the soaring melodies of operetta called for more classical vocal technique. Eventually, American songwriters such as Kern and Rodgers began to develop a more natural and idiomatic approach to songwriting in order to express the psychological and emotional world of the characters in a musical. In an effort to better express the meaning of the lyrics, they composed less ornate and melismatic melodies. Broadway composers such as Vincent

Youmans constructed entire melodies out of small motivic cells. Youmans's "Tea for Two" from *No, No, Nanette*, for example, states the opening three-note motive no fewer than twenty-four times during the course of the thirty-two-bar refrain (AA'AA") (see Chapter 5). Such tight-knit motivic design rarely obtains in operetta composition. As popular songs began to absorb features from jazz and incorporate colloquial lyrics, composers and singers began to prefer a lower tessitura (the mean or average range), a narrower range, and from the thirties onward the chest voice.

Singing in the chest voice engages the full length of the vocal muscles, called the vocal folds or vocal chords. It is closer in quality to the speaking voice than the beautifully "pear-shaped tones" of legitimate vocal technique. Belting involves pushing the chest voice beyond the natural break between it and the head voice. The vocal tension associated with belting energizes the music and produces the intensity and excitement associated with the musical comedy genre. Before the thirties, belting and other forms of "non-legit" singing were confined to less mainstream venues and genres than Broadway musical theater, especially those with ethnic associations, such as Irish folk music and African American traditions. In contrast to mainstream white female vocalists, who emphasized their upper register, black artists and white "coon shouters" relied on their chest register and began to develop the practice of belting.

At the turn of the century, George M. Cohan (see Chapter 3) adopted a type of vocal delivery akin to "talk-singing" and based on the performance style of Edward Harrigan (see Chapter 2). Although Cohan regularly sang in chest voice, he never developed the exciting belt of many later Broadway stars. Cohan's fame as a performer was based on the sum of several parts, including his dancing, self-assuredness, and identity as a hard-working Irish American. Although Cohan eventually turned to writing, his stage persona and reputation paved the way for the rise of the Broadway star. A glance at a few of Broadway's earliest musical theater celebrities will help set the stage for Ethel Merman, the focus of this chapter.

AL JOLSON

Al Jolson's legacy has suffered more than that of any other performer from the early days of musical comedy, but at the height of his career, Jolson was considered "the greatest showman on earth," as he liked to claim. His reputation will forever be tarnished by his egomania and his continued and offensive use of blackface long after its heyday (see Chapter 2), not to mention several sordid details from his personal life. Today, the name Jolson conjures up the image of a white performer in blackface makeup, down on one knee, rolling his eyes, flapping his arms, clapping, and whistling. Jolson married four times and was allegedly an abusive husband. The size of his ego matched that of his fame, and he insisted on being the center of attention whenever and wherever he appeared.

Born Asa Yoelson (1886–1950), the son of Jewish immigrants from Lithuania, Jolson grew up in New York. His father, who earned a living slaughtering animals for kosher butchers, dreamed that his son would become a cantor in a synagogue. As a child, though, Jolson performed on the streets. He, his brother, and a friend appeared as a trio in vaudeville. It was at this time that he began performing in

Al Jolson as Jack Robin (a.k.a. Jackie Rabinowitz) in blackface in the film *The Jazz Singer. Courtesy Library of Congress Prints and Photographs Division, Washington, DC.*

blackface. He appropriated the old minstrel trope of the Northern black man singing nostalgically about his mammy and the Swanee River. After a few years with the trio, Jolson struck out on his own, and by the mid-teens, he had become a major Broadway star. Attesting to his fame, when Warner Bros. was preparing to shoot the landmark film *The Jazz Singer*, the first major full-length "talkie," the studio hired Jolson for the leading role of Jakie Rabinowitz (although only after Eddie Cantor and George Jessel, who had played the role in the stage version, turned it down).

Jolson, according to Mark Grant, "liberated the musical comedy voice from the legitimate voice." He developed a style of talk-singing that merged legitimate, Irish ballad, and black consonantal singing. In fact, some called Jolson a "Jewish Irish" tenor, and critic George Jean Nathan referred to him as a "Jewish Negro." Jolson was able to project his voice and physicality to the rear balcony seats in the days before amplification. His were not the refined performances of the concert stage. He incorporated his entire body, interjected grace notes and mordents into his singing, and delivered songs with intensity and raw emotionalism, which appealed to his immigrant fans.

No one mistook Jolson for a great actor. Regardless of the role, every one of Jolson's performances was a variation of the same personality that audiences expected of him. His signature role was a schemer named Gus Jackson. Gus appeared in several Jolson musicals, including *Bombo* (1921). Surviving film footage of Jolson conveys his dynamism, but it does not make it any easy for modern audiences to share his fans' enthusiasm. As Robert Viagas describes, "There he is, down on one knee grotesquely made up in blackface, white-gloved hands outstretched imploringly, sobbing, 'Do ya hear me, Mammy?' How could something so offensive and excessive have been so massively popular?" It is no wonder that none of the many attempts to create a bio-musical about Jolson has ever panned out.

Jolson's singing style was geared for live performance in large venues. By contrast, the controlled environment of the recording studio allowed vocalists such as Bing Crosby (1903–1977) to experiment with crooning and close-mike techniques. According to Mark Grant, Jolson "enlivened show music's capacity to be dramatic art; Crosby put the voice in a box." Eventually, rock and pop music introduced the microphone into musical theater, and today it is ubiquitous.

MARILYN MILLER

Marilyn Miller had a much shorter career than Jolson, but her reputation has remained untarnished. In the decade of the so-called Cinderella musical (see Chapter 5), Miller reigned as the darling of Broadway. She epitomized the wanting heroine of the twenties, and real-life events reinforced her onstage persona. Like Cohan, Miller too grew up in a show-business family, appearing as "Mademoiselle Sugarlump." When Miller was in her teens, the Shuberts and Florenz Ziegfeld competed for her talents, but shortly thereafter she suffered several major setbacks. Miller's husband died in an auto accident, leaving her a widow at the age of twenty-one. To make matters worse, Ziegfeld, who was in love with her, caused her emotional distress. He produced *Sally* as a star vehicle for Miller, but he allowed his personal feelings to get in the way of his professional relationship with her. During *Sally*, Miller sang "Look for the Silver Lining," Kern's paean to American optimism. The fragile, recently widowed Miller singing her heart out resonated with audiences who had just survived World War I and the 1918 influenza epidemic. Miller eventually walked out on Ziegfeld and appeared in two musicals produced by Charles Dillingham, *Peter Pan* and *Sunny*. By then, she had remarried, but the marriage ended quickly in divorce, after which Miller returned to Ziegfeld's employ for *Rosalie* (1920). She repeated her stage roles in the film versions of *Sally* (1929) and *Sunny* (1930), which were among the first wave of Hollywood adaptations of Broadway musicals. In the early thirties, Miller's life spiraled further out of control, and in 1936 she died nearly a penniless alcoholic.

THE "MERM"

Background

During the twenties, Marilyn Miller's attractiveness, dancing, and pluck helped her to forge a sentimental bond with audiences. In the thirties, audiences embraced a less classically feminine type of female star, Ethel Merman (1908–1984), whose temperament and vocal style were closer to Jolson's than to Miller's. Merman not only legitimized belting on Broadway, but she also altered the comportment of leading lady characters in musical comedy. Before Merman, leading ladies were genteel, as epitomized by their legitimate soprano voice. By contrast, belters, such as May Irwin (1862–1938) and Sophie Tucker (1887–1966), were blues singers, hog callers, or white "coon shouters"—in other words, ethnic performers.

Merman's career provides an ideal case study for examining the musical theater star because it straddles the first phase of Broadway stardom, the Golden Age of the integrated musical, and the early rock era. It coincides with Porter's and Gershwin's most creative years, extends into the Rodgers and Hammerstein era, and winds down around the time that the first post–Rodgers and Hammerstein generation was making its initial mark on Broadway. Merman's career reads like the proverbial show-biz success story: young secretary accepts singing engagements during her free evenings, is discovered by a major Broadway producer, appears in her first Broadway show, and becomes a star overnight.

Ethel Zimmermann, Merman's original name, was born in Astoria, Queens. As a young girl, she performed at various local events and entertained troops stationed on Long Island. Merman's cultural background was decidedly lowbrow. Her parents took her to movies and vaudeville but rarely to a Broadway musical, let alone an opera. They never gave her formal voice lessons, as in their minds music was not a viable career option for their daughter. She, on the other hand, had her heart set on a singing career. To placate her parents, in high school she acquired good stenographic skills, and found office work almost immediately after graduating. Before long, though, she was accepting singing engagements in Manhattan, and by 1927, she had a regular fifteen-minute spot on a radio station in Hoboken, New Jersey. By this time, Ethel had shortened "Zimmermann" to Merman. While playing a two-week engagement at the Little Russian on 57th Street in Manhattan, she met the theatrical agent Lou Irwin, who got her a contract with Warner Bros. and, after the studio failed to come up with any good projects for her, secured her an engagement at the Palace Theatre, New York's premiere vaudeville house, where she earned a whopping $500 a week. The Broadway producer Vinton Freedley (see Chapter 6), who along with his partner, Alex Aarons, was in the process of producing *Girl Crazy*, their sixth Gershwin musical, caught Merman's act. Within days, Merman found herself at George Gershwin's apartment, where she auditioned and landed a part in the show.

Girl Crazy is a quintessential thirties musical comedy about a *bon vivant* New Yorker whose father sends him to tend to the family ranch in Arizona. He transforms the property into a dude ranch with chorus girls transported from New York. Merman's character, Frisco Kate, is hired to manage the ranch's gambling room. Merman told gags and belted her way through three songs: "I Got Rhythm," "Sam and Delilah," and "Boy, What Love Has Done to Me." Her rendition of "I Got Rhythm" is the stuff of Broadway legend: during the second chorus, she belted out

Situated in the borough of Queens just a short subway ride from Times Square, Astoria is one of New York's densely ethnic neighborhoods. In the late nineteenth century, it was a point of destination for German and Irish working-class immigrants. Later, Italians and Jews became the dominant immigrant groups, followed by Greeks and then Arabs.

Ethel Merman (center) as Kate Fothergill backed by 30 chorus girls in Gershwin's *Girl Crazy. Courtesy KB Archives.*

sustained high notes while the orchestra played the now famous syncopated melody. After the curtain fell, an excited George Gershwin rushed to her dressing room and exclaimed, "Ethel, do you know what's happened? Do you know what you've done? You've just been made a star!"

From the start of her Broadway career, Merman was considered a wisecracking comic and belter rather than a romantic ingénue with a sweet, lyrical voice, such as Marilyn Miller. Like Jolson, she also physicalized the act of singing, using her hands, arms, and animated facial gestures. She rarely wandered far from center stage, and she sang directly to the audience. It was still the pre-amplification era, and Merman had no trouble reaching the last row of the theater.

In her book *A Problem Like Maria*, Stacy Wolf, a theater historian and feminist scholar, argues that Merman's "butch style" separated her from other female stars of her day and permits a queer reading of her performance in *Gypsy* (Rose Hovick was Jewish and a lesbian): "Merman's strong and masculine body and the ways in which it was described by the media presented a highly unusual image of femininity for the time." Merman's assertiveness and professional drive, moreover, were stereotypical traits of Jews. The perception that Merman was Jewish, lesbian, and working class complicated notions of the feminine diva and "excludes her from the category of 'woman.'" Wolf ultimately concludes that "Merman's star persona makes more sense as a 'lesbian' one" than as the traditional female persona associated with stars such as Marilyn Miller. After all, *Gypsy* "refuses a musical's expected heterosexual romantic resolution. Instead, the musical eschews heterosexual marriage for a gynocentric world, comes forth as a star vehicle for a single woman's performance, and develops a primary relationship between two women." Lastly, Merman's portrayal of Rose can be seen as a "refreshing queer image of femininity."

Merman's persona and demeanor placed her outside the mainstream middle class. Her powerful belting voice marked her as an ethnic female, and critics read her physical appearance as being more Semitic than Anglican, more Sophie Tucker than the typical white female singer. Merman was a practicing Episcopalian, but many people believed she was Jewish, which she resented. In fact, she told Jewish jokes, perhaps as a defense mechanism against what she interpreted as an insult. Likewise, Merman's reputation for being an aggressive, outspoken New Yorker and independent woman gave rise to the belief that she was a lesbian. Further, in several respects Merman's stage persona resembled a child. As Caryl Flinn points out, "not romantic, not adult, and with a frankness about sex, Ethel's image had something perennially childlike about it, something that would shape perceptions of her off-stage." Merman never became a sex symbol. She acquired "an almost asexual veneer that made her actual romantic entanglements almost uninteresting" to the public.

The public narrative about Merman painted her as a *nouveau riche*, straight-talking dame who lacked sophistication but had vulgarity in spades. However, the press turned a blind eye when it came to Merman's most offensive personality traits, such as her crassness and alleged homophobia. Journalists smoothed over her lack of social graces by emphasizing her affinity with the working class. Merman and Rosie the Riveter went hand in hand, and their independence and professional success played into the positive image of women during the war. That Merman had achieved stardom without the benefit of formal training only furthered the mythology. The press also avoided the most sordid and tragic details of her private life, including her four marriages and the premature death of her daughter due to depression.

The Porter Shows

Cole Porter wrote *Anything Goes* (1934), another Freedley production, specifically for Merman and four more musicals for her after that (see Chapter 6). Porter admired Merman, but he and his book writers felt that her range was limited. She played working women in all of these musicals (nightclub owner or singer, beautician, war department employee), and three of these characters gain wealth through an inheritance. A military base provides the backdrop for two of these shows, and in both cases Merman's character saves the day. *Anything Goes* intensified Merman's reputation as a comic and a belter, and it made her a genuine celebrity. The show provided product sponsors a marketing platform, and it even inspired a short-lived dance craze called "The Merman." In her next Porter show, *Red, Hot and Blue!* (1936), Merman played "Nails" O'Reilly Duquesne, a former manicurist who has inherited a fortune. Nails helps Bob Hale, played by her co-star Bob Hope, to find his childhood sweetheart. They discover her whereabouts when they recognize a distinct scar on her backside (which she got from sitting on a waffle iron, thus the title). Ultimately, Hope chooses Merman over her. Merman's character in Porter's *DuBarry Was a Lady* (1939) goes from rags to riches. She starts out a nightclub singer. When the club's washroom attendant (Bert Lahr), who is in love with her, inadvertently drinks the Mickey Finn that he prepared for the man who has stolen her heart, he dreams that he is Louis XV and that she is the Duchesse Marie-Caroline de Barry (Madame du Barry). The humor is based on the fish-out-of-water premise: a non-sophisticate suddenly finds herself in an aristocratic milieu and struggles to negotiate unfamiliar territory. In *Panama Hattie* (1940), Merman played the owner of a nightclub in the Panama Canal Zone. As Merman noted in her autobiography, *Merman* (written with George Eels), Hattie Maloney is "a brassy broad who hung out with sailors and didn't speak correct." Hattie also falls in love with a wealthy Navy officer stationed there. Conflicts arise when his eight-year-old daughter belittles her about her lack of sophistication. Merman/Hattie eventually wins her over.

Merman made little effort to adapt her acting or singing style to the aesthetic changes wrought by *Oklahoma!*, but she nevertheless sailed through the forties and fifties unscathed by limiting herself to musical comedy, which required less emotional depth from performers than the more demanding musical play. When *Oklahoma!* opened in 1943, Merman was appearing in Porter's *Something for the Boys*, the last bastion of the star-dominated musical comedy (see Chapter 1) (again she played a nightclub singer). Her first Broadway appearance after *Oklahoma!* was in *Annie Get Your Gun*, Irving Berlin's initial response to the Rodgers and Hammerstein revolution. Merman's fiery temperament and unrefined disposition served her well in *Annie Get Your Gun*. She played the historical figure of Annie Oakley, who also came from humble origins and landed in the middle of high-class society. The cast album of *Annie Get Your Gun* increased Merman's national exposure and reinforced her image as a straight-talking dame without airs or graces. She employed a slight twang, limited vibrato, and grace notes on certain words, such as "doin" in "Doin' What Comes Natur'lly," all of which seemed natural for the unrefined and unworldly Oakley. Despite Merman's triumph in the role, MGM hired Betty Hutton (originally Judy Garland) to play Annie in the film version, adding to Merman's long list of snubs from Hollywood.

Beginning with *South Pacific*, Rodgers and Hammerstein produced or co-produced their own musicals, thus exercising total control over their work as well as maximizing their profits. They also produced a few spoken plays and the musical *Annie Get Your Gun*, which they originally offered to Jerome Kern, who died before he could start work on the score.

The film medium did not complement Merman, who was known for playing to the back row of gargantuan theaters, not the camera lens a few feet away. She often boasted, perhaps defensively, that New York was superior to Hollywood: "New York's the place for me, and anybody that's got the swing of it like I have can't break out of it so easily."

Irving Berlin also composed Merman's next show, *Call Me Madam* (1950). She played Sally Adams, a wealthy widow appointed ambassador to the small fictional country of Lichtenburg. The role of Sally Adams, a more refined and educated character than Merman's earlier roles, bestowed a modicum of sophistication on Merman's image. Despite the show's diplomatic milieu, the story emphasized romance over politics, and Sally's party affiliation is never openly stated. (Merman was herself a life-long Republican, and she appeared regularly at GOP events—and at an occasional Democratic one.) *Call Me Madam* marks a highpoint in Merman's career. By this time, her name on a marquee meant brisk ticket sales at the box office. The producers knew this, so when Merman made stiff contractual demands, they did not hesitate to agree to 8% of the show's gross in addition to 10% ownership of the property, and a $5,000-a-week salary during the run of the show. Indeed, the show had the biggest advance for a Broadway musical up to that point. Even 20th Century-Fox recognized Merman's popularity at the time and hired her to recreate her role of Sally Adams in the film version of *Call Me Madam* (1953).

Merman spent the next five years living in Denver with her third husband, Robert Six, president of Continental Airlines. She returned to Broadway in 1956 for *Happy Hunting*. The couple's production company, MerSix, put up most of the show's $360,000 financial backing. Merman played Liz Livingstone, a role conspicuously similar to Sally Adams: a wealthy American widow in Europe hoping to find a suitable husband for her daughter. They travel to Monaco to attend Grace Kelly and Prince Rainer's wedding. However, *Happy Hunting* marks the nadir of Merman's career. The show's premise and topicality had the makings of a good musical comedy, but the weak script could not be overcome. Brooks Atkinson complained, "the chief purpose of the book is to get Miss Merman out there in center stage." To make matters worse, personality conflicts plagued the production.

Merman's male co-star, Fernando Lamas, provided the press with plenty of mud to sling. In an interview, he quipped, "Have you ever kissed Ethel Merman? It's somewhere between kissing your uncle and a Sherman tank."

Moreover, by the mid fifties Merman's voice had begun to take on some idiosyncratic features (e.g., untoward grace notes and a twang). She blamed the show's failure on its relatively unknown composer, Harold Karr (a dentist by trade), and lyricist, Matt Dubey. She would never have agreed to do the show in the first place had Six not pressured her to do so. His business acumen paid off, however, as advance ticket sales surpassed $1.5 million. But *Happy Hunting* paled in comparison to several other musicals playing at the time, including *My Fair Lady*, *Candide*, and *Li'l Abner*.

GYPSY AND MAMA ROSE

Background

After the *Happy Hunting* debacle, Merman was eager to find a project that would repair the damage that her image had suffered. She stopped looking as soon as Gypsy Rose Lee's memoir reached *The New York Times* bestseller list in 1957. Lee's memoir recounts her life on the road with her mother, Rose Hovick. Merman knew Lee personally and during a cocktail party announced, "I've read your book. I love it. I want to do it. I'm going to do it. And I'll shoot anyone else who gets the part." The producer David Merrick obtained the musical rights and assembled a top-notch creative team: director-choreographer Jerome Robbins, book writer Arthur Laurents, lyricist Stephen Sondheim (all of them fresh from *West Side Story*), and composer Jule Styne. Sondheim was eager to write both the words and music for *Gypsy*, but Merman, still feeling the sting of *Happy Hunting*, refused to bet on another unproven composer. She was willing to let Sondheim write the lyrics but insisted on Styne for the music. Sondheim agreed, but only after Oscar Hammerstein convinced him that it was in his best interests to do so. Laurents steered the show in a more serious direction than most other writers at the time would have done. Given the intrinsic backstage-musical framework of *Gypsy*, people expected a broad comedy with lots of entertaining presentational numbers, but Laurents constructed the story around the mother–daughter conflict and the generational codependency that it engenders. In his version of the story, the bond between Rose and Louise substitutes for the "marriage trope", as Raymond Knapp calls it, of traditional musical comedy and relegates the younger, more romantic characters in the show to the background. Rose and Louise desperately need self-validation and look for it from each other.

    Gypsy was not Merman's final Broadway musical, but Rose was her last original role, and it was the crowning achievement of her career. Indeed, Merman's

PLOT OF GYPSY

Rose Hovick steals a gold retirement plate from her father in order to put together a vaudeville act for her two young daughters. She builds the act around June and sticks Louise, her less talented daughter, into the boys' chorus. During an audition, Rose encounters a friendly candy salesman named Herbie. Tempted by Rose's cajoling and flirting, Herbie agrees to represent her daughters' act. The act does well until the girls begin to outgrow their parts. Herbie manages to get them booked onto the Orpheum Circuit and meanwhile continues to pester Rose about marrying him. Eventually, June and Tulsa, one of the chorus boys, elope and abandon the act. Rose decides to rebuild the act around Louise. However, the glory days of vaudeville are over, and soon engagements for the new act dwindle. Out of desperation, Herbie books the act into a burlesque house. Rose is aghast, but when one of the strippers fails to show up, she volunteers Louise as her replacement. Louise is a sensation, and her new career as a stripper takes off. When Louise receives top billing at Minsky's Burlesque in New York, Rose begins to feel rejected and unneeded. Louise still appreciates her mother, although now from a distance.

performance put to rest any doubts about her acting abilities. Before *Gypsy*, the issue never came up. But Rose is the most complex, taxing, and coveted female role in the musical theater repertory. She dominates the action and sings seven songs. The role requires a stentorian vocal instrument, emotional maturity and resilience, physical stamina, a sense of humor, and even a little sex appeal. *Gypsy* elevated the strong-willed female character to diva status and presented the American heroine at her most problematic and mature state. Rose is part maternal nurturer and part monster. Her refusal to accept society's gender expectations—that she be an ordinary housewife and mother—explains why *Gypsy* has remained a popular diva musical and by extension why it has had a long history with gay culture.

Rose's Three Turns

Rose's three major solos ("Some People," "Everything's Coming Up Roses," and "Rose's Turn") occur toward the beginning, middle, and end of the show, respectively, and determine the emotional pulse of the story.

"Some People"

"Some People," Rose's wanting song, establishes her motivation, single-minded ambition, and insuppressible nature. As Stacy Wolf points out, Rose distances herself from the typical American mother and housewife, crassly putting down "people"—meaning women—who knit sweaters, play bingo, and "sit on their butts." Rose's eventual decision not to marry Herbie does not signify a rejection of him so much as his idea—and, by extension, fifties America's idea of the perfect woman. The song also introduces recurring musical themes. The opening phrase begins with a stinging appoggiatura and then strives upward, spanning more than an octave in the course of four short measures (Example 17.1). The initial harmony implies the key of D minor, but the song vacillates between it and the relative F major. The arduous opening line, restless harmony, and unstable tonality are musical analogues for Rose's nomadic existence in vaudeville. The next phrase drags the first half of the opening theme through a series of ascending sequences, driving toward a half-cadence on "alive!" In the B phrase ("But I"), Rose demands her father's (and our) undivided attention, as she leaps up a minor seventh to the highest note in the song up to this point and holds it out for two and a half measures. This gesture recalls Merman's performance of "I Got Rhythm" in 1930, which Styne must have had in mind. The next segment introduces an exciting new musical idea in stop-time. The accompaniment drops out except for an occasional accented chord that punctuates the staccato melody. It is a tightly wound, syncopated theme in the style of a tap-dance break. The opening theme returns but cadences on F on "ain't me," initiating an ostinato in the orchestra, which has the forward thrust of a train at full speed: a repeated quarter-note pattern comprising parallel chords rising and falling by step. Over this ostinato Rose belts out a new theme on "I had a dream": the interval of a fourth followed by a fifth in quarter-note triplets set against the quarter-note ostinato in the accompaniment. Raymond Knapp aptly labels this theme the "inspiration anthem." The triplet rhythms and relatively large intervals are emblematic of Rose's indestructible

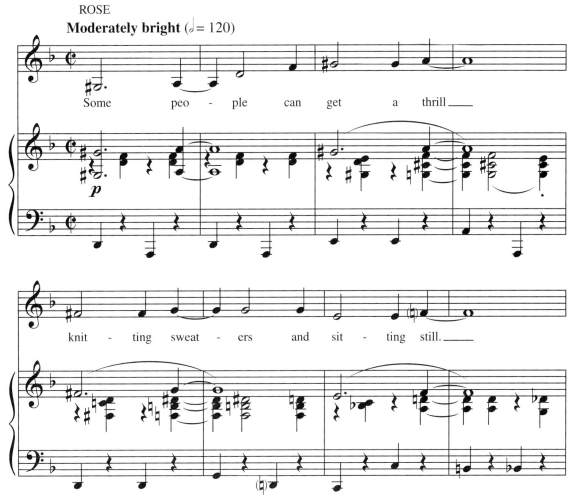

EXAMPLE 17.1. "Some People," first phrase

idealism. The different rhythmic spheres (triplets in the voice and even quarter notes in the orchestra) capture the two contradictory sides of Rose: her ability to dream big for her kids and her practical approach to the nitty-gritty details of life on the road. On "a wonderful dream," she sings a minor seventh, harkening back to the first interval of the B phrase. A pedal point in the bass creates a dreamy aura. As Rose retreats further into her fantasy world, her melody becomes more rhythmically detached from the accompaniment. She snaps out of it, though, when her father refuses to fork over money for what he considers a fool's errand. The song builds to a flashy finish reminiscent of the peppy exit music for vaude-ville comedians.

"Some People" is a powerful establishing number, but the first notes that Rose sings do match the emotional intensity of the spoken dialogue leading up to the song. Most recordings of *Gypsy* include a bit of this dialogue: "If I die, it won't be from sitting. It'll be from fightin' to get up and get out!" Such a high-pitched song cue should, according to Sondheim, be followed by a high note that matches the intensity of the speech. Instead, the song begins at the bottom of Rose's vocal range. The first note, a dissonance, fits the sentiment, but it is registrally pitched too low. Styne and Sondheim wrote an introductory section to compensate for the false start, but it destroyed the emotional effect achieved in the opening phrase. More-over, Merman balked. According to Sondheim, "In [the verse] Rose told Poppa to go to hell, but Ethel refused to sing it because, she claimed, her fans would never forgive her for cursing her father."

"Everything's Coming Up Roses"

Styne and Sondheim intentionally gave "Everything's Coming Up Roses" the style of a "typical Merman number," such as "Blow, Gabriel, Blow" from *Anything Goes*. However, the song's simple duple-time melody disguises a thick layer of dramatic irony. Left to her own devices, however, Merman would probably not have discov-ered the song's dramatic undercurrent. As Sondheim observed, Merman was known for her blunt delivery, not nuance:

> The problem was that Ethel had been brought up in farce musicals as a low comedienne . . . and had never been tested as an actress. We had no reason to believe she could do anything but bray her way through a show. I decided therefore to utilize that quality for the railroad scene and suggested to Jule that we write her a typical Merman number . . . something she could easily sing while the performer playing Herbie and Louise, being actors first and singers second, could express the horror of the moment.

To Sondheim's surprise, Merman "was able to tap into the reserve of anger that fuels every comedian, high or low."

What turns the seemingly straightforward Broadway showstopper into a rivet-ing, even tragic, *tour de force* is the clever rhythmic treatment of the title line: the first six syllables are set to even half-notes in triple meter (Example 17.2). The metri-cal shift disrupts the otherwise strong duple meter of the refrain, and ultimately accounts for why the song transcends its lowbrow roots. As Knapp observes, "[T]he song seems genetically restless, moving between a broadly scaled syncopated turn (a generic 'Broadway' style . . .) and a more urgent, highly repetitive motive that will resurface." Most "pop" versions of "Everything's Coming Up Roses" flatten out the rhythm by substituting the metrical change with two consecutive triplets over a two-beat-per-measure march. The elongated "show" version forces the actress playing Rose to struggle harder to get through the phrase. Triple meter returns in the coda, during which Rose rattles off a long list of positive images on a series of four repeated phrases, each one consisting of three measures in triple meter plus one in duple (uneven units of eleven beats). Knapp observes, "it is as if the triplets—the emblem of her 'dreams'—are fighting to emerge, to impose themselves on the reality of the duple, generic 'Broadway' style of the rest of the song." Indeed, Rose ultimately bends the music to her will. Sondheim and Styne wanted Rose to

EXAMPLE 17.2. "Everything's Coming Up Roses," title line

maintain her optimistic outlook throughout "Everything's Coming Up Roses." Merman certainly did. But several actresses push Rose to the brink of tears, playing against her sentiment in the lines that lead up to the song, "This time I'm not crying."

"Everything's Coming Up Roses" became a crossover hit, but when performed out of its original context (and without its metrical shifts), it loses its dramatic irony and comes across as a generic, albeit effective, paean to optimism. Over the years, the song has been appropriated for television commercials and political campaigns. Merman herself sang the song for John Lindsey's 1965 New York mayoral campaign, albeit with altered lyrics ("With Lindsay it's coming up roses") and during President Ronald Reagan's inaugural ceremony in 1981.

"Rose's Turn"

"Rose's Turn" was conceived not as a coherent, melodically unified song but rather as the musical equivalent of a mental breakdown. In it, Rose sings snippets of songs heard earlier: "Some People," "Everything's Coming Up Roses," and "Momma's Talkin' Soft." ("Momma's Talkin' Soft," in which Louise and June mock their mother, was ultimately dropped from the show, but by that time "Rose's Turn" was firmly in place, making it impractical to expunge any traces of the cut song.) Jerome Robbins had originally envisioned "Rose's Turn" as a "surreal ballet" in which Rose encounters all the important people in her life, but due to time constraints he ended up asking Styne and Sondheim to write a song. One evening after rehearsal, Sondheim and Robbins brainstormed ideas (Styne was engaged elsewhere). As Sondheim describes it, "the setting was excessively theatrical: everyone had gone home and there was no light in the auditorium except, on the stage, a ghost light. . . . It was like every shimmering nighttime rehearsal scene I'd ever loved in the movies." Sondheim suggested that Rose sing fragments of her earlier songs. Sondheim and Robbins's after-hours brainstorming session gave birth to one of musical theater's most haunting metatheatrical moments: alone on a bare stage and looking out at the empty theater, Rose faces the truth about herself. If she were so talented, why did she herself not become a star? Was she no better than the women she criticizes in "Some People"? Rose also questions the wisdom of how she raised her daughters. Sondheim recalled, "As I pounded out variations on the burlesque music, Jerry clambered onto the stage and started to move back and forth across it like a stripper, but a clumsy one: like Rose doing a strip. That was the beginning of three exhilarating hours of musical and choreographic improvisation, as we shaped and constructed the number to be a summary for the score."

One could easily play "Rose's Turn" as a mental breakdown, as Patti LuPone did (see below). Merman's Rose reached an emotional high point but was entirely in control of herself. In fact, Robbins had to teach Merman by rote how to act out parts of the song. He never even attempted to encourage her to "probe for subtleties or subtext." Merman's voice, as Laurents recalls, was "a trumpet call to Armageddon," and it did the song's emotional work all by itself. "When she hit that last 'For me!' it was Ethel Merman triumphant. She knew all about a show being for her."

Merman's Turn

Merman's performance helped to make *Gypsy* a hit. In fact, the critics reserved their highest praise for her at the expense of the show's creators. Some of the critics, however, were taken aback by Rose's brashness, vulgarity, and self-centeredness, but they found Merman's portrayal enthralling. Merman relied on the stage technique and instincts that came from years of experience. She did not attempt to unpack Rose's emotionally complex psyche. There was no question of the psychological nuances associated with method acting or the sense of irony that later actresses have attempted to bring to the role. In fact, Merman did not consider Rose to be a monster: "She yells and screams but she loves her children. Everything she does, she does because she loves too much."

As a star, Merman could count on the writers of her shows to tailor the material to her unique talents. Indeed, the composers wrote songs that complemented her range, timbre, and straightforward mode of delivery. The book writers heard her inflection and cadence when they wrote her dialogue, and they played up her comic timing rather than tap into her emotional reservoir, which did not run very deep. Although Merman's musicals were star vehicles built around her, it is a testament to their artistic quality that many of them are still performed today. By contrast, the star vehicles from earlier decades, such as literally all of Jolson's shows, were simply forgotten once they served their utilitarian purpose. Without Jolson, a Jolson vehicle generated little interest. At the peak of Merman's career, writers began to write better plots and scores and more complex and interesting characters. Their efforts led to the creation of a musical theater canon and standard repertory. *Gypsy*, notwithstanding Merman's hold on the role of Rose, continues to be performed today. However, even more than a half a century after the original production, actresses playing Rose must still contend with Merman's legacy and her association with the part.

Recreating a Merman role was not an enviable job and being her understudy meant sitting in the wings night after night, for she usually remained in a show for its entire Broadway run, including the 1,147 performances of *Annie Get Your Gun* (1946), and she rarely missed a performance. On those rare occasions that Merman could not go on, her understudy had to face a disappointed audience that would have rather seen the star. During *Gypsy*, throat problems forced Merman to miss seven performances. Her understudy, Jane Romano, did her professional best and came through the experience unscathed, but ticket sales dipped from $82,900 to $71,800 during Merman's absence. Commentators have attributed Merman's long runs to her incorruptible sense of professionalism and loyalty, but a sense of ownership, not to mention the financial remuneration from appearing on Broadway, no

THE ROSES

The list of actresses who played Rose in touring and regional productions of *Gypsy* during the sixties is quite long: Kaye Ballard, Vivian Blaine, Yvonne De Carlo, Susan Johnson, Gisele MacKenzie, Mary McCarty, Jane Morgan, Ann Sothern, Margaret Whiting, and Julie Wilson. In the seventies, Dolores Gray (1973, 1976, and 1982) and Mimi Hines (1977) played the part. In recent years, several notable actresses have joined the list of women who have played Rose: Linda Lavin (who replaced Tyne Daly), Karen Morrow (1992), Betty Buckley (1992, 1998), Judy Kaye (2001), Lorna Luft (2002), Andrea McArdle (2004), Joyce DeWitt (2005), Tovah Feldshuh (2011), Leslie Uggams (the first African American Rose in a professional production) (2014), and Imelda Staunton (2015).

doubt had something to do with her stick-to-it-iveness. Today, successful Broadway musicals run not for years but for decades, making it virtually impossible for an actor to remain with a show from opening night to closing night.

A Rose by Any Other Name

Gypsy is no ordinary star vehicle, and no role has spurred more competition than Rose. Few other female characters in the repertory test the full range of an actress's vocal and dramatic skills as much as Rose does. In 1960, Mama Rose was nearly synonymous with Merman, so when Merman declined to bring *Gypsy* to England, the producers simply canceled plans for the London production. In America, no one dared bring *Gypsy* back to Broadway until more than a decade after the original production closed, but several Merman-less touring and regional productions of *Gypsy* played around the country. *Gypsy* has remained one of the most popular musicals in the repertory, with four full-scale Broadway revivals, one Hollywood film, and one television movie. These versions have generated no fewer than seven commercial recordings, inviting comparison of the different performances and drawing attention to the built-in competitive nature of playing Mama Rose (Table 17.1). According to Arthur Laurents, who directed three of the four Broadway revivals, "Every production is ipso facto going to be different from every other because a different actress is going to be playing Rose, and the production takes its character from her." For instance, Merman set a "breezy tone" for the original production.

Like Merman, the other major actresses in Table 17.1 brought the experience of playing strong, outspoken women to the role of Rose. Rosalind Russell epitomized the fast-talking urbane women of screwball comedy. Angela Lansbury's versatile career includes the calculating Mrs. Eleanor Iselin in the Cold War film thriller *The Manchurian Candidate* (1962). Tyne Daly played a tough street cop in the popular television police drama *Cagney & Lacy* (1981–1988). Bette Midler's role in the film *The Rose* (1979), which was suggested by the life of Janis Joplin, established her ability to convey vulnerability and toughness simultaneously. Bernadette Peters

TABLE 17.1. The Mama Roses of Broadway Productions and Movie Versions of *Gypsy*

Ethel Merman	Broadway, 1959	702 performances
Rosalind Russell	Hollywood film, 1962	–
Angela Lansbury	London, 1973; Broadway 1974 (limited engagement)	300 performances; 120 performances
Tyne Daly	Broadway, 1989	476 performances
Bette Milder	Television movie, 1993	–
Bernadette Peters	Broadway, 2003	451 performances
Patti LuPone	Broadway, 2008	332 performances

TABLE 17.2. Other Musical Theater Roles in Common Among the Mama Rose Actresses

	ETHEL MERMAN	ROSALIND RUSSELL	ANGELA LANSBURY	TYNE DALY	BERNADETTE PETERS	PATTI LUPONE
Rose	✓	✓	✓	✓	✓	✓
Sally Adams	✓			✓		
Annie Oakley	✓				✓	
Mrs. Lovett			✓			✓
Auntie Mame		✓	✓			
Reno Sweeney	✓					✓

originated the role of the Witch in *Into the Woods* (1987) Patti LuPone achieved stardom for her portrayal of Eva Perón, the most ruthless female protagonist in the musical theater repertory. Apart from Midler, each of these actresses had also rec-reated one of Merman's other roles, and they also played some of each other's roles (Table 17.2).

The role of Rose exposes the fault line between acting and singing. It is the quintessential belting role and requires considerable acting ability. Prior to *Gypsy*, Merman's reputation rested purely on her singing, without which she surely would not have had much of a stage career. Neither Merman nor any other Rose por-trayer possesses a particularly pleasant vocal timbre. Few belters do, as belting emphasizes muscular strength, raw emotion, dramatic verve, and clarity of dic-tion. Merman's voice, it is worth noting, has been described as "tune-walloping," "twangy," and "unschooled," but these attributions were intended as positive qual-ities. A belter's singing voice is an extension of her speaking voice. Belters bare their souls through their voices, often without the honed technique of legitimate singing. Broadway divas such as Merman, Gwen Verdon, Judy Holliday, and Carol Channing were idiosyncratic performers with larger-than-life personalities that they never entirely submerged into the characters they played.

The tempo, key, musicality, and dramatic interpretation of Rose's songs vary considerably from performer to performer. Technical precision, musicality, pitch accuracy, tonal consistency, and vocal endurance also vary. As a testament to the sheer strength of her voice, Merman uniformly sings Rose's songs in higher keys than any of the other Roses (Table 17.3). Although she also adopts the slowest tempos, her singing does not lack for zeal or impeccable diction. Rosalind Russell, the first post-Merman Rose, falls at the opposite end of the spectrum, singing in lower keys than anyone else.

Rosalind Russell
Merman fans are still scratching their heads over the fact that she lost the Tony Award in 1960 to Mary Martin, who won for her performance of Maria von Trapp in *The Sound of Music*. That the nun won over the pushy stage mother with

TABLE 17.3. Approximate Timings and Keys of Rose's Three Turns

	"SOME PEOPLE"	"EVERYTHING'S COMING UP ROSES"	"ROSE'S TURN"
Ethel Merman	3:22 (G)	3:02 (ends in C)	4:20 (B flat)
Rosalind Russell	3:17 (B flat)	3:00 (A/D: verse and refrain are in different keys)	4:07 (F)
Angela Lansbury	3:21 (E flat)	3:00 (A)	3:53 (G)
Tyne Daly	3:01 (F)	2:49 (B flat)	3:55 (A flat)
Bette Midler	3:08 (F)	2:44 (B)	4:02 (A)
Bernadette Peters	2:58 (F)	3:03 (B)	4:22 (A)
Patti LuPone	3:03 (F)	2:44 (B flat)	4:12 (A flat)

These figures are based on the commercial recordings, which (the film versions excluded) were made shortly after the Broadway opening. Performance issues such as tempo can vary from night to night and can change over the run of a show.

questionable morals reflects the country's conservative values in the late fifties. But however disappointing the loss was to Merman, it pales in comparison to events surrounding the film version of *Gypsy*. Freddie Brisson, Rosalind Russell's husband, was involved in the film deal and had the clout to get his wife the leading role. The news that she had lost the part to Russsell came as a major blow to Merman.

Rosalind Russell (1907–1976) is best remembered as the eponymous heroine in the stage and screen versions of Patrick Dennis's *Auntie Mame*. Singing was never Russell's strongest suit (although she studied to become an opera singer and starred in Leonard Bernstein's 1953 *Wonderful Town*), but her domineering personality made her a strong candidate for Rose. Ironically, the studio brought in the Broadway singer Lisa Kirk (1925–1990) to dub most of Rose's songs. Kirk performs the music with less urgency than she might have done in the theater. Her rendition, recorded in the safety and comfort of a recording studio, lacks the spontaneity and energy of a live performance. The film was poorly received. It did not help that the critics compared Russell to Merman, whose fans were in no mood to forgive Russell for stealing a role that they felt rightly belonged to Merman. Russell's performance, however, is not without its merits: her Rose has vim and verve and arouses sympathy.

Angela Lansbury

In the early seventies, theatergoers in England finally got their first opportunity to see *Gypsy* when two Americans, Fritz Holt and Barry Brown, decided to produce the show there. They hoped to get Merman to repeat her role, but again she declined to go to London, claiming that she could not abandon her ailing parents. The

Rosalind Russell (right) as Rose, singing "Everything's Coming up Roses" to Natalie Wood as Louise in the 1962 film of *Gypsy. Courtesy Photofest.*

producers eventually offered the role to Angela Lansbury. Lansbury (b. 1925) had became a major musical theater celebrity when she starred in *Mame* in 1966. However, following *Mame* she appeared in two highly visible flops. She was therefore eager to find a show that would revitalize her musical theater reputation, but the memory of Merman as Rose intimidated her. Lansbury realized that her voice could never compete with Merman's, but once she realized that she could construct her performance on her acting abilities, which were never in question, she agreed to play the role.

Lansbury's Rose was gentler albeit more intense than Merman's, but no one ever doubted that she was a desperate stage mother. She saw Rose as "a pathetic person, but her guts make her riveting, exciting, and extremely stage-worthy." For many people, Lansbury's Rose evoked more pathos than Merman's. Merman was second to none in terms of vocal excitement, but Lansbury produced more tears. She did a lot with a rather limited voice, bringing great intensity to Rose's songs. For instance, she takes "Some People" at a fast clip and reaches a near-breakdown during the course of the number. She rips through the repeated eighth notes in the stop-time section with seething anger. Arthur Laurents, who directed the London production, considered Lansbury's interpretation the most "probing yet deftly comedic . . . [a Rose] in conflict with herself." He gave the show an additional

ANGELA LANSBURY

Typical American audiences are most familiar with the British-born actress Angela Lansbury as the sleuth Jessica Fletcher in the long-running television series *Murder, She Wrote* and as Mrs. Potts in the animated film *Beauty and the Beast*. Theatergoers, however, know Lansbury as the recipient of five Tony Awards, a record that was only recently broken by Audra McDonald, who won her sixth Tony in 2014. In 1964, Lansbury appeared in her first Broadway musical, Stephen Sondheim and Arthur Laurents's *Anyone Can Whistle* (see Chapter 9). In recent years, the octogenarian Lansbury has appeared on Broadway in spoken plays as well as the 2010 revival of Sondheim's *A Little Night Music*.

element of gravitas by inventing a new ending for Rose's bow at the end of "Rose's Turn." He turned this moment into a "stunning mad scene" by directing Rose to continue bowing even after the applause had died down. The London production received such glowing notices that the producers transferred the production to Broadway in 1974, for which Lansbury won a Tony Award.

Tyne Daly
Nearly a decade and a half transpired between the first and second Broadway revivals of *Gypsy*. This version starred Tyne Daly (b. 1946), who was known primarily for her television work. However, Daly's lack of musical theater credentials worked in her favor, as audiences had no preconceived notion of how she might interpret the role. Critics and audiences admired Daly's performance, and they forgave her weak singing. Frank Rich wrote, "[T]his fiercely committed actress tears into . . . Mama Rose . . . with a vengeance that exposes the darkness of the heart of 'Gypsy' as it hasn't been since Merman." Daly's Rose was self-centered and, according to Laurents, the most "savage." Her vocal limitations are particularly apparent in "Rose's Turn." Shouting rather than singing her lines, she effectively renders the number a monologue with musical accompaniment. Although Daly's voice was a liability, she was honest, intense, and sexually provocative, and she too won a Tony Award for her performance.

Bette Midler
When Bette Midler was introduced to Ethel Merman at an awards ceremony in 1973, she exclaimed, "Mama, this is fabulous. I'm so thrilled to meet you." There is no record of Merman's response. Midler (b. 1945) burst onto the scene in the mid-sixties, and people at the time saw her as a throwback to Merman. Like Merman, Midler also identified as a singer and comedian rather than as an actress. As Caryl Flinn puts it, "There is also the near-constant twinkle in [Midler's]

Herbie, Rose, and Louise singing "Together" in the 1989 Broadway revival of *Gypsy. From l to r*: Jonathan Hadary, Tyne Daly, and Crista Moore. *Courtesy Photofest.*

eye and her readiness for a naughty joke: after marrying German performance artist Martin Von Haselberg, Midler told the press, 'Every night I get dressed up like Poland and he invades me.'" Midler revels in sexual innuendo, and she shares some of Merman's crassness. However, Midler's open recognition of her gay following and her successful film career distinguish her from Merman. Her portrayal of a self-destructive rocker in the film *The Rose* (no connection to Mama Rose) catapulted her to stardom and earned her an Academy Award nomination as well as a reputation for pluckiness. On the other hand, she, like Merman, has had bad luck with television sitcoms. Midler's series *Bette* (2000), in which she played a diva with an adoring fan base, was canceled after a single season. More memorable is her appearance in a *Seinfeld* episode in which she played herself as the star of a fictional Broadway musical called *Rochelle, Rochelle* (in an episode entitled "The Understudy"). Midler's appearances on the *Tonight Show Starring Johnny Carson* (including a prominent spot on his farewell show) revealed a sympathetic side of her personality.

Midler, who was born in Honolulu, Hawaii, landed in New York in 1965. She made her Broadway debut when she took over the role of Tzeitel during the original run of *Fiddler on the Roof* (see Chapter 9). She then appeared in several rock musicals, which were gaining popularity at the time. In the seventies, she

Bette Midler as Rose performing "Rose's Turn." *Courtesy Photofest.*

performed at the Continental Baths, a well-known gay club. Shortly thereafter, she built a following as a solo artist and began to appear in films. Recently, Midler toured with her act titled *Kiss My Brass*. She returned to Broadway in 2011 as a producer, putting her clout behind *Priscilla, Queen of the Desert*. In 2013, she appeared in John Logan's play *I'll Eat You Last*. Midler founded the charitable organization New York Restoration Project in 1995 and remains its principal fundraiser.

Midler's *Gypsy*, a made-for-television movie, earned her a Golden Globe Award for Best Actress. As John O'Connor noted, "The special Merman imprint lingered as a kind of theatrical Everest that would never be scaled in quite the same way again. Until now." Midler's beaming smile, optimism, and sheer desire to please make her Rose a relatively likeable stage mother. She generated more empathy for Rose than any of the earlier incarnations and was "more of the sad woman who has been rejected by three husbands and even by her own parents." Milder did justice to Rose's songs, although her voice lacks the clarity and power of Merman's.

Bernadette Peters

When Bernadette Peters (b. 1948) was three, her mother got her onto the television show *Juvenile Jury*. Peters made her New York stage debut in the 1959 revival of *The Most Happy Fella* and her Broadway debut in 1967 in *Johnny No-Trump*, which lasted one performance. She played opposite Joel Grey in the 1968 Broadway musical *George M!* Her performance in the Off Broadway musical *Dames at Sea* the same year earned her a Drama Desk Award. In the eighties, Peters starred in Sondheim's *Sunday in the Park with George* and *Into the Woods*. In recent years, Peters has dedicated much of her time to the animal charity Broadway Barks (which she co-founded with Mary Tyler Moore).

Peters was cast as Rose for the next Broadway revival of *Gypsy* (2003). Herself a child actress with an eager stage mother, her first experience with *Gypsy* was playing one of the "Hollywood Blondes" (and understudying the role of Dainty June) in the second national touring production (1961). Peters maintained her youthful appearance and sexy figure into her sixties, which served her well in the part of Rose, although the inherent hoarse and pinched quality of Peters's voice has worsened with age. Peters is not naturally suited to the role of Rose, as critics went out of their way to remind readers. She had played several abused or put-upon women (e.g., Mabel in *Mack and Mabel* (1974) and Dot in *Sunday in the Park with George*).

Rose demanded much more from her as an actress. The director of the production, Sam Mendes, had approached Patti LuPone for the role, but he ended up going with Peters because of pressure from Arthur Laurents.

Throughout Peters's career, critics have fawned over her while downplaying her limitations as an actress and singer. *Gypsy* was no exception. For instance, Ed Brantley proclaimed that her performance was "the most complex and compelling portrait of her long career"—which is not the same thing as saying that it was the most complex and compelling portrait of Rose. The critics' idolatry of Peters in *Gypsy* mirrors the loyalty of her fans and is historically ungrounded. Critics seemed to forget Lansbury's acclaimed performance twenty years earlier, not to mention Daly's rendition. Peters made some odd musical choices and took some extreme liberties with tempo and rhythm. On the recording of the production, she delivers "Some People" nearly twenty seconds faster than Merman, although Daly, Midler, and LuPone come in close behind. On the other hand, she adopts Merman's slow tempo for "Everything's Coming Up Roses" and "Rose's Turn."

Peters's life in the theater should have translated into her performance of "Rose's Turn," but, according to Arthur Laurents, Mendes limited her emotionally and physically. The other actresses, Merman included, strutted across the stage and expressed their anger physically as well as vocally. The production garnered mixed reviews, which Arthur Laurents blamed squarely on Mendes. He claimed that the director's cynical and dark approach to the material robbed the story of its intrinsic humor. Set against a stark Depression-era bleakness, Peters's Rose seemed to effuse a "crazed optimism." The revival did poorly at the box office. Peters missed several performances due to illness, and she could not keep the show open long enough to recoup much more than half of its $8.5 million capitalization.

Patti LuPone

An appearance on *The Ted Mack Original Amateur Hour* at the age of thirteen put Patti LuPone on the path to a stage career. A few years later (1968), she joined the first class of the new Drama Division of the Juilliard School, which was founded by John Houseman and Michel Saint-Denis. After graduation, LuPone joined Houseman's Acting Company, which specialized in the classics. LuPone received her first Tony Award nomination for the Acting Company's limited-run production of the musical *The Robber Bridegroom*, but her involvement with the show precipitated the first of several scandals that have plagued her career. When producers decided to bring the production back to Broadway for an extended commercial run, they insisted that LuPone re-audition for her role. She refused and subsequently lost the part and left the Acting Company.

For many years, Arthur Laurents held a grudge against Patti LuPone and prohibited any work of his to be produced in New York with her in it. LuPone (b. 1949), who yearned to play Rose, eventually appealed to Laurents and convinced him to lift his ban. He even decided to direct her in the part. They both published accounts about the indulgently protracted rehearsal period for this revival of *Gypsy* and the personal satisfaction they derived from it. The production was riveting musically and dramatically, but for the director and star, their own involvement in the daily process of putting the show together was as important as the final product

Patti LuPone's reputation as a temperamental diva is legendary and deserved. She wears the label unabashedly and demands an equally high degree of professionalism from herself and her colleagues. For instance, when Mendes cast Peters instead of LuPone as Rose in the 2003 revival of *Gypsy*, without ever informing her of his decision, LuPone wrote him: "this [decision] isn't a question or good or bad, it's a question of right or wrong. Please reconsider. Never heard from him [after that]. And then they did that production [the Peters revival]. Fuck you." LuPone justifies her occasional public outbursts and unforgiving disposition in the name of art. For *Gypsy*, in addition to her financial remuneration, LuPone received several perks, including a daily massage. LuPone caused a stir during a performance of *Gypsy* when she brought the show to a screeching halt in order to admonish a man for taking photographs during "Rose's Turn." (Merman, it should be noted, once stopped a show in order to usher a rude male member of the audience out of the theater.) LuPone refused to continue with the performance until the offender had left the theater. The exchange, captured on a cellphone, went viral online. LuPone's outspokenness has been misinterpreted as arrogance and has cost her roles. The perception that she is difficult stems back to Andrew Lloyd Webber's *Evita*, for which she earned a Tony Award as well as a reputation for being a prima donna. She took a stand against the poor working conditions backstage, and it has haunted her ever since. "I was made difficult. I wasn't born difficult," she insists.

LuPone possesses some of Merman's raw star quality, but she also has formal acting training and prepared for a career as a classical actress. Her dramatic craft has informed all of her musical theater roles. Although LuPone has done some film and television work, she, like Merman before her, has found greater success on stage, playing some of the most challenging roles in the musical theater repertory, including Mrs. Lovett in *Sweeney Todd*. She first played Rose in a staged version at the Chicago Ravinia Festival in 2006. The City Center "Encores!" series remounted this version during its summer series the following year, and this production in turn led to a full-scale Broadway revival. LuPone's Chicago performance was, according to *The New York Times*, "not a fully integrated one" and too fraught with "mannerism." The essence of the character still eluded her during the Encores! production. Ben Brantley detected a "preliminary sketch," a "first-rate Momma Rose waiting to emerge." She fulfilled Brantley's prediction half a year later when the production opened on Broadway. "Watch out, New York," he exclaimed, "Patti LuPone has found her focus." It was a "single, highly disciplined interpretation that combines explosively contradictory elements into a single, deceptively ordinary-looking package."

Interpreting Rose's Songs

Merman, who was a highly disciplined performer, sings Rose's music mostly as written, taking very few artistic liberties. By contrast, LuPone places dramatic verisimilitude ahead of musical exactitude. One exception to LuPone's freewheeling approach occurs in "Everything's Coming Up Roses," which poses several musical challenges, in particular the metrical shift on the title line. LuPone turns in the quickest version of this song. In the published score, the triple measures are marked "poco allargando" and the duple meter "a tempo." No two singers execute this passage alike, and few do it entirely correctly. The rubric "poco allargando" implies a gradual stretching of the tempo. Only LuPone sings the meter change as the score dictates (although this detail varied in performance). Merman hits the downbeat of the first 3/2 measure at a slower tempo and maintains it right up to the "a tempo" two measures later. Lansbury barely slows down at all for these measures, maintaining a nearly steady pulse throughout. Daly and Midler emulate Merman's performance, although Midler anticipates the "a tempo" before the downbeat. Peters slows down to the point of distorting the beat altogether during the triple measures, and her treatment of the hemiolas destroys the subtle musical effect written into the score.

LuPone's performance of "Rose's Turn" reaches a near-manic level, the first hint of which comes in the form of a crazed giggle during the orchestral lead-in. The histrionics notwithstanding, LuPone's rendition was "a portrait of a woman finally understanding her whole life, rather than a complete implosion," according to Robert Viagas. However, her Rose does not roll over quietly. She mocks her daughter's striptease routine, delivers a desperate, throaty cry on "Mama's gotta let go," and transforms the long final note of the song into an hysterical shriek.

Final Assessment

Anecdotes, reviews, and surviving film footage reveal additional differences between these seven portrayals of Rose. No two readings are alike, and no actress since 1959 has attempted to imitate Merman's indomitable portrayal and "breezy tone." Merman is the most direct, Lansbury the most desperate, Daly the earthiest, Midler the neediest, Peters the most feminine, and LuPone the most overwrought. Each actress brings her own assets and temperament to the role. Moreover, every production of *Gypsy* is a *Gypsy* for a specific historical moment. Merman's straightforward portrayal lacks irony and the subtle shading of character that would help today's audiences to understand Rose's abusive parenting and self-obsession. Conversely, Patti LuPone's Rose would have come off as too shrill and psychologically terrifying for audiences in the late fifties. Each era's critics and theatergoers instinctively view the latest version of *Gypsy* as the best version of *Gypsy* and their favorite diva as the best Rose. Diva worship requires blind devotion.

BROADWAY STARS TODAY

Broadway is still a place where stars are born, albeit rarely of the same stature as stage legends such as Merman. New York today is teeming with extraordinarily talented performers, but few are able to construct an entire career on Broadway musicals alone. Young performers study voice, acting, and dance at esteemed conservatories and academic institutions. Degree programs in musical theater performance have proliferated, and opera programs have expanded their curricula to include musical theater. But opportunities have not kept pace with the expansion of the talent pool. In their day, Cohan and Merman learned their craft on the job, and there was plenty of work to keep them busy. Were it the twenties, a talent such as Kristin Chenoweth (b. 1968) would be appearing regularly in Cinderella musicals and giving Marilyn Miller stiff competition as Broadway's sweetheart. Instead, Chenoweth, despite her remarkable vocal range, formidable comic timing, and admirable acting ability, has not enjoyed the sort of sustained Broadway career that someone with her talent would have had in an earlier era. Chenoweth last originated a Broadway role in 2003, Galinda in *Wicked*, for a total of three. (Merman originated over twelve.) Since then she has starred in two Broadway revivals, *Promises, Promises* (2010) and *On the Twentieth Century* (2015).

Other changes have affected the very nature of musical theater performance. Years ago, musical theater stars were, according to Ethan Mordden, "great eccentrics, visitors from Mars." Today, technical skill has replaced unique personality. There are exceptions, of course, such as Nathan Lane. Lane has assumed the mantle of legendary stage comics such as Phil Silvers and Bert Lahr. Belting continues to be the dominant mode of singing on Broadway, but musical theater today suffers from a vocal sameness, as young singers especially emulate the peppy belting style of contemporary popular music. During the eleven years that *Wicked* has been playing on Broadway and touring the country, scores of young women have played Glinda and Elphaba, delivering technically polished but indistinguishable performances. Glinda and Elphaba are major diva roles, but only the two actresses who created them for the original production, Chenoweth and Idina Menzel, have the name recognition that once went hand in hand with Broadway stardom. The homogeneity of the subsequent performers is the desired end product of musical theater franchising.

The twenty-first century has witnessed a proliferation of memoir musicals in which a famous star recounts the highpoints of her or his career, mostly the former, and sings some of the songs associated with it. *Lena Horne: The Lady and Her Music* (1981) is an early example of this special category of star vehicle. *Martin Short: Fame Becomes Me* (2006) parodied these star showcases.

The economic reality of Broadway today does not foster the type of symbiotic relationship that once existed between stars and writers, such as that of Merman and Porter, and between stars and producers, such as Miller and Ziegfeld. Because it can take years to shepherd a musical from its original inception to opening night, actors cannot count on producers for steady work, and in turn producers do not want to be beholden to a star's availability. Producers will put money into a revival with a star attached (e.g., Daniel Radcliffe in *How to Succeed in Business Without Really Trying* [2011]), but they are far less likely to risk money on an original musical even when it features a star. The recent *If/Then* (2014), which starred Idina Menzel, is a rare instance of a new star-oriented Broadway musical.

In the forties, the improved literary quality of musicals affected the perception of musical theater as a star vehicle and lightened the dependency of the genre on celebrities. *Oklahoma!*, it will be recalled, achieved hit status without a single star. Stars still matter, and without them and their ability to energize a musical, Broadway would be a dimmer place. A celebrity with the popularity of Hugh Jackman can still sell enough tickets to keep a critically panned show (such as the 2003 *Man from Oz*) in the black long enough for it to generate a profit, as Merman did for *Happy Hunting* in the fifties. On the other hand, talented actors, even those with limited national visibility, can still be a valuable asset. Len Cariou (b. 1939), a highly respected Broadway actor in the seventies but hardly a household name, turned in a breathtaking and memorable performance as the eponymous protagonist of *Sweeney Todd*. He sang the part effectively and brought a horrific unpredictability to one of the repertory's most deliciously repulsive roles.

MERMAN'S LEGACY

After *Gypsy*, Merman gave concerts and appeared in films and television specials. In 1963 alone, she performed an act in Las Vegas, appeared in the film *It's a Mad, Mad, Mad, Mad World*, attempted to get a television sitcom off the ground, and appeared on Judy Garland's television show beside Barbra Streisand. In 1966, at the request of Irving Berlin, a fifty-eight-year-old Merman returned to the stage as Annie Oakley. In 1970 she took over the role of Dolly Levi in *Hello, Dolly!*, a role that was originally written for her but that she had turned down. Merman remained active during the seventies, mainly giving concerts. But Merman's vocal mannerisms and physical appearance during the twilight of her career became a source of ridicule. Her voice developed a distinct wobble, and her vibrato grew increasingly large, as did her hair. Instead of exiting tastefully from the public eye, she put out *The Ethel Merman Disco Album*.

The year 2007 saw the publication of two Merman biographies, which attest to her remarkable life but do little to give people unfamiliar with the star an appreciation of her onstage magnetism. Film footage of Merman fails to present her in the best possible light, making it difficult to understand her popularity during the most important decades of musical theater history. As Brian Kellow eulogized,

> Throughout her career Ethel had been the embodiment of the rambunctious, audacious spirit of New York as it was expressed in the music of Gershwin and Porter and Berlin. . . . The great age of personalities had long since faded, and although Ethel's vocal powers had miraculously never abandoned her until her final illness, she came face-to-face with a different sort of march of time, one that ran parallel to the actual passing of the years.

There will no doubt be more revivals and more recordings of *Gypsy*. The latest commercial recording is of the 2015 London revival starring Imelda Staunton. For a long time, rumors of a new film version starring Barbra Streisand circulated, but as the years pass such a gift to her fans becomes increasingly unlikely to materialize. Sooner or later, Merman's association with Mama Rose will fade. Already, few young musical theater fans are aware that she created the parts of Reno Sweeney in *Anything Goes* and Annie Oakley in *Annie Get Your Gun*. That is the fleeting nature of stardom.

AND BEAR IN MIND

Fine and Dandy *(1930, Globe Theatre, 441 performances)*

Music by Kay Swift
Lyrics by Paul James
Book by Donald Ogden Stewart

Kay Swift is best remembered for her romantic involvement with George Gershwin. Far more significant, however, is her status as the first female composer to write an entire Broadway musical, the 1930 hit *Fine and Dandy*. James Paul Warburg (1896–1969), scion of a major Jewish banking family and her husband at the time, wrote the lyrics under the pseudonym Paul James. Despite the show's top-notch score, *Fine and Dandy* was known primarily as a star vehicle for Joe Cook (1890–1959).

From left, Dave Chasen as Wiffington and Joe Cook as Joe Squibb in *Fine and Dandy.* The machine in the background is part of the set for the Fordyce Drop Forge and Tool Works factory. *Courtesy Photofest.*

In fact, *The New York Times* announced the show as "Joe Cook's latest piece of revelry, masquerading under the name of 'Fine and Dandy.'" In vaudeville, Cook (born Joe Lopez in Evansville, Indiana) earned a reputation for absurd Rube Goldberg–like inventions and amusing nonsensical stories, skills that served him well in *Fine and Dandy*. The reviewer Brooks Atkinson compared Cook in *Fine and Dandy* to Leonardo da Vinci and the Marx Brothers.

The script of *Fine and Dandy*, by the left-leaning satirist Donald Ogden Stewart (1894–1980), is a pretext for Cook's antics and the jazzy score. The story is set at the Fordyce Drop Forge and Tool Works. Cook played Joe Squibb, the factory foreman. Squibb receives a promotion, but his pro-labor stance does not put him in good stead with management. Things turn out fine, though, and he ends up marrying the boss's daughter.

The white-collar characters are preoccupied with upward mobility, Yale and Princeton, golf, trans-Atlantic crossings, organized labor, the League of Nations, Joan of Arc, Bolshevism, and President Hoover. The satirical elements, though, are tame compared to those of the decade's more famous musical satires such as *Of Thee I Sing* and *The Cradle Will Rock* (see Chapter 6).

Fine and Dandy reflects the short distance between vaudeville and musical comedy during the pre-*Oklahoma!* era. As vaudeville performers saw their industry dry up, many of them attempted to make the leap to Broadway, but for every Cook, there were several out-of-work vaudevillians.

* *

NAMES, TERMS, AND CONCEPTS

Anything Goes	Jolson, Al
Annie Get Your Gun	Laurents, Arthur
Benay Venuta	LuPone, Patti
Berlin, Irving	Martin, Mary
Chenoweth, Kristin	Mendes, Sam
chest voice and head voice	Midler, Bette
Daly, Tyne	Miller, Marilyn
diva	Peters, Bernadette
Girl Crazy	Porter, Cole
Happy Hunting	Robbins, Jerome
The Jazz Singer	Russell, Rosalind

DISCUSSION QUESTIONS

1. How did the growing presence of belting on Broadway in the thirties and forties affect the character of musical theater?

2. How does Al Jolson's career reflect the complicated relation between Jews and African Americans in the twentieth century?

3. Discuss the dramatic context and function of Rose's three principal solo turns.

4. What are the challenges that Broadway actors face today?

BIBLIOGRAPHY

All of the titles listed in this bibliography have informed the writing of *American Musical Theater*. The primary sources consulted (scripts, scores, recordings, newspaper articles, and archival manuscripts) are not listed here.

Adler, Richard, with Lee Davis. *"You Gotta Have Heart": An Autobiography*. New York: Donald I. Fine, 1990.

Adler, Steven. *On Broadway: Art and Commerce on the Great White Way*. Carbondale: Southern Illinois University Press, 2004.

Alonso, Harriet Hyman. *Yip Harburg: Legendary Lyricist and Human Rights Activist*. Middletown, CT: Wesleyan University Press, 2012.

Altman, Richard, with Mervyn D. Kaufman. *The Making of a Musical:* Fiddler on the Roof. New York: Crown, 1971.

Baker, Hilary. "From Broadway to Vegas: The Triumphs and Tribulations of *Avenue Q*." *Studies in Musical Theatre* 5 (2011): 71–83.

Banfield, Stephen. *Jerome Kern*. Yale Broadway Masters. New Haven, CT: Yale University Press, 2006.

_____. *Sondheim's Broadway Musicals*. Ann Arbor: University of Michigan Press, 1993.

Beggs, Anne. "'For Urinetown in Your Town. . .': The Fringes of Broadway." *Theatre Journal* 62 (2010): 41–56.

Berg, James J., and Chris Freeman, eds. *The Isherwood Century: Essays on the Life and Work of Christopher Isherwood*. Madison: University of Wisconsin Press, 2000.

Berger, Glen. *Song of Spider-Man: The Inside Story of the Most Controversial Musical in Broadway History*. New York: Simon & Schuster, 2013.

Berson, Misha. *Something's Coming, Something Good:* West Side Story *and the American Imagination*. New York: Applause Theatre and Cinema Books, 2011.

Blades, Joe. "The Evolution of *Cabaret*." *Literature/Film Quarterly* 1 (1973): 226–238.

Block, Geoffrey, ed. *Enchanted Evenings: The Broadway Musical from* Show Boat *to Sondheim and Lloyd Webber*. 2d ed. New York: Oxford University Press, 2009.

_____. *Richard Rodgers*. Yale Broadway Masters. New Haven, CT: Yale University Press, 2003.

_____, ed. *The Richard Rodgers Reader*. New York: Oxford University Press, 2002.

Bordman, Gerald. *American Musical Comedy: From* Adonis *to* Dreamgirls. New York: Oxford University Press, 1982.

_____. *Jerome Kern: His Life and Music*. New York: Oxford University Press, 1980.

Brengle, Linda K. "Divine Decadence, Darling!: The Sixty-Year History of the Kit Kat Klub." *Journal of Popular Culture* 34 (2000): 147–154.

Bristow, Eugene K., and J. Kevin Butler. "*Company*, About Face!: The Show That Revolutionized the American Musical." *American Music* 5 (1987): 241–254.

Burston, Jonathan. "Performance Review of *The Producers*." *Theatre Journal* 54 (2002): 467–469.

Carter, Tim. Oklahoma!: *The Making of an American Musical*. New Haven, CT: Yale University Press, 2007.

Chapin, Ted. *Everything Was Possible: The Birth of the Musical* Follies. New York: Alfred A. Knopf, 2003.

Citron, Stephen. *Jerry Herman: Poet of the Showtune*. New Haven, CT: Yale University Press, 2004.

_____. *Sondheim and Lloyd-Webber: The New Musical*. New York: Oxford University Press, 2001.

Clark, Randy. "Bending the Genre: The Stage and Screen Versions of *Cabaret*." *Literature/Film Quarterly* 19 (1991): 51–59.

Clum, John M. *Something for the Boys: Musical Theater and Gay Culture*. New York: St. Martin's, 1999.

Coleman, Bud, and Judith A. Sebesta. *Women in American Musical Theatre: Essays on Composers, Lyricists, Librettists, Arrangers, Choreographers, Designers, Directors, Producers and Performance Artist*s. Jefferson, NC: McFarland, 2008.

Copeland, Roger. "*Cabaret* at the End of the World." *American Theatre* 16 (1999): 25–28, 88–90.

Crohn Schmitt, Natalie. "A Popular Contemporary Work: *A Chorus Line*." In *Actors and Onlookers: Theater and Twentieth-Century Scientific Views of Nature*, 77–91. Evanston, IL: Northwestern University Press, 1990.

Dash, Irene G. *Shakespeare and the American Musical*. Bloomington: Indiana University Press, 2010.

Davis, Lee. *Bolton and Wodehouse and Kern: The Men Who Made Musical Comedy*. New York: James H. Heineman, 1993.

Davis, Lorrie. *Letting Down My Hair: Two Years with the Love Rock Tribe—From Dawning to Downing of Aquarius*. New York: A. Fields Books, 1973.

Decker, Todd. Show Boat: *Performing Race in an American Musical*. Broadway Legacies. New York: Oxford University Press, 2013.

De Giere, Carol. *Defying Gravity: The Creative Career of Stephen Schwartz from* Godspell *to* Wicked. New York: Applause Theatre & Cinema Books, 2008.

_____. *The* Godspell *Experience: Inside a Transformative Musical*. Bethel, CT: Scene 1 Publishing, 2014.

Dormon, James H. "Ethnic Cultures of the Mind: The Harrigan-Hart Mosaic." *American Studies* 33, no. 2 (1992): 21–40.

Dunn, Don. *The Making of* No, No, Nanette. Secaucus, NJ: Citadel, 1972.

Eells, George, *The Life That Late He Led: A Biography of Cole Porter*. New York: G.P. Putnam's Sons, 1967.

Elicker, Martina, "Rock Opera—Opera on the Rocks?" In *Essays in Honor of Steven Paul Scher and on Cultural Identity and the Musical Stage*, edited by Suzanne M. Lodato, Suzanne Aspden, and Walter Bernhart, 299–314. Word and Music Studies, vol. 4. Amsterdam: Rodopi, 2002.

Engel, Lehman. *The American Musical Theater*. Rev. ed. New York: Macmillan, 1975.

Everett, William. *Rudolf Friml*. American Composers. Urbana: University of Illinois Press, 2008.

_____. *Sigmund Romberg*. Yale Broadway Masters. New Haven, CT: Yale University Press, 2007.

Everett, William A., and Paul R. Laird, eds. *The Cambridge Companion to the Musical*. 2d ed. Cambridge: Cambridge University Press, 2008.

Ewen, David. *The Cole Porter Story*. New York: Holt, Rinehart and Winston, 1965.

_____. *Richard Rodgers*. New York: Henry Holt, 1957.

_____. *With a Song in His Heart: The Story of Richard Rodgers*. New York: Holt, Rinehart and Winston, 1963.

Farber, Donald C., and Robert Viagas. *The Amazing Story of* The Fantasticks: *America's Longest-Running Play*. Secaucus: N.J.: Citadel, 1991.

Fermaglich, Kirsten. "Mel Brooks' *The Producers:* Tracing American Jewish Culture Through Comedy, 1967–2007." *American Studies* 48, no. 4 (2007): 59–87.

Feuer, Cy, with Ken Gross. *I Got the Show Right Here: The Amazing, True Story of How an Obscure Brooklyn Horn Player Became the Last Great Broadway Showman*. New York: Simon & Schuster, 2003.

Filichia, Peter. *Strippers, Showgirls, and Sharks: A Very Opinionated History of the Broadway Musicals That Did Not Win the Tony Award*. New York: St. Martin's, 2013.

Flinn, Caryl. *Brass Diva: The Life and Legends of Ethel Merman*. Berkeley: University of California Press, 2007.

Flinn, Denny Martin. *Little Musicals for Little Theatres: A Reference Guide to the Musicals that Don't Need Chandeliers or Helicopters to Succeed*. Pompton Plains, NJ: Limelight Editions: 2006.

_____. *Musical! A Grand Tour: The Rise, Glory, and Fall of an American Institution*. New York: Schirmer Books, 1997.

Forte, Allen. *The American Popular Ballad of the Golden Era: 1924–1950*. Princeton, NJ: Princeton University Press, 1995.

_____. "The Twentieth Century: Secrets of Melody: Line and Design in the Songs of Cole Porter." *The Musical Quarterly* 77 (1993): 607–647.

Fraser, Barbara. "The Dream Shattered: America's Seventies Musicals." *Journal of American Culture* 12 (1989–1990): 31–37.

Furia, Philip. *Ira Gershwin: The Art of the Lyricist*. New York: Oxford University Press, 1996.

Ganzl, Kurt. *The Musical: A Concise History*. New York: Schirmer Books, 1989.

Garebian, Keith. *The Making of* Cabaret. 2d ed. New York: Oxford University Press, 2011.

_____. *The Making of* Guys and Dolls. Oakville, Canada: Mosaic, 2002.

_____. *The Making of* Gypsy. Toronto: ECW Press 1994; Reprint, Oakville, Canada: Mosaic, 1998.

_____. *The Making of* My Fair Lady. Toronto: ECW Press, 1993; Reprint, Oakville, Canada: Mosaic, 1998.

_____. *The Making of* West Side Story. Toronto: ECW Press, 1995; Reprint, Oakville, Canada: Mosaic, 1998.

Gill, Brendan. *Cole: A Biographical Essay*. Edited by Robert Kimball. New York: Holt, Rinehart & Winston, 1972.

Gilvey, John Anthony. *Before the Parade Passes By: Gower Champion and the Glorious American Musical*. New York: St. Martin's, 2005.

Goodhard, Sandor. "Happily Ever After: The Criticism of Stephen Sondheim." *Ars Lyrica* 8 (1994): 43–48.

_____, ed. *Reading Stephen Sondheim: A Collection of Critical Essays*. New York: Garland, 2000.

Gordon, Joanne, ed. *Stephen Sondheim: A Casebook*. New York: Garland, 1997.

Gordon, Robert. *The Oxford Handbook of Sondheim Studies*. New York: Oxford University Press, 2014.

Gottfried, Martin. *All His Jazz: The Life and Death of Bob Fosse*. New York: Bantam, 1990.

_____. *Broadway Musicals*. New York: H. N. Abrams, 1979.

Gould, Neil. *Victor Herbert*. New York: Fordham University Press, 2008.

Grant, Mark N. *The Rise and Fall of the Broadway Musical*. Boston: Northeastern University Press, 2004.

Green, Stanley. *The Rodgers and Hammerstein Story*. New York: John Day, 1963.

Greenspan, Charlotte. *Pick Yourself Up: Dorothy Fields and the American Musical*. Broadway Legacies. New York: Oxford University Press, 2010.

Hammerstein, Oscar Andrew. *The Hammersteins: A Musical Theatre Family*. New York: Black Dog & Leventhal Publishers, 2010.

Harrigan, Edward, and David Braham. *Collected Songs: II. 1883–1896*. Edited by Jon W. Finson. Recent Researches in American Music, vol. 28; Music of the United States America, vol. 7. Madison, WI: A-R Editions, 1997.

Heale, M. J. *The Sixties in America: History, Politics and Protest*. Chicago, Fitzroy Dearborn, 2001.

Hinton, Steven. *Weill's Musical Theater: Stages of Reform*. Berkeley: University of California Press, 2012.

Hirsch, Foster. *Harold Prince and the American Musical Theatre*. Expanded ed. New York: Applause Theatre and Cinema Books, 2005.

Hischak, Thomas S. *Boy Loses Girl: Broadway Librettists*. Lanham, MD: Scarecrow, 2002.

_____. *The Boys from Syracuse: The Shuberts' Theatrical Empire*. New York: Cooper Square, 2000.

_____. *Off-Broadway Musicals Since 1919: From* Greenwich Village Follies *to* The Toxic Avenger. Lanham, MD: Scarecrow, 2011.

_____. *Through the Screen Door: What Happened to the Broadway Musical When It Went to Hollywood*. Lanham, MD: Scarecrow, 2004.

_____. *Word Crazy: Broadway Lyricists from Cohan to Sondheim*. New York: Praeger, 1991.

Hoffman, Warren. *The Great White Way: Race and the Broadway Musical*. New Brunswick, NJ: Rutgers University Press, 2014.

Horn, Barbara Lee, *The Age of* Hair: *Evolution and Impact of Broadway's First Rock Musical*. New York: Greenwood, 1991.

Horowitz, Mark Eden. *Sondheim on Music: Minor Details and Major Decisions*. Lanham, MD: Scarecrow, 2003.

Huber, Eugene Roberts. "Stephen Sondheim and Harold Prince: Collaborative Contributions to the Development of the Modern Concept Musical, 1970–1981." Ph.D. diss., New York University, 1990.

Hyland, William G. *Richard Rodgers*. New Haven, CT: Yale University Press, 1998.

Isenberg, Barbara. *Tradition: The Highly Improbable, Ultimately Triumphant Broadway-to-Hollywood Story of* Fiddler on the Roof, *the World's Most Beloved Musical*. New York: St. Martin's, 2014.

Jablonski, Edward. *Alan Jay Lerner: A Biography*. New York: Henry Holt, 1996.

Jenkins, Jeffrey Eric. "Through a Glass, Nostalgically: The Death and Life of Broadway." *American Literary History* (2006): 191–210.

Johnson, Jonathon. *Good Hair Days: A Personal Journey with the American Tribal Love-Rock Musical* Hair. Lincoln, Nebraska: iUniverse, 2004.

Jones, John Bush. *Our Musicals, Ourselves: A Social History of the American Musical Theatre*. Hanover, NH: Brandeis University Press, 2003.

Jones, Tom, and Harvey Schmidt. The Fantasticks: *The Complete Illustrated Text Plus the Official* Fantasticks *Scrapbook and History of the Musical*. New York: Applause Theatre Book Publishers, 1990.

Kander, John, and Fred Ebb as told to Greg Lawrence. *Colored Lights: Forty Years of Words and Music, Show Biz, Collaboration, and All that Jazz*. New York: Faber and Faber, 2003.

Kellow, Brian. *Ethel Merman: A Life*. New York: Viking, 2007.

Kenrick, John. *Musical Theatre: A History*. New York: Bloomsbury Academic, 2010.

Kirle, Bruce. *Unfinished Show Business: Broadway Musicals as Works-in-Process*. Carbondale: Southern Illinois University Press, 2005.

Kislan, Richard. *Hoofing on Broadway: A History of Show Dancing*. New York: Prentice Hall, 1987.

_____. *The Musical: A Look at the American Musical Theater*. Englewood Cliffs, NJ: Prentice-Hall, 1980.

Kissel, Howard. *David Merrick: The Abominable Showman: The Unauthorized Biography*. New York: Applause Books, 1993.

Klein, Christina. *Cold War Orientalism: Asia in the Middlebrow Imagination, 1945–1961*. Berkeley, University of California Press, 2003.

Knapp, Raymond. *The American Musical and the Formation of National Identity*. Princeton, NJ: Princeton University Press, 2005.

_____. *The American Musical and the Performance of Personal Identity*. Princeton, NJ: Princeton University Press, 2005.

Knapp, Raymond, Mitchell Morris, and Stacy Wolf, eds. *The Oxford Handbook of the American Musical*. New York: Oxford University Press, 2011.

Kowalke, Kim H. "Theorizing the Golden Age Musical: Genre, Structure, Syntax." *Gamut: Online Journal of the Music Theory Society of the Mid-Atlantic* 6, no. 2 (2013): 133–184.

Kreuger, Miles. Show Boat: *The Story of a Classic American Musical*. New York: Oxford University Press, 1977.

Laird, Paul R. Wicked: *A Musical Biography*. Lanham, MD: Scarecrow, 2011.

Lambert, Philip. *To Broadway, To Life!: The Musical Theater of Bock and Harnick*. Broadway Legacies. New York: Oxford University Press, 2011.

Laurents, Arthur. *Mainly on Directing:* Gypsy, West Side Story, *and Other Musicals*. New York: Alfred A. Knopf, 2009.

_____. *The Rest of the Story: A Life Completed*. New York: Applause Theatre & Cinema Books, 2011.

Lees, Gene. *Inventing Champagne: The Worlds of Lerner and Loewe*. New York: St. Martin's, 1990.

Lerner, Alan Jay. *The Street Where I Live*. New York: W.W. Norton, 1980.

Leve, James. *Kander and Ebb*. Yale Broadway Masters. New Haven, CT: Yale University Press, 2009.

Loney, Glenn, ed. *Musical Theatre in America: Papers and Proceedings of the Conference on the Musical Theatre in America*. Contributions in Drama and Theatre Studies, ed. Joseph Donohue, vol. 8. Westport, CT: Greenwood, 1984.

Lovensheimer, Jim. South Pacific: *Paradise Rewritten*. Broadway Legacies. New York: Oxford University Press, 2010.

LuPone, Patti, with Digby Diehl. *Patti LuPone: A Memoir*. New York: Crown, 2010.

Magee, Jeffrey. "'Everybody Step': Irving Berlin, Jazz, and Broadway in the 1920s." *Journal of the American Musicological Society* 59 (2006): 697–732.

_____. *Irving Berlin's American Musical Theater*. Broadway Legacies. New York: Oxford University Press, 2012.

Mandelbaum, Ken. A Chorus Line *and the Musicals of Michael Bennett*. New York: St. Martins, 1989.

_____. *Not Since* Carrie: *40 Years of Broadway Musical Flops*. New York: St. Martin's, 1991.

Marmorstein, Gary. *The Life of Lorenz Hart: A Ship Without a Sail*. New York: Simon & Schuster, 2012.

Martin, Andrew. *All for the Best: How* Godspell *Transferred from Stage to Screen*. Albany, GA: Bear Manor Media, 2012.

Martin, Philip John. "Development and Interpretation of the Elements of Integration in the Princess Theatre Musicals." Ph.D. diss., University of Utah, 1993.

Marx, Samuel, and Jan Clayton. *Rodgers & Hart: Bewitched, Bothered, and Bedeviled*. New York: G.P. Putnam's Sons, 1976.

Mates, Julian. *America's Musical Stage: Two Hundred Years of Musical Theatre*. Contributions in Drama and Theatre Studies, vol. 18. Westport, CT: Greenwood, 1985.

McBrien, William. *Cole Porter: A Biography*. New York: Alfred A. Knopf, 1998.

McCabe, John. *George M. Cohan: The Man Who Owned Broadway*. Garden City, NJ: Doubleday, 1973.

McClung, Bruce D. Lady in the Dark: *Biography of a Musical*. New York: Oxford University Press, 2007.

McConachie, Bruce A. "The 'Oriental' Musicals of Rodgers and Hammerstein and the U.S. War in Southeast Asia." *Theatre Journal* 46 (1994): 385–406.

McHugh, Dominic, ed. *Alan Jay Lerner: A Lyricist's Letters*. New York: Oxford University Press, 2014.

_____. *Loverly: The Life & Times of* My Fair Lady. Broadway Legacies. New York: Oxford Press, 2012.

McMillin, Scott. *The Musical as Drama: A Study of the Principles and Conventions Behind Musical Shows from Kern to Sondheim*. Princeton, NJ: Princeton University Press, 2006.

Miller, Scott. *Deconstructing Harold Hill: An Insider's Guide to Musical Theatre*. Portsmouth, NH: Heinemann, 2000.

_____. *From* Assassins *to* West Side Story: *The Director's Guide to Musical Theatre*. Portsmouth, NH: Heinemann, 1996.

_____. *Let the Sun Shine In: The Genius of* Hair. Portsmouth, NH: Heinemann, 2003.

_____. *Rebels with Applause: Broadway's Groundbreaking Musicals.* New York: Applause Books, 2001.

_____. *Sex, Drugs, Rock & Roll, and Musicals.* Boston: Northeastern University Press, 2013.

_____. *Strike Up the Band: A New History of Musical Theatre.* Portsmouth, NH: Heinemann, 2006.

Moody, Richard. *Ned Harrigan: From Corlear's Hook to Herald Square.* Chicago: Nelson-Hall, 1980.

Mordden, Ethan. *Anything Goes: A History of American Musical Theatre.* New York: Oxford University Press, 2013.

_____. *Beautiful Mornin': The Broadway Musical in the 1940s.* New York: Oxford Press, 1999.

_____. *Better Foot Forward: The History of American Musical Theatre.* New York: Grossman, 1976.

_____. *Broadway Babies: The People Who Made the American Musical.* New York: Oxford University Press, 1983.

_____. *Coming Up Roses: The Broadway Musical in the 1950s.* New York: Oxford University Press, 1998.

_____. *The Happiest Corpse I've Ever Seen: The Last Twenty-Five Years of the Broadway Musical.* New York: Palgrave Macmillan, 2004.

_____. *Make Believe: The Broadway Musical in the 1920s.* New York: Oxford University Press, 1997.

_____. *One More Kiss: The Broadway Musical in the 1970s.* New York: Palgrave Macmillan, 2001.

_____. *Open a New Window: The Broadway Musical in the 1960s.* New York: Palgrave, 2003.

_____. *Rodgers and Hammerstein.* New York: H.N. Abrams, 1992.

_____. *Sing for Your Supper: The Broadway Musical in the 1930s.* New York: Palgrave MacMillan, 2005.

Morehouse, Ward. *George M. Cohan: Prince of the American Theater.* Westport, CT: Greenwood, 1943.

Morella, Joseph, and George Mazzei. *Genius and Lust: The Creativity and Sexuality of Cole Porter and Noel Coward.* New York: Carroll & Graf, 1995.

Morris, Mitchell. "*Cabaret*, America's Weimar, and Mythologies of the Gay Subject." *American Music* 22 (2004): 147–157.

Most, Andrea. *Making Americans: Jews and the Broadway Musical.* Cambridge, MA: Harvard University Press, 2004.

_____. "The Politics of Race in *South Pacific*." *Theatre Journal* 52 (2000): 307–337.

_____. "'We Know We Belong to the Land': The Theatricality of Assimilation in Rodgers and Hammerstein's *Oklahoma!*" *PMLA* 113 (1998): 77–89.

Napolitano, Mark. *Oliver!: A Dickensian Musical.* New York: Oxford University Press, 2014.

Nicholls, David. "Virtual Opera, or Opera Between the Ears." *Royal Musical Association* 129 (2004): 100–142.

Nisbet, Ian. "Transposition in Jonathan Larson's *Rent*." *Studies in Musical Theatre* 5 (2011): 225–244.

Nolan, Frederick, *The Sound of Their Music: The Story of Rodgers and Hammerstein.* New York: Walker, 1978.

Noonan, Ellen. *The Strange Career of* Porgy & Bess: *Race, Culture, and America's Most Famous Opera.* Chapel Hill: University of North Carolina Press, 2012.

Oates, Bill. *Meredith Willson—America's Music Man: The Whole Broadway-Symphonic-Radio-Motion Picture Story.* Bloomington, IL: Author House, 2005.

Ohl, Vicki. *Fine and Dandy: The Life and Work of Kay Swift.* New Haven, CT: Yale University Press, 2004.

_____. *Bernstein Meets Broadway: Collaborative Art in a Time of War.* Broadway Legacies. New York: Oxford University Press, 2014.

Oja, Carol J. "*West Side Story* and *The Music Man*: Whiteness, Immigration, and Race in the US during the Late 1950s." *Studies in Musical Theater* 3 (2009): 13–30.

O'Leary, James. "*Oklahoma!*, 'Lousy Publicity,' and the Politics of Formal Integration in the American Musical Theater." *The Journal of Musicology* 31 (2014): 139–182.

Our Story: Jets and Sharks: Then and Now. Denver, CO: Outskirts, 2011.

Porter, Cole. *The Complete Lyrics of Cole Porter.* Edited by Robert Kimball. New York: Knopf, 1983.

Prince, Hal. *Contradictions: Notes of Twenty-Six Years in the Theatre.* New York: Dodd, Mead, 1974.

Propst, Andy. *You Fascinate Me So: The Life and Times of Cy Coleman.* New York: Applause Theatre & Cinema Books, 2015.

Randall, James Kenneth. "Becoming Jerome Kern: The Early Songs and Shows, 1903–1915." Ph.D. diss., University of Illinois at Urbana-Champaign, 2004.

Riis, Thomas L., ed. *The Music and Scripts of* In Dahomey. Recent Researches in American Music, vol. 25; Music in the United States, vol. 5. Madison, WI: Published for the American Musicological Society by A-R Editions, 1996.

Riis, Thomas L. *Frank Loesser.* Yale Broadway Masters. New Haven, CT: Yale University Press, 2008.

_____. *Just Before Jazz: Black Musical Theater in New York, 1890–1915.* Washington, DC: Smithsonian Institution Press, 1989.

Rodgers, Richard, *Musical Stages: An Autobiography.* New York: Random House, 1975; Reprint, with a new introduction by Mary Rodgers, New York: Da Capo, 1995.

Rosenberg, Bernard, and Ernest Harburg. *The Broadway Musical: Collaboration in Commerce and Art.* New York: New York University Press, 1993.

Schwartz, Charles. *Cole Porter: A Biography.* New York: Dial Press, 1977.

Schwartz, Michael. *Broadway and Corporate Capitalism: The Rise of the Professional-Managerial Class, 1900–1920.* Palgrave Studies in Theatre and Performance History. New York: Palgrave Macmillan, 2009.

Sears, Benjamin, ed. *The Irving Berlin Reader.* New York: New York University Press, 2012.

Sebesta, Judith. "From Celluloid to Stage: The 'Movical,' *The Producers*, and the Postmodern." *The Theatre Annual* 56 (2003): 97–112.

_____. "Of Fire, Death, and Desire": Transgression and Carnival in Jonathan Larson's *Rent*." *Contemporary Theatre Review* 16 (2006): 419–438.

Secrest, Meryle. *Somewhere for Me: A Biography of Richard Rodgers.* New York: Alfred A. Knopf, 2001.

_____. *Sondheim: A Life*. New York: Alfred A. Knopf, 1998.

Shapiro, Eddie. *Nothing Like a Dame: Conversations with the Great Women of Musical Theater*. New York: Oxford University Press, 2014.

Singer, Barry. *Ever After: The Last Years of Musical Theater and Beyond*. New York: Applause Theatre & Cinema Books, 2004.

Skipper, John C. *Meredith Willson: The Unsinkable Music Man*. Mason City, IA: Savas, 2000.

Smart, Jeffrey Hilton. "The Internal Development of the Princess Theatre Musical Shows." Ph.D. diss., University of Missouri-Columbia, 1991.

Smith, Cecil, and Glenn Litton. *Musical Comedy in America: From* The Black Crook *to* South Pacific, *From* The King and I *to* Sweeney Todd. New York: Theatre Arts Books, 1981; Reprint, Abingdon, England: Routledge, 1991.

Solomon, Alisa. *Wonder of Wonders: A Cultural History of* Fiddler on the Roof. New York: Metropolitan Books, 2013.

Sondheim, Stephen. *Finishing the Hat: Collected Lyrics (1954–1981) with Attendant Comments, Principles, Heresies, Grudges, Whines and Anecdotes*. New York: Alfred A. Knopf, 2010.

_____. *Look, I Made a Hat: Collected Lyrics (1981–2011) with Attendant Comments, Amplifications, Dogmas, Harangues, Digressions, Anecdotes and Miscellany*. New York: Alfred A. Knopf, 2011.

Stafford, David, and Caroline Stafford. *Fings Ain't Wot They Used T'Be: The Lionel Bart Story*. London: Omnibus, 2011.

Starr, Larry. *George Gershwin*. Yale Broadway Masters. New Haven, CT: Yale University Press, 2011.

Stempel, Larry. *Showtime: A History of the Broadway Musical Theater*. New York: W.W. Norton, 2010.

Sternfeld, Jessica. *The Megamusical*. Bloomington: Indiana University Press, 2006.

Steyn, Mark. *Broadway Babies Say Goodnight: Musicals Then and Now*. New York: Routledge, 1999.

Strum, Rebecca W. "Elisabeth Marbury, 1856–1933: Her Life and Work." Ph.D. diss., New York University, 1989.

Summers, Claude J. *Christopher Isherwood*. New York: Frederick Ungar, 1980.

Sunshine, Linda. *Introduction to* Cabaret *by Joe Masteroff*. New York: Newmarket, 1999.

Suskin, Steven. *Second Act Trouble: Behind the Scenes at Broadway's Big Musical Bombs*. New York: Applause Theatre & Cinema Books, 2006.

_____. *Show Tunes, 1905–1985: The Songs, Shows, and Careers of Broadway's Major Composers*. 4th ed. New York: Oxford University Press, 2010.

_____. *The Sound of Broadway Music: A Book of Orchestrators and Orchestrations*. New York: Oxford University Press, 2009.

Swain, Joseph P. *The Broadway Musical: A Critical and Musical Survey*. New York: Oxford University Press, 1990.

Swayne, Steve. *How Sondheim Found His Sound*. Ann Arbor: University of Michigan Press, 2005.

Symonds, Dominic. *We'll Have Manhattan: The Early Work of Rodgers and Hart*. Broadway Legacies. New York: Oxford University Press, 2015.

Symons, Alex. "An Audience for Mel Brooks's *The Producers:* The Avant-garde of the Masses." *Journal of Popular Film and Television* 34 (2006): 24–32.

Taylor, Mille. *Musical Theatre, Realism and Entertainment.* Ashgate Interdisciplinary Studies in Opera. Farnham, England: Ashgate, 2012.

Thelen, Lawrence. *The Show Makers: Great Directors of the American Musical Theatre.* New York: Routledge, 2000.

Traubner, Richard. *Operetta: A Theatrical History.* Rev. ed. New York: Routledge, 2003.

Vernette, Margaret. *The Musical World of Boublil and Schönberg.* New York: Applause Theatre & Cinema Books, 2006.

Viagas, Robert. *I'm the Greatest Star: Broadway's Top Musical Legends from 1900 to Today.* New York: Applause Theatre & Cinema Books, 2009.

Viagas, Robert, Baayork Lee, and Thommie Walsh. *On the Line: The Creation of* A Chorus Line. New York: William Morrow, 1990.

Walsh, David F., and Len Platt. *Musical Theater and American Culture.* Westport, CT: Praeger Publishers, 2003.

Wasserman, Dale. *The Impossible Musical.* New York: Applause Theatre & Cinema Books, 2003.

Wasson, Sam. *Fosse.* New York: Houghton Mifflin Harcourt, 2013.

Wells, Elizabeth A. West Side Story: *Cultural Perspectives on an American Musical.* Lanham, MD: Scarecrow, 2011.

Wilder, Alec, *American Popular Song: The Great Innovators, 1900–1950.* New York: Oxford University Press, 1972.

Wilk, Max. *OK!, The Story of* Oklahoma!: *A Celebration of America's Most Loved Musical.* New York: Applause Theatre & Cinema Books, 2002.

Willson, Meredith. *"But He Doesn't Know the Territory": The Making of Meredith Willson's* The Music Man. New York: G. P. Putnam's Sons, 1959; Reprint, Minneapolis: University of Minnesota Press, 2009.

Wolf, Stacy. *Changed for Good: A Feminist History of the Broadway Musical.* New York: Oxford University Press, 2011.

_____. *A Problem Like Maria: Gender and Sexuality in the American Musical.* Ann Arbor: University of Michigan Press, 2002.

Woll, Allen L. *Black Musical Theatre: From* Coontown *to* Dreamgirls. Baton Rouge: Louisiana State University Press, 1989.

_____. *The Hollywood Musical Goes to War.* Chicago: Nelson-Hall, 1983.

Wollman, Elizabeth L. *Hard Times: The Adult Musical in 1970s New York City.* New York: Oxford University Press, 2013.

_____. *The Theater Will Rock: History of the Rock Musical, from* Hair *to* Hedwig. Ann Arbor: University of Michigan Press, 2006.

Young, Kay. "'Every Day a Little Death': Sondheim's Un-Musicaling of Marriage." *Ars Lyrica* 8 (1994): 63–74.

Zandan, Craig. *Sondheim & Co.* 2d ed. New York: Harper & Row, 1986.

Zimmers, Tighe E. *Lyrical Satirical Harold Rome: A Biography of the Broadway Composer-Lyricist.* Jefferson, NC: McFarland, 2014.

CREDITS

All I Ask of You

from THE PHANTOM OF THE OPERA
Music by Andrew Lloyd Webber
Lyrics by Charles Hart
Additional Lyrics by Richard Stilgoe
© Copyright 1986 Andrew Lloyd Webber
   licensed to The Really Useful Group Ltd.
This arrangement © Copyright 2014
   Andrew Lloyd Webber licensed to
   The Really Useful Group Ltd.
   International Copyright Secured All
   Rights Reserved
*Reprinted by Permission of Hal Leonard
   Corporation.*

All I Ask of You

from THE PHANTOM OF THE OPERA
Music by Andrew Lloyd Webber
Lyrics by Charles Hart
Additional Lyrics by Richard Stilgoe
© Copyright 1986 Andrew Lloyd Webber
   licensed to The Really Useful Group
   Limited.
This Arrangement © Copyright 2015 The
   Really Useful Group Limited.
All Rights Reserved. International Copyright
   Secured.
Used by Permission of Music Sales
   Limited.

Cotton Blossom

from SHOW BOAT
Words by Oscar Hammerstein II
Music by Jerome Kern
Copyright © 1927, 1928 UNIVERSAL –
   POLYGRAM INTERNATIONAL
   PUBLISHING, INC.
Copyright Renewed
This arrangement Copyright © 2014
   UNIVERSAL – POLYGRAM
   INTERNATIONAL PUBLISHING, INC.
All Rights Reserved. Used by Permission.
*Reprinted by Permission of Hal Leonard
   Corporation.*

Cotton Blossom

Words by Oscar Hammerstein II
Music by Jerome Kern
© Copyright 1927 T.B. Harms & Company
   Incorporated, USA.
Universal Music Publishing Limited.
This Arrangement © Copyright 2015
   T B Harms Company.
All Rights Reserved. International Copyright
   Secured.
Used by Permission of Music Sales Limited.

Ease on Down the Road

from THE WIZ
Words and Music by CHARLIE SMALLS
© 1974 (Renewed) WARNER-TAMERLANE
   PUBLISHING CORP. and MIJAC MUSIC
All Rights Reserved.
Used by Permission of ALFRED MUSIC.

Ease on Down the Road

Words and Music by Charlie Smalls
© Copyright 1974, 1978 Mijac Music.
Sony/ATV Music Publishing.
This Arrangement © Copyright 2015 Mijac
   Music.
All Rights Reserved. International Copyright
   Secured.
Used by Permission of Music Sales Limited.

Ease on Down the Road

Words and Music by Charlie Smalls
© 1974 (Renewed) WARNER-TAMERLANE
   PUBLISHING CORP. and MTJAC MUSIC
This arrangement © 2014 WARNER-
   TAMERLANE PUBLISHING CORP. and
   MIJAC MUSIC
All Rights on behalf of MIJAC MUSIC
   Administered by SONY/ATV MUSIC
   PUBLISHING LLC, 424 Church Street,
   Suite 1200, Nashville, TN 37219
All Rights Reserved. Used by Permission.
*Reprinted by Permission of Hal Leonard
   Corporation.*

The Light in the Piazza

from THE LIGHT IN THE PIAZZA
Music and Lyrics by Adam Guettel

The Music of the Night

from THE PHANTOM OF THE OPERA
Music by Andrew Lloyd Webber
Lyrics by Charles Hart
Additional Lyrics by Richard Stilgoe

The Music of the Night

from THE PHANTOM OF THE OPERA
Music by Andrew Lloyd Webber
Lyrics by Charles Hart
Additional Lyrics by Richard Stilgoe

The Surrey With the Fringe on Top

from OKLAHOMA!
Lyrics by Oscar Hammerstein II
Music by Richard Rodgers

Think of Me

from THE PHANTOM OF THE OPERA
Music by Andrew Lloyd Webber
Lyrics by Charles Hart
Additional Lyrics by Richard Stilgoe

Think of Me

from THE PHANTOM OF THE OPERA
Music by Andrew Lloyd Webber
Lyrics by Charles Hart

Thirteen Collar

from VERY GOOD EDDIE
Words by Schuyler Greene
Music by Jerome Kern

Thirteen Collar

Words by Schuyler Greene
Music by Jerome Kern

Willkommen

from the Musical CABARET
Words by Fred Ebb
Music by John Kander

Yankee Doodle Dandy Give My Regards to Broadway

Written by George M. Cohan

INDEX